Alexander the Great

Alexander the Great

A New History

Edited by
Waldemar Heckel and Lawrence A. Tritle

WILEY-BLACKWELL

A John Wiley & Sons, Ltd., Publication

This edition first published 2009
© 2009 Blackwell Publishing Ltd

Blackwell Publishing was acquired by John Wiley & Sons in February 2007. Blackwell's publishing program has been merged with Wiley's global Scientific, Technical, and Medical business to form Wiley-Blackwell.

Registered Office
John Wiley & Sons Ltd, The Atrium, Southern Gate, Chichester, West Sussex, PO19 8SQ, United Kingdom

Editorial Offices
350 Main Street, Malden, MA 02148–5020, USA
9600 Garsington Road, Oxford, OX4 2DQ, UK
The Atrium, Southern Gate, Chichester, West Sussex, PO19 8SQ, UK

For details of our global editorial offices, for customer services, and for information about how to apply for permission to reuse the copyright material in this book please see our website at www.wiley.com/wiley-blackwell.

The right of Waldemar Heckel and Lawrence A. Tritle to be identified as the authors of the editorial material in this work has been asserted in accordance with the Copyright, Designs and Patents Act 1988.

Wiley also publishes its books in a variety of electronic formats. Some content that appears in print may not be available in electronic books.

Designations used by companies to distinguish their products are often claimed as trademarks. All brand names and product names used in this book are trade names, service marks, trademarks or registered trademarks of their respective owners. The publisher is not associated with any product or vendor mentioned in this book. This publication is designed to provide accurate and authoritative information in regard to the subject matter covered. It is sold on the understanding that the publisher is not engaged in rendering professional services. If professional advice or other expert assistance is required, the services of a competent professional should be sought.

Library of Congress Cataloging-in-Publication Data

Alexander the Great : a new history / edited by Waldemar Heckel and Lawrence A. Tritle.
    p.   cm.
  Includes bibliographical references and index.
  ISBN 978-1-4051-3081-3 (hardcover : alk. paper) – ISBN 978-1-4051-3082-0 (pbk. : alk. paper)
   1. Alexander, the Great, 356-323 B.C.   2. Greece–History–Macedonian Expansion, 359-323 B.C.   3. Greece–Kings and rulers–Biography.   4. Generals–Greece–Biography.   I. Heckel, Waldemar, 1949–   II. Tritle, Lawrence A., 1946–
  DF234.A4857 2009
  938′.07092–dc22
  [B]

                                       2008026394

A catalogue record for this book is available from the British Library.

Set in 10.5/13 Minion by SNP Best-set Typesetter Ltd., Hong Kong
Printed in Singapore by Ho Printing Singapore Pte Ltd

01   2009

Contents

Figures

Contributors

E. J. Baynham, Professor of Classics and Ancient History, University of Newcastle

Pierre Briant, Professor of History, Collége de France, Paris

Elizabeth D. Carney, Professor of History, Clemson University, South Carolina

Boris Dreyer, Ancient History Seminar, University of Göttingen

Waldemar Heckel, Professor of Ancient History, University of Calgary

Alexander Meeus, Faculty of Arts, Ancient History, Catholic University of Louvain

Catie Mihalopoulos, Assistant Professor of Art and Archaeology, California State University, Channel Islands

Daniel Ogden, Department of Classics, University of Exeter

Elisabetta Poddighe, Department of Classical Philology and Ancient History, University of Cagliari

Diana Spencer, Institute of Archaeology and Antiquity, University of Birmingham

Lawrence A. Tritle, Professor of History, Loyola Marymount University, Los Angeles

Gregor Weber, Professor and Chair of Ancient History, University of Augsburg

Patrick Wheatley, Lecturer, Department of Classics, University of Otago

Michael Zahrnt, Emeritus Professor of Ancient History, University of Cologne

Chronology

All dates are BC unless indicated otherwise.

c.498–454		Reign of Alexander I "Philhellene."
c.454–413		Reign of Perdiccas II.
413–399		Reign of Archelaus I.
393–369		Reign of Amyntas III.
360/59–336		Reign of Philip II.
359–338		Reign of Artaxerxes III of Persia.
357		Marriage of Philip II to Olympias of Epirus.
356		Philip founds Philippi. Victory at Olympic Games.
356	c. July 20	Birth of Alexander.
356–346		Third Sacred War.
352		Philip acquires control of Thessaly.
348		Philip sacks Olynthus.
346		Peace of Philocrates. Philip celebrates Pythian Games.
344/3		Persia reconquers Egypt (in revolt since 404).
343		Aristotle tutors Alexander at Mieza.
342–339		Philip gains control of Thrace.
340/39		Alexander, as regent during Philip's absence at siege of Byzantium, defeats the Maedians and founds Alexandroupolis.
338	August	Philip defeats Greek coalition led by Athens and Thebes at Chaeroneia.
337	spring	Philip founds League of Corinth, is chosen leader of Panhellenic expedition against Persian empire.

336		Accession of Darius III of Persia. Philip dispatches forces under Parmenion to Asia Minor.
336	?Oct.	Philip assassinated at Aegae.
336–323		Reign of Alexander III the Great.
336/5		Alexander recognized as Philip's successor as head of League of Corinth and commander of Persian expedition.
335	late spring	Alexander campaigns in Thrace against Triballi and in Danube region.
	June–Aug.	Campaigns against the Illyrian chieftains Cleitus and Glaucias.
	early Oct.	Destruction of Thebes.
334	spring	Alexander's army crosses into Asia.
	May	Battle of the river Granicus.
	May–Aug.	Campaigns in western Asia Minor; Greek-Macedonian fleet disbanded.
	Aug.–Sept.	Siege of Halicarnassus.
	autumn–winter	Campaigns in Caria, Lycia, Pamphylia.
333	spring	Advance to Great Phrygia (Gordian Knot incident).
	summer	To Ancyra, through Cilician Gates; to Tarsus and Soli.
	Nov.	Battle of Issus in Cilicia.
	Dec.	Parmenion captures Damascus.
332	Jan.–July/Aug.	Siege of Tyre.
	Sept.–Nov.	Siege of Gaza.
	Nov.	Alexander recognized as pharaoh of Egypt.
331	Jan.–Mar.	Foundation of (Egyptian) Alexandria (official "birthday" April 7).
		Consultation of oracle of Ammon at Siwah oasis.
	spring	From Memphis to Tyre, reorganization of financial administration.
	July–Aug.	To Thapsacus.
	autumn	"Battle of Mice" (Antipater defeats Spartan king, Agis III, at Megalopolis).
	Sept. 20	Evening eclipse of moon.
	Oct. 1	Battle of Gaugamela.
	Oct.–Dec.	Progress through Babylonia and Sittacene (military reorganization) to Persepolis (Uxian campaign and battle at the Persian Gates).
330	spring	Campaign in interior of Iran.
	Apr./May	Return to Persepolis, burning of palace, and departure for Media.
	early June	Allied Greek contingents dismissed at Ecbatana.

	June	To Rhagae (ancient Teheran) and Caspian Gates.
	July	Capture of Darius III's body. Advance to border of Hyrcania. Reception of Nabazarnes and Phrataphernes. Visit of the Amazon queen (alleged). Advance to Zadracarta. Alexander starts acting as Great King; adopts mixed oriental dress.
	Aug.	Toward Bactria, then diversion to Artacoana (Herat). Revolt of Satibarzanes.
	Sept.	Trial and execution of Philotas, followed by murder of Parmenion. Trial of Amyntas and his brothers.
	winter	Through land of Drangaeans and Ariaspians, into Arachosia; through Paropamisadae to foot of Hindu Kush.
330/29	winter	Foundation of Alexandria-by-the-Caucasus (near Begram and Charikar).
329	spring	Crossing of Hindu Kush, to Drapsaca (Kunduz) and Bactra; older men and Thessalian volunteers sent home. Crossing of Oxus river.
	summer	Capture of Bessus (Persian pretender) by Ptolemy; punishment of Bessus. Advance to Maracanda (Samarkand), summer capital of Sogdiana, to river Jaxartes (Syr-darya). Foundation of Alexandria Eschate (Khodjend). Revolt of local Scythian tribesmen and of Sogdians, campaign against defected Spitamenes.
329/8	winter	At Bactra Alexander receives embassies from Scythians and Chorasmians. Capture of the Rock of Sogdiana (Rock of Arimazes).
328	spring	Systematic pacification of Sogdiana begins; guerrilla warfare against Massagetae of Turkestan steppes and against Spitamenes.
	late summer	Return to Maracanda.
	Nov.	Alexander murders Cleitus at Maracanda. Spitamenes killed by Massagetae.
328/7	winter	Alexander quarters at Nautaca.
327	spring	Capture of Rock of Chorienes (Koh-i-Nor). Alexander marries Roxane, daughter of Oxyartes. Return to Bactria; defeat of last opposition. *Proskynesis* episode; Pages' Conspiracy; arrest and execution of Callisthenes.

	late spring	Departure from Bactria; recrossing of Hindu Kush to Alexandria by-the-Caucasus.
	late	Invasion of India begins.
327/6	winter	Alexander among the Assacenians (Swat and Buner); capture of Massaga. Advance to Indus river and Rock of Aornus (Pir-Sar).
326		Progress to Taxila
	May	Battle of the Hydaspes (Jhelum) against Porus (rajah of the Pauravas).
	May–June	Halt in Porus's kingdom.
	late June	Advance to Acesines river and Hyphasis (Beas) river. The army refuses to advance beyond the Hyphasis. Return to the Hydaspes. Death of Coenus. Fleets prepared.
	Nov.	Beginning of descent of Indus river system.
325		Reduction of Mallian tribe; near-fatal wounding of Alexander. Journey to the Indian Ocean.
	July	Pattala (?Hyderabad) reached.
	Aug.	Descent from Pattala begins.
	Aug.–Nov.	Approach to march through Gedrosian desert (Makran).
	Sept.	Alexander reaches Oreitae.
	Sept./Oct.	Nearchus leaves with fleet; Alexander marches through Gedrosia and reaches Pura.
	mid Dec.	Nearchus reaches Hormozeia (Hormuz).
	late Dec.	Alexander and Nearchus reunited in Carmania (?at Gulashird).
325/4	winter	Executions of satraps and generals; flight of Harpalus.
324	Jan.–Mar.	Nearchus leaves Hormozeia, then enters Arabian Gulf.
	?Jan.	Alexander reaches Pasargadae.
	Mar.	Alexander and Nearchus reunite at Susa.
	Apr.	Susa weddings. Paying off of soldiers' debts. Voyage up Tigris.
	June	Mutiny at Opis (Baghdad). Banquet of reconciliation.
	July	Harpalus arrives at Athens, hands over 700 talents.
	Aug.	Promulgation by Nicanor of Alexander's Exiles' Decree at Olympic Games.
	Oct.	Death of Hephaestion at Ecbatana.
324/3	winter	Campaign against Cossaean nomads.

323	early	Alexander in Babylon. Preparations for Arabian expedition. Visits of Greek envoys acknowledging Alexander's divinity.
	June 11	Alexander dies at Babylon, aged nearly 33, having reigned just over twelve and a half years
323/2		Lamian War in Greece.
320		Political settlement at Triparadeisus (northern Syria).
319		Death of Antipater. Beginning of the struggle for power between Cassander and Polyperchon.
317		Deaths of Philip III and Adea-Eurydice. Eumenes betrayed to Antigonus at Gabiene; his death.
316		Death of Alexander's mother, Olympias.
310		Death of Alexander IV at Amphipolis.
306		Battle of Salamis. Antigonus and Demetrius assume the royal title; other Successors follow suit.
301		Battle of Ipsus. Death of Antigonus the One-Eyed.

Preface and Acknowledgments

One of the strengths of this volume is that it includes contributions by scholars outside the English-speaking world, whose views on the reign of Alexander often do not receive due notice and attention. The Editors are grateful to Al Bertrand and to Blackwell Publishing who realized that such contributions would enhance the volume's importance and so supported the work of our translators. We would thus like to acknowledge the following contributions: Dr. John Nicholson (Loyola University Chicago Rome Center) who translated Elisabetta Poddighe's chapter on Alexander and the Greeks; Dr. Reyes Bertolin-Cebrian (University of Calgary) who translated Gregor Weber's chapter on Alexander's court; Ms. Sandra Colantonio who translated Pierre Briant's discussion of the historiography of Alexander and the Persian empire. Their efforts were supported additionally by Anneli Purchase and Wouter Henkleman (P. Briant's assistant) who were no less important in this work.

The Editors are also grateful to Al Bertrand and Blackwell for their generous decision to illustrate this volume lavishly with some of the more important examples of the art and imagery of the reign of Alexander. Humberto DeLuigi at Art Resource New York located a number of the images illustrated here; his efforts were assisted by Blackwell's Leanda Shrimpton who found several others and arranged for the Charles Le Brun artwork as well.

Abbreviations

Names of ancient authors and titles of works are abbreviated after H. G. Liddell and R. Scott, *A Greek–English Lexicon*, 9th edn., rev. by Sir H. S. Jones and R. McKenzie (Oxford, 1940), pp. xvi–xxxviii, or as listed in *OCD*[3] (cited below). For standard reference works, the usual abbreviations are followed, e.g., *CAH* = *Cambridge Ancient History*, ed. by J. B. Bury et al., 1st edn., 12 vols. (Cambridge, 1923–39; 2nd and 3rd editions in progress).

ADAB	J. Naveh and S. Shaked, *Aramaic Documents from Ancient Bactria*, Corpus Inscriptionum Iranicarum 1.V (London, 2009)
Austin	M. M. Austin, *The Hellenistic World from Alexander to the Roman Conquest* (Cambridge, 1981)
Beloch	K. J. Beloch, *Griechische Geschichte*, 2nd edn., 4 vols. (Strasbourg, Berlin, Leipzig, 1912–27)
Berve	H. Berve, *Das Alexanderreich auf prospographischer Grundlage*, 2 vols. (Munich, 1926)
BHAch I	P. Briant, *Bulletin d'Histoire Achéménide*, vol. i, *Topoi* suppl. 1 (1997), pp. 5–127
BHAch II	P. Briant, *Bulletin d'histoire Achéménide*, vol. ii (Paris, 2001)
CAH	*Cambridge Ancient History*
CAH[2]	*Cambridge Ancient History*, 2nd edn.
CDCC	G. Shipley, J. Vanderspoel, D. Mattingly, and L. Foxhall (eds.), *The Cambridge Dictionary of Classical Civilization* (Cambridge, 200)
CIG	*Corpus Inscriptorium Graecarum* (Berlin, 1825–1977)
FdX	H. Metzger et al., *Fouilles de Xanthos*, vol. vi : *La stèle trilingue du Létôon* (Paris, 1973)

FGrH	F. Jacoby, *Die Fragmente der griechischen Historiker*, vols. i–ii (Berlin, 1923–6); vol. iii (Leiden, 1940–58)
Hammond–Griffith	N. G. L. Hammond and G. T. Griffith, *A History of Macedonia*, vol. ii: *555–336 BC* (Oxford, 1979)
Hammond–Walbank	N. G. L. Hammond and F. W. Walbank, *A History of Macedonia*, vol. iii: *336–167 BC* (Oxford, 1988)
Heckel	W. Heckel, *Who's Who in the Age of Alexander the Great* (Oxford, 2006)
HPE	P. Briant, *From Cyrus to Alexander: A History of the Persian Empire* (Winona Lake, IN, 2002)
IG	*Inscriptiones Graecae*
IGR	*Inscriptiones Graecae ad res Romanas pertinentes* (Paris, 1911–27)
ISE	L. Moretti (ed.), *Iscrizioni storiche ellenistiche* (Florence, 1967–76)
*OCD*³	*Oxford Classical Dictionary*, 3rd edn., rev. by S. Hornblower and A. Spawforth (Oxford, 2003)
OGIS	W. Dittenberger, *Orientis Graeci Inscriptiones Selectae*, 2 vols. (Leipzig, 1903–5)
P. Köln	*Kölner Papyri* (Opladen, 1976–)
P. Oxy	*The Oxyrhynchus Papyri* (London, 1898–)
RC	C. Bradford Welles, *Royal Correspondence in the Hellenistic Period* (London, 1934)
RE	Pauly-Wissowa-Kroll, *Realencyclopedaedia der classischen Altertumswissenschaft* (Stuttgart, 1894–1980)
Rhodes–Osborne	P. J. Rhodes and R. Osborne (eds.), *Greek Historical Inscriptions, 404–323 BC* (Oxford, 2003)
RTP	P. Briant, *Rois, tributs et paysans* (Paris, 1982)
SEG	*Supplementum Epigraphicum Graecum* (Leiden, 1923–)
*SIG*³	W. Dittenberger, *Sylloge Inscriptionum Graecarum*, 3rd edn., 4 vols. (Leipzig, 1921–4)
Tarn	W. W. Tarn, *Alexander the Great*, 2 vols. (Cambridge, 1948)
Tod	M. N. Tod, *A Selection of Greek Historical Inscriptions*, 2 vols. (Oxford, 1933–48)

Journal and Serial Abbreviations

Titles of periodical literature are generally abbreviated in accordance with those listed in *L'Année philologique*.

A&A	*Antike und Abendland*
AAWW	*Anzeiger der Österreicheschen Akademie der Wisenschaften in Wien*
ABull	*Art Bulletin*
AC	*L'Antiquité classique*
AchH	*Achaemenid History*
AClass	*Acta Classica*
AFLFB	*Annali della Facoltà di Lettere e Filosofia, Università degli Studi di Bari*
AFP	*Archiv für Papyrusforschung*
AHB	*The Ancient History Bulletin*
AHR	*American Historical Review*
AJA	*American Journal of Archaeology*
AJAH	*American Journal of Ancient History*
AJN	*American Journal of Numismatics*
AJPh	*American Journal of Philology*
AK	*Antike Kunst*
AKG	*Archiv für Kulturgeschichte*
AM	*Ancient Macedonia*
AMIT	*Archäologische Mitteilungen aus Iran*
AncSoc	*Ancient Society*
AncW	*Ancient World*
Annales (HSS)	*Annales: histoire, sciences, sociales*
ANRW	*Aufstieg und Niedergang der römischen Welt*
AOAT	Alter Orient und Altes Testament

AOS	American Oriental Society
ASNP	*Annali della Scuola Normale Superiore di Pisa*
BCH	*Bulletin de correspondance hellénique*
BiOr	*Bibliotheca Orientalis*
BMCR	*Bryn Mawr Classical Review*
Bullsoc Arch. Alex.	*Bulletin de la Société Archéologique d' Alexandrie*
CA	*Classical Antiquity*
C&M	*Classica et Medievalia*
CISA	*Contributi dell'Istituto di Storia Antica*
CJ	*Classical Journal*
CPh	*Classical Philology*
CQ	*Classical Quarterly*
CR	*Classical Review*
CRAI	*Comptes Rendus de l'Académie des Inscriptions et Belles-Lettres*
DHA	*Dialogues d'histoire ancienne*
EA	*Epigraphica Anatolica*
EVO	*Egitto e Vicino Oriente*
G&R	*Greece and Rome*
GJ	*Geographical Journal*
GRBS	*Greek, Roman and Byzantine Studies*
HSCPh	*Harvard Studies in Classical Philology*
IA	*Iranica Antiqua*
ICS	*Illinois Classical Studies*
IEJ	*Israel Exploration Journal*
INJ	*Israel Numismatic Journal*
JAOS	*Journal of the American Oriental Society*
JBerlMus	*Jahrbuch der Berliner Museen*
JCS	*Journal of Cuneiform Studies*
JDAI	*Jahrbuch des Deutschen Archäologischen Instituts*
JHS	*Journal of Hellenic Studies*
JNES	*Journal of Near Eastern Studies*
JNFA	*Journal of Numismatic Fine Arts*
JS	*Journal des Savants*
LCM	*Liverpool Classical Monthly*
MAAR	*Memoirs of the American Academy in Rome*
MDAI(A)	*Mitteilungen des Deutschen Archäologischen Instituts (Athen)*
MDAI(R)	*Mitteilungen des Deutschen Archäologischen Instituts (Rom)*
NC	*Numismatic Chronicle*
OLP	*Orientalia Lovaniensia Periodica*
OLZ	*Orientalistische Literaturzeitung*
P&P	*Past and Present*
PACA	*Proceedings of the African Classical Association*
PAPhS	*Proceedings of the American Philosophical Society*
PBA	*Proceedings of the British Academy*

PEQ	*Palestine Exploration Quarterly*
PP	*La parola del passato*
QS	*Quaderni di storia*
QUCC	*Quaderni urbinati di cultura classica*
RA	*Revue archéologique*
REA	*Revue des études anciennes*
RF	*Rivista di filosofia*
RFIC	*Rivista di filologia e di istruzione classica*
RhM	*Rheinisches Museum für Philologie*
RIDA	*Revue Internationale des Droits de l'Antiquité*
RPh	*Revue de Philologie*
SIFC	*Studi Italiani di filologia classica*
SOsl	*Symbolae Osloenses*
StudClas	*Studia Classica*
TAPhA	*Transactions of the American Philological Association*
Trans.	*Transeuphratène*
YClS	*Yale Classical Studies*
ZA	*Zeitschrift für Assyriologie*
ZDPV	*Zeitschrift des deutschen Palästina-Vereins*
ZPE	*Zeitschrift für Papyrologie und Epigraphik*

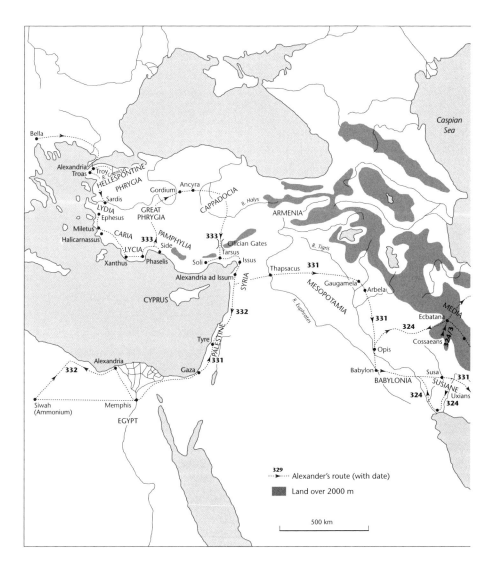

Caspian
Sea

Bella

Alexandria
Troas
Troy
R. Granicus
HELLESPONTINE
PHRYGIA
Sardis
LYDIA
Ephesus
GREAT
PHRYGIA
Gordium
Ancyra
CAPPADOCIA
R. Halys
ARMENIA

Miletus
Halicarnassus
CARIA
LYCIA
Xanthus
Phaselis
PAMPHYLIA
Side
333
333
Cilician Gates
Tarsus
Soli
Issus
R. Tigris
Thapsacus
331
Gaugamela
Arbela
MESOPOTAMIA
MEDIA
Ecbatana

Alexandria ad Issum

CYPRUS

SYRIA

332
R. Euphrates

331
Opis
Cossaeans

Tyre
PALESTINE
331
Gaza

Alexandria
Memphis
Babylon
BABYLONIA
Susa
SUSIANE
Uxians
331

332
Siwah
(Ammonium)
EGYPT
324
324
324

329
········► Alexander's route (with date)

▓▓▓ Land over 2000 m

500 km

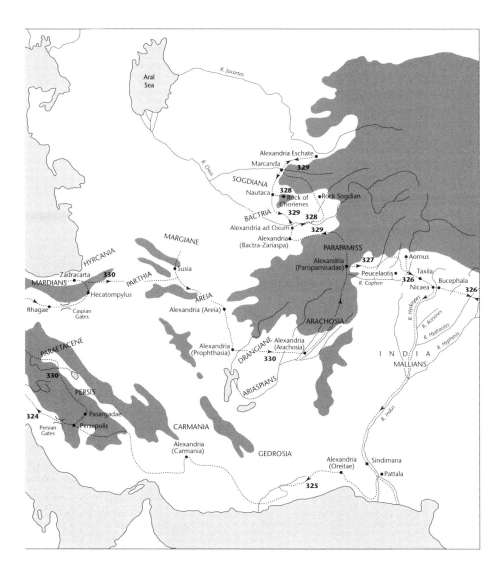

Aral
Sea

R. Jaxartes

R. Oxus

Alexandria Eschate
Marcanda
329
SOGDIANA
Nautaca
328
Rock of
Chorienes
Rock Sogdian
BACTRIA
329
328
Alexandria ad Oxum
329
Alexandria
(Bactra-Zariaspa)
MARGIANE
PARAPAMISS
Alexandria
(Paropamisadae)
327
Aornus
HYRCANIA
Susia
Peucelaotis
Taxila
Zadracarta
330
PARTHIA
R. Cophen
326
Nicaea
Bucephala
MARDIANS
AREIA
326
Hecatompylus
Rhagae
Caspian
Gates
Alexandria (Areia)
ARACHOSIA
R. Hydaspes
R. Acesines
R. Hydraotes
R. Hyphasis
Alexandria
(Prophthasia)
DRANGIANE
Alexandria
(Arachosia)
I N D I A
PARAETACENE
330
MALLIANS
330
PERSIS
ARIASPIANS
Pasargadae
R. Indus
324
Persian
Gates
Persepolis
CARMANIA
Alexandria
(Carmania)
GEDROSIA
Alexandria
(Oreitae)
Sindimana
Pattala
325

Introduction

When Blackwell's Al Bertrand first suggested that I edit a volume of new papers on Alexander the Great, it was believed that a "Guide" or "Companion" to the study of the famous conqueror would serve as a useful background for readers attracted to the subject by the appearance of Oliver Stone's film *Alexander*. For once, my habitual lethargy proved beneficial; for the anticipated triumph of Stone's epic never materialized – and I leave it to readers to decide for themselves why this was so. The volume's title thus mutated into *Alexander the Great*: *A New History*, a change that is neither subtle nor unimportant. What, one may ask, is *new* in this *New History*? Is it even possible to say anything new? Again, readers will have or at least may form their own opinions, but some observations are worth making at the outset.

First of all, this book offers a collection of views on aspects of the history and life of Alexander, as well as on the kingdom from which he emerged and the empire he conquered, by a wide range of scholars – some providing a synthesis of arguments developed over many years of engagement with the subject (or, on occasion, of "engaging the enemy more closely" – for we are not all admirers of his alleged "greatness"), others presenting fresh new approaches to topics both familiar and less so. Neither the contributors nor the editors would agree in every case (or even whole-heartedly) with the conclusions reached in some or perhaps most of the chapters in this book, but all will recognize that the arguments presented here are based on reasoned interpretations of the (often complex) evidence. And it is precisely this healthy difference of opinion that keeps the study of Alexander fresh and, dare I say, new. The newness and appeal of this volume are, thus, to be found in its diversity and its combination of novel insights with breadth of coverage, of in-depth investigation with an appreciation of universal truths. The individual chapters are not intended primarily as surveys of scholarship, although they often provide this very thing; instead they offer thought-provoking insights into much discussed problems as well as new areas of study. Furthermore,

I have in recent months debated with myself whether it is not somewhat disingenuous to claim as "new" contributions which in some cases have been sitting on my desk for over four years, but again the newness resides in the arguments and their presentation rather than in the speed with which they have found their way into print.

This leads me to comment briefly on the evolution of this particular volume. As I mentioned above, the proposal came originally from Al Bertrand to me, but I soon found it desirable to invite – perhaps "beg" would be the more appropriate word – my friend Larry Tritle to join me as co-editor. We commissioned articles by German, French, and Italian scholars, and the need to translate these brought with it concomitant delays in publication. When it came to contributors who wrote in English, some withdrew – reluctantly and with apologies and ample warning – and another simply did not deliver or bother to forewarn the editors or offer an excuse. Hence, a further delay. Nevertheless, the final collection vindicates the adage that "good things come to those who wait," even when this means waiting for *A New History*. The volume, in its final form, combines narrative[1] with special studies, background and context with specific details, and a survey of older literature with the promise of new approaches. Some contributors have examined new areas without resorting to what might be considered "trendy" or being seduced by the need to be "sexy"; nor is there an excessive use of jargon (though, in one case, I would venture to say that one man's jargon is another woman's precision). Others have taken traditional approaches to subjects previously neglected. And, for those with a craving for scholarship so profound that only foreign expressions will suffice to define it, this volume offers *Quellenforschung*, *Wissenschaftsgeschichte*, and *Nachleben* in healthy doses. The book's range is geographically expansive and it stretches chronologically from the formative years of Persia and Macedon to the *annus mirabilis*, 2004, which witnessed the tragic non-event of Stone's *Alexander*, the inspiration for the countless "new" volumes that sounded to publishers very much like the clinking of "money in the bank," but proved to be nothing more than the echoing of an empty vault. Indeed, we have arrived too late to jump on the bandwagon. Just as well, for I would rather rock on my own than sink with the Stone.

                                                                          WH

Works on Alexander the Great, his life and times, his military achievements, are legion – scholarly, popular, military, and most recently cinematographic – and all this points to the ongoing interest in one of the ancient world's great figures, perhaps the greatest. All of this might prompt the question, What more could be said, can anything be new? The answer to this must be yes, as scholars and authors continually respond to Alexander from the perspective of their own time.

---

[1]   I would acknowledge, without a twinge of guilt, that my own contribution to the narrative section is the least new, being in fact a very slight reworking (by prearrangement with the publisher) of my contribution to K. Kinzl (ed.), *A Companion to the Classical Greek World* (Oxford: Blackwell, 2006).

I

In the early modern era, Alexander was a subject of interest to many authors as well as translators. Niccolò Machiavelli in *The Prince* refers to the Macedonian king and conqueror, titling one chapter (4) after him and elsewhere citing his generosity while also referring to his imitation of Achilles just as Caesar would imitate him.[2] The earliest translations of Plutarch's *Lives* including the *Alexander*, began in the sixteenth century, first into Latin (e.g., Politan, Melanchthon, on the continent; in England Sir John Cheke and Richard Pace) and then followed not long after by vernacular translations in virtually all the major European languages. Of these those of Jacques Amyot in France and Thomas North in England were perhaps most important as they made available as never before the life of Alexander, whose achievements would inspire others to great deeds.[3] At the same time, additional historical accounts, particularly those of Quintus Curtius (1470/1) and Arrian (1535) provided even more information which stimulated further the study of Alexander's life and achievements.[4]

The first detailed and modern scholarly treatment of Alexander appeared with the 1833 publication of Gustav Droysen's study of Alexander.[5] Droysen continued revisions to this work through the nineteenth century, and to the present day it is widely regarded that he not only single-handedly revolutionized the study of Alexander, but in doing so created a whole new field of ancient history, the Age of Hellenistic.[6] This view is now in need of revision, as Pierre Briant convincingly demonstrates in the pages that follow. A few years later in England, banker and parliamentarian George Grote began to publish *A History of Greece* in 1846, a work that concluded with an entire volume on Alexander that continues to be cited today.[7] Though a pronounced contemporary liberal temper and middle-class ethic characterizes his work, Grote weighs the evidence of the ancient authors carefully and his judgments are generally judicious.

[2] Machiavelli 1992: 12, 42, 45. Written in 1513 and published (officially) in 1532, Machiavelli's source for Alexander was the recently printed text of Q. Curtius (see below n. 3).

[3] On the translations and their publication see Russell 1973: 147–52. For detailed commentary to Plutarch's *Alexander* see Hamilton 1969. An accessible edition of Plutarch's *Alexander* (and related texts) is Scott-Kilvert 1973.

[4] Curtius: first edition is that of Spirensis (1470/1), possibly that which Machiavelli read for his references to Alexander in *The Prince* (see Whitfield in Machiavelli 1992: 198); many editions followed including those of Hedicke 1931 and Rolfe 1946, the latter with English translation. See also the English translation of Yardley and Heckel 1984. Arrian: first edition is that of Trincavalius (1535); many editions followed, including those of Roos and Wirth 1967–80 and Brunt 1976–83 (with English translation). Another readily available English translation of Arrian is de Sélincourt 1971.

[5] Readers might consult the introductions of Bosworth and Baynham 2000 and Bosworth 2002 which summarize the nature of the evidence for the study of Alexander and provide a historical overview. Cf. Roisman 2003a which offers neither.

[6] Droysen 1833, 1877. In this newly created field of Hellenistic civilization, see especially the work of Rostovtzeff 1941 and Green 1990.

[7] Grote 1846–56; citation is usually made from the 1888 "new" edn.

Since Droysen and Grote, their many contemporaries and students, research into Alexander has continued to explore the king's life and times, going beyond the mere military achievement and finding whole new subjects to consider. In the English-speaking world, scholars including E. Badian, A. B. Bosworth, E. D. Carney, P. Green, N. G. L. Hammond, W. Heckel, and W. W. Tarn have made numerous contributions to this investigation, as have P. Briant and P. Goukowsky (in French), H. Berve, F. Schachermeyr, U. Wilcken, and G. Wirth (in German).[8] The present collection of essays offers both a broad survey of the reign and conquests of Alexander, Greeks and Persians, as well as focused studies of his life and impact on those who followed.

II

We begin with the background of ancient Macedonia and Greece, and its world well beyond Alexander's life and reign. The historical narrative of Michael Zahrnt, Waldemar Heckel, and Patrick Wheatley examines the formation of the Macedonian kingdom under Philip and his immediate predecessors (Zahrnt), the conquests of Alexander (Heckel), and the Hellenistic world of Alexander's successors, the Diadochi (Wheatley). The story of Alexander's battles and conquests has certainly been told many times, but Heckel's narrative is at once familiar yet also refreshing and insightful. Alexander's death in Babylon led to a tumultuous and violent era that is often so confusing to students that it is dismissed as simply beyond comprehension. Pat Wheatley provides a concise discussion of this immensely difficult subject. He manages at the same time to give an overview of the sources for this period, including recent scholarly work on long neglected sources from the Near East that shed light on the notoriously difficult chronology of the period. New ideas of kingship that formed at this time are also examined.

Alexander could have accomplished nothing without one of the great armies of all time, and Waldemar Heckel, in a second essay, and Gregor Weber offer stimulating treatments of Alexander, his army, and court. Exploring the nature of the army – where its men came from and also the relationship between commander and commanded – Heckel offers an interpretation of Alexander's leadership and command abilities that readers will find stimulating and provocative. Alexander also inherited a court from his father Philip, and Weber shows how, during the course of his reign and conquest, this court changed along with the king. Persian institutions as well as representation entered the Macedonian court, making it different. The court also became permanent as the source of power of a monarch who is at once Greek and Macedonian as he is also Persian.

Alexander inherited not only his kingdom from his father but also a complex web of connections to the Greeks whom Philip had defeated at Chaeronea in 338/7.

---

[8]   Readers can find references to the works of these scholars in the bibliography to this book.

These relationships are examined by Elisabetta Poddighe and Lawrence Tritle, looking at two very different dimensions of these. As Philip planned his attack on the Persian empire, he established an alliance and league, what we now know as the Corinthian League, to create stability and order in Greece while campaigning. Leadership of this fell to Alexander, inheriting his father's title as *hegemon*. Poddighe examines the sometimes sensitive dealings between king and League, arguing that Alexander mostly maintained a diplomatically proper relationship with the Greeks. This changed somewhat upon his return to Babylon in 324, especially for Athens which disputed the king's call for "freedom" in Greece which for Athens meant loss of the island of Samos as its exiled population would now return home. Not all Greeks, however, saw Alexander and the Macedonians as oppressors. Many, thousands even, benefited and profited from Alexander and the Macedonian conquests, and participated in the great adventure into the Persian east, joining Alexander as soldiers and bureaucrats, artists and entertainers, of all kinds. Tritle identifies these, discussing and analyzing their associations with Alexander and his army.

The Persians, of course, suffered defeat and ignominy at Alexander's hands. Pierre Briant sheds light on this defeat, first looking at the state of affairs in the empire as Alexander invaded, then turns to history of the history of Alexander's Persian conquest. R. G. Collingwood in his *Idea of History* (1946) discussed what he called "second order history," or the history of history, and how present ideas shaped understanding of the past. In a penetrating study, Briant traces the origins of many of the ideas common to Alexander studies, placing them within the context of European intellectual history from before the Enlightenment to the twentieth century.

Conquering an empire is the work of great men, and few compare with Alexander. But what kind of a man was he? Three essays examine Alexander's family life and his transition from man to virtually godlike stature. Elizabeth Carney and Daniel Ogden look at the man Alexander, but from very different perspectives. Carney investigates Alexander's relations with his mother Olympias and her formative influences upon him. Slightly different is Ogden's approach, which examines Alexander's sexuality, placing it in the wider context of what sex in the ancient world was all about and what it would have meant to Alexander. Whatever one might say of Alexander's relationship with his mother and with men and women, there is certainty in his heroics on the battlefield and in his conquests. These clearly set him apart from those around him and during his reign and conquests his heroic stature grew by leaps and bounds. Along with this rise in his larger-than-life status, there came to be established in his honor, and to enable his rule over those he conquered, many cults and festivals throughout the lands he touched. Boris Dreyer traces the evolution of the man to demigod status, and the establishment of his cults and festivals, many of which continued to be observed for hundreds of years after his death and those of his successors.

This heroic stature survives into our own time. The impact and tradition of Alexander into later times is the subject of four essays by Alexander Meeus, Diana

Spencer, Catie Mihalopoulos, and Elizabeth Baynham, all examining later images of Alexander. Meeus begins with a stimulating reinterpretation of the image of Alexander that was already taking shape in the era of the Successors. This continued, as Spencer shows, with the Romans who were at once appalled and amazed at what Alexander had achieved. Best known perhaps is the famous antagonist of Julius Caesar, Pompey "the Great" who styled himself after Alexander as seen in his portrait and in literature, particularly Plutarch's *Life of Pompey*. On a much broader level, Mihalopoulos investigates Alexander's impact on portraiture and what would become known as Hellenistic art as seen the surviving body of Greek originals and Roman copies. Finally, the Romans were just the beginning of later generations' fascination with Alexander. Alexander's accomplishments and person, Baynham shows, influenced the art and court of Louis XIV as seen in the famous paintings of Charles LeBrun which the Sun King commissioned. No less influential is the powerful allure of Alexander in modern film. The interpretation of Alexander screened by Oliver Stone early in the twenty-first century, despite its commercial failure, makes plain not only the ongoing public interest in history and one of its biggest stars, but also the constant presence of the past.[9]

LAT

---

[9]   While Oliver Stone's film may be deserving of criticism, its depictions of the Macedonian phalanx and cavalry deploying at Gaugamela, the drunken brawl that cost Cleitus the Black his life at Alexander's hands, are exemplary. This is in contrast to the 1956 film *Alexander the Great*, starring Richard Burton.

1

The Macedonian Background

Michael Zahrnt

"No Alexander if not for Philip" is true in more than just biological terms. Alexander's triumphant conquests would not have been possible without Philip's achievements, namely, the enormous expansion and consolidation of the Macedonian kingdom, with the removal of any danger posed by the Greek states or neighboring barbarians, and the development of an army ready to strike and a capable and loyal officer corps.[1] But Philip did not create Macedonia from nothing, despite what ancient authors and modern scholars suggest: he inherited a kingdom which while it had experienced many ups and downs over three centuries had always survived and – given stable internal affairs and favorable external circumstances – represented a power that was recognized and at times even courted by others.[2]

It all started from small beginnings around the middle of the seventh century, south of that part of the Thermaic Gulf which in those days extended far west inland.[3] There, on both sides of the Haliacmon, lay a region called Makedonis and within it – on the northern slopes of the Pierian mountains – the original Macedonian capital Aegae. It was from here that the Macedonians conquered Pieria, the coastal plain east of the Pierian mountains and the Olympus, as well as Bottiaea, the region extending west and north of the Thermaic Gulf up to the Axius, with the future capital Pella. Next they crossed the Axius and occupied the plain between this river and present-day Thessaloniki. Thus they established control over the whole area around the Gulf and finally, just before the end of the sixth century, they also took over the regions of Eordaea and Almopia which bordered the central plain on the western and northwestern sides. The capture of Eordaea, beyond the mountain ridge sealing off the plain to the west, allowed the Macedonian kings to

[1]   The author wishes to thank Dr. Kathrin Lüddecke for the English translation.
[2]   For more recent studies of Macedonian history up to the time of Philip II see Hammond 1972; Hammond–Griffith; Errington 1990; Borza 1990, 1999.
[3]   Zahrnt 1984.

Figure 1.1   Bust of Alexander the Great, *c.*340–330 BC (copy?), as a youth. Acropolis Museum, Athens. Photo: Scala/Art Resource, New York.

reach further into upper Macedonia, where the regions of Lyncus, Orestis, and Elimeia lay, enclosed by mountains and with their own rulers, whose adherence to the Macedonian kingdom was dependent on the strength of its central rule at any one time. It is impossible now to ascertain when the Macedonian kings first approached these mountain areas, while the further expansion toward the east falls into the period after the failure of Xerxes' campaign.

The early days of Macedonian history are obscure. The first certain reports relate to the time of Persian rule on European soil: around 510 the Persian general Megabazus conquered the area along the northern coast of the Aegean and accepted the surrender of the Macedonian king Amyntas I. During the Ionian Revolt the Macedonians too shook off Persian sovereignty, which was restored as early as 492. Amyntas' son Alexander I therefore participated in Xerxes' campaign as a subject of the Great King.[4] Immediately after the Persian defeat at Plataea, Alexander defected and took possession of the regions of Anthemus, Mygdonia, Crestonia, and Bisaltia which lay between the Axius and Strymon. However, in the final years of his reign he sustained losses on the western banks of the Strymon.

---

[4]   On Macedonia during the Persian Wars see Zahrnt 1992.

His successor, Perdiccas II, who ruled until 413, was not only unable to reverse the losses in the east but also had to contend with the endeavors of the rulers of upper Macedonia to establish independence. Moreover, in his time Macedonia was impeded by the Athenian naval empire and drawn into the conflicts of the Peloponnesian War. But Perdiccas was able to maneuver a way through the warring factions fairly successfully and thus for the most part to maintain the independence of his kingdom.

His son Archelaus was destined for a happier rule, since Athenian pressure had eased after the Sicilian disaster. Relations with the Athenians were virtually reversed as they relied on Macedonian timber for shipbuilding. Archelaus' real contributions lay in domestic politics, his cultural efforts and military reforms. Not only did he accelerate the extension of the road network, but he also initiated the development of a heavily armed infantry which, as shown by the events of the Peloponnesian War, was yet lacking in Macedonia. In the final years of his rule Archelaus was able even to intervene in Thessaly in favor of the imperiled noble family of the Aleuadae, to gain territory and secure his influence in Larisa.[5] The right conditions for further extending Macedonian control were therefore in place when Archelaus was murdered in 399.

"Macedonian kings tended to die with their boots on"[6] – and indeed the years from 399 to 359 were marked by turmoil and disputed successions during which the position that Macedonia had gained under Archelaus could not be retained. It was only in the latter half of these forty years that Macedonia was once more strengthened internally and enjoyed a degree of external authority, and we shall see when and why this became possible.

However, before that period, the Macedonians saw no fewer than four rulers within the six years, of whom we know little except that most of them came to a violent end and that the kingdom lost territories under them, at least in the east. We can picture Macedonia's troubles more clearly in the first years of the rule of Amyntas III, who ascended the throne in 393.[7] Soon after, Amyntas came under threat from the Illyrians and entered into a defensive alliance with the Chalcidian League which had become an important power on the north coast of the Aegean; he paid for this by ceding the Anthemus, the fertile valley southeast of present-day Thessaloniki. This alliance, however, did not save him from being temporarily expelled from his country. Only in the second half of the 380s was Amyntas secure enough to reclaim from the Chalcidians the land that he had ceded. Not only did they refuse to return it, but they for their part intervened in Macedonian affairs and forced Amyntas to turn to the Spartans who sent an army north in 382. The Olynthian War which began thus was, according to Xenophon's report, fought mainly by the Spartans and their allies. The Macedonians did not contribute any military force worth mentioning, although Derdas, ruler of the Elimeia, and his

[5]   Westlake 1935: 51–9.
[6]   Carney 1983: 260.
[7]   On Amyntas III see Zahrnt, forthcoming.

cavalry provided useful support. Derdas and his territory are portrayed as being independent of the Macedonian king, and the other upper Macedonian kingdoms appear to have broken away at that time. In 379 the Chalcidian League was dissolved. Amyntas regained the Anthemus, but, according to Xenophon, the Spartans did little otherwise to strengthen the rule of the Macedonian king.[8]

Isocrates, a slightly older contemporary of Xenophon, however, took quite a different view. In his *Panegyricus*, published in 380, he castigates Spartan politics of the time with harsh words, introducing as one example among others that the Spartans had helped to extend the rule of the Macedonian king Amyntas, the Sicilian tyrant Dionysius, and the Great King (126). If Isocrates wished to remain credible in his condemnation of Spartan politics, he could not have included a completely insignificant Macedonian king in his trio of those then in power on the boundaries of the world of the Greek *poleis*. Therefore in 380 Amyntas must have been a political power not to be despised, even if in previous years he had suffered domestic and external problems. Isocrates also had something to say about this when he published his *Archidamus* in the 360s. Here Amyntas serves as a perfect example of what can be achieved by sheer determination: after he had been vanquished by his barbarian neighbors and robbed of all Macedonia, he regained his whole realm within three months and ruled without interruption into ripe old age (46). Isocrates could make such an assertion only if Amyntas was recognized as a ruler to be reckoned with even after his death.

In the context of a trial in 343, the Athenian Aeschines similarly identifies Amyntas as a political figure of some significance, when he records that Amyntas had been represented by a delegate at a Panhellenic congress (of which there were three between 375 and 371) but had full power over that delegate's vote (2.32). According to this, Amyntas III was regarded as a full member of the community of Greek states at least toward the end of the 370s. The Athenians had already regarded him as such a little earlier in the 370s when they entered into an alliance with him (*SIG*[3] 157; Tod 129), the details of which unfortunately are not known, but which was probably connected to the expansion of Athenian naval power at the time. We know that in the year 375 the ship timber required came from Macedonia (Xen. *Hell.* 6.1.11). Macedonian ship timber was clearly once more in demand, and therefore the initiative to reach an agreement is likely to have come from the Athenians. In any case this agreement provides additional evidence that Macedonia had again joined the circle of states able to pursue their own policies.

Amyntas' son Philip II is unwittingly responsible for the negative picture which both later sources and modern scholars have painted of him. In fact, Philip not only eclipsed the achievements of his predecessors, but also induced contemporary writers such as Theopompus, and later universal historians like Diodorus and modern historians, to portray him as almost the god-sent savior of a Macedonia sunk into chaos. Amyntas, with his stamina and energy, had already slowly overcome the disorder following Archelaus' murder, although he also benefited from

---

[8] Xen. *Hell.* 5.2.11–24, 37–43; 3.1–9, 18–19, 26; cf. D.S. 15.20.3–23.3.

the shifts in power around Macedonia, and he left his sons a fairly well-secured kingdom when he died in 370/69.

The general state of affairs remained essentially favorable to the further rise of Macedonian power for his successors. But inner stability and continuity in the succession were needed as well as favorable external conditions. That it had taken Amyntas more than ten years to rebuild the kingdom, and that previously six years of disputes over the succession had been sufficient to bring Macedonia to the brink of disaster, show how quickly what had been achieved could be jeopardized. However, at this point a period of internal turmoil and struggle for the throne, as well of major external interference, soon commenced once more.

The succession of 370/69 went smoothly: Alexander II, the eldest son from Amyntas' marriage to Eurydice, came to the throne, which in itself shows that Amyntas had again established order. The Illyrians, however, were of a different mind and invaded Macedonia. Pausanias, a relation of the ruling house who lived in exile, used the resulting absence of the young king to invade the country from the east. In this predicament the king's mother Eurydice turned to the Athenian general Iphicrates who had been dispatched to win back Amphipolis and asked him for help. Iphicrates, gladly taking the opportunity to place the Macedonian king under an obligation, succeeded in expelling Pausanias.[9]

With this Alexander's rule was secured, particularly since he had managed to ward off the Illyrian threat. The young king also began to assume the external status his father had achieved in his last year of rule, for the Thessalian Aleuadae called on his support against the tyrant Alexander of Pherae. The Macedonian king appeared with his army in Larisa, was allowed to enter the town, and took the castle after a short siege. Crannon likewise fell into his hands shortly afterward. But instead of handing over the towns to the Thessalian nobility, he kept them himself and installed garrisons in them. This turn of events was not what the Thessalian nobles had expected; they therefore turned to the Thebans who sent Pelopidas to their aid. Pelopidas marched north with an army and liberated Crannon and Larisa from Macedonian rule.

In the mean time Alexander II had been forced to return to Macedonia, for his brother-in-law Ptolemaeus had risen against him. Both parties turned to Pelopidas and called on him to be the arbiter. In order to insure that his arrangements would last and to retain a bargaining tool against the Macedonian king, Pelopidas received Alexander's youngest brother Philip and thirty sons from the leading families as hostages. Thus the position of power gained under Amyntas III and inherited by Alexander II was quickly lost again and the country once more came under the influence of the then predominant power in Greece, but this was also due to their own mistakes. The state of affairs was to continue for some time. As soon as Pelopidas departed after settling the internal dispute, Alexander II was killed in the winter of 369/8.

---

[9]   On the history of Macedonia during the Theban hegemony see Hatzopoulos 1985.

As one of the closest male relatives, Ptolemaeus became guardian of Perdiccas, Alexander's younger brother, and assumed the reins of government. The friends of the murdered ruler, however, regarded him as a usurper and in the summer of 368 turned to Pelopidas, who once more entered Macedonia. Ptolemaeus was forced to declare himself ready to come to an arrangement and to undertake to safeguard the rule for Alexander's brothers, Perdiccas and Philip. Moreover, he had to agree to an alliance with Thebes and surrender his son and fifty nobles as hostages to guarantee his loyalty. Once more Macedonia was at the mercy of external forces, and again as a result of internal turmoil.

In 365 Perdiccas III succeeded in ridding himself of his guardian Ptolemaeus. Soon after assuming his rule, he decided to make common cause with the Athenians, to work with their commander Timotheus who was operating off the Macedonian coastline, and to take joint action with him against the Chalcidians and Amphipolis. Timotheus gained Potidaea and Torone on the Chalcidian peninsula, but was unable to achieve anything against Amphipolis. Soon afterward, the Athenians sent a cleruchy to Potidaea in order to secure his new acquisition, which occupied a strategic position.

Working with Timotheus is likely to have opened the Macedonian king's eyes to the Athenians' political ambitions for power and their by this time very limited capabilities, and to have strengthened his self-confidence, for he soon defected from them and secured Amphipolis through a garrison. Thus Perdiccas ended up on hostile terms with both the Athenians and the Chalcidians, who were themselves also at war with each other, and Athens' power continued to wane. Overall Macedonia was again on the rise, after the rightful ruler had assumed the throne in Perdiccas and overcome initial problems. He was now able to begin to consolidate the kingdom and to secure it externally. As part of this, he also appears to have reasserted control over the upper Macedonian kingdoms. He also resolved to stop the Illyrians, who had plagued Macedonia since the times of Amyntas III, but was at last defeated in a great battle and fell with 4,000 of his men.

In this situation Perdiccas' brother Philip proceeded with determination, military ability, and diplomatic skill, first to stabilize Macedonia, and then to pursue a course of expansion by making the most of each opportunity as it presented itself.[10] He was able to eliminate the pretenders to the throne who almost always quickly appeared in Macedonia in such circumstances; his next step was to secure the borders of the kingdom and their immediate approaches. In this he benefited from the situation in Greece: the Spartans, who acted as if they had been the masters of Greece for some time and had even intervened in the years 382–379 in favor of the

---

[10]   On Philip II and the sources for his reign see (in addition to the works cited above): Ellis 1976; Cawkwell 1978; Griffith in Hammond–Griffith 210–726; Hatzopoulos and Loukopoulou 1980; Hammond 1994b: 11–17; Bradford 1992; McQueen 1995; Hammond 1994a. Since no continuous account of Philip's history exists apart from the incomplete report in Diodorus' sixteenth book and Justin's rather unreliable statements (books 7–9), the evidence has to be collated from the most diverse ancient sources; therefore these references are not provided when discussing diplomatic and military events, and readers are referred instead to the studies mentioned.

then Macedonian king, had been eliminated as a leading power since their defeat at Leuctra (371) and limited to the Peloponnese in their political ambitions. From 357 to 355 the Athenians were entangled in conflicts with some of their allies, and the Second Athenian Confederacy was falling apart. The Thebans' power likewise was crumbling: where ten years earlier they had still exerted crucial influence as far as Macedonia and even on the Peloponnese, now even their attempt at chastising the insubordinate Phocians failed. Instead, these occupied the sanctuary of Delphi in the early summer of 356 and proceeded to form a large army of mercenaries with the help of its treasures and to hold their own against the other members of the Amphictyony. Finally, the situation in Thrace was also advantageous for Philip after its king Cotys, who had succeeded in reuniting the kingdom, was murdered in the summer of 360 and Thrace was broken up into three parts in the subsequent battle for the succession. Thus the 350s saw convincing successes by Philip on all borders of his kingdom.

The borders to the west and north caused the fewest problems: Philip had already marched against the Illyrians in the early summer of 358, forcing them to cede substantial territories up to Lake Ochrid. When two years later the Illyrian king allied himself with the Paeonians, Thracians, and Athenians against Philip, it was sufficient for Philip to send the experienced general Parmenion against him. After that the region was quiet for more than ten years, especially after another safeguard had been put in place toward the end of the 350s when Philip installed his brother-in-law Alexander as ruler in Epirus, turned the country into something resembling a satellite kingdom, and annexed the region of Parauaea, located between Epirus and Macedonia.[11] The Paeonians, who had settled midway on either side of the Axius, were neighbors who had hoped to gain at the expense of Macedon following the defeat of Perdiccas III. At the beginning Philip induced them to maintain peace by making both payments and promises but soon after he attacked, defeated, and brought them into line. In 356 the king of the Paeonians joined the coalition (see above), and shortly afterward his country was finally subjugated.

Philip began to turn east and to round off the area under his rule along the Macedonian coastline in 357. First, he captured Amphipolis, with its deposits of precious metals and timber, which controlled both the crossing over the Strymon and access to the interior of the country, and secured his new acquisition with a garrison; soon after he attacked Pydna on the Macedonian coast. The Athenians who at that time held Pydna and laid claim to Amphipolis declared war against him, but Philip responded to this by approaching the Chalcidian League, promising to acquire for them the Athenian cleruchy of Potidaea.[12] This was meant to happen in 356, but while still laying siege to the town Philip received a request for help from the Greek colony of Crenides, which lay in the hinterland of Neapolis (present-day Kavala), and which saw itself threatened by a Thracian king. Philip placed a

[11] On Philip's intervention in Epirus, see Errington 1976.
[12] On Amphipolis see Hatzopoulos 1991: 62ff., and on relations between Philip and the Chalcidian League Zahrnt 1971: 104ff.

garrison in the town which he refounded under the name of Philippi. By this he gained not only another foothold in the east, but also the opportunity to exploit the Pangaeum's rich deposits of precious metal.[13] The Thracian king in whose territory Philippi lay naturally joined the coalition, with the result that by the end of the year he was a vassal of Philip and the latter had extended his rule up to the Nestus. In the autumn of 355 Philip attacked Methone, Athens' last remaining foothold on his shores, and succeeded in forcing it to surrender after a prolonged siege. This represented not only a material but also a public relations victory, for the Athenians had not offered the town any help even though they had the means after the Social War came to an end. As a result, Philip thought a second attempt worth his while: in the spring of 353 he was active east of the Nestus, presumably in order to harm the Greek towns along the coast that were allied to Athens and to make an impression on the Thracian king who ruled this region. The outcome of this test, which was of limited duration, appears to have satisfied Philip: in the autumn of 352 he returned to Thrace and marched rapidly in stages across the Hebrus against Cersebleptes, who ruled the most easterly of the three Thracian kingdoms, and forced him to subordinate himself as vassal. We do not know to what extent this expedition was also aimed at the Athenian territories on the Thracian Chersonese, for Philip fell ill and had to curtail the campaign.

These activities served for the most part to safeguard and expand the Macedonian kingdom and were directed against Athens only among the Greek states. However, what secured a decisive influence over central Greece for Philip occurred between the two campaigns into middle and eastern Thrace. The energetic kings among his predecessors had always pursued three aims: to subjugate the rulers of upper Macedonia; to reach the mouth of the Strymon in order to secure the Bisaltia, which was rich in precious metals, and to alleviate the possibility of Athenian pressure on the coasts of their kingdom; and to extend their influence into Thessaly. Philip achieved the first two goals relatively quickly, and even surpassed his predecessors by not only placing the upper Macedonian territories under his rule, but also pushing the western border of Macedonia up to Lake Ochrid, and by reaching not only the Strymon in the east but as far as the Nestus, and bringing the precious metal deposits of the Pangaeum and of the Bisaltia under his control. He also gave his attention to the third objective and brought his influence to bear in Thessaly.[14] In this he was able to exploit the tensions between the Aleuadae in Larisa and the Thessalian League on the one hand and the tyrants of Pherae on the other: a first intervention took place as early as 358 and secured the position of his newly won friends among the Thessalian nobility. Philip intervened a second time in 355 in favor of the Thessalian League and thereby made it possible for it to commence a Sacred War jointly with the Thebans against the Phocians, who by now had been in Delphi for over a year without punishment. It appears that Philip had clearly understood that getting involved in central Greece might open up an opportunity

[13] On Philippi, Collart 1937 is still worth reading.
[14] Cf. Griffith 1970.

for him to gain influence by intervening personally, an influence which could then perhaps also be brought to bear against the Athenians.[15]

But the Sacred War came to an end in the autumn of 354. Philip saw no chance of personally intervening in it and turned against Thrace in the spring of 353. Then the hoped-for turn of events in central Greece did occur after all, in the form of an offensive by the Phocians under Onomarchus and a rekindling of the conflict between the Thessalians and the tyrants of Pherae. The latter turned to the Phocians, and the Thessalians to Philip. At first Philip experienced some success but then he suffered two defeats by Onomarchus and had to retreat to Macedonia. He returned in 352, had supreme command over the armies of the Thessalian League transferred to himself, and routed Onomarchus. Soon afterward Pherae and its port Pagasae fell; the *tyrannis* there came to an end. It would have been natural for Philip to use his military successes so far to legitimize his position as Thessalian supreme commander, and he therefore marched his troops against the Thermopylae which were being held by the Phocians, in order to deal a decisive blow against the temple robbers. However, this was no longer an issue which concerned only Philip, the Thessalians, and the Thebans on the one hand and the Phocians on the other. Control of the Thermopylae would have opened up the way south for the Macedonian king, and thus he found the pass occupied by troops of the Phocians, Athenians, Achaeans, and Spartans, as well as the tyrants who had been expelled from Pherae with their mercenaries. Philip had to withdraw again, and as a result the battles in central Greece continued without him, and the enemies wore each other out in these conflicts to his advantage. Thus he turned for some years to other issues in the north, to the situation in Thrace and Epirus and to his relations with the Chalcidian League, which had long ago ceased to be Philip's ally in his war against the Athenians and had become an alien element in the much enlarged Macedonia. The folly of alerting Philip to this fact through insubordination presented him with a reason to intervene and led to the destruction of Olynthus in 348, the dissolution of the League, and the annexation of its territory. A military alliance with the Athenians, sealed in the summer of 349, was not enough to save the Chalcidians.

Indeed, throughout these years the Athenians had not managed to achieve military success against Philip. He for his part had not only refrained from seriously pursuing the Athenians, but had even repeatedly signaled his desire for peace by indications to this effect or even clear offers. However, his military activities decreased noticeably after 352, without his relinquishing his aim to wield decisive influence in Greece. But Philip could afford to wait. When the Phocians at last conceded defeat in 346, they informed him of their capitulation, and it was owing to him that the conditions turned out to be less harsh than had been demanded by some members of the Amphictyony.[16] Philip could believe that he had resolved the situation in central Greece in a manner beneficial to himself. He was already assured of lasting influence in the region by his having been given both of the Phocian votes

---

[15] On the so-called Third Sacred War, see Buckler 1989.
[16] On the Phocians' contract of capitulation with Philip II, see Bengtson 1975: ii. 318–19.

in the Amphictyonic council and by also being able to call on those of the Thessalians and their neighbors.

Shortly before this, in the spring of 346, peace had also been agreed with the Athenians, on the basis of the status quo.[17] The Athenians thus had to concede Amphipolis and other places along the Macedonian–Thracian coast that had been lost; in return Philip guaranteed their ownership of the Thracian Chersonese which was crucial to Athenian survival. He demonstrated to the Athenians that this was very obliging of him while yet negotiating the Peace of Philocrates: as deliberations about the conditions he had proposed at Pella took place in Athens, he led a surprise campaign against Cersebleptes and forced him again to acknowledge Macedonian sovereignty. From here it would have been a stone's throw to the Chersonese. Despite having once more demonstrated his military supremacy, Philip granted the Athenians a comparatively favorable peace in 346.[18]

However, it soon become apparent that Philip's expectations of the Peace of 346 had been too high and that it was impossible for him to strengthen his own influence in Greece at the same time as developing good relations with the Athenians.[19] On the face of it, over the next years he limited himself to securing and consolidating his rule in the north: in 345 he led a campaign against the Illyrians, and in 344 he executed some military operations in Thessaly. In the winter of 343/2 he arrived in Epirus, took some Greek cities on the coast for its ruler and thus bound him to himself more closely. Next, administrative reforms were implemented in Thessaly which allowed Philip to exert an even tighter grip on the country. Once the south (i.e., Thessaly), the southwest (i.e., Epirus), and the northwest (i.e., the Illyrian border) had been secured, the Thracian campaign of the years 342/1 could commence.

South of Thessaly Philip had not looked to expand the territory over which he ruled, yet he did not abstain from extending his influence there as well. At the same time he continued to court the Athenians and endeavored to avoid coming into conflict with them. He proved this for the first time in the autumn of 346 when the Athenians did not contribute to his campaign against the Phocians despite their alliance with him, did not send a representative to the Amphictyonic council, and offered an even greater provocation by omitting to send an official delegation to the Pythian Games which were being held under Philip's stewardship for the first time. In view of the Athenians' pro-Phocian attitude during the ten-year-long

---

[17] Overview of the sources in Bengtson 1975: ii. 312ff.

[18] According to Markle 1974 and Ellis 1982, Philip even had the intention of weakening the Thebans in favor of the Athenians in 346 (which, as we shall see later, did indeed happen after the battle at Chaeroneia), but these plans had been thwarted by the machinations of Athenian politicians. The two speeches that Demosthenes and Aeschines made three years later during the trial against the latter are our main sources for the agreement of the Peace of Philocrates; and since they both spoke on their own behalf and were not always particular about the truth, even in later statements, we cannot discover Philip's real intentions with certainty, but, as we shall see later, the Macedonian king was already at pains to be on friendly terms with the Athenians even at the time.

[19] On what follows see Wüst 1938, as well as Perlman 1973; Ryder 1994.

Sacred War and the general sentiment among the Amphictyons, it would have been easy for Philip to decide in favor of another Sacred War, this time against the Athenians. However, Philip not only refrained from a military advance against the Athenians, but even secured a resolution by the Amphictyonic council a little later which took their interests into account. On the other hand in 344 he supported Sparta's enemies in the Peloponnese both financially and by dispatching mercenaries, which provoked an Athenian counter-delegation to the Peloponnese led by Demosthenes.

This illustrates Philip's dilemma which finally led him to change his approach. Developing a good understanding with the Athenians was not easy after the blows they had been dealt over the years. His attempts to extend his own influence in Greece also cast a shadow over relations with the Athenians and hindered a *rapprochement*. Philip began by courting them, and in the winter of 344/3 offered to negotiate with them in revising the peace treaty of 346, but the negotiations foundered on the Athenians' exaggerated demands. Philip reacted in the following year, 343, by once again exerting influence over the internal affairs of Greek cities, that is, Elis, Megara and Euboea, two of which lay in close proximity to Athens. He followed this warning shot by approaching the Athenians in early 342 with a renewed offer to improve relations. When he was again rebuffed he realized that an encounter to settle the matter once and for all could not be avoided, but he insured that he would determine the circumstances in which this was to take place. He proceeded to conquer Thrace, which until then had stood in a relation of loose dependency upon Macedonia, in order to annex the whole region up to the straits. With it under his control, it was possible to bring the Athenians to their knees.

However, the campaign against Thrace was aimed not only at the Athenians. In 344 the Great King had regained Cyprus, in 343 Phoenicia, and news of Persian military preparations that came to Philip led him to expect a reconquest of Egypt.[20] While this was not an alarming prospect, given the reputation of the Persian empire in recent decades, which appeared to pose no threat to Macedonia, a newly consolidated Persian empire might well change the equilibrium of power in the Aegean. By expanding his own authority up to the straits, Philip thought to prevent this. In the summer of 341 the conquest of Thrace was complete, but Philip appears to have remained in this country for another winter in order to implement administrative measures.

Philip was not the only one who thought the decisive confrontation with the Athenians was unavoidable, however little he relished the prospect. Demosthenes likewise saw no other solution but war, but, in contrast to Philip, he purposefully worked toward it. He inflamed the situation by provocation and finally in the spring of 340 managed to establish a Hellenic League directed against Philip; besides Athens, this (purely defensive) alliance included the cities of Euboea, Megara, Corinth with its colonies Leucas and Corcyra, as well as Achaea and Acarnania.

---

[20] On the situation in the Persian empire at the time, see Zahrnt 1983.

In the mean time Philip led his troops against Perinthus which he was unable to take, in particular because it received support from the Byzantians and the Persian satraps on the eastern shore of the Propontis. In the autumn of 340 he attempted a raid on Byzantium with part of his troops. In his vicinity cruised the Athenian general Chares, whose task was to provide safe conduct into and through the Aegean for the grain ships arriving from the Black Sea region, and who met with the Persian generals for a conference while this fleet assembled. By now Philip must have been convinced that war was inevitable, and the fleet that was so easily within his reach was so tempting that he could not wait for another such opportunity for an entire year. He seized it during Chares' absence and thereby – in addition to gaining rich booty – provoked the Athenian declaration of war. That this would be the consequence must have been obvious to him. The question is only whether he wished to overcome the Athenians in battle or whether, by striking against the grain fleet, he did not also wish to convince them of their inferiority at sea. In any case, he did not at first concern himself with the Athenians but continued his maneuvers against Byzantium. This city, however, was now successfully supported by the Athenians, and Philip was forced to put an end to his operations in early 339. But instead of marching against the Athenians he campaigned against the Scythians near the mouth of the Danube to safeguard his new conquest, Thrace, from this direction as well, and then returned to Macedonia through the territory of the Triballians. Here a call for help from his friends in central Greece soon reached him.

For, of course, Philip had not forgotten the Athenians. They had so far been unable to mobilize their allies against him and he now attempted to isolate them further by inducing others to bring a charge against them in the Amphictyonic council. The allegation against them was cleverly chosen: during the Phocian War the Athenians had put up votive offerings, intended as a memorial of their victory over the Persians and Thebans in the year 479, in the as yet unconsecrated temple of Apollo in Delphi. That it was sacrilege was clear and it was expected that the city would be ordered to pay a large fine, if only because of Philip's majority in the Amphictyonic council. Naturally, the Athenians would not comply, and the Thebans were unable to avoid participating in the Sacred War which would then have to be waged, if only because of its cause. This extremely skillful plan failed, because Aeschines of all people represented Athenian interests in Delphi at the time and was able to redirect the anger of the Amphictyons against the small city of Amphissa with a clever counter-accusation, with the result that a Sacred War did ensue but followed a different course from that Philip had intended. The Thebans, whom Philip had planned to employ in his interests, indeed even in his place against the Athenians, did not only back up the Amphissaeans, but turned against Philip and snatched control of the Thermopylae from him. Thus it became impossible for the other Amphictyons to lead their troops south and to proceed with a military campaign against Amphissa, and in the autumn of 339 they had to call on Philip who had just returned from the Danube.

In this way the war in central Greece, which Philip had first attempted to avoid and then had to fight and which he continued to try to resolve after it had broken out by repeatedly offering to enter into negotiations, erupted after all. But a military decision could not be avoided, and it came at the beginning of August 338 at Chaeroneia unequivocally in favor of the Macedonian king. He was again able to begin to order his relations with the Greeks and to set the direction for his next undertaking.[21]

His longstanding ally Thebes received a heavy punishment for having defected to the enemy: a Macedonian occupying force was stationed in the Cadmeia and those who had been exiled were allowed to return; this brought Philip's friends into power and led to a change of government. The Boeotian League was not dissolved; in this way the Thebans who now lost their positions of power in Boeotia were meant to be held in check. Refounding the Boeotian cities which the Thebans had destroyed during their rule served the same purpose. All these measures had only one aim: Thebes was to be weakened as a land power and subject to the control of hostile neighbors.

In 346 the Athenians had obtained a fairly favorable peace and entered into an alliance with Philip. The peace and alliance were later extended to Philip's successors and thus declared to be everlasting. We saw earlier Philip's courting of the Athenians in subsequent years as well as Demosthenes' attempts to sabotage any rapprochement, to build up an alliance of Greek cities against Philip, and finally to bring about a decisive battle. In Philip's eyes the Athenians were therefore more than guilty and let others become culpable, and did not deserve any leniency because of their stubbornness. And yet they received it in greater measure than could have been expected. Philip did not touch Athenian democracy despite all his bad experiences with it, and he did not even invade Attica. Moreover, the Athenians were allowed to retain their possessions abroad, Lemnos, Imbros, Skyros, and Samos, and had to cede only the Thracian Chersonese to Philip. Since the Athenians depended on the cereal imports from the Black Sea region, the loss of the Thracian Chersonese meant that they were obliged to conduct themselves well toward Philip or face the possibility of a blockade of the Hellespont. The Athenians were also to be deprived of any opportunity to prepare for or wage a war against Philip at sea, and therefore the Second Athenian Confederacy, or what remained of it, was dissolved.[22]

We know barely anything about how other Greek states fared, especially those that had sent troops to Chaeroneia. Corinth and Ambracia had to accept a Macedonian garrison.[23] Together with the Theban Cadmeia, this made for three bases, which appear to have been sufficient for Philip. The distribution of these garrisons was well chosen: the one in Corinth controlled access to the Peloponnese, and the arrangements which were made here soon afterward guaranteed the good behavior of the peninsula. Ambracia controlled northwestern Greece and was situated

[21]   On the measures then taken, see Roebuck 1948.
[22]   On the peace and alliance between Philip and Athens, see Schmitt 1969: iii. 1–7, an overview of the sources and discussion of previous literature.
[23]   Chalcis is often supposed to have been the fourth base but there is no evidence at all for this.

strategically between Epirus and Aetolia, two new rising states who had thus far been promoted by Philip but could not be trusted. Lastly, Philip knew the Thebans personally and was aware of their ambitions to rule over central Greece. In order to prevent this, his friends kept hold of the reins in the city and, since they were relatively few in number and were opposed by the demos, they had to be safe-guarded by a Macedonian garrison. In some states the outcome of the war appears to have brought friends of the Macedonians into power, without our having to assume a direct intervention by Philip in their internal affairs.

These were the measures taken immediately following the decision at Chaeroneia, which demonstrate a great divergence between the conditions for peace and in which the treatment of his former enemies is at times strangely dispropor-tionate to their actual guilt. Something similar is true of Philip's actions in the Peloponnese. Members of the erstwhile coalition of enemies in the north of the peninsula were spared, but Sparta, which had remained neutral, was significantly weakened in that it had to cede frontier areas to its hostile neighbors Messenia, Megalopolis, Tegea, and Argos. The aim of this was not to eliminate Sparta com-pletely, but to strengthen its neighbors at its expense, with the result that none of these states was in a position to develop a hegemony over the whole Peloponnese. They owed their territorial expansion to Philip, and as long as Sparta continued to exist and to hope to regain what it had been forced to cede, these states were not allowed to forget who their friend and ally was.

With these arrangements Philip made sure that the former principal Greek powers would not again be in a position to assume a role that would compete with his. All three were significantly weakened, and care was taken to keep them under control for the future: the Thebans by the change in government, the gar-rison in the Cadmeia, and the strengthening as well as multiplication of the individual cities of the Boeotian League; the Spartans by territorial losses and the mistrust of the hostile states which surrounded them; and the Athenians by the loss of the Thracian Chersonese and the dissolution of the meager remainder of the Confederacy. The differences in treatment become even more obvious when we consider what the Athenians held onto and what comparable potential had been taken from the other states. Thebes and Sparta were land powers and as such had clearly been weakened. The might of the Athenians lay in their fleet which Philip allowed them to keep, even though he had nothing comparable to set against it.

The sparing treatment of the Athenians is astonishing, and attempts have been made to interpret it. For instance, Philip may have wished to retain the Athenian fleet in order to be able to deploy it in a war against the Persian empire.[24] This would also explain his courting of the Athenians from 348 onward, which is an indisput-able fact, and, as we saw earlier, a certain forbearance toward the Athenians could be observed even before that date.

---

[24]   See, e.g., Griffith 1979: 619–20. Ellis 1976: 11–12, 92 and Cawkwell 1978: 111ff. assume this even already for the time of the Peace of Philocrates.

This leads to the question as to when Philip began seriously to toy with the thought of marching against the Persian empire and when his politics on the southern Balkan peninsula were colored by it. In the sources the notion of a Persian campaign first appears for the year 346, although this is in a later source. After his report of the end of the Phocian War, Diodorus speaks of Philip's wish to be appointed commander of the Greeks entrusted to lead the war against the Persians (16.60.5). Diodorus or his source knew that this wish, ascribed to the king in 346, became a reality later and may have dated it wrongly to an earlier period. On the other hand, planning a war against the Great King in 346 was not unrealistic if we consider the situation in the Persian empire as Isocrates describes it in his letter addressed to the Macedonian king in the summer of that year.[25] With it, he hoped to win Philip for a military campaign against the Persian empire. Isocrates could propose such a plan only if he were confident that such a proposal would be thought feasible because of the power structure in the eastern Aegean and the state of affairs within the Persian empire at the time. It was also not the first time that Isocrates publicly proposed a Persian war. As early as in the *Panegyricus* of the year 380 he had lobbied for a reconciliation between the Greeks and a campaign against the Persian empire, and he could not have hoped to achieve anything with this pamphlet if his readers had been convinced that a war against the Great King was impossible.

The tyrant Jason of Pherae who represented the strongest power in central Greece toward the end of the 370s must have been among his readers; he was given credence when he announced that he would march against the Persian empire. That this claim is historical is certain: for one, Isocrates refers to it in 346 in his letter to Philip (119–20), then we have a guarantor of Jason's ambitions in Xenophon who was no longer alive at the time when the *Philippus* was being composed and who has the tyrant argue as follows:

> You are surely aware that the Persian king too owes being the richest man in the world to income not from the islands but from the mainland. To make him a subject of mine is a plan which I believe to be able to realize more easily than to subject Hellas to me. For I know . . . by what kind of army – and this is true as much for Cyrus' troops during his march inland as for those of Agesilaus – the Persian king has already been brought to the verge of ruin (Xen. *Hell.* 6.1.12).

Xenophon himself had participated in the military operations to which he makes Jason refer in the above passage. Isocrates had already employed these examples in 380 (*Panegyricus* 142–9), and the historian Polybius also made use of them in the second century when he traced Philip's planned campaign against the Great King back to the proven ineffectiveness of the Persians when faced with Greek armies (3.6.9–14). Polybius does not say when the Macedonian king decided on this plan for he is concerned purely with the preconditions for it. These had already been in place since the beginning of the fourth century. Since the successful retreat of the

[25] *Philippos* 99–104; cf. Zahrnt 1983: 278–9.

10,000 Greek mercenaries and even more since Agesilaus' maneuvers in western Asia Minor, the weakness and military inferiority of the Persians had become blatantly obvious. Consequently it was by all means realistic when Isocrates spoke of a joint campaign against the Great King by all Greeks in his *Panegyricus* in 380. Likewise, the tyrant Jason of Pherae was able publicly to consider pursuing a Persian war without having to fear being laughed at. And that even tough Jason at the time represented no more than the greatest land power in central Greece, the region over which Philip became supreme commander in 352. And this was basically only an annex to the then consolidated Macedonia which had been expanded in all directions. In contrast, the picture presented by the Persian empire in the first years of Philip's rule was such that it was even more inviting to invade than it had been at the beginning of the century. This was even more so after the end of the second phase of Macedon's rise, which extended from 352 to 346 and at which conclusion Isocrates asked the Macedonian king in an open letter to march against the Persian empire. Such an undertaking could reasonably be seen to promise even greater chances of success. The overview of Philip's actions and movements should have demonstrated that he had been interested in power, and in extending it, all his life. With this attitude the notion of a Persian war may already have entered into his considerations at a fairly early stage. In conclusion we have to ask at what point it was first conceived, when it may have taken shape, and how far it determined his policies on the Balkan peninsula.

Before assuming the throne Philip had spent some years as a hostage in Thebes at the house of the general Pammenes. In early 353 the latter was sent to Asia Minor with 5,000 soldiers to aid the insurgent satrap Artabazus. Philip facilitated the passage through Macedonia and Thrace for him and therefore knew how large a force was considered sufficient to be deployed against an army of the Great King. Philip also heard of Pammenes' successes after Artabazus had fallen out with him and fled to Macedonia, if not before.[26] It may thus easily be imagined that as early as the end of the 350s Philip was toying with the idea of a future war to be fought against the Persians. But the circumstances for such an undertaking and the prolonged absence it necessitated were not yet favorable. He was at war with the naval power Athens, and even if the Athenians had so far been unable to harm him – they have actually lost one stronghold after another to him – as potential allies of the Great King they could certainly become an irritant for him. Likewise, while he had secured Thessaly in 352 against the tyrants of Pherae and the advancing Phocians, Philip had not succeeded in occupying the Thermopylae. Thus the opportunity to exert a decisive influence over central and southern Greece did not yet exist.

But Philip could prepare for a Persian war in another way. Immediately following the retreat from the Thermopylae, he led his army against Thrace and up to the Propontis. Of course this march also served as a display for the Athenians to

---

[26] In this context Amminapes must also be mentioned, a noble Parthian, who, at some point which can no longer be ascertained and for reasons unknown, was exiled by the Persian king Artaxerxes III Ochus, came to Philip's court, and apparently became a friend of the Macedonians (see Heckel 22).

demonstrate that he would always be able to threaten their grain supply routes and their possessions on the Chersonese. At the same time the subjection of Cersebleptes as vassal, and Philip's alliance with Byzantium and possibly other coastal cities, safeguarded a territory that would some day prove useful when he was required to lead land forces against Asia Minor. The notion of such a campaign, which must have been a factor in Philip's deliberations, must have seemed even more attractive a short time later when not only did the Great King fail once again to regain Egypt, but unrest broke out in the satrapies bordering Egypt as a result of the defeat. It does not appear to be a coincidence that for a year and a half from the autumn of 351 nothing is heard of any actions against Athens, and that these were resumed only in the context of Philip moving against the Chalcidian League, and even then he offered peace. Therefore much points to Philip having conceived the plan of a war against the Persian empire as early as in the late 350s and that he let it guide his policies in Greece. These were most likely based on the following consideration: for a Persian campaign he needed the Greeks, if not as fellow combatants, at least as sympathetic neutral powers, and he had to insure that they could not be incited by the Persian king behind his back and cause him difficulties. The latter related primarily to Athens where the city and harbor represented fortifications that were difficult to capture and could not under any circumstances be allowed to be turned into a Persian base on the European mainland. It would of course be even better to win over to his side the Athenians with their naval power and nautical expertise, so as to meet the Persian fleet with a force that could match it.[27]

If we accept that these were Philip's intentions, his approach toward the various Greek states, which was very different from his approach toward the barbarians of Illyria and Thrace, against whom he campaigned more than once and whom he treated without squeamishness, becomes more comprehensible. With the Greeks, Philip intervened only when absolutely necessary, and then with such force that one strike was sufficient. After victory he would show carefully measured leniency. He preferred, if possible, not to strike against the Greeks at all. This had proved to be illusory, but after the victory at Chaeroneia Philip again proceeded to put in order his relations with the Greeks and to set the direction for his further plans once and for all. Philip's aim to create the right conditions for a safe prolonged absence and

[27] This is also the view of the scholars mentioned in n. 24: Ellis 1976 has the Macedonian king toy with the notion of a Persian war as early as the late 350s, while Cawkwell 1978 and Griffith 1979 consider that such a plan can be regarded as proven with any certainty only for the time of the Peace of Philocrates. Such a consensus among more recent scholars may of course not remain unchallenged, and thus Errington 1981 has dismissed all three estimated timings and has Philip conceive the idea of a Persian war only just before the battle at Chaeroneia. After his diplomacy in central Greece had failed, Philip had wished to reconcile the Greeks to Macedonian authority by making a dramatic Greek gesture in proposing a Persian war, in other words, he made a national concern his own. For Buckler 1996, Philip's possible attempts to develop a hegemony over Greece have left no traces at all, and we can only speculate about his ambitions toward the Persian empire, and his actual target right until the end was the Athenians. In view of the arguments in this chapter, a rebuttal appears superfluous.

a successful attack on the Persian empire was served by the measures implemented directly after Chaeroneia, which become understandable in view of the background on which light has now been shed. That the Athenians were for the most part spared accorded with Philip's interest as did the harsh treatment of the Thebans. The participation of the Theban hoplites in the Persian war, in comparison to the Athenian fleet, appeared to be less important. Philip was able to recruit infantry soldiers in sufficient numbers from Macedonia. On the other hand, the Thebans remained the strongest Greek land power and could become a threat because of their ambitions by upsetting the peace in central Greece during Philip's absence.

With the exception of the Thebans, Philip granted most of his opponents in war lenient conditions, but, for all his moderation, in dealing thus with them he also laid solid foundations for establishing a Macedonian hegemony over Greece. Moreover, in the Spartans he weakened a neutral but potentially dangerous power. Finally, shifting the balance of power within a state was one of the measures to secure his rule. In the end these were all individual measures, and Philip was justified in doubting whether, taken together, they represented a solid basis for controlling Greece. To achieve this required an order to incorporate all states that was not immediately seen as an instrument of Macedonian rule. A set of tools that had by now become established in Greece, without being connected to the hegemonial models of the Athenians, Spartans, or Thebans, was ideal.

Thus Philip secured the arrangements contractually with a Panhellenic peace treaty (*koine eirene*), the so-called Corinthian League, which was also to serve as the basis for Alexander's relations to the Greek states.[28] In the first half of 337 representatives of the Greek states assembled in Corinth at Philip's invitation and agreed the freedom and autonomy of all Greeks as in previous *koine eirene* treaties. Not only was any military attack on a member of the peace treaty prohibited and a court of arbitration, it seems, established for territorial disputes, but in addition to guaranteeing the states' current territorial possessions the treaty likewise protected their current constitutions from being overthrown in any way. Furthermore, the treaty obliged every member of the peace treaty to provide military aid to victims of aggression and to consider as an enemy anyone disturbing the peace. Earlier peace treaties had contained similar regulations, but the problem had always been how to ascertain bindingly who had broken the peace and how to set in motion disciplinary measures. Now for the first time institutions were created that not only insured the regulations were being kept to, but could if necessary enforce them and thus rebuild the order that had been disturbed. At the heart of this *koine eirene* was a *synedrion*, a body at which all participating powers were represented by delegates and whose decisions were binding on all member states. In order to execute the decisions of the *synedrion*, the office of *hegemon* was introduced. In military operations, the *hegemon* determined the size of each contingent and was in command.

---

[28]   Overview and detailed analysis of the sources in Schmitt 1969: iii. 3–7. The standard study of the Corinthian League of Philip II is now Jehne 1994: 139ff.; see Perlman 1985 on the background of the interstate relations during the fourth century. See Poddighe, ch. 6.

As expected, Philip, who belonged to the League in his own right and not as Macedonian king, was voted to the office.

With the Corinthian League Philip created a legal basis for his hegemony in Greece and thus sealed Macedonia's rise under international law. To this end he had adopted a type of treaty which the Greeks had by now become accustomed to, but continued to develop it by creating an overseeing and decision-making body and by introducing the office of the commander of the League's forces to implement its decisions. The best orders and contractual regulations would have been worthless if the *hegemon* did not represent a power no one would have dared to contradict, even if there had been no treaty on the southern Balkan peninsula.

The Corinthian League created by Philip was no doubt the most effective of all general peace treaties on land that had been agreed so far and appeared to stand the best chance of guaranteeing that the peace would be kept. Although this peace had been imposed by the victor and was a means of consolidating his supremacy and securing his hegemony in Greece, he had skillfully veiled it in the form of a *koine eirene*, acceptable to all states, which many had tried in vain to establish in Greece for fifty years. In particular, it was likely that the smaller states would welcome the new order, for it guaranteed them protection against their more powerful neighbors. Internal peace across Greece now appeared to have been secured, and in return many a state may have been willing to accept a degree of loss of its own independence. The status quo was, however, guaranteed primarily by the person of the *hegemon* – and therefore the oath of the *koine eirene*, part of which is transmitted epigraphically, also included the obligation not to abolish the rule of Philip and his successors. In all this Philip's intention was not to develop direct rule over the Greek states but simply to govern them indirectly as a precondition for the Persian war, which it seems he had already decided to pursue from the late 350s. That he had to postpone these plans time and again had been due to his enemies in Greece, foremost Athens. Now there was nothing to hold him back any longer.

Following a motion by Philip, the *synedrion* agreed the war against the Persian empire and granted the *hegemon* additional powers for the duration of the campaign. As early as spring 336 a Macedonian army of 10,000 men crossed the Hellespont under Parmenion and his son-in-law Attalus, in order first to cause the Greek cities of Asia Minor to defect. Philip intended to follow as soon as military preparations had been completed, but it did not happen, for he was murdered in the autumn of 336. This time the succession in Macedonia went smoothly and the new ruler Alexander III also secured the hegemony in Greece despite some difficulties with the Thebans. As he set out on his campaign against the Persian empire in early 334, Alexander was able to do so trusting fully in the foundations laid by his father, and when he later began to be called "the Great," it was overlooked that he was the son of an even greater man.

2

Alexander's Conquest of Asia

Waldemar Heckel

On the seventh day of the Attic month Metageitnion (August 2) 338, Philip II, with his son Alexander commanding the cavalry on the left, defeated a coalition of Thebans and Athenians at Chaeroneia, destroying the vaunted Theban Sacred Band and, as many writers of the nineteenth and twentieth centuries have commented, dealing the fatal blow to "Greek liberty." Today we may be more circumspect about the nature of Greek "freedom," but the fact remains that Chaeroneia was a turning point in Greek history. Philip promptly consolidated his gains on the battlefield by forging the League of Corinth,[1] which he was designated to lead as its *hegemon* in a crusade of vengeance against Persia. But dynastic politics, following on the heels of personal misjudgment, supervened, and in 336 the Macedonian king fell victim to an assassin's dagger before he could witness his statue carried into the theater at Aegae (Vergina) along with those of the twelve Olympians.[2] The ceremony was to have been a fitting tribute to a descendant of Heracles about to embark upon a Panhellenic war of conquest. The undertaking and the greatness that its fulfillment held in promise were to be Alexander's inheritance.

Straightaway, it was necessary for the new king to establish his authority. Rivals for the throne, and their supporters, were swiftly dispatched: first of all, two sons of Lyncestian Aëropus, Arrhabaeus and Heromenes, were publicly executed on charges of complicity in the assassination (Arr. 1.25.1). The murderer himself, Pausanias of Orestis, had been killed in flight by the king's bodyguards. If there was any truth to the charge that the Lyncestians had conspired with him,[3] they appear to have given little help (unless they supplied the horses that were meant to facilitate his escape), nor was it clear if they sought the throne for a member of their own family, or for Amyntas son of Perdiccas (Plu. *Mor.* 327c). The vagueness in the reporting of their

---

[1] Rhodes–Osborne, no. 76.
[2] Willrich 1899; Badian 1963; Bosworth 1971b; Kraft 1971: 11–42; Fears 1975; Develin 1981; Heckel 1981.
[3] Bosworth 1971b.

alleged crime is doubtless Alexander's doing: it suited his purpose to eliminate all contenders, including the hapless Amyntas. Indeed, it is hard to credit the existence of such a conspiracy without dismissing its perpetrators as inept, if not downright stupid. The Lyncestians ought to have secured the support of Antipater, the powerful father-in-law of their brother Alexander. But clearly they did not. Alexander was reportedly the first to proclaim Alexander king, doubtless at the urging of Antipater, who proved his own loyalty and bought the life of his daughter's husband by abandoning Arrhabaeus and Heromenes. Even in later years, when distrust had tainted the relationship between king and viceroy, no charge of conspiring to kill Philip or prevent Alexander's accession was ever leveled against him. Amyntas son of Perdiccas, too, appears to have been eliminated swiftly – certainly he was dead by the spring of 335 (Arr. 1.5.4). A companion of his, Amyntas son of Antiochus, fled Macedonia and took service with the Persian king, but it is unlikely that this occurred *before* the death of Perdiccas' son. The latter was a nephew of Philip II and rightful heir to throne, whose claims the state, in need of strong leadership to combat external foes, had swept aside in the years that followed the death of Perdiccas III in 360/59.[4] Married to Philip's daughter by an Illyrian wife, the discarded heir had lived quietly, without incurring suspicion; in all likelihood, he became the victim of the aspirations of others and of his own bloodline.[5]

Elsewhere, Attalus, guardian of Philip's last wife Cleopatra-Eurydice, may have been perceived as a threat. But, in this case as well, stories that Attalus was conniving with the Athenian Demosthenes and other Greeks (D.S. 17.5.1), if they are true, point only to the desperation of his situation. So weak was his position that he could not even persuade his own father-in-law, Parmenion, to side with him, though together they commanded a substantial force in northwestern Asia Minor. Alexander's agent, Hecataeus, secured Attalus' elimination, something that could not have been achieved without Parmenion's acquiescence. Some scholars have been misled into attributing too much power to Attalus; for his influence with Philip must be explained by the fact of his relationship to Cleopatra-Eurydice.[6] His remark at the wedding feast in 337, that the marriage would produce "legitimate heirs" to the throne, marked him for execution when Alexander became king. It was the tactless utterance of a drunken man, but fatal nonetheless. His relatives by blood and marriage, though hardly contemptible, could do little to save him and found it expedient not to try. Parmenion obtained a more suitable husband for his widowed daughter in the taxiarch, Coenus son of Polemocrates. The father-in-law and his sons received high offices in the expeditionary force.[7]

---

[4]   Hammond–Griffith 208–9.

[5]   See, however, Ellis 1971, rejected by Prandi 1998; but see Worthington 2003: 76–9. Weber (ch. 5 in this volume) believes that Amyntas was, in fact, a very serious threat to Alexander's succession.

[6]   Heckel 1986b: 297–8. For the details of her life and death see Heckel 89–90; Whitehorne 1994: 30–42; Ogden 1999: 20–2; Carney 2000b: 72–5. The woman is referred to as Cleopatra in all sources except Arr. 3.6.5, where she appears as Eurydice (see Heckel 1978). I have used the compound name for the sake of clarity, to distinguish her from Alexander's sister Cleopatra.

[7]   Heckel 1992: 13–33, 299–300.

Domestic problems were, moreover, balanced by defection in the south and challenges on the northern and western marches of the kingdom. In western Greece, Acarnania, Ambracia, and Aetolia openly declared themselves hostile to Philip's settlement;[8] the Peloponnesians too evinced widespread disaffection. But Alexander made a rapid foray into Thessaly, effected by means of cutting steps into Mt. Ossa ("Alexander's Ladder"), and induced the Thessalians to recognize him as Philip's heir as *archon* of their Thessalian League, thereby also gaining a voice in the Amphictyonic Council. With the added moral authority, the new king granted independence to the Ambraciots, and then moved south into Boeotia preempting military action there. The Athenians saw to their defenses and sent an embassy to Alexander; Demosthenes was said to have abandoned the embassy at Cithaeron, fearing the king's wrath.[9] Now, too, the League of Corinth declared Alexander its *hegemon*, but the sparks of disaffection were yet to ignite into full-scale rebellion.

In the north, Alexander turned against the so-called "autonomous" Thracians and the Triballians, tribes dwelling near the Haemus range and beyond to the Danube. South of the Haemus, the Thracians sought to blockade Alexander's force by occupying the high ground and fortifying their position with wagons. Unable to resist the attacking Macedonians, even after pushing the empty wagons into the path of the oncoming enemy, they were dispersed with heavy casualties. The Triballians responded by transferring their women and children to the Danubian island of Peuce, which their king, Syrmus, defended with a small but adequate force. The remainder of the Triballians evaded the Macedonian army as it hastened north, and occupied a wooded area near the river Lyginus, less than a day's march from the Danube. But Alexander turned back and dealt with them, using his skirmishers to dislodge the Triballians from the forest before catching them between two detachments of cavalry and attacking their center with the phalanx. Some 3,000 were killed; the remainder escaped into the safety of the woods.

An attempt on Peuce failed: the ships which Alexander had brought up from the Black Sea were insufficient in numbers and the banks of the island too well defended. Instead the Macedonians launched an attack on the Getae who lived on the north bank of the river. After destroying their town and devastating their crops, they forced the Getae to come to terms. Syrmus too sent a delegation asking for terms; possibly, Alexander demanded that he contribute a contingent to serve in his expeditionary army, in which some 7,000 Illyrians, Odrysians, and Triballians are found in 334.

To the west, the Illyrians, inveterate enemies of Macedon, threatened the kingdom's borders as Glaucias son of Bardylis allied himself with the Taulantian chief Cleitus. At Pellium Alexander displayed what a superior army led by a brilliant tactician could do. The campaign was a textbook example of speed and maneuver: the discipline of Alexander's troops mesmerized the Illyrians, outwitting them with a display of drill that turned them into spectators when they ought to have been

---

[8] Roebuck 1948: 76–7.
[9] D.S. 17.4.6–7; cf. Plu. *Dem.* 23.3, in the context of Alexander's destruction of Thebes.

taking counter-measures.[10] But the preoccupation with northern affairs gave new impetus to the anti-Macedonian party in central Greece. The reckoning was long overdue, and the consequences for Thebes devastating.

Encouraged by rumors that Alexander had been killed in Illyria and by the false hope of Athenian aid, the Thebans besieged the Macedonian garrison established on the Cadmeia after Chaeroneia.[11] The king's response was swift, far more so than they could have imagined; for Alexander bypassed Thermopylae and arrived before the gates of Thebes within two weeks. Negotiations amounted to little more than posturing by both sides and Thebes, abandoned by the very Athenians who had incited the rebellion, was quickly taken, though not without great blood-shed. The city was razed and the survivors enslaved, all as later – and doubtless contemporary – apologists claimed by the decision of a council of Alexander's allies. Many of these were Boeotians and Phocians with a long history of enmity toward the city, but it could also be argued that it was condign punishment for a century and a half of collaboration with Persians (*medismos* or "Medism"). So it proved both a warning to other cities in Greece that Alexander would not tolerate rebellion and a symbolic beginning of the campaign against the true enemy of Greece and its supporters.

The Athenians, for their part, hastened to display contrition, foremost among them the very self-serving politicians who had fomented the uprising from the safety of the *bema*. Nevertheless, their prominence diverted the young king's wrath from the common citizens: instead he demanded the surrender of ten orators and generals. In the event, only the implacable Charidemus was punished with exile, although Ephialtes fled to Asia Minor in the company of Thrasybulus; several of the others outlived Alexander to rally their citizens to another disastrous undertaking in 323/2. It is important to note, however, that whereas the destruction of Thebes could be justified with reference to the city's history of Medism, any hostile act against the Athenian state as a whole would have undermined Alexander's Panhellenic propaganda.[12]

The Asiatic campaign began in spring 334: in fact, it was a continuation of the initiative launched in spring 336 but postponed by Philip's murder and the unrest in Greece. The advance force under Parmenion, Attalus, and Amyntas had faltered and was now clinging to its bases on the Asiatic side of the Hellespont. Attalus' execution had doubtless undermined the morale of the army, but the setback had as much to do with the vigorous resistance by the forces of Memnon the Rhodian.[13] Cities that had proclaimed their support of Philip – some with extravagant honors for the Macedonian king – reverted to a pro-Persian stance (Rhodes and Osborne 83–5), and it was doubtless the lackluster performance of the first Macedonian wave that persuaded Darius III that a coalition of satraps from Asia Minor was sufficient

[10] Fuller 1960: 225.
[11] Wüst 1938: 169; Roebuck 1948: 77–80.
[12] Will 1983: 37–45; Habicht 1997: 13–15.
[13] Judeich 1892: 302–6; Ruzicka 1985 and 1997: 124–5.

to confront the invaders. For Darius, in addition to securing his claim to the Persian throne, had been preoccupied with an uprising in Egypt.[14]

The army that crossed the Hellespont comprised 12,000 Macedonian heavy infantry, along with 7,000 allies and 5,000 mercenaries; the light infantry were supplied by Odrysians, Thracians, and Illyrians, to the number of 7,000, as well as 1,000 archers and the Agrianes, for a grand total of 32,000. To these were added 5,100 cavalry (thus D.S. 17.17.3–4; but other estimates range from 34,000 to 48,000 in all). At the Granicus River,[15] to which the coalition of satraps had advanced after their council of war in Zeleia, the "allied" forces confronted a Persian army that included a large contingent of Greek mercenaries. By choosing to stand with the Persian forces they had disregarded an order of the League and committed high treason, and Alexander was determined to make an example of them (Arr. 1.16.6). Distrusted by their employers, the mercenaries were not engaged until the battle was already lost (McCoy 1989). Nevertheless, they paid a heavy price in the butchery that followed, and those who surrendered were sent to hard labor camps in Macedonia, stigmatized as traitors to a noble cause and denied whatever rights might be granted prisoners of war. This stood in sharp contrast to Alexander's clemency on other occasions, and it would be almost three years before he relented and authorized their release. For their part, the Persian cavalry and light infantry fled as the victors turned to deal with the mercenaries. Arsites, in whose satrapy the disaster had taken place, escaped and thus bought enough time to die by his own hand. Panoplies from the battle were sent to Athens with the dedication, "from Alexander son of Philip and all the Greeks, except the Lacedaemonians," maintaining the pretense of a common cause while directing criticism at the Spartans for their refusal to join the League.

Victory at the Granicus cleared the path for the conquest of the Aegean littoral. Many states came over voluntarily, while others were prevented by the presence of Persian forces from declaring for the Macedonian conqueror. This should not be seen as enthusiasm for Macedonian "liberation" but rather as an opportunity for the enemies of the existing regimes to overthrow their political masters. Far different was the case of Mithrenes, the *hyparchos* of Sardis, who surrendered the city despite its superb natural defenses (Briant 1993a: 14–17). The death of Spithridates at the Granicus had left Lydia without a satrap (cf. Egypt after the death of Sauaces at Issus), and Mithrenes, making a realistic appraisal of the Persian military collapse in Asia Minor, was motivated by self-preservation and the hope of favorable treatment. Alexander received him honorably, although it would be late 331 before he reaped as his reward the unenviable task of ruling Armenia. To the Aeolic cities, not directly in the army's path, the king sent Alcimachus – a prominent Macedonian and, apparently, a brother of Lysimachus – to establish democracies. Alexander meanwhile turned his attention to Miletus and Halicarnassus, where resistance continued; for the Persian navy still dominated the eastern Aegean and Darius'

[14] Anson 1989; Garvin 2003: 94–5; but *HPE* 1042 urges caution; on Khababash see Burstein 2000.
[15] For the battle see D.S. 17.19–21; Arr. 1.13–16; Plu. *Alex.* 16; Just. 11.6.8–15.

Figure 2.1 Bronze equestrian statue of Alexander the Great, found at Herculaneum. Museo Archeologico Nazionale, Naples. Photo: Foto Marburg/Art Resource, New York.

general Memnon had concentrated his forces in that area. Miletus was taken with relative ease, when the Macedonians controlled the access to the harbor before the Persian fleet could arrive.[16] Nevertheless, Alexander decided at this point to disband his fleet – its strength, quality, and loyalty were all suspect – and concentrate on engagements by land. The decision, though baffling to some at the time, would prove to be a wise strategic move and an economic blessing.

At Halicarnassus, Memnon and Orontopates directed a stubborn defense, inflicting casualties on the besiegers and setting fire to their siege-towers.[17] But the city was quickly cordoned off and eventually taken; for Alexander found a less costly, political means of gaining control of Caria. He had received envoys from

[16] Arr. 1.19; D.S. 17.22.1–23.3; Plu. *Alex.* 17.2.
[17] Arr. 1.20.2 ff.; D.S. 17.23.4 ff.; Plu. *Alex.* 17.2; Fuller 1960: 200–6; Romane 1994: 69–75.

neighboring Alinda, where Ada, the aging sister of Maussolus, and rightful queen of Halicarnassus, was residing. Some time after the death of her husband (also her brother), Idrieus, Ada had been deposed by yet another brother, Pixodarus.[18] When Pixodarus died shortly before the Macedonian invasion, the administration of the satrapy was given to Orontopates, who appears to have married the younger Ada, a bride once offered to Alexander's half-witted sibling, Arrhidaeus.[19] By restoring the former queen to her kingdom, and by accepting her as his adoptive mother, Alexander earned the goodwill of the Carians. Sufficient forces were left with Ada to compel the eventual surrender of Halicarnassus, thus freeing Alexander to proceed into Pamphylia. But the act of reinstating Ada, like the king's treatment of Mithrenes, was a departure from the official policy of hostility to the barbarian. Few in the conquering army will have cared about the Hecatomnid record of philhellenism.

Over the winter of 334/3, Alexander campaigned in Lycia and Pamphylia, rounding Mt. Climax where the sea receded, as if it were doing obeisance (*proskynesis*) to the future king of Asia (Callisthenes, *FGrH* 124 F31), just as the Euphrates had lowered its waters for the younger Cyrus in 401 (Xen. *Anab.* 1.4.18). This apparent foreshadowing gained credence in spring 333 when Alexander slashed through the Gordian knot with his sword and claimed to have fulfilled the prophecy that foretold dominion over Asia for the man who could undo it. While prophecies could be carefully scripted by the spin-doctors, mastery over Asia would require military victory over Darius III, who, by the time Alexander entered Cilicia, had amassed an army on the plains of northern Mesopotamia at Sochi. Alexander's own advance had been methodical, aiming clearly at the coastal regions that might give succor to the Persian fleet and the satrapal capitals with their administrative centers and treasure houses. Near Tarsus he fell ill, collapsing in the cold waters of the river Cydnus, perhaps stricken with malaria.[20] That Darius interpreted the Macedonian's failure to emerge from Cilicia as cowardice (Curt. 3.8.10–11) may be attributable to the sources who wished to depict the Persian king as a vainglorious potentate whose actions in the field belied his boastful pronouncements. On the other hand, it is not unlikely that the Persians had a genuine expectation of victory – after all, a larger army under the younger Cyrus had been crushed at Cunaxa in 401 despite the valor of the Ten Thousand (Xen. *Anab.* 1) – and underestimated both the Macedonian army and its youthful commander. Impatient and eager to force a decision upon an enemy he regarded as shirking battle, Darius entered Cilicia via the so-called Amanic Gates and placed himself astride Alexander's lines of communication. By doing so, the Persian king abandoned the more extensive plains which offered him the chance of deploying the mobile troops that could most harm the enemy and negated his numerical superiority by leading his forces into the narrow coastal plain between the Gulf of Issus and the mountains.

---

[18] Hornblower 1982: 41–50; *HPE* 706–7; for Ada in particular Özet 1994.
[19] Plu. *Alex.* 10.1–3; French and Dixon 1986.
[20] Engels 1978b: 225–6.

Figure 2.2 The Alexander Mosaic, from the House of the Faun, Pompeii. Museo Archeologico Nazionale, Naples. Photo: Scala/Art Resource, New York.

Alexander, who had advanced south of the Beilan Pass (Pillar of Jonah)[21] and approached what would in the Middle Ages be known as Alexandretta (Iskenderum), now turned about to confront the Persian army, marching first in column and then spreading out to occupy the plain south of the Pinarus river. Despite his initial error in allowing himself to be lured onto a battlefield more favorable to the smaller Macedonian army, Darius made good use of the terrain, which he strengthened in one spot by means of a palisade. The Greek mercenaries gave a good account of themselves, as did the cavalry posted by the sea, but the battle was decided on the Persian left, where Alexander broke the Persian line and advanced directly upon Darius. The Great King was soon turned in flight, a move that signaled defeat and *sauve qui peut*. The slaughter was great, but the enemy leader escaped, ultimately, to the center of his empire to regroup and fight another day.[22]

The fortunes and paths of the two kings now moved in different directions. Darius returned to Mesopotamia, intent upon saving the heart of the empire and rebuilding his army. For this purpose, he summoned levies from the upper satrapies, which had not been called up in 333, perhaps from overconfidence that the victory would be easily won without them. Alexander meanwhile stuck doggedly to his strategy of depriving the Persian fleet of its bases and gaining control of the lands that supplied ships and rowers. For it was clear that most served Persia under

[21] For the topography see Hammond 1994a. For the battle see Arr. 2.8–11; Curt. 3.9–11; D.S. 17.33–4; Plu. *Alex.* 20.5–10; Just. 11.9.1–10; *POxy* 1798 §44 = *FGrH* 148.
[22] Seibert 1988: 450–1 dismisses charges of "cowardice"; see also Nylander 1993; Badian 2000b; and the comments of Briant in ch. 9.

Figure 2.3 The Alexander Sarcophagus, late fourth century BC. Detail of a helmeted Alexander on horseback. Marble, 195 × 318 × 167 cm. Inv. 370T. Archaeological Museum, Istanbul. Photo: Erich Lessing/Art Resource, New York.

Figure 2.4 The Alexander Sarcophagus. View of the entire sarcophagus. Photo: Erich Lessing/Art Resource, New York.

Figure 2.5 The Alexander Sarcophagus. View of the long battle side. Photo: Erich Lessing/ Art Resource, New York.

compulsion and would defect once their home governments had acknowledged the power of the conqueror. Tyre proved a stubborn exception – not out of loyalty to Persia, but rather in hope of gaining true independence as a neutral state. But Alexander could not afford to leave so prominent and powerful an island city unconquered. The siege and capture of Tyre were one of the king's greatest achievements and a monument to his determination and military brilliance. After seven months, the city succumbed to a combined attack of the infantry on the causeway, built with great effort and loss of life, and a seaborne assault on the weakest point of the walls. The king's naval strategy was already paying dividends; for the Cypriot rulers had by now defected and joined with the other Phoenicians to blockade the Tyrian ships in their harbor, while a second flotilla carrying soldiers and battering rams gained undisputed access to the walls. The defenders repelled an attack after the initial breach was achieved, but they were soon overwhelmed and the city paid a heavy price for its defiance of Alexander.[23]

To the south, Gaza represented the final obstacle to the Macedonian strategy. It too was captured after a two-month siege. Its garrison commander, Batis, was allegedly dragged around the city by Alexander in imitation of Achilles' punishment

[23] For the siege of Tyre see Arr. 2.16–24.5; Curt. 4.2–4; D.S. 17.40.2–46.5; Plu. *Alex.* 24–5; Just. 12.10.10–14; Polyaen. *Strat.* 4.3.3–4; 4.13; *FGrH* 151 §7; Fuller 1960: 206–16; Romane 1987.

of Hector. This has generally been dismissed as fiction, though perhaps unjustly. The form of punishment and Alexander's personal role may well be literary invention on the part of Cleitarchus, if not of Callisthenes of Olynthus, but there is a strong suspicion that behind this story there lurks an element of truth: Batis was doubtless subjected to cruel punishment for his opposition to Alexander (and we might add that Alexander was twice wounded in the engagement), just as later Ariamazes was crucified for his defiance.

In Egypt, the Macedonian army faced no resistance, since Persian authority in the satrapy had collapsed.[24] If the populace welcomed Alexander as liberator, they did so out of hatred for Persia, which had harshly reintegrated Egypt into the Persian empire after roughly sixty years of independence under the kings of the Twenty-Eighth to Thirtieth Dynasties, and because, like the native populations of other regions, they were helpless to do otherwise. Alexander himself was recognized as the legitimate pharaoh – whether or not an official crowning took place in Memphis[25] – and the earthly son of Amun, both in the Nile Delta and by the high priest of the god at Siwah in the Libyan Desert. Thus Egypt began a new era of foreign rule. The pharaonic titles were accepted by Alexander, just as they were conferred by his subjects, as recognition of the irresistible conqueror and his achievement. Neither side was truly deceived, but the process reaffirmed order and the continuation of the patterns of everyday life; for Alexander, like his Persian predecessors, would reside elsewhere and govern through satraps and nomarchs. The reality was clear to both Alexander and the Egyptians, but for the Macedonians Alexander's new role and the nature of his relationship with Amun were deeply disturbing.

The journey to the oracle of Amun at Siwah in the Libyan Desert represents a critical point not only in Alexander's personal development but also in the king's relationship with his men – common soldiers and officers alike. Although there is a tradition that Alexander was "seized by an urge" (*pothos*) to visit the oracle and thus emulate his mythical ancestors, Perseus and Heracles, the journey cannot have been an impulsive act. Some have argued that the king sought divine approval for his new city on the Canopic mouth of the Nile. It is most likely that the journey was in some way connected with Alexander's role as pharaoh, and such an interpretation finds curious support in Herodotus' account of Cambyses. Certainly the story that the Persian king sent an army to destroy the shrine, and that this army was buried in the desert sands (Hdt. 3.26; Plu. *Alex.* 26.12), is as apocryphal as the one about his killing of the Apis calf – a patent fabrication that still commands the belief of some Classical scholars. The kernel of truth is surely that Cambyses consulted the oracle once he became master of Egypt. Whatever the fate of his envoys, the Herodotean account defies credulity. But Alexander must have known that, as pharaoh, he would be recognized as son of Amun. Whether the trip was made solely to consolidate his position in Egypt, or for a more ambitious purpose, cannot be

[24]   *HPE* 861.
[25]   Burstein 1991.

determined. What is certain is that his men soon equated his acceptance of Amun as his divine father with a rejection of Philip (see Hamilton 1953). The first rumblings of discontent occurred before the army left Egypt; in the coming years, as the army made its weary progress eastward, Alexander's apparent repudiation of his Macedonian origins was to become a recurring cause of complaint.

The conquest of the Levantine coast and Egypt had given Darius time to regroup. In 331 he moved his army from Babylon, keeping the Tigris river on his right and then crossing it south of Arbela, where he deposited his baggage. From here he marched north, bridging the river Lycus, and then encamped by the Boumelus (Khazir) in the vicinity of Gaugamela. As the Persian king was choosing his battle-field, Mazaeus, who had once been satrap of Abarnahara (the land beyond the river), approached the Euphrates near Thapsacus with some 6,000 men. This force was far too small to prevent Alexander's crossing and was probably intended to harass and observe the enemy, and Mazaeus quickly withdrew in the direction of the Tigris. Alexander, for his part, had been informed by spies about Darius' location and the size of his army; at any rate, he had banished any thought of proceeding directly to Babylon, a move which would have created supply problems and allowed Darius to position himself astride his lines of communication for a second time. Furthermore, Alexander was eager for a decisive engagement.[26]

In 331, Darius was not Alexander's only worry. During his second visit to Tyre, on the return from Egypt, the king received word of unrest in Europe, where the Spartan king Agis III had organized a coalition and defeated Antipater's *strategos* in the Peloponnese, Corrhagus.[27] Agis was besieging Megalopolis with an army of 22,000 just as Antipater was attempting to suppress a rebellion by Memnon, *strategos* of Thrace. Despite the timing, there is no good reason for suspecting that the uprisings were coordinated, or that Memnon had been in communication with Agis (*pace* Badian 1967). In fact, Antipater was able to come to terms with Memnon far too quickly for the Thracian rebellion to benefit Agis. Nor can the actions of the *strategos* have been regarded as treasonous; for the truce allowed him to retain his position, and Alexander appears to have taken no retaliatory action against him. Freed from distractions in the north, Antipater led his forces to Megalopolis and reestablished Macedonian authority with heavy bloodshed: 3,500 Macedonians lay dead, and 5,300 of the enemy, including Agis himself. But when Alexander confronted Darius at Gaugamela the affairs of Europe were only beginning to unravel.[28]

In his address to the troops, Alexander told them that they would be facing the same men they had defeated twice before in battle, but in fact the composition of the Persian army at Gaugamela was radically different and included the skilled horsemen of the eastern satrapies. And, this time, the Persians would be fighting

---

[26] For the battle of Gaugamela see Arr. 3.11–15; Plu. *Alex.* 31.6–33.11; D.S. 17.57–61; Curt. 4.13–16; Just. 11.13.1–14.7; Polyaen. *Strat.* 4.3.6, 17.

[27] For the background to the war see McQueen 1978.

[28] Borza 1971; Wirth 1971; Lock 1972; Badian 1994.

on terrain of their own choosing. With vastly superior numbers, Darius expected to outflank and envelop the much smaller Macedonian army, which numbered only 47,000. Furthermore, the Macedonians were confronted by scythe chariots and elephants. But the Macedonians advanced *en echelon*, with the cavalry on the far right wing deployed to prevent an outflanking maneuver there; behind the main battalions of the *pezhetairoi*, Alexander stationed troops to guard against envelopment. By thrusting with his Companions against the Persian left, Alexander disrupted the enemy formation as the heavy infantry surged ahead to strike at the center. But in so doing, the infantry created a gap, which the Scythian and Indian horsemen were prompt to exploit. But the barbarians rode straight to the baggage of the field camp, eager for plunder and acting as if their victory was assured. Had they struck instead at the Macedonian left, where Mazaeus was putting fear-some pressure on the Thessalian cavalry under Parmenion's command, they might have turned the tide of battle. Instead they were soon following their king in flight, struggling to escape the slaughter that emboldens the victor.

Defeat at Gaugamela left the heart of the empire and the Achaemenid capitals at the mercy of the invader. Mazaeus, who had fled to Babylon, now surrendered the city and its treasures to Alexander, thus earning his own reward. The king retained him as satrap of Babylonia, though he took the precaution of installing Macedonian troops and overseers in the city. The administrative arrangements, like the ceremonial handing over of the city, were the same as those at Sardis, except that at that uncertain time Alexander was not yet ready to entrust the Iranian nobility with higher offices. In Susa, the king confirmed the Persian satrap Abulites, who had made formal surrender after Gaugamela: but again native rule was fettered by military occupation as its Persian commandant Mazarus was replaced by the Macedonian Xenophilus.[29]

In the closing months of 331, anxiety about Agis' war in the Peloponnese helped to buy the Persians time. The need to await news of events in the west kept Alexander in Babylonia and Elam longer than he had planned, a delay exploited by the Persian satrap, Ariobarzanes, who occupied the so-called Persian Gates[30] with an army of perhaps 25,000 (40,000 infantry and 700 horse, according to Arrian 3.18.2). But his efforts, like those of the Uxians shortly before, proved futile. Alexander circumvented the enemies' position and was soon reconstructing the bridge across the Araxes, which the Persians had destroyed in an effort to buy time. Perhaps the intention was to facilitate the removal or even the destruction of the city's treasure; for the best Ariobarzanes could do was delay Alexander's force while Parmenion took the heavier troops and the siege equipment along the more southerly wagon road to Persepolis. But no such measures were taken, and Tiridates surrendered the city and its wealth to the conqueror.

Vengeance had been the theme exploited, first by Philip and then by Alexander, and the war against Persia the justification for allied service under the Macedonian

---

[29]   Heckel 2002a.
[30]   For location and topography, see MacDermot and Shippmann 1999; Speck 2002.

hegemon. The mandate of the League could be enforced before the troops even reached Asian soil. Thebes, which had a long history of Medism, was accused once again of collaboration with Persia, and indeed of advocating alliance with the Great King to overthrow the tyrant who was oppressing Greece, Alexander (D.S. 17.9.5). The city's destruction was at once an act of terror and vengeance. On similar grounds, Parmenion had destroyed Gryneium on the Aegean coast and enslaved its population.[31] And, not surprisingly, Alexander's propagandists depicted the crossing into Asia as the beginning of another chapter in the ongoing struggle between east and west. The king sacrificed to various gods and heroes associated with the Trojan War, including an *apotropaic* sacrifice to Protesilaus, the first of the Achaeans to leap ashore and to meet his fate there. Thereafter he hurled his spear into Asian soil, and leaping onto the Asian shore, proclaimed it "spear-won land."[32] The message was unmistakable: more than a mere punitive expedition, this was to be a war of conquest, and it was to be a Panhellenic effort.[33] But Alexander had no sooner embarked on this fine-sounding mission than it became clear to him that propaganda and expediency were destined to clash. Slogans might prove useful for the enlistment of troops or creating ardor among the rank and file, but victory over the enemies' military forces did not guarantee the political acquiescence of the conquered peoples.

Hardly had he consigned Greeks who had served as mercenaries of the Great King to hard labor camps, for their collaboration with the enemy, before he accepted the surrender of Sardis by the Persian Mithrenes, whom he treated with respect and kept in his entourage. It was a clear indication of what could be accomplished without recourse to battle, and the friendly treatment of the defector would induce others to follow his example. In the same campaigning season, Alexander dismissed the allied fleet. Militarily and economically, this was a good move, but the political implications were otherwise. The leader of the League of Corinth had rejected the participation of one of its most powerful members. Furthermore, he followed this gesture with an equally confounding one when he allowed Ada to return to Halicarnassus as its rightful queen and accepted her as his adoptive mother. From the very beginning, Alexander had recognized that he might conquer without reaching an accommodation with the barbarian, but he would do so more easily and rule the empire more securely if he did so. Hence, the orientalizing tendencies of the king, which were to cause so much anxiety in the years that followed Darius' death, were already in evidence in 334/3. But Alexander was doing little more than applying the methods of Philip to the Asiatic sphere.

For the conservative Macedonians and Greeks, it was a disturbing trend, but Alexander's progressive moves reveal a political talent that rivaled his military genius. No opportunity was wasted. The decision to send the newly-weds back to Macedonia, where they could kindle the enthusiasm of their countrymen for the

---

[31] D.S. 17.7.8; Bosworth 1988a: 250.
[32] Mehl 1980–1; Zahrnt 1996.
[33] Seibert 1998; Flower 2000.

war and return with reinforcements, was a fine public relations exercise, to say nothing of its impact on the Macedonian birth rate. In spring 333, Alexander was quick to exploit the prophecy of the Gordian knot, even if his rashness forced him to find a desperate solution. After the king's death there were those who said that he had cheated by cutting the knot with his sword, but no one said so at the time. The respectful treatment of the Persian women captured at Issus showed that Alexander was the consummate master of propaganda, whether it was directed toward the Greeks, the Macedonians, or the barbarians. Not every victory would be gained on the battlefield. So much was clear to the young conqueror, although the soldiers and the majority of their commanders failed to appreciate their leader's approach. Whatever political advantages accompanied the king's recognition as "Son of Amun," the troops saw only the rejection of Philip II and the inflated ego of a man to whom success came too soon and too easily.

It would indeed be easy to reduce the king's actions to those of a young man corrupted by fortune; for thus he is represented in some of the extant accounts. But this is to deny Alexander an awareness of the political reality. He more than anyone understood that the rhetoric which had fueled the campaign in the first place must give way to a policy of *rapprochement* if the fruits of his military successes were not to be squandered. Nevertheless, he was prepared to employ different forms of propaganda in his dealings with two conflicting groups – the victors and the vanquished. But, when the fighting stopped, the consequences of this studied duplicity would confront him.

In truth, that confrontation occurred even before the war was officially ended. The flight of Darius from Gaugamela and the surrender of Babylon and Susa made Alexander *de facto* ruler of the Persian empire. Although one final attempt was made to impede the king's progress at the Persian Gates, the capture of Persepolis was more or less symbolic. Indeed, for the Greeks, the entry into the city was, like that of the armies of the First Crusade into Jerusalem in 1099, the culmination of the campaign and the fulfillment of the purpose for which they had crossed into Asia. But for Alexander it was a public relations nightmare. As long as Darius lived and continued to be recognized as Great King, the war remained unfinished and the eastern half of the empire unconquered. Greek allies, mindful of the League's propaganda, demanded the destruction of the city in the hope of sating their hunger for revenge and booty. Victorious and laden with spoils, they expected to be demobilized. To deny the soldiers of League, as well as his Macedonian veterans, the right to plunder would be a failure to acknowledge their sacrifices, but Parmenion rightly advised that Alexander should not destroy what was now his (Arr. 3.18.11). Hence the king compromised, allowing his troops to pillage while still reserving the greatest treasures for himself; for even in the suburbs there were enough spoils to go around. But, if the destruction of the palace was an act of policy, it was an unfortunate miscalculation. Alexander may have attempted to limit the physical destruction while satisfying the expectations of the Greeks back home; the symbolism of the act was, however, seared into the hearts of Iranians for centuries.[34]

[34]   Balcer 1978; Shabazi 2003: 19–20.

In vain Darius summoned reinforcements from the upper satrapies, despite the fact that Alexander was delayed at Persepolis awaiting news of the outcome of Agis' war and the clearing of the passes through the Zagros. When in May 330 Alexander finally crossed the Zagros into Media, Darius had little choice but to retreat to the solitudes of Central Asia, following the caravan route (later to be known as the Silk Road) that led from Rhagae through the Caspian Gates (the Sar-i-Darreh pass) between the Great Salt Desert and the Elburz mountains. But the cumbersome train of women and eunuchs, and the other *impedimenta* of royalty, made slow progress, while Alexander closed the distance between himself and his prey. Darius thus felt compelled to decide the matter in battle, with an army that had dwindled to fewer than 40,000 barbarian troops and 4,000 Greeks. And these lacked the fighting spirit or the leadership to decide the matter on the battlefield: Bessus, satrap of Bactria and Sogdiana, and the chiliarch Nabarzanes were intent upon flight to Bactra (Balkh), where new forces could be enlisted for a guerrilla war against Alexander; Darius had lost all authority. He was arrested and placed in chains, allegedly of gold, as if to mitigate the crime, and his remaining followers slipped away to make submission to the advancing conqueror. Finally, in a vain hope of buying time or winning Alexander's goodwill, the conspirators murdered their king and left him by the roadside. Arrian dates Darius' death to the month Hecatombaeon in the archonship of Aristophon, that is, July 330 (Arr. 3.22.2; Bosworth 1980b: 346 suggests a miscalculation and postpones the event to August). Not long after, Alexander reached Hecatompylus and dismissed the remainder of his allied troops. The pressure to declare an end to the Panhellenic war had been mounting since the fall of Persepolis, and some forces had been sent home from Ecbatana. Despite the loss of the allied contingents, there was still a ready supply of mercenary soldiers and regular reinforcements from Macedonia and Thrace. Furthermore, since the king was anxious to bring about an accommodation with the Persian aristocracy, and indeed to present himself as the legitimate successor of Darius III, it was necessary to abandon the slogans of Panhellenism and vengeance.

Those who supported Bessus hastened in the direction of the Merv Oasis and the upper satrapies of Bactria and Sogdiana. Others, however, rejected Bessus and his clique. Bagisthanes, Antibelus (or, as Curt. 5.13.11 renders the name in Latin, Brochubelus) son of Mazaeus, and Melon, the king's interpreter, had surrendered even before the conspirators seized Darius. Now, upon Bessus' usurpation, the number and importance of these defectors increased: Phrataphernes, Autophradates, Artabazus and his sons, all found their way to Alexander's camp. The king did not disappoint them, assigning to Phrataphernes the rule of the Parthians, and Autophradates the Tapurians. Artabazus and his sons remained with Alexander – he had known them since they had taken refuge at Philip's court, and would reward them later. Even the regicide Nabarzanes surrendered to Alexander and was pardoned through the efforts of the younger Bagoas, an attractive eunuch who found favor with Alexander.[35] Perhaps he lived out his life in obscurity, although it is

---

[35] Badian 1958b (the paper is a methodological study arguing against the views of Tarn 2.320–3); for Bagoas' life see Heckel 68; for his relationship with Alexander see Ogden, ch. 11.

possible that the "Barzanes" who attempted to gain control of Parthia and Hyrcania, and was subsequently arrested and executed, was in fact the former chiliarch.[36]

It soon became known that the regicide Bessus had assumed the upright tiara and styled himself Artaxerxes V, and it is perhaps no mere coincidence that Alexander adopted Persian dress at about the same time (Plu. 45.1–3). At Susia (Tus), Alexander accepted the surrender of Satibarzanes, whom he confirmed as satrap of the Areians and sent back to his satrapy (in the vicinity of modern Herat) accompanied by forty javelin men under Anaxippus. These were soon butchered by Satibarzanes' forces and Alexander, who had set out for Margiana, was forced to divert his army to Artacoana. Caught off-guard by the suddenness of his arrival, the treacherous satrap fled to Bactria with 2,000 horsemen, but he soon returned to challenge the Persian Arsaces, whom Alexander had installed in his place. Not much later, Satibarzanes was killed in single combat with Erigyius.

Alexander himself followed the Helmand river valley eastward in the direction of Arachosia. On the way, he encountered the Ariaspians, a people known also as the "Benefactors" (*euergetae*) for the aid they gave Cyrus the Great in the 530s; now they provisioned another great conqueror over the winter of 330/29. In Arachosia, in the vicinity of modern Kandahar (but see Vogelsang 1985: 60 for pre-Alexandrian settlement), the king founded yet another Alexandria in the satrapy abandoned by the regicide Barsaentes, whom Sambus now sheltered. The Macedonians then entered Bactria via the Khawak Pass, which led to Drapsaca (Qunduz). Their speed and determination were beginning to take a toll on the barbarian leaders, who sought reprieve by surrendering Bessus. The regicide was arrested, stripped naked, and left in chains to be taken (by Ptolemy) to Alexander, but the conspirators who betrayed him were not yet ready to test the conqueror's mercy.

The punishment of Bessus – Alexander sent him back to Ecbatana to be mutilated in Persian fashion (which involved cutting off the ears and nose) and then executed – should have ended the affair. But the northeastern frontier was unstable, and the semi-nomadic peoples there were inclined to trust the vastness of its open spaces and its seemingly unassailable mountain fortresses. Furthermore, Alexander's campaign to the Iaxartes, and the establishment of Alexandria Eschate to replace the old outpost of Cyropolis, threatened the old patterns of life and trade in Sogdiana.[37] Hence the local dynasts, Spitamenes, Sisimithres, Oxyartes, Arimazes, took up the fight, and two years of guerrilla warfare followed before the political marriage of Alexander and Oxyartes' daughter, Roxane, could bring stability to the region.

Alexander's treatment of Bessus had perhaps sent the wrong message: the rebels should expect no clemency from the conqueror. Invited to a council at Bactra (Zariaspa), the chieftains of Bactria and Sogdiana suspected treachery and renewed their opposition. Spitamenes, perhaps an Achaemenid, emerged as the leader of the resistance, striking at Maracanda while Alexander carried the war beyond the

---

[36]   Heckel 1981: 66–7.
[37]   Holt 1988: 54–9.

Iaxartes. Next he caught the force sent to relieve the town in an ambush at the Polytimetus, inflicting heavy casualties and inspiring the natives' hopes. But the following year, he was hemmed in by the contingents of Craterus and Coenus and eventually betrayed by his Scythian allies, who sent his head to the Macedonian camp while they themselves made good their escape into the desert.

In the late autumn of 328, large numbers of rebels and their families took refuge with Sisimithres on the so-called "Rock of Chorienes," now known as Koh-i-nor,[38] frighteningly high and of even more imposing circumference and surrounded by a deep ravine. But Alexander induced his surrender through the agency of Oxyartes, who must have defected to the Macedonians in the hope of saving his family. By his voluntary submission Sisimithres averted a fate similar to that of Ariamazes, and he was allowed to retain his territory (probably the region of Gazaba), although his two sons were retained as hostages in Alexander's army. In early 327, Sisimithres was able to provision Alexander's army with supplies for two months, "a large number of pack-animals, 2000 camels, and flocks of sheep and herds of cattle" (Curt. 8.4.19). Alexander repaid the favor by plundering the territory of the Sacae and offering Sisimithres a gift of 30,000 head of cattle. It was almost certainly at this point that the banquet at which Roxane was introduced to Alexander occurred, and the king took his first oriental bride.

Alexander had never entirely trusted mercenaries – perhaps he had bitter memories of their betrayal of Philip (Curt. 8.1.24) – and he found it convenient to settle not fewer than 10,000 of them in military outposts beyond the Oxus (Amu-darya). The king had, of course, founded numerous "cities" throughout the east – several, though not all, named for himself – and would continue to do so in India: Plutarch (*Mor.* 328e = *de fort. Al.* 1.5) speaks of more than seventy, but many of these involved either the resettling of old cities (e.g., Alexandreia Troas, or Prophthasia at Phrada, modern Farah) or the establishment of military colonies (*katoikiai*), though some twelve to eighteen Alexandreias deserve serious attention.[39] In Bactria and Sogdiana, the short-term prognosis for these settlements was not good: for the mercenaries felt abandoned in the solitudes of Central Asia and, prompted by the false news of Alexander's death in India, considered a bold escape to the west – thus imitating on a grander scale the achievement of the Ten Thousand – but the plan was suppressed in 326/5 and again, with great slaughter, in 323/2.[40] Paradoxically, Bactria and Sogdiana were destined to become an outpost of Hellenism between the Mauryan kingdom in the east and the Parthians in the west.

The opposition to Alexander that manifested itself at the time of Philip's death had been silenced by swift and decisive measures, but the opponents remained. In the first year of the Asiatic campaign, the king found evidence of secret negotiations between Alexander Lyncestes and representatives of the Great King. In winter 334/3,

---

[38] Chorienes was, in all likelihood, Sisimithres' official name: Heckel 1986a; but see Bosworth 1981; 1995: 124–39.

[39] Stephanus of Byzantium, s.v. "Alexandreiai"; Fraser 1996; Tarn 1997: ii. 232–59.

[40] Holt 1988; Tarn 1997.

the Lyncestian was arrested on information divulged by a Persian agent named Sisenes (Arr. 1.25). The theory that he had not been in treasonous contact with the chiliarch Nabarzanes and the exile Amyntas son of Antiochus, but was himself the victim of conspiracy devised by Alexander (thus Badian 2000a), is unconvincing (see Heckel 2003b). At the time, however, Alexander's position was far from secure, and he was reluctant to test the loyalty of Antipater by executing his son-in-law. The Lyncestian was nevertheless kept in chains for three years before being brought to trial.

Further dissatisfaction resulted from the king's acceptance of his "divine birth" at Siwah. For the conquest and administration of the satrapy, Alexander's recognition by the priests of Amun was a political expedient. But the subtleties of politics were wasted on the conservative Macedonian aristocracy, which had grown to regard its king as first among equals. Like the king's later orientalisms, the decision to exploit native sentiment was regarded by the conquerors as a demotion of the victors and their practices. Hegelochus, perhaps a relative of Philip's last wife Cleopatra, appears to have plotted against the king in Egypt, but the plan came to naught and was disclosed only in 330, more than a year after the conspirator's death at Gaugamela. Philotas had also voiced his displeasure in Egypt, treasonous activity for a lesser man. His claim that Alexander's military success was due primarily to Parmenion's generalship did not sit well with the son of Philip of Macedon, perhaps because there was some truth in it. Before the final decision at Gaugamela, the remark was ignored but not forgotten. The echo of Philotas' boast would resound in Phrada in 330, when Parmenion had been left behind in Ecbatana.

In Alexander's camp there now occurred the first open signs of opposition to the king's authority and policies (see also ch. 4). The so-called "conspiracy of Philotas" in the autumn of 330 was, if anything, an indication that some of the most prominent *hetairoi* had begun to question Alexander's leadership. At that time, a relatively unknown individual named Dimnus either instigated or was party to a conspiracy to murder the king. The details of this plot he revealed to his lover Nicomachus, and by him they were transmitted to Nicomachus' brother Cebalinus and ultimately to Alexander himself. Philotas' role is at best obscure: what we do know is that Cebalinus reported the plot to him and that he did not pass it on, later alleging that he did not take it seriously. He could perhaps point to the humiliation endured by his father, Parmenion, who falsely accused Philip of Acarnania of planning to poison the king in Cilicia. But the fact remains that Philotas was already on record as having made boastful remarks which exaggerated his own achievements, and those of his father, and cast aspersions on Alexander's generalship (Arr. 3.26.1; Plu. *Alex.* 48.1–49.2 provides the details). That this occurred in Egypt, after Alexander's acceptance of his role as "Son of Amun," is significant; for it is a clear sign of how the orientalizing policies of the king were alienating the conservative commanders of the army. Hegelochus son of Hippostratus, as has been noted, harbored treasonous ambitions at this time (Curt. 6.11.22–9). Furthermore, in the deadly world of Macedonian politics, where assassination was a regular and effective tool, it was easily believed that anyone who knowingly suppressed knowledge of a conspiracy must in some way have approved of it. This, at least, was the substance of the charge against Philotas and, combined with his previous record of disloyalty, it was sufficient to bring about his condemnation and execution. Alexander nevertheless was careful to give the impression of legality to his actions, for he knew that the execution of the son would have to be followed by the father's murder. Charges were laid against Parmenion, and Polydamas the Thessalian was sent in disguise to Ecbatana, where the murder was carried out swiftly by men Alexander felt he could trust.[41]

The deaths of Philotas and his father gave Alexander the opportunity to eliminate Alexander Lyncestes, who, if he was no longer a danger to the king, remained a political embarrassment. Antipater appears not to have protested against the imprisonment of his son-in-law, and the king, who had now become truly the master of his growing domain, felt secure enough to execute the traitor. A lengthy incarceration will have given the Lyncestian time to rehearse a defense, but the hopelessness of his position rendered him confused and all but speechless.

The elimination of Philotas required a restructuring of the command of the Companion Cavalry. The king had learned that it was unwise to entrust so important an office to a single individual, and his solution was designed to limit the power of the hipparch while making conciliatory gestures to the old guard. Philotas' command was thus divided between Black Cleitus, who had saved the king's life at the Granicus and whose sister had been Alexander's wet nurse, and the untried but unquestionably loyal Hephaestion. The latter appointment proved to be not merely a case of nepotism but an unsound military decision, and within two years the Companions were divided into at least five hipparchies, of which only one remained under Hephaestion's command.

The strain of combat and campaigning under the harshest conditions took its toll on soldiers and commanders alike. In summer 328, at a drinking party in Maracanda, the stress of combat mixed with personal resentment and political outlook into a deadly brew. The event that precipitated a quarrel between Alexander and Black Cleitus, the former commander of the "Royal Squadron" (*ile basilike*) of the Companion Cavalry, was, on the face of it, innocent enough. A certain Pierion or Pranichus, who belonged to the king's entourage of artists, recited a poem that appears to have been a mock epic about one of their own – the harpist Aristonicus (see Tritle, ch. 7) – who died in battle against Spitamenes.[42] But the veteran warrior, Cleitus, took umbrage and faulted Alexander for allowing Greek nonmilitary men to ridicule a Macedonian defeat at a function that included barbarians. And we must assume that there were greater issues at play: Cleitus had watched Alexander's transformation from a traditional Macedonian ruler to an orientalizing despot with disapproval, and the argument that ensued was as much a clash of generations and ideologies as the machismo of two battle-scarred veterans under the influence of alcohol.

---

[41] See Badian 1960; Heckel 1977; Adams 2003.
[42] Holt 1988: 78–9 n. 118, plausibly.

The underlying tensions were not to subside. If anything, the marriage of Alexander to Roxane in winter 328/7, which had done so much to reconcile the barbarians with their conquerors, proved immensely unpopular with the army and its commanders – even more so, if there is any truth to claim that Alexander arranged for similar mixed marriages between his *hetairoi* and Bactrian women (*Metz Epit.* 31; D.S. 17 index λ). Furthermore, the king's attempt to introduce the Persian practice of obeisance known as *proskynesis* at the court, for both barbarians and Macedonians, not only proved a dismal failure but increased the alienation of the Macedonian aristocracy.

Many scholars have seen Alexander's unsuccessful experiment with *proskynesis* as a thinly veiled demand for recognition of his divine status. This is, however, highly unlikely; for the Greeks themselves knew that the Great King was never regarded as divine and that *proskynesis* was merely part of the court protocol. That they considered it an inappropriate way of addressing a mortal ruler is another matter. If hostile sources chose to equate Alexander's adoption of the practice with a request for divine honors, that was a misinterpretation – either deliberate or unintentional – of the king's motives. (In view of his later demands, this is not entirely surprising.) Furthermore, the claim that *proskynesis* required the Macedonians to prostrate themselves before their king is equally nonsensical. Herodotus, in a famous passage concerning the practice (1.134.1), makes it clear that the extent of debasement was directly proportional to the status of the individual and was not restricted to the greeting of the Great King (see also Xen. *Anab.* 1.6.10). If Macedonians like Leonnatus ridiculed the Persians for abasing themselves, it demonstrates merely that the conquered peoples approached their new sovereign as suppliants, thus humbling themselves before Alexander in a way that would not have been required of them at the court of Darius, where the hierarchy was clearly established. The position of Persian nobles at the court of Alexander was yet to be determined and obsequious behavior was a form of self-preservation. By contrast, Alexander would have required of his *hetairoi* little more than a kiss on the lips or the cheek, and it is perhaps a misunderstanding of this practice that led contemporary historians to claim that Alexander gave a kiss to his *hetairoi* only if they had previously performed *proskynesis*, when in fact the kiss and the *proskynesis* were synonymous. What is certain, however, is that the ceremony, which was intended to put the Persian and Macedonian on a roughly equal footing (Balsdon 1950: 382), and which suited Alexander's new role as Great King, was rejected by the Greeks and Macedonians, and that Callisthenes of Olynthus was among the most vocal of those who voiced their objections. Nor is it difficult to understand that the nobles who had long regarded their ruler as *primus inter pares* would be reluctant to acknowledge that they, like the conquered enemy, were now "slaves" (*douloi*) of the Great King.

The extent of the alienation can be seen in the so-called "Conspiracy of the Pages." The plot had its origins in a personal humiliation: Hermolaus son of Sopolis, while hunting with the king, had anticipated Alexander in striking a boar, an act of *lèse-majesté*.[43] For this he was flogged. But the view that he plotted to murder the king in order to avenge this outrage is simplistic, and it was recognized even at the time that there were larger issues at play. The Pages were the sons of prominent *hetairoi*, and their hostility toward Alexander was doubtless a reflection of the Macedonian aristocracy's reaction to his policies. The conspiracy itself came to naught: Eurylochus, a brother of one of the Pages, brought the news of the plot to the *somatophylakes* Ptolemy and Leonnatus, and the conspirators were arrested, tried, and executed. But the episode revealed once again the extent of disaffection among the Macedonian aristocracy. The elimination of the conspirators also gave Alexander the opportunity of ridding himself of Callisthenes (Aristotle's nephew), the official historian who, over the course of the campaign, had developed too sharp a tongue for the king's liking and played no small part in sabotaging the introduction of *proskynesis*. As tutor of the Pages, he could be held responsible for their political attitudes, and, although there was no clear evidence to incriminate him, the suspicion of ill-will toward the king was sufficient to bring him down. If the king's friendship with Aristotle, perhaps already strained, mattered, he may indeed have intended to keep Callisthenes in custody until his fate could be decided by a vote of the League of Corinth. The conflicting stories of the nature of his death reflect at least two layers of *apologia*. In the version given by Ptolemy, he was tortured and hanged, a punishment at once barbaric and appropriate to traitors (Arr. 4.14.3; Bosworth 1995: 100); Chares of Mytilene says that he was incarcerated for seven months and died of obesity and a disease of lice (see Africa 1982: 4) before he could stand trial (Plu. *Alex.* 55.9 = Chares, *FGrHist* 125 F15).

In spring 327, Alexander recrossed the Hindu Kush and began his invasion of India, the easternmost limits of the Achaemenid empire. The extent of Persian rule in Gandhara and the Punjab had doubtless declined since the age of Darius I, but the response of the local dynasts to Alexander's demands for submission shows that they continued to recognize some form of Achaemenid overlordship (hence Arrian's use of the term *hyparchoi*), that is, they regarded Alexander's authority as legitimate (see Bosworth 1995: 147–9). Not all came over willingly. In Bajaur, the Aspasians, who dwelt in the Kunar or Chitral valley, fled to the hills after abandoning and burning Arigaeum (Nawagai); nevertheless the Macedonians captured 40,000 men and 230,000 oxen. More obstinate was the resistance of the Assaceni, who fielded 2,000 cavalry, 30,000 infantry, and thirty elephants. After the death of Assacenus, who may have been killed in the initial skirmish with Alexander, Massaga in the Katgala Pass relied for its defense on Cleophis, the mother (or possibly widow) of Assacenus. Soon Cleophis sent a herald to Alexander to discuss terms of surrender, gaining as a result the reputation of "harlot queen"; for she was said to have retained her kingdom through sexual favors (Just. 12.7.9–11). The story that she later bore a son named Alexander is perhaps an invention of the late first century

---

[43] But see Roisman 2003b: 315–16.

and an allusion to Cleopatra VII and Caesarion.[44] Ora (Udegram) and Beira or Bazeira (Bir-kot), other strongholds of the Assaceni, fell in rapid succession. But a more strenuous effort was required to capture the rock of Aornus, which abutted on its eastern side the banks of the Indus river. Hence, it is probable that its identification with Pir-Sar by Sir Aurel Stein is correct, though recently others have suggested Mt. Ilam.[45]

In the mean time, the king had sent an advance force to bridge the Indus and secure Peucelaotis (modern Charsadda) with a Macedonian garrison. Ambhi (whom the Greeks called Omphis or Mophis), the ruler of Taxila – the region between the Indus and the Hydaspes – had already sent out diplomatic feelers to Alexander and he now welcomed the Macedonian army near his capital (in the vicinity of modern Islamabad); for he was prepared to exchange recognition of Alexander's overlordship for military help against his enemies, Abisares and Porus, who ruled the northern and eastern regions respectively. In return for Macedonian support, Philip son of Machatas was appointed as overseer of the region, with Ambhi (under the official name of "Taxiles") as nominal head of the kingdom.

Abisares had known of Alexander's advance since at least winter 327/6, when he sent reinforcements to Ora. After the fall of Aornus in 326, natives from the region between Dyrta and the Indus fled to him, and he renewed his alliance with Porus. Though clearly the weaker partner in this relationship, Abisares could nevertheless muster an army of comparable size; hence Alexander planned to attack Porus before Abisares could join forces with him. In the event, Porus looked in vain for reinforcements, as Abisares made (token?) submission to Alexander and awaited the outcome of events. After the Macedonian victory at the Hydaspes, Abisares sent a second delegation, led by his own brother and bringing money and forty elephants as gifts. Despite his failure to present himself in person, as had been required of him, Abisares retained his kingdom, to which was added the hyparchy of Arsaces; he was, however, assessed an annual tribute and closely watched by the satrap, Philip son of Machatas. Although Abisares is referred to as "satrap" by Arrian, his son doubtless followed an independent course of action after Alexander's return to the west.

Porus meanwhile prepared to face the invader and his traditional enemy, Taxiles, at the Hydaspes (Jhelum), probably near modern Haranpur.[46] Here, Alexander positioned Craterus with a holding force directly opposite Porus and stationed a smaller contingent under Meleager and Gorgias farther upstream; he himself conducted regular feints along the river bank before marching, under the cover of night and a torrential downpour, to ford the river some 26 km north of the main crossing point, catching Porus' son, who had been posted upstream,

[44] Gutschmid 1882: 553–4; Seel 1971: 181–2.

[45] Stein 1929; Bosworth 1995: 178–80. For Mt. Ilam: Eggermont 1970: 191–200; Badian 1987: 117 n. 1.

[46] Stein 1932; Wood 1997: 184–7; Fuller 1960: 180–4 for earlier theories. For the battle see Arr. 5.8.4–18.5; Curt. 8.13.5–14, 33; D.S. 17.87–8; Plu. *Alex.* 60; Just. 12.8.1–8; Polyaen. *Strat.* 4.3.9, 22; Frontin. *Strat.* 1.4.9; *Metz Epit.* 53–62.

off his guard. This was near modern Jalalpur and the wooded island of Admana. The main engagement was a particularly hard-fought and bloody one,[47] in which the Indian ruler distinguished himself by his bravery. The valiant enemy earned Alexander's respect, and was allowed to retain his kingdom. It had not always been so: Alexander had not always been so generous in his treatment of stubborn adversaries. The greater challenge lay, however, in the attempt to bring about lasting peace between the Indian rivals. Curtius claims that an alliance between Taxiles and Porus was sealed by marriage, the common currency in such transactions. But the arrangement was never entirely satisfactory. Though Taxiles was perhaps more to be trusted than Porus, Alexander needed a strong ruler in what would be the buffer zone at the eastern edge of his empire (see Breloer 1941).

Despite the popular view of Alexander as a man obsessed with conquest and intent upon reaching the eastern edge of the world – a view which will persist because the legend of Alexander has become so firmly rooted that it defies all rational attempts to change it – Alexander abandoned thoughts of acquiring new territory after his hard-fought victory over Porus. What he needed now was security, and he worked with his new ally himself to bring the neighboring dynasts under Porus' authority. The Glausae were reduced by Alexander and their realm added to that of Porus, while Hephaestion annexed the kingdom of the so-called "cowardly" Porus, between the Acesines (Chenab) and Hydraotes (Ravi) rivers. Garrisons were established in the region, but they comprised Indian troops and were responsible to Porus, not Alexander. Beyond the Ravi, the campaigns were either punitive or preemptive, depending on how Porus in his discussions with the king assessed their power or reported their activities. Sangala, indeed, was stubborn in its resistance, and the attackers paid a heavy price in casualties; but Sophytes (Saubhuti) made peace, perhaps relieved by the conqueror's suppression of the neighboring Kshatriyas.

Nevertheless, the Hyphasis (Beas) marked the end of the eastward march – and Alexander knew it. He had, in truth, already determined to take the army elsewhere. After the victory at the Hydaspes, the king had established two cities, Bucephala and Nicaea, as outposts of his realm, and sent men into the hills to cut down trees for the construction of a fleet that would sail down the Hydaspes to the Indus delta, thus following a route known to the Greeks since the exploits of Scylax of Caryanda during the reign of Darius I (Hdt. 5.44). His reasons for campaigning in the eastern Punjab were simple and practical enough. It was essential that Porus should control a strong vassal kingdom on the edge of Alexander's empire, and it was important to keep the men occupied and to place the burden of feeding his troops on the hostile tribes in that region rather than on his newly acquired friend Porus. Alexander's behavior at the Hyphasis, when he withdrew into his tent and sulked because his troops would not follow him to the Ganges, was as a much an act of dissembling as the larger-than-life structures that were erected at the river, designed

---

[47] Hamilton 1956; cf. Devine 1987.

to deceive posterity into thinking that the Macedonian invaders had been more than mere humans.[48]

For Alexander the path to the Ocean was still open, but the need to secure the empire was not forgotten: the descent of the Indus waterway, conducted by land as well as on the river, shows that Alexander intended a systematic reduction of the area which would insure Macedonian rule in the Punjab (Breloer 1941). The expedition was a show of force on the eastern side of the Indus to support Macedonian claims to rule the western lands adjacent to the river (Bosworth 1983). The Sibi, allegedly descendants of Heracles, were woven into the fabric of the Alexander legend more securely than into that of the empire. The Kshudrakas (Oxydracae or Sudracae) and Malavas (Mallians) were deadly foes and long-time enemies of both Porus and Abisares. The sack of one of their towns – probably located at or near modern Multan (Wood 1997: 199–200) – nearly cost the king his life, and from this point, he was conveyed downstream by ship, displayed to the troops, in an attempt to stifle rumors that he had died and the "truth" was being kept from them by the generals.

When the king recovered his strength, he turned his attention to Musicanus, whose kingdom beyond the confluence of the Chenab is probably to be identified with ancient Alor. Musicanus, surprised by the enemy's approach, surrendered and accepted a garrison. But Oxicanus (or Oxycanus), a nomarch of upper Sind (Eggermont 1975: 12 locates him at Azeika), resisted the invader and was eventually captured and, presumably, executed. Porticanus, ruler of Pardabathra, suffered a similar fate, but the arguments for identifying the two rulers as one and the same, as many scholars do (Smith 1914: 101 n. 3; Berve ii. 293), are not compelling (Eggermont 1975: 9–10, 12). At Sindimana, the capital of the dynast Sambus, whom Alexander had appointed satrap of the hill country west of the Indus, the inhabitants opened their gates to receive the Macedonians, but Sambus himself fled. Musicanus, too, on the advice of the Brahmans, had rebelled soon after the king's departure, only to be hunted down by Peithon son of Agenor and brought to Alexander, who crucified Musicanus and other leaders of the insurrection. What became of Sambus we do not know, but Craterus' return to the west through the Bolan Pass may have been intended to root out the remaining insurgents; for it appears that Sambus controlled the profitable trade route between Alor and Kandahar (Eggermont 1975: 22).

From Sind, Alexander explored the area of Patalene and the Indus delta before sailing into the Indian Ocean, where he sacrificed to the same sea deities whom he had propitiated at the Hellespont. But the road home, through the lands of the Oreitae and the Gedrosian desert (for the route: Stein 1943; Strasburger 1952; Engels 1978a: 135–43; Seibert 1985: 171–8; see Hamilton 1972 for the Oreitae), would be a hard one, especially for the ill-provisioned camp followers who had swollen the numbers of the Macedonian army. But the march was necessary if the king was to keep in contact with Nearchus' fleet, which had been instructed to sail

---

[48] Spann 1999; Heckel 2003a.

from the delta to the straits of Hormuz (for early travel from the Persian Gulf to India, see Casson 1974: 30–1, 45) and ultimately to the mouth of the Tigris; for at that time the river flowed directly into the sea, rather than joining the Euphrates, as it does today. The privations of the army were aggravated by the failure of certain satraps to provide the requisitioned supplies. The king's angry gesture of tossing Abulites' coins at the feet of his horses (Plu. *Alex.* 68.7) may suggest that the satrap had sent money instead of provisions. Nevertheless, Alexander reunited with Nearchus in Carmania and later again at the Tigris. The infamous Dionysiac procession, accepted or rejected by scholars (according to their personal views of Alexander) as evidence of his degeneration, may have been nothing more than well-deserved "R & R" for the troops (Tarn i. 109, typically, "a necessary holiday which legend perverted into a story of Alexander . . . reeling through Carmania at the head of a drunken rout").

Alexander's lengthy absence in Central Asia and the Indus valley had raised doubts about whether he would return, and in the heartland of the empire the administration of the lands and treasures was conducted with little regard for the king's pleasure or the empire's well-being. Among the worst offenders was Harpalus, the treasurer who had moved his headquarters from Ecbatana to Babylon, where he lavished gifts and titles upon first one Athenian courtesan, Pythionice, and after her death another, Glycera. Other charges against him involved sexual debauchery and illegal treatment of the native population. When he learned of Alexander's reemergence from India, Harpalus fled westward, first to Cilicia and then on to Athens, taking with him Glycera and no small amount of the king's treasure. But Harpalus was only the most famous of the offenders and perhaps the most sensational in his offenses. Others were quickly called to account, tried, and in many cases deposed or executed. One scholar has labeled the actions a "reign of terror" (Badian 1961) and the phrase is now employed by many scholars as a convenient shorthand for the events that followed the king's unexpected return from the east. Alexander's restoration of order is frequently interpreted as abuse of power, and criminals as "scapegoats," and not all were executed or deposed from office. It is hardly surprising that the king, after a lengthy absence, should conduct an investigation into their affairs.[49]

The house cleaning was accompanied by further orientalizing policies: at Susa, mass marriages of prominent *hetairoi* to the daughters of noble Persians were celebrated in conjunction with the legitimization of the thousands of informal unions of Macedonian soldiers with barbarian women. Not a "policy of fusion," to be sure, or the creation of a "mixed race," but rather a blueprint for political stability,[50] if carried through by a capable leader committed to this vision of a new empire. This ceremony was soon followed by further integration of orientals into the military and the demobilization of some 10,000 Macedonian veterans. The process was regarded as an insult, even by those most eager to return home, and at Opis, for

[49]   For a more balanced picture: Higgins 1980; cf. Müller 2003: 194–6; Worthington 2004b: 172–3.
[50]   Bosworth 1980a.

the first time, there was a genuine mutiny within the army. Once again Alexander showed himself a worthy son of Philip II, combining soothing words with largesse, while executing the ringleaders of the sedition. Notions of an appeal for universal brotherhood have, rightly, been debunked,[51] but Alexander did not back away from his orientalizing policies; for he must now have given thought to establishing an administrative center in Asia – possibly in Babylon[52] – and it appears that he elevated his best friend Hephaestion to the rank of *chiliarchos* or "Grand Vizier" (on the chiliarchy see Collins 2001).

As it turned out, the *Alexanderreich*, buffeted by political storms and weighed down by the king's grandiose schemes, proved too flimsy a structure. Nor was the man himself emotionally prepared for what was to come. In the summer of 324, Nicanor of Stageira had proclaimed the Exiles' Decree at the Olympic festival (D.S. 18.8.2–6; Zahrnt 2003), its demands far exceeding Alexander's prerogatives as *hegemon* of the League and their implications catastrophic for many states, Athens in particular. The danger of war with Macedon was heightened by the arrival of Harpalus and the lure of his money. But Alexander himself was soon plunged into personal tragedy, as Hephaestion died of fever and excessive drinking in Ecbatana (October 324). The king's grief knew no bounds and, although genuine, its Homeric displays were all too familiar. Anger was eventually directed against the Cossaean rebels, and mercy was in short supply. And in the months that followed, as he awaited the unfolding of events in Europe, including the possible confrontation between Antipater and Craterus, who had been sent to replace him, Alexander turned his thoughts to funeral monuments, a hero cult for Hephaestion, and a demand for his own recognition as a divinity (Habicht 1970: 28–36). In June 323 he too died of illness in Babylon without designating an heir. It would not have mattered, for only three male relatives of the king remained, one of them as yet unborn, and the marshals of the empire had taken too equal a share in the burden of conquest to relinquish overall power to one of their own number. Even as he was destroying the empire's equilibrium, Alexander had been planning new expeditions to Carthage and Arabia.[53] Thus his exit from life, and history, was at the same time an evasion of responsibility. Alexander (the Great) was as fortunate in death as he had been in life, as the burden of dealing with the consequences of his superhuman achievements fell on the shoulders of his all too human successors.

[51]   Badian 1958a, against Tarn 1933 and 1997: ii. 434–49.
[52]   Schachermeyr 1970, and Weber, ch. 5.
[53]   D.S. 18.4.4; Högemann 1985.

3

The Diadochi, or Successors to Alexander

Patrick Wheatley

The line it is drawn, the curse it is cast
The slow one now will later be fast
As the present now will later be past
The order is rapidly fadin'
And the first one now will later be last
For the times they are a-changin'

Bob Dylan

Alexander's death at about 4.30 in the afternoon of June 11, 323[1] resounded across the empire that he had captured in eleven short years from the Persian kings.[2] There was no heir, and no obvious successor. A constitutional crisis ensued among the Macedonians, with no hope of an untroubled transmission of power. Within months, two major revolts against the Macedonian hegemony would erupt in opposite corners of the empire: Greek mercenaries garrisoned in Bactria would attempt to march back to Europe, and the Athenians tried again to shake off the Macedonian yoke from Greece in the revolt which became known as the Lamian War.[3] Within twelve more years, the marshals fought themselves to a fruitless standstill in three successive so-called Diadoch Wars and by 306, two essential

---

[1] The date of Alexander's death, which until recently had veered back and forth in scholarship between June 10 and 13, has finally been fixed by the testimony of a contemporary Babylonian Astronomical document (Diary I, pp. 206–7, No. -322 B Obv. 8´; for full discussion, assembling the chronographic evidence from several traditions, see Depuydt 1997.

[2] I thank my colleagues Jon Hall and John Walsh for help and encouragement while writing this essay.

[3] On the Bactrian revolts: D.S. 17.99.5–6; 18.4–8; cf. Babylonian Astronomical Diary I, p. 211, No. -322 D Obv. 22. On the Lamian War: Arr. *Succ.* 1.9; D.S. 17.111; 18.8–19; Plu. *Dem.* 27; *Phoc.* 23–8; Hyp. *Epit.* 10–20; Just. 13.5; Paus. 1.25.3–5, 29.13; Str. 9.5.10; Polyaen. 4.4.2; Plb. 9.29.2; with Mathieu 1929; Lepore 1955; Errington 1975; Ashton 1983, 1984; Lehmann 1988; Morrison 1987; Schmitt 1992; Bosworth 2003a.

energies had materialized, which sought diametrically opposite outcomes for Alexander's stolen domains. The ambitions of the Antigonids were always centripetal – to reestablish a centralized hegemony over the Greco-Persian possessions – but the ambitions of Ptolemy Soter, Cassander, Lysimachus, and Seleucus were centrifugal: to carve themselves significant gobbets of the so-called "great carcass." The metaphor is apt, and was used by Plutarch (*Demetr.* 30.1) in his description of the situation after the great battle of Ipsus in 301. Moreover, it is as suitable for modern analysis as it was for the ancient writers. There were inevitable irruptions by brilliant and talented individuals, such as Demetrius the Besieger, and at least two of the kingdoms would fail to survive, but by the time four decades had passed after the fateful afternoon of June 11, 323, the Greco-Persian world would settle into reformed geopolitical parameters, and would have to face threatening new movements of Celtic peoples from the depths of Europe.

This transitional forty-year period is without doubt one of the most curious and fascinating in ancient history. It is marked by the utter chaos of the historiographical tradition, the chronography, the prosopography, and the received historical narrative, and yet it is crucial to our understanding of all the succeeding major events, including the rise and dominance of the Roman republic, and the cultural ramifications for the modern world of the ensuing religious developments in the Near East.[4] Within the parameters of the present essay, it is not possible to cover satisfactorily all aspects of the events of these years; I shall therefore discuss in some detail four critical thematic facets of the decades following Alexander's demise. These will include some explication of the source tradition which preserves the history of the period; scrutiny of the centralist/separatist dichotomy among the Successors, which naturally links to an analysis of the conceptual evolution of the kingship or *basileia* in the Macedonian dominated world; and, finally, some brief remarks on the extraordinary and pernicious chronographic difficulties that bedevil study of the Diadochi.

First, the source tradition. The Alexandro-centric nature of both the primary and secondary Classical sources tends to cast a shadow over the documentation of the Diadochi, and the one contemporary writer and participant who did cover the aftermath in detail, Hieronymus of Cardia, is lost.[5] However, Hieronymus is generally acknowledged to be the foundation for what literary accounts we do have for the Successors, in particular books 18–20 of the first-century Diodorus Siculus, the most complete extant account of the years 323–301. The difficulties in supplementing this work are quickly evident when it is revealed that historians must turn to Plutarch's relevant *Parallel Lives*, such works as Polyaenus' *Stratagems*, and the generalized or largely lost epitomes of Pompeius Trogus (by Justin), and Arrian's *Events after Alexander* (by Photius and Dexippus). A number of minor works

---

[4]   Useful modern treatments of the period include Tarn 1913: 1–138 (aging, but still very helpful); Hammond–Walbank 95–258; Bosworth 1988a: 174–81; 2002; Green 1990: 1–134; Heckel 1992; Habicht 1997: 36–97; Shipley 2000: 33–47; Huss 2001: 79–262; Chamoux 2003: 39–54.

[5]   On Hieronymus, see Brown 1947; Hornblower 1981; Bosworth 2002: 169–209; Anson 2004: 2–11.

contain snippets and fragments: Nepos, Appian, Athenaeus, Pausanias; and, of the Alexander sources, book 10 of Curtius contains the most detail on the settlement at Babylon and the weeks after June 11, 323.[6]

This quite varied, but desperately fragmentary and incomplete corpus may be supplemented by material from other genres, especially coinage and epigraphy. One of the results of Alexander's *anabasis* was the creation of an international *fiscus* covering the Greco-Persian world, and Alexander-type coinage continued to be minted posthumously for some two centuries after his death.[7] Thus a very large body of primary source material is available for historical analysis though, unfortunately, the disciplines of numismatics and ancient history are not as closely allied as is desirable, and coinage is not as regularly integrated into historical reconstruction as it might be. Epigraphic evidence is also extant wherever Greek cities are founded, and this, too, may be mined for historical data. It is particularly valuable in the spheres of the large Greek mainland *poleis*, such as Athens, and for the period after 301, when the continuous narrative of Diodorus cuts off, and literary sources become extremely sparse.

So much for the Classical sources, but to these may be added an alternative tradition: Babylonian cuneiform texts, including chronicles, astronomical diaries, and economic texts. These primary documents, the Babylonian equivalent of original Greek sources, are of incalculable value to Classicists and Assyriologists alike. The key text is Chronicle 10, the so-called Babylonian Chronicle of the Diadochi.[8] This cryptic document has fueled massive ongoing controversy among scholars and generally defied precise integration with the Classical sources. However, though these texts are extremely significant, they must be interpreted with an awareness of their narcissistic nature: events are recorded from an entirely Babylonian domestic perspective, with little thought for the wider historical picture (a criticism that can also at times be leveled against the Classical sources). Therefore, while they do provide precise dates, and even times, for some nodal events, there are often difficulties in meshing these events with other types of source material. Babylonian astronomical diaries are also critical in dating (and sometimes timing) vital events, such as the death of Alexander (see n. 1 above), and the sheer precision of these documents from a distance of well over two millennia is awe-inspiring to the modern researcher.[9]

So we have a chaotic source tradition to record one of the most chaotic and poorly understood periods in ancient history. Nevertheless, certain themes obtrude. One of these is the overarching tension between centralist and separatist ambitions

[6]   For a recent, lucid, essay on the source tradition for the Diadochi, see Bosworth 2002: 19–28.

[7]   On the Alexander-type coinage of the Successors, see Newell 1927; Bellinger 1963: 81–130; Mørkholm 1991: 55–96; Price 1991; Houghton and Lorber 2002.

[8]   First published by S. Smith in 1924, but now updated in several languages and editions: Grayson 1975; Glassner 1993; Del Monte 1997: 183–94.

[9]   More recently the work of J. Lendering and certain Assyriologists such as T. Boiy, R. J. van der Spek, and the ongoing Babylonian Chronicles of the Hellenistic Period (BCHP) project, has helped bridge the gap between Classical and Near Eastern scholars.

among Alexander's marshals, which informs events down to 281, but especially impacts on the actions of these individuals up to the great battle of Ipsus in spring, 301. This tension was always inevitable in the event of Alexander's untimely death because of his failure to secure the succession, and was immediately evident in the settlement at Babylon in the weeks after June 11. Perdiccas, who received the chiliarchy after Hephaestion's death in 324, is the first marshal to manifest centrist tendencies.[10] However, he appears to have lacked the confidence to make an overt bid for sole power, and although initially he emerged dominant, one of his first acts, the distribution of the satrapies, supplied the seeds for his later undoing.[11] Perdiccas continued to focus on establishing and deposing satraps, provoking the so-called First Diadoch War, until he overreached himself at the Pelusiac branch of the Nile in 321 or 320 (the chronology is disputed), and was assassinated by his lieutenants.[12] Thus ensued the second conference in two years to settle the power hierarchy of the empire, this time at Triparadeisus in northern Syria. At this venue the power-broker was the aging Antipater, Alexander's regent in Macedonia during the *anabasis*. Antipater was aided by the surprise emergence of the marshal who would become the greatest centralist figure among the Diadochi: Antigonus Monophthalmus ("The One-Eyed"). Antipater's preeminence was short-lived, as the last epitomized fragments of Arrian's *Events after Alexander* describe his humiliation in the winter of 320/19 by the Perdiccan general, Eumenes of Cardia, and his return to Macedonia after April 1, 319.[13]

From this point on, it becomes clear that Antigonus' ambitions were dynastic: to dominate the Macedonian dominions and reforge them into a single political entity under the rule of his family. His sons, Demetrius (later Poliorcetes, "The Besieger of Cities") and Philip, were adolescents, and his grandson, the future Antigonus Gonatas, was born in 319.[14] He first set about eradicating the remnants of the Perdiccan faction in Anatolia, and thus began the Second Diadoch War. This conflict was to last for three full years, and though Antigonus had swift success

---

[10] He also received Alexander's ring from the dying king: Curt. 10.5.4; cf. 10.6.4. On the chiliarchy, see Collins 2001.

[11] By rewarding his rivals with plum satrapies (Just. 13.4.9), Perdiccas made his own quest for supreme power intrinsically far more difficult. On the satrapy distribution, see Curt. 10.10.1–4; D.S. 18.3.1–3; Just. 13.4.9–25; Arr. *Succ.* 1.5–7; cf. Dexippus, *FGrH* 100 F8 §§2–6; *Heid. Epit.* 1; *Liber de Morte* 115–22; cf. Oros. 3.23.7–13; Paus. 1.6.2; with Julien 1914; Lehmann-Haupt, *RE* 2R. ii (1921). 82–188, s.v. "satrap"; Berve i. 253–84; Leuze 1935; Heckel 1988: 108–9; Klinkott 2000.

[12] Installation of Eumenes: D.S. 18.16.1–3, 22.1; Arr. *Succ.* 1.11; Just. 13.6.1–3; Plu. *Eum.* 3.12–13; App. *Mith.* 8; with Schäfer 2002: 60–6; Anson 2004: 65–79. Deposition of Antigonus: D.S. 18.23.3–4, 25.3; Arr. *Succ.* 1.24; Just. 13.6.8; with Billows 1990: 59–60. Campaign against Ptolemy: D.S. 18.29.1, 33.1–36.5; Arr. *Succ.* 1.28–9; Just. 13.8.1–2; Plu. *Eum.* 8.2–3; Polyaen. 4.19; Front. *Strat.* 4.7.20. See, in general, Briant 1973a; Hauben 1977; Billows 1990: 64–71; Heckel 1992: 154–63; Heckel 199–202; Anson 2004: 77–116.

[13] Precision is enabled by a juxtaposition of three diverse ancient references: D.S. 18.40.1; Arr. *Succ.* F1.45 (cf. Göteborg Palimpsest 73v.11–12); Babylonian *Chronicle* 10, Obv. 7′–8′ (= BCHP 3. 26–7).

[14] He died an octogenarian in 239: [Lucian], *Macrob.* 11; Porphyry, *FGrH* 260 F3[12]; with Tarn 1913: 15; Hammond–Walbank 313, 581–2; Bosworth 1994b: 61.

against Attalus, Alcetas, Polemon, and Docimus, and the alliance between Arrhidaeus, the satrap of Hellespontine Phrygia, and the Macedonian admiral Cleitus the White, he was confounded by the stubbornness and wiles of Eumenes. Moreover, the matter of the relative allegiance to the royal house of the warring marshals became critical. Perceived loyalty to the two cipher-kings, the mentally challenged Philip III Arrhidaeus and the child Alexander IV, had become a deciding factor in gaining the commitment of the Macedonian soldiery. The kings, whether physically present or not, became cards in the hands of the marshals, and they were at first, ironically, best exploited (remotely) by the Greek Eumenes.[15] The epic running campaign of 318–317 across Babylonia to Iran is chronicled in great detail by Diodorus, drawing on the eyewitness reports of Hieronymus, who was present at the critical battles of the Coprates river and Paraetacene, and was wounded and captured by Antigonus after the deciding engagement of Gabiene in January 316.[16] At this juncture, Antigonus, like Perdiccas before him, had achieved preeminence among the marshals, and was already regarded as a king in the Iranian satrapies.[17]

The illusion was soon shattered. Before a year was out, in a pattern which was to be repeated regularly for the next three decades, Antigonus received an ultimatum from the other great Diadochi.[18] Cassander, Lysimachus, and Ptolemy, urged on by the fugitive Seleucus, demanded shares of the spoils from the Second Diadoch War: Antigonus' scorn signaled the immediate commencement of the Third Diadoch War. Now the notional centralist–separatist tension became geographically manifest. The Antigonid possessions included the heartlands of the empire: Anatolia, the Levant, and all satrapies east. But they were encircled by Ptolemy to the south, Cassander to the west, and Lysimachus to the northwest. The Antigonid strategic equation would seem simple: isolate each opponent, and crush them one by one. In practice, it proved impossible. The five marshals had fought each other to exhaustion by late 311, and the only real winner was Seleucus, who had successfully retaken his satrapy of Babylonia in the aftermath of the battle of Gaza in late 312.[19] The other protagonists agreed to an intermission in the famous Peace of the Dynasts in late 311 or early 310, from which Seleucus appears to have been excluded.[20] But the peace was a chimaera. It is doubtful whether any of the signatories intended using the lull for anything but rearming and remobilizing. In a remarkable campaign largely hidden from the classical sources, Antigonus waged a separate war,

---

[15]   With a mixture of genuine and forged correspondence: Plu. *Eum.* 13.1–4; D.S. 19.23.3; Polyaen. 4.8.3; with Bosworth 1992b: 69–71; 2002: 122–4; Anson 2004: 142–9, 172–5.

[16]   D.S. 19.44.3. On the battle of Gabiene, see the accounts of Billows 1990: 99–105; Bosworth 2002: 146–60; Schäfer 2002: 155–64; Anson 2004: 184–8. The chronology is hotly disputed: see, for instance, Anson 2006; *contra* Bosworth 1992a.

[17]   D.S. 19.48.1; 55.2; Polyaen. 4.6.13; but see Bosworth 2002: 162.

[18]   D.S. 19.57.1; App. *Syr.* 53; Just. 15.1.2; with Aucello 1957; Grainger 1990: 55–6.

[19]   D.S. 19.90.1; App. *Syr.* 54; Mehl 1986: 89–120; Grainger 1990: 72–81; Bosworth 2002: 216–17, 230–40. Scholars have reached no agreement about the timing of the battle of Gaza; for an overview of the situation with some new evidence, see Wheatley 2003; *contra* Bosworth 2002: 217–30.

[20]   On the Peace, see *OGIS* 5; D.S. 19.105.1; with Simpson 1952; Landucci Gattinoni 1985; Billows 1990: 132–6; Grainger 1990: 85–7; Lund 1992: 60–2.

this time unsuccessfully, against Seleucus in Babylonia,[21] and Ptolemy commenced an offensive in Cilicia, Caria, and the Peloponnese. The defeat of Antigonus seems to have satisfied the Coalition, and the Diadochi in the west returned to petty bickering among themselves. However, it is arguably from this point that Seleucus, who had originally been the catalyst for the alliance against the unifying energy of Antigonus, entered onto the path of centralism himself. He appears to have spent much of 308–302 coalescing the satrapies east of Babylonia into the nucleus of the future Seleucid empire, and he reappeared on the scene in the west once again in 302 with stunning effect.[22] His centralist drive reached its apogee in the campaign against Lysimachus in 282, and just as he appeared to be on the threshold of realizing the old Perdiccan and Antigonid dream, he himself was eliminated through the treachery of Ptolemy Ceraunus later in 281.[23]

In the mean time, returning from Babylonia in 309 or 308, Antigonus prepared his next offensive. This time, in mid 307, he deployed his energetic son, Demetrius, to lead an expeditionary force against Athens.[24] Demetrius easily ended the decade-long hegemony over the city of Cassander's agent, Demetrius of Phalerum, bringing the charisma of Macedonian nobility to subvert the ideals of Greek democracy. While the sources revel in the astonishing Athenian sycophancy to Demetrius, then and later from 304 to 302, a greater Antigonid strategic purpose may be discerned. Monophthalmus had been building himself a capital city in northern Syria,[25] and it seems he had envisaged his reformation of the empire based on twin capitals: Antigoneia-on-the-Orontes, and Athens, no doubt ruled by himself and Demetrius respectively. These would serve as long as necessary as bastions against Cassander and Lysimachus in Europe, and Seleucus and Ptolemy in Asia, though it is certain that the Antigonids always intended to totally eradicate their rivals. Seleucus in 309–308, Ptolemy in 306, and Cassander in 302 knew this beyond doubt,[26] and

---

[21]   For a reconstruction from the vestigial source tradition, see Wheatley 2002.

[22]   For the progress of Seleucus in the east from 308 to 302, see Schober 1981: 140–93; Mehl 1986: 134–214; Grainger 1990: 95–119. Seleucus reappeared in Anatolia in late 302 for the battle of Ipsus the following spring (D.S. 20.113.4; Just. 15.4.1), bringing with him the resource which proved decisive in the battle: 480 elephants for which he had surrendered his claims on the far eastern and Indian satrapies to Chandragupta, founder of the Mauryan dynasty (Just. 15.4.12–21; Plu. *Alex.* 62.4; App. *Syr.* 55; Str. 15.2.9, 16.2.10). On the campaign of Ipsus see Plu. *Demetr.* 28–30; *Pyrrh.* 4.4–5; D.S. 20.111–13, 21.1.4; Just. 15.2.15–17; 15.4.21–2; [Lucian], *Macrob.* 11 (= Hieronymus, *FGrH* 154 F 8); App. *Syr.* 55; Plb. 5.67.8; Nepos, *de Regibus* 3.2; cf. Trogus, *Prol.* 15; Lib. *Or.* 11.84; Oros. 3.23.46; with Bar-Kochva 1976: 105–10; Billows 1990: 173–85.

[23]   Mehl 1986: 318–22; Hammond–Walbank 239–44; Grainger 1990: 189–91; Landucci Gattinoni 1992: 214–21; Lund 1992: 205–6; Franco 1993: 63–4; Habicht 1997: 66–72.

[24]   Plu. *Demetr.* 8–10; D.S. 20.45–46.4; Polyaen. 4.7.6; with Billows 1990: 148–51.

[25]   The exact location of Antigoneia, some 7.3 km from Antioch (Lib. *Or.* 11.85 says 40 stadia), and apparently inland (Dio. 40.29.1) is today uncertain, but it was probably situated in a defensible position between the modern lake Amik and the rivers Asi (Orontes) and Kara Su, perhaps 31 km from the river mouth today; for detailed topography, see esp. Downey 1961: 60–61; also Billows 1990: 297.

[26]   On these campaigns, see respectively Wheatley 2002; Hauben 1975–6; Billows 1990: 173–4.

the hard-line attitude carried the seeds which always undid Antigonid centralist ambitions. As soon as the other Diadochi perceived any serious Antigonid strategic build-up of resources and munitions, they united to negate it,[27] and incidentally to reify the original satrapy distributions of Babylon and Triparadeisus.

While it may appear that all hope of reunification for Alexander's empire was shattered at Ipsus in 301, even the resulting rearrangement in the status quo was insufficient to quench the centralist flame. Demetrius' fortunes were kept alive by the bickering and maneuvering of the victors, especially Ptolemy and Seleucus, and fortune delivered him the kingdom of Macedonia in 294. The restless Demetrius, irrevocably infected by his father's grand ambition, and his own desire to be another Alexander, was found rearming Macedonia for a second *anabasis* by 289. The Diadochi reverted to pattern. Ptolemy, Lysimachus, and Seleucus induced a new player, Pyrrhus, king of Molossia, to join in ousting Demetrius, and the Antigonid dream was extinguished.

We have already observed the ultimate fling of centralist Diadoch energies in the form of Seleucus' victory over Lysimachus at Corupedium in early 281, and for a brief few months the Achaemenid–Macedonian empire was as close to reunification as it would ever come. But this dream also was swiftly shattered by the dagger of Ptolemy Ceraunus at Cardia, and a new energy quickly supervened: the Celtic invasions from the north. The old Diadoch drive to repair the Humpty Dumpty of their empire dissipated in the pyrrhic offensive in Italy to awaken Rome, the final nemesis of Macedonian hegemony, and a two-century-long stalemate between the Seleucid and Ptolemaic empires.[28]

It is arguable that Alexander the Great saw to it in his own lifetime that he was the tallest among tall poppies, and that in the event of his premature death, there would inevitably be a leadership vacuum. The attrition rate among the great marshals and satraps was always likely to be high, given the propensity of the Macedonian court to conspiracy, coupled with the king's increasing paranoia as the reign progressed. It was unlucky for the continuity of the empire that the Successors at Babylon were either too indecisive (Perdiccas), or intentionally separatist (Ptolemy, Peithon). But the marshals with the charisma and power to keep the empire together (Antipater, Craterus, Antigonus) were all absent. Later, some of the marshals may have aspired to primacy (Leonnatus in 322, Peithon in 318, perhaps even the foreigner Eumenes), but aside from Antigonus, the next generation of Diadochi – Cassander, Lysimachus, and Seleucus – were content to consolidate their splinter kingdoms. Perhaps there was a fleeting phantasm of preeminence: Ptolemy in 310, Seleucus in 282, but the reality of a united – and expanding – Macedonian empire died with Alexander.

---

[27] This occurred in 315 (D.S. 19.57.1; Just. 15.1.2; App. *Syr.* 53), and 302 (D.S. 20.106). Even as late as 289 the other Diadochi perceived Demetrius' grand preparations with alarm, and forestalled them with a broad alliance: Plu. *Demetr.* 43.3–44; *Pyrrh.* 10–12; Just. 16.2.1–3.

[28] On the events from 301 to 280, see the treatments of, for instance, Tarn 1913: 10–138; Hammond–Walbank 199–249; Green 1990: 119–34; Grainger 1990: 114–91; Lund 1992: 80–206; Shipley 2000; Huss 2001: 198–212.

The Successors' desires to unite or divide the Macedonian conquests pivot on their conceptions of *basileia*. Alexander was an autocrat, very young at his accession, and cultivated his personal myth of *aniketos*: invincibility. Though reason would suggest to his marshals that his reckless disregard for human life – including his own – could end his reign peremptorily, only Antipater and Parmenion seem to have been concerned for the succession.[29] His death far from Europe, whether the result of conspiracy or not, launched the Macedonian nation into uncharted waters. The hereditary field of candidates for the kingship was even slimmer than usual, and those with a real or imagined link (Leonnatus, Craterus, Ptolemy) with the Argead house eyed their chances. But this was a time in which *military* expertise was of paramount importance to a ruler,[30] and in this regard, the circumstances were little different from those surrounding Philip II's accession. Perdiccas had military seniority and preeminence in Babylon, and, despite some indecisiveness, emerged dominant. The lesson was clear, though, and the great marshals proceeded to adapt their game to the evolving rules.

Leonnatus was possibly the first. His successful rescue of Antipater in the Lamian War, terminating in a way reminiscent of the unfortunate Cyrus the Younger, was likely the first step toward a claim to the throne predicated on both traditional pillars: legitimacy and military prowess. Antipater's luck held – as always – and Leonnatus was defeated and killed in battle against the Greeks, leaving Antipater his largely intact army, but no unwelcome rivalry for primacy, and releasing the old regent from the siege at Lamia.[31]

Craterus, we are told, also gave himself royal airs,[32] but delayed acting on the second stage of his orders from Alexander, tarrying in Cilicia for a considerable time.[33] He finally moved when an appeal for aid against the Greeks came from Antipater, and he reached a ready accommodation with the latter.[34] Diodorus informs us in two dislocated passages that, having concluded the Lamian War hostilities, Craterus was preparing to return to Asia (D.S. 18.18.7–8). But curiously, he is next found on a winter campaign against the Aetolians, when Antigonus and his son Demetrius arrive with the news of Perdiccas' designs on the royal title (D.S. 18.25). Thus began the First Diadoch War, fought overtly for the *basileia*. Perdiccas' fate has been recorded, and the reason for his murder is unequivocal in the sources: his defeat at the Fort of Camels in Egypt sparked mutiny among his senior officers. Perdiccas' regal aspirations, and his life, were truncated.[35]

---

[29] D.S. 17.16.2; with Baynham 1998b.

[30] *Suda* s.v. "basileia" (2); translations: Austin, no. 37; Sherwin-White and Kuhrt 1993: 119–20; with Rostovtzeff 1941: iii. 1346–7.

[31] D.S. 18.14.4–15.7; Arr. *Succ.* 1.9. Just. 13.5.14–16, digesting Pompeius Trogus' source, is especially trenchant: "[Antipater] was nevertheless glad at Leonnatus' death, congratulating himself on the simultaneous removal of his rival and acquisition of the latter's forces."

[32] *Suda* s.v. "Krateros" (= Arr. *Succ.* F19); with Ashton 1992; Bosworth 2002: 10–11, 31, cf. 276, 278.

[33] Badian 1961: 41; Bosworth 1988b: 207–11; 2002: 31.

[34] D.S. 18.16.4; Arr. *Succ.* 1.12; Plu. *Phoc.* 26.1; with Goralski 1989: 87–8; Heckel 98. Bosworth is cautionary regarding the ready *rapprochement* between the two great marshals (2002: 10–11).

[35] D.S. 18.36.5; Just. 13.8.10; Arr. *Succ.* 1.28; with Heckel 202.

The attrition among the great marshals continued, and by late 319, Antigonus was the sole survivor of the senior generals from Philip II's generation. The sources record that it was at this point that he began aspiring to the kingship.[36] As we have already observed, he was treated as royalty in Persia after his victory over Eumenes in 316; even before that, in 322/1, he is noted for his dynamism, intelligence, and daring,[37] and after Triparadeisus, his ambitious nature was clearly discerned by Antipater.[38] The scope of his vision was obvious to the other marshals during the Second Diadoch War, but the setbacks of the years 312–309 perhaps dampened his hopes. With the removal of the last of Alexander's heirs between 310 and 308, however, the way was cleared for the appropriation of the royal title, and Diodorus clearly states that, from this point on, the dynasts "entertained hopes of royal power" and ruled their territories as "spear-won" kingdoms (D.S. 19.105.4). But nothing overt was attempted while some balance prevailed in the power dynamics between the Diadochs, and the catalyst was, inevitably, military. In June 306, Demetrius inflicted a shattering naval defeat on Ptolemy at Salamis in Cyprus, and in the aftermath Antigonus finally published his intentions by declaring himself and his son to be kings.[39] A startling domino effect was initiated. Within two years, Ptolemy, Seleucus, Lysimachus, Cassander, and even Agathocles in Sicily, and perhaps Dionysius of Heraclea Pontica, followed suit and arrogated the royal title.

The pattern is clear. While no individual dynast had any advantage and the status quo was maintained, the kingship remained in abeyance, but once a single dynast could force a military victory, political dominance followed immediately, and the *basileia* itself was snatched, like the geographical territories, as a "spear-won" right. The response of both the defeated dynast and the onlookers is also informative. Ptolemy recouped some of his prestige by his second successful defense of Egypt, this time against an ill-judged Antigonid invasion in autumn of 306,[40] and then, perhaps still in damage control, took the royal title himself late in 305.[41] The setbacks Demetrius suffered early in his famous siege of Rhodes would have provided an excellent backdrop for the maneuver, as Ptolemy provided considerable support for the Rhodians throughout their year-long ordeal.[42] Notably, late in the siege, a certain Rhodian captain named Damophilus sent seized purple clothing belonging

---

[36]   D.S. 18.50.2; 58.4; Plu. *Eum.* 12.1–2; *Heid. Epit.*, FGrH 155 F3.2; with Bosworth 2000a: 237–8.

[37]   D.S. 18.23.3–4: *praktikos, sunesis, tolma.*

[38]   D.S. 18.39.7; cf. Cassander's suspicions of Antigonus at Arr. *Succ.* 1.43.

[39]   Battle of Salamis: D.S. 20.49–52; Just. 15.2.6–9; Plu. *Demetr.* 16–17.1; Polyaen. 4.7.7; Paus. 1.6.6; App. *Syr.* 54; Parian Marble, *FGrH* 239 F B21; with Wheatley 2001. Declaration of kingship: Plu. *Demetr.* 17.2–18.7; D.S. 20.53.1–2; App. *Syr.* 54; Nepos, *de Regibus* 3.1; *Heid. Epit.*, FGrH 155 F1.7.

[40]   D.S. 20.73–6; Plu. *Demetr.* 19.1–3; Paus. 1.6.6; with Seibert 1969: 207–24; Hauben 1975–6; Huss 2001: 185–91.

[41]   D.S. 20.53.3; Just. 15.2.11; Plu. *Demetr.* 18.2; App. *Syr.* 54; *P. Köln* vi, no. 247; *Heid. Epit.*, FGrH 155 F1.7; Parian Marble, *FGrH* 239 F B23; Porphyry, *FGrH* 260 F2.2, 9; Syncellus, *Chron.* 321; with Gruen 1985: 257–8; Huss 2001: 190–1. Significantly, Justin and Appian indicate that Ptolemy received the title by acclamation from his army.

[42]   D.S. 20.81.4, 84.1, 88.9, 94.3, 96.1–2, 99.2–3, 100.3–4; see also Seibert 1969: 225–30; with Gruen 1985: 257–8.

to Demetrius directly to Ptolemy as being "proper for a king" (D.S. 20.93.4; cf. Plu. *Demetr.* 22.1), probably indicating that the latter took the title before the siege was over, and this may be confirmed by the order of events in the Parian Marble (*FGrH* 239 F B23). According to most of our sources, Seleucus also appears to have promoted himself to royal status around the same time,[43] and indeed, cuneiform texts in Babylonia begin to be dated to "Seleucus, King" from 305/4 onwards.[44] Seleucid coinage also began to bear the legend ΒΑΣΙΛΕΩΣ ΣΕΛΕΥΚΟΥ at some point after 305.[45]

Cassander, however, was once thought to have been the exception. Plutarch (*Demetr.* 18.2) claims that Cassander did not employ the royal title in his correspondence, although he was accorded it by the other dynasts. His name is usually last on the list of royal title claimants (D.S. 20.53.4; Nep. *Eum.* 13.3), and is not specifically named by Appian or the *Heidelberg Epitome*. But other evidence indicates that Cassander arrogated the title as eagerly as anyone. Certainly, he was entertaining royal ambitions and assuming regal prerogatives from at least 316,[46] and the title *Basileus Makedonon Kassandros* appears on an inscription which may date to the foundation of Cassandria.[47] A statue base from Dium with the same caption is also extant, and bronze coinage was produced with the legend ΒΑΣΙΛΕΩΣ ΚΑΣΣΑΝΔΡΟΥ.[48] However, none of the evidence can be dated securely, and Cassander must have moved as carefully toward a public statement as his peers. He may have been idiosyncratic in his use of the royal style, or have been curbed by local political considerations and sensibilities (especially as news of the royal murders leaked out). A reasonable interpretation, on the basis of the evidence, and of the historical context, would be that Cassander began using the title openly by mid 304, perhaps a little after Ptolemy, and at about the same time Demetrius abandoned his siege of Rhodes.[49]

In the light of his close association with Cassander,[50] the above conclusions may be applied equally well to Lysimachus, who is likely to have taken the title at

---

[43]   D.S. 20.53.4; Nep. *Eum.* 13.3; App. *Syr.* 55; *Heid. Epit.*, *FGrH* 155 F1.7; Justin omits him altogether. Plutarch inserts the rider that Seleucus now began affecting royal trappings in his dealings with Greeks (*Demetr.* 18.3); likely a confirmation that he was already using the title among his eastern subjects.

[44]   For the chronographic technicalities, with earlier bibliography, see Boiy 2000; 2002a; 2002b. In general: Mehl 1986: 147–55; Grainger 1990: 109–13.

[45]   See Houghton and Lorber 2002: 35–6, 77–8, and *passim*.

[46]   Syncellus, *Chron.* 320; D.S. 19.52.5; cf. Just. 14.6.13. On Cassander and the kingship, see now Landucci Gattinoni 2003: 124–37.

[47]   *SIG* 332; so Errington 1974: 23–5; Landucci Gattinoni 2003: 137.

[48]   Statue base: *SEG* xxxiv. 620; see Hammond–Walbank 174. Coinage: Errington 1974: 25; Hammond–Walbank 174, pl. If; Mørkholm 1991: 59–60, 79, pl. V. 71–2; Ehrhardt 1973; Miller 1991; Landucci Gattinoni 2003: 136–7.

[49]   D.S. 20.100.2; with Ritter 1965: 107, where the grateful Rhodians erect statues of King Cassander and King Lysimachus after the siege.

[50]   D.S. 20.106.2–3; 18.72.9; 19.77.7; Just. 15.2.12, 17; with Lund 1992: 55–7, 66–70; but cf. Plu. *Demetr.* 31.3–4.

approximately the same time and in the same context as his neighbor.[51] Soon after this ΒΑΣΙΛΕΩΣ ΛΥ began appearing on his coinage from Lysimacheia.[52] In addition, news of events in the east also inspired Agathocles, the tyrant of Syracuse, to adopt the royal style,[53] and it is possible that Dionysius, the tyrant of Heraclea Pontica, also took the title (so Memnon, *FGrH* 434 F4.6), although this raises chronographic difficulties, as Diodorus (20.77.1; cf. 16.88.5) reports that he died in 306/5.[54]

It would seem, therefore, that the Diadochi observed a decent period of mourning between the extinction of the Argead house and their arrogation of the *basileia*, but nothing could be more misleading. Although Justin asserts that they had "all refrained from adopting the trappings of royalty" (15.2.13), numerous examples of the royal style or title being attributed to, or used by, the Successors prior to 306 appear in the ancient literature. Craterus, Leonnatus, Perdiccas, Eumenes, Seleucus, Antigonus, Demetrius, Ptolemy, and Cassander all appear to display anachronistic regal pretensions, or are referred to with royal terminology between 322 and 306.[55] The only hint of reticence with regard to the royal regalia comes in the cases of Cassander and Agathocles.[56]

From this we might conclude that aspirations to primacy among the Diadochi were always endemic, perhaps ebbing and flowing with the quirky fortunes of these individuals. Achievement of the dream was always stymied prior to 309 by the existence of Alexander's legitimate heirs, and after that year by military stalemate. But it is abundantly evident from the ancient sources that this did not prevent the dynasts from playing the king in their own territories, and among their own companions. However, to take the next logical step, a clear military advantage had to be achieved. This was done by Demetrius at Salamis in 306, and a watershed public assertion followed.

[51] So Landucci Gattinoni 1992: 133 (who proposes spring 304); Lund 1992: 156–7 (summer 304). Billows 1990: 156 asserts that Lysimachus certainly followed Cassander's lead in this, rather than vice versa.

[52] See Thompson 1968; Hadley 1974: 55; Landucci Gattinoni 1992: 45–50; Mørkholm 1991: 60–1, 81–2, pl. V. 78–9; and, in general, Ritter 1965: 105–8; Landucci Gattinoni 1992: 129–34; Lund 1992: 153–61; cf. Just. 15.3.13–14.

[53] D.S. 20.54.1; 19.9.7; Plu. *Demetr.* 25.7; *Mor.* 823c–d; Phylarchus, *FGrH* 81 F31 = Athen. 6.261b.

[54] It is possible that Dionysius either died later than is generally thought, or from an earlier stage was "king" in the minor key (cf. Porphyry, *FGrH* 260 F41), in the same manner as the local dynasts of Phoenicia and Cyprus. The matter of Dionysius' kingship has not been resolved satisfactorily; for discussion, see Berve ii. 144–5, no. 276; Burstein 1976: 77; Gruen 1985: 268–9 n. 44; Billows 1990: 66–7, 113, 380–1.

[55] Craterus: *Suda* s.v. (= Arr. *Succ.* F19 [Roos]); Leonnatus: *Suda* s.v. (= Arr. *Succ.* F12 [Roos]); Perdiccas: D.S. 18.23.3, 25.3; Eumenes: Plu. *Eum.* 8.12; cf. Athen. 12.539–60; Seleucus: Plu. *Demetr.* 18.3; D.S. 19.90.4, 92.5; Antigonus: D.S. 19.48.1, 55.2; Polyaen. 4.6.13; D.S. 18.58.4, 20.73.1; *Heid. Epit.*, *FGrH* 155 F3.2; Demetrius: D.S. 19.81.3–4, 85.3, 93.4, 97.3; Ptolemy: D.S. 18.21.9, 20.27.1; Plu. *Demetr.* 17.6 (with Bosworth 2000a: 228–41); and Cassander: D.S. 19.52.1–5; see also Errington 1974: 23–5.

[56] Plu. *Demetr.* 18.4; D.S. 19.9.7, 20.54.1; and cf. Perdiccas: Curt. 10.6.16–20.

The Antigonids were therefore the first, but how did they conceive their king-ship? Did they see themselves as sole heirs to Alexander's empire, with the brief to achieve its reunification under their own rule, or did they in reality partake of the same schismatic tendencies generally attributed to the other dynasts?[57] Certainly, the spirit of Alexander seems to have devolved more fully on the Antigonids than on their rivals: nearly forty years after his death, Demetrius was *again* constructing an armada to invade Asia, and yet another coalition of his opponents was needed to suppress him. However, in 306 the Antigonids were certainly not close to reunit-ing Alexander's empire or controlling Macedonia itself, even if they did consider that their self-proclaimed dynasty entitled them to inherit the Argead mantle. Like their rivals, they clearly regarded themselves as kings of the territory they already held, and of any more they could conquer, and had done so for some time.[58] But by their very nature, and because of the power vacuum left by Alexander, the Successors ruled kingdoms built on opportunity, and were engaged in a continual struggle for ascendancy over one another. That the Antigonid domain – whatever parameters its architects envisaged for it – would no longer be Eurocentric is evident in that the process of constructing a new Asian capital had already begun. The strategic central siting of this foundation may in itself be proof of Antigonid inten-tions, for an empire of this scope would need to be ruled from the hub, not the periphery.[59] The celerity with which they sought to eliminate Ptolemy later in the year is also significant, but, again, whether this was a purely opportunistic response or part of a master plan is impossible to tell. At least one source specifically asserts that Antigonus' ambitions extended to the reformation of Alexander's empire,[60] but after 306 the old man had abandoned the territory east of Syria at least, and seems to have been settling into semi-retirement.[61]

However, if the father's dream had faded by 305, the torch had certainly been taken up by the son, and indeed, because of his vicissitudes, Demetrius provides the best case study for the evolution of a king in early Hellenistic times. It is likely that the evergreen son of Antigonus always harbored the ambition to be another Alexander, and indeed, he would become arguably the most fervent Alexander impersonator among the Diadochi. He had been born in the year that Alexander had ascended the throne, and raised in the years of his *anabasis*. The initial struggles of the marshals had formed the backdrop of his adolescence, and he had grown to

---

[57] For early bibliography, see Seibert 1983: 136–40. For some useful recent discussions of Hellenistic kingship, see Gruen 1985: 253; Austin 1986; Lund 1992: 155–65; Sherwin-White and Kuhrt 1993: 114–40; Billows 1995; Bosworth 2002: 246–78.

[58] Ptolemy certainly regarded Egypt as his "prize of war" after repelling Antigonus and Demetrius in November 306: D.S. 20.76.7; cf. D.S. 19.105.3–4.

[59] D.S. 20.47.5 spells out the purpose and strategic advantages of Antigoneia's position; see further n. 24 above.

[60] *P. Köln* VI, no. 247, col. I, ll. 18–27; with Lehmann 1988; Billows 1990: 351–2; Bosworth 2000. See also Plu. *Demetr.* 15.3; *Eum.* 12.1; D.S. 18.50.2.

[61] Plu. *Demetr.* 19.3 states that after the Egyptian expedition Antigonus increasingly delegated the running of the kingdom to Demetrius, being himself to some degree incapacitated by age, obesity, and perhaps illness as well; see Plu. *Mor.* 182b with Billows 1990: 161. See also Polman 1974: 175.

manhood just as his father had risen to bestride the wreckage of the empire.[62] From this point on, his own expectation had been to overtake his rivals, and, it seems, even to reach for the highest office. In 306, for the first time, the royal title was deployed as a weapon in the contest. Its effectiveness is readily apparent, in that the other dynasts were forced to follow suit. But for Demetrius, I would argue that the title meant more than the ratification of his claim to suzerainty over a geographical realm. In reality, his power and achievements were not comparable in scope to Alexander's, nor would they ever be. However, his assumption of the kingship multiplied his potential exponentially. It must surely be acknowledged in historical retrospect that Demetrius had the will, resources, and desire to reunite the empire, and the royal title provided the vehicle for the enterprise. The crucial factor in the milieu of the Successors, however, was not so much whether he desired to achieve this feat, but whether he would be given the opportunity to do so. Time would also test his aptitude for the task, and find it wanting.

One further aspect of the kingship, as Demetrius and Antigonus conceived it in 306, was that it not only had territorial implications, but was the statement of a personal evolution.[63] The Antigonids were widely regarded as kings, had exhibited the prerequisite royal attributes, and were demonstrably preeminent among their peers. All that was lacking was the official act of appointment and recognition, and the charade described by Plutarch (*Demetr.* 17) in the aftermath of the battle of Salamis supplied it. Demetrius' case supports the notion of "personal monarchy": he retained the style of "king" for the rest of his life, even though his roller-coaster fortunes meant that at various stages (such as after Ipsus in 301) he held only minimal territory, and in fact "ruled" a thalassocracy from his flagship.[64] Even later, in 285 at the end of his career, and with only small forces at his disposal, he retained his royal status, and was still regarded as a king by Seleucus, who ordered his generals to provide him with "royal maintenance," and termed him "the most violent of the kings, and the most given to grand designs" (Plu. *Demetr.* 47.4). At the final confrontation, Demetrius' troops went over to Seleucus, hailing *him* as king, as if transferring Demetrius' title to the latter (Plu. *Demetr.* 49.4).

Nevertheless, Seleucus entertained the captive Demetrius with regal trappings and magnificence, and eventually consigned him to a gilded royal captivity (Plu. *Demetr.* 50.1–2, 8–9). Although he died shamefully in captivity, having apparently

---

[62] On Demetrius' early life, see Wheatley 1999.

[63] Billows 1990: 158–60 is persuasive in stating this case. For earlier bibliography with some cautionary discussion, see Sherwin-White and Kuhrt 1993: 118–120 and n. 1. See also Errington 1974, whose analysis from epigraphy supports the investiture of supreme power and prerogative in the person of the Macedonian monarch, rather than in his status vis-à-vis his territory or subjects.

[64] Plu. *Demetr.* 45.4 records the sole occasion on which he relinquished his royal status. This occurred in the winter of 288/7, following his deposition from the throne of Macedonia and the resulting suicide of Phila, which evidently plunged him into deep depression. Plu. *Demetr.* 46.1, however, relates how he rebounded from this nadir, and resumed his royal career and trappings. For the date, see Wheatley 1997: 21–2; also Tarn 1913: 97.

abdicated to clear the way for the accession of his son,[65] Plutarch describes his funeral as that of a king, with the funerary vase adorned with royal purple and a diadem.[66] From the moment when Demetrius received his first *diadema* in 306, and the letter from his father addressing him as *basileus*, the process was complete and apparently irreversible. The title, like a university degree, was personal, and could not be revoked. Demetrius ended his life as an "unemployed" king, but the reality of his vocation was never diminished by the occasional absence of a kingdom to rule. From 306 onward, whatever his circumstance, he lived and died a king.

Finally, it must be noted that the chronology of the Diadoch period is an especially vexatious problem which persists to the deaths of the first-generation Successors. The problem is rooted in the ancient source tradition and it is highly likely that the ancient writers themselves were confused – this, at any rate, is certainly evident from the narrative of Diodorus.[67] Moreover, coinage and epigraphy, which are especially useful in establishing chronographic frameworks for the period, often fail to mesh with the literary tradition. Essentially, two schools of thought regarding the chronology of the Successors have evolved over the last eighty years. These reflect the progressive construction since 1949 of two separate chronographic schemes for the period 322–310, conveniently labeled the "High" chronology, and the "Low" chronology. Most scholars who concern themselves with such matters espouse either one scheme or the other, often with considerable tenacity.[68]

The feasibility of two separate chronographic schemes for the years after Alexander is remarkable, and merits some scrutiny. Essentially, the pattern of events tends to form itself into "bubbles," which center on the three separate so-called Diadoch Wars fought from 322 to 311. Within these "bubbles" are contained certain mutable nodal events, around which scholars are polarized. Curiously, by interpretation of the sources alone, these nodal events can be persuasively dated and arranged to fit either chronographic scheme. As a result, two perfectly feasible parallel historical reconstructions can be generated which do little or no violence to the source tradition. The nodal events in question with their "High" and "Low" chronology dating are as follows:

First Diadoch War
The deaths of Craterus and Perdiccas and the conference at Triparadeisus ("High": 321; "Low": 320).

---

[65] Plu. *Demetr.* 51.1; cf. *Mor.* 183c. For discussion of this apparent abdication, see Wheatley 1997: 27. Demetrius' situation by this time was analogous to Alexander IV's after 316, when Cassander divested him of his royal trappings and incarcerated him in Amphipolis for the remainder of his life (D.S. 19.52.4; cf. 105.2). Both kings retained their royal titles in captivity, but in real terms their status was disregarded.

[66] Plu. *Demetr.* 53.4; Macurdy 1932: 68.

[67] See, for instance, the analysis of book 19 in Wheatley 1998: 261–8.

[68] For a convenient summary of the earlier scholarship, see Bosworth 1992c: 55 n. 1. Significant treatments since then include Bosworth 1992b; 2002: 279–84; Wheatley 1995, 1998, 2003; Boiy 2000, 2002a, 2002b; Anson 2002–3, 2005a, 2006. For an overview of the problem, representing an assortment of scholarly opinions, see now the essays of Wheatley, Anson, Boiy, and Dreyer in Heckel et al. 2007.

Second Diadoch War

The battle of Gabiene and death of Eumenes; the siege of Pydna and death of Olympias ("High": winter 317/16; "Low": winter 316/15).

Third Diadoch War

The death of Eumenes and flight of Seleucus to Egypt (as for Second Diadoch War); the battle of Gaza ("High": spring 312; "Low": autumn 312); the return of Seleucus to Babylonia ("High": summer 312; "Low": spring 311).

The problem is all the more vexing in that we have a number of reliable fixed points for the period, beginning with the battle of Crannon (August 322) and ending with Ptolemy's control of Phoenicia and Palestine by February 22, 311, and a good number of these pegs are agreed on by scholars of either persuasion. Moreover (and this is pernicious), for most of the years 319 and 318, both chronologies overlap and are in complete agreement,[69] and in theory one might wonder how the problem persists. If the events from the historical narrative are integrated into the framework of the chronological fixed points, a scheme should emerge. Not so, unfortunately. Where the so-called nodal events impinge on the historical narrative, agreement is impossible, and one may enter an almost science-fiction-like world of parallel timelines. To further compound the problem, the nature of the separate "bubble" chronographic structure enables scholars to take a limited "mix and match" option in espousing the two chronological schemes. It is, for instance, possible to accept the "Low" scheme for the First Diadoch War to 320, then the "High" chronology through the consensus years of 319 and 318 through to 312, where one could accept a "Low" date for the battle of Gaza. Equally, one might accept the "High" scheme for the First Diadoch War and follow the "Low" scheme through to 311. These possibilities, however, do have some historical limitations. The Second and Third Diadoch Wars hinge around certain nodal events (the deaths of Eumenes and Olympias), and must therefore comprise a unit: if the "Low" chronology is accepted for the Second Diadoch War, it must also be imposed on the Third Diadoch War, and vice versa. Similarly, there would seem to be no room for a "High" date for Gaza in the "Low" chronology, as the timelines become too compressed, and lose feasibility.[70] Finally, it is notable that, in their efforts to resolve the issues, researchers regularly introduce minor refinements of their own into the equations, and put forward small subvariants within the greater chronographic schemes. The result is a veritable Gordian Knot, of both modern scholarship and ancient historiography.

The source of the dilemma lies in the fact that, while in modern thought the conflicts during the period are generally segregated, there was actually only one Diadoch War. The fighting was in reality continuous, with the seeds of one war igniting – usually immediately – the next conflagration. Thus it is always moot to discern at which point in time one war ends and the next begins. The settlement at

[69] Finally recognized, in a most lucid synthesis, by Boiy 2007b.
[70] But see Schober 1981: 97 n. 1.

Triparadeisus, whether in 321 or 320, while ending the First Diadoch War, contained the imperatives which immediately began the Second Diadoch War. The victory of Antigonus and the aftermath of this war instantly sparked the Third Diadoch War, which was ended – in name at least – by the Peace of the Dynasts late in 311 or early in 310. There is, therefore, a blending of these events, which defies the imposition of chronological specificity. The problem is aggravated by the need to synchronize events in several far-flung geographical areas, notably in Asia or Europe, but with numerous substrands requiring precise integration. If one concentrates on tracing the movements of a particular group of characters, or events in one geographical region, it is easy enough to map out a feasible itinerary, but this is only ever done at the expense of precipitating other characters or regions into utter chaos: the so-called "butterfly effect" comes into play.

Clearly, what is needed is a synthesis: a chronographic scheme built around fixed and ineluctable points, which takes into account the potential activities of all the actors and meshes the parallel events of Europe and Asia in relation to each other, while – and this is paramount – maintaining the integrity of the rich primary and secondary source traditions. Is this achievable? The sheer volume and variety of source material suggests that it should be possible, and new discoveries that settle the matter may be hoped for,[71] yet the key to this puzzle continues to elude researchers.

Scholars who propose to enter the field of study of the Diadochi must swiftly become cognizant of several dire problems. The primary sources must be assimilated and sifted according to their idiosyncrasies; the matter of the dichotomic centralist/separatist ambitions of the marshals must be probed; the way in which the dynasts conceived the *basileia* must be understood; and perhaps most crucial of all, a bizarre chronographic and chronological labyrinth must be negotiated. When these critical matters are digested, then true inquiry into this most remarkable of historical milieux may be commenced.

---

[71]   Though such material often complicates rather than simplifies. This has been vividly illustrated in the lively recent discussions (not all yet published) of the newly collated Aramaean ostraca from Idumaea, as well as the increasing corpus of numismatic evidence from the Levant. For representative discussions, see Eph'al and Naveh 1996; Wheatley 2003; Anson 2005a; Porten and Yardeni, forthcoming.

4

A King and His Army

Waldemar Heckel

The rivalry among Alexander's commanders is clear from the very fact of the wars of the Successors, which reflect not only the natural reluctance of talented, ambitious men to subordinate themselves to their perceived equals or inferiors but also the fact that, during his lifetime, the king established a system of checks and balances, thus preventing the development of a clear hierarchy of command (Heckel 2002b).[1] The frictions within the army and at the court are discussed in more general terms by Gregor Weber (see ch. 5) and are illustrated by some of the best-known episodes in the Alexander historians: the affairs of Philotas, Cleitus, and Callisthenes (including the conspiracy of Hermolaus). Each case is different, but all have in common the tension between certain officers – along with their families or adherents – and the king, as well as that within the circle of command. To some scholars, these episodes are manifestations of deep-rooted resentment toward Alexander, going back to the time of Philip's reign, but exacerbated by the king's orientalizing policies; for one writer in particular they illustrate that Alexander was not only capable of, but actually engaged in, plotting against his own men.[2]

The fall of Philotas and Parmenion, the murder of Cleitus, and the affair of Callisthenes and the Pages have all been dealt with in the introductory narrative. The aim of this discussion is to consider the significance of these episodes for Alexander's relationship with the army; for the officers and the court represented a layer of command and organization separating the king from the common soldier. Nevertheless, there was a bond between Alexander and the army that was both direct and genuine, and this was not due solely to the young king's charisma, though it did play a part. Curtius Rufus remarks that:

[1] This discussion is meant to supplement rather than supersede Heckel 2003b.
[2] Badian 2000a.

The Macedonians have a natural tendency to venerate their royalty, but even taking that into account, the extent of their admiration, or their burning affection, for this particular king is difficult to describe. First of all, they thought his every enterprise had divine aid. Fortune was with him at every turn and so even his rashness had produced glorious results. His age gave added luster to all his achievements for, though hardly old enough for undertakings of such magnitude, he was well up to them. Then there are the things generally regarded as rather unimportant but which tend to find greater approval among soldiers, the fact that he exercised with his men, that he made his appearance and dress little different from an ordinary soldier's, that he had the energy of a soldier. These characteristics, whether they were natural or consciously cultivated, had made him in the eyes of his men as much an object of affection as of awe (3.6.18–20).[3]

A state engaged in the conquest of a neighboring area usually sends out from its homeland an army considered capable of accomplishing the undertaking. When this aggressor state has legally constituted assemblies or councils, the separation of military and civil powers is usually clear and the leader of the army and the head of state are often not the same individuals. Even when the army was led by the state's chief executive officer (or officers, as when both consuls of Rome were with the army), the civil government and, to some extent, the conduct of the war remained in the hands of the elected assemblies or a Senate with traditional *auctoritas*. Monarchy presents a different set of problems and solutions. Not all kings were military leaders, and these relied on generals to implement their foreign policies, often with great risk to the security of their rule. Others, like Alexander, were warriors and strategists of the first order, but they relied heavily on the skill, leadership, and, what is more, the loyalty of their commanders.

Alexander's "partners in conquest" played no insignificant role in the shaping of world history, and their interactions with one another and their king provide a fascinating subtext to the well-known story of his subjugation of the east. Two aspects of the Macedonian politico-military system are vital to our understanding of these interrelationships. The first is the geographic (or territorial) basis on which the majority of the native troops and their leaders were recruited, which meant that the bond between troops and *taxis* commanders was greater than that between the men and the general officers. The latter were, in effect, middle managers charged with implementing the king's orders. As such, they were more expendable than the taxiarchs and ilarchs, and more prone to resent the fact that credit for victory inevitably went to the king.[4] But it was this very perception of the king as author

---

[3]   Here and elsewhere I have used the Penguin translation of Curtius by J. C. Yardley (Yardley and Heckel 1984).

[4]   "... as a young man will often talk freely in vaunting and martial strain to his mistress and in his cups, Philotas used to tell her [Antigone] that the greatest achievements were performed by himself and his father, and would call Alexander a stripling who through their efforts enjoyed the title of ruler" (Plu. *Alex.* 48.5, trans. B. Perrin 1986). Compare Curt. 8.1.28–9: "Then Cleitus ... turned to the men reclining below him and recited a passage from Euripides so that the king could catch the tone without fully hearing the words. The gist of the passage was that the Greeks had established a bad practice in

of an unbroken chain of victories that earned him the affection and admiration of the troops.

Secondly, Macedonian kings, from the time of Philip II, if not earlier, had learned to counterbalance territorial loyalties through the practice of raising the sons of the Macedonian aristocracy (many of them scions of the once independent, royal houses of Upper Macedonia) at the court in Pella. This institution, which joined *somatophylakia* (*custodia corporis*) and *therapeia*, "served the Macedonians as a kind of seminary for their officers and generals" (Curt. 8.6.6); for "such was the upbringing and training of those who would be great generals and leaders" (Curt. 5.1.42).[5] It was a system which fostered at once loyalty and competition, leadership and obedience, and it served as a kind of West Point from which graduating officers took their places as leaders of units comprising neighbors and kinsmen accustomed over the generations to follow the aristocrats of their region. So, again, there was an exceptional bond between the officer and his men, a companionship of commander and king, and finally a strong and overriding love and respect on the part of the men for the monarchy. A large number of the important regional commanders, already at the outset of the expedition, were Alexander's men, his friends and *syntrophoi*.

Hence, despite the notoriety of a small number of "conspiracies" that occurred within Alexander's reign, the king was remarkably secure in his position and the aspirations of his political enemies limited by the reality of what they were capable of achieving. These limits were imposed by the special bond and nature of the king's *hetairoi* (especially those of his generation, his *syntrophoi*) and by the mood and composition of the army itself. In the expedition against Persia, Alexander was their commander, their guide, their shining example, in short, their hero. They had acknowledged him in 336 as their king – even though the practice amounted to the endorsement of a decision made by the nobility – and it would take a remarkable man indeed to supplant him, even if he were the worst of kings, which certainly he was not.[6] Ability and charisma play their part in the relationship between the general and his men, but Alexander was more than a Robert E. Lee or an Erwin Rommel: through his veins flowed the very lifeblood of the Macedonian army, and there were few of his officers who did not understand or who underestimated the potency of the idea.

---

inscribing their trophies with only their kings' names, for the kings were thus appropriating to themselves glory that was won by the blood of others." This is not a far cry from Homer's *Iliad*, where Achilles upbraids Agamemnon: "The heat and burden of the fighting fall on me, but when it comes to dealing out the spoils, it is you that takes the lion's share, leaving me to return to my ships, exhausted from battle, with some pathetic portion to call my own" (1.165–8; trans. E. V. Rieu 1950).

[5] For the menial nature of their service to the king see Curt. 8.6.2 (*munia haud multum servilibus ministeriis abhorrentia*).

[6] Hence, although Alexander may have feared the power of Parmenion after Philotas' execution, the likelihood of a rebellion by the troops under his command was probably not great. One need only think of the reaction of Adea-Eurydice's Macedonians who, when they learned that Olympias was with the opposing army, immediately defected (D.S. 19.11.2); and similarly the very appearance of the legitimate king Antiochus III foiled the rebellion of Molon (Plb. 5.54.1).

Once he had recovered sufficiently from his close call with death in the town of the Mallians, he was visited by his officers.[7]

> Craterus, who had been charged with the task of conveying to him the entreaties of his friends, [remarked]: "Do you think that an enemy advance – even supposing they were now standing on our rampart – would cause us more anxiety than does our concern for your health, on which, as matters now stand, you set little value? No matter how powerful an army unite against us from the world over; no matter though it fill the entire earth with arms and men or pave the seas over with ships or bring strange monsters against us – *you* will make us invincible. But which of the gods can guarantee that this mainstay, this star of Macedon will long continue when you are so ready to expose yourself to obvious danger, unaware that you draw the lives of so many of your fellow-citizens into disaster? Who wants to survive you? Who is able to? Following your authority and your command, we have reached a place from which returning home without your leadership is impossible for any of us" (Curt. 9.6.6–9).

For all its dramatic touches, this is neither delusional hero-worship or sycophancy, but rather a realistic assessment of the importance of the king to the success and well-being of his army and its leaders. Though militarily capable of stepping into his shoes, the marshals were constitutionally[8] barred and restrained by the command structure from becoming second Alexanders. Thus like the common soldier who took his cue from his every nod, or judged the prospects of success or failure by the king's mood or facial expression, his officers knew – and few were the times when the truth was even temporarily forgotten – that "without Alexander they were nothing." The sentiments of the Macedonians are echoed in the words of Ambroise, in his history of the Third Crusade, where the troops tell Richard the Lionheart: "When you want to damage the Turks take a large company with you *for our life is in your hands, for when the head of the body falls, the body cannot survive alone.*"[9]

It is in the light of this peculiar balance of king, commander, and common soldier, of regional and national interests, that we must consider the politics of Alexander's officers, the workings of conspirators, and the counter-measures of the king and his supporters. Factions certainly existed, and their primary aim was the advancement of their own positions, either as a group or as individuals.[10] But those

---

[7]   The troops were taken by surprise by the king's rashness and, once they saw that he was placing himself in grave danger, they unwittingly overloaded the ladders, which broke under the strain. It is fatuous to use this catastrophe as an indication of the army's reluctance to support their king after the Hyphasis incident.

[8]   Macedon did not, of course, have a written constitution, but there were strong traditions, ceremonies, and obligations connected with the governing of the state that needed to be adhered to. See, e.g., Hammond 1989b: 21–4, 166–77.

[9]   Quoted by Gillingham 1999: 181 (emphasis added). Cf. the Confederate troops who, in times of heavy fighting were wont to shout "General Lee to the rear!" (Freeman 1993: 385–6).

[10] Consider the cynical remarks of Oliver Goldsmith: "He [Polydamas] was one of Parmenio's most intimate friends, if we may give that name to courtiers, who study only their own fortunes" (1825: ii. 129).

who sought the death of the king, and these were but a few officers and "cadets," deluded themselves if they thought they could gain the support of the troops. Hence, any conspiracy that actually succeeded in killing Alexander would undoubtedly have led to exactly the kind of contest for power that followed his death from "natural" causes in 323. The fact that the soldiery preferred an idiot to any of the marshals – no matter how much these played up or invented familial relationships with Philip and Alexander – speaks volumes. The popular Alexander tradition speaks of a "disciplinary unit" (*ataktoi*) made up of disgruntled supporters of the house of Parmenion. This should not surprise, for even the most isolated or fanatical individuals have their supporters. What does deserve emphasis is that there were very few men who, despite their personal affection for their officers, were willing to support them in an act of treason against the king. Even at the Hyphasis the reaction of the troops was *secessio*, which threatened only the plans (if these were, in fact, genuine[11]) and not the person of the king. Nor can one justly speak of conspiracies initiated by the king or a genuine "loneliness of power." The demands of leadership can isolate a ruler from his men, but in a world of lonely rulers Alexander was far less lonely than most.

Who were the men who constituted serious threats to Alexander's kingship and life? Attalus, of course, though most likely in an attempt to preempt the ruin he had brought upon himself. He knew well that Alexander would never forgive the (not too subtly) implied insult of his drunken remark (Satyrus *ap.* Athen. 13.557d–e; Plu. *Alex.* 9.6–7; Just. 9.7.12). But his only hope of safety lay in the mobilization of the Greek enemy against Macedon[12] – though, again, we cannot be sure of Diodorus' claim (17.5.1) that he communicated with Demosthenes – and his elimination was sanctioned (if not carried out) by his own father-in-law, Parmenion. To what extent Amyntas son of Perdiccas III sought to revive his claims to the throne, or whether he was a front for the ambitions of others (namely the sons of Aëropus), is unclear. Philip had pushed him aside with the support of the army, and Alexander could confidently terminate his existence by invoking state security.

The aspirations of the Lyncestians, if they sought anything more than revenge, were also clearly deluded; the king retained the services of Alexander Lyncestes[13] and his nephew Amyntas son of Arrhabaeus, at least until the winter of 334/3, when the Lyncestian was arrested for treasonable communication with the Persian king. Amphoterus, the brother of Craterus, traveled to Parmenion's camp, where the Lyncestian and his Thessalian troops were in winter quarters, in disguise – not out of fear of a general uprising of the troops, who had no reason to be provoked by his arrival, but to avoid tipping off the conspirator and allowing him to escape.[14]

---

[11]   Spann 1999; Heckel 2003a.

[12]   A similar act of desperation was attempted in 324 by Harpalus.

[13]   It is generally (and probably correctly) assumed that he was saved through the efforts of his father-in-law, Antipater, and by the fact that he was the first to hail Alexander as king.

[14]   Craterus and his phalanx battalion were probably in Parmenion's camp. He is not mentioned in the accounts of Alexander's campaigns over the winter of 334/3.

Lyncestes' troops were, at any rate, not Macedonians, and Parmenion once again supported his king in the affair. The arrest and eventual execution of Alexander Lyncestes concluded the purge of those who threatened Alexander's title in 336. The troops, it seems, shed few tears for them,[15] and the royal council (*consilium amicorum* or *synedrion*; on which see also Weber, ch. 5) voiced its opinion that the king should have rid himself of the third Lyncestian long ago.[16]

Discontent arose once more in 332/1, after Alexander's visit to Siwah and his recognition as "Son of Amun," but neither the men nor their leaders went beyond voicing dissatisfaction in private. Philotas son of Parmenion is supposed to have made his feelings known to his mistress, Antigone, a Greek woman captured at Damascus shortly after Issus (see n. 4 above). But what she heard and passed on to her friends reached Alexander in the form of hearsay, and Craterus' attempt to gather damning evidence against his fellow commander points more to the rivalries within the system than to a serious threat to the king. Alexander, at any rate, excused his conduct.

In 330 Philotas, under torture, is said to have revealed that in Egypt Hegelochus son of Hippostratus (apparently a relative of Cleopatra-Eurydice and Attalus) had urged Parmenion to overthrow Alexander.[17] That Philotas made such a confession can neither be proved nor disproved, but the story may well have been fabricated to justify Parmenion's execution. Certainly, Hegelochus was no longer alive to refute the claim, and his family connection with Attalus rendered the charge plausible. There is certainly no basis for the claim that Curtius himself invented the story, for the details clearly go back to a primary source who knew something about

---

[15]   In Curtius' speech by Hermolaus, Alexander is reproached with the death of Alexander Lyncestes (8.7.4). This has a dramatic purpose in that it allows Alexander in his point-by-point refutation of Hermolaus' remarks to emphasize how he had been lenient with the Lyncestian far too long and to his own detriment.

[16]   Arr. 1.25.5. Plu. *Mor.* 327c says that the Macedonians were looking toward Amyntas IV and the Lyncestians, but we do not actually know much about the aspirations of the latter (see Hammond and Griffith 15–16). Had their bloodline truly entitled them to consideration for the kingship, the actions of Antipater, who was Alexander Lyncestes' father-in-law, become harder to explain. Perhaps he feared Arrhabaeus and Heromenes. Habicht 1977 identifies Arrhabaeus, the father of Cassander, with the son of Alexander Lyncestes and Antipater's daughter. We do not know, however, when the marriage took place or how many children this unnamed daughter produced. One would be tempted, however, to estimate the relative importance of the two families by the name of the first son, if there was, in fact, an older brother of this Arrhabaeus. Aëropus, the other father-in-law, appears to have been no longer alive (for no one mentions his execution or exile) – no one, that is, except perhaps Polyaen. *Strat.* 4.2.3, who says that Philip, on the eve of Chaeroneia, punished two *hegemones*, Aëropus and Damasippus, with exile for disobeying his orders and bringing a female harpist into the camp. Now Philip was said to have executed a Page named Archedamus for disobeying his orders (Ael. *VH* 14.48), but the banishment of officers for what was the equivalent of "curfew violation" strikes me as excessive. Hence, I am inclined to believe that it was the status and identity of the offender that mattered more than the nature of the offense. Philip may have used the opportunity to rid himself of an unwelcome presence (see Heckel 5). This is speculative, at best, and one would dearly like to know something about the identity of his "colleague," Damasippus.

[17]   For Hegelochus' "conspiracy" see Curt. 6.11.22–9; Heckel 1992: 6–12.

the factions within the army – the details of which Curtius could hardly have concocted.[18] But the mark of the Roman author can be found in the thinking he imputes to Parmenion:

> With Darius still alive, Parmenion thought the plan premature, since killing Alexander would benefit the enemy, not themselves, whereas with Darius removed the reward of killing the king that would fall to his assassins would be Asia and all of the east (Curt. 6.11.29).

In the late republic and early empire such usurpations of power by generals were routine, but the idea of giving power to a non-member of the Argead house would not have occurred to the Macedonians. It would certainly have been incumbent upon Antipater to secure the throne for an Argead – even if this meant crowning the pathetic Arrhidaeus – and punish the regicides.[19]

Hence, the argument that the army would rally around Parmenion makes sense only in the short run. The military body, deprived of its head, would need to be extricated from the unfinished war in Asia. But Parmenion had no regal aspirations, and no claim to them. All this makes the question of Philotas' behavior in 330 difficult to understand. At Phrada (Farah, in what is now Afghanistan), he was informed by a certain Cebalinus, whose brother had been coerced into joining a plot by his lover, Dimnus, of a threat to the king's life. Philotas' crime amounted to little more than failing to pass on the information. He claimed he had not taken it seriously – and, many historians have pointed out that the conspirators were virtual nonentities. This is true, for the most part, but the alleged involvement of Demetrius the Bodyguard is particularly disturbing. We do not know what motivated him to throw in his lot with the others – it is, in fact, his participation that lends credence to the existence of the plot – since his identity cannot be established.[20] His grievances may have been entirely personal. Like Pausanias, who assassinated Philip II, Demetrius may have been blind to the consequences of regicide for the army and the state. He may have belonged to a group of conservative Macedonians who opposed Alexander's orientalism and wished to return home. That he ran the risk of execution, he knew well, and so he must have considered the attempt on the king's life worth it. Nevertheless, here was a man of high standing, well placed to murder the king.[21]

---

[18] Hegelochus is alleged to have remarked that Alexander pardoned his father's killer, which must be a reference to Alexander the Lyncestian (Curt. 6.11.26). The remark also emphasizes the tension between the factions of Parmenion and Antipater.

[19] Alexander was criticized by contemporaries (and by modern scholars) for not producing an heir before he left Macedonia. Ironically, if he had taken a (Macedonian) son with him to Asia, this prince might have become a puppet for a mutinous general.

[20] See Heckel 108 [2].

[21] Those who decry the fate of Philotas or assume that the Dimnus conspiracy was a fabrication appear to be untroubled by the execution of Demetrius. Since we know that Dimnus was one of the *hetairoi* and from Chalaestra, he was clearly of some importance, and influential enough to win the support of Demetrius.

Possibly, Philotas' failure to report the incident was an attempt to protect Deme-trius, though one would expect him to have warned the Bodyguard about the security leak. Under these circumstances, Philotas' inaction amounted to a serious case of negligence; and certainly he neglected to factor in the hostility of his political rivals and their determination to bring him down.

A conspiracy at this point of the campaign should not come as a surprise. All heads of state run the risk of being targeted by malcontents, even the least threaten-ing or competent.[22] Nevertheless, some scholars have regarded Philotas as an inno-cent victim, subjected to a show trial in which a carefully orchestrated prosecution stirred up the emotions of the mob – so that the punitive measures that the king had already determined to take would seem to have been forced upon him by the popular will. The weaknesses of the theory that Philotas was "framed" have been discussed on several occasions by "another scholar," and need not be repeated here. But, even if the conspiracy theorists are right, their case would provide eloquent testimony to the hold that Alexander had over the army and the futility of any act of rebellion. The trial of Philotas occurred at a time when the insurrections of Satibarzanes and Bessus made it clear that the campaign was destined to drag on and lead the troops into the solitudes of Central Asia. It occurred at a time when Alexander's adoption of the trappings of Persian royalty appeared as a betrayal of the very principles for which Greeks and Macedonians had fought. Philotas, despite ample opportunity to speak in his own defense, was incapable of exploiting feelings of discontentment, unable to sway the opinion of the army. For them, all com-plaints against the king's behavior or the burdens of campaigning were silenced by the horror of regicide.

Some scholars have compared Alexander to Hitler and Stalin (whom Richard Overy has called the "twin demons of the twentieth century"[23]), an unfortunate choice, since a comparison of Hitler and Stalin themselves does not stand up to close scrutiny. As Overy points out, the most obvious parallels in the lives of these dictators involve characteristics and circumstances they shared with many other figures of their age.[24] It has become fashionable to categorize enemies of the west or of western ideologies as "evil" and to stereotype Idi Amin, Saddam Hussein, Kim Jong-il, and others as arch-villains through simplistic comparisons with Hitler or Stalin.[25] The detractors of Alexander have fallen into

[22] There were two attempts on the life of President Gerald Ford, neither motivated by political fac-tions. Like Demetrius' colleagues, Ford's would-be assassins were relative nonentities: only Lynette "Squeaky" Fromme's connections to Charles Manson gave her a measure of notoriety. Anarchist Sara Jane Moore won her fifteen minutes of fame, and a lifetime behind bars, by actually firing her gun.

[23] Overy 2004: xxxi.

[24] Family life, brutal corporal punishment, periods of imprisonment, hostility to religion and intel-lectuals, etc.

[25] Despite the body count attributed to Idi Amin, it would, indeed, be hard to find anyone who genu-inely deserved comparison in terms of cruelty to his own people (least of all that other "man of steel," Temujin), though Pol Pot might be a strong candidate. Certainly he suits Overy's description of leaders who were responsible for "the construction of a social utopia on a mountain of corpses" (2004: xxxiv).

line.[26] But attempts to compare Philotas with one of the many victims of Stalin's show trials miss the point entirely. Stalin had none of the legitimacy of a Macedonian king,[27] and was in constant fear of losing his position to rivals.[28] These were broken by unrelenting torture in the Lubianka prison until they confessed their fictitious crimes. Philotas, at his trial, did not implicate himself in the Dimnus conspiracy. Rather he openly proclaimed his innocence, admitting only his failure to take the news of Dimnus' plot seriously. That was, indeed, his undoing, and the true nature of his crime. The dangers of such action (or rather inaction) were apparent to his listeners. In a time of crisis the mere hint of treason sufficed to convict a man and negligence was interpreted as approbation. The army reflected also upon the virtues of their king, whose hero cult they had themselves helped to create, contrasting them with the arrogance of the defendant. It is in the nature of humans, particularly in groups, to overlook even major crimes committed by those whom they idolize and yet to dwell upon the minor faults of those they despise.[29] No wonder that Alexander the Lyncestian lacked words to defend himself. If the army had been quick to condemn the negligence of Philotas, what hope was there of deflecting their hostility in a clear-cut case of treason?

The Cleitus episode can be dealt with quickly. This was a personal matter, although it played out in public in the form of a drunken quarrel, the sort of thing all too common among the Macedonians. It ended tragically in murder. In the course of the argument, Cleitus gave voice to his own dissatisfaction with Alexander's conduct, but his concerns were shared by many of those at the banquet table, especially those of Cleitus' generation. Lawrence Tritle (2003) has made a

[26] See, e.g., Hanson 2001: 89–90. For a much needed antidote, see the sensible comments of Rogers 2004: 280–3. I am, in general, of the opinion that valuable insights into ancient history can be gained from historical analogies (provided these are not pushed too far), but Hitler and Stalin have become icons whose very names are synonymous with unspeakable evil and calculated mass murder. To invoke these names is tantamount to applying an inappropriate adjective to the subject of the discussion. I am reminded of the words of Demetrius (*De eloc.* 304): "Often objects which are themselves full of charm lose their attractiveness owing to the choice of words. Cleitarchus, for instance, when describing the wasp, an insect like a bee, says: 'It lays waste the hill-country, and dashes into the hollow oaks.' This might have served for a description of some wild ox, or of the Erymanthian boar, rather than a species of bee. The result is that the passage is both repellent and frigid" (*FGrH* 137 T10, trans. W. R. Roberts in Robinson 1953).

[27] Lenin himself had expressed serious concerns about his leadership and his fitness to lead the state. In recent years a number of excellent studies of Stalin have appeared: in addition to Overy 2004, see Sebag-Montefiore 2003; Rayfield 2004; Service 2004.

[28] The power struggle at Alexander's court, within his inner circle, involved the subordinate positions. No one was, to put it colloquially, "after Alexander's job."

[29] Thus Curt. 6.11.1–7 attributes to a certain Bolon a speech reminding the men that Philotas had ejected them from their assigned quarters to make room for his own slaves. A similar act of arrogance is attributed by Antiphanes to Amyntas son of Andromenes (Curt. 7.1.15–17). For the blindness of hero-worshipers we need only look at the disbelief that greeted charges against Michael Jackson or Martha Stewart, or the reaction of the African-American community to the indictment of O. J. Simpson. On the political level, consider the failure to hold Henry Kissinger accountable for crimes against humanity (see Hitchens 2001).

strong case for combat fatigue and Post-Traumatic Stress Disorder (PTSD) as contributing factors. If Alexander under the influence of alcohol displayed signs of paranoia, this is hardly surprising. The victim of the crime might have been any other Macedonian, accustomed to speaking frankly to his king, but there can be no doubt that Cleitus' sense of honor – probably also his displeasure at being assigned the remote satrapy of Bactria – made him unlikely to suffer the king's boastful remarks in silence. His anger was directed as much against the court sycophants as the king himself, and Alexander, for his part, had doubtless come to resent Cleitus' repeated reminders of how he had saved his life at the Granicus. What matters, for our purpose, is that the army was quick to excuse Alexander's conduct and was concerned about his mental state and suicidal tendencies.

Alexander's drunken outburst in Maracanda is hardly unique in the annals of history, though its consequences were particularly tragic. Philip II himself attacked his own son with drawn sword, thus sullying his own wedding banquet, and similar scenes have been acted out in other societies, where the heavy consumption of alcohol mixes unhappily with *machismo*. In 1698 Johann Georg Korb, who was with the Austrian ambassador at the court of Peter the Great, recorded in his *Diarium itineris in Moscoviam* a confrontation between the Tsar and his military commander Alexis Shein. Peter had left the room after a heated engagement:

> When he returned a short time later, his rage had increased to such an extent that he drew his sword out of its scabbard and, in front of the General-in-Chief, struck the table and threatened: "Thus shall I strike you and put an end to your command." Foaming with righteous anger, he stepped up to Prince Romadanowsky and Mikitin Moseiwitsch; but as he sensed that they were excusing the general, he went into such a smouldering rage that, through repeated and undirected thrusts of the cold steel, he transported all the guests into a state of panic. Romodanowsky received a slight wound on his finger, another a cut to the head, and as he brought his sword backward he injured Mikitin Moseiwitsch on the hand.
>
> He aimed a far more deadly blow against the General-in-Chief, who would doubtless have been stretched out in his own blood at the hands of the Tsar, had not General Lefort – probably the only one who would have dared the deed – clutched the hand of the Tsar and pulled it back and thereby prevented a wound. But angered by the fact that there was someone who prevented the fulfillment of his justified rage, the Tsar turned and dealt the uninvited interloper a hard blow on the back.[30]

The intervention nevertheless prevented Peter from murdering Shein as Alexander had killed Cleitus. Both episodes, however, bring into focus the fine line between familiarity and autocracy. In Peter's case, his frequent drinking parties and buffoonery had eroded the traditional divide between tsar and subject, whereas

[30] Leingärtner 1968: 79. The *Diarium itineris in Moscoviam* (1698) has been translated into several languages. The English version of Count MacDonnel (1863; repr 1968) is awkward and dated. Since the Latin text was unavailable to me at the time of writing, I have supplied my own translation of Leingärtner's German version.

Alexander, through his imitation of the Great King and his growing aloofness, had begun to stifle the liberties of the Macedonian *hetairoi*.[31]

It was this changing relationship between king and courtiers – and the orientalizing program contributed to it – that formed the backdrop to the so-called Conspiracy of the Pages. Like many conflicts, this plot had its immediate origins in a private grievance: Hermolaus son of Sopolis, one of the king's Pages, was flogged for anticipating the king in a boar hunt and striking the animal first. Alexander was certainly within his rights; for it was the king's prerogative to punish those of the *paides basilikoi* for disobeying orders, and we may assume that it was an unwritten (perhaps even unspoken) rule that the first attempt on the prey belonged to the king. The humiliation of the punishment brought to mind other complaints, and it may well be that the Pages had heard their fathers comment on the changing nature of the Macedonian kingship. But ideological differences generally take a back seat to personal injury and revenge is easily cloaked in moral indignation.[32]

It is unfortunate that the Hermolaus affair followed so closely on the heels of Alexander's attempted introduction of *proskynesis*. Although Hermolaus, at his trial, listed among the king's offenses his wish to receive obeisance, the conspiracy had little if anything to do with *proskynesis*. It did, however, prove fatal for Callisthenes of Olynthus, who served both as official historian of the campaign and tutor of the Pages. As far as the army was concerned, Hermolaus and his fellow conspirators were guilty of treason and deserving of punishment. If Callisthenes had, in any way, influenced their thinking or taught them that tyrannicide was a noble act, he too merited execution. But again the underlying issues were of little concern to the common soldier, who looked only to the security of his commander and the maintenance of proper order. In this instance, and as the campaign progressed, it became increasingly clear that although he disliked the policy – indeed, he was hurt by it – he nevertheless loved the king. Like Craterus, who held dear the traditions of Macedonia, the common soldier remained *philobasileus*.[33]

It was in the political world between the king and his army, in the sheltered environment of the royal tent, that the drama of the court played itself out. As Robin Lane Fox has noted, the experiment with *proskynesis* was conducted under very controlled circumstances, with a limited number of participants, all of them

---

[31] Curt. 8.4.30 typically exaggerates when he speaks of "the suspension of free speech following Cleitus' murder." If this had been the case, Meleager suffered no more than the king's ill-will when he spoke his mind in India (8.12.17). For Curtius' inconsistency, compare Darius' treatment of Charidemus (3.2.17–19) with his subsequent comment that "Nobody's life should be forfeit for making stupid recommendations" (3.8.6).

[32] One might compare the nature of the offense that motivated Harmodius and Aristogeiton to conspire against the Athenian "tyrants" (Arist. *AP* 18.2; Thuc. 6.56.1). In more prosaic terms, the perceived importance of a situation may be likened to the modern saying, "A recession is when your neighbor is out of work; a depression is when you yourself are out of work."

[33] See also Lane Fox 1973: 325.

courtiers or officers – and surprisingly successful.[34] Of course, some of the more
conservative leaders, like Craterus and Polyperchon, were absent from the camp at
the time. It is an exaggeration to say that Callisthenes was responsible for scuttling
the experiment. He did indeed make his objections known and incurred the king's
wrath, but it was probably the mockery of the process by high-ranking *hetairoi*
(notably Leonnatus) that contributed most to the failure. Callisthenes' self-
righteousness would come back to haunt him; when the Pages led by Hermolaus
son of Sopolis, plotted against the king, it was inevitable that Callisthenes should
be suspected of inciting them. That he was guilty of "seditious teachings" is highly
likely; but his complicity in the actual conspiracy cannot be proved. Unless the
report that he died of obesity and a disease of lice is *apologia*, it appears that his
case was indeed being postponed until a Greek court could decide.

The first serious clash between king and army occurred at the Hyphasis (Beas)
river, when Alexander proposed to lead his troops against the Gangetic kingdom
of the Nandas. For the first time, Alexander was guilty of misjudging the enemy
and his chances of success. For the first time, he failed to use the motivational tools
that form the arsenal of every good general. Some scholars have argued that his
ambitious plans and recklessness were simply in keeping with his character and
his heroic *ethos* – as if it were possible to look 2,400 years into the past and psycho-
analyze any historical character, but especially an enigma such as Alexander. What
we can do, and what has been done since ancient times, is evaluate the actions of
the general. And what Alexander proposed at the Hyphasis, how he went about
pitching the campaign to his men, and the way he failed to control public opinion
suggest that his skills as a general were sadly lacking. But this is true only if we
believe that Alexander genuinely wished to continue beyond the Hyphasis, and this
defies credulity. The problems have been discussed elsewhere (see ch. 2; and Heckel
2003a; 2007: 120–5; Spann 1999). But what is interesting is that even in the most
extreme situation, when the men were exhausted and their uniforms were literally
rotted off their bodies, their spokesman, Coenus, could express the following
sentiment:

> May the gods keep disloyal thoughts from us! And, indeed, they do so. Your men are
> as willing as ever to go wherever you command, to fight, to face danger, to shed our
> blood in order to transmit your name to posterity. So, *if you are going on, we shall
> follow* or go before you wherever you wish, even though we be unarmed, naked and
> exhausted (Curt. 9.3.5).

These are not the words of mutineers but of men who are begging their king
to consider their plight. They continued to call upon Alexander as "their king,
their father, their lord" (Curt. 9.3.16). Now we need not take everything that
Curtius puts in his speeches as genuine, but it is clear that each speech supplies the

---

[34] Lane Fox 1973: 323: "The plan could hardly have been tried more reasonably and despite
the indignation of Romans, philosophers and others since who have missed its Persian background,
Alexander came out of it all remarkably well."

sentiments required by the situation – what Thucydides called *ta deonta*. Even in Arrian's version of Coenus' speech, where the emphasis is on age, exhaustion, and the unwillingness of the soldiers to go on, the emphasis is still on the hope that Alexander will take pity on those who have done so much to win him glory. But, as I have argued elsewhere,[35] Alexander (unless we are prepared to question his leadership skills and his intelligence) was merely attempting to lay the responsibility for turning back on the men. He gave them sufficient reasons for refusing his request to advance, and they responded as he hoped they would.

Little needs to be said about the absurdity that Alexander was deliberately exposed to danger in the town of the Mallians by troops who no longer wished to follow him. Even less convincing is the idea that the march through the Gedrosia was a form of punishment. Indeed, if anything, the shared experience of the Gedrosian march created an even stronger bond between the king and his men. History may pass harsh judgments on the execution of Antony's Parthian or Napoleon's Russian campaigns, but the bond between commander and soldier was never stronger. Napoleon had more to fear from the politicians at home than from the rank and file. So too Alexander's army was allowed to frolic in Carmania, while the king turned his mind to the abuses of his provincial governors. But the Gedrosian ordeal was an affirmation of shared trust, exemplified by Alexander's refusal to accept a gift of water while his men suffered from thirst (Arr. 6.26.1–3). Would such a man actually have led his men to ignominious destruction on the banks of the Ganges?

The Opis mutiny, in its own strange way, confirmed rather than questioned Alexander's power over the army. The underlying issue was, as so often before, the king's orientalism. The men resented the incorporation of barbarians into the army, and the rabble-rousers told him to wage war with his new recruits, and with his father Amun. But it was the king's apparent rejection of them – his claim not to need their services – that devastated them. Suddenly they were content to see the leaders of the sedition executed for proffering bad advice, perhaps even for verbally abusing the king, as if they had not all taken part. They no longer thought of wounded pride or the justice of their case: instead they begged forgiveness, like children who had angered a parent and sought reassurance. Curtius' comments underscore the mood of Alexander's troops and their relationship with their king:

> Who would have believed that a gathering fiercely hostile moments before could be paralyzed with sudden panic at the sight of men being dragged off for punishment whose actions had been no worse than the others? They were terror-stricken, whether from respect for the title of king, for which people living in a monarchy have a divine reverence, or from respect for Alexander personally; or perhaps it was because of the confidence with which he so forcefully exerted his authority. At all events they were the very model of submissiveness: when, towards evening, they learned of their comrades' execution, so far from being infuriated at the punishment, they did everything to express individually their increased loyalty and devotion.[36]

[35] See Heckel 2003a; 2007: 120–5.
[36] Curt. 10.3.1–4; trans. J. C. Yardley.

The reaffirmation of this bond was as important to the commander as it was for his men. As a boy, Alexander read a speech attributed by Xenophon to Clearchus, the conclusion of which proclaimed:

> I will follow you and endure what has to be. This is because it is you I think of as being my country and my friends and my allies; when I am with you I think I shall have honor wherever I may be; but apart from you I don't think I shall be able either to do good to a friend or harm an enemy. So you can make up your minds that I am going to go wherever you go (Xen. *Anab.* 1.3; trans. R. Warner 1972).

Perhaps he understood that Clearchus was being disingenuous – if not, his tutors probably told him so – but he learned nevertheless that this is what troops want to hear, that this is what they believe and what keeps them loyal. It is, like strategy, tactics, and personal leadership, an essential component of the art of command.

5

The Court of Alexander the Great as Social System

Gregor Weber

In his discussion of events that followed Alexander's march through Hyrcania (summer 330), Plutarch gives a succinct summary of the king's conduct and reports the clash of his closest friends, Hephaestion and Craterus (*Alex.* 47.5.9–11).[1] The passage belongs in the context of Alexander's adoption of the traditions and trappings of the dead Persian Great King (Fredricksmeyer 2000; Brosius 2003a), although the conflict between the two generals dates to the time of the Indian campaign (probably 326). It reveals not only that Alexander was subtly in tune with the attitudes of his closest friends, but also that his changes elicited varied responses from the members of his circle. Their relationships with each other were based on rivalry, something Alexander – as Plutarch's wording suggests – actively encouraged. But it is also reported that Alexander made an effort to bring about a lasting reconciliation of the two friends, who had attacked each other with swords, and drawn their respective troops into the fray. To do so, he had to marshal "all his resources" (Hamilton 1969: 128–31) from gestures of affection to death threats.

These circumstances invite the question: what was the structural relevance of such an episode beyond the mutual antagonism of Hephaestion and Craterus? For these were not minor protagonists, but rather men of the upper echelon of the new Macedonian-Persian empire, with whose help Alexander had advanced his conquest ever further and exercised his power (Berve nos. 357, 446; Heckel 1992: 65–90, 107–33). This power required a concrete organization: the core that was formed around Alexander needed to fulfill specific personal and institutional demands in order to function successfully. For our purposes, the phenomenon of "court" is defined as the extended house of a monarch, the central functions of which can be

---

[1] Editors' note: Professor Weber completed this chapter before the appearance of A. J. S. Spawforth's "The Court of Alexander the Great between Europe and Asia," in A. J. S. Spawforth (ed.), *The Court and Court Society in Ancient Monarchies* (Cambridge, 2007), 82–120, and was unable to take his observations into account.

regarded as interaction, representation, and power. Alexander's court and the court society around him were rooted in a double tradition: elements emanating from the traditions of the Macedonian monarchy, which Philip more than anyone had influenced, and Persian ceremonies, which were added incrementally until, by the time of Alexander's death, a new court life had come into being as a result of the king's residence in Babylon.

An analysis of the court from 336 to 323 must take into account three factors. The first is the manner in which Alexander's court presented itself primarily as an itinerant military camp, renouncing a permanent geographic place. Hence, as a social configuration, the court was a dynamic institution, whose evolution ran parallel to the development of the monarchy itself (Borza 1990: 236–41; Hatzopoulos 1996: i. 37–42). Second, it is difficult to make a critical assessment of Alexander's court in its final form, since the king's early death and the ensuing turmoil of the Diadoch age prevented any continuation of this type of court. Therefore, one cannot put it to the test or consider the consolidation or modification of its form. Third, as far as the Alexander historians are concerned, the topic of the "court" is inextricably tied to the problem of how Alexander influenced the primary authors and how these reported the king's methods of communication and interaction on a scale that reflected their own personal involvement. On the other hand, the later or secondary authors were steeped in the terminology and concepts of the courts of the later Hellenistic kings and Roman emperors. Finally, it is difficult to make an adequate assessment of corresponding practices in the Achaemenid empire: these are derived mostly from Greek fragments (quotations or paraphrases selected for completely different purposes) – at a distance of hundreds of years – which suggest too great a degree of continuity.

Although the courts of the Hellenistic kings have aroused the interest of researchers in recent times (Weber 1997; Meissner 2000; Savalli-Lestrade 2003), for the court of Alexander there are only detailed studies on specific aspects of the theme (Berve i. 11–84; Heckel 1986b, 2003b; Völcker-Janssen 1993). Therefore, it is necessary first to explain the concept of court in terms of typology and to clear up matters of terminology. Then the court of Alexander will be treated not as a closed unit, but one in which the key categories – interaction, representation, and power – can be analyzed over the period of time spanning its starting and end points. Finally, in the last part essential developmental factors will be mentioned.

Concept of the Court and Terminology

The concept of "court" designates, in the first instance, a spatial center in the sense of an extended house (*oikos*), which was inhabited by a ruler (*basileus, monarchos*) and from which he directed the political government and administration of his realm. This *oikos*, generally situated in a central place, could be enhanced architecturally in a specific manner as a palace, since it had to accommodate the ruler's increased need for display. With this, one should also include the staging of sumptuous festivities and demonstrations of wealth. The court was also an "extended house" because not only the family of the ruler in the strictest sense gathered in it, but also the social elite with whom the ruler interacted. The relationship between ruler and elite had either an informal character, if it involved the ruler's trusted men (*hetairoi* (companions), *philoi* (friends)), or a hierarchical organization with a system of court titles. One could call this group, which included also the service staff in charge of the practical organization, the closer or inner court. The determining criterion for membership in the inner court is the real or titular proximity to the ruler. There is a farther or outer court to be distinguished from the first one, which comprises guests, foreign ambassadors, and civil servants who are temporary visitors at the court. The two groups of court society were not hermetically sealed from each other, but permeable. The interaction of their members, especially members of the ruler's family or confidants, deserves close examination. Similar attention must be given to the composition of the second group with regard to their geographical and ethnic background (Macedonians, Greeks, Persians, et al.), prosopographic connections and competence (military, intellectual, etc.), which determined the selection of particular individuals.

There is no clear, specifically coined Greek term for the concept of "court" or "court society." Instead, there are several – *oikia, to basileion, ta basileia,* and *aule* – which are difficult to separate from one another, but all have a local connotation in the sense of residence. They describe various parts of the abode or emphasize different aspects of access or exclusion (Arr. 7.25). It seems that the term *aule* is first used to describe the Hellenistic courts, and designates not only the actual court of the monarch, but also court society, including servants and the entire court management (Funck 1996: 52–4). The ruler's permanent presence was not always required in order for a residence to be considered a court – on the contrary, permanent habitation was impossible in an empire like that of the Persians, with its many residences and a Great King who, subject to seasonal and military demands, moved constantly about (Briant 1988; Nielsen 1994; Boucharlat 2001). Each of these residences constituted for a period of time a "court" along with a court management.

Basically, however, the court was located wherever the Great King or Alexander happened to be (Briant 1996: 200–4, 292–5; *HPE* 187–91, 280–3). In time of war the court was perforce a mobile headquarters. To that end, the royal tent (*skene*), equipped for organization and display, became a significant center. After the baggage of Darius fell into Alexander's hands at Issus, he took over the use of the tent and was able to host many guests. His resources were augmented by the spoils taken at Damascus by Parmenion (Arr. 2.11.10). The ancient authors make it clear that the pomp of Alexander's court was now greater than what was normal in Macedonia. Thus, practical demands and the need for ostentation could be met at the same time (Arr. 2.12.3–4, 2.20.10; Briant 1988: 265–9).

Alexander's Court at the Start of the Persian Campaign

When Alexander acceded to the Macedonian throne, he inherited Philip's court. As the probable heir to the kingdom, he had become familiar with the structure of the court, its strengths and weaknesses. The personal interactions at the court reflected the nature of the Macedonian aristocracy, which comprised three groups: first, those who belonged to the branches of the Argead dynasty, then members of powerful Macedonian noble clans (Borza 1990: 237–8; Heckel 2003b: 200–3), and finally the so-called coeval companions (*syntrophoi*) of the new king, who had grown up with him (Heckel 1986b: 301–2; 2003: 203–5). It is important to remember that the interaction of these groups among themselves and with Alexander was rooted in the reign of Philip (Gehrke 2003a: 156).

That Alexander, born in 356, could successfully assume the succession of his father is anything but self-evident. Philip too had not begun his reign as rightful heir to the throne, but as guardian of his nephew, Amyntas. Neither had he decided on *one* marriage and *one* successor. Instead, according to Macedonian custom, he was polygamous: Philip contracted seven marriages, all of which appear to have had political implications (Kienast 1973: 30–1; Goukowsky 1991: 60–5; Carney 2003b: 228–9). Although Philip undoubtedly "trained" Alexander to be his successor for a long time, his marriage to the Macedonian noblewoman Cleopatra in 337 must have had an alarming effect on Alexander, inasmuch as his legitimacy to the throne was placed in doubt (Ogden 1999: 20–2; Müller 2003: 27–34). That Philip was strongly inclined toward his nephew Amyntas and married him to his half-Illyrian daughter Cynane pointed in the same direction. On top of this, he planned to marry off Alexander's sister Cleopatra to Alexander I, king of Molossia in Epirus and brother of Olympias, Alexander's mother – undoubtedly in order to isolate the latter (D.S. 16.91.4–92.1). These procedures show a king who was able to subordinate the members of his dynasty to his strategic demands. Even Olympias, ambitious as she might have been, often had no way to oppose these machinations (Carney 2003b: 229–334).

Philip's position seemed to be so secure that the Macedonian aristocracy imposed few, if any, limitations on him. On the contrary, his efforts toward integration had proved effective. Presumably inspired by a corresponding Persian practice (Borza 1990: 248–9), he was successful in bringing the sons of the clan chiefs from all of Macedonia into the court as "king's pages" (*basilikoi paides*). These fulfilled various obligations toward the king and represented their families at court – to say nothing of their role as hostages. Also, as a result of the practice, the barons of the Macedonian highlands experienced a "bonding" (Arr. 4.13.1; D.S. 17.65.1; Heckel 1986c: 279–85). Philip surrounded himself with a group of Macedonian nobles, the *hetairoi* (Hammond 1989b: 141–8),[2] among them Attalus (Cleopatra's guardian),

---

[2]   Philip had, according to Theopompus (*FGrH* 115 F225b = Ath. 6.260d–261a), 800 *hetairoi* equipped with land. Alexander is credited with 2,800 *hetairoi* around 334, in reference to the *hetairoi* cavalcade.

Parmenion and his son Philotas, Cleitus the Black, Antipater, and Antigonus the One-Eyed (Monophthalmos) (Heckel 1992: 3–64). Although one cannot in all cases ascertain the exact provenance of these persons, their prosopographic connections and careers, they must nevertheless have been those whom Philip trusted with the most important duties. From this group the seven royal bodyguards (*somato-phylakes*) were chosen (Heckel 1986c: 288–93; Heckel 2003b: 205–8). Evidently, they were all endowed with appropriate military competence and experience in organization and administration (Errington 1990: 99–102).

Nothing is known about housing arrangements, whether the *hetairoi* (and their families) lived at the court itself or in its proximity. Also unknown is the selection process: how did they come to be part of Philip's circle? Philip could have inherited at least some of them from his predecessor(s). We are not dealing here with an aristocracy related to the ruler, nor with nobility based solely on family status, but with a group that satisfied the Macedonian code of values and which the king could put together from among the aristocracy (on game hunting see Briant 1991: 217–22; Briant 1993b: 273–4; Carney 2002: 62–5). The individual members did not carry out, as far as we can discern, a specific function: there was no link between belonging to the group, actual title, and prescribed duty. The king employed each man according to his abilities, as the occasion demanded.

When Amyntas did not succeed Philip after his murder, it was due, thanks in no small measure, to the decision of Antipater and his family to support Alexander (Baynham 1998b: 146–8); Parmenion and Attalus followed suit – the latter against his family obligations. Alexander himself secured his power in three ways, which essentially depended on court dynamics. First, he eliminated those members of the Argead dynasty who were potential rivals for the throne (Bosworth 1988a: 25–6), and thereby preempted the creation within the court of factions around other aspirants to the kingship. Second, he did not marry before the Persian campaign, especially not a Macedonian, because it would have implied a preference for one aristocratic family and because to leave an heir in Macedonia would have created an incalculable risk (Carney 2003b: 230). Third, he trusted people who had already been loyal to his father and conducted other campaigns together with them. By not granting blatant privileges he kept the *hetairoi* in balance so that existing groupings were neutralized. This meant that the third-mentioned group of aristocrats, the *syntrophoi*, did not receive their anticipated rewards until much later, as Alexander consciously opted for tradition and continuity. In the event, his decision was vindicated. The young king also succeeded in winning the loyalty and acquiescence of his helpers through selective preferment and personal acquaintance.

Serious rivalries among the members of the court could pose a danger to the king, as the famous quarrel between Hephaestion and Craterus shows. Certainly, it would be wrong to paint too harmonious a picture. It is more proper to assume permanent competition for the favor of the king and lasting (re-)creation of factions (Heckel 1986b: 305). The circumstances attendant upon Philip's murder demonstrate that there were critical voices among the members of the court and also against the king. As well, one has to take into account the opportunistic behavior of some *hetairoi* when it came to securing or improving their own positions.

Antipater's decision to support Alexander must have been made after carefully weighing the chances of survival and acceptance of the various candidates to the throne.

What then was relationship of the king to the court groupings? In general, one can assume that the communications among the Macedonian aristocracy were not based on rules of order and obedience. Under such conditions, there developed a stronger dependence on the person of the king: he, as integrative focal point, granted favor, the privileges associated with which were worth striving for (Berve i. 34–6). Certainly, it must have made a difference for *hetairoi* in their sixties and seventies whether they dealt with Philip or with Alexander. For the young king too, his relationship to the *hetairoi* closer to his own age was a different one, based strongly on common education, undertakings, and friendships.

Members of the aristocracy had no recourse to the social system if they wanted to keep or improve their position, except withdrawal to their family estates/ancestral lands. Nor did they have access to other courts, such as those of Epirus or Thrace, even less so that of the Persian Great King, unless they were prepared to engage in open rebellion and treason. In the world of the Greek *polis* a Macedonian was not necessarily well received, even if there was no doubt about the orientation of the Macedonian court toward Greece (Borza 1996, 1999; Baynham 1998b: 142–3). Since social opportunities at the court were monopolized, there was a reciprocal interest in collaboration – more so after the Macedonian court had developed into a power center in the second half of the fourth century. There were also embassies from the *poleis*, from the Persian satraps and the Great King, as well as exiles from the Persian empire (Plu. *Alex.* 5.1, 10.1; D.S. 17.2.2).

Macedonian custom required that the king be accessible and a role model: he had to be receptive to the claims of the inhabitants of the land and he conducted war not from a safe distance, but alongside his men in the front lines. Life at the court and access to the king were doubtless tempered by certain rules. One has to assume that royal audiences were regulated by established court ceremonial practices.[3] The king met for advice with his closest circle at the royal council (*synedrion*), but he was apparently reasonably free to determine the composition of this scarcely formalized "guild," which drew upon the most important *hetairoi* and *philoi* (D.S. 17.16.1–2; Corradi 1929: 235–8; Hatzopoulos 1996: i. 323–59). It is highly probable that the members of the *synedrion* were recognizable by their distinctive dress including the wearing of purple clothing, which thereby projected their status. Sources also relate the communal drinking sessions (*symposion, potos*) of the king and his companions, which were of great importance and rooted in Macedonian tradition (Borza 1983; Völcker-Janssen 1993; Murray 1996; Nielsen 1998; Vössing 2004). Here the king's companions could make informal agreements and establish their positions and status in personal and social terms. For the king himself this

[3] On possible Persian models see Kienast 1973: 28–30; cf. Briant 1996: 950; *HPE* 924–5. On the presence of Barsine and her family at the Macedonian court (D.S. 16.52.3; Curt. 6.5.2–3) see McQueen 1995: 117.

was an effective means of extracting obligations from his followers and of interacting with them as equals (Borza 1983: 52–4; Müller 2003: 254–5).

A complex interdependence between the king and older and younger aristocracy is obvious: on the one hand, the king relied upon particular groups of people; on the other, he was in a position as ruler of the court to share wealth, prestige, and access to power. Success within this system depended primarily on the person of the king himself, particularly on his charisma and his ability to gain acceptance.

The representation of the kingdom took place on two levels: on one level, through the embodiment of monarchy and the monarch through delegates and representatives outside the court ambience, as, for example, at places of Panhellenic significance such as Delos, Olympia, or Delphi (Bringmann and von Steuben 1995: s.v. "Philip II");[4] on the second level, in the projected image of the monarchy at the court and the capital city, such as in feasts for the court itself or for people outside of the court, for example, in the palaces of Pella and Aegae or in mobile structures if the king was traveling. The archaeological findings do not give a conclusive picture of this, nor have we learned a great deal about Alexander's living quarters (Arr. 1.17.4, 1.27.2; Plu. *Alex.* 9.3). Primarily, it seems that the Macedonian court was equipped for feasts only on a small scale, such as the above-mentioned *symposia*. Events on a larger scale required other venues: the wedding of Cleopatra to Alexander of Epirus was celebrated in the theater of Aegae, which lay in the vicinity of the palace (D.S. 16.91.4–95.5; Drougou 1997). Diodorus informs us, under the year 335/4, that before the departure to Persia there was a nine-day-long *panegyris* organized in Macedonian Dion with sacrifices and dramatic *agones*, in which the participants – *philoi*, *hegemones*, and *presbeis* – were served in a banqueting tent with 100 recliners (D.S. 17.16.4; Aneziri 2003: 57; Vössing 2004: 69–70).

Already under King Archelaus poets were patronized. Philip and Alexander continued this tradition even if big names and actual works are lacking (Plu. *Alex.* 4; 10.2–3; Weber 1993: 44–51). One did not publicly seek prestige through the fostering of intellectuals or individual scientific fields. Thus, the residence of Aristotle at the court in Pella (343–340) was dependent upon his role as educator of the successor to the throne (Plu. *Alex.* 5; Rubinsohn 1993; Scholz 1998: 153–65; Alonso 2000; Carney 2003a). Aristotle's nephew Callisthenes is exceptional in that he performed the function of official historian of the Persian campaign, but there were also various philosophers and poets whose exact duties, apart from intellectual conversation on different occasions, remain unclear.[5] One may assume that some intellectuals joined the expedition voluntarily, or on the recommendation of others, and endured the hardships of campaigning in order to gain financial profit and prestige (see Tritle, ch. 7).[6]

[4]   According to Plu. *Alex.* 4.9 Philip had his Olympic victory in the chariot race coined. On the golden staters see Le Rider 1977: 413 with pls. 53–6.

[5]   For Agis of Argos, Aischrion, Anaxarchus of Abdera, Anaximenes of Lampsacus, Pranichus of Pierion, Pyrrhon of Elis, and Choerilus of Iasos, see Berve i. 66–72; Weber 1992: 68–9; Carney 2003a: 53–61.

[6]   On an alleged reward for Pyrrhon (or Choerilus) with 10,000 gold coins for a poem of praise (Sext. Emp. *Adv. Gramm.* 282b), see Decleva Caizzi 1981: 136ff.; Brunschwig 1992: 59–60.

The court provided an organizational framework for the exercise of power. The *synedrion* of the king and his companions played a role in its operation; there was also a royal treasury[7] as well as a royal chancellery. The latter fulfilled diverse functions, primarily the completion of private and official written correspondence, the compilation of important individual notifications, and the keeping of the royal diaries. One must assume that there were many free and non-free civil servants, besides the *basilikoi paides* (Berve i. 39–42; Scholl 1987). Their names or job descriptions are not known to us for want of evidence, but they fall into the general category of "service" (*therapeia*: Berve i. 25). This service met the personal needs of the king and those demands which were necessary for the successful accomplishment of different external relations (Berve i. 55–64; Hatzopoulos 1997). In short, it was more than merely a power structure for the maintenance of the rule over the different parts of the empire. The king rather had to deal with euergetic demands: here one notes Alexander's benefactions to individual cities in Asia Minor which went beyond the pure rhetoric of freedom and changes in internal politics. They consisted of land and monetary donations, as well as freedom from taxation or compulsory contributions.[8] Little is known about the settlement of the corresponding regulations or the involvement of courtly structures and their staff (Alfieri Tonini 2002; Faraguna 2003).

Alexander's Court in Babylon

After his return from the east, Alexander dwelt again in the nucleus of the Persian empire, Susa and Babylon. Here he had at his disposal the Great King's palaces and their infrastructure, which implied an end to the mobile camp structure and new possibilities for royal representation (Funck 1996: 46–52; von Hesberg 1996: 84–5; Brosius 2003a: 181–7).

The interactive relations within the court's society and its composition changed in three ways. First, Alexander's inner circle was no longer restricted to Macedonians alone; there were now Sogdianians, Bactrians, and especially Iranians, either from the aristocracy or the Great King's family, for example, Oxyathres (brother of Darius) and Oxyartes (Roxane's father) among the *hetairoi* (Berve, nos. 586, 587; Collins 2001: 263–4).[9] Following Persian custom, "relatives" (*syngeneis*) of the king were added to the original all-Macedonian group. The implied proximity to the king, expressed by the bestowal of the diadem, was accompanied by duties and privileges (Arr. 7.11.2–6; Gauger 1977: 157; Vössing 2004: 49–50, 86; otherwise Briant 1996: 321–2; Jacobs 1996: 275, 283; *HPE* 309–10). These could be attached

---

[7]   On Harpalus see Berve i. 303–4; ii. 75–80, no. 143; Hammond 1989b: 187–92.

[8]   On the sending of spoils to cities and temples in Greece see Bringmann and von Steuben 1995: s.v. "Alexander d. Gr."; Whitby 2004: 35–7. On the probable return of art objects which were stolen by the Persians see Bringmann and von Steuben 1995: no. 319.

[9]   The only Greeks who were among the *hetairoi* of Alexander from before were Eumenes and Nearchus. Alexander continued the practice of Philip: Völcker-Janssen 1993: 39–40.

to various functions outside of the court, such as with the administration of a satrapy (Briant 1996: 350–9; *HPE* 338–47). It is hard to say on what basis Alexander selected individuals. In essence it seems that it was the relationship of these persons to their predecessors. It is also not known "how the Persians regarded their role in the corps of Alexander's bodyguards and the Companions" (Brosius 2003a: 176). Nevertheless, Alexander tried to expand his circle of helpers by integrating some of the Achaemenid elite and, in this way, to preempt any tendency toward resistance or disintegration (Högemann 1992: 344–51).

The significance of this step does not end with the change in the membership of the king's circle. More decisive was the very fact of the adoption of Persian traditions of court and kingship (Wiesehöfer 1994: 149–51). The relationship of the Great King to his circle was *not* characterized by the usual Macedonian accessibility, but rather by restriction of access (Briant 1996: 270–1; *HPE* 258–9). Whereas an elevated position befitted the Great King in his appearances, the Persian elite exercised a different type of social contact with the king. Not only did the nobility hold titles that were more honorific than functional, but the distance between the Great King and the elite was manifest in the practice of *proskynesis* (Wiemer 2005: 137–40). The position of the Great King was recognized in the ritual of hand-kissing and bowing. The failure of Alexander's attempt in 327 to introduce and impose this ritual was due to the resistance of his Macedonian friends. While Alexander submitted to the wishes of the elite on this offensive Achaemenid ceremonial, he tried to strengthen his position by cultivating his own image (Wirth 1993: 355–61). Significantly, there were no Persians among the *somatophylakes*: this may suggest that not all members of the Persian elite acknowledged Alexander's status or wanted to collaborate with him. Alexander could have pressed for greater consideration from the Persians, but he would have run into massive resistance from the Macedonians in whom he had the greatest confidence. The native elite was denied immediate and responsible participation in the victories of Alexander.

The dynamic at Alexander's court also changed as the forces of war and conquest brought new men into the circle of Macedonians around the king. Gone were the men of the old guard: Antipater functioned as the king's representative in Macedonia and Greece, but exercised no immediate influence on the court or Alexander's inner circle (Carney 1995: 371–2). The same was true of Antigonus, left behind as satrap of Phrygia. Attalus, Parmenion, Philotas, and Cleitus were murdered either at the beginning or during the course of the campaign (Müller 2003: 55–133). The latter three were not receptive to Alexander's orientalizing policies (Heckel 2003b: 215, 221–2). But these did not have an influential and open advocate to express their resistance, while Alexander had the possibility of disengaging himself from traditional Macedonian circles. New opportunities opened up especially for younger *hetairoi*, mostly for the group of persons to whom Alexander was already close and to which Coenus, Hephaestion, Leonnatus, Craterus, and Perdiccas belonged. The same was true for other friends of Alexander's youth, such as Laomedon, Harpalus, Ptolemy, and Nearchus. From this pool, the seven *somatophylakes* were taken. Criteria for membership in that group are not entirely clear (Berve 25–30; Rubinsohn 1977: 415; Gehrke 2003a: 66–7). This was a sworn community, welded together by numerous shared experiences and exertions but also under tremendous pressure of competition and inclined to be jealous of one another. The abilities and skills of these individuals lay again in the military and organizational area, but there were also specialties: for instance, Peucestas, through contact with the native elite and population, possessed a special linguistic ability (Berve, no. 634; Heckel 1986c: 290–1; Brosius 2003a: 177–8). But in other respects, intellectual abilities or prestige in literature, science, and art were not of great importance at the time for the *hetairoi*, even if Eumenes, Ptolemy, and others could demonstrate their competence in them (von Hesberg 1998: 205–10).

Generally, personal acquaintance with Alexander, absolute loyalty to him, and the faithful execution of duties, especially military, played the decisive role in bringing individuals into his circle. Alexander imposed mostly his own opinions, especially in personal matters. Apparently, even toward Hephaestion he made it clear that he was the source of each and every privilege (Plu. *Alex.* 47.9; Müller 2003: 258–9). With the increasing size of his empire, Alexander was dependent on a rising number of trusted helpers. He took some of them, at least, from his circle of Persian followers. Lastly, the Macedonian *hetairoi* were left with even fewer alternatives than before, unless they wanted to lose their status or even their lives, other than to work together with Alexander and in accordance with his wishes – something which was not always disadvantageous (Plu. *Eum.* 2.5–6; Hatzopoulos 1996: i. 335).

Finally, Alexander's marriages and the procreation of heirs also changed his status and position at the court from what it had been at the beginning of the campaign. It is true that the consequences of this change in behavior did not become clear until the war for his inheritance which followed his death. Nevertheless, already during his lifetime, his actions took on more than merely symbolic importance. The marriage to Roxane bypassed the Achaemenid (and, of course, also the Macedonian) elite, and Alexander could thereby retain a measure of independence – which he clearly did.[10] On the other hand, the multiple weddings at Susa in 324, when he married Stateira, the daughter of Darius III, who had been taken captive after the battle of Issus, and also Parysatis, the daughter of Artaxerxes III (Ogden 1999: 44–5; Carney 2000b: 108–11), sent a different signal. Now it was about creating a broader elite for the empire. For this reason Alexander appeared no longer (only) as a Macedonian king, even if Macedonian custom predominated. He took a clear leading role and, here too, his trusted Macedonians were left with no alternative but to cooperate. These weddings strengthened the ties of the Persian "relatives" with the king. None of the women took an active role, not even a visibly political one.[11] At the end of his life Alexander placed less and less importance on

---

[10]   On Alexander and Barsine see Ogden 1999: 42–3, 47–8; Carney 2000b: 101–5. On Alexander and Roxane see Ogden 1999: 43–4; Carney 2000b: 105–7.

[11]   For Olympias and Cleopatra in Macedonia and Epirus see Miron 2000: 37–8; Carney 2003b: 231–4, 250–1; for the legendary exaggeration of Olympias' behavior see Hammond 1989b: 34–5; Carney 1995: 383. On the Achaemenid queens see Brosius 1996: 105–19, and on the activities of Roxane, Ogden 1999: 46–7.

his relationship with the Argead dynasty and the considerations of the Macedonian nobility linked to it.

The preceding discussion of the inner workings of court society makes it clear that we are dealing with a new, artificially created elite. At the beginning of his reign Alexander had to accept the trusted men of his father and the Macedonian clan chiefs, but as time progressed they were removed from the inner circle and military office and replaced by friends of Alexander's youth. Their destiny was inextricably linked to that of their king. Moreover, his position was so strong that he could not only impose his will on them, which they enforced in concert with him, but also demand that they accept the increasing integration of the Iranian elite into the military and command structure. Even if Alexander surrounded himself mostly with Macedonians, the *hetairoi* were threatened by the ongoing integration of the Iranian elite and their connections through marriage. The deaths of Parmenion, Philotas, and Cleitus made it clear – regardless of the circumstances – who monopolized the violence. Some, like Craterus, were torn between loyalty to the king and conservative principles, and opted for silence. Finally the king's dependence on members of his aristocracy declined, particularly as distance and extended absence from the homeland weakened links to Macedonia. Even though they ruled together, considered each other *hetairoi*, and recognized a connection with each other and the king (Stagakis 1970: 99–100; Gehrke 2003a: 92–3), Alexander represented the focal point of a "personal kingdom." It was not by coincidence that he designated his friend Hephaestion chiliarch and – as vizier in the Persian style – second man in the new empire (Wirth 1993: 345–7; Collins 2001: 259–62, 268–74).

Access to the king, especially at the audiences, was now subject to stricter regulations and court ceremonies which made clear the personal nature and style of the monarchy. The *somatophylakes* decided who was allowed to see the king, and when (Berve 18–20, 27–8; Collins 2001). This process of increasing ceremony was in accordance with the fact that by 330 Alexander had already taken over not only parts of the ornamentation of the Persian Great King (Ritter 1965), but also his court system with its great number of offices and dignitaries, countless servants and concubines (D.S. 17.77.4; Scholl 1987; Briant 1989). Among the servants, slaves, and especially eunuchs, unattested at the Macedonian court (Tougher 2002b), played a great role: they belonged in their institutionalized organization to the outward appearances of court ceremony. This also prevented the concentration of power in the hands of one family (Briant 1996: 279–88; 2002d: 268–77): staff disposition implied a different kind of dependence and personal relation to the king (Llewellyn-Jones 2002).

The increase in ceremony becomes clear in the use of the royal tent architecture: to arrive there, as Phylarchus describes, one had to pass rows of elite troops (Ath. 12.539d–e = *FGrH* 81 F41; Briant 1996: 246–9; *HPE* 234–7). It is clear from the passage that purple clothing was a distinction and an external sign of royal favor (Ritter 1965; Blum 1998: 49–65, 191–210). Ephippus informs us that the clothing of the king represented a mixture of Macedonian and Persian elements: "on almost all other occasions he had for daily use, a purple cloak and a white and purple undergarment and the wide-brimmed hat with the royal diadem" (Ath. 12.537e–f = *FGrH* 126 F5).[12] Ephippus also asserts that Alexander, in his closest circle, dressed as he saw fit, sometimes appearing as Ammon or Artemis, another time as Hermes or Heracles. The use of costumes is informative inasmuch as it shows Alexander striving to direct his image to a specific point of acceptance through the temporary assumption of a divine role. Whether there was an explicit demand for divinity linked with it is impossible to say. In any case, Alexander reacted sensitively to the reactions of his circle. The fact that he had to play many roles created greater difficulties than one would expect – the costume was among other things a good protection.

External appearances were also important among the *hetairoi*: the ancient authors stress that "the followers of Alexander, too, lived more than luxuriously," though it is not always clear whether this behavior was exhibited during or after the king's lifetime. "One of these was Hagnon. He had golden nails in his boots. When Cleitus 'the White' dealt with state affairs he did business with those who came to him, while he walked around on purple rugs" (Phylarchus and Agatharchides in Ath. 12.539c = *FGrH* 81 F41 and 86 F3; Plu. *Alex.* 40.1; von Hesberg 1996: 88; Carney 2002: 62). Other extravagant behaviors do not seem to have been an exception. They provided the opportunity for the *hetairoi* to make their status visible outside Alexander's circle.

In addition to official appearances, Alexander interacted with his *hetairoi* in the *synedrion* and in particular in the symposium, which also had a corresponding Persian tradition in the form of royal banquets (Ath. 4.143–6: Briant 1996: 297–309; Murray 1996: 18–20; *HPE* 286–97; Vössing 2004: 38–51). Discussions and drinking bouts with members of the inner circle were features of court culture right up to Alexander's death. They occurred within a representative framework and ideally with freedom of speech – when the king tolerated it (Ephippus in Ath. 12.537d = *FGrH* 126 F4; Nielsen 1998: 117–18). Alexander also participated in other symposia which were hosted by the *hetairoi* in their living quarters (Arr. 7.24.4–25.1; Ael. *VH* 3.23). Equality among the participants remained important, although some Persian elements, perhaps such as the seating order, pursued a contrary tendency (Vössing 2004: 90–2).

The court became increasingly more important as a center of power and co-ordination. As with the *somatophylakes*, many of the *hetairoi* were continuously on the road with commissions. These forms of interaction promoted an ever stronger dynamic of competition among the *hetairoi*, who were responsible for insuring that no resistance against Alexander was successful (Rubinsohn 1977: 418–19; Badian 2000a). Also for this period there is no indication of the granting of secondary favors through the members of Alexander's circle. No danger threatened the king in this

---

[12]   On the diadem and Kausia see Ritter 1965: 55–62; Bosworth 1988a: 158. For its significance see von Hesberg 1999: 68–9; Collins 2001: 260–1; Gehrke 2003a: 154.

way. He was capable of imposing himself and in spite of equality marked the differences in rank and status with merciless punishments (Plu. *Alex.* 57.3; Berve no. 502; Müller 2003: 194–202). It does not come as a surprise that this effected a more strict opportunistic behavior, criticized in the Greek sources as flattery (*kolakeia*) and which stands out all the more sharply against the background of the resistance of a few. The Conspiracy of the Pages and the events that led to the murder of Callisthenes made this clear to everyone (Gehrke 2003a: 73; Virgilio 2003: 41–2).

The reactions of Cassander, who in 324 arrived in Babylon as a representative of his father, Antipater, provide an important confirmation of the changes that had taken place at court. Much that he witnessed he found highly irritating and, according to Plutarch, frequently angered Alexander with his ill-timed laughter. In fact, he was so roughly treated by the king that for years afterward he could not look upon even an image of Alexander without experiencing physical tremors (Plu. *Alex.* 74.1–6; Berve no. 414; Wirth 1989: 204–5, 213; but see Meeus, ch. 13, p. 250). It is no wonder that rumor held the family of Antipater and Cassander responsible for poisoning Alexander (Landucci Gattinoni 2003).

Representation at the court (i.e., display of wealth and power) remained important until the end of Alexander's power, particularly because this was a very significant element in the tradition of the Persian monarchy. In the words of Nicobule (Ath. 12.537d = *FGrH* 127 F2), "during meals, all possible artists were occupied with competing to provide pleasure for the king. Even during his last meal Alexander recited from memory and played out a certain scene of Euripides' *Andromeda* and then drank unmixed wine with a passion, inciting others to do the same" (see also Weber 1992: 68; von Hesberg 1999: 69). Greek elements were fostered as before. Poets and philosophers followed the court, but no quality works were produced, which took the king as their theme (Arr. 1.12.2; Weber 1993: 49–50). Instead, conflicts arose between Macedonians of the closest court society and those intellectuals who were too compliant were dismissed as flatterers (Curt. 8.5.7–8; Völcker-Janssen 1993: 81–4); even among the intellectuals themselves there was conflict (Brunschwig 1992: 66ff.; Müller 2003: 124–31, 138–40). That Callisthenes' role as promulgator of deeds of Alexander for a Greek and Macedonian audience was not assigned to anyone else after his death can be explained by the changed necessities (Golan 1988; Faraguna 2003).

In reports such as those of Nicobule one can discern the essence of royal daily life. The mass marriage in Susa in 324 constituted an outstanding event, whose extravagance, described in detail by Chares of Mytilene, undoubtedly corresponded with its function of impressing both participants and spectators (Ath. 12. 538c–d = *FGrH* 125 F4; Murray 1996: 19–20; Vössing 2004: 82–4). Along with the description we have a list of the invited artists. Chares, a participant in the campaigns and an eyewitness of the events he described, is a valuable source for the organization of the audiences and ceremonial occasions (*eisangeleus*). The feast took place in a tent, probably the tent of the Great King (Hammond 1989b: 219–20; Schäfer 2002: 21ff.): mobility and transience underscored its uniqueness.

Another event for which great expenditures are attested is the banquet at Opis, with its 9,000 participants, in the summer of 324. For the purpose of this discussion Alexander's immediate political intentions are not important (Arr. 7.11.8–9; Vössing 2004: 84–6); what is noteworthy is the fact that great care was taken with the representative process – the seating order of the people (Llewellyn-Jones 2002: 26) and the religious ceremonies in the Greek manner. The target group of this extravagance was not the inner court society. The court opened itself up to special subjects: the Macedonian soldiers. Alexander's conciliatory gesture compensated for the troops' evident decline in importance, for it was no longer about a Macedonian kingdom with Macedonian elite troops, but the domination of Asia, which could be maintained, if necessary, by native forces on location (Fredricksmeyer 2000).

The presentational aspect became stronger again during the sojourn in Ecbatana (winter 324/3). Here Alexander organized athletic and music competitions (Arr. 3.1.4; Bloedow 1998), as he had done before, only on this occasion with 3,000 athletes and artists who came by sea and overland from Greece. Furthermore, he gave continuous banquets for his inner circle (Arr. 7.14.10; Plu. *Alex.* 72.1; Borza 1983: 50–1). Above all, the 10,000 talents allegedly spent for the games on the occasion of Hephaestion's burial and his monumental tomb in Babylon, still unfinished at the time of Alexander's own death, must be mentioned (Völcker-Janssen 1993: 100–16; Borchhardt 1993; for its historicity see Palagia 2000; McKechnie 1995). It is important to note that these tombs were not planned for Ecbatana or Macedonia, but for Babylon. If one considers the artistic arrangements and their effect on the participants in the funeral feast, especially the *hetairoi* and Macedonian soldiers, then Hephaestion's memorial looms large. That Alexander buried there in the grandest and most extravagant manner (Völcker-Janssen 1993: 103–5) the one *hetairos* who had most supported his plans shows clearly that it was Babylon that Alexander considered as the center of his new empire.

As far as the *hetairoi* are concerned, one can conclude that they were integrated into the framework of power, whether as satraps or military commanders or in other roles demanded by the occasion. It is true that there was no external threat to the empire, yet the transition from the Achaemenid to Macedonian power was anything but easy. For the transition, the banquet played a pivotal role as a central place for the exchange of gifts, which exemplifies the reciprocity so essential to the Persian system of benefaction (Wiesehöfer 1980: 8–11, 17–18). Moreover, an important part of the transition was Alexander's conduct toward the *poleis* in Greece and Asia Minor, in whose internal affairs he intervened massively with the decree regarding the repatriation of the exiles (D.S. 18.8; Wiemer 2005: 160–4; Zahrnt 2003; see below Poddighe, ch. 6).

Alexander could fall back on the administrative structures of the Achaemenids in much stronger measure than before. They were all the more necessary since the empire, with its immense expansion, demanded a high level of organization (Koch 1990: 217–18; Klinkott 2000). This was true, as well, for the royal chancellery and the royal treasury, whose resources served not only for the exhibition of wealth, but also for the financing of new enterprises, such as the planned Arabian campaign (Koch 1990: 235ff.).

Balance: Factors of the Evolution

There are differences and commonalities in the two phases described above, and in how the court and court society represented itself. The courtly interaction between Alexander and the aristocracy in the first phase is characterized by an attempt to accommodate different groups. Alexander was still greatly dependent on Macedonian tradition. His behavior toward the inner circle was characterized by friendship and intelligent calculation, which gave individuals influence without their own families becoming a threatening factor. At the end of Alexander's life the Macedonian aristocracy around him was more homogeneous. Nevertheless, it had to accept a "strengthening" from the Persian elite. Opportunistic behavior increased, especially after all attempts at resistance to the king failed and there was no alternative for Greeks or Macedonians – nor even the Persians – in his entourage except collaboration. Numerous reports (despite their anecdotal character) of intrigue at the court, including men who were in his confidence, reflect the high potential for conflict in such relationships. The concentration around the king had not revealed, at least at Alexander's death, the delegation of power as a structural weakness. Alexander's circle was not ordered in fixed ranks except for the Achaemenid structures to which Hephaestion's official position belonged. This followed not least from the circumstance that the representation of ruler and court served not only exorbitantly the integrative self-depiction of the ruling society, but also enabled the collaborators to depict themselves within it without touching the actual leading role – the king was without an alternative. At first, the representation proceeded in the rather modest ways of the Macedonians and carried with it a minimum of ornate ceremony, overlaid with the outward appearance of equality within the elite. For feasts of greater dimensions, one had to call upon auxiliary constructions. Achaemenid traditions brought new qualities and dimensions to the ceremonial matters. The representation of the ruling society to different groups of subjects played a decisive role. Exhibitions of immense wealth in quantity and quality took on a special significance. The tradition of a certain intellectual style of the court society, which in the meanwhile was established in Macedonia, found no parallel in its Persian counterpart (Briant 1996: 339–42; *HPE* 327–30; van der Spek 2003).

Since the administrative and military threads run together in the court, it also served to secure power. The lack of institutions competing with the court meant there was neither an alternative to it nor a threat. Neither were there threats from the population of a capital city, as occurred in the later Hellenistic empires. The assumption of the corresponding Achaemenid organizational units made the practical change easier. With the passing of time, Greek and Macedonian affairs became less interesting and were displaced by current demands and future plans.

Under Alexander the Great there was a convergence of Macedonian and Achaemenid traditions in the monarchy. This assimilation was consciously orchestrated; it was throughout a carefully measured experiment and, above all, a selective one. The basic receptivity to the "other" led to something new, which was individually tailored for Alexander. Its character is not least recognizable by the fact that Alexander's successors gave up many of its elements again. The unity of extreme opposites, which are represented at different levels in the persons and attitudes of Hephaestion and Craterus, was possible only in the person of Alexander himself.

On the other hand, Alexander was successful in organizing the composition of his circle in a way that furthered his goals and supported *his* cause with all its strength and considerable abilities at different levels. This implied more than a mere exchange of individuals: it had its foundations in the composition of courtly structures that were decisively fostered by Philip and in changes introduced by Alexander.

The self-reinforcing tendencies of war and military success, resolutely fostered by allies such as Hephaestion and Craterus, combined with continuous military campaigns, allowed the elite to become a "closed society." All participants were completely cut off from other links (such as the Macedonian homeland) and were closely attached to each other in their administrative and military duties. It is true that this ruling society was not hermetically sealed, but in essence its members kept to themselves. The almost permanent state of exception, which became the daily life of the court, is symbolized best by the tent of the king, which only at the end of Alexander's life was replaced by fixed structures and nevertheless was still in use (von Hesberg 1996: 89). The "itinerant court" distinguished itself from the static residence not because the circle of persons who were present or the range of actions which started there were different. Alexander's "itinerant court" lacked fixed structures in the periphery. He ran out of time to establish them in Mesopotamia.

6

Alexander and the Greeks

The Corinthian League

Elisabetta Poddighe

During Alexander's reign relations between the Greeks and the Macedonian kingdom were regulated by the charter of the "Corinthian League." This modern expression refers to the political and military pact between Philip II and the Greeks ratified at Corinth after the defeat of the allied Greeks at Chaeroneia, and then renewed by Alexander in 336. The pact set the seal on a design for establishing Macedonian hegemony that would insure control over Greece and unite it in a war against Persia. It achieved its purpose because Alexander, in his relations with the Greeks, constantly sought to emphasize the legitimacy of his leadership: on the basis of traditional Greek hegemonic practice, Alexander regulated his political activity in Greece and used key themes of Greek propaganda as a catalyst against his opponents, and by turning their opposition to tyranny and their concern for freedom to his own advantage.

Alexander's Accession to Leadership of the Corinthian League

After Philip's assassination at Aegae in 336, Alexander inherited, together with the Macedonian kingdom, his father's Panhellenic project to lead the Greeks in the conquest of Persia. Part of this legacy was the Corinthian League, founded for this purpose by Philip. This was a league of autonomous Greek states (excluding Sparta) that in early 337 proclaimed peace and autonomy for the Greeks who swore not to attack the kingdom of Macedonia. The peace required recognition of the conditions established in the postwar period, that is, the complete political and/or territorial reorganization of the cities that had challenged Macedonia for hegemony in Greece (Athens, Sparta, and Thebes), now policed by garrisons stationed in Corinth,

Ambracia, Thebes, and Chalcis.[1] A common council (*koinon synedrion*) of the Greeks was established at Corinth, hence the name "Corinthian League." Voting rights were assigned to the member states on a proportional basis; these also conceded supreme command (*hegemonia*) to Philip (and to his descendants) in the event of war.[2] It had been agreed in advance that action must be taken against Persia, the common enemy, and predictably perhaps, the delegates consented to the proclamation of a war of revenge for the outrages committed against the Greeks in the Great Persian Wars of the fifth century, more than 150 years before (D.S. 16.89.2; Plb. 3.6.13).[3] This consent (*eunoia*), which confirmed the "Greekness" of the war of revenge, legitimized the leadership role of the Macedonian kingdom, though Philip did not live to exploit it. Yet there can be no doubt that Philip's most important legacy, though always a fragile one, was Greek adherence to the Panhellenic project.

The Lawful Inheritance

In the meeting with the Greek delegations after Philip's death, Alexander demanded the consent of the Greeks as his paternal inheritance (D.S. 17.2.2), clearly *the* consent won by his father when he promised to lead the Greeks in a war against Persia. Later, when Alexander moved south into Greece, he demanded once again hegemony over Greece as part of his father's legacy (D.S. 17.4.1), and once again, as we shall see, he stressed the Panhellenic character of this undertaking. Both demands underlined a key concept: the Macedonian kingdom was the legitimate leader of the Greeks against the barbarians and Alexander, as Philip's heir in all respects, was determined to confirm the legitimacy of his leadership and status.[4]

Although the claim to Philip's position as leader of the Greeks was juridically founded, many Greeks did not intend to acknowledge it. The Athenians and the Thebans proclaimed that "they did not want to concede hegemony over the Greeks to the Macedonians" (D.S. 17.3.2, 4). Athenian negotiations with the Persian king Darius III demonstrated that many Athenians saw the Macedonian king as a more dangerous and "common" enemy than the Persian, a warning already delivered by Demosthenes ([Dem.] 10.33–4; D.S. 17.4.8). Peace appeared especially precarious

---

[1]   The battle and postwar period: Hammond–Griffith 596–614; Buckler 2003: 500–11. Garrisons: D.S. 17.3.3, 8.7; Arr. 1.7; Plu. *Arat.* 23; Din. 1.18; Bosworth 1994a, 1994b; Buckler 2003: 511ff. The case of Chalcis (Plb. 38.3.3) is uncertain: Bosworth 1998: 48 n. 6; Faraguna 2003: 100 n. 4.

[2]   The oath sworn by the Greeks, preserved in a fragmentary inscription (Tod 1946: no. 177 = Rhodes and Osborne, no. 76), concedes hegemony to the Macedonian kingdom on a dynastic basis (l. 11; cf. Arr. 3.24.5): Perlman 1985: 170ff.; Hammond–Walbank 571; Hatzopoulos 1996: 297; Mari 2002: 113 n. 2.

[3]   Philip emphasized the prospect of the advantages involved in this (D.S. 16.89.3; Plb. 3.6.12): Hammond–Griffith 631. On the passage from Polybius: Walbank 1967: 307ff.; Seibert 1998: 27ff.

[4]   On Alexander's inheritance of authority, see Hammond–Walbank 16 n. 2; Squillace 2004: 20.

in the places where, after the surrender to Philip, compliant regimes and military garrisons had been installed. It was these interventions in the cause of "pacification" that surely precipitated the first revolt against Alexander (336): the Aetolians debated recalling the exiles proscribed by Philip; the Ambracians drove out the Macedonian garrison and set up a democratic regime; the Thebans decreed the removal of their garrison; and, probably at this stage, the Philiades were deposed at Messene (D.S. 17.3.3–5; [Dem.] 17.4).

Alexander's determination to follow Philip's path of mediation in the pursuit of supreme leadership in Greece is certainly indicated by his policy of intervening in the Greek world only on a firm legitimate basis. Diodorus strongly emphasized this when he pointed out how the Greeks had legitimized Philip's hegemonic aspirations, not only on the basis of Macedonian military superiority demonstrated at Chaeroneia (16.89.1), but also as a result of the discussions and meetings "in the cities" that convinced the Greeks to endorse the Persian campaign (16.89.2–3). The contents of those discussions are unknown, but it is certain that the language used was precisely the Panhellenic rhetoric that claimed the Greek (and Macedonian) right to territorial expansion and to the civilizing of the non-Hellenic peoples (cf. Isoc. 5.16.111–16).[5] The Greeks could tolerate – sometimes defend – Macedonian leadership only in terms of "antibarbarian" rhetoric (Aeschin. 3.132; Plu. *Phoc.* 17.7). Therefore, it was a foregone conclusion that Alexander would request a *formal* reconfirmation of his supreme command and undertake *formal* negotiations with the Greeks (D.S. 17.4.1–9) by reiterating the Panhellenic grounds for the anti-Persian crusade (Ael. *VH* 13.11).

The Panhellenic Crusade and Acknowledgment of Hegemony over Greece

Negotiations with the Greeks insured, first of all, that the Thessalian and Delphic Amphictyonies (*koina*) recognized Alexander's hegemony (D.S. 17.4.1–2). According to the sources, Alexander persuaded the Thessalian League to grant him the double title of *hegemon* and *archon*. This he claimed by appealing to the common descent (*syggeneia*) of the Argeads and of the Aleuads, the ruling dynasty of Larissa, from Heracles and Achilles whose exploits prefigured the Asian campaign (D.S. 17.4.1; Just. 11.3.1–2).[6] It would seem that the Aleuad connection was also the basis for the Amphictyonic council's concession of hegemony over Greece to Alexander (D.S. 17.4.2). Indeed, a reevaluation of the Aleuads was linked to exploiting the

---

[5]   On Panhellenism in Macedonian propaganda see Seibert 1998: 7–58; Flower 2000: 96–135. On the invention of an ancient enmity between Macedonians and Persians see Brosius 2003. Her undervaluation, however, of the expansionistic aims of the undertaking is unacceptable. Cf. Sakellariou 1980: 136ff.; Fredricksmeyer 1982: 85ff.; Bosworth 1988a: 17ff.; J. R. Ellis 1994: 784ff.; Seibert 1998: 28ff.

[6]   Sordi 1984a: 10 n. 5; Harris 1995: 175ff.; Helly 1995: 59ff.; Sanchez 2001: 253; Squillace 2004: 47ff. For a different view: Heckel 1997: 90ff.

myth of the Aeacidae[7] whose cult was an essential ingredient in Delphic propaganda. Alexander's visit to the sanctuary at Delphi, possibly confirmed by an inscription (*SIG*[3] 1. 251), is perfectly coherent with this diplomatic policy (Plu. *Alex*. 14.6).[8] Presumably the Panhellenic grounds for the war against Persia were also confirmed in negotiations with the Amphictyonies which, according to the *Alexander Romance*, were incited to make war against the "barbarians" (Ps. Call. 1.25.1). In any case, their acknowledgment of the hegemony confronted the Corinthian *synedrion* with a *fait accompli* by emphasizing the principle of dynastic hegemony ratified at Delphi in 346 (D.S. 16.60.4–5) and at Corinth in 337, thereby legitimizing Macedonia's hegemonic role.[9] It is significant that the Panhellenic sanctuaries were delegated, later, to inform the allied Greek cities of federal decisions and to host the federal assemblies (see below).[10] This procedure would later be repeated in the League of 302 promoted by Antigonus I (Monophthalmus) and Demetrius, which attributed a kind of "foundation act" to an amphyctictyonic *psephisma* (Lefèvre 1998: 97). This ordered too that, in peacetime, the federal assemblies were to be held during the sacred games (Moretti 1967, no. 44, ll. 65ff.).[11]

The glorification of cultural and religious themes most likely to promote Greek participation in the campaign was also a determining factor in negotiations with the states that refused to acknowledge Macedonian hegemony (D.S. 17.4.3–6). Once again, the criteria were the same as those adopted by Philip after Chaeroneia. In Boeotia, Alexander ruled with an iron hand (D.S. 17.4.4; Just. 11.2.9), continuing Philip's policy which had imposed an oligarchic junta and a Macedonian garrison on this traditional hotbed of Persian sympathizers. At the same time, he favored the other Boeotian cities, especially Plataea, because its forefathers had provided the field of battle where the Persians were defeated in 479.[12] Now on the eve of the Panhellenic crusade, Plataea welcomed home its exiles. This was a decisive step for Macedonian propaganda which would soon portray Alexander as the champion of the Plataean cause (see below).

At Athens, which had hurriedly sent ambassadors to Boeotia to request pardon for not having conceded hegemony immediately,[13] favorable conditions for peace

---

[7]   The symbols on a commemorative Larisean drachma are evidence of this: Sordi 1996: 38ff.; Squillace 2004: 48; cf. Just. 11.3.1.

[8]   Plutarch places the visit in 335: Sordi 1984a: 9.

[9]   Sordi 1984a: 9–13; Hammond–Walbank 14ff.; Lefèvre 1998: 94; Mari 2002: 221ff. Sanchez 2001: 253ff., however, distinguishes between Amphictyonic and Corinthian hegemony.

[10]   The reconstruction of Plataea and Thebes was announced at the Olympic (Plu. *Alex*. 34.2; see below) and Isthmean Games (Ps. Call. 1.47.1–7). The *synedrion* seems to have met at the Isthmus in 332 (D.S. 17.48.6; Curt. 4.5.11) and in 330 at the Pythian Games (Aeschin. 3.254).

[11]   Helly 1995: 66; Sanchez 2001: 246; Mari 2002: 222. The relevance of the League of 302 to Philip and Alexander remains under discussion: Moretti 1967: 116ff.; Bosworth 1988a: 190ff.; Mari 2002: 135ff., 222ff.; Buckler 2003: 516 n. 26; Rhodes–Osborne 379.

[12]   D.S. 16.87.3, 17.8.3; Arr. 1.7.1; Just. 9.4.7–8; Paus. 4.27.10, 9.1.8, 6.5; *Anth. Pal.* 6.344; Dio Chrys. 37.42; Gullath 1982: 12ff.; Heckel 1997: 92.

[13]   According to Diodorus (17.4.5–8) Demosthenes was among them, but other sources give a different date for the episode (Aeschin. 3.160–1; Plu. *Dem*. 23.2–3).

and the alliance sealed with Philip were confirmed (D.S. 16.87.3; Plu. *Phoc.* 16.5).[14] Ratification came under Athena's protection, to which anti-Persian propaganda reserved a determining role (Mari 2002: 260ff.). Macedonian officers "in charge of the common defense" later set up an inscription in Athena's sanctuary at Pydna recording Athenian contributions to Alexander's army; a copy of this was, in turn, displayed on the Athenian acropolis (*IG* II[2] 329, ll. 12ff.).[15]

It must be noted that the agreements were reached without threat of sanctions. Thessaly's resolution to retaliate militarily against Athens (Aeschin. 3.161) would seem to belong to another context,[16] and it is highly improbable that Alexander, as *hegemon* of the League, would assume responsibility for a measure such as this. As long as the *synedrion* had not legitimized his role, Alexander was determined not to punish violations of the peace.

From Corinth 337 to Corinth 336: The Letter and the Spirit of the Agreements with Alexander

At Corinth the Greeks definitively recognized Alexander's legitimacy. The same delegates who had met in 337 confirmed Alexander's functions as *hegemon* and *strategos autokrator* (D.S. 17.4.9; Arr. 1.1.1–3; Plu. *Alex.* 14.1; Just. 11.2.5);[17] it seems that they also met in the same place, the city or the sanctuary of Isthmia,[18] symbolic sites associated with the first anti-Persian Greek federation of 480 (Hdt. 7.145). The roll of those taking the oath must also have included the cities and states of continental Greece (except Sparta) together with some of the Aegean and Ionian islands (Rhodes-Osborne, no. 76b, ll. 2ff.).

Several clauses of the treaty (*synthekai*) are preserved in the Demosthenic oration *On the Treaty with Alexander*, possibly delivered by Hypereides.[19] There is general

---

[14]   The dissolution of the Second Athenian League (Paus. 1.25.3) was counterbalanced by the transfer of Oropus (Hyp. 3.16; [Demad.] *Concerning the Twelve Years* 9; [D.] 17.26; [Arist.] *Ath. Pol.* 61.6, 62.2; D.S. 18.56.6–7; Plu. *Alex.* 28.1–2; Just. 9.4–5; Plb. 5.10.1, 4; Paus. 1.34. 1; Brun 2000: 58 n. 11; Whitehead 2000: 207ff.; Faraguna 2003: 100 n. 4).

[15]   Heisserer 1980: 23; Voutiras 1998: 116; Rhodes–Osborne 379. Against: Tronson 1985: 15ff. On the "defense officers" see Hammond–Griffith 639ff.; Culasso Gustaldi 1984: 67ff.

[16]   In 335, so Sanchez 2001: 245ff.; Mari 2002: 135; Hammond–Walbank 15.

[17]   The functions of *hegemon* and *strategos autokrator*, considered distinct by Diodorus (17.4.9; cf. Heckel 1997: 85ff.), appear to be interchangeable elsewhere and hegemony seems to include command of the expedition or campaign (*strateia*: Aeschin. 3.132; Arr. 1.1.2, 2.14.4, 7.9.5; Plu. *Alex.* 14.1; Just. 11.2.5). Even Philip is defined as *strategos autokrator* (D.S. 16.89.1–3; *FGrH* 255, ll. 24–5; Just. 9.5.4) or *hegemon* of the *strateia* (D.S. 16. 91.2; Plu. *Mor.* 240a; Plb. 9.33.7): Bosworth 1980b: 48ff.; Jehne 1994: 181ff.; Hammond 1999a; Sisti 2001: 306ff.

[18]   D.S. 17.4.9; Just. 11.2.5 (Corinth); Plu. *Alex.* 14.1 (Isthmia, but in 335). The place chosen by Philip is uncertain (Mari 2002: 193 n. 3).

[19]   According to the traditional chronology of Demosthenes' speeches, the oration was given in 336/5 (Debord 1999: 469; some think 333 more probable: Will 1982: 202–3; Sordi 1984b: 23ff.) or 331 in the

agreement that the treaty completely renewed the agreements with Philip (Buckler 2003: 516). The allies swore to guarantee the peace (*eirene/koine eirene*),[20] that is, the autonomy and freedom of the Greeks ([Dem.] 17. 8), based on provisions tested in recent peace and alliance treaties such as the Peace of Antalcidas (387/6), the charter of the Second Athenian League (377), and the Athenian *koine eirene* of 371. The parameters of autonomy were defined with formulas preserved on inscriptions and in fourth-century historical accounts; on the negative side these stated what was forbidden: namely, not to attack states that had sworn to the peace and not to overthrow existing regimes (Rhodes–Osborne, no. 76, ll. 8–14; [Dem.] 17.10.14).[21] Other stipulations defined the right to political and territorial sovereignty[22] and obliged the Greeks to maintain the social status quo; illegal executions and banishment were prohibited as were the confiscation and redistribution of land, the remission of debts, the freeing of slaves, and the restoration of exiles to their home cities ([Dem.] 17.10, 15–16). Even in this case, however, the ban on fomenting revolution (*neoterismos*) was limited to improving a clause in the charter of the Second Athenian League that urged the allies "to live at peace" (Rhodes–Osborne, no. 22, ll. 10–11). The result was that the Greeks guaranteed preservation of the status quo on the basis of principles elaborated during their long experience with hegemony and that the rights of the dominant state were safeguarded precisely on the basis of these formal guarantees.

Even the administrative machinery delegated to safeguard the regulations and their activation were regulated by criteria that gave only formal guarantees to the allies. The common council assigned the seats and votes to the delegates according to objective factors such as population and military strength;[23] it appears that councilors could not be prosecuted in their home states for their decisions (cf. Moretti 1967: no. 44, ll. 75ff.). The council's wide authority encompassed arbitration,[24] protection of the social order, and ratification of war but, in the crucial areas, it was firmly controlled by the Macedonian state. In maintaining social order, it was the Macedonian military, "the board in charge of common defense," that assisted the *synedrion* ([Dem.] 17.15; Bosworth 1992a: 148) and it was the role of the *hegemon*

---

context of the debate following the revolt of Agis III (Cawkwell 1961; Bosworth 1994a: 847; Habicht 1997: 21; Blackwell 1999: 58 n. 79; Brun 2000: 78 n. 29). Differing are Culasso Gustaldi 1984: 159ff. (after 330) and Squillace 2004: 64 (335/4). Bosworth 1992a: 148 n. 17 attributes the oration to Hypereides, as does Whitehead 2000: 7 n. 26, on stylistic grounds. In the discussion below, the orator will simply be referred to as the "anonymous Athenian."

[20]   On the question of terminology: Buckler 1994: 114; Rhodes–Osborne 376.

[21]   Perlman 1985: 156ff.; Lanzillotta 2000: 144ff.; Musti 2000: 172ff.; Buckler 2003: 511ff. See also Sakellariou 1980: 142; J. R. Ellis 1994: 784; Rhodes–Osborne 378.

[22]   Extended also to territorial waters: [D.] 17.19–21; Alonso 1997: 186ff.; Lanzillotta 2000: 152.

[23]   Hammond–Griffith 632ff.; Buckler 2003: 514; Rhodes–Osborne 378.

[24]   There is epigraphic evidence of arbitration between the islands of Melos and Cimolos for the possession of three islets in the Melos group (Tod 1946: no. 179; Ager 1997: no. 3; Magnetto 1997: no. 1; Rhodes–Osborne, no. 82). The verdict (in favor of Cimolos) seems to have been delivered by Argos on the authority of a "*synedrion* of the Hellenes" (ll. 3–5) that seems identifiable as the Corinthian *synedrion*; cf. Ager 1996: 40ff., Rhodes–Osborne 404.

to propose to the council that it declare war against transgressors of the agreements.

In this case Greek diplomatic tradition also provided the principles that were to be followed. Armed intervention was regulated by a guarantee (or sanction) clause that had long been tested in fifth- and fourth-century treaties between the Greek states. In the Peace of Athens of 371 such a clause had demonstrated its potential, one capable of guaranteeing an alliance between signatories without ratification of a distinct treaty of *symmachia* (Alonso 2003b: 355ff.).[25] That the clause was to be activated only at the victim's request (Rhodes–Osborne, no. 76, ll. 18–19, Alonso 1997: 186) broadened its legitimate basis. The report of a clear abuse was sufficient for declaring war. The twofold role of the *hegemon* as advocate of peace (Arr. 2.14.6) and leader of the alliance, and the fact that peace was not guaranteed by the stamp of an external authority,[26] insured that the *hegemon* determined when sanctions would be declared.

Philip had activated the machinery for sanctions in 337: he had proposed that the *synedrion* declare war against the Persians in revenge for the sacrileges against the Greek temples in 480 (D.S. 16.89.2; Plb. 3.6.13), and declared afterward that he also wanted to liberate the Greeks in Asia (D.S. 16.91.2). Alexander repeated this procedure (Just. 11.5.6; D.S. 17.24.1). The Greeks and Macedonians could easily portray themselves as the victims of these earlier offenses that required punishment and thus the war could be interpreted as one of just retribution. In his letter to Darius III after Issus, Alexander referred to the offenses committed in 480 and denounced those of more recent date, namely, the plot against Philip and, after his death, the attempt to break up the peace among the Greeks (Arr. 2.14.4–6; Curt. 4.1.10–14).[27] The transgression of law and decency (*paranomia*) by the Persians was evident in both cases (D.S. 16.89.2; Plb. 3.6.13): the violation of the laws of war regarding respect for sanctuaries (Ilari 1980: 258ff.) and the infringement of the norms regulating relations between states (Ryder 1965: 147). Even the Greek judgment that Greek autonomy in Asia entailed freedom for Greeks everywhere provided a legitimate basis for action against the Persians (Musti 2000: 176). There is no reason, however, to believe that the non-allied Greeks of Asia made a formal request for help;[28] rather it was the allies of Corinthian League who were the injured party (*adikoumenoi*).

---

[25]   The alliance, explicitly defined by Arrian (3.24.5), was provided for by the *synthekai* (Bosworth 1980b: 46–51; Hammond–Walbank 571ff.; Hatzopoulos 1996: 297; Blackwell 1999: 49; Buckler 2003: 513ff.). See also Magnetto 1994: 283ff. The absence of the term *symmachia* from the text of the Greeks' oath (Rhodes–Osborne 376), however, seems decisive for those who deny the existence of the alliance (Ryder 1965: 158; Hammond–Griffith 628; Jehne 1994: 157ff.; Faraguna 2003: 102), or else they admit it in a stage successive to the oath (Tod 1948: 177, 229; Heisserer 1980: 16; Sakellariou 1980: 145).

[26]   Differently from the Peace of 386: Schmidt 1999: 92ff.; Buckler 2003: 512.

[27]   Atkinson 2000: 332 defends the historicity of the letter. Cf. Bosworth 1980b: 277ff.; Squillace 2004: 102ff.

[28]   Thus Jehne 1994: 157ff. and Faraguna 2003: 102. Seibert 1998: 15ff. rightly emphasizes that the liberation theme only applied to operations undertaken in place (D.S. 16.1.5–6, 91.2; 17. 24). Moreover, even once they were liberated the Ionian cities remained outside the League either as allies (Rhodes–Osborne 379) or as subjects (Bosworth 1998: 63).

Once war was declared, the prerogatives of the *hegemon* were renewed and everything was readied for the campaign. With an army of about 40,000 men Alexander renewed the expedition that Philip had earlier sent to Asia (D.S. 16.91.2). Less than a quarter of the army came from cities belonging to the League.[29] In this context, the *hegemon* had a legitimate basis for dealing with (predictable) Greek resistance. The *synedrion*'s resolution to punish any Greek who fought on the Persian side (Arr. 1.16.6, 3.23.8), a resolution inspired by the "oath of Plataea" sworn at Corinth in 480,[30] would permit Alexander not only to punish the numerous[31] mercenaries recruited by Darius III, but all Persian sympathizers.

Modern scholars have often seen in Alexander's approach to the Persian sympathizers,[32] and in general his relations with the Greeks, evidence of an early and growing indifference to the League's charter.[33] Analysis of actual cases, however, demonstrates that the League was in fact what it claimed to be: an instrument for exercising control over the allies in the hands of the *hegemon* who used it according to his prerogatives throughout his entire reign.

Alexander and the Greeks of the Corinthian League in the Context of the Persian War

The ideological profile of the campaign against the Persians and the network of relations with the allies justified the hegemonic role of the Macedonian king. As enforcer of the *eunoia* of the Greeks, Alexander's duty was to assert the primacy of civilization over barbarism; once elected *hegemon*, he was able to exercise his prerogatives in order to achieve his purpose.

On the other hand, many Greeks felt that Macedonian hegemony was an attack on the freedom of the *poleis*.[34] Although in hostile cities such as Athens reaction to these conditions took different forms, ranging from pragmatic acceptance of the new political reality (Aeschin. 2.164–5; Plu. *Phoc.* 16.7[35]) to pursuit of their own claims to hegemony (Dem. 18.60–72), the resolve to oppose the Macedonian tyrant usually prevailed. Opponents' demands followed a constant pattern that emphasized those elements of the treaty guaranteeing the freedom and autonomy of the allies, while obscuring the campaign, the alliance, and the powers ascribed to its leader. But it was precisely the "emergency powers"[36] decreed by the *synedrion* for

---

[29]   D.S. 17.17.3–5; Just. 11.6.2; Plu. *Alex.* 15.1; Arr. 1.11.3.

[30]   Hdt. 7.132; Lycurg. *Leoc.* 81; D.S. 9.3.1–3; Bosworth 1988a: 189ff.

[31]   According to the sources (Curt. 5.11.5; Paus. 8.52.5) there were 50,000: Green 1991: 157ff.

[32]   Arr. 1.16.6, 19.6, 29.5; 3.6.2, 23.8; Curt. 3.1.9.

[33]   Already during the *strateia*: Prandi 1983: 32; Errington 1990: 82ff.; Blackwell 1999: 77ff. After 330: Heisserer 1980: 233ff. After 325/4: Bosworth 1988a: 220ff.; 1998: 73ff.

[34]   For an evaluation of the survival of the free *poleis* after Chaeronea: Price 1988: 324ff.; Green 1990: xx–xxi, 24ff., 196ff.; Bencivenni 2003: 1ff.

[35]   On the views of Aeschines and Phocion: Tritle 1988: 123ff.; 1995. Against: Bearzot 1985: 135ff.

[36]   Hammond–Walbank 79; against: Blackwell 1999: 43 n. 37.

conquering the Persian empire that were to be used against rebellious Greeks who, as Persian sympathizers, were the enemies of peace.

Panhellenism and the Exercise of Hegemony against Theban Resistance

The war against Thebes is a striking example of resistance by the more hostile Greek allies (Thebes and Athens) to Macedonian leadership and the determination of the *hegemon* to oppose it on legal grounds. In the case of Thebes, sanctions had to demonstrate that defection from the accords would not be tolerated (D.S. 17.9.4; Plu. *Alex.* 11.17); at the same time it also had to emphasize that intervention was legitimate. Therefore, rebels had to be punished on the basis of League accords and wartime propaganda.

Late in the summer of 335, the exiles proscribed by Philip after Chaeroneia returned. After attacking and isolating the Macedonian garrison on the Cadmea, the Thebans installed a democratic regime, overthrowing the 300-member *politeuma* that had been set up two years before.[37] The rebels were convinced that Alexander had died in battle against the Illyrians. When this news turned out to be false, the majority of the Thebans resolved to hold fast to their original intentions.[38] The rebellion, which violated several clauses of the League charter, rapidly spread to the rest of Greece: the Arcadians revived their league and sent an army to the Isthmus; the Eleans exiled the pro-Macedonian party; the Athenians ordered the deployment of their forces. The rebellious Thebans invited the Greeks to return to the peace terms agreed in 387/6 with Persia which was financing the rebellion.

As *hegemon* Alexander intervened to punish the defection and collaboration with the Persians.[39] The legitimacy of the intervention took on a distinctive character as Greek forces joined Alexander's army during its march to Boeotia from Illyria where news of the rebellion had reached him (Arr. 1.7.5–7).[40] These forces included Phocians and Thessalians, but especially Orchomenians, Thespians, and Plataeans, all Boeotians and all enemies of Thebes. As the only Boeotians who had opposed the "barbarian" during the Persians wars (Hdt. 7.132.1) they guaranteed legitimacy to federal sanctions. The support of these "champions" of Greek liberty[41] compensated for the massive abstention of other allies in the war, the legality of which, in

---

[37] Just. 9.4.7–8 (Gullath 1982: 10; Heckel 1997: 92). Possibly the *politeuma* excluded manual workers (Arist. *Pol.* 1278a25; Poddighe 2002: 83, 98ff.).

[38] The Thebans opposed to this were spared by Alexander after the battle (Plu. *Alex.* 11.12).

[39] Aeschin. 3. 239–40; Din. 1.18–21; D.S. 17.8–14; Arr. 1.7–10; Just. 11.3.6–4, 8; Plu. *Alex.* 11; *Dem.* 20.4–5; Bosworth 1980: 73ff.; Gullath 1982: 20ff.; Hammond–Walbank 56ff.; Worthington 1992: 162ff.; Heckel 1997: 87ff.; Blackwell 1999: 46ff.; Brun 2000: 71ff.; Sisti 2001: 321ff.; Squillace 2004: 112ff.

[40] Bosworth 1980b: 76ff.; Green 1991: 142; Sisti 2001: 323ff.

[41] Hdt. 8.34, 8.50, 9.16, 25; Squillace 2004: 124ff.

this and other cases, was no less serious an issue.[42] The case of the Arcadians demonstrates this: declaring themselves ready to support the Theban revolt, they were persuaded to accept the *hegemon*'s decision by not being required to furnish troops (Din. 1.18–20).[43]

The exemplary purpose of sanctions required an exemplary use of the *hegemon*'s prerogatives and, in fact, this was guaranteed. The herald's proclamation that traditionally announced an ultimatum invited the Thebans to accept the offer of peace; this also emphasized the "constitutionality" of the punitive war. Only after the Theban counter-proclamation, which invited violation of the accords, did punitive war (*timoria*) against the rebels begin.[44]

The *hegemon* also exercised his prerogatives after the battle which ended rapidly with the foreseeable defeat of the Thebans (Bosworth 1988a: 32ff.). On the basis of the rule that allowed the federal authority to select the *synedrion*'s meeting place, the allied council did not gather at Corinth as usual, but probably in Alexander's camp.[45] Here, the fate of the defeated, usually reserved to the *hegemon* (Alonso 2003a: 353), was delegated to the allies (Arr. 1.9.9); this was certainly intended to emphasize that Alexander would not be responsible for the anticipated vengeful decisions of Thebes' neighbors, and to use the *synedrion* against Persian sympathizers. Once military action had punished the defection, the campaign's propaganda apparatus conditioned debate among the allies about the final sentence. Thebes' earlier and more recent Persian sympathies, along with abuses committed against the Boeotian cities and Athens, placed the sentence firmly within a Panhellenic context. The decision to destroy Thebes, to sell the prisoners into slavery, and to banish the exiles from everywhere in Greece was just retaliation for the damage done by the Thebans to Plataea in 374/3 and Orchomenus in 364. The *synedrion*'s decision to link the destruction of Thebes with the reconstruction of Plataea, along with Alexander's pledge to carry this out, was an appropriate recognition of the Panhellenic status of the city that, in 479, had sacrificed its territory in the name of freedom.[46] The execution of a cruel sentence seemed legitimate from a Panhellenic point of view (Aeschin. 3.133), and the "just" condemnation of Thebes echoes later in the *Alexander Romance* where a personified Mt. Cithaeron exults at the city's destruction (Ps. Call. 1.46.1; Gargiulo 2004: 109ff.).

[42]   The penalties imposed in 302 for failure to send a military contingent (Moretti 1967: no. 44, ll. 95ff.) are evidence that there was frequent abstention. The sanctions (20 drachmas per day for each hoplite) were imposed whenever a contingent was required from a city.

[43]   Only those who supported the revolt were punished (Bosworth 1980b: 92).

[44]   D.S. 17.9.5–6; Plu. *Alex.* 11.7–9; Alonso 1995: 211ff.; Squillace 2004: 122ff.

[45]   There is evidence for normal procedures only in 302 (Moretti 1967: no. 44, ll. 70ff.). The place (Borza 1989: 128; Blackwell 1999: 46) and composition of the meeting is uncertain; either the victorious (Arr. 1.9.9; Just. 11.3.8) or all the delegates to the *synedrion* (D.S. 17.14.1); Bosworth 1980b: 89ff.; Heckel 1997: 94.

[46]   Arr. 1.9.9; D.S. 17.14.2–4; Just. 11.3.9–11; Plu. *Alex.* 11.11. On Theban responsibility with respect to Athens, Plataea, and Orchomenus: Isocr. *Plat.* 31; Arr. 1.9.7; D.S. 15.46.5–6, 79.3–6. On the measures in favor of Plataea: Arr. 1.9.10; Plu. *Arist.* 11.3–9; *Alex.* 34. 2; Prandi 1988: 138ff. On the significance of the condemnation: Plu. *Alex.* 11.11; Plb. 4.23.8, 5.10.6, 9.28.8, 38. 2.13–4; Heckel 1997: 92ff.

The Athenians, instigators of the revolt and Persian accomplices as well, paid a less drastic price for their crimes. Alexander directed the negotiations in person. The demand that those anti-Macedonian politicians most heavily involved in the revolt be turned over to the *synedrion* was reformulated in bilateral negotiations with Demades and Phocion (Arr. 1.10.3–6; Plu. *Phoc.* 9.10–17). Condemnation was reserved for those generals who had most compromised themselves with the Persians and who had fled Greece to fight on the side of Darius III.[47] The need to move quickly into Asia (Arr. 1.10.6) and to be moderate in his treatment of Athens convinced Alexander that he had to assume the role of final judge in deciding the fate of Persian sympathizers. This operating principle was used for the first time now and would be repeated at Chios and Sparta (see below).

Alexander's Exercise of Absolute Sovereignty after his Departure for Asia

Even after Alexander's arrival in Asia in spring 334, intervention among the allied cities appeared to be consistent with the League's mission. The visit to the tombs of the Greek heroes, Protesilaus, Ajax, and Achilles, leaders of the mythical first campaign in Asia, and sacrifices at the sanctuary of Athena Ilias, symbolically emphasized the significance of Alexander's presence in Asia and his campaign.[48] It was soon clear that Alexander was in a position to lead the alliance in pursuit of its objectives, not only in defeating the Persian army, but also by punishing those Greek mercenaries who fought for the Persians. He also exerted pressure on allied cities that impeded the war's success. In each case the appeal to the League's mission was formal in nature.

After the first victory over the Persians at the Granicus in summer 334, the "spoils of war captured from the barbarians in Asia" were offered to Athena in the name of the League (Arr. 1.16.7; Plu. *Alex.* 16.17–18); captured Greek mercenaries were sentenced to hard labor in Macedonia for having fought "against Greece" (Arr. 1.16.6, 1.29.5–6). Soon after, the imposition of pro-Macedonian regimes in the allied cities of the Peloponnesus and the Aegean islands followed. These, the anonymous Athenian orator tells, were based on ideological principles governing the League's actions: in Greece the principles of status quo and *homonoia* and, in Asia, the battle against despotism prevailed ([Dem.] 17.4, 7, 10). The anonymous orator went on to condemn constitutional upheavals that violated the accords – "as if Alexander's absolute sovereignty extended over perjury also" (12) – and also pointed out that they did not even have a consistent ideological basis: on the one

---

[47] The sources differ on the number and identity of the Athenians (Arr. 1.10.4; Plu. *Phoc.* 17.2; *Dem.* 23.4; *Suda* s.v. "Antipater"; Heckel 1997: 102ff.; Sisti 2001: 334ff.) and on the final decisions (Arr. 1.10.6; Just. 1. 4.11; Landucci Gattinoni 1994: 60; Heckel 1997: 103; Brun 2000: 73ff.).

[48] D.S. 17.17.1–3; Plu. *Alex.* 15.4; Arr. 1.11.3–7; Just. 11.5.12; Flower 2000: 108ff.

hand (at Messene) the installation of tyrants was legitimate because they were in power "before" the accords (7); on the other hand (at Lesbos) the tyrants, though in power "before" the accords, were deposed with the "laughable" justification that they were detestable.[49] It is evident, however, that in both cases intervention punished defecting allies and helped achieve success in the war.

This intervention must be placed within the context of war against the attempted Persian reconquest of the Aegean;[50] this engaged Macedonian and League forces from the spring of 333 to the spring and summer of 332. The victories of the satraps Pharnabazus and Autophradates fed anti-Macedonian ferment in the island states of Chios and Lesbos, who now allied themselves with the Persians; on the Greek mainland Autophradates' support of Agis of Sparta resulted in certain countermeasures also mentioned by the anonymous Athenian orator ([Dem.] 17.4, 7, 10). Alexander's victory at Issus in the autumn of 333 helped considerably in rallying the temporary support of most mainland Greeks and placated their hostility. At the Isthmian Games in 332, the delegates of the Corinthian League decreed a golden crown for Alexander. In the same year, the king, in his letter to Darius III, officially confirmed the League's resolve to avenge fifth-century Persian offenses against the Greeks (see above), and dealt exemplary punishments to those island communities that had defected.

The *Hegemon* and the Allies Chios and Lesbos after their Defection from the Accords: The Imposition of Democracies and Readmission to the League

The Macedonian reconquest of the islands (Arr. 3.2.3–7) was sanctioned by agreements defined by the sources as *homologiai*.[51] As reported by the anonymous orator, the oligarchs' treachery was punished by removal from office. The oligarchies had probably already been in power when the League was formed in 337. They were accepted at first and then deposed after their defection (Bosworth 1988a: 192; Lott 1996: 38). Removing the oligarchies as an effective anti-Persian measure had been demonstrated during the "liberation" of the Greek cities in Aeolia and Ionia. In the summer of 334, after the victory at the Granicus, Alexander had sent his agent Alcimachus to depose the oligarchies in those cities and install democratic regimes, thereby insuring their autonomy and remission from paying Persian tribute (Arr. 1.18.1–2). Obviously, it would be consistent to extend this measure to those allied cities that had left the alliance and joined the Persians. Experience with the

---

[49]   The pacts (*synthekai*) and the accords (*homologiai*) ratified in 336 and 332 (see below). Against: Debord 1999: 469ff.

[50]   Arr. 2.1.1–5, 13.4–5, 3.2.3–7; Curt. 3.1.19–20, 4.1.36–7, 5.14–21; D.S. 17.29.1–4; Bosworth 1988a: 52ff.; Debord 1999: 466ff.; Rhodes–Osborne 416ff.

[51]   [D.] 17.7; Arr. 3.2.6. See Rhodes–Osborne, no. 85b, l. 35.

non-allied cities of Ephesus, Priene, Aspendus, and Soli had already shown that institutional democratization did not necessarily guarantee effective freedom or a common juridical status; instead it satisfied in different ways the various military, propaganda, and financial needs of the war.[52] Furthermore, the democratic model was a part of Greek political culture and therefore ideal for reuniting the islands to the anti-Persian league.

Some inscriptions of uncertain date (*c*.332?) from Chios and Lesbos probably refer to this institutional reorganization.[53] The best evidence of the numerous juridical instruments at the disposal of the *hegemon* are Alexander's so-called first[54] and second letter to the Chians.[55] These contain, respectively, a constitutional plan for Chios and a message to its inhabitants regarding some questions arising from the first measure. The first letter probably referred to an edict (*diagramma*) issued after the reconquest of the island.[56] The royal decree installed a democratic regime and reintegrated the pro-Macedonian exiles into civic life. The presence of a temporary garrison insured the application of the prescribed measures. A board of scribes was to draw up and revise the laws so that they would be in harmony with the democratic regime and the return of the exiles. These norms, whether amended or written, were to be submitted to Alexander. As king and supreme commander, Alexander would oversee the application of the measures. As supreme commander, he ordered that Chios provide twenty triremes as part of the "fleet of the Hellenes," this probably the fleet equipped by Hegelochus in 333.[57] Moreover, in conformity with the decrees already voted by the *synedrion*, he decided the fate of Persian sympathizers: he proclaimed the banishment and arrest of those who had fled the city; he deferred judgment of Persian sympathizers remaining on the island to the *synedrion*; and, finally, he mediated in the dispute between the Chians and Persian sympathizers who had returned home. In line with this role of direct mediation, already used in dealing with Athenian Persian sympathizers, Alexander decided the

[52]   Bosworth 1998: 61ff.; Debord 1999: 476ff.; Mossé 2001: 52ff.; Faraguna 2003: 113ff. Epigraphic documentation on Alexander's intervention at Priene in Rhodes–Osborne, no. 86. Cf. Bosworth 1998: 64ff.; Debord 1999: 439ff.; Faraguna 2003: 109ff.; Squillace 2004: 155ff.; Hansen and Nielsen 2004: 1092ff. On Aspendos: Magnetto 1997: 24ff.; Bosworth 1998: 62ff.; Faraguna: 2003: 112.

[53]   Prandi 1983: 27; Bosworth 1988a: 192ff.; Hammond–Walbank 73ff.; Lott 1996: 26ff.; Brun 2000: 85ff.; Faraguna 2003: 109ff.; Hansen and Nielsen 2004: 1023ff., 1028, 1067ff. According to a different reconstruction (Heisserer 1980: 27ff.; Labarre 1996 25ff.; Rhodes–Osborne 414ff.; Squillace 2004: 64), the inscriptions would be evidence for earlier constitutional changes. This theory is founded on the hypothesis that, on the islands allied to the League in 336 following the operations of Parmenio and Attalus (Diod. 16.91.2), democracies had already been installed, then deposed after the insurrection led by Memnon of Rhodes in 335 (D.S. 17.7.2–3, 8–10) and reinstated by Alexander in 334. It seems, however, that the islands were not involved in Parmenios's operations nor in Memnon's insurrection (Hammond–Walbank 73 n. 2; Green 1991: 139ff. Against: Labarre 1996: 24ff.).

[54]   *SIG*³ 283 = Rhodes–Osborne, no. 84a = Bencivenni 2003: no. 1.

[55]   *SEG* xxii. 506 = Rhodes–Osborne, no. 84b.

[56]   Bencivenni 2003: 18ff. The hypothesis of a preventive document (Bosworth 1980b: 268) is discussed by Prandi 1983: 26ff. Cf. Bosworth 1988a: 193ff.; Debord 1999: 466ff.; Faraguna 2003: 113ff.; Hansen and Nielsen 2004: 1067ff.

[57]   Arr. 2.2.3; Curt. 3.1.19–20; Hauben 1976: 84ff.; Prandi 1983: 26 n. 10; Debord 1999: 466ff.

fate of the Persian sympathizers who had been captured on the island later. Taken to Egypt by Hegelochus (possibly after being judged by the *synedrion*), these were then sent by Alexander to Elephantine (Curt. 4.5.17; Arr. 3.2.3–7).[58]

The anonymous writer reports ([Dem.] 17.7), and the epigraphic record indirectly confirms, that intervention in the cities of Lesbos was equally drastic. A group of documents from Eresus[59] gives an account of the judicial proceedings against the tyrants Agonippus and Eurysilaus, guilty of collaborating with the Persians during the Aegean war, and then tried and exiled in 332. In this case, once again, a *diagramma* probably established the democratic regime that tried and exiled the two tyrants, a democratic regime whose judicial proceedings regarding the exile of Persian sympathizers had to conform to the decisions (*kriseis*) of Alexander and his successors.[60]

The installation of a democratic government and the forced civic reorganization at Mytilene (perhaps an ally since 337[61]) were probably also a result of the desertion in 333. Two decrees from the city[62] record the measures issued by the deliberative democratic organs (the *bolla* and the *damos*) installed by Alexander after Hegelochus' reconquest of Lesbos in 332 (Arr. 2.2.6; Worthington 1990: 207).[63] These measures were probably based on a *diagramma* (Bencivenni 2003: 47) that ordered, in the name of the king, the return of the exiles, the installation of a democratic regime, and civic reconciliation between the pro-Macedonian exiles and the Persian sympathizers. Once again Alexander oversaw the difficult civil reconciliation and the fate of the Persian sympathizers, apparently without the intervention of the *synedrion*.

The "New" Peloponnesian Tyrants and Loyalty to the Corinthian Accords

The constitutional changes in the Peloponnesian cities, coordinated by Antipater,[64] Alexander's deputy for Greek affairs, and in his absence, by Corrhagus the garrison commander of Acrocorinth, appear justified by the need to insure control over

---

[58]   Bosworth 1980b: 268; 1988a: 193; Hammond, in Hammond–Walbank 74. Against: Prandi 1983: 28.

[59]   Rhodes–Osborne no. 83 = Bencivenni 2003: no. 3.

[60]   Bosworth 1988a: 192; Debord 1999: 468 ff.; Hansen and Nielsen 2004: 1023ff.

[61]   Arrian (2.1.4) records an alliance with Alexander (Bosworth 1980b: 181; Hammond–Walbank 73 n. 1) but this might be short for "alliance with Alexander and the Greeks" (as it is for Tenedos: Arr. 2.2.2.): Prandi 1983: 28; Sisti: 2001: 395. Cf. also Badian 1966a: 50; Debord 1999: 472 n. 397.

[62]   Rhodes–Osborne, no. 85a–b = Bencivenni 2003: no. 2. Debord 1999: 467ff.; Hansen and Nielsen 2004: 1028.

[63]   For other dates (334, 324, or 319): Rhodes–Osborne 430; Bencivenni 2003: 45ff.

[64]   Arr. 1.11.3; D.S. 17.17.5; Blackwell 1999: 53 ff.

Greece in the years when Agis of Sparta was preparing war against Macedonia (see below). Both acted autonomously, that is, apparently without consulting the *synedrion*, and both appealed to the statutory principles of the status quo and (possibly) of civil concord (*homonoia*).

In about 333, during the first phase of negotiations between Agis and the Persians, the Philiades, tyrants overthrown in the disorders following Philip's death, were brought back to Messene ([Dem.] 17.7).[65] Their restoration to power was formally legitimate, but at this point it functioned especially to reinforce control over Sparta's eastern borders and, therefore, was linked to the measures adopted at Sicyon and Pellene for securing Sparta's northern borders. At Sicyon, an anonymous tyrant, known in Athens as "the *paidotribes*" ("the professional trainer") was brought back from exile ([Dem.] 17.16; possibly he was Aristratus (Poddighe 2004: 187ff.)). His return had been imposed by an edict (*prostagma*), probably on the grounds of institutional continuity. At Pellene, however, soon before Agis' revolt and with the support of Corrhagus,[66] the tyrant Chaeron replaced the preceding regime which the anonymous Athenian orator thought democratic ([Dem.] 17.10). The historical circumstances of his installation are obscure, as Chaeron's supposed tyrannical ambitions derive from a *topos* elaborated by Athenian democratic propaganda, probably shaped by Demochares (Marasco 1985: 113ff.), and still recognizable in Pausanias in the second century AD (7.27.7).[67] The hypothesis based on Athenaeus (11.509b; cf. Marasco 1984: 163ff.), however, that the deposed regime was not democratic and that wide support for Chaeron's action resulted from serious social conflicts would suggest that intervention was based on the need to insure social order (*homonoia*) which would explain the *synedrion*'s silence. Moreover, it cannot be excluded that Alexander's intentions to suspend tyrannical regimes, once Asia had been conquered, had a reassuring effect on the *synedrion*. Furthermore, the consolidation of relations between Antipater and the Peloponnesian tyrants, though worrisome, could be tolerated for strategic reasons.[68] In any case, the effectiveness of the intervention at Pallene became evident when, soon afterward, Pellene was the only Achaean city that did not join Agis' anti-Macedonian revolt, the ultimate Greek threat to the war against Persia.[69]

---

[65]　Bosworth 1988a: 188. For 333: Walbank 1967: 567. The years 336 and 335 are proposed respectively by Debord 1999: 469 and Squillace 2004: 64 n. 89.

[66]　*Acad. index Herc.*, cols. 11, 28ff., 32ff; Culasso Gastaldi 1984: 54ff.; Bosworth 1988a: 194, 201.

[67]　Pausanias refers the *topos* to Alexander. For Pausanias' use of Demochares: Bearzot 1992: 111ff.; Culasso Gastaldi 1984: 54ff., 159ff. attributes the pseudo-Demosthenic oration to Demochares.

[68]　Bosworth 1988a: 162; Badian 1994: 269; Baynham 1994: 343, 346; Blackwell 1999: 76.

[69]　Aeschin. 3.163, 165–7; Din. 1.34; D.S. 17.48.1–2, 62–3; Plu. *Mor.* 219b; *Dem.* 24.1; *Agis.* 3; Curt. 4.1.39–40, 6.1.1–21; Arr. 2.13.4–6, 3.16.10; Just. 12.1.4–11; McQueen 1978: 40ff.; Bosworth 1988a: 198ff.; Badian 1994: 258ff.; Baynham 1994: 339ff.; Heckel 1997: 183ff.; Blackwell 1999: 53ff.; Brun 2000: 85ff.; Worthington 2000: 189; Squillace 2004: 131ff. The much discussed chronology of the war places its outbreak in mid 331 (Bosworth 1988a: 200).

Anti-Macedonian Resistance during Alexander's Absence

The territorial reorganization imposed on Sparta after Chaeroneia kept the city out of the League.[70] Alexander called attention to this when, in 334, he dedicated the arms taken at the Granicus to Athena for the Greeks "except the Spartans" (Arr. 1.16.7; Plu. *Alex.* 16.17–18). Spartan determination to modify this territorial arrangement, secured by Macedonian garrisons, may well have helped spark Agis' revolt; but there were appeals also to antityrannical rhetoric and such slogans as "freedom for the Greeks" (D.S. 17.62.1–63.3; Just. 12.1.6). Moreover, the agreements with the Persian king meant that the rebels were seen as enemies of peace and of the campaign against Persia. During the conflict, however, the league charter operated as it was set up and it is important to note these procedures.

We know from Arrian that after the battle of Issus, Agis obtained ships (ten triremes) and money (thirty talents) from Autophradates (2.13.4–6). Enlisting 8,000 mercenaries dismissed by Darius, he reestablished Persian control over most of Crete. Victory over Corrhagus, who commanded Macedonian forces in the Peloponnesus while Antipater was engaged in Thrace against Memnon, followed his operations on Crete (Aeschin. 3.165). At this point some of the allies joined the revolt: the Achaeans (except for Pellene), the Eleans, and the Arcadians (except for Megalopolis).[71] Yet the adherence of these and "other" Greeks recorded by Diodorus (17.62.7) probably had no significant effect, and Agis began the siege of Megalopolis with an army totaling some 32,000 men.[72]

League sanctions brought the support of a number of Greek allies in this punitive war and these joined Antipater's army during its march to the Peloponnesus. The percentage and the composition of the Greek allies are much discussed (D.S. 17.63.1); the size of the Macedonian force Alexander entrusted to Antipater in 334, whether 12,000 or 4,000/5,000, is also uncertain.[73] The federal army, however, included troops from Corinth, Messenia, Argos, Megalopolis, as well as from Boeotia and Thessaly.[74] The composition of the *hegemon*'s de facto allies (and also Sparta's traditional enemies), and the fact that there was apparently no preliminary meeting of the *synedrion*, suggests that the response taken now followed that of the Theban crisis of 335. But unless we believe that the charter was non-operative from the beginning, we have no reason to consider the 331 intervention as anomalous. The absence of allies was common to both punitive wars. For most Greeks, but especially the more hostile Aetolians and Athenians (Aeschin. 3.165; D.S. 17.62.7),

---

[70] Laconia's borders were "rearranged" to the advantage of the Argives, Arcadians, and Messenians (D. 18.64–5, 295; Plb. 9.28.6–7, 33.8–12; Paus. 2.20.1, 38.5, 7.11.2, 8.7.4) and therefore Sparta remained outside the League (Just. 9.5.3; Arr. 1.16.7; Plu. *Alex.* 16.18; D.S. 17.3.4–5): McQueen 1978: 40ff.; Hammond–Griffith 613ff.; Magnetto 1994: 283ff.; Buckler 2003: 507ff.

[71] Aeschin. 3.165; Din. 1.34; D.S. 17.62.6–63.4; Curt. 6.1.20; Paus. 7.27.7; Just. 12.1.6.

[72] Din. 1.34; McQueen 1978: 52ff.; Bosworth 1988a: 203.

[73] Badian 1994: 261ff. (12,000); Bosworth 2002: 65ff. (4,000/5,000).

[74] Bosworth 1988a: 203; Baynham 1994: 340; Heckel 1997: 187; Blackwell 1999: 56.

the option of neutrality seemed legitimate. The Aetolian decision to abstain was perhaps due to good relations with Antipater (Plu. *Alex.* 49.8) who, in exchange for neutrality in the face of Agis' revolt, tolerated the Aetolian occupation of Oeniadae (Mendels 1984: 132ff.; cf. below). In the case of Athens, however, the decision to respect the federal sanction was the outcome of heated debate. There has been a useless attempt to question this by accepting Diodorus's claim (17.62.7) that Athenian neutrality was a response to Alexander's benevolent treatment (Sawada 1996: 88ff.),[75] or by denying the strength of the interventionist position (Brun 2000: 88 ff.), or even by refusing to recognize the force of the Corinthian charter (Blackwell 1999: 58ff.). Instead, respect for the treaty was the fundamental criterion for evaluating the legality of the assembly's decisions ([Dem.] 17.1, 5, 7, 11–12, 14, 17–19). These decisions determined the outcome of the revolt. Agis' army was defeated near Megalopolis (dated to spring 330) and Agis himself was killed.

Even when the war was over, the charter operated regularly. Antipater entrusted all decisions to the federal *synedrion* which met with its regular membership at Corinth (Curt. 6.1.19; D.S. 17.73.5). The fact that the meeting was not limited only to allies is evidence that Antipater was worried that an autocratic approach to the question would arouse Alexander's resentment, a concern indicated by the sources and which cannot be considered unfounded.[76] The *synedrion* legitimately discussed both the allies who had defected (Eleans, Achaeans, and Arcadians) and the Spartans. Those who had been in contact with the Persians (Arr. 2.15.2; Curt. 3.13.15) were guilty of treason. For this, the *synedrion* could take action against any Greek, even those who were not members of the League. After imposing a fine on the Eleans and the Achaeans (obliged to pay 120 talents for damage caused by the siege) and banishing only the guilty Tegeans, the *synedrion* also discussed at length the case of Sparta.[77] Because consensus among the delegates was impossible, in spite of the arguments for and against, the *synedrion* entrusted the matter to Alexander while giving the Spartans the option of sending their own delegates to the king to ask for pardon (D.S. 17.73.5–6; Curt. 6.1.20). This decision was based on precedents where the defendants were to be judged at the highest level: in the case of Athens as an alternative to the *synedrion*'s judgment and in the case of Chios apparently following the *synedrion*'s judgment. The intervention on the number and composition of the hostages handed over to Antipater pending the final sentence is consistent with the three-way negotiations from which the *synedrion* was excluded (McQueen 1978: 53ff.). Alexander's decision is not recorded; but the hypothesis of Sparta's forcible enrollment in the League is probable and testifies to a strong interest in the League as late as 330.[78]

[75] Evidence of this is Iphicrates' mission to Darius III (Arr. 2.15.2; Curt. 3.13.15; Bosworth 1980b: 233ff.) and the ratification of an *epidosis* of 4,000 drachmas (Tod 1946: no. 198; Faraguna 1992: 256; Rhodes–Osborne, no. 94; against: Brun 2000: 88 n. 20). The abstentionist position, however, backed by Demosthenes and Demades prevailed: Badian 1994: 259; Blackwell 1999: 63.

[76] Curt. 6.1.18–19; Baynham 1994: 341–2; Blackwell 1999: 72.

[77] Differing: Bosworth 1988a: 203; Blackwell 1999: 70; Worthington 2000: 189.

[78] McQueen 1978: 56; Bosworth 1988a: 204; Hammond 1988: 78.

After Gaugamela: Alexander, the League, and "Greek Freedom"

The campaign's ideological profile and its relationship with the allies changed after Gaugamela when the conquest of the Persian capitals (Babylon, Susa, Persepolis, Ecbatana) and the discharge of the Greek contingents in Alexander's army signaled the end of the war of revenge.[79] The catalyst for rallying consent then became "Greek freedom." This principle satisfied several needs. Ideologically, it consolidated Greek association with the Asian campaign once the destruction of Persepolis had satisfied the desire for revenge (Flower 2000: 115ff.); it also governed relations with the allied states. In this latter area, although long empty of juridical content,[80] the principle of freedom supported Alexander's leadership aspirations more than the binding principle of autonomy. It was also a more effective answer to the antityrannical views of his Greek opponents.

If we are to believe Plutarch, immediately after his coronation as "King of Asia," Alexander provided factual proof that the principle of freedom was important for his political activity. He wrote to the Greeks informing them that tyranny had ended and autonomy had begun for the Greeks in Asia (*Alex.* 34.2; Hamilton 1969: 91). In this context, he promised the citizens of Plataea that he would rebuild their city as compensation for their forefathers' sacrifices in providing the battleground for the Greeks in the fight "for freedom"; he sent a portion of the spoils of war to the Crotonians in Italy so that they could honor the memory of Phayllus, who had fought at Salamis (480) with the single ship given by western Greeks in the Hellenic cause (Hdt. 8.47; Plu. *Alex.* 34.2–4). Alexander rallied greater consensus in the years following 330 by exalting the principle of freedom for the Greeks (Flower 2000: 118ff.), and it is not surprising that this seems to be defended in the contemporary *Letter to Alexander* that has been attributed to Aristotle.[81] On two occasions the freedom of the Greeks was extolled with a public proclamation. The rebuilding of Plataea, that "martyr" to freedom, was announced by a herald at the Olympic Games of 328 (Plu. *Arist.* 11.9; cf. Fredricksmeyer 2000: 138). In a similar manner, at the Olympic Games of 324, the return of the exiles was announced to the Greeks. This latter act is a striking example of the impact of the freedom principle on Alexander's Greek policy.[82]

---

[79]   Arr. 3.11.1–15.7, 19.5; Curt 4.12.1–16.9; Plu. *Alex.* 33.8–11; Bosworth 1980b: 329ff.; Sisti 2001: 518ff.

[80]   Karavites 1984: 191. On *eleutheria* and autonomy in the fourth century: Bosworth 1992a: 122ff.; Musti 2000: 176ff.; Bertoli 2003: 87ff.

[81]   Faraguna 2003: 116–18; Squillace 2004: 23ff. (with fuller bibliography).

[82]   Hyp. *Dem.*, cols. 18–19; Din. 1.81–2; D.S. 17.109.1–2, 18.8.2–7; Curt. 10.2.4–7; Just. 13.5.1–5; Bosworth 1988a: 220ff.; 1998: 73ff.; Hammond–Walbank 80ff.; Blackwell 1999: 145ff.; Flower 2000: 126ff.; Faraguna 2003: 124ff.

The Exiles' Decree, Greek Freedom, and the Corinthian League

At Opis in Mesopotamia, in the spring of 324, Alexander proclaimed the Exiles' Decree to his army in which many exiles were serving. One of the objectives of the Decree was to reinstate mercenaries in their native cities, a measure that took care of their needs and provided the king with a strong base of support in the Greek cities (Green 1991: 449ff.; Landucci Gattinoni 1995: 63ff.). The Decree's impact on life in the city-states was predictable and it also explains Craterus' return to Europe. He was given the task of bringing Macedonian veterans back home and a new assignment as Antipater's replacement as administrator of Macedonia, Thrace, Thessaly, and of "Greek freedom" (Arr. 7.12.4).[83] It is possible that Alexander intended to extend the Asian experiment in "liberation" to the mainland Greeks and that the exiles' return was a preliminary to the type of institutional democratization that took place in 319 following Polyperchon's *diagramma* (Heckel 1999: 492ff.).[84] But whatever Alexander's plans were, it is clear that the Exiles' Decree was intended as a reaffirmation of his *own* political procedures and an improvement on those of Philip and Antipater. This policy was consistent with his new role as King of Asia and ruler of all the Greeks ([Plu.] *Vit. X or.* 852d).[85]

The important fact, however, is that Alexander intended to adapt the juridical instrument at his disposal for this purpose, namely, the Corinthian League. Violating or ignoring its charter was neither useful nor necessary.[86] On the contrary, Alexander was anxious to legitimize the Decree: by insuring an effective flow of information and adjusting its content to previous decisions of the League, and by entrusting its application to recognized authorities, that is, Antipater and eventually to the allies (D.S. 18.8.4; Just. 13.5.7). The choice of the Olympic Games as a platform points to a hegemonic voice that permitted an exchange of information without any meeting of the *synedrion*.

The Decree was promulgated at the beginning of the Olympic Games between the end of July and the beginning of August. The emissary, Nicanor of Stageira, delivered an open letter to the winner of the herald's competition who read it to the more than 20,000 exiles present at Olympia (D.S. 18.8.2–5; Just 13.5.1–3).[87]

---

[83]   Bosworth 1994a: 856 n. 24; Sisti and Zambrini 2004: 610.
[84]   On the *diagramma* of Polyperchon (D.S. 18.56), cf. Poddighe 2002: 171ff.; Dixon 2007.
[85]   Culasso Gustaldi 2003: 69ff. (with fuller bibliography).
[86]   The following judge the Decree to be legitimate: Bikerman 1940: 29 n. 3; Hammond–Walbank 80ff.; Green 1991: 451ff. Against: Heisserer 1980: 233ff.; Errington 1990: 96ff.; Blackwell 1999: 146ff. suggests a provision that had nothing to do with the treaty.
[87]   Diodorus' source: for Hieronymus (Bosworth 1988a: 220; Heckel 1999: 491; Flower 2000: 127) or Duris (Prandi 1996: 89; Blackwell 1999: 146 n. 30). It is also discussed whether the 20,000 represented all of the beneficiaries (McKechnie 1989: 26) or only those present at Olympia (Worthington 1990: 201).

Delegates from the cities, including Demosthenes, were also present in the audience (Din. 1.82).[88] The Decree ordered the return of all Greek exiles, with the exception of those guilty of sacrilege and murder, and required the cities to apply the measures under threat of military reprisal (D.S. 17.109.1, 18.8.2–4). In the text, as read by the herald, it appeared that everyone was to benefit from the Decree. But it is certain that the cases of application and exemption, as well as the procedures governing the exiles' reinstatement in their native cities, were contained in a more ample document than the proclamation, probably a *diagramma*. Plutarch clearly indicates that there were exceptions such as the Thebans (*Mor.* 221a); Diodorus also records categories of exiles that, in 324, did not benefit from the return because they had been proscribed by the generals (Antipater) after Alexander had crossed into Asia (18.56.4).[89] These few but significant exceptions confirmed the federal measures against Thebes, Tegea, and Pellene. Confirmation of these sentences created a dangerous difference in the fate of the cities in the regions to which they belonged (Arcadia, Achaea, and Boeotia), and, in view of possible resistance from the regional leagues, a second rescript was issued that Nicanor himself brought into Greece (Hyp. 5, col. 18). This might have been a warning to the Achaean and Arcadian (and possibly Boeotian[90]) leagues regarding debate about or military opposition to its application (Worthington 1986: 115ff.), or it might have been a measure ordering their dissolution (Bosworth 1988a: 77; Whitehead 2000: 415). In any case it was a measure conceived to insure the security of the return of the exiles (*kathodos*), as well as the office that had been entrusted to Antipater (D.S. 18.8.4).

Arcadian Tegea seems to be the "exception to the exception" in that it allowed the return of exiles proscribed after 334; an inscription in Delphi, datable probably to 324, is evidence for this (Bencivenni 2003: no. 4; Rhodes–Osborne, no. 101). This exception can be explained by the concentration of hostile mercenaries on nearby Cape Taenarum.[91] This threat led to the reinstatement of most exiles including those recently condemned and who had been unable to attend public festivals (ll. 21–4),[92] and those of longer date (for whom Alexander was especially concerned) including possibly the Tegeans who had been proscribed during the civil war that brought the establishment of the Arcadian *koinon* (Xen. *Hell.* 6.5.10; D.S. 14.34.3, 5; McKechnie 1989: 26). The economic difficulties of integrating exiles[93] are evidence that the royal decree forced the integration of estranged groups and explains the decision to display the document at Delphi, a procedure usually reserved for inter-state treaties (Bencivenni 2003: 97).

[88]   Din. 1.82–3, 103; Plu. *Dem.* 9. 1; Worthington 1992: 253; Landucci Gattinoni 1995: 70.
[89]   Bosworth 1988a: 224; Brun 2000: 104; Poddighe 2002: 186. Against: Jehne 1994: 248 n. 338.
[90]   The name of the Boeotians is not clearly legible: Bosworth 1988a: 222 n. 39.
[91]   Heisserer 1980: 221ff.; Worthington 1993: 63ff.; Blackwell 1999: 150; Bencivenni 2003: 95. On their composition: Green 1991: 449ff.; Landucci Gattinoni 1995: 66ff.
[92]   Probably sanctions for ceremonies that had not been paid for: Bencivenni 2003: 99.
[93]   *SIG*[3] 312; Heisserer 1980: 182; Bosworth 1998: 75ff.

Athens, Samos, and Greek Freedom

The Exiles' Decree arose from the determination to deal with different kinds of cases (Cargill 1995: 41–2; Bosworth 1998: 76). For some of these, Alexander was under strong pressure at court. Examples include the exiles from Oeniadae in Acarnania and from Samos, the victims respectively of Aetolian and Athenian colonialism. The fact that individual cases were not mentioned in the text of the Decree proves, according to some, that initially Alexander was indifferent;[94] but this is no argument since the text of the Decree, as read by the herald, did not mention any specific cases. The Oenidaean and Samian cases were, however, crucial from the Macedonian perspective. The exiles banished by the Aetolians and the Athenians belonged to the category of those whose exile was unjust and longstanding and whose reinstatement demanded the allies' support (D.S. 18.8.2–4; Just. 13.5.4, 7). In about 330 (D.S. 18.8.6–7; Jehne 1994: 241ff.), the Aetolians had occupied Oeniadae during a controversial campaign of expansion (Landucci Gattinoni 2004: 112ff.). Alexander certainly promised to punish this abuse and perhaps too the understanding between the Aetolians and Antipater (Plu. *Alex.* 49.8) who had tolerated their aggression (Mendels 1984: 131).

The Decree had an even stronger impact on Athens which was obliged "to return Samos to the Samians" as we read on the cast of a now lost Samian inscription (*SIG*³ 312, ll. 11–14; Hallof 1999: 392ff.). The Samians had been expelled by Athenian cleruchs established on the island beginning in 365[95] and the Athenians were not disposed to allow their return (D.S. 18.8.7). Even when, shortly before the king's death, groups of Samian exiles tried to return to the island from their base on Anaea, Athenian reaction was very firm; clearly, the island was a possession not to be surrendered (Badian 1976: 289ff.). Alexander's position, strengthened by pressure from the supporters of the Samian cause such as Gorgus of Iasus, did not allow for indecision.[96] Alexander's hostility was already clear in the autumn of 324 when, during the annual sacrifice to Dionysus at Ecbatana, the prospect of a siege and war against Athens seems to have discussed (Ephippus of Olynthus, *FGrH* 126 F5, preserved in Athen. 12.538a–b). Resentment grew further that summer when Harpalus, Alexander's treasurer, fled to Athens with a considerable portion of the royal treasury.[97] Harpalus was later mocked in a satyr play, which also reflected hostility toward Athens (Ath. 13.596a; Gadaleta 2001: 109ff.).

The Exiles' Decree was primarily intended for political exiles, but also for so many others who had been forced from their homes on account of poverty and who had, as in the case of a number of Athenians, taken up mercenary service

---

[94] Mendels 1984: 147; Worthington 1992: 60.
[95] Numbers and places of exile: Shipley 1987: 141ff.; Landucci Gattinoni 1997: 11ff.
[96] *SIG*³ 312; Heisserer 1980: 182; Bosworth 1998: 75ff.
[97] D.S. 17.108.4; Plu. *Dem.* 25.1–2; *Phoc.* 21.3; Curt. 10.2.1–3; Bosworth 1988a: 215ff.; Worthington 1994a: 307ff.; Blackwell 1999: 134ff.

(Landucci Gattinoni 1995: 61ff.). The prospect, however, of dispossessed Athenian cleruchs returning to Athens was upsetting, as these amounted to a third of all adult (male) Athenian citizens (Habicht 1996: 401). In this light, the Samian question is paradigmatic for understanding the social meaning of the Decree and the reasons for Athenian opposition to it on behalf of freedom.

According to Curtius (10.2.6), Athens claimed the role of *vindex publicae libertatis* against Alexander, emphasizing that the Decree's social consequences would be to bring back the "dregs" (*purgamenta*) of the city. Athenian accusations against Alexander, expressed in typically antityrannical language, do not appear explicitly related to the return of the Samian cleruchs. This should not be surprising: the Samian issue was a clear case of colonialism (Shipley 1987: 166), embarrassing to the cause of freedom and therefore ignored, as seen in the total silence of the Athenian sources.[98] However, it is probable that Curtius' reference to the "dregs" concerns the cleruchs of Samos whom the orator Demades (in Athenaeus) characterized as the "deposit of the dregs" of the city (Ath. 3.99d; see Brun 2000: 105 n. 38; Poddighe 2007).

Alexander's death delayed the decision regarding Samos and only when Perdiccas raised the question again after the Lamian War (a war strongly motivated by the Exiles' Decree), were the Samians restored (D.S. 18.18.9).[99] But Alexander's conduct of the matter is evidence that he had a perfect grasp of the Greek interpretation of freedom. In a letter to the Athenians, Alexander "returned to sender" the accusation of despotism when he called attention to the theme of Samian freedom in the following statement:[100] "I would not have given you that *free* and admirable city: you have it, having received it from him . . . who was said to be my father" (Plu. *Alex.* 28.2). Hypothetically, the context of the letter could be that referred to by Ephippus (see above). In both cases, there was a reference to the king's divine descent, a very topical issue in 324[101] in the context of the confrontation with Athens. Clearly, Alexander intended to defend the rights of the Samians by turning against Athens the very theme of freedom by which it claimed its right to the island.

---

[98] In this perspective, silence does not prove either that the Athenians found the problem insoluble (Landucci Gattinoni 1995: 75ff.) or that it would arise later (Worthington 1992: 63).

[99] Poddighe 2002: 186.

[100] This is a text differently dated and translated (Rosen 1978: 20ff.; Hammond 1993: 174ff.; Jehne 1994: 254 n. 374). For 324: Hamilton 1969: 74; Heisserer 1980: 187 n. 44. For the proposed translation: Bikerman 1940: 34; Cargill 1995: 41.

[101] Brun 2000: 104; Mari 2002: 239ff.

7

Alexander and the Greeks

Artists and Soldiers, Friends and Enemies

Lawrence A. Tritle

Babylon, 323: Alexander's death has left his great army leaderless and dissension grows in the ranks, particularly between the cavalry elite and infantry rank and file. Relations between the contending factions are tense, negotiations difficult. In this crisis three individuals emerge to defuse the situation and work out a solution: Damis of Megalopolis, Pasas of Thessaly, and Perilaus, all Greeks, all surely occupying positions of influence in Alexander's army or court (Curt. 10.8.15).[1]

Alexander's relations with the Greeks has been the subject of several notable discussions. E. Badian in a well-known essay touched on the subject noting *inter alia* that Alexander's program of "liberating" the Greeks of Asia had a profound impact on subsequent relations between these cities and the monarchs of the Hellenistic age (Badian 1966a: 61). This treatment updated an earlier discussion by V. Ehrenberg (the honoree of Badian's essay) who in 1938 contributed a sweeping survey of the topic, attempting to solve such longstanding issues as the place of the island communities Chios, Lesbos, and Rhodes in the Corinthian League (Ehrenberg 1938: 16–17). Since Badian's essay, now nearly forty years old, more recent discussions by A. B. Bosworth and C. Habicht recently supplemented by a collection of papers edited by O. Palagia and S. V. Tracy have added to the subject of Alexander and the Greeks.[2] In the present volume, E. Poddighe contributes to the topic, examining the issues and commenting on them with particular attention to the evidence preserved on inscriptions (ch. 6).

In all of these there will be fine points of argument mostly focusing on institutions and "official" relations between Alexander and the Greek cities. The approach taken in this essay will be somewhat different: to discuss those Greeks who in some fashion were associated with Alexander on the march to India, and back, or who

---

[1] Plu. *Eum*. 3.1 claims that Eumenes, Alexander's secretary, also became involved in the discussions but this seems to have occurred later.

[2] Bosworth 1988a; Habicht 1997; Palagia and Tracy 2003.

otherwise served in the administration of his empire or military forces. The analysis will also shed some light on a longstanding debate regarding Greeks and Macedonians, namely the issue of "pro-" and "anti-Macedonian" Greeks, and the reasons why some Greeks joined Alexander's cause, while others vigorously opposed him just as they had his father Philip.

Artists and Athletes with Alexander

In spring 328/7 Alexander focused his attention on "pacifying" Sogdiana and Bactria and ending the insurrection of Spitamenes.[3] This led him to disperse his troops over a wide area and in doing so he became vulnerable to the hit-and-run warfare practiced in this region. Strengthened with tribesmen recruited among the Massagetae, Spitamenes attacked several of Alexander's isolated garrisons, among them Bactra where he had left behind his sick and injured to recover, including several Companions, placing in command over them a court official, Peithon. Prodded by Spitamenes' attack, Peithon and the Companions launched a retaliatory attack that miscarried as the Macedonians fell into an ambush. A hundred men were lost, among them Aristonicus, a harpist of long standing at the Macedonian court. Arrian, who records this incident, remarks that Aristonicus died fighting, not as a harpist but as a good and brave man (Arr. 4.16.6–7).[4]

The heroic death of Aristonicus reveals one of the more interesting and esoteric group of Greeks found in the company of Alexander – the musicians, artists, and athletes – who accompanied him in the march east. In itself Spitamenes' little victory was no more than a bee sting, but the death of Aristonicus did upset the king. A well-known musician, Aristonicus seems to have been a member of Philip's entourage since Chaeroneia (his Olynthian background suggests this) and was thus closely connected to Alexander and the Macedonian cause. It has been argued that Aristonicus had been in Alexander's court since the crossing into Asia, and all of this may explain why Alexander ordered a statue to be set up in his honor at Delphi, depicting him with a lyre in one hand, a spear in the other (Plu. *Mor.* 334e–f).[5] That Aristonicus also played a military role sheds light on the sometimes difficult conditions faced by Alexander's army: that in an emergency every able-bodied man might be pressed into service, not unlike, for example, those Europeans in the legations and elsewhere in China who were caught up in the Boxer Rebellion, or even the artists and poets who so happily enlisted in the European armies of 1914. Aristonicus' heroic death suggests that those in the sources casually identified as "musicians," "actors," or "athletes" were capable of other roles, including military and diplomatic, and in fact performed these.

---

[3] On the brutal nature of this campaign see Holt 2005.

[4] See Bosworth 1995: 115–17 for more detailed treatment; note that Bactra is also Zariaspa.

[5] See sources and discussion in Heckel 49; Bosworth 1995: 116 (who notes Berve's (no. 132) suggestion that Aristonicus had been with Alexander since 334).

That actors in the life and reign of Alexander played roles other than those on stage can be amply demonstrated. Two tragic actors, Aristocritus and Thessalus, figure at the beginning and end of the king's life. Early on, one of the acts that earned the young prince Philip's wrath was his meddling in the dynastic marriage offered Philip by the Carian dynast Pixodarus (Plu. *Alex.* 10.1). Evidently Aristocritus carried Philip's counter-proposal that Pixodarus' daughter marry his son Arrhidaeus. Stung that he had been passed over by his father, the young Alexander complicated the negotiations by sending his own envoy, Thessalus, a Corinthian actor, with the proposal that he marry Pixodarus' daughter.[6] In the end no marriage came from all this diplomatic activity and king and prince were temporarily estranged. The two actors, however, must have conducted themselves competently and faithfully, for they remained in Alexander's service until the end of his reign, participating in the festivities that were part of the great wedding celebration at Susa in 324 (Chares, *FGrH* 125 F4 = Athen. 12.583f).

The diplomatic activities of Aristocritus and Thessalus are by no means uncommon and other actors served in similar roles. In 324 Alexander's lifelong friend Harpalus fled from his administrative post in Babylon, taking with him a large sum of money as well as a large contingent of mercenaries and other followers.[7] Harpalus eventually made his way to Athens where in the end he was rebuffed, though a number of prominent Athenians were entangled in his web of corruption and intrigue. In a speech attacking Demosthenes, Hypereides claimed that Demosthenes had persuaded an Athenian dancer named Mnesitheus to find out how much money Harpalus had brought with him (Hyp. 5, col. 9).[8] It seems unlikely that someone unacquainted with Harpalus could learn such information, which suggests that Mnesitheus had accompanied Harpalus in his flight. As will be discussed below, large numbers of actors, artists, and musicians were already flocking to the east in search of work, and Mnesitheus might have been one of these. This is further evident in the selection of two actors, Ephialtes and Cittus, recruited to bring the news of Harpalus' defection to Alexander. These actors must have been in or around Babylon and sent on their mission by those who assumed Harpalus' duties. On hearing their report the two actors were imprisoned for a time, the king refusing to accept that they were telling the truth (Plu. *Alex.* 41.8).[9]

While the dramatic talents of actors account for their use as envoys, other artists who performed similar political activities were the star athletes of the day. Among these was Chaeron of Pellene, victor in both the Nemean and Olympic Games. Chaeron's fame won him the attention of Alexander who empowered him as tyrant

[6] Plu. *Alex.* 10.2 states that Philip ordered the Corinthians to send Thessalus to him in chains, which may suggest that he was a native of that city. Alternatively, Philip perhaps attempted to use the judicial procedures of the Corinthian League in order to extradite him. See also Heckel 265.

[7] On this see Bosworth 1988a: 149–50; Tritle 1988: 119–22.

[8] See Heckel 169 for other sources and discussion.

[9] Heckel 118 suggests that Ephialtes was an actor, noting the evidence (*IG* ii² 2418) attesting this career for Cittus.

of his home town.[10] In doing so, Alexander ignored the statutes of the Corinthian League, created by Philip in 337 and whose founding principles technically restricted such meddling in the affairs of member states. Pellene, however, was one of the Peloponnesian communities by which the Macedonians attempted to control Sparta, which had refused to join the League on its establishment. In 331 the Spartan king Agis III challenged Macedonian power, only to be defeated by Antipater, Alexander's regent in Macedonia and Greece, who destroyed his army at Megalopolis. Pellene, led by Chaeron, remained loyal to the Macedonian cause and so played a small but important part in insuring Agis' defeat (see Poddighe, ch. 6). As Heckel notes, Chaeron's support of the Macedonian cause certainly accounts for the negative picture of him in the ancient sources.

Not all athletes who found themselves in Alexander's elite circle, however, were as successful or as essential as Chaeron. A case in point is the Athenian Dioxippus, star pankratiast and Olympic champion.[11] A flagrant flatterer of Alexander (he once claimed that Alexander's blood was like the *ichor* of the gods), Dioxippus is found in Alexander's entourage by 326/5 when he achieved some fame in defeating the veteran Macedonian soldier Corrhagus, evidently one of Alexander's *hetairoi*, in single combat (and not to the death as is sometimes claimed). Challenged to a duel by Corrhagus, Dioxippus met the Macedonian nude and armed with only a club and a robe over his arm. According to Curtius (9.7.21–2), one of the sources that recounts this story, Dioxippus successfully dodged Corrhagus' javelin, then closed with his opponent quickly, disarmed him, and threw him to the ground. Dioxippus was ready to finish off the stunned Macedonian with his club when Alexander intervened and saved Corrhagus' life. Curtius (9.7.18) and Diodorus (17.100.4) tell that a sports-like atmosphere colored the match, the Greeks cheering on Dioxippus, the Macedonians Corrhagus. Winning at Macedonian cost, however, came with a price and in Dioxippus' case it was a false accusation of theft which ultimately drove him to suicide (Curt. 9.7.23–6).[12]

Several problems complicate the interpretation of this incident, ranging from the Roman-style weapons and manner of fighting that Curtius ascribes to Corrhagus, to the reason for the duel in the first place. The first of these may be explained simply by a Roman author writing for a Roman audience who is not concerned with matters of authenticity. Curtius relates a duel in terms his readers would understand, and that is enough for him. The reason for the duel is a bit more complicated. Curtius (9.7.18) makes much of the supposed laziness and gluttony of athletes who are of little use, whereas soldiers face many dangers on the battlefield (an attitude that might well be found in some modern circles). Truesdell Brown accepts this explanation, agreeing that it is a typical soldier's attitude. But the

---

[10]   Heckel 82–3.

[11]   Heckel 115, 308 for discussion and evidence.

[12]   Brown 1977: 76–88 extensively examines the little that is known of this incident. See Heckel 34, 49, 100 for other athletes noted in Alexander's camp: Antigonus (Amphipolis), Aristonicus (2) (Carystus), and Crison (Himera/Sicily). Bracketed numbers appearing after names are Heckel's; multiple examples are listed in alphabetic order throughout.

conclusion that follows from this argument – that soldiers like Corrhagus viewed athletes with "mixed feelings of envy and contempt," that star athletes like "jugglers, tragic actors and musicians . . . went out to the front [only] as entertainers" – goes too far.[13] Here it is useful to recall the story of Aristonicus, the harpist who died fighting alongside Macedonian soldiers and whose heroic death was immortalized at Delphi. This argues again that those in Alexander's entourage – including the athletes – and probably more often than we know, participated in both military and political/diplomatic activities.

Alexander's flatterers, however, were not restricted to star athletes such as Dioxippus. Among them as well was Gorgus of Iasus, *hoplophylax*, literally armorer, but more accurately arms merchant, to Alexander.[14] While the sources describe him as a flatterer, there should be little doubt that he worked for the benefit of those lacking power or influence, though like lobbyists today this was not generated by compassion or generosity. This is evident in Gorgus' promise to Alexander that, were the king to attack Athens, he would provide 10,000 sets of armor and an equal number of catapults and other weapons as well (Athen. 12.538b).[15] With his brother Minnion, Gorgus facilitated the return of disputed water rights to Iasus, and the repatriation of Samian exiles homeward, this in connection with Alexander's Exiles' Decree of 324. He also assisted the city of Epidaurus with several petitions made to Alexander, the exact nature of which is no longer known. His lobbying on behalf of his native city, Samian exiles, and Epidaurus point to a well-connected and influential figure whose supplying of arms, no doubt punctuated by well-placed gifts, enabled him to influence decision-making at the highest level.

Possibly the most interesting group of actors, musicians, and other entertainers are the twenty-two known individuals who were among the 3,000 "artists from Greece" who performed at the great weddings at Susa in 324. The source identifying these entertainers is Chares of Mitylene, himself a Greek in Alexander's service from the beginning of the Asian campaign, who eventually became *eisangeleus*, or "royal usher," at Alexander's court.[16] Such a position enabled Chares to learn some of the names of these entertainers, which survive in the accounts of later writers Athenaeus (12.538b–539a) and Aelian (*VH* 8.7). These individuals came from all corners of the Greek world.[17] They include:

---

[13]   Brown 1977: 88. Curtius' comments may also reflect later Roman attitudes regarding professional athletes.

[14]   See Heckel 127 for discussion and evidence.

[15]   Gorgus' offer may have been made during the dispute between Athens and Alexander over Samos, which followed on the announcement of the Exiles' Decree (see Poddidghe, ch. 6, for further discussion). Athenaeus' source for this appears to be Ephippus of Olynthus, a contemporary historian.

[16]   Chares' *History of Alexander* (*FGrH* 125 F4 records the names of the artists) ranks among the chief sources for Alexander's reign, though its surviving fragments are chiefly of social and cultural value.

[17]   Two other musicians, both flutists, might be mentioned, Timotheus and Xenophantus (Heckel 268, 272). Timotheus, first mentioned performing at Philip's court, joined Alexander in Egypt and later performed at Susa. It is not clear if he is Greek or Macedonian. Xenophantus played at the funeral of Demetrius Poliorcetes forty years later; Heckel seems right in arguing against any association with Alexander.

Western Greeks (4)

  Tarentum: Alexis, rhapsode; Heraclitus, harpist; Scymnus, juggler

  Syracuse: Philistides, juggler[18]

Eastern Greeks (5)

  Cyzicus: Hyperbolus, flutist

  Heraclea: Dionysius, flutist

  Lesbos: Cratinus, psilokitharist from Methymna; Heraclitus, juggler from
    Mytilene

  Teos: Athenodorus, harpist[19]

Mainland Greeks (7)

  Athens: Aristonymus, harpist; Athenodorus (4), tragic actor;[20] Phormion,
    comic actor (?)

  Corinth (?): Thessalus, tragic actor

  Chalcis (Euboea): Evius, flutist

  Locris: Lycon, comic actor

  Thebes: Aristocrates, harpist[21]

Unidentified origins (6)

  Aristocritus, tragic actor; Ariston (4), comic actor; Caphisias, flutist;
    Diophantus (1), flutist; Phasimelus, harpist; Phrynichus, flutist[22]

A short time later, in summer 324, most of these artists appeared again at Ecbatana where events ran for more than a week before the death of Hephaestion intervened and ended them.[23] Soon after, these same performers played at Hephaestion's funeral and, a short time later, at Alexander's (Arr. 7.14.10).

But the appearance of this great horde of actors, musicians, and other entertainers in Susa and Ecbatana is not unprecedented. In spring 331, after establishing his authority over Egypt, Alexander returned to Phoenicia to continue his campaign against Darius. At Tyre a second round of athletic and literary contests were held, events sponsored in part by the Cypriot kings Nicocreon of Salamis and Pasicrates of Soli.[24] Among the performers were Thessalus, the same actor who had earlier served as Alexander's agent in the marriage negotiations with Pixodarus, and his rival Athenodorus. Much to the king's disappointment, the judges awarded the prize of victory to Athenodorus: Plutarch records (Plu. *Alex.* 29.3) Alexander saying he would have given up part of his empire to see Thessalus win.

---

[18] Heckel 21, 138, 246, 215.

[19] Heckel 141, 114, 100, 137–8, 60.

[20] Heckel 61 declines to identify Athenodorus' origin; see the discussion below.

[21] Heckel 50, 61, 222, 265, 124, 152, 47.

[22] Heckel 47, 49, 78, 114, 207, 223.

[23] Arr. 7.14.1; Plu. *Alex.* 72.1, 3. Alexander's grief at Hephaestion's death led to the cancellation of the performances and he specifically forbade the playing of musical instruments in camp, which surely ended the festivities.

[24] Arr. 2.24.6 records the first contests, celebrated after the fall of Tyre in August 332 (on the date see Bosworth 1980b: 255).

Both Athenodorus and Thessalus were among the performers participating in the events held in Susa and Ecbatana. At some point Athenodorus returned to Athens where he competed in the dramatic contests, winning a prize in 329; the Athenians, however, fined him for his absences from the city which led him to ask Alexander to pay his fine. The king declined, though he did provide him with the money to do so.[25] Thessalus does not appear in the sources again until 324, which suggests that he remained with Alexander on the expedition, not only as the king's favorite actor but also as trusted emissary.

What is of interest first is the number of these individuals in the midst of Alexander's empire. Aristocritus, Aristonicus, Thessalus (and perhaps Athenodorus) point to the various real world functions that musicians and actors performed at Alexander's court. Second, the wide geographic range of this group, from Syracuse and Tarentum in the far-off Greek west to the eastern Aegean, also gives us some idea of the attraction for adventure and wealth that joining Alexander's expedition offered to the bold or the ambitious and greedy, as the case may be.

Among Alexander's artistic entourage were also a number of poets. At least seven or eight writers of verse accompanied Alexander in order to tell the tale of his great expedition. Little information of these individuals is known beyond their name and a few basic facts, such as the tragic poet Neophron of Sicyon, who accompanied his friend Callisthenes of Olynthus, nephew of Aristotle and perhaps the "official" historian of the expedition.[26] Neophron also shared Callisthenes' fate, execution, when Callisthenes, who had a penchant for annoying Alexander with his free speech, finally ran afoul of the king in the so-called Pages' Conspiracy and was put to death.[27] Another Aristotelian contact was the poet Aeschrion of Mytilene who also came to sing Alexander's praises. Nothing that he wrote, however, survived for later sources to record.[28]

Poets who made some impression in the historical record were Pierion and Pranichus, the catalysts perhaps in one of the more celebrated incidents in Alexander's expedition, his murder of his long-time friend Cleitus the Black.[29] Pierion and/or Pranichus achieved some notoriety for composing some doggerel verse that, with black humor, joked about the deaths of some hundreds of Greek and Macedonian soldiers killed by Spitamenes in 328 near Maracanda (Arr. 4.5.2–6.7). Pierion-Pranichus recited this poetry at a symposium in Maracanda

[25] Plu. *Alex.* 29.5. That Athenodorus could be fined suggests his citizenship (see Harrison 1971: 4–7 and fines levied by magistrates). Pickard-Cambridge 1988: 280 n. 7 passes over Athenodorus' origin; Kirchner 1901: 1, 19–20 lists several contemporary homonyms.

[26] Heckel 174.

[27] Callisthenes, the nephew of the philosopher Aristotle, was the "official" historian of Alexander's expedition, but his habit of sharing his thoughts too frankly, something Aristotle recognized (D.L. 50.5.4–5), led to his falling out of favor with Alexander, followed by his death. See Heckel 76–7, also *FGrH* 124.

[28] Heckel 6. Other poets also known only by name are Agis (Argos), Choerilus, and Sopater; see Heckel 8, 85, 252 for references.

[29] Plu. *Alex.* 50.8 notes that sources confused the names, calling Pranichus Pierion. See also Hamilton 1969: 141, Heckel 223, 232.

attended by Alexander and a number of his officers, including Cleitus, who was about to assume command over Bactria, and several newly arrived Greek visitors. The sarcastic humor infected the audience darkly, and soon some of the partiers were making disparaging comments about Philip and the older generation of Macedonians while praising Alexander and the "new" generation. All this proved too much for Cleitus, who reminded Alexander that he had saved his life, and that the king's accomplishments were not his alone but achieved with much help from the Macedonians, including Philip. Both men, drunk and prone to violence, became engaged in a heated argument which finally left Cleitus dead on the end of a sarissa wielded by Alexander.[30]

As noted above, another friend of Alexander's who came to grief was Harpalus, and his downfall was the subject of a play by Python of Catane (or Byzantium).[31] At a date likely to be *c.*324, Python staged a satyr play entitled *Agên* which satirized Harpalus and his affair with the courtesan Pythonice, whom he had treated as a queen in Babylon as he had access to the wealth of an empire – the Persian empire, now Alexander's.[32] The location of the play's performance is obscure, and scholars have argued for venues from India to Persia. But two references suggest an Athenian debut. Python refers to the poverty of Attica (13.596a) and a gift of grain made by Harpalus to the Athenians that won him a grant of citizenship (Ath. 13.596b).[33] An Athenian debut also seems likely from Athenaeus' reference to Python performing the play at a Dionysian festival (Ath. 13.595e).[34] Harpalus' arrival in Athens, and his bribes of high-ranking Athenians which provoked bitter political feuding, rocked the city. Python's play, however, regarding extravagant luxury and tyranny, issues that would have been in the minds of many Athenians and Greeks at the time, would have provided some good laughs, at both Harpalus' and Alexander's expense.

The artists and athletes who accompanied Alexander's expedition performed functions that to the casual reader might seem outside the scope of their vocations. As argued above, however, the abilities of the actors actually enabled them to carry out duties essential to the administration of a state, whether for Philip or Alexander. Additionally, the sources and the artists identified suggest that many of these individuals moved easily between their homes and Alexander's army. The Athenian

[30] For discussion of this incident and the sources see Tritle 2003.
[31] Ath. 2.50f, 13.595e. Python's identity is uncertain nor is it clear that he was part of Alexander's entourage (Athenaeus' obscure reference suggests the possibility that he was Athenian: Kirchner 1901: ii. 242–4 lists thirteen known Athenians so named). Even in the fifth century, non-Attic poets competed in Athens and this may have become more common in the fourth (see Henderson 2007: 179). Additionally, some 500 years separate Athenaeus from Python and it is not impossible that a number of details became confused.
[32] Ath. 595e–596a; see also the discussion in Heckel 240.
[33] Osborne 1981–3: iii. 79 also notes Harpalus' gift of grain that earned him citizenship some time between 327 and 324.
[34] With the details so obscure, it is nearly impossible to determine which Dionysian festival might be involved. In Athens there were three such festivals, the City, Rural, and Lenaea, but other festivals were also dedicated to Dionysus. See *OCD*³ 476 for discussion and references.

athlete Dioxippus, for example, was not with Alexander from the beginning of the conquest of Asia, but joined Alexander when he was far to the east.[35] Another artist, the dancer Theodorus from Tarentum became involved in a scandal with Philoxenus, a financial officer in Asia Minor, who wanted to buy his two slave boys for the king (Plu. *Alex.* 22.1–2; Athen. 1.22d).[36] While Alexander rebuked Philoxenus for procuring for him, it is to be emphasized that a Greek dancer was traveling from Sicily to the east to find work and make a mark for himself.[37]

The movement of literally thousands of artists of all kinds from across the Greek world to Alexander's army and empire says much about the lucrative profit there was to be had in making such a trip. As news of Alexander's conquests spread, but more importantly, the stories of vast wealth, an entrepreneurial spirit encouraged many enterprising Greeks to head east looking for Alexander's army, knowing that from time to time athletic and artistic competitions of all kinds were held and that the king was generous.[38] And it may not have been difficult to find Alexander and his army either. Contingents of troops, including replacements from Greece, as well as numerous couriers were surely familiar sights on the roads across Asia and to and from the king's camp. Aside from the usual dangers inherent in travel, artists and musicians would not have had a difficult time finding their way to Alexander, or in supporting themselves with impromptu shows along the way until they reached Alexander and hit the proverbial jackpot. It is this that explains how 3,000 entertainers came to be at Susa, ready to perform when the time was right. Such travels and the search for wealth and opportunity give a broader and different meaning to the old phrase "the impact of Alexander."

Soldiers, Bureaucrats, and Alexander

Athens, 323: Alexander is really dead, not supposedly as in 335 when he arrived before a rebellious Thebes soon to destroy it. Two generals, one old, the other young, debate before the Athenian assembly the proposal to go to war with the Macedonians and recover their lost freedom. In as sharp a rebuke as might be found, the old general, Phocion, says to the younger, Leosthenes: "Boy, your words are like cypresses – tall, stately, and barren of fruit!"[39] Their clash certainly

---

[35]   Heckel 115.

[36]   Heckel 263.

[37]   Also involved in this affair was another dancer, Chrysippus, perhaps Theodorus' traveling companion (see Heckel 85).

[38]   Pickard-Cambridge 1988: 281–305 notes that artist guilds and regulations for them date to the early third century. This suggests that artists who traveled east during Alexander's expedition did so as individuals, perhaps occasionally as ad hoc companies, but not in the way of organized troupes.

[39]   Plu. *Phoc.* 23.1, with Tritle 1988: 125, explaining Phocion's description of Leosthenes as boy, or *meirakion*. Phocion was a powerful speaker, one even Demosthenes dreaded in the give and take of assembly debate (see Plu. *Phoc.* 5.9).

represents something of a generational conflict. But there were other issues at stake, namely the choices many Greeks made in deciding to accept or reject friendship and association with Alexander and what that meant for themselves and their communities.

Leosthenes' military service during Alexander's conquests illustrates nicely the activities of those Greeks fighting with and against the king. In his case, however, the story is only a little better known as well as more complicated. The complication comes in the person of Leosthenes' father, also named Leosthenes, who was exiled from Athens following his misconduct (accepting bribes) in leading an expedition against the Thessalian tyrant Alexander of Pherae in 362/1.[40] This led to his exile from Athens, a dishonor that brought loss of political rights not only to him but to his son as well.[41]

The elder Leosthenes frequented the court of Philip of Macedon, perhaps remaining there until his death, and it is this that suggests that it was with Alexander and the Macedonians that the younger Leosthenes initially served.[42] Shortly after Alexander's death, Leosthenes returned to Greece, where the Athenians clearly reinstated him, electing him to the *strategia*, the board of generals. About the same time he contributed money to at least one liturgy and a costly one – support and maintenance of a warship – which argues that military service in the east had been profitable.[43] While the money might have come from Persian service, his father's Macedonian connection argues that Leosthenes' military career began with Alexander and the Macedonians and ended some time around 331 when many Greek troops were discharged. Eastern service, either with the Macedonians or Persians (or both), is the likeliest explanation of Leosthenes' wealth, which, together with his military service and volatile times, enabled him to return to Athens and immediately assume a position of influence.

Leosthenes thus represents those Greeks who soldiered in the army of Alexander. Some fought alongside him, such as the cavalrymen from Boeotian Orchomenus who returned home when the campaign against the Persians was declared to be over (see below, p. 131). Others, such as Damis of Megalopolis and the Thessalian Pasas remained on active duty right up to the king's death. The Greeks fighting for Alexander include:

Aeschylus, Rhodes (*epsikopos* of mercenaries, Egypt)
Agathocles, Samos (*taxiarches*, of allied troops)

---

[40] D.S. 15.95, and other sources cited in Davies 1971: 342. Note that early discussions of Leosthenes (e.g., Parke 1933: 203–4; Griffith 1935: 34–5) had no knowledge of his father and family connections.

[41] On the loss of rights, or *atimia*, see Harrison 1971: ii. 169–70.

[42] *Pace* Davies 1971: 342. It would not be the first time that a son had rebelled and rejected his father's actions.

[43] Davies 1971: 342 notes that Leosthenes contributed money to a trierarchy during the Lamian War. See sources cited there.

Alcias, Elis (cavalry commander)

Cyrsilaus, Pharsalus/Thessaly (Thessalian cavalry?)

Holcias, Illyria (? – troop commander)

Moschion, Elis (allied cavalry)

Pasas, Thessaly

Philon (2), of the Aenianes[44]

Polydamas, Thessaly[45]

Philotas (3), Augaea, Chalcidice[46]

Plato, Athens (troop commander)[47]

Socrates, Apollonia (ilarch)[48]

Other Greeks mentioned in the sources but without identification are:

Andromachus (1) (mercenary cavalry commander), Apollonides (2) (cavalry commander?), Ephippus (1), (*episkopos* of mercenaries, Egypt), Eudamas (= (2)?)[49]

The activities of those Greeks on the "enemy" side are much more complex and certainly murkier.[50] More certain are cases such as the mercenary leaders Glaucus (Aetolia) and Patron (Phocis) who surrendered to Alexander after Gaugamela and who, with the remnants of their forces, were probably integrated into Alexander's army.[51] There is no evidence this happened, but what was Alexander to do with them? Place them in a prisoner-of-war camp, send them to the "rear" under guard when he needed every available man for fighting?[52] The capture of the Persian "capitals" of Ecbatana, Persepolis, and Susa brought the great crusade against Persia to an end. Soon after, Alexander discharged the contingents of Greek allies in his army and sent them home. Evidence of this is to be found in the inscription from Boeotian Orchomenus which lists the surviving members of a cavalry unit which

---

[44]   Heckel 6–7, 9, 101, 140–1, 170, 192.

[45]   Heckel 225–6, noting that Polydamas carried the secret orders for the murder of Parmenion (Arr. 3.26.3).

[46]   Heckel 216 suggests now that Augaeus in Curtius' text may be a corruption of Aegaeus, a man from the old Macedonian capital; this would make Philotas Macedonian, not Greek.

[47]   Curt. 5.7.12; Heckel 252, following Berve ii. 367, suggests that later source traditions may have confused the philosophic names Plato and Socrates and exchanged Socrates (of Apollonia) for Plato. But see Kirchner 1901: ii. 203–6 who lists seven fourth-century Athenian "Platos" which suggests that Curtius' reference is no less a possibility than Berve's suggestion.

[48]   Heckel 252, with preceding note.

[49]   Heckel 28, 41, 118, 120, 215–16.

[50]   Cf. the case of Aristomedes, the Thessalian (Pherae) mercenary general, who was among those Greek mercenaries who abandoned the Persian cause after Issus, fleeing to Cyprus and Egypt. See the discussion in Heckel 47–8.

[51]   Heckel 126.

[52]   That Alexander was short on troops may be inferred from the musician Aristonicus volunteering for battle when Spitamenes attacked Bactra in 328. See discussion and n. 3 above.

made the long journey home.[53] While certainly not capable of proof, the mustering out of the Greek allies would have left only those "volunteering" in his army and these would have been too few to account for the thousands of Greeks who attempted to return home after the king's death.[54] Those mercenaries like Glaucus and Patron (and the men serving under them) who surrendered then were most likely incorporated into Alexander's army and used (mostly?) for garrison duty, incidentally perhaps the most irksome duty imposed on a soldier, which might also explain why these men so willingly abandoned their posts.

In the months following Alexander's death there were numerous clashes between the Greeks desiring to return home and Alexander's successors attempting to maintain the integrity and control of his empire. Many were killed and it seems likely that few ever saw home again. Among these are:

Aristomenes, Thessaly (Pherae?) (mercenary commander)[55]
Bianor, Acarnania (mercenary commander)
Glaucus, Aetolia (mercenary commander)
Leosthenes, Athens (mercenary)
Lycidas, Aetolia (mercenary commander, Egypt)
Mnasicles, Crete (mercenary commander)
Nicon, Athens (mercenary commander)
Ombrion, Crete (*toxarches*)
Patron, Phocis (mercenary commander)
Phoenix (2), Tenedos (mercenary cavalry commander)
Thibron, Sparta (mercenary commander)[56]

Additionally, there are several others mentioned in the sources but whose origins are not recorded. These include Athenodorus (3), Bion, Biton, and Letodorus.[57]

Related to the "army" men are the navy commanders and sailors. A number of these are the Greek Cypriote kings and their sons, who first served with the Persian fleet in its Aegean operations but then submitted to Alexander after his victory at Issus in 332. Some of these joined him and participated in the siege of Tyre (August 332) and then accompanied him to the east. Their known activities include the

[53] *IG* vii. 3206, now in Heckel 345. The names of twenty-three men survive. While the number of survivors originally listed is uncertain, as also the strength of the force when it went on the expedition, the relative brevity of the inscription might reveal something as to the losses such a unit took while fighting for Alexander.
[54] The number of mercenaries serving with Alexander is difficult to assess. D.S. 18.7.2 reports that 20,000 infantry and 3,000 cavalry followed Philon the Aenian in attempting to fight their way home. All that may be safely said perhaps is that there were many. Cf. Parke 1933: 202–3 and Griffith 1935: 9–32.
[55] Aristomenes and Nicon of Athens (also listed here) appear on an inscription (*IG* v. 948) found on the island of Antikythera (ancient Aegilia). My thanks to N. Sekunda for the reference; he plans to discuss these individuals in a forthcoming study of the Persian Aegean counter-offensive of 333–330.
[56] Heckel 72, 126, 151, 152, 169, 183, 193, 265.
[57] Heckel 60, 72–3, 151, 162.

hosting of literary and dramatic competitions in Phoenicia, and command of the Hydaspes fleet in its Indian Ocean voyage.[58] The Greek Cypriote royalty include:

Androcles, Amathus
Nicocles (1), Soli
Nicocreon, Salamis
Nithaphon, Salamis
Pasicrates (1), Curium
Pasicrates (2), Soli
Pnytagoras, Salamis[59]

There were, however, a large number of naval commanders, technicians, and sailors from around the Greek world who also went east with Alexander, and, like the artists and musicians, were surely attracted by the prospect of financial gain and opportunity. These sailors include:

Andromachus (3), Cyprus (nauarch)
Androsthenes, Thasos/Amphipolis (trierarch, Hydaspes fleet)[60]
Critobulus, Cos (trierarch, Hydaspes fleet)
Eumenes, Cardia (trierarch, Hydaspes fleet)
Evagoras, Corinth (*grammateus*, Hydaspes fleet)
Hagnon, Teos (trierarch, Hydaspes fleet)
Hieron, Soli/Cyprus (sailor)
Maeander, Magnesia (trierarch, Hydaspes fleet)
Medius, Larissa/Thessaly (trierarch, Hydaspes fleet)
Miccalus, Clazomenae (naval recruiter)
Nicocles (1), Soli/Cyprus (trierarch, Hydaspes fleet)
Nithaphon, Salamis/Cyprus (trierarch, Hydaspes fleet)
Onesicritus, Aegina/Astypalaea (helmsman)
Thoas, Magnesia-on-the-Maeander (trierarch, Hydaspes fleet)[61]

Related to both groups are the military technicians and support personnel. Their valuable knowledge positioned them to see and hear things which they later recorded. Among these were the engineer Aristobulus whose account ultimately influenced Arrian's, the future and surviving historian of Alexander's campaign. Several others, however, also wrote specialist military books, including Damis of Megalopolis, the same who negotiated the settlement after Alexander's death, who wrote a study on the use of war elephants. Other specialized studies included works on harbors

---

[58] On the competitions see Arr. 3.6.1; Curt. 4.8.16; Plu. *Alex.* 29.1–4; on Cypriote participation in the Hydaspes fleet see below.
[59] Heckel 28, 179–80, 193, 224.
[60] Brunt 1983: ii. 357, commenting on Arr. *Ind.* 18.3, notes that trierarch is honorific. It may be too that Arrian archaizes. In any case it seems likely that the term essentially means ship's captain.
[61] Heckel 29, 100, 120, 124, 128, 139, 156, 158, 167, 179–80, 183–4, 266.

(Cleon of Syracuse) and sieges (Charias and Diades of Thessaly). These support personnel and technicians include:

Aristobulus, Cassandreia (engineer)
Charias, Thessaly(?) (engineer)
Cleon, Syracuse (expert on harbors and water/irrigation?)
Crates, Chalcis (engineer)
Cretheus, Collatis/Black Sea (supply)
Damis (2), Megalopolis (military adviser/elephants)
Deinocrates, Rhodes (architect)
Diades, Thessaly (engineer)
Diocles, Rhegium (engineer)
Diognetus, Erythrae (surveyor)
Gorgus (1), Iasus (arms supply)
Gorgus (2), mining expert
Philonides, Chersonessus/Crete (surveyor)

Related to the military and naval figures and the military technocrats are those Greeks who found work ruling Alexander's empire. While sixteen of these are identified in the sources, the origins of fewer than half are known. Of the seven whose local origin is known, three were Greeks from Egypt (Cleomenes) or Cypriote Greeks (Stasander and Stasanor). Perhaps of interest here is that, as "eastern" Greeks, these individuals might have had knowledge of local languages and customs which might explain their appointments to administrative positions.

Known origins[62]
Antimenes, Rhodes (financial official)
Cleomenes, Naucratis/Egypt (governor of Egypt)
Ophellas (1), Olynthus (finances)
Stasander, Cyprus (governor of Aria-Drangiana)
Stasanor, Soli/Cyprus (troop supplier; governor of Bactria-Sogdiana)
Unknown origins[63]
Apollonius (governor in Egypt; finances)
Asclepiodorus (3) (finances)
Callicrates (finances)
Megasthenes
Mentor (Eumenes' staff?)
Nicias (finances)
Nicocles (3) (=Nicocles (1)?, envoy)
Proxenus (royal household)
Tauriscus (Harpalus' staff)
Thersippus (envoy)

---

[62] Heckel 34–5, 88–9, 184, 255.
[63] Heckel 41, 58, 75, 167, 179, 234, 260, 264.

The final category of Greeks working or otherwise performing some duty in Alexander's camp are those classified as his Companions, friends, intellectuals, court officials, and medical staff. These include:

Companions (or hetairoi)[64]
Ariston (2), Pharsalus/Thessaly
Cyrsilaus, Thessaly
Demaratus (1), Corinth
Hagnon, Teos
Medius, Larissa/Thessaly
Nearchus, Crete/Amphipolis
Polydamas, Thessaly
Nicocles (1), Soli/Cyprus
Polydamas, Thessaly
Stasanor, Soli/Cyprus

Friends[65]
Alcimachus (2), Chios
Gorgus (1), Iasus

Intellectuals[66]
Anaxarchus, Abdera
Anaximenes, Lampsacus
Callisthenes, Olynthus
Polycleitus, Thessaly
Pyrrhon, Elis

Court officials and staff[67]
Aristander, Telmissus (seer)
Artemius, Colophon
Athenophanes, Athens
Chares (2), Mytilene
Charon, Chalcis
Cleomenes (2), Sparta (seer)
Diodotus, Erythrae
Eumenes, Cardia
Heracleides (4), Thrace
Xenodochus, Cardia[69]

Physicians[68]
Critobulus, Cos
Dracon, Cos
Hippocrates, Cos
Philip (9), Acarnania

---

[64] Heckel 48, 101, 107, 128, 158, 171–3, 179, 225–6, 255.
[65] Heckel 10, 127.
[66] Heckel 27, 76–7, 225, 239.
[67] Heckel 45–6, 56, 61, 83, 84, 89, 113, 120–1, 137, 272.
[68] Heckel 100, 116, 140, 213–14.
[69] Xenodochus and Artemius of Colophon are mentioned as present the evening that Alexander killed Cleitus (Plu. *Alex.* 51.4). While they might belong to Alexander's court, it seems just as possible that they were present as visiting diplomats. At one point during the argument, Alexander turned and asked them if they did not think the Greeks godlike compared to the bestiality of the Macedonians. If accurately reported (and this is a big if), the remark seems an odd thing for Alexander to say to familiars in his court (who would have been familiar with such Macedonian antics), but not to strangers.

The following Greeks also appear at Alexander's court, but their place of origin is unrecorded:

Companion: Perilaus (1)
Court officials: Callicrates, Melon, Mentor, Nicesias
Physicians: Androcydes, Glaucias (3)
Seer: Demophon (1)[70]

For centuries before Alexander, Greeks had served abroad as soldiers and in many other capacities as well. Those who lacked the artistic talents of an Aristonicus or Thessalus offered their bodies, and as H. W. Parke noted long ago, "Alexander's ever-increasing demands for new recruits must have contrived almost to drain Greece of soldiers, just as it actually did drain Macedon of citizens."[71]

The Problem of Macedonian Friends and Enemies

Since scholars began studying relations between the Greeks and Philip and Alexander of Macedon in the mid nineteenth century, it has become a common-place that the Greeks aligned themselves into two competing factions, pro- and anti-Macedonian.[72] While Brian Bosworth once observed that "it has long been accepted that the labels pro- and anti-Macedonian are seriously misleading,"[73] scholars have continued to adhere to this nineteenth-century dogma in postulating this schism among the Greeks.

The problem is rooted in historiography, that is, how one goes about writing history, as well as how one looks to the present to interpret the past. It is well known that historians, like laymen, must from time to time generalize while advancing an argument. We generalize in order to summarize an argument, we select bits of evidence from all that we find and present those that best support the argument we wish to make. But a generalization or select evidence, while convenient, may and sometimes does too easily obscure a multiplicity of factors and results in a distortion of historical reality and the dilemmas people faced.[74] So in the matter of those Greeks labeled pro- and anti-Macedonian, the complexities of the economic and political realities they faced, as well as the bitter nature of domestic political battles

---

[70] Heckel 202–3, 75, 161, 167, 179, 28, 126, 109–110.

[71] Parke 1933: 202.

[72] See, e.g., Schaefer 1885–7: i. 206–7; iii. 33 for examples of this schematization (see also his index which includes the entry "makedonische Partei") and the more recent authors noted and discussed below.

[73] Bosworth 1985.

[74] See Marwick 1971: 224, who notes that "many of the well-worn labels and generalizations, unhappily, stand as barriers between the historian and his reader on one side and the real texture of the past on the other. . . . The trick to be used here, and whenever such phrases come to hand, is to switch on the mental television set, to endeavor to visualize the concrete realities implied in the phrase."

of which they were a part, becomes lost in the labels. Moreover, such a simplified notion as pro- and anti-Macedonian as applied to Athenian politics at this time, fails to do justice to the hard choices confronting the Athenians.

The problem of pro- and anti-Macedonian is also rooted in the nature of nineteenth-century European politics and their divisions. It is no accident then that the alignment of Athenian politics around (supposed) support or hatred for Macedon, or Philip and Alexander, or both, is encountered in Arnold Schaefer's study noted earlier.[75] Similar schematization of Athenian politics continued in Chiara Pecorella Longo's 1971 study of Athenian politics, followed by George Cawkwell (1978), Wolfgang Will (1983), and Peter Green (2003).[76] Some scholars, however, have discounted the idea: Raphael Sealey (1993) and Edward Harris (1995) have both critiqued the notion, with Harris asserting that "to divide the politicians of Greece into two monolithic parties of pro-Macedonians and anti-Macedonians does not do justice to the rich variety of opinion in Greece at the time."[77] Since Harris's and Sealey's arguments have generally failed to discourage such schematization, it seems worthwhile to revisit the concept, and the supposed Macedonian sympathies of perhaps the longest serving Athenian general ever, Phocion, provide an excellent test case.[78]

The debate over Athens' decision to go to war with Macedon after Alexander's death, briefly mentioned above, included the pointed exchange between Phocion and Leosthenes, both well-known military men. At the time some 80 years old, Phocion had surely outlived most of his contemporaries, or was visiting the few who were still alive in nursing homes or their equivalent.[79] Age and an extensive military record are not without relevance in examining Phocion's actions and conduct.[80]

Against Philip himself or his Greek allies in such places as Euboea and Megara, Phocion led Athenian military forces during at least five campaigning seasons (348, 343, 341/40, 340/39, 339/8). In these he succeeded in discouraging Philip from attacking Byzantium, overthrew Philip's allies in Euboea (twice) and Megara, and

---

[75] See n. 72.

[76] Pecorella Longo 1971: 83; Cawkwell 1978: 118–23; Will 1983: 9–11; Green 2003: 2–3.

[77] Harris 1995: 154 (with Tritle 1997: 700); also Sealey 1993: 163–5.

[78] Plu. *Phoc.* 8.2 notes that the Athenians elected Phocion forty-five times; see Tritle 1992 for discussion.

[79] While Phocion's age is often noted in discussions, little attention – one might even say none – is paid to the issues of aging and how these, combined with stressful times, might have influenced and affected his judgment.

[80] This seems necessary following Green 2003 and Kralli 2006: 682. Kralli states that Phocion assumed prominence only after Chaeroneia, which begs the question of how he earned the respect first of Philip then Alexander; Kralli also argues that Phocion preferred a passive policy for Athens, but nowhere notes his military service (at 80!) in the Lamian War; finally Kralli states that Phocion's actions were treasonous and "criminally negligent," ignoring completely the political and military realities of Macedonian-occupied Athens. No less problematic is the argument (first made by de Sainte Croix 1981: 609 n. 2), analogizing Phocion to French World War I general and hero, and World War II traitor, Marshal Pétain. Argument by analogy, while it does help to inform the reader, does not amount to proof.

harried the Macedonian coast, undoubtedly making things difficult for the Macedonian king.[81] These earned Phocion Philip's respect, for after his death his officers made it a point to make Phocion known to young Alexander (Plu. *Phoc.* 17.6).[82] After Philip's assassination there was much celebration in Athens, which prompted Phocion to remind the Athenians that the army that had beaten them at Chaeroneia was reduced by only one man (Plu. *Phoc.* 16.8). Phocion's assessment reflects that of a veteran commander able to analyze a military situation and see it for what it is – in this case all too dominating.

The old general and young king maintained a relationship, as far as can be discerned in Plutarch, of mutual respect, with Phocion refusing every gift Alexander offered him (Plu. *Phoc.* 18.1–7).[83] This friendship, while formal and political in nature, was only one enjoyed by a number of Athenians and Macedonians. Phocion enjoyed a similar relationship with Antipater, a friendship that later proved a great liability. Demades, Phocion's contemporary, an influential orator and politician in Athens, also counted Antipater a friend, though it seems that Demades was more interested in his wealth than friendship. Antipater is said to have remarked that of his Athenian friends, Phocion and Demades, he could not persuade the first to accept any gift while the second was insatiable (Plu. *Phoc.* 30.2). Also among Antipater's friends was Alexander's old teacher Aristotle, who while not Athenian was a major intellectual presence in Athens.[84] Demosthenes appears to have had some sort of relationship with Hephaestion, and Waldemar Heckel has plausibly suggested that Hephaestion, Alexander's closest boyhood friend and companion, may even have held Athenian citizenship thanks to its grant to his father Amyntor.[85] Relationships such as these surely complicate categories such as pro- and anti-Macedonian.[86]

---

[81]   See sources and discussion in Tritle 1988: 76–96.

[82]   Kralli 2006: 682 dismisses Phocion's military record, neither paying attention to the many source problems of the fourth century, nor to Phocion's service as a mercenary general in Cyprus (*c*.351? see D.S. 16.42.3–9, 46.1–3, and Tritle 1988: 152–6, 215–18), in an era when such service was common – and not seeing that incompetent commanders do not find employers.

[83]   Plu. *Phoc.* 17.9 notes that Alexander made Phocion his *xenos*, a term synonymous with *proxenos* or guest-friend (see Tritle 1988: 194 n. 16 for discussion). Phocion did take advantage of his relationship, but not for himself. He used his influence to secure the release of several political prisoners (Plu. *Phoc.* 18.6–7).

[84]   On this relationship see Paus. 6.4.8; Plu. *Alex.* 74.4, 77.3; and the discussion in Berve ii. 74.

[85]   Heckel 1991. Heckel 133 notes additionally that in summer 332 Hephaestion commanded the Macedonian fleet and its Athenian contingent in moving the army's siege train from Tyre to Gaza (Curt. 4.5.10). As an Athenian citizen (through his father's honorary grant), Hephaestion's command would be politically expedient.

[86]   This becomes even clearer when the Harpalus affair is examined. Harpalus arrived in Athens with a huge sum of money and badly in need of refuge. Appealing to the Athenians as a suppliant, Harpalus bribed lavishly in the hope of winning support from prominent Athenians. Among these was Demosthenes, perhaps the most "anti-Macedonian" of all Athenians, who was prosecuted by Hypereides, no less "anti-Macedonian" in his politics ([Plu.] *Mor.* 846b–c); also caught up in the affair was Phocion's son-in-law Charicles (Plu. *Phoc.* 21.3, 22.4), who unwisely befriended Harpalus. The confused nature of this affair cautions against the oversimplification of Athenian politics along pro- and anti-Macedonian lines.

Alexander's death in Babylon ignited a political storm in Greece that many believed would end the fifteen-year-long Macedonian domination. Nowhere was the debate more intense than in Athens, the most powerful of the Greek states. Many Athenians now saw an opportunity to reclaim the hegemony lost to Macedon at Chaeroneia. In the debate at Athens Phocion played a role, attempting to get his fellow citizens to see that deciding to fight was easy, but finding a winning strategy more difficult. For this appeal Phocion has been condemned as pro-Macedonian, a member of the peace party, but in fact his rationale seems rooted in his long experience as a soldier, questioning the apparently easy decision to go to war.[87] In the end he accepted the collective wisdom of his fellow Athenians and the command of citizen forces entrusted to him; with these he acquitted himself, repulsing a Macedonian invasion of Attica (Plu. *Phoc.* 25.1–4). The fact that he undertook this command at age 80 should argue, if the circumstances are examined critically, that his loyalty and commitment to the democracy cannot be challenged.

Macedonian victory brought with it an army onto Attic soil, something that Phocion had feared as the citizen soldiers of the Greek city-states proved no match for the experienced Macedonian veterans who had conquered the east. A personal relationship with Antipater enabled Phocion to blunt Macedonian demands, but only that (Plu. *Phoc.* 26.5–7). Antipater evidently agreed not to bring his army into Attica and forage as a favor to Phocion, undoubtedly an act that would have inflicted major losses upon the Athenians. But he also forced other conditions upon the Athenians, conditions for which Phocion has been condemned as accepting as *philanthropous*, "generous" or "humane" (Plu. *Phoc.* 27.5).

Peter Green has criticized my interpretation of all this, namely that Phocion did not just "tolerate" what Antipater demanded, but did so gladly. Yet with the victorious Macedonian army standing ready to attack should the Athenians become uncooperative, and with the once mighty Athenian fleet now destroyed or unmanned, it seems difficult to see what Phocion could have done differently. A defense of the city was impossible and Antipater was in no mood to negotiate.[88] In the recent war Leosthenes, commander of the allied Greek army, had trapped the old general in Lamia and pressed him hard. Leosthenes rejected Antipater's overtures for peace and simply demanded unconditional surrender. Now Antipater returned the favor to the Athenians (Plu. *Phoc.* 26.7). Clearly Antipater had a score to settle and this left Phocion and his fellow ambassadors little maneuvering room in their negotiations. Finally, it is not irrelevant that Philip had similarly moved against Thebes after the Greek defeat at Chaeroneia in 338. With its military power all but destroyed, Philip forced Thebes to accept a new constitution and garrison, exile enemies of Macedon, and pay an indemnity. Students of these affairs need look no

---

[87]   A modern parallel may be seen in US Army general Eric Shinseki, a critic of the US plan to invade Iraq in 2003. I doubt that General Shinseki could be called "pro-Iraqi" or "pro-Saddam" simply on account of his criticism of the Bush administration's war plans.

[88]   Green 2003: 3, on Tritle 1988: 130. Critics of Phocion, and those seeking to understand the problems faced by the Athenians in the aftermath of Antipater's victory, could better appreciate their situation by looking at events in Baghdad and Iraq since 2003. Cf. Sealey 1993 for another view.

further for Antipater's model: his "peace" for Athens simply followed Philip's earlier handling of Thebes.[89]

Finally, Green's understanding of Plutarch's use of *philanthropia* ignores generations of scholarship that has demonstrated how Plutarch, writing 500 years after the events he discussed and little understanding them, read his sources' accounts of events and then rewrote them with the moral and philosophical vocabulary with which he wished to influence his reader's approach to living life.[90] While incapable of proof, a likelier reading of Phocion's supposed *philanthropia* is that Plutarch read in a source that Phocion grudgingly accepted what Antipater demanded because he had no other choice.[91] This Plutarch then rendered as *philanthropous*, "tolerated," a term that in his vocabulary carries a philosophical and moral connotation that was surely absent in his source.

Athenians committed to resisting the Macedonians blamed the envoys including Phocion for accepting that which they did not approve, and surely considered the resulting regime as "oligarchic," hence such references to it in contemporary sources. As these critics grew in number, they found ready listeners in the contending Macedonian factions – Cassander attempting to take his father's place, Polyperchon representing Philip III Arridaeus and himself, and other interested Macedonians farther afield. These were little concerned with those Athenians like Phocion, who by 318 found themselves snared in the intrigues of greater forces. The frailties of his eighty-four years finally caught up with him, and Phocion was sacrificed on the altar of power politics.[92]

Conclusions

Available evidence suggests that many Greeks saw Alexander and service to him as a means to prosperity and greater social stature, familiar ambitions in any age. Many of these, like the flatterers who abounded at his court, were apolitical and saw service with Alexander only as a means of surviving the hardships of life. Others, however, joined Alexander, as many had earlier flocked to his father Philip, seeing in him not only a benefactor, but also the leader and maker of a new age.

---

[89]   Arr. 1.7.1; D.S. 16.87.3; Paus. 9.1.8 (garrison); Just. 9.4.7–8 (exiles); see also Hammond–Griffith 610–11; Bosworth 1980b: 74. That the Macedonians were sophisticated enough to comprehend the inner workings of Greek political life is a position that scholars seem reluctant to accept. Yet by this time several generations of Macedonians had absorbed Greek culture extensively, and at least one, Cleitus the Black, went to his death quoting lines of Greek drama. If such learning were possible, why not details of *polis* life?

[90]   See Martin 1961: 164–75, preceded by Hirzel 1912: 23–32.

[91]   See also Lamberton 2003: 11, who notes Plutarch's description of Phocion's "mild" (*praos*) rule over Athens. *Praos/praotes* is yet another philosophical term Plutarch injects into his *Lives* and readers need to treat it as cautiously as *philanthropia*. See Martin 1960: 65–73.

[92]   These events properly belong to the history of the Successors and so are only summed up here. Readers might consult the collection of papers in Palagia and Tracy 2003 for further discussion.

8

The Empire of Darius III
in Perspective

Pierre Briant

1 Sources and Problems: The Empire in Short- and Middle-Term Perspective

1.1 Darius and his empire

Until recently, Achaemenid historiography did not show much interest in the reign of Darius III, or in the state of the empire at the time Alexander set foot in Asia Minor. It sufficed to explain everything by the convenient thesis of the "colossus with feet of clay" that had become irreversibly undermined by disorganization, overtaxation, and rebellious subjects.[1] This thesis was, in itself, deemed sufficient to explain the Persian defeat in confrontations with the Macedonian armies.[2] From its origins, Alexander historiography has developed two visions on the Persian adversary. One is found in handbooks and the most recent conference proceedings: that the Achaemenid empire is evanescent to such a degree that it does not even represent one of two players in the game about to be played on the Near Eastern chessboard: time passes "as if Alexander were alone . . . when he faced his personal quest."[3] In contrast, other historians have attempted to reevaluate the military and strategic capacities of the last Great King.[4]

---

[1] My warmest thanks to Wouter Henkelman (Collège de France) who translated my text into English.

[2] See below, ch. 9.

[3] Cf. Briant 2005c: 26 [=1974: 27], 36, 39–4; also Briant 2003a: 567–8. The necessity of presenting the Achaemenid empire in courses on the history of Alexander is sometimes explicitly acknowledged (e.g., Flower 2007: 420), but has not really been taken into account in more recent syntheses.

[4] See, e.g., Seibert 1988; Badian 2000; Garvin 2003 and compare the earlier publication by Murison 1972 (followed by Briant 1974: 50 n. 2). See also Nylander 1993 (with my remarks in Briant 2003a: 242–4, 530–1, 577).

This double orientation in modern historiography is, to some extent, the latest avatar of a double-sided image of Darius handed down by the Greco-Roman tradition and continuously running through modern European historiography: Darius is either portrayed as a despot characterized by weakness and lack of drive, a man incapable of facing the danger that the Macedonian invasion presented to his throne and his empire; or he is glorified as a king possessing virtues and all kinds of admirable qualities, yet confronted by an enemy of such overwhelming strength that he stood no chance of gaining victory over him.[5] This second image, of a man both capable and courageous but overcome by a peerless adversary (presented by Bossuet as early as 1681), was adopted by Droysen from 1833 on, and the same conclusion is reached by a recent study by Badian (2000b: 265).[6]

This observation certainly does not imply that since Bossuet the historian's attitude toward his sources has not been redefined in terms of methodological rigor. It simply illustrates that, when scholars keep posing the same questions concerning Darius's "merit," there is a risk of falling into an epistemological trap, that is, to be obliged to choose between the "vices" and the "virtues" of Darius, a choice preconditioned by the ideological presuppositions and literary attitudes of the Classical authors.[7] Today, the historian's task should not be to "rehabilitate" Darius, nor to summon Alexander before an international court of justice to charge him with his "crimes."[8]

The question of the political aptitude and strategic abilities of Darius should indeed not be ignored and, apart from a few exceptions (e.g., Strauss and Ober 1990), there is nowadays agreement among scholars that the king was not an incapable strategist. Yet, on the one hand, such an observation reduces the historical analysis to its military aspects, at the cost of the political aspects of the Persian–Macedonian conflict, while, on the other hand, the analysis may not be subordinated to a teleological approach predetermined by the Achaemenid defeats. The empire lived its own life and its rulers did not have their eyes fixed on what Classical and modern historiography has presented as a conquest that, if not determined by fate, was in any case inevitable. Consequently, it is better to avoid the term "pre-Hellenistic" (German: *Vorhellenismus*), informed as it is by an a priori vision (*RTP* 320–3). Contrary to what a celebrated Iranian philologist in a commentary on the Xanthus Trilingual asserts, Asia Minor in the third quarter of the fourth century BC was not situated "between the death throes of the Persian Empire and the Hellenistic Spring," or "in a dying world, plunged into the shadows," a world waiting for "the charismatic, still uncertain light of Alexander."[9] When interpreted without such prejudices, the epigraphical document suggests a rather different assessment of the state of the empire (see below §3.1).

[5]   See Briant 2003a: 85–130, 567–9.
[6]   "This man of demonstrated courage . . . found himself facing one of the greatest military leaders. What might have sufficed against an Agesilaus proved totally inadequate against Alexander."
[7]   Briant 2003a: *passim*.
[8]   Briant 2003a: 126–30; Briant 2005c: 49–62.
[9]   Mayrhofer 1976; the same scholar participated in the premier edition: *FdX* 181–5.

In order not to reduce a complex and evolving reality to the "shadow of Alexander," and to avoid an Aegeocentric approach,[10] it is helpful to analyze the Achaemenid empire, in geographical terms, as an entity stretching from Central Asia to the Aegean and, in terms of chronology, from a middle-term perspective, that is, the period roughly defined by the last part of Artaxerxes II's reign and the death of Darius III (*c.*365–330).[11] By reinserting Darius' short reign into the imperial context that precedes it, and from which it proceeds, one creates the conditions necessary for understanding the distinctiveness of the empire's internal situation.[12]

Evidently, an analysis of the kind just described would exceed the bounds of a chapter like the present one. I shall therefore only point out a number of particularly notable historical and methodological features, more precisely with evidence that, though still not fully published, are accessible to the historians of the empire. Many of these corpora continue into the beginnings of the Hellenistic period, but rather than treating the entire period of transition (see Briant and Joannès 2006), I aim simply to shed light on a period sometimes characterised as a Dark Age.

1.2   Greco-Roman literary sources

The Greco-Roman sources are, it should be stressed, a constituent part of the documentation that we have at our disposal. But they must be considered within the context of Achaemenid reality. Such evidence is so deeply enshrined in the Greco-Roman perspective that it is severely distorted. To give only one especially striking example: new analysis of Greco-Roman texts relating to the inhabitants of the Zagros (Uxians and Cossaeans) and to the καταρράκται in the Tigris demonstrates that, contrary to long established opinion based on superficial evaluation, the royal residences in the empire's core were not in Darius III's time at risk from the double threat of mountain "brigands" and Persian Gulf "pirates."[13]

[10]   I sensed this approach already in *CAH²* vi (1994), which includes several chapters that are excellent syntheses, but lacks chapters on the regions beyond Mesopotamia. The very recent case of the *Cambridge Economic History of the Graeco-Roman World* (2007) is distinctly worse. The chapter "The Persian Near East" (Bedford 2007) is included in a volume the title of which clearly announces its Aegeocentric orientation. Despite the deceptive map (304–5), an incomprehensible editorial bias has in fact reduced "the Persian Empire" to Mesopotamia and Syria-Palestine, i.e., to the Near East, in an extraordinarily restrictive sense that excludes Asia Minor and Egypt, as well as the regions east of the Tigris. Furthermore, recently published documentation (such as the Idumean ostraca; cf. 312–13, 315–16) are neither mentioned nor used. As to the Persepolis tablets, these are barely referred to in the course of a bibliographical note (315, with n. 47). Against the background of the *longue durée* of Achaemenid historiography, such a chapter and the conception that informed it represent a perplexing step backward.
[11]   Extensive discussions of the subject are already to be found in *HPE* 691–871, 1007–50; updates are given in *BHAch* I. 57–63 and II. 92–100.
[12]   Military operations as such need not be discussed again within this perspective, except where they can clarify the structural analysis (see *HPE* 817–71, 1042–50).
[13]   See Briant 1976 and 1982: 57–112 (*HPE* 726–33, 1022: Zagros); *HPE* 1019–20 and Briant 2006c, 2008 (καταρράκται). Compare also, on the Uxians and Cossaeans and their connections with the royal administration, the interesting proposals by Henkelman 2005: 159–64.

At the same time, and despite grave omissions and biases, it is clear that the historian should not minimize the testimonies of the Classical authors, as long as necessary methodological precautions are taken.[14] It is by these sources, for example, that we are informed about the violent dynastic conflicts that emerged, one after another, between the murder of Artaxerxes III (end of 338) and that of Darius III (July 330), including the brutal elimination of Arses by Bagoas followed by the rise of Codomannus/Artašata under the name of Darius (end of 336). When comparing such episodes with the numerous comparable cases since the death of Cambyses (522), it is easy to appreciate that they do not allow the conclusion of increasing decadence in Persian politics (Briant 2002b). The very same documentation clearly suggests that the accession of Darius occurred along familiar lines, with the new king assuming the robe of Cyrus, as Artaxerxes II had done before (*HPE* 769–80, 1033–4). Also, it is generally implied in the sources that Darius managed to impose his authority: it is under his supreme command that Arsites was charged, in 334, with the command of the satrapal contingents from Asia Minor (*HPE* 820–3); from that moment until the fall of the royal residences (November 331–January 330) and the subsequent conspiracy instigated by Bessus under very special circumstances (331/30) no internal crises are detectable, nor any revolt within the Persian and Iranian nobility who held the reins of royal power.[15] One need only follow the ancient testimonies step by step to realize that, on the contrary, the leading officers, with very few exceptions (Mithrenes at Sardes), displayed an exemplary loyalty toward the crown, even after the first two defeats at the Granicus and at Issus (*HPE* 780–3, 842–52).

The Greco-Roman texts also allow, albeit only partially, the reconstruction of a relief map of Achaemenid lands, showing their specific aspects and traits at the moment they were crossed and conquered by Alexander's armies: they show that there were satrapies, palaces, treasuries, and fortresses, plains, streams, and natural resources, populations, villages, and towns, but also regulations and administrations at the level of cities and regions, tribute and taxes, as well as an overarching system of managing expenses and revenues. From this perspective, especially when

---

[14]   See Briant, *RTP* 141–5, 491–506, the resolved methodological reminder in *HPE* 693–5 and chs. 16–17, devoted to a detailed analysis of the empire. See also Briant 1999: 1131–8 and 2003a: 16–18; cf. below §4. I cannot see why Garvin (2003: 89 n. 11) would assume that I dismissed "the Greek sources on account of their biases," or why Brosius (*Gnomon* 2006), in a very positivist review of Briant 2003a, assumes that I have denied any reality to the Greek and Latin literary texts about Alexander. The method that I have consistently promoted and defended is rather more complex and elaborate (see, e.g., Briant 2006c and 2008 on the καταρράκται of the Tigris): it is not about simplistically reasoning by exclusives (yes/no), but about understanding that the literary Classical tradition is *at the same time* useful and deforming.

[15]   The thesis that holds the contrary finds its origins in Macedonian circles (*HPE* 842–3 and esp. Briant 2003a: 177–81); via the biased lens of the *Alexander Romance* the idea was redeveloped in medieval Arab-Persian literature in order to make an "evil king" out of Dārā (2003a: 461–3, 475–86).

considering the period under discussion, one cannot emphasize enough the importance of Ps.-Aristotle's *Oeconomica*.[16]

It is also thanks to the same sources that we have access to information on the military organization, on the mustering of the royal armies, on the rites that precede the entry and exit of the king's retinue, on many other aspects of Achaemenid aulic practice, and on the composition of the highest ranks in the imperial government. In general, it cannot be denied that our knowledge about the last phase of Achaemenid history would be diminished if we did not possess the conqueror's perspective, if only because we lack the perspective of the conquered.

1.3 The Achaemenid documentation: illuminating life in the provinces

Still, a type of documentation like that offered by the Greco-Roman sources could never suffice; one is obliged to gather, as far as possible, a range of sources from the lands that formed the Achaemenid empire, whether they are textual (in whatever language and script), archaeological, numismatic, or iconographic. Until recently, the period under discussion ranked among the most unknown of Achaemenid imperial history. The reign of Darius II (424–405/4) is the last one that is relatively well documented, and even this reign stands out much less distinctly than the reigns of Darius I (522–486), Xerxes (486–465), and Artaxerxes I (465–425/4).[17] In the case of Darius II, royal presence and activity is attested at Persepolis (inscriptions and constructions), Ecbatana, and Susa. Life in the provinces can be studied in detail on the basis of the abundant Babylonian documentation (in particular the corpus of tablets from the Murašû firm), the exceptional Aramaic documentation from Egypt, biblical and a number of Anatolian sources (*HPE* 600–11, 981–4). The study of the reign of Artaxerxes II (405/4–359/8) still profits from a reasonably favorable documentary situation, particularly through the epigraphical and archaeological sources from Susa (construction of the Palace of Chaour) and the other royal residences.[18] At the same time one has to observe that Aramaic documentation from Egypt has disappeared (the Nile valley became independent again *c.*400) and that the Babylonian documentation has become both less abundant and more difficult to use as a result of the frequent difficulty of distinguishing between the different kings named Artaxerxes or Darius.[19] In the absence of substantial and precisely dated bodies of evidence from the provinces, and with the importance of the Greek

---

[16] See *HPE*, *passim*, esp. 389–90, 451–6, and index, 1125–6; see also below §4 and the numerous studies on the subject by Descat, the latest being 2006: 365–71. The recent commentary by Zoepffel 2006 is, unfortunately, badly informed on current debates in Achaemenid and Hellenistic history.

[17] It is to these three reigns that the documents from Persepolis are dated (*HPE* 422–3, 938–9). On the unequal spread of the sources see also *HPE* 8–10, 518, 569–70, 612–15.

[18] On Susa, see the surveys by Boucharlat 2006: 443–50 and forthcoming.

[19] *HPE* 613–14, 675–81, 986–7, 998–1003; see also Boiy 2006: 45–7.

material (particularly Plutarch, Xenophon, and Diodorus), narrative history focused on western affairs once again takes precedence. Even in that particular area uncertainty reigns, however, especially with respect to the evidence for the satrapal revolts, which has always held a decisive place in the evaluation of the empire's relative strength or fragility in the course of the fourth century.[20]

Confronting the Greek sources with those from the Achaemenid world does not always yield decisive results, since the relevance of a certain comparison is sometimes hard to demonstrate.[21] As to the economic and commercial revival occasionally deduced from Artaxerxes III's mintings (Mildenberg 1998, 1999), the proposed interpretation is both disputable and less original than it appears.[22] In some cases the ambiguities in our documentation are such that we are, for example, still neither capable of telling whether the new Egyptian revolt under pharaoh Khababbash was put down by Darius III,[23] nor of reconstructing the conditions under which the land again came to be governed by the satrap Sabaces who, like his predecessor Mazdaces, is known from the coins he struck in Egypt.[24]

Some of the imperial lands are very well known. Such is the case for Babylonia (Briant and Joannès 2006: 17–306) and Asia Minor (Briant 2006a). Other regions elude detailed analysis on account of lacunae in the documentary record (Egypt).[25] Fortunately, our knowledge of the Achaemenid world is not fixed, but expanded by an evolving corpus of new discoveries and publications.[26] As a result, two regions of very different importance, Bactria and Idumea, merit revisiting.

The recently (but not completely) published corpora from the vast Central Asiatic satrapy and the little Palestinian district are both parts of archives written in Aramaic and brought to light by illegal excavations. With the exception of a few texts,[27] they were drafted in a time frame defined by the last decades

---

[20] See *HPE*, chs. 14–15, with the corresponding notes (972–1006); see also Briant 1984: 76–80 (Bactria).

[21] With regard to the revolt of Datames, the Babylonian explanation suggested by Van der Spek 1998: 253–5 seems very speculative to me (see *BHAch* II. 93–5). The postulated connection between Datames and the Tarkumuwa known from Cilician mintings has met with skepticism from several scholars, myself included (*BHAch* I. 59–61; II. 94–5).

[22] See the doubts expressed by Le Rider 2001: 223–6. On the traditional glorification of the figure of Artaxerxes III, in contrast to the negative image of Darius (so Mildenberg 1998: 283), see Briant 2003a: 108–12.

[23] On the Satrap Stele, see the bibliography and discussion in *HPE* 1017–18; *BHAch* I. 58; and Briant 2003a: 65–70, 563; most recently: Schäfer, forthcoming.

[24] See Nicolet-Pierre 1979 (*HPE* 1017) and, most recently, Van Alfen 2002; images in Briant 2003a: 76–7.

[25] The influx of new material (see Briant 2003c: 39–46) does not pertain to the period under discussion. On the documents relating to the second Persian domination (between 343 and 332), see Devauchelle 1995; on the documents from the transition period see Chauveau and Thiers 2006.

[26] See *HPE* 693–768, 1007–32, particularly the comments on 1029–32, as well as the updates in *BHAch* I and II, and the synthesis in Briant 2003b.

[27] Two texts from Bactria are palaeographically dated to the fifth century (Shaked 2004: 13, 22; 2006; *ADAB* 16 [B10]); two ostraca of Maresha are dated to the same century (Kloner and Stern 2007: 142).

of Achaemenid history and the beginnings of the Hellenistic age: from Artaxerxes III to Alexander (358[28]–324) in Bactria, and from Artaxerxes II (362) to Ptolemy (post 306) in Idumea.[29] Incidentally, it may be noted that, thanks to the Bactrian corpus, the number of texts dated after the last Darius has grown spectacularly.[30]

The space reserved in this survey for the Aramaic documents from Bactria and Idumea can easily be justified by simple reference to an appropriate methodological remark made by Eph'al during the presentation of a preliminary synthesis of the new Palestinian sources:

> A historical picture based on non-literary sources may be likened to a mosaic, put together from tiny stones, rather than large blocks, as it is generally the case with literary sources . . . A meticulous analysis of the entire corpus should help to accord the Persian period its proper place in the history of Palestine and its environs, as a substantial link between the Ancient Near East and the Hellenistic period. (Eph'al 1998: 109, 119)

Such documentation enables the historian to leave political and dynastic history for what it is and to concentrate on history from below. As has been remarked by another editor of the corpus (Lemaire 2002: 232–3), the Idumean documentation invites a modest kind of history, "a social and economical history on a local level where a small group of tax collectors and scribes do their best to manage levies in kind and in silver from taxpayers who, for the most, are peasants." What is true for the Idumean documents also pertains to the Bactrian corpus, with the difference that the latter is more readily accessible since it includes texts in literary (epistolary) format. Documents of that type are completely absent from the minute accounts written and abbreviated on the Idumean ostraca.

---

[28]   The date depends on the dating of text C1. The dating formula reads, "In the month of Kislev, in year 1 of king Artaxerxes." As the editors read the name of "Bessus," receiving "supplies as he went from Bactra to Varnu," they conclude that the texts is from the first regnal year of Bessus-Artaxerxes V or November–December 330 (Shaked 2003; 2004: 16–17; *ADAB* 180). The interpretation seems disputable, however (on this point I share the skepticism expressed by Lane Fox 2007: 297), since, apart from the difficulties in the reading "Bessus," I fail to see how, in one and the same document, the same individual could be referred to as "king" and as private person receiving travel rations. If the text indeed dates to the first year of a certain ruler, it may pertain to year 1 of Arses-Artaxerxes IV (336/5) or, more plausibly, to year 1 of Artaxerxes III, i.e., 358 (this hypothesis is considered but rejected by Shaked 2003: 1521 on the basis of arguments that do not seem to be decisive).

[29]   A recently published ostracon (Ahituv and Yardeni 2004: 9, 19–20) dates to Ptolemy ("Talmaios the king"), but see cautioning remarks on the identity of this Ptolemy by Lemaire 2006c: 417 n. 96: "Cet ostracon fragmentaire devra être revu et interprété . . . pour savoir s'il faut le rattacher au groupe principal ou aux ostraca du IIIe siècle."

[30]   On the few Babylonian documents dating to Darius III, see Joannès 2001: 250, 255 and Boiy 2006: 45–7; see also Dušek 2007: 118–19 (Samaria; accession year of Darius, corresponding to the second regnal year of his predecessor, i.e., March 335).

2   From Bactria to Idumea

2.1   Bactria–Sogdiana from Artaxerxes III to Alexander

Recently acquired from London dealers and purportedly coming from Afghanistan, the Khalili collection[31] includes thirty documents written on parchment and eighteen on "wooden sticks" (small wooden boards), all inscribed in Aramaic; nine additional documents have up to this point come to light – of which five are usable and date to the same period – but these texts so far remain unedited (Shaked 2006). All are dated to the third regnal year of Darius III (333/2). The wooden boards carry brief inscriptions and are acknowledgments of debts (*ADAB*, D1–18, pp. 31–3, 231–57). The parchment documents, on the other hand, are letters and lists of allocations. One recognizes the names of the leading officials of the satrapy such as Bagavant, whose designation is *peḥat* (governor) of the town of Khulmi (modern Khulm) and who corresponds with his superior Akhvamazda. The latter could be considered the satrap in Bactria, but no text confers that title on him. An elusive reference to a treasurer/*ganzabara* is found on a fragment (B10).[32] The name of Bactra is twice attested, again in fragmentary texts (A7, A8). As the corpus testifies, the responsibilities of Akhvamazda and Bagavant were not limited strictly to Bactria.[33] Bagavant's assignment was to administer the collection of crop revenues in storages, and, additionally, the distribution of rations to various groups; additional duties included the maintenance of buildings and the construction of fortifications in Sogdiana. In 348 or 347, Bagavant, at this time in Khulmi, received a letter from Akhvamazda, telling him that he had been assigned a contingent from the local troops (*hyl' mt*) in order to construct a wall and a ditch in the town of Nikhshapaya (A4, pp. 93–9). Another letter, sent to Bagavant and to other officials, conveys Akhvamazda's renewed insistence that his orders be carried out strictly and that the wall be constructed in conformity with regulations. This time the letter is to be delivered by a messenger (*zgnd'*; compare Gk. ἀστάνδης) and Akhvamazda's foreman (**frataraka-*); it concerns the town of Kiš (A5). Other texts mention more individuals and toponyms and allow tentative descriptions of the status of the garrison troops, apparently part-soldier, part-peasant.[34]

---

[31]   See the preliminary but precise presentations in Shaked 2003, 2004, who kindly entrusted me with an advance copy of the premier edition (*ADAB*, forthcoming): I express my warmest thanks to him and his co-author.

[32]   Text dated to the middle of the fifth century by palaeographical criteria (*ADAB* 16). On administrative structures and practices see *ADAB* 22–6, 27–9.

[33]   As stressed by Shaked (2003: 1528–30), it is certainly remarkable that the administration's authority stretched into Sogdiana, across the Oxus: the two regions seem to form a single unit, as was the case during Darius III (cf. Berve ii. 267–8; I am not sure whether I understand correctly the construction suggested by Jacobs 1994: 213–14 in this regard). On the strategic responsibilities of the satrap of Bactria, see also Briant 1984: 71–6.

[34]   This is at any rate what is suggested by text A4 (letter from Akhvamazda to Bagavant at Khulmi): upon the request to that effect received from "Spaita, the magistrates and others (of) the garrison" of

The range of different rations in document C1 (Shaked 2003: 1522–4; 2004: 40–2; *ADAB* 177–85) allows glimpses of the richness of the production in livestock (sheep, goats, cattle, donkeys, geese, chicken),[35] animal products (cheese, milk), crops, and agricultural products (fruits, spices, flour of various qualities, oil, spices, vinegar), as well as the magnitude of the reserves kept in the administration's storehouses (fodder; see also A10a). In addition, this document is part of a group of texts that yield pertinent details on the organization of official missions and the rations given to travelers at state-run halting places (C5). One finds a technical terminology known from the Aramaic documents from Egypt and the Elamite tablets from Persepolis (e.g., *baššabara* = **pasābara-*, "travel provisions" – *ADAB* 197). Other documents again list products, such as barley, wheat, and millet disbursed as rations (*ptp*) to laborers and to the administration's personnel; the quality of the products allocated is clearly a function of the social rank of the recipient (B2). As for the term used for "ration," *ptp*, it is the same that is found at Elephantine as well as at Persepolis, in Babylonia (*HPE*, index, 1174) and now in Idumea (see below). One of the suppliers of rations holds an Iranian designation, rendered in Aramaic as *ptpkn* (*<*piθfakāna-*).[36]

In the Bactrian corpus, one also discerns clearly the transfer of commodities from one locality to another, by means of the officials that collect them and transport them to those responsible for its distribution (C4, dated to year 7 of Alexander: *ADAB* 203–12). The meticulousness of the accounting of commodities entering and leaving the storehouses seems to equal procedures known from Persepolis (e.g., C3).

Apart from donkeys (C1, B4, B6), camels were reared (B8) and used for transports. Some of these animals were labeled "camels of the king" (A1:3: *gmln zy mlk'*), again an expression known from Persepolis, where it is used to refer to king's assets per se (as opposed to the institution's assets in general).[37] The situation undoubtedly was the same in Bactria. Camel-keepers (**uštrapāna-*) enjoyed a special fiscal status and were exempt from certain taxes. One letter relates that, at one occasion, they were unjustly surcharged, and even detained by Bagavant, his foreman (**frataraka-*) and the magistrates (*dyny'*), upon which Akhvamazda had to intervene on several occasions in order to make sure that his orders were followed by Bagavant and the other officials of the district (*ADAB* 68–75, A1). The document also gives some specifications on the taxes (here: *ḥlk*). In an unfortunately broken context, another document refers to "the king's tribute" (*mndt'mlk'*: A8: 2).[38]

Nikhshapaya, Akhvamazda gives his authorization to interrupt their construction work temporarily so that the "troops" may return to gather the harvest under threat of a locust plague; after having completed harvesting, "they will build that wall and ditch."

[35] See the list of animal and plant species in *ADAB* 33–5.

[36] See *ADAB*, C4:10; 28, 55.

[37] See discussion in *HPE*, 463–71 and 945–7; Henkelman, forthcoming.

[38] On the different meanings of *mandattu*, see *HPE* 385 (a tax levied on commercial cargo entering the Nile); 405, 462 (taxes levied on Egyptian domains); 441 (in a Treasury text from Persepolis); 942.

Akhmavazda himself seems to have owned property in the province under his control. One text refers to commodities taken out "from [his] house" (*byt'zylk*: A2), but it is possible that the expression relates to assets that are *ex officio* under the satrap's control (see *HPE* 463). In another letter (A6), Akhvamazda reproaches Bagavant, this time for not having followed his instruction (*handarz*) to roof two old houses (located in two villages), and to bring wheat and sesame for sowing as seed to the granary in accordance with his instructions. If Bagavant remains reluctant to effectuate the order, he risks having to pay for the whole amount "from your own house" (*byt'*). Here again, Akhvamazda refers to the buildings, the houses, and the granary as belonging to him. Are these his private property, or domains of which he, in his capacity as satrap, was the usufruct, like Aršāma a century before in Egypt? Note that, like his Egyptian colleague, Akhvamazda had a steward (*paqdu*) who managed his assets, and who denounced Bagavant's culpable behavior (A6: 1). As to the threat that hangs over the latter's head, the expression used ("from your own house"), is reminiscent of the expenditures by other administrators or Persian military commanders, whose responsibility makes them liable, if necessary, "from their own possessions" (ἐκ τῶν ἰδίων: *HPE* 595–6).

The new documentation also yields information on religious practices (Shaked 2004: 42–47; *ADAB* 35–7) and on Old Iranian onomastics (partly from local origin, such as the names built on the base *whšw* (**vaxšu-*), the name of the river known in Greek as the Oxus: *ADAB* 57–60). One even finds, on a rolled document (C2), the impression of a magnificent Achaemenid seal: a horseman holds up a lance and faces a rampant lion; he is accompanied by a second figure on foot who, his head covered by a *bashlyk*, holds a pike, ready to help the horseman if necessary.

A first encounter with the said documentation inspires amazement at the fact that it was found in a region that, until now, was a little-known territory that appeared in two quite disparate groups of sources: the Greco-Roman corpus of Classical and Hellenistic texts on the one hand, and the massive amount of data gathered in years of surveys in northern Afghanistan on the other. Archaeologists have always insisted on the "particularly Bactrian" character of the hydraulic structures attested in the area since the third millennium. From their point of view, the extent of these structures and their continuity into the Achaemenid period suggest the existence, persisting during the reigns of the Great Kings, of what is invariably referred to, with a somewhat hazy description, as a "Bactrian entity," or a "pre-Achaemenid Palaeo-Bactrian entity." In this model, the focus lies on Bactrian continuities still existing after the Achaemenid conquest, which, by contrast, would not have left conspicuous traces.

This view raises several questions. That the construction of systems of irrigation canals was a phenomenon occurring throughout the third, second, and first millennia is not to be doubted. But should one deduce from the existence of an inherited "characteristically Bactrian" technique – and from that alone – that, after the Persian conquest, the Achaemenid administration never intervened in this complex? Would that not be an overinterpretation of the absence of Achaemenid textual evidence? For many reasons (including the find of an Elamite Persepolis-type administrative tablet in the Achaemenid layers of Old Kandahar[39]), which I have advanced since the start of the debate, the validity of such a rigid interpretation may be doubted.[40] From my point of view, it would seem preferable to leave open the possibility that, one day, a textual documentation from the Achaemenid period would come to light from this region.[41] This is exactly the point proved by the corpus currently being published. Obviously, the texts do not answer all the questions, but they will at least show that, contrary to well-established opinion, Bactria did not constitute a special case within the whole of the Achaemenid empire. The region was, unmistakably, a satrapy in the full sense of the word, a province where the royal administration carried out the same tasks that it had assigned itself in other parts of the empire. One is struck in particular by the formal and functional similarities between the Bactrian documentation on the one hand, and the Elamite tablets from Persepolis and the Aramaic documentation from Egypt on the other.

Another characteristic of the Bactrian administration is that it is written in a form of Aramaic very close in morphology, syntax, and redaction to that known from Achaemenid Egypt (Shaked 2004: 22–9; *ADAB* 39–51). It is fascinating to note that the hypothesis of a diffusion of *Reichsaramaïsch* throughout the lands of the Iranian plateau during the reigns of the Great Kings had already been posed with much vigor by Benveniste as early as 1958 in his edition of the Aramaic version of the Kandahar Bilingual, that is, on the basis of a document dating well into the Hellenistic period. There, he demonstrated the close links in terms of language and redaction, as evidenced by the presence of a host of Iranian loans, with the Elephantine documents dated to Artaxerxes I and Darius II. "Nous sommes en réalité dans une province iranienne où s'étaient maintenues les traditions des chancelleries achéménides," Benveniste concluded, speaking of the borders between the Iranian Plateau and the Indus lands.[42] This is precisely what the Aramaic documents from Bactria are now confirming. As the great number of Iranian terms they include shows (*ADAB* 281–3), it is absolutely clear that the use of Aramaic in the Bactrian documents should be related to the installation and functioning of the imperial administration of the Great Kings.

[39]   Briant 1984: 59; *HPE* 753, 764; most recently *BHAch* II. 73, and Stolper-Tavernier, www.achemenet. com/document/2007.001-Stolper-Tavernier. pdf). Note that recent archaeological research has identified new important sites dating to the Achaemenid period (communication by Roland Besenval).

[40]   On the debate with archaeologists see Briant, *RTP* 314–18, and esp. Briant 1984; cf. *HPE* 752–4, 1027–8; Gardin 1997; Lyonnet 1997: 118–19; Francfort and Lecomte 2002: 659–66 – the last three adopting a more flexible approach, with recognition of the limits of the archaeological documentation. See also *BHAch* II. 162–4 and Briant 2002a (where the future publication of the Aramaic documents from Bactria and their integration in the ongoing debate is announced: 522 n. 20).

[41]   See Briant 1984, esp. ch. 2, where, objecting to the *argumentum a silentio*, I introduced the idea and the conviction that "les autorités achéménides de Bactriane maniaient les archives avec autant de constance et de persévérance que leurs collègues des régions babyloniennes et égéennes" (59; on satrapal archives see *RTP* 209); see also *HPE* 754: "It is safe to say that the discussion is not over."

[42]   References in Briant 1984: 59–60 (see n. 7 on the Aramaic documents found at Ai-Khanum); see also my introduction to Shaked 2004: 5–8. Benveniste's study is, surprisingly, not mentioned by Graf 2000.

2.2   Idumea, a province in the Trans-Euphrates satrapy between Artaxerxes II and Darius III

The period discussed in the previous section is also illuminated by material from the other end of the empire: Idumea, at the frontiers of the Negev. In the context of the attack by one of Antigonus' generals against the city of Petra at the beginning of the Hellenistic era, Diodorus refers to the eparchy as well as to the satrapy of Idumea, centered on Lake Asphaltites (the Dead Sea).[43] At that point, Idumea served as a military base for the Macedonian troops (19.95.2, 98.1). Regardless of the term used for it, one observes that the area constituted the territory of a provincial government; its capital, during the Persian period, may have been Hebron or Lachish. The new Aramaic documentation, which is currently being published,[44] will give new impetus to the debate on the region's status during both the last phase of imperial Achaemenid history and the period of transition and the establishment of the Hellenistic kingdoms.

The size of the corpus is considerable;[45] however, it is mutilated as a result of the illegal character of the excavations that brought it to light and its subsequent dispersal, in smaller lots, between a number of museums and private collections (since *c.*1985). Nevertheless, the Aramaic ostraca from Idumea bring new insights into one of the least-known regions of the Achaemenid Trans-Euphratean lands.[46] The texts, which are extremely difficult to read, are very short and may be drafts of partial accounts, possibly destined to be included in longer documents that would have been kept in the regional archive.

Though some documents have no date at all, many mention a month name and some a regnal year. Fortunately, a few texts also provide a royal name: Artaxerxes,

[43]   The expression found in D.S. 19.98.1, "in the middle" (κατὰ μέσην τὴν σατραπείαν), does not have a strictly geographical meaning: cf. Bartlett 1999: 106; on the excavation see the survey in Stern 2001: 443–54 as well as Grabbe in Lipschits et al. 2007: 125–44.

[44]   The new documentation is briefly introduced in *BHAch* I. 31; II. 56–7, and announced in *HPE* 1017. Three volumes, comprising 201, 199, and 384 texts, have been published: one by Eph'al and Naveh (1996), and two by Lemaire (1996, 2002). The publications of Lemaire 1996 and Eph'al and Naveh 1996 have been discussed also by, e.g., Amadasi-Guzzo 1998: 532–8. Since these publications, a number of isolated documents have been published in various articles partial list: see esp. Lozachmeur and Lemaire 1996; Lemaire 1999b, 2006a; Ahituv and Yardeni 2004; Porten and Yardeni 2003, 2004, 2006 (these last three articles contain the most sophisticated interpretation of the archives). A great number of documents, dispersed over various private and public collections, are yet to be edited (a history of the successive discoveries is found in Porten and Yardeni 2003: 207–9; 2006: 457–9); an encompassing publication with continuously numbered texts, under the direction of Porten, is in preparation (see Porten and Yardeni 2003). Among (necessarily provisional) syntheses see, e.g., Eph'al 1998; Lemaire 1999a; 2006a; 2006b: 416–19; and Kloner and Stern 2007.

[45]   According to the latest estimate by Porten and Yardeni 2006: 458, 1,900 items, of which about 1,700 are legible.

[46]   On Trans-Euphrates in this period see *HPE* 716–17, 1016–7, as well as the regular surveys published in *Transeuphratène* (Elayi and Sapin 2000; *Transeuphratène* 32 [2006], 191–4) and, most recently, Lemaire 2006c.

Alexander, Philip, and also Antigonus. The last three names may be those of Alexander IV (?),[47] Philip Arrhidaeus and Antigonus Monophthalmus (see also Wheatley, ch. 3).[48] The Achaemenid part of the chronology of the ostraca is established by the occurrence of the royal name Artaxerxes which can be associated with certain years and sometimes interpreted more precisely thanks to identification of individual dossiers within the corpus (Porten and Yardeni 2003, 2004, 2006). Given that there is a series of documents dating to years 42–46, it is certain that part of the corpus is from the reign of Artaxerxes II (the only king of that name who ruled for so many years), and that ostraca from years higher than 21 may be assigned to the reign of the same king. Identifying documents dating to Artaxerxes II's successors is often more complicated: Arses can be referred to only by his first or second regnal year, and Darius III by years 1–3 (until the loss of Syria), but years 1–3 may also refer to Artaxerxes III (which is, in fact, often the case[49]), Philip or Alexander.[50] Be that as it may, the beginning of the Aramaic Idumean documentation, as far as we know at present, may be fixed to 362, during the reign of Artaxerxes II.[51] None of the documents is explicitly dated to the reign of Darius III.

The ostraca are silent with regard to the designations and functions of those active in the region's administration,[52] but they imply that products were collected, undoubtedly as taxes, from the land, that they were registered and subsequently redistributed from storehouses[53] that must be those controlled by the provincial administration. Some of these are located at Maqqedah (Kirbet-el Qom, 14 km west of Hebron) and Maresha (well known from the Hellenistic period, from the correspondence of Zeno, among other sources).[54]

The texts are dockets that, after a date, mention one or several commodities, the quantity delivered, the measure in which it is counted, and a proper name. They supply, in the first place, information on the resources of a region that, manifestly, was being extensively developed in the period. Apart from cereals, flour, and straw,

---

[47]   There are some differences in opinion with regards to this Alexander: contrary to Eph'al and Naveh 1996, Lemaire argues that he cannot be Alexander IV, but must be Alexander the Great. To support this, he has devised the hypothesis that there was a different year count in Palestine in this period (1996: 41–5; 2002: 199–201; repeated in 2006b: 418 n. 98). Anson 2005a chooses Lemaire's chronology without hesitation, whereas Porten and Yardeni 2006: 484–6 seem to remain undecided. That the documents refer to Alexander IV is forcefully asserted by Boiy 2006: 58–61; see also his reflections in Boiy 2005 (on the Lydian inscriptions).

[48]   On the chronology of the ostraca dated to Antigonus, see now Boiy 2006: 73–4.

[49]   See the chronological charts in Porten and Yardeni 2006: 462–3, 468–70; see also Porten and Yardeni 2003 and 2004.

[50]   See the remarks of Eph'al and Naveh 1996:16–17 and Lemaire 1996: 11–13.

[51]   See Lemaire 2002: no. 1 (pp. 11, 199): a document dated to Tammuz 27, year 43, i.e., July 20, 362.

[52]   It may be mentioned, however, that Lemaire 2002: 227–8 proposes to read the term GZBR' (*ganzabara*, "treasurer") on an ostracon found at Tel 'Ira.

[53]   From this perspective, the documentation under discussion presents a number of functional resemblances with the Aramaic texts from Persepolis (see the remark by Eph'al and Naveh 1996: 14–15).

[54]   On the history of Maresha in the Achaemenid period on the basis of the ostraca, see the remarks by Eshel 2007. On Zeno's voyages in the region see Durand 1997.

one finds wine, olive oil, wood, and hay (measured in fodder loads) as well as all kinds of livestock (camels, donkeys, cattle, sheep/goats, pigeons).[55] Some documents refer to the handling of silver (*ksp*), perhaps measured in shekels,[56] others to some form of cadastral register, or at any rate a registry of fields, which are, as elsewhere (*HPE* 414), sometimes measured by the amount of seed necessary for cultivation.[57] More than forty texts also speak of "workers," plausibly day laborers, each of whom was registered on a document. It is particularly difficult, however, to establish under what conditions such workers were recruited, and by which authority.[58]

The Idumean corpus also yields a good deal of information on the organization in "clans" ("house," *byt*) or "families" ("son of," *bny*), on the coexistence of populations with different origins in the same region during the Achaemenid period (Arabs, Arameans, Judeans, Phoenicians, etc.),[59] on the temples, and on the cults.[60] Finally, a few Iranian terms are recognizable in their Aramaic form, such as "paradise, garden" (*prds*) and "rations" (*ptp*).[61]

It is essential to compare the Idumean ostraca with other corpora discovered, in regular excavations, at other sites in southern Palestine, especially those of Arad and Beersheba.[62] The Arad ostraca, published in 1981, carry very short texts written in ink. They document deliveries of staple goods (barley, barley grits, straw) as fodder for animals (horses, donkeys). The texts are not dated, but may be situated, on palaeographic grounds, in the middle of the fourth century, that is, in the late Achaemenid period (Naveh 1981). The same is true for the Beersheba ostraca, which do, however, mention regnal years (from 1 to 12) that belong either to Artaxerxes II or to Artaxerxes III (the latter is more likely according to the editor: Naveh 1973, 1979). Some twelve documents may be considered as dockets that register deposits of certain quantities of barley and wheat, and that mention proper names (as in Idumea and Arad): these texts may pertain to the delivery to a central storage facility of taxes collected from farms scattered in the countryside. Based on such evidence, it appears that Beersheba must, at this date, have been one of the most importance centers (perhaps the capital?) of the Negev.

Even though the ostraca currently being published are silent on the ranks of the administration, there is no doubt that the circulation of commodities as evidenced by these tiny documents bears witness to a system well known from Persepolis, that

---

[55] Eph'al and Naveh 1996: 10–13; Lemaire 1996: 142–6; 2002: 203–8, 223–9.

[56] See the interpretations suggested by Lemaire 2002: 223–9.

[57] Eph'al and Naveh 1996: 13; Lemaire 2002: 206.

[58] On this point see esp. the exposition by Porten and Yardeni 2006: 473–82; see also Lemaire 2006b: 443, who raises the question of forced labor.

[59] Kloner and Stern 2007: 142–3; a small number of Iranian anthroponyms have been noted (see table on p. 143); on Maresha, see Eshel 2007.

[60] See, e.g., Lemaire 2002: 221–3.

[61] Lemaire 2002: 208 (the term *ptp* is known from Bactria, Elephantine, Babylonia, and Persepolis).

[62] So already Eph'al and Naveh 1996: 11. Note that the reconstruction of administrative processes in Idumea, as proposed by Lemaire (1996, 2002), is clearly directly inspired by the model drawn by Naveh for Arad and Beersheba.

is, that of levies, storage, and redistribution.[63] As to the utilization of the reserves, the Arad ostraca may give a possible answer: the rations given to animals and their caretakers can probably be related to the disposition of guard posts (with an organization in contingents (*degelin*), as in Elephantine), as well as to the existence of official halting stations along a road (Naveh 1981: 175–6)[64] – these are elements well known from the Persepolis tablets, from a famous Aramaic document from Egypt, and from the Greco-Roman sources (*RTP* 505; *HPE* 364–5).[65]

The Idumean ostraca now accessible illustrate imperial realities that, though situated in a micro-region, are far from insignificant. The chronological convergence of the various text groups seems to allow for the conclusion that the region was being reorganized during the later part of the reign of Artaxerxes II, resulting in a relatively dense occupation of the available space under the aegis of the imperial authorities and their local representatives.[66] It is therefore possible that our documentation bears witness to the origin of the province of Idumea as attested later by Diodorus when using the terms *satrapeia* and *eparchia*. We can scarcely go beyond that conclusion, though it is tempting to establish a link with the strategic situation of this region within the empire at the time, until 343, that the Achaemenid armies were led in counter-offensives against Egypt.[67]

3   From Halicarnassus to Sidon, via Xanthus and Tarsus: Two Achaemenid Satraps between Artaxerxes III and Darius III

It is not a novel observation that an inventory of satrapies constituting the empire of Darius III and a list of holders of satrapal positions can be given on the basis of Greco-Roman accounts of Alexander's expedition.[68] Yet, even when connected to episodes from earlier periods, these texts yield limited concrete and precise evidence on either the regular or the special missions of Achaemenid satraps. As shown by the Egyptian and Babylonian examples (sixth to fourth centuries) and that of

---

[63]   *HPE*, ch. 11; these are the "revenues" (εἰσαγώγιμα) and "expenses" (ἐξαγώγιμα) of Ps.-Arist. *Oec.* 2.1.2 (*HPE* 452–3, 943–4).

[64]   This interpretation by Naveh has met with some opposition (see *HPE* 928).

[65]   On the strategic aspect of fodder reserves in this region (and certainly in others too, e.g., in Bactria: *ADAB*, A10, C1, C3), compare the famous travel voucher given by the Egyptian satrap Aršāma to his intendant (*HPE* 362–3) or the measures taken by the Sidonian rebels against the Persians (D.S. 16.41).

[66]   On this point see also *HPE* 716–17; 1016–17.

[67]   So Lemaire 1996: 151; 2002: 231–2; see also Sapin 2004.

[68]   See Berve i. 253–73, and the name entries in vol. ii; cf. Jacobs 1993. On the functions of satraps see Berve i. 273–83 and, recently, Klinkott 2005; Henkelman, forthcoming, esp. §5. On the satraps and satrapies in Asia Minor, see the recent synthesis by Debord 1999, whose analysis has the merit of integrating numismatic sources in all their diversity and complexity. To my knowledge, Casabonne 2004 is the only recent monograph on Achaemenid Cilicia.

Akhvamazda in Bactria during the reign of Artaxerxes III, those persons whom
we would term "satraps" are not necessarily designated as such in documents
pertaining to regular administrative practice.[69] Moreover, it is much less from
the Classical texts than from Achaemenid evidence (textual or numismatic;
Elamite, Akkadian, Aramaic, etc.) that we may gather pieces of information on the
specifics and the nature of the satraps' interventions in the daily life in the provinces,
as well as on the prerogatives granted to them by the central authorities in
times both of peace and war. What is true for the satraps of Egypt,[70] Babylonia, or
Bactria applies also to the satraps of Asia Minor and Syria under the last Achaemenid kings. This is demonstrated by the examples of Pixodarus and Mazaeus/Mazday,
selected here because of the variety of available sources and the insights they offer
on how the provincial administrations represented and managed the imperial
interests.

3.1   Pixodarus at Xanthus: satrapal power and local elites

In contrast to the case of the satrap Mausolus, whose links to the crown can be
studied on the basis of a number of (largely epigraphical) sources,[71] the same type
of research was rather difficult in the case of Pixodarus until recently.[72] The youngest son of Hecatomnus and brother of Mausolus, Artemisia, Hidrieus, and Ada (the
last being the famous dynast/satrap of Caria), Pixodarus was born *c*.400; he died in
336/5, shortly after the accession of Darius III. Pixodarus was succeeded, as satrap
in Caria, by Orontobates, who was sent not long before to Halicarnassus by the
Great King and had married his predecessor's daughter, Ada the Younger.[73] The
literary sources also inform us on the obscure episode of negotiations with Philip
II ("the Pixodarus affair").[74]

Apart from a few inscriptions that illustrate his administrative measures in Caria
and Lycia (*HPE* 709), Pixodarus used to be known particularly for his remarkable
coin issues, struck in his own name.[75] He has become even more well known,
however, since the French mission at Xanthus uncovered, in 1973, and published
the now famous trilingual inscription, a document that continues to arouse diver-

[69]   See Stolper 1987 and 1989b (Babylonian terminology); Briant 2000c: 268 (Aramaic and Demotic terminology).
[70]   On the coins struck by the last two satraps in Egypt under Darius III, see Nicolet-Pierre 1989 and Van Alfen 2002.
[71]   See Hornblower 1982: 137–70; *HPE* 667–70, 995; on his double status ("king of the Carians" and satrap), see *HPE* 767–8, 1032.
[72]   Overview of the sources in Berve ii, no. 640; see also Ruzicka 1992: 100–55 and Debord 1999: 400–6.
[73]   Arr. *Anab.* 1.23.7–8; Str. 14.2.17; on the name Orontobates (written Rhoontopates on the coins), see Schmitt 2006: 257–60; on the later history of this individual see also *HPE* 1043–4.
[74]   See Plu. *Alex.* 10.1–5 (e.g., Ruzicka 1992: 120–34).
[75]   See Konuk 1998: 161–83 (gold coinage: 178–83); 2002.

gent, if not conflicting interpretations.[76] Though technically a trilingual inscription (Lycian, Greek, Aramaic), the stele in fact carries the text of *two* resolutions: first, the decision taken by the inhabitants of Xanthus, expressed in Lycian and Greek, inscribed on the sides of the monument; second, the intervention of the satrap Pixodarus documented in an Aramaic text on the edge of the stele.

The evidence can be summarized as follows: the Xanthians decided to institute a regular cult for Basileus Kaunios and Arkesimas. Accordingly, appropriate measures were taken concerning the erection of an altar (βωμός), the selection of a priest (ἱερεύς) both for the present and for the future, an exemption from taxes (ἀτέλεια) for the priest, and the allocation of land, the revenues of which would finance the cults. Furthermore, the income of the sanctuary would be provided by an annual sum levied from the Xanthians and a tax incumbent on freed slaves. The inscription ends with a traditional curse formula aimed at any future violator of the rules; the text also includes a direct appeal to Pixodarus, who is to punish anyone who violates the "law" (*datah*):[77] "May Pixodarus be its guarantor!" (Πιξώταρος δὲ κύριος ἔστω).

The trilingual document poses some formidable problems in terms of satrapal chronology and imperial history, which will be touched on only briefly. The Aramaic text opens with an absolute dating formula: "In the month of Sivan in year 1 of King Artaxerxes, in the citadel of Orna, Pixoda[ro] son of Katomno, the satrap of Caria and Lycia, said . . .". In the eyes of the editors, this could refer only to Artaxerxes III, that is, in the year 358. In an attempt to solve certain difficulties, Badian (1977) has, however, proposed to date the text to the first regnal year of Artaxerxes IV, that is, according to the author, Arses, in 337. Despite the critique expressed by the editors vis-à-vis this view (*FdX* 166 n. 1), Badian's proposal has been accepted by a number of scholars.[78] If correct, it would imply that the Xanthus Trilingual is the only official text dated to Artaxerxes IV[79] – the existence of this king has hitherto not unambiguously been confirmed by the Babylonian texts.[80] According to a third hypothesis (Maddoli 2006), the chronology behind the carving of the different versions of the text is more complex than previously assumed: in summary, Pixodarus

[76] Since its preliminary presentation in *CRAI* 1974 and its premier edition in 1979 (*FdX*), the document has provoked a considerable number of studies, listed and discussed in 1996: 707–9 (text on 708), 1011–12, and particularly in my specialized study, Briant 1998 (and, subsequently, in *BHAch* II. 179–82). In this context I refer only to the most recent studies. Text of the Lycian version: Melchert 2000; text of the Aramaic version: Kottsieper 2002.

[77] On the term (used in the Aramaic version and in many other imperial corpora), see *HPE* 510–1, 956–7; *BHAch* I. 96–7; ii. 143, 177; Briant 1999: 1135.

[78] See, e.g., Briant 1998: 305–6 n. 3.

[79] An Aramaic document from the Wadi Daliyeh, published by Cross in 1985 and republished by Gropp in 1986 (*HPE* 1033) and Dušek (2007: 118–19), is dated to the accession year of Darius (III) and the second regnal year of his predecessor (March 19, 335); unfortunately neither his personal name (Arses) nor his throne name are mentioned.

[80] See recently Boiy 2006: 45–7, whose argumentation on the basis of the unique and only decisive tablet reveals that the "fact" is still to be established firmly.

would have become satrap of Lycia *only* in the first regnal year of Artaxerxes III (358)[81] while Mausolus was still satrap of Caria and would only later, from 341 onward, control Caria as well (the situation known from other sources).

Regardless of how the dating issue is to be solved, the exceptional document at any rate informs us on what constituted a "satrap" in the period between Artaxerxes III and Darius III in a micro-region of the empire, on his prerogatives and capacity to intervene in the local affairs of the territories of his assignment. Given the evident intricacies of jurisdictions involved in the decision to introduce a new cult at Xanthus, the Trilingual bears an exceptional contribution to the debate on the relationship between imperial authority and local rule.

All this explains why, throughout the last quarter-century, the document has more or less been adopted by specialists of postexilic Judah. This tradition is actually older than the discovery of the Trilingual, since, in 1896 Eduard Meyer had already used the *Letter from Darius to Gadatas* (published 1888) as an argument supporting the purported authenticity of the decrees contained in the book of Ezra (Briant 2003b: 110–11). As the number of archaeological discoveries and textual publications increased, the case of Judah gradually became integrated in a dossier containing a documentation as varied as the *Cyrus Cylinder* (Akkadian), the Aramaic papyri from Egypt, the hieroglyphic inscriptions of Udjahorresnet, the correspondence of Pherendates with the authorities of the temple of Khnūm (Demotic and Aramaic), the "Decree of Cambyses," and the codification of Egyptian laws at the initiative of Darius (Demotic). In one and the same assemblage, one finds, from Asia Minor, the *Letter from Darius to Gadatas* as well as (since the 1970s) the inscription of Droaphernes at Sardes and the Xanthus Trilingual, but also some other epigraphical documents from Lydia (the so-called "Inscription of Sacrileges"), from Ionia (arbitration by Struses: *HPE* 495, 646) and from Caria, and even a passage from Herodotus on the tribute reforms by Artaphernes (*HPE* 494–7). It is on the basis of this dossier that, in recent years, the status of Judah has been reexamined, often in the light of the Xanthus Trilingual. In an attempt to clarify the texts by means of other texts in the same corpus, they have been included in more general interpretations at the level of the empire, resulting in sharply contrasting views: either that of an extremely potent and interventionist empire of the kind defined by Eisenstadt,[82] or an empire that grants local communities far-reaching autonomy and that even lends its "imperial ratification" (*Reichsautorisation*) to decisions taken locally (see Frei 1996, 1996²). As a result of this debate on the status of Judah, the Xanthus Trilingual has acquired the rank of an essential comparative reference.[83] It shares this position

---

[81]   On the date formula that opens the Lycian and the Greek version (ἐπεὶ Λυκίας ξαδράπης ἐγένετο Πιξώδαρος), see discussion in Briant 1998: 320–5, and the meticulous study by Cau 1999–2000.

[82]   A thesis defended throughout by Fried 2004 (see 4–5), following Eisenstadt 1969 (frequently cited). On the subject see my remarks in *BHAch* II. 184–5 n. 396 (on the basis of the 2000 typescript, published largely unaltered, as Fried 2004).

[83]   See esp. Frei 1996: 39–47; in the first edition of this book (1983), the Trilingual already held a strategic importance. See also Fried 2004: ch. 4 (140–54 on the Trilingual); Watts 2001 (see index, 222, and the high number of references to the Trilingual in the papers of the contributors); Bedford 2001:

with some other epigraphical documents from Asia Minor, including texts of doubtful authenticity[84] or of debatable relevance for the discussion at hand.[85]

In itself, approaching a problem at the level of the empire is a perfectly sound method. At the same time, it should be observed that an all-encompassing comparatist view tends to construct or postulate a global model that in turn is applied, without the necessary precautions, to a regional or micro-regional case to the detriment of its specific traits. The consequence is, all too often, that the epigraphical material from Asia Minor is used within a "dossier" that is so heterogeneous that one risks pushing the independent voice of individual inscriptions into deadlocked generalizations.[86]

A more fruitful approach would be to revisit the historical and institutional context of the Xanthus Trilingual, a context that can explain its genesis and that shows its particularities. To start with: what relations existed between the satrap and the city of Xanthus? Two possible answers, which are not mutually exclusive, suggest themselves. First, it may be reiterated that there should be no doubt that Lycia and Xanthus were subjected: Pixodarus appointed two *archontes* in the land, and an ἐπιμελητής at Xanthus. In addition, it was the satrap's prerogative to impose certain taxes (customs) or to proclaim a fiscal exemption (TL 45).[87] Furthermore, though referred to as πόλις in the Greek version (l. 12), Xanthus appears, under its Lycian name Orna, as a *birtha* in the Aramaic version of the Trilingual; *birtha*, "citadel," appears as a generic term in several Aramaic corpora of the imperial administration (Elephantine, Samaria, Sardes, Kiršu-Meydancıkkale, and even Persepolis: Briant 1993a: 21; *HPE* 433).

At the same time, Xanthus is not defined by its status as subject city alone. The decision to found a new sanctuary, to organize the performance and material conditions of the cult, was actually taken by "the Xanthians and the perioeci" (ἔδοξε δὴ Ξανθίοις καὶ τοῖς περιοίκοις); it is this community that "selects a priest" (εἵλοντο ἱερέα) and that makes an oath to effect all that it has pledged in the stele. Also, it is the πόλις that allocates (ἔδωκαν) lands and fields (ἀγρόν) for the support of the new cult. It can therefore not be denied that, whatever the precise institutional

---

132–57 (143–5 on the Trilingual); Kratz 2002: 174, 194; Grabbe 2004: 107–9; 213–4; Grabbe in: Lipschits and Oeming 2006: 538–9.

[84]　On the *Letter of Darius to Gadatas*, see Briant 2003b; Lane Fox 2006 does not respond to any of the arguments and analysis advanced in it (despite his postscript, 169–71); the same is true for Fried 2004: 108–19.

[85]　See, on the Droaphernes inscription, my remarks in *BHAch* II. 177–9, and, on the "Inscription of Sacrileges," Briant 2000a: 242 n. 32 and *BHAch* II. 179.

[86]　See on this problem Kuhrt 1987 and 2001: 171–2, where she stresses the "crucial" character of the Trilingual in Frei's argumentation and reaches the conclusion that "in sum, then, none of Frei's examples provides instance of *Reischsautorisation* in the sense needed to sustain the argument." On the risks of comparative history, see also Briant 2000a: "L'histoire comparatiste ne peut aboutir à des résultats fondés que si chacun des exemples … a été minutieusement étudié préalablement *per se*" (242); cf. *BHAch* II. 157–9.

[87]　See *HPE* 709, and compare other Achaemenid texts such as the papyrus on the custom duties of Egypt: *HPE* 384–7, 930.

contexts, the text refers to a community that exerts some kind of autonomy. As to the closing formula, "May Pixodarus be its guarantor!" (κύριος ἔστω), it certainly does not imply that the whole process, from the beginning to the end, is placed under the satrap's supervision. Already under the threat of divine wrath, the offenders will also have to account for their acts before the satrap, if the Xanthians decide to refer a complaint to his authority. From that moment onward, it is the satrap's responsibility to preserve or restore the sanctuary's interests, including the economic conditions that insure its sustenance.[88]

In the eyes of several commentators, however, the formula κύριος ἔστω, well attested in Greek cities, could not have had the same meaning in a Lycian context, since Xanthus was not a democratic Greek city.[89] The objections seem hardly decisive (*BHAch* II. 179–82). In fact, both the concept and the reality of a "deliberating community," whatever the basis of the selection of the "citizens," are not exclusively Greek,[90] and in this case it is clearly "the Xanthians and the *perioeci*." In addition, the recently published Carian–Greek document from Caunus demonstrates that the Caunians were perfectly able to develop a political vocabulary and political concepts without slavishly adopting a Greek model (Marek 2006: 122–3).

The Xanthus Trilingual also informs us about the coexistence of Lycians and Greeks in the Lycia in the second half of the fourth century and the preservation of the local language. It is certainly remarkable that it was on the basis of the Lycian text that the Greek version could be restored, and not the other way around. Despite the advance of Greek as the preferred language for official inscriptions in Lycia, Lycian remained very much present throughout the period of Achaemenid domination. Recently enriched by the Caunus Bilingual, evidence of the intercultural and interlingual contacts in southern Asia Minor at the end of the Achaemenid period keeps expanding and grows more promising – all this despite the uncertain datings which complicate interpretation (Briant 2006a: 322–7).

3.2 "Mazday who is over Trans-Euphrates and Cilicia"

Attention may be drawn to another satrap of Darius III, a man known from the Classical sources as Mazaeus, a grecism of the Persian Mazday, as found on coins.

---

[88] I have developed this interpretation in Briant 1998, esp. 330–6; it has, basically, been followed by Maddoli 2006: 607.

[89] See, independently, Fried 2004: 151–2 and Le Roy 2005; see also Debord 1999: 66–7 (the comparison with the Droaphernes inscription seems unfortunate: *BHAch* II. 153).

[90] See Briant 1993a: 19–23, on Sardis and its internal organization, with a comparison with the case of Xanthus (21–2); see also the connections rightly established between the Xanthus Trilingual and the Caro-Greek Bilingual from Caunus (SEG xlvii: no. 1568; Marek 2006: 120–1). In both cases, what I call the "civic version" (a terminology accepted by Frei) is introduced by ἔδοξε Καυνίοις/Ξανθίοις καὶ τοῖς περιοίκοις. See most recently Briant 2006a: 322, and compare Debord 1999: 67, who also speaks of a "décision politique . . . consistant en la création d'un culte poliade." A firm stand to the same effect is also taken by Domingo Gygax (2001): 102–3, 195–9; see the discussions summarized in *SEG* li: no. 1824, and *SEG* lii: no. 1424–5.

There is no doubt that this individual enjoyed a very high prestige in the king's entourage.[91] Nothing can be said about his family background, but we do know that he had already been charged with certain responsibilities under Artaxerxes III. In his long and rather imprecise description of the revolts of the lands between Syria and Egypt,[92] Diodorus notes that Artaxerxes himself took supreme command and that, on the march from Babylonia to Phoenicia, he was joined, "by Belesys, satrap of Syria, and by Mazaeus, governor of Cilicia [Βέλεσυς ὁ τῆς Συρίας σατράπης καὶ Μαζαῖος ὁ τῆς Κιλικίας ἄρχων], who had opened the campaign directed against the Phoenicians" (16.42.1). As so often with a testimony from Diodorus, we find ourselves confronted with several difficulties: one relating to its terminology, the other to its chronology.

What, then, was the division of authority between Belesys (I) and Mazday? Was it just that of different provinces: Trans-Euphrates (Belesys) and Cilicia (Mazday)? Or was it a difference in rank (σατράπης/ἄρχων) within the same administrative division? Nothing is known of Belesys, but it is tempting to connect him with a homonymous individual who, around 400, governed Syria (τοῦ Συρίας ἄρξαντος) and who, on the basis of that position, could dispose of a residence (βασίλεια) and a paradise (παράδεισος) at the sources of the Dardas (near Aleppo).[93] The latter Belesys (IIa) is certainly the same person who, in the Babylonian sources, has a Babylonian name (Belšunu; IIb) and patronymic (Bel-usuršu), who, from 407 to 401, held the title of "governor (*pīḫātu*) of Ebir-Nāri" and who, under Darius II (between 421 and 414), held the title of "governor (*pīḫātu*) of Babylon" (Stolper 1987). Another (?) Belšunu has the title of satrap (*aḫšadrapanu*) in a text dated to 429? (IIc). This text, among others, attests that Babylonian terminology for satrap/ governor is as variable as that found in Greek texts, but the document does not allow the conclusion that the "satrap" Belesys (IIc) is identical to the Belesys (IIb) who is qualified as "governor of Syria" (Βέλεσυος . . . τοῦ Συρίας ἄρξαντος) by Xenophon (Stolper 1989a: 291; *HPE* 601–2, 981). Apart from the hypothesis of his Babylonian origins, the anthroponyms and the terminology used tell us nothing about the identity and functions of the Belesys (I) of Diodorus. One cannot there-fore reliably interpret his Greek titulature (τῆς Συρίας σατράπης) in the light of one of the titles of the Babylonian Belšunu (*pīḫātu* of Ebir-Nāri; IIa). Nor is it pos-sible to advance a hypothesis on the functions assigned to Mazday in Cilicia: whether it is that of a plenipotentiary governor, or that of a subordinate of Belesys.[94]

---

[91]   Μαζαίου δὲ τοῦ μεγίστου παρὰ Δαρείῳ γενομένου (Plu. *Alex.* 39.9); he was one of the Friends (τῶν φίλων) of the king (D.S. 17.55.1) and a *vir illustris* who became even more celebrated on account of his behavior at Gaugamela (Curt. 5.1.18).

[92]   On the enormous difficulties in the reconstruction and interpretation of Diodorus narrations see *HPE* 656–75, 993–8 (Artaxerxes II); 681–8, 1003–5 (Artaxerxes III).

[93]   Xen. *Anab.* 1.4.10.

[94]   A host of different hypotheses was already extensively analyzed by Leuze 1935: 193–235, without any real progress.

It is only on the basis of numismatic evidence that we can proceed from here, but only with due caution since the interpretive uncertainties are impressive and persistent. Series of coins struck at Tarsus, already known for a long time, often display on the obverse a seated figure on a throne at right and an Aramaic inscription at left: "Baal of Tarsus." The reverse has the well-known theme of lion and prey (very familiar in Achaemenid art). Certain series also have an Aramaic inscription above the lion that may be translated as "Mazday who is over (governing) Trans-Euphrates and Cilicia."[95] Comparison with the situation deduced from Diodorus' testimony suggests that, at some point, Mazday united Cilicia and Trans-Euphrates under a single governorship,[96] and that Belesys disappeared from the scene (or our sources).

Unfortunately, the chronology of the mintings is highly uncertain as a result of divergent dates (355 or 346) assigned to the revolt and the surrender of Sidon to Artaxerxes III and his generals. The latter event is fixed to year 4 or 14 of Artaxerxes on the basis of a Babylonian chronicle, which cites the arrival of Sidonian prisoners in the royal palace at Babylon at that time.[97] Finally, the entire argument is connected to mintings by Mazday at Sidon; the coins from these mintings bear his name in Aramaic (MZD) on the reverse, sometimes accompanied by an official scene representing the king or the city god in a chariot.[98] There are some disagreements, however, on the counting system used by the satrap on the coins: if we are dealing with year numbers from the reign of Artaxerxes III (years 1–21: 353–333?), his mintings could indicate that Mazday became satrap of Cilicia and Trans-Euphrates in 356, and kept his post until 333.[99]

In any case, there is scarcely any doubt that Mazday was, as a governor, assisted by a host of local subordinates such as, possibly, his son Brochubelus in Syria proper.[100] There were, additionally, a governor of Damascus,[101] local dynasts at Sidon (Elayi 2005), Jerusalem, or Samaria (Dušek 2007), and no doubt also a governor of Idumea.

---

[95]   Ever since Six 1884, Mazday's coinage has often been studied; see Mildenberg 1990–1; Debord 1999: 412–16; Le Rider 2001: 211–3, 226–8; Casabonne 2004: 207–23. In these publications detailed analyses are given for each minting. On the Aramaic titulature see Lemaire 2000: 134–8, and my own remarks in Briant 2000c: 268.

[96]   A coin, published in 1998, from Menbig in Syria (the coinage of which is otherwise well known) has the Aramaic inscription "Mazday who is over Ebir-Nāri." The document has engendered quite some conflicting interpretations (*BHAch* I. 29; Lemaire 2000: 135–7; Casabonne 2004: 210). Much caution remains warranted and this includes reckoning with the possibility of a fake (so Elayi and Sapin 2000: 173–5).

[97]   *HPE* 683–4, 1004 (year 345); since then, Elayi 2005: 129–32 has reaffirmed his conviction that the date is indeed year 4 of Artaxerxes III, i.e., 355.

[98]   The historical implications are debated: is it a purely Sidonian scene (Elayi and Elayi 2004b; 2005: 6974), or one that marks the Great King's imprint on the city (*HPE* 606–8, 983, with caution)?

[99]   Such is the position defended by Elayi and Elayi 2004b and Elayi 2005: 132–5, 139–41; a number of questions remain unanswered, however.

[100]   See Curt. 5.13.11: *Brochubelus, Mazaei filius, Syriae quondam praetor* (*HPE* 1013).

[101]   Curt. 3.12.3: *praefectus Damasci.*

3.3   From Lycia to Cilicia: the imperial hold

On a general level, the examples from Lycia and Cilicia are remarkably instructive concerning the empire that Darius III inherited. In Cilicia, leaving aside the chronological debate, the literary (Diodorus) and especially the numismatic evidence demonstrates two essential facts. One is that a new, vast administrative division was created, encompassing Cilicia and Trans-Euphrates. This measure was not without logic since Cilicia had long been oriented toward Syria and Mesopotamia, and its culture included a number of common and similar characteristics. In addition, Mazday was not the first imperial grandee to have struck coins in Cilicia: his predecessors, Persian military commanders, minted coins in the context of short-term military operations in the region. But Mazday was the first to coin silver as a standing territorial responsibility in his capacity as "governor of Cilicia and Trans-Euphrates." He was also the first to include his name and titulature on the coinage. Simultaneously, yet without abolishing the royal coinages, Mazday introduced his name on a series of mintings at Sidon – another means of asserting, even more distinctly, Achaemenid sovereignty over the region.

As for Lycia, the Xanthus Trilingual fits in the history of Carian–Lycian relations since at least the reign of Mausolus, and illustrates the constant tendency of the lords of Halicarnassus to extend their sway to Lycia. It is possible that the introduction of divinities whose origins lie in Caria (more precisely in the border region with Lycia) corresponded, at least partially, with the wishes of the Hecatomnid satrap. Yet, in these circumstances, the introduction of Hecatomnid power in the region was not brought about against the empire's interests. Quite the contrary: it was rather to strengthen control over Lycia that, under Artaxerxes III, the region was first defined as an autonomous satrapy and confined to Pixodarus, and subsequently included in a larger Carian-Lycian satrapy from 341 onward. When one takes into consideration that Pixodarus' harmonious relations with the central court brought Orontobates to Halicarnassus and that the latter succeeded him upon his death (336/5), one discerns in the developments described a reinforcement of Achaemenid imperial hold on the southwestern regions of Asia Minor between Artaxerxes III and Darius III (see *HPE* 666–73, 707).

The case of Cilicia is thus joined by that of Lycia, in the sense that one witnesses the disappearance of local dynasts: in the course of Artaxerxes III's reign, Lycia and Caria were, as it were, "satrapized" to a greater extent than before. Changes in the territories assigned to satraps were a frequent and constant feature in these regions: hence, it is quite possible that the death of Pixodarus led Darius III to take measures to effect a territorial and tributary organization in Lycia and the adjacent regions.[102] Altogether, if we add the cases of Bactria and Idumea (§2.1–2), the Lycian and Cilician examples (§3.1–2) confirm the reality of Achaemenid imperial domination, both in its unity (e.g., the use of Aramaic) and in its regional diversity.

---

[102]   Arr. *Anab.* 1.24.5, with my comments in *HPE* 706 and 1011.

4   At the Empire's Center: Indications of Dynastical and Imperial Continuity

Greek texts abound in details on the dynastic conflicts that took place between Artaxerxes III and Darius III, on the "decadent luxury" of Darius III's court.[103] The documentation on the center of the empire as such is less informative, even though there are some particularly important insights into the daily administrative organization of life at court.[104]

According to Plutarch (*Alex.* 69.1–2), Artaxerxes III never went to Pasargadae in order to avoid the royal custom that demanded that at such occasions the king gave Persian women a piece of gold. Evidently, the anecdote has been reworked by Plutarch (Stadter 1965: 53–6), who wanted to contrast Alexander and Artaxerxes and to portray the former as the one who revitalized the tradition of the "giving king." At the same time, Arses and Darius III may not have left any material or epigraphical trace at Persepolis or any other residence,[105] but their immediate predecessors certainly did. The royal tombs (V and VI) overlooking the platform and seen by Diodorus' source (17.71.7) are attributed to Artaxerxes II and Artaxerxes III. Though we do not know the reasons prompting their choice of Persepolis rather than Naqš-i Rustam, the site of the four earlier royal tombs, it is at any rate clear that the later tombs followed a model that had been used without interruption since the first rock tomb, that of Darius I (Schmidt 1970: 99–107). With the exception of a few details, the motif of subject peoples represented as throne bearers and identified by means of captions (A^3Pb) is repeated exactly. The same loyalty to dynastic traditions can be observed in an inscription by Artaxerxes III (A^3Pa), found in different fragmentary copies on that part of the Persepolis platform where early constructions (Artaxerxes I) had become dilapidated (Palace G).[106] As he himself records, Artaxerxes III ordered the construction of a staircase and the execution of reliefs, the sequencing of which evinces a development from earlier models of representing delegations of subject peoples.[107] The inscription A^3Pb (on his tomb) reproduces (ll. 1–8) part of the inscription that may be described as the "Prince's Own Mirror" and was carved on the tomb of Darius I (*DNa*), and it proceeds according to the well-known model of the royal genealogy (ll. 8–21). The captions that identify the thirty throne bearers on Artaxerxes III's tomb duplicate almost exactly the captions of inscription *DNe*, at Naqš-i Rustam. It may also be noted that, as Artaxerxes II had done before him, Artaxerxes III explicitly included Mithra among the gods whose protection he implores for himself and his constructions.

---

[103]   See Briant 2003a: 347–419.
[104]   Esp. Polyaen. *Strat.* 4.3.32, on which see *HPE* 286–92, 921, as well as the recent seminal study by Amigues 2003.
[105]   On Darius III, see Briant 2003a: 40–52.
[106]   See esp. Tilia 1972: 243–4; Roaf 1983: 127–31, 140–1.
[107]   See Calmeyer 1990a: 12–13; *HPE* 734. The inscriptions A^3Pa and A^3Pb have been edited by Schmitt 1990: 114–22 (with specialized bibliography).

Despite the persistent uncertainties involved, it is clear that the royal inscriptions attest that ideological-religious traditions continued, but underwent evolution and adaptation throughout the Achaemenid period (*HPE* 676–9, 998–1001). Several testimonies by the Alexander biographers show that Darius III still invoked the protection of Mithra in his prayers (*HPE* 243, 253).

The persistence of religious and dynastic traditions during the reign of Darius III is also shown by the descriptions given by the classical authors of Alexander's second visit to Pasargadae after his return from India. One detail in these reports, as given by Arrian, that demonstrates the importance that the tomb and the memory of Cyrus the Great had for Alexander (*RTP* 386–393) should be singled out:

> Within the enclosure and by the ascent to the tomb itself there is a small building (οἴκημα σμικρόν) put up for the Magians who used to guard Cyrus' tomb, from as long ago as Cambyses, son of Cyrus (ἔτι ἀπὸ Καμβύσου τοῦ Κύρου), an office transmitted from father to son (παῖς παρὰ πατρὸς ἐκδεχόμενος). The king used to give them a sheep a day, a fixed amount of meal and wine, and a horse each month to sacrifice to Cyrus (καὶ τούτοις πρόβατόν τε ἐς ἡμέραν ἐδίδοτο ἐκ βασιλέως καὶ ἀλεύρων τε καὶ οἴνου τεταγμένα καὶ ἵππος κατὰ μῆνα ἐς θυσίαν τῷ Κύρῳ). (6.29.7; trans. P. A. Brunt)

This passage not only shows unequivocally the continuity of the dynastic and religious tradition in Fārs under Darius III (and even five years after the death of the last Great King), but it also, and especially, informs the debate on the economic bases of the monarchy at this period. In fact, the testimony of Arrian evokes in a compelling way the functioning of a "royal economy" as we know it from the reigns of Darius I, Xerxes, and Artaxerxes I thanks to the Persepolis archives (*HPE* 422–71). Part of this documentation deals with the allocation of various commodities (flour, cereals, livestock) to officiants administering different cults. These allocations are made, on the orders of the king and the highest representatives of the crown, from the institution's stores and/or from the House of the King (Henkelman 2003, 2006). Such is certainly the case here, in the context described by Arrian.[108]

The testimony just cited and the commentary to be added to it on the basis of the Persepolis material open up a different approach for historians of the reign of Darius III. In the absence of any Achaemenid documentation in the proper sense, the Greco-Roman texts on Alexander and the Diadochi, when analyzed against the background outlined above, indicate the persistence of an institutional economy, with its organized means of production and intricate administration, in Fārs throughout the Achaemenid period. Echoes of Achaemenid administrative practice are, for example, clearly discernible in an anecdote (set in 322) related by Plutarch in his *Life of Eumenes* (8.5).[109] Another example, pertaining to a few years earlier

---

[108] As demonstrated in *HPE* 95–6 and 895; 734–6; my interpretation was subsequently followed and elaborated by Henkelman 2003: 152–4, who also comments (153) on a slightly divergent passage in Str. 15.3.7.

[109] See my comments in *RTP* 209 and *HPE* 452.

(325/4) and this time situated in Babylonia, is that of the financial stratagems recorded in the *Oeconomica* of Ps.-Aristotle (2.2.38), which introduce a certain Antimenes. This individual was undoubtedly Alexander's director of finances[110] and it is in this capacity that he issues orders to satraps.[111] He reminds them that their task is to retain a constant level of reserves (ἀναπληροῦν) in the supply stations situated along the royal roads (τοὺς θησαυροὺς τοὺς παρὰ τὰς ὁδοὺς τὰς βασιλικάς) – the places where traveling groups on official business could receive rations, doubtless upon presentation of an authorized travel voucher. The striking similarity with the well-known organization of the road system at the time of the Great Kings unmistakably shows that the orders given by Antimenes were not an innovation; rather, they reflect an Achaemenid heritage (cf. κατὰ τὸν νόμον τὸν τῆς χώρας).[112] The same is true for another measure taken: Antimenes imposed the tithe on all caravans entering Babylon, including "those who bring numerous presents (δῶρα πολλά) <to the king>." In doing so, he reintroduced a regulation that had existed for a long time in Babylon (νόμου . . . ἐν Βαβυλωνίᾳ παλαιοῦ), but that had fallen into disuse (2.2.34). A third measure (2.2.34), another of Antimenes' expedients to replenish Alexander's funds, was to demand that slave owners in the armies register the value of their slaves (ἀνεγράψατο) and pay a specific tax. It is tempting to relate this information to what we know about the taxes levied on slave sales in Babylonia since the reign of Darius I: here too, the royal registries (*karammaru ša šarri*) were in charge of controlling the slave rolls and levying the tax.[113]

Such connections allow the deduction that the material, productive, and administrative basis of taxation and redistributions had continued in more or less the

---

[110] In *Oec.* 2.2.34, Ps.-Aristotle calls him ἡμίολος (conj.; ἡμιόδιος ms.), an appellative that has long been disputed (e.g., Zoepffel 2006: 629–30). Based on the context of his activities, Le Rider 2003: 304–5 has proposed considering him as the official charged with the finances of Babylonia after Harpalus' flight. Müller 2005, in turn, based his analysis on recently published inscription from Asia Minor (*SEG* xlvii: no. 1745) and concludes that Antimenes was Alexander's director of finances. The tentative comparison suggested (381), with the position of Parnakka in the Fortification texts from Persepolis is a bit bold, but certainly suggestive in terms of possible continuities between Achaemenid financial administration and that of Alexander.

[111] See *Oec.* 2.2.38: ἐκέλευε τοὺς σατράπας. Similarly 2.2.34: Antimenes orders the satraps to recover runaway slaves (ἐκέλευσε τὸν σατράπην . . .).

[112] See *HPE* 364–5; 406 (on the term θησαυροί); 364–5 and 453 (on the ambiguous role of Antimenes – but the passage merits a detailed reevaluation); see also Le Rider 2003: 304–10 (analysis of each of the stratagems related in the *Oeconomica*), and 316–19 (Antimenes and the coinage of Alexander).

[113] The existence of this tax in Babylonian has been demonstrated by Stolper 1989b (see *HPE* 413, 935). Comparison with this material allows, in my view, a better understanding of the passage in Ps.-Aristotle, including the clause on the flight of slaves. In a very rigid line of argumentation that, necessarily, is not made explicit, Lane Fox 2007: 290 decides that there has been no continuity, erroneously assuming that the tax was only imposed under Darius I (undoubtedly he misread *HPE* 413). In fact, Stolper's unmistakably shows that the tax is especially known from texts postdating Darius (probably from the reigns of Artaxerxes II and III: 82 n. 2), and that it is subsequently amply attested in the Seleucid period. As the author demonstrates very clearly, we are dealing with a remarkable case of Achaemenid–Hellenistic continuity via Alexander (90–1).

same form into the reigns of the last Great Kings. Only the sustaining (even if only partially) of these traditions, administrative modes, and practices makes it possible to understand how, at the end of the Achaemenid period, the richness and the prosperity of the Persian lands struck eyewitnesses in the way they did: the agricultural wealth was not simply the result of advantageous climatic conditions, but rather that of organized development.[114] This is also the only context that allows us to appreciate how the kings of the fourth century could continue with their building programs, as well as with the reconstruction and maintenance of Persepolis and other royal residences (*HPE* 734–5), or how Alexander could gather enormous herds of pack animals for the transport of the royal treasure.[115] As the measures taken by Antimenes reveal, it was evidently in the best interest of the conqueror to retain in force all the traditions and regulations, since he was the de facto heir of the Persian House of the King (*ulhi sunkina*) in the economic sense that the expression already had in Achaemenid context (*HPE* 463–71, 445–6, 945–7).[116]

Against the above background, one can better understand the episode of the herdsman who, in the winter of 331/30, guided Alexander round the Persian Gates. Plausibly, the son of a mixed marriage and deported to Persia after a Lycian defeat against the Persians, the herdsman is but one of many individuals who constituted the labor force in the service of the institutional economy, those whom the Persepolis tablets call, in generic terminology, the *kurtaš*. These *kurtaš* were recruited from all the empire's populations (one of the most frequently mentioned ethnonyms is that of the *Turmilap* (Τερμίλαι)). A number of them were active in the administration's craft centers where production was organized and closely supervised (*HPE* 433). If we disregard the romantic overtones of the contexts in which they appear, the status of the Greeks "liberated" by Alexander from the *ergastula* of Persepolis, seems perfectly comparable.[117] Other *kurtaš* worked on the fields and on pastures. The tablets also provide documentation on flocks of livestock and their herdsmen (*batera*) whose status undoubtedly was the same as that of the Lycian who guided Alexander at the end of the year 331 through the Persian mountains.[118]

One simply cannot avoid acknowledging that what has been called the "sudden interruption" of the Persepolis archives is an illusory phenomenon, a distorting

---

[114] See esp. D.S. 17.67.3; 19.21.3; Arr. *Ind.* 40.2–3; Str. 15.3.6 (*RTP* 338, *HPE* 733–4). On Arr. *Ind.* 42.5; cf. Briant, forthcoming: 70.

[115] See, e.g., Plu. *Alex.* 37.4; D.S. 17.71.1 (on the numbers see de Callataÿ, *REA* 1989: 263); the pack animals partly came from the royal herds, and partly from subject peoples (cf., e.g., Arr. *Anab.* 3.17.6, with the comments by Henkelman 2005: 159–64).

[116] As Arr. *Anab.* 3.18.11 remarks (through Parmenion), that a lasting conquest cannot be defined by military victories and plundering alone: Alexander would also have to let the economical and fiscal heritage of Darius, to which his victories had given him access, yield profit since he now possessed these as "his own property" (αὐτοῦ κτήματα), both in the present and in the future.

[117] *RTP* 223 n. 353; 329 n. 161; 344 n. 73; *HPE* 735–6.

[118] On the *kurtaš*, see *HPE* 429–39, 456–63; on the episode with the Lycian herdsman see my suggestions in *RTP* 343–4; cf. *HPE* 735.

perspective due to the intrinsically uncertain history of the modes of archiving.[119] It is, at any rate, certainly not the expression of an abrupt annihilation of the "royal economy" evidenced by the texts. Other bureaucratic methods (involving more perishable documents? *HPE* 423) and/or chance preservation suffice to explain "archival silence" after 458.

Once reunited in a single dossier, the texts cited above, as well as others, allow the conclusion that, under Darius III, there was, on the regional level of the Persis as well as on the general level of the empire, still an economic and administrative organization with a logical coherence that was comparable overall with the elaborately documented structures in place during the reign of Darius I.[120] It is thanks to the ample documentation of those "bureaucratic" systems (*RTP* 209) inherited by later kings that we are able to pinpoint their echoes in the Greco-Roman sources on the reigns of Darius III and Alexander. Altogether the daily and/or monthly allocations to the magi at Pasargadae are only the tip of an iceberg of Achaemenid documentation that will, perhaps, one day be revealed more completely.

5   From Darius to Alexander: Empire(s) in Transition

As observed by one of the editors of the Idumean ostraca, "the arrival of Alexander did not result in a sudden disruption of economic life in this region. Aramaic continued to be used and one only replaced the name of the Persian king with that of Alexander."[121] The Aramaic documents from Bactria invite a similar reflection: a list of rations (C4) documents, for a period of three months (June–August), the allocation of cereals (barley, millet, wheat) to various groups. The text itself is dated to "the 15th of Sivan, year 7 of Alexander," that is, July 324; it constitutes one of the proofs that, from one domination to another, the administrative processes and their textual and linguistic expression remained the same, at least in the short term.[122] In this sense, these documents on economic practice nourish the discussion on the continuities and adaptations that mark the transition from the administration of the Great Kings to that of Alexander.

Let us, in conclusion, return to Mazday. At the time that this individual continued to fight at Darius' side (November 333 to November 331), Alexander had

---

[119]   Pending the publication of the international Paris symposium on the Persepolis archives (Briant et al., forthcoming), see the reflections of Henkelman 2006: 96–116, who suggests that the excavated part of the archive was already dormant during the Achaemenid period (and preserved precisely because of that circumstance).

[120]   See already my explicit reflections to this regard in *RTP* 208 and 223 n. 353; 344; 329 (the documentation "suggère le maintien (total ou partiel) de l'organisation sociale et économique achéménide dans le Fārs du vivant d'Alexandre"); see *HPE* 734–6.

[121]   Lemaire 1996: 152; the remark remains valid, independent of the identity of the "Alexander" of the ostraca; see also my remarks in *BHAch* I. 62.

[122]   Shaked 2003: 1526–9; 2004: 17–8; *ADAB* 202–12. Paradoxically, to say the least, the very same document is advanced by Lane Fox 2007: 297 as support for his skepticism on the assumed continuities between the Achaemenids and Alexander!

Figure 8.1   Coin of Mazaeus/Mazday, struck at Tarsus, *c*.350–333 BC. Photo: Dominique Gerin.

his first imperial coinage struck at Tarsus: a coinage that displays undisrupted continuity from the coinages struck by Darius' satrap, if not the rehiring of artists from the satrapal workshops.[123] Thanks to a now celebrated astronomical tablet (*ADRTB*-330), we know that about a month after Gaugamela, and after negotiations with the Babylonians, Alexander appeared before the walls of the imposing Mesopotamian metropolis (November 331). Arrian and Curtius, each in his own style, describe the welcome organized for the conqueror outside the city walls, with representatives of the local elites as well as the Persian leaders: Bagophanes, the *custos* of the royal fortune, and Mazaeus/Mazday. Having fled to the city after the battle, Mazday met Alexander "as a suppliant, with his mature children, and surrendered the city and himself."[124] Next, Mazday was given the post of satrap in

[123]   See Le Rider 2003: 161–5, with my comments in Briant 2006a: 312–17.
[124]   Curt. 5.1.17; on the circumstances of Alexander's entry into Babylon see *HPE* 840–2, 845–50, 1045–6. Despite Lane Fox 2007: 275–7, 297–8 n. 60, the available documentation, when taken together, does indeed show clearly that there had been negotiations (see also Le Rider 2003: 275–6). As to the official entrance into Babylon and other places (*HPE* 189–95), this was, again despite Lane Fox (2007), surely an Achaemenid ceremonial protocol, which in turn was adapted from an Assyro-Babylonian model (Kuhrt 1990). The necessary logistics are clearly referred to in a Babylonian text (official entrance of Artaxerxes II at Susa in 398; text in Joannès 2004: 217–18; see Briant forthcoming. On the use of the image of Mazday in the Napoleonic period see Calmeyer 1990b (see Briant 2003c: 33).

Babylonia, the first appointment of this kind, which was, at the same time, a sign of the continuity of an Iranian policy conceived by Alexander from the moment he embarked on his expedition.[125]

The poorly documented satrapal administration of Mazday (331–328) does not concern us directly in this context, except for one point: numismatic evidence shows not only that, among Alexander's satraps, Mazday was the only one to have minted his own coinage in the province under his control, but also that the types used copied those from the earlier coin series he had struck at Tarsus at the time of the Great Kings. The Babylonian tetradrachms of Mazday bear, on the reverse, his name in Aramaic (MZDY), inscribed over a lion; on the obverse, one finds again a Tarsian motif, that of a figure seated on a throne and the name of the god (Baaltars) inscribed in Aramaic (BLTRZ). Only the standing censer (*thymiaterion*) of the Cilician coinages has disappeared.[126] In other words: these Babylonian mintings provide most eloquent comments on the question of the transition of the empire(s) from Darius to Alexander, and they bear witness to the intermediary role played by a man like Mazday.

[125] Briant 1993a and *HPE* 842–4.
[126] On this complex see the remarkable study by Nicolet-Pierre 1999; see also Le Rider 2003: 274–6 (Mazday himself, in the course of the negotiations that resulted in his coming over to Alexander's side, obtained from the latter the right to coin money with his own name and his own mint types), and Mildenberg 1990–1 = 1998: 9–23. After 328, the motifs are still the same, but they have been partially Hellenized: Babylonian documents from the time of Antigonus refer to the coins as "lion staters."

9

Alexander and the Persian Empire, between "Decline" and "Renovation"

History and Historiography

Pierre Briant

In the late 1970s I first attempted to clarify a debate that dated back to Droysen concerning the question of the continuity, adaptations, and transformations that marked the history, societies, and economy of the regions between the Mediterranean and Central Asia as a result of the conquests of Alexander (Briant 1979a). That study endeavored to promote the idea that Alexander's conquests could not really be understood without a knowledge of the history of the Achaemenid-Persian empire that is as precise and intimate as possible. The unprecedented development of the discipline of Achaemenid history since then has only reinforced my conviction.[1] New collections of sources have come to the light and been published that are powerful incentives to relocate the history of the Macedonian conquest into the middle- to long-term context of first-millennium Near Eastern history.[2]

I have revisited the above theme frequently since 1979a[3] – if only to emphasize that Rostovtzeff had previously pleaded strongly for this approach (Briant 2000d). If I again address the question here, within the framework of a necessarily concise contribution, it is to organize my reflections about the history of a well-defined theme: the economic transformations brought to the Middle East by the Macedonian conquest. The traditional error (and one which I too have not escaped[4]) is to consider Droysen's 1833 study, followed by updated editions until 1877, as the obligatory and exclusive starting point for any investigation of this type.[5]

---

[1]   On this progress, see my assessments, 2003c and *BHAch* I.

[2]   See, e.g., Shaked 2004 and the papers in Briant and Joannès 2006.

[3]   See in particular Briant 2000b, 2003d, 2005–6, 2006a; *HPE* 1007–8. In his recent article (kindly given me by the author), Lane Fox 2006 offers a counter-argument to my past studies, including skeptical remarks on the expression I used in 1979 ("the last of the Achemenids"); but I had already emphasized that it was just a metaphor.

[4]   I explored the eighteenth-century historiography of Alexander in my lectures at the Collège de France in 2004–5 (see 2005d), to which I have returned. See Briant 2005a, 2006c, 2007a, 2007b.

[5]   See, *inter alia*, Borza 1967: xii: "It may be said that modern scholarship began in 1833 with the initial publication of a biography by Johann Gustav Droysen. Droysen was a product of a nineteenth century

Admittedly, Droysen developed his theses about the profound transformations that Alexander would have introduced in the lands of the Achaemenid empire, and these theses, in turn, were either embraced enthusiastically or contested without the slightest reserve by his peers and successors. But as E. Bikerman (1944–5: 382)[6] and A. Momigliano (1952: 364–6) both suggested, the debate on the nature and the extent of the transformations introduced by Alexander's conquests started well before 1833.[7] Between the eighteenth and nineteenth centuries, it was generally assumed that "Achaemenid decline" and "Asian stagnation" were followed by a phase of profound "economic regeneration" that was initiated by Alexander and resulted from the Macedonian conquest. The aim of the following pages is to identify the origins and foundations of this view and the variations thereof.

I

During the seventeenth and eighteenth centuries historians and scholars collected the heritage of Classical antiquity, a corpus in which, traditionally, Greek vigor and Macedonian strength were contrasted with the weakness of the Persian empire. The latter was usually defined by its state of political and territorial disorganization, by its corrupting luxury, and by its irreversible military inferiority, in short by, to use the traditional expression, "Achaemenid decadence." According to a tenacious stereotype, which can be traced back to Greek authors, this empire was wealthy and weak at the same time.[8] It suffices to examine a single example, the *Histoire ancienne* by Charles Rollin, which was published from 1730 onward to exceptional acclaim in all European states. Influenced by Bossuet (1681), Rollin developed a catastrophic view of the Persian enemy and its continuous decline from Xerxes to Darius III. Based on the same pedagogical and political presuppositions (the values to be impressed upon a prince), Rollin condemned Alexander's excesses, which he saw corrupted by Asian luxuries:[9] "In imitation of the Persian kings he turned his palace into a seraglio, filling it with three hundred and sixty concubines (the same number Darius kept) and with bands of eunuchs, of all mankind the most infamous" (Rollin 1791: 168).

As the polemic brought forth by the Abbé Mably (1709–85) against Montesquieu (1689–1755) shows, two opposing visions developed on the consequences of Alexander's victories. Referring to Machiavellian authority (*The Prince*, ch. 4), the

---

school of German historiography which had developed the principles of modern critical method." In fact, Droysen is also the conscious heir of the discussions and reflections that had been going on about Alexander in Europe since the Enlightenment (see Briant 2005a, 2005–6, 2006c).

[6]   On Bikerman's review article, too often omitted in recent studies, see my comments in Briant 2005b: 42–9.

[7]   See in particular Briant 2005a, 2005b, 2005–6, 2006c.

[8]   See Hdt. 5.49 and my discussion in *HPE* 691–876.

[9]   Rollin 1821: vi. 346–71; see Briant 2003d.

former argued that Alexander did not change anything essential in an empire characterized by its gigantic structures, its despotism, and its decadence. In his eyes, it is the same despotism that was maintained before and after the conquest: "The revolution that passed the crown of Darius on to Alexander's head was not a revolution for the state, it remained in the same condition" (Mably 1766: 226). As a contrasting perspective, starting with Montesquieu, we see a profound evolution in Alexander's image. He appears more and more as an organizing conqueror and a man of exceptional political talent, who transformed the structures of an empire that, at the same time, he was both conquering and adapting.

The role Alexander played in opening new commercial routes was in fact pointed out prior to Montesquieu. The competition among the great powers which led to the creation of the various oriental Indian companies (England, France, Holland, etc.), prompted political leaders to order reports on the nature of the Indian trade since antiquity. It was thus on Colbert's urgent demands that the bishop P.-D. Huet wrote his *Histoire du commerce et de la navigation dans l'Antiquité* (published in 1713), a work that was subsequently translated into every European language and in turn inspired the publication of many similar works in many different languages throughout that century.[10] Among the major steps in the evolution of the paradigm is Huet's strong emphasis on the transformations that were brought by Alexander, himself totally unlike the Great Kings, who were uninterested in anything connected with the sea and navigation after the middle of the fifth century BC:

> Things were in that state when Alexander attacked the Persian Empire; by this conquest, so to speak, the face of the world was changed and a great revolution in commercial affairs was brought about. One must thus look at this conquest, and particularly the capture of Tyre and the foundation of Alexandria, as a new era in commerce. The change in the way of governing and in the interests of the populations, having opened new ports and passages, he gave a new route for the conduct of trade. (Huet 1713: 91–2)

Although deeply hostile toward Alexander, Rollin, following Huet, attributed to him too "the great revolution in commercial affairs," as a result of the destruction of Tyre and the foundation of Alexandria (1821: vi. 469). Huet's formula was also taken up by Montesquieu, but this time it was integrated into a coherent and global vision of the Macedonian conquest, already introduced in the 1748 edition of his *Esprit des Lois* (xxi. 7) and particularly developed in the posthumous edition of 1757.[11] Though Huet and Montesquieu differed on the reasons for the lack of interest in maritime commerce attributed to the Persians,[12] and on the final aims of

---

[10] On the forgotten place of Huet in the historiography of Alexander, see in particular Larrère 2002; Briant 2006c: 17–26; among many other works of the same type, see Schlözer 1761; Ameilhon 1766; Berghaus 1797.

[11] See Volpilhac-Auger 2002; Briant 2005–6.

[12] For Huet, the explanation must be sought in the constraints imposed on the Persians in defending immense frontiers; for Montesquieu, religious precepts prohibited the Persians from dedicating

Alexander,[13] they agreed on a more fundamental level. Managed according to meticulously prepared plans, and accompanied by a political friendship with the Persians and the local populations (x. 13–14), the Macedonian conquest brought about major disruptions in commercial exchanges, in particular by the opening of a direct route between the Indus river valley and Babylon via the Persian Gulf:

> Four events occurred under Alexander that produced a great revolution in commerce: the capture of Tyre, the conquest of Egypt, that of the Indies, and the discovery of the sea to the south of that country . . . He had scarcely arrived in the Indies when he had new fleets built and set sail on the Eulaeus, the Tigris, the Euphrates and the sea; he removed the cataracts the Persians had put in these rivers; he discovered that the Persian Gulf was a gulf of the ocean. As he set out to explore this sea, in the same way he had explored that of the Indies, as he had a port for a thousand vessels and arsenals built in Babylon, as he sent five hundred talents to Phoenicia and Syria in order to attract pilots whom he wanted to settle in the colonies that he built along the coasts, and finally, as he did immense work on the Euphrates and the other Assyrian rivers, one cannot doubt that his design was to engage in commerce with the Indies through Babylon and the Persian Gulf.[14]

Several historians from the second half of the eighteenth century insisted on the establishment of commerce between east and west. Even if it cannot be reduced to a single explanation, it seems clear that this new historiographical orientation is to be linked directly with the interests of the European superpowers in the east, and particularly with the profits derived from commerce, after the Portuguese had opened a new direct route to India via the Cape of Good Hope (1498). It is at this time that Arrian's *Indica* was rediscovered, considered by its first commentators as a vade mecum for navigators and explorers coming from Europe.[15] It is on Arrian that Montesquieu essentially founded the revised edition of the *Esprit des Lois*.

Influenced by Montesquieu, the work written by William Vincent in 1797 on the voyage of Nearchus is again very clear in its outlook. Not only did the author emphasize the assistance to his research he had received from the employees of the East India Company (x–xii), but he also established a direct link between Nearchus' voyage in the Persian Gulf and the expansionist and commercial enterprises of modern Europe:

> Historical facts demand our attention in proportion to the interest we feel, or the consequences we derive from them; and the consequences of this voyage as such, that is, in the first instance, it opened a communication between Europe and the most distant countries of Asia, so, at a later period, was it the sources and the origin of the

---

themselves to the navigation of rivers and the sea (an explanation endorsed later on only by W. Robertson 1791: 201): see Briant 2006c: 20–33.

[13]   Contrary to Huet, Montesquieu did not consider that Alexander was fighting for the *monarchie universelle*: see Volpilhac-Auger 2002 and Larrère 2002.

[14]   Montesquieu 1989: 364–7.

[15]   This image is already in place with Ramusio in 1563.

Portuguese discoveries, the foundation of the greatest commercial system ever introduced into the world; and consequently, the primary cause, however remote, of the British establishments in India. (Vincent 1797: 2–3)[16]

The positive transformation brought by Alexander in the history of commercial relations were emphasized by other authors as well, for example, by William Robertson in his work on India (1791–2; cf. Briant 2005a), and John Gillies in his famous study on the history of Greece, published in 1786:

> His only remaining care was to improve and consolidate his conquest. For these important purposes, he carefully examined the course of the Eulaeus, the Tigris, and the Euphrates; and the indefatigable industry of his troops was judiciously employed in removing the weirs or dams, by which the timid ignorance of the Assyrian and Persian kings had obstructed the navigation of these great rivers. But Alexander, having no reason to dread fleets of war, wished to invite those to commerce. The harbors were repaired; arsenals were constructed; a bason was formed at Babylon sufficient to contain a thousand galleys. By these and similar improvements, he expected to facilitate internal intercourse among his central provinces, while, by opening new channels of communication, he hoped to unite the wealthy countries of Egypt and the East, with the most remote regions of the earth. (Gillies 1831[1786]: 430)

Introduced by Gillies and reiterated by W. Robertson following Huet and Montesquieu, the theme of the destruction of the cataracts would become a metaphor for change throughout the nineteenth and twentieth centuries: the installation of these obstacles ("weirs", "dams") across the Tigris and Euphrates during the Persian era, and then their removal by Alexander, then symbolized the passage from a closed economy to an open economy (Briant 2006c; 2008).

The vision set forth by Huet and Montesquieu found an especially determined opponent in the person of the Baron Sainte-Croix. When, in the first edition of his book (1775: 252–3), the author, following Huet, admits that "Nearchus left memoirs of the expeditions that were useful for war and commerce," he also opposed Montesquieu's views regarding Alexander's colonies and their supposed commercial functions. He surmised that the speed of the military marches were incompatible with the conception and the application of a long-term policy (96–8). His criticism is even more detailed and firm in the second edition, and it also targets W. Robertson and W. Vincent. Sainte-Croix vigorously reiterates his doubts on the existence of the "scheme" attributed to Alexander "of expanding geographical knowledge and multiplying commercial relations that could unite the different parts of the world," and he issues a final judgment: "One makes of the victor of Darius and Porus an armed merchant, and one gives to the emulator of Hercules the ideas of a factory chief . . . To attribute to Alexander, in this state of frenzy, great

---

[16]   See also the commentaries of Heeren (1830: 357 and n. 1): "[Nearchus] gave us an exact description that is still used to this day by navigators. . . . This comparison of relations by the English captains and the accounts of Alexander's admiral that were advantageous to the latter: it has confirmed almost every detail."

views of commerce, isn't that creating a debased form of history?" (1804: 416, 418). In spite of the renown of Sainte-Croix and his work, his restrictive interpretation was not widely echoed. The larger part of historiography at the end of the eighteenth and the beginning of the nineteenth centuries continued to see Alexander as the first to have opened Europe up to the riches of Egypt, Mesopotamia, and India, decidedly striving to trigger profound transformations in these parts. This tendency goes hand in hand with a persistent lack of knowledge about the Persian empire, still considered as an empire undermined by despotism, lack of unity, and decadence. Even though an author like Arnold Heeren describes how entire regions of the Persian empire were developed thanks to irrigation, he does not directly infer that the Great Kings had made productive investments, positive results of which were still observed well into the Hellenistic era. Heeren, citing Polybius (10.28) and James Morier (1812: 163), is one of the few to mention the importance of the underground canals of the Persians,[17] but he first draws the lesson that these facilities could have been destroyed by any of the many invasions that the country witnessed (Heeren 1830: 89).

II

When the young Droysen (born in 1808) began to write his book on Alexander in the fall of 1831, he benefited from the historiographic advances of the previous generations. Proceeding from these, he too would present the great economic successes of Alexander, namely, the minting of the immobile treasures of Persia and their reintegration into the economic and commercial circuits (1883: 360, 687–9);[18] the abolishment of all levies in kind, and the transformation of the royal court into a locus that was rather creating and diffusing wealth (689–90); the grand works in Greece and Asia (690); the creation of new commercial routes by removing the cataracts in the Tigris (650–1), and by the opening up of direct contacts between the Indus and Babylon (597–603). In Droysen's view, there is no doubt that this is a totally innovative set of policies, consciously developed by the Macedonian conqueror:

> All of these are enough to show the importance of the commercial successes of Alexander from an economic point of view. Perhaps, from this perspective, we have never seen one man's influence producing such a sudden transformation, so profound and on such an immense territory. This transformation was not the result of mere accidental circumstances, but, as much as one can judge, it was wanted and pursued with full intention to fulfill its goal. (Droysen 1877: ii. 296–7; 1883: 690–1)

---

[17]   See Briant 2001b. The first author to use Polybius in the same sense was Montesquieu 1989: 289; see Briant 2007b.

[18]   I am working from the French translation of 1883 (published in a German edition 1877: ii. 255–7; 290–8); on this point, the 1877 text has almost no changes from that of 1833 (507–9; 538–45).

Like his predecessors, Droysen (1877: ii. 296 n. 1; 1883: 690 n. 4) simply refers, at this point, to *De fortuna Alexandri* (1.5, 18), where Plutarch aims to present Alexander not as a conqueror coming to ravage Asia like a brigand, but as a civilizer coming to promote world unity on the basis of Greek values. Altogether, Droysen's analysis has nothing profoundly original. Described by B. Bravo (1968: 136 n. 164), as "a rational, lucid, political, methodical hero crafting grandiose plans," Droysen's Alexander is very similar to the Alexander of Montesquieu and his followers. This is particularly evident in the pages dedicated to the creation of the route to India and the reopening of waterways in Babylon (Briant 2006c, 2007b), but similar observations can be made concerning other aspects. Take, for example, what Droysen writes about the profound transformations that, according to him, Alexander brought to the fiscal system in force under the Great Kings, and the inferences he draws from this regarding the resulting economic boom:

> What was most harmful, amongst the Persians, was the infinite number of duties in kind; for the royal court alone, they were estimated at 13000 talents a year, and each satrap and dynasty followed, in his region, the example of the Great King. Certain clues point to Alexander actually abolishing this system of payments of kind . . . The sojourn of the royal court now came to boast the prosperity of a city or a country just as much as the presence of the Great King had previously exhausted it. The pomp that the king was surrounded by, particularly in the later years, no longer bore down on the peoples, but created to the contrary, growth and prosperity of commerce . . . (1877: ii. 295; 1883: 689–90)

Two references in the Pseudo-Aristotelian text *Oeconomica* (2.32, 39) seem to justify the hypothesis on the removal of levies in kind (1877: ii. 295 n. 2; 1883: 689 n. 2). The first introduces a certain Antimenes, who was selling to soldiers merchandise saved in storage units (*thesauroi*) situated along the royal roads; Droysen argues that another anecdote is supposed to confirm this system of "voluntary services obtained through force."[19]

From a historiographic point of view, the important thing is to observe that debate on payment in kind in the Persian empire had already been started by A. Heeren and Fr. Schlosser. In relation to the mode of remuneration of the officers and the administrators of the Great Kings (Heeren 1830: 514–24), the former cites the passage in Athenaeus (4.146) related to the Great King's table: he saw in it the typical expression of a despotic regime, whose principle it is to live at the expense of its subject peoples (Heeren 1830: 514; 1824: 262). As for Schlosser, he too cites Athenaeus extensively (1828: 2 n. 2) in order to show to what extent the contributions made for the king's table were constricting; he also refers to Polyaenus (4.3.32) to illustrate, as a contrast, the relief measures taken by Alexander.[20] In addition,

---

[19] The text (2.32) is also cited in the 1833 edition: 541–2; on its place in more recent discussions see *HPE* 364–5, 453; Le Rider 2003: 303–10.

[20] Schlosser 1828: 2: "Alexander, one can say, tipped a bronze column that was an edict to this subject; but it was no doubt due to simply to the fact that the edict was unreasonable, and not to disprove the luxuriousness of the Persian kings." For this passage of Polyaenus, see *HPE* 286–92 and Amigues 2003.

speaking of the imperial administration that was put in place, Schlosser does not fail to comment on the passages in Pseudo-Aristotle on "Philoxenus and Cleomenes" (1828: 12–18). In 1812, B.-G. Niebuhr had already emphasized the interest and the importance of the Pseudo-Aristotelian text, which he saw originating in western Asia Minor in the entourage of satraps of the Hellenistic era (Niebuhr 1828[1812]). Although Droysen never cites Niebuhr, Heeren, or Schlosser, there is no doubt that any German student of ancient history had read these authors during his course of study at the university – particularly Droysen who had taken Boeckh's seminars in Berlin.

Droysen's treatment of the theme of "Alexander the renovator of the economy," provokes two additional reflections. It is clear, first, that the insistence on this aspect of Alexander's politics results from the assumption – accepted without reserve in Europe at that time and still destined for a long life (see Briant 2003d: 116–26) – that conquered Asia was in a state of stagnation and enslaved by its own despotic regime. Thus, at Alexander's arrival, "the Persian Empire had reached the point at which it had exhausted the constituent elements of the power that lay at the base of its successes; it looked as though it could only maintain itself thanks to the inert force of the established fact" (Droysen 1883: 48). It is from Xerxes' reign onward that "one started to notice the signs of stagnation and decline, to which the empire, incapable of internal development, had to succumb as soon as it would cease to grow through its victories and conquests" (Droysen 1883: 53–4). Without utilizing the expression, Droysen in fact analyzes the Persian empire through the "predatory state" model, in which the political and social elites nourish themselves from tributary levies of any sort, to the detriment of any productive investment. Such a state is necessarily hit by stagnation as soon as it can no longer increase the number of its subjects. At the same time, stagnation accentuates even more the harshness of these levies, and it feeds the hostile sentiments among the subject states. Hence the enormous change brought about by Alexander, by whose actions the immense riches held by the Great Kings for more than two centuries, hoarded away in their citadels and treasuries, were given back to commercial circulation and regained their productive power:

> One of the most energetic fermenting agents that was working this world in a state of formation must have been the immense mass of precious metals that the conquest of Asia had put into Alexander's hands. . . . When the new royal power which reigned in Asia now gave flight to these hidden riches, when it let them overflow from his breast, like the heart pumps out blood, it is easy to understand that work and commerce began to spread them, by an ever increasing speed of circulation, through the longtime tired limbs of the empire; one can see how, by these means, the economic life of the peoples, which the Persian domination had sucked out their strengths like a vampire, revived and prospered . . . (Droysen 1883: 687)[21]

---

[21]   See also Droysen 1833: 537; 1877: ii. 294; on the Droysenian concept of monetary circulation and its links with the economic theories of the eighteenth century, see the comments in Briant 2005d: 593–4.

With the above, Droysen took up his position in a debate that had started over a century before in Europe, and that was to develop further. In his opinion, there is no doubt that Alexander was not simply a war leader; he also kept in mind the well-being of the inhabitants of the empire that he was conquering and transforming. In fact, for Droysen, ever since the battle of Gaugamela Alexander was convinced that "his power . . . had to find in the good deeds that it brought to the defeated his apology, and through the adhesion of the people his support and his future" (1883: 346). The same reflection is attributed to Alexander when he was in the Indus Delta a few years later: "His power, which for the first time put in direct contact people from furthest lands, had not to be simply founded on the strength of the weapons, but more on the interests of the people themselves" (1883: 597). And here is how Droysen finally introduces the work of the builder during the last two years of the reign: "And it was from there, one could conclude, that started the second part of the task that Alexander imposed on himself, the peaceful work, which, harder than the victories of arms, had to justify them by strengthening the results and assuring them a future" (1883: 684). In this assessment, Droysen is in agreement with the philosophers and historians of the eighteenth and early nineteenth centuries who felt that the grandeur of a king should not be evaluated on the basis of his military victories, but rather on the basis of the happiness of his people. The historiography of Alexander was itself split between groups of historians: those who condemned him for having spread terror and bloodshed for his sole glory, including the destruction of an existing economy,[22] and those who praised him for having introduced the agents of a positive transformation in the countries previously dominated by the Persians: it is this second perspective that Droysen so clearly illustrates.

III

In Germany, reviews of Droysen's book took a rather critical tone, either because the reviewers emphasized what they considered a questionable use of sources, or because they questioned the too favorable portrait of the Macedonian conqueror. The reception was also mixed in England, as shown by the contrasting responses by Connop Thirlwall and George Grote,[23] including that on the question of economic transformations brought forth (or not) by Alexander. Thirlwall repeated Droysen's views unaltered:

> His main object undoubtedly was to found a solid and flourishing empire. . . .
> The mere circulation of the immense treasures accumulated [by the Great Kings] . . .

[22] See the interesting example offered by the popular book by J. Abbott still in print today: "He was, throughout most of his career, a destroyer. He roamed over the world to interrupt commerce, to break in upon and to disturb the peaceful pursuits of industry, to batter down city walls, and burn dwellings, and kill men" (Abbott 1848: 162).

[23] On these two authors and their context and thoughts on Alexander, see Briant 2005b: 18–27.

was doubtless attended by innumerable happy results: by a great immediate increase
of the general well-being, by a salutary excitement of industry and commercial activity.
The spirit of commerce was ... more directly roused ... by the foundation of new
cities ..., by the opening of new channels of communication between opposite
extremities of empire, and the removals of obstructions [across the rivers] arising
from the feebleness and wantonness of the ancient government ..., by the confidence
inspired by the new order of things ... (Thirlwall 1839: vii. 110–11)

Grote, on the other hand, accepted that the opening of new channels for commerce
and the geographical exploration resulted in positive transformations in countries
now dominated by the Macedonians; he says nothing, however, of the consequences
of the circulation of Persian treasures, nor of the destructions of the cataracts when
he mentions (1862: viii. 451–2) Alexander's navigation on the Tigris and refers to
the crucial passage in Arrian (7.7). The line of argument is simple. Grote does not
believe that Alexander had any project which targeted economic development. In
imagining what could have been the later career of the conqueror, he strongly takes
position against the image that Montesquieu had created and which Droysen later
developed, and instead adopts the thesis of a pure and simple continuity in terms
of despotism and levy of tribute:

We see nothing in prospect except years of ever-repeated aggression and
conquest. ... The acquisition of universal dominion ... was the master passion of his
soul. ... The mere task of acquiring and maintaining, – of keeping satraps and tribute-
gatherers in authority as well as in subordination–, of suppressing resistances ever
liable to recur in regions distant by months of march, – would occupy the whole life
of a world-conqueror, without leaving any leisure for the improvements suited to
peace and stability, if we give him credit for such purposes in theory. But even this
last is more than can be granted. Alexander's acts indicate that he desired nothing
better than to take up the traditions of the Persian empire: a tribute-levying and army-
levying system, under Macedonians, in large proportion, as his instruments; yet partly
also under the very same Persians who had administered before, provided they submitted to him. (1862: viii. 468–9)

The clash between Droysen's thesis on the one side and Grote's on the other
continued without interruption during the nineteenth and twentieth centuries
(Briant 2005b: 27–61). The success of the image of Alexander as the "great economist" is due, it seems to me, to the conjunction of two historiographic currents: the
scientific prestige of the position taken by Wilcken, on the one hand, and the influence of "colonial geography" on the other.

As a renowned scholar,[24] Ulrich Wilcken (1862–1944) showed a particular admiration for Droysen. When, in 1893–4, two volumes of Droysen's *Kleine Schriften*
were published, the editor asked Wilcken to add his own reading notes and critical
comments to a new edition of Droysen's 1831 thesis. These notes span more
than ten tightly packed pages (ii. 432–43). They are introduced by an eulogistic

[24]   See the short presentation by Borza 1967: xix–xxi.

appreciation: "More than sixty years after its publication, the work of the young Droysen . . . remains to this day the starting point for any new treatment of the theme." The formula was repeated in *Alexander der Große* which appeared in 1931, and which was explicitly presented by its author as the continuation of Droysen's monograph, a pioneering book, "fundamental and inspiring" (Wilcken 1931: vii; 1967: xxix, 325).

Actually, in this work one can recognize all of Droysen's theses on the developments set into motion by Alexander's conquests, but they are hereafter in a way legitimated by the indisputable scientific prestige of a scholar who dedicated himself to the analysis of the ancient economy. One distinguishes this tendency particularly in the last three chapters of the book. Wilcken revisits several times Alexander's grandiose plans:

> He kept in view the great plan of finding a way by sea from the Indus to the Tigris and Euphrates, and if he succeeded, of forming a connection between the western empire and his new colonial empire in India. . . . The trade of India would be connected with that of Hither Asia, and wide perspectives opened to world-commerce throughout his Empire. (Wilcken 1967: 194)

The destruction of the cataracts (dams) in the Tigris was one element of that great plan, since it permitted accessibility to a river that the Persians had closed off to commerce (218, 255). For this and other reasons, Wilcken holds a view on Alexander that was already Droysen's:

> We see Alexander too as an economist who knew already what he was aiming at, when we recall what he has already related in detail about his development of trade and intercourse. . . . All these are achievements and designs of colossal dimensions, which display a genius at work, who intended to divert into the paths he regarded as right the world commerce of his world-empire. (255)

He returns to this notion in his last chapter, which is dedicated to the legacy of Alexander's conquests:

> The economic revolutions which have been described as brought about by Alexander's conquest of Asia and Egypt, and which confronted the Greek merchant and industrialist in the East, in process of time increasingly influenced the economic development of Greece itself; the whole foundation indeed of Greek trade in the Mediterranean was changed . . . (293–4)

The power of conviction expressed by Wilcken in these analyses is even more notable in that he never ceased to insist on them throughout his career. They had already been clearly presented in a 1921 article, which made a lasting impression on the minds of historians: the study, which was explicitly in the same vein as Droysen's (very often cited in the footnotes), seemed to establish with certitude the decisive role played by Alexander in the economic disruption of the world

(Wilcken 1931: 349–61), the impact of which was followed by the author down to the evolutions of Ptolemaic and Roman Egypt. Wilcken's strong support, on the whole, would play a decisive role in relaying and legitimizing the thesis expressed a century earlier by Droysen.

The historiographical influence of Ulrich Wilcken's vision was of an astonishingly fruitful kind. Even those who contested the existence of a minute and scrupulous design planned by Alexander were ready to admit that, "for centuries, the global economy of antiquity was determined by this twelve year work."[25] It would be easy to mention numerous later authors who cite him favorably. In 1939, R. Cohen, while admitting that "the documentary evidence is particularly rare and subject to almost contradictory interpretations" (434), brings forward very firm propositions regarding the politics of economic transformations conducted by Alexander:

> To update procedures of a thousand years old culture: to plant in Asia the trees that have made the fortune of Greece; to install at the crossroads of trails marked by nature and local customs, citadels under the shade of which the merchants can peacefully trade; to fix canals that had become impassable; to improve the course of rivers; in short, to help everywhere in the development of prosperity . . . (1939b: 417)

The same author calls Alexander "a great economist" and concludes his account in the following manner: "What more is needed to assure him of an immense place in the history of universal economics?" (1939a: 248).[26] In the same period, one can cite M. Rostovtzeff who, in his conclusion, specifically addresses the issue of the "reclaimed land" (1941: ii. 1160–2). Aside from the drainage works documented for Greece itself and the improvements conducted in Ptolemaic Egypt, Rostovtzeff did not fail, by citing Arrian, Aristobulus, Wilcken, and Cohen (iii. 1609 n. 96), to mention explicitly and as parallels the works undertaken by Alexander in Babylonia, including those on the Tigris (1160–1).

This very "modernist" point of view presented by both Droysen and Wilcken,[27] taken and developed in the reference books on Alexander and/or on the ancient economy, was even more easily adopted since it was consistent with the vision of the world as seen through the history of European colonization. In this context, Alexander had been styled a model colonial, according to a very simple rationale: from Alexander to the present, Europe has brought economic progress to countries that had fallen into profound lethargy and were stuck in structural stagnation

---

[25]   As expressed by P. Roussel (1932: 53) in his overlapping reviews of Wilcken 1931 and Radet 1931, where he calls into question "the systematic characterization" of the administrative organization of the empire postulated by Wilcken; precisely as Radet had done (1931: 413, 422), Roussel cited Montesquieu and the rational image he gave of Alexander (Montesquieu 1989: 148–51), but, altogether, he nevertheless felt that many of Alexander's decisions "escape . . . analysis" (60).

[26]   In these two cases, Cohen refers to Wilcken (Cohen 1939a: 246 n. 145, 247 n. 156; 1939b: 434–5).

[27]   For Droysen's modern vision of the economy, see the apt comments by Bravo 1968: 355–7.

(see Briant 1979b). Among many other examples, let us simply cite V. Duruy's assessment of Alexander's economic achievements, from a manual for young students:

> Commerce, the link between nations, developed on an immense scale and met with routes either new or pacified that Alexander had opened; – the ports, building sites, places of refuge or way stations that he had prepared; – the industry vividly solicited by these immense treasures previously sterile, now brought into circulation from the lavish hand of the conqueror. (Duruy 1858)

The vision of the conquest would also fit within a discipline that the French geographer Albert Demangeon would baptize in 1923 as "colonial geography," starting from the example of the British empire.[28] Here is how the author defines it, separating it from two other disciplines, history and regional geography:

> Our main object is to study the effects arising from the contact between two types of peoples who are called upon to associate with each other in a colony: the one civilized, well provided with capital and material goods, in search of new wealth, thoroughly mobile, and alive to the spirit of enterprise and adventure, the strange and the unknown; the other isolated and self-centered, faithful to its ancient modes of living, with a limited outlook, and ill equipped with weapons and tools. Our task is to explain how the colonizing race has gone to work to exploit his new territory, to create wealth, and to rule and employ natives . . . (Demangeon 1925: 11–12)

The author introduces the chapter entitled "The Weapons of British Colonization" (105–50) as follows:

> To colonize a country is to increase its trading capacity, to link it up with the world system of communications, to make its soil bring forth crops by giving it or restoring to it its fertility, to exploit its resources in the matter of labor, to break down those forces of inertia which hold it bound, and to inoculate its organism with the vital ferment prepared in the hothouses of Europe. (Demangeon 1925: 105)

The author studies successively: (1) means of transport; (2) irrigation works; (3) British capital; (4) scientific investigation and research. Of course, as indicated by item 3, Demangeon was not thinking about antiquity or Alexander. But what one sees is that the proposed conceptual framework adapts itself very well to the European vision of Alexander's conquests: the development of means of transportation, the integration of the east into a global commercial network, the irrigation works that will increase tenfold the profitability of the land, and the enterprises of discovery. The words and expressions used by Demangeon are identical to those used by historians who like to present Alexander's conquests as a scientific enterprise:

---

[28] Demangeon's work (1923) was translated immediately into English by E. F. Row, without any change (Demangeon 1925: 5); that translation is cited here.

The power of material resources is not sufficient in itself to endow a colony with life. In most cases material exploitation needs to be directed by a preliminary process of methodological inquiry and scientific research. The art of colonization does not consist merely in the crude appropriations of wealth. It presupposes also an intellectual appropriation of the colonial territory, – a knowledge of the general conditions of relief, climate, flora, fauna, and inhabitants of the country in question. A man cannot live without knowledge of its surroundings and it is only when he has this knowledge that he can arrange and adapt them to its use. (Demangeon 1925: 119)

Demangeon's definitions are not particularly original; fundamentally, they put into focus ideas and images that, since the seventeenth and eighteenth centuries, the discipline of geography had already partially brought forward. Indeed, one cannot emphasize enough the role played by geography, and geographers and cartographers, in the process of making the geo-historiography of Alexander. The history of Alexander finds itself at the crossroads of the history of discoveries, the history of geography, the history of commerce, and the history of European colonization. The systematic nature of Demangeon's study clearly demonstrates how this body of doctrine has now become largely accepted, including by historians who are interested in the conquests of Alexander and its consequences in economic terms.

IV

In a 1966 attempt to offer a synthesis of major recent studies, G. T. Griffith did not include any article that, in his eyes, would have contained new approaches to the matter of the profound transformations brought about by Alexander's conquest. He clearly explained this in the volume's introduction, and his reasons deserve to be cited in their entirety:

The administration of his empire, though our record of it is very defective, and consequently a subject for controversy, raises only one question that is absolutely vital, namely how far if all at all Alexander changed the system which he found existing in it already. The answer to this question goes some way, perhaps much of the way, towards answering how far if at all Alexander was a man of reflection and a planner, and not predominantly a man of action in war and of improvisation in the art of peace. This approach to him has not yet been made, so far as I know, in any study of a scope for inclusion in this selection (perhaps it is not possible); if it were possible, it would be a valuable step forwards arriving at our final view of the essential Alexander. (Griffith 1966: ix)

Forty years later, an overall evaluation risks not being much more optimistic. Having taken into account the bibliographical surveys published between 1950 and

1993 and the thematic volumes published in the past ten years,[29] one can only state, in fact, that the economic consequences of the Macedonian conquest do not raise much interest among historians. It is not mentioned in the work of Seibert (1972),[30] and one of the most recent manuals simply refers, with regard to these questions, to Wilcken 1931 and Rostovtzeff 1941 (Wiemer 2005: 176–7, 222), exactly as Schachermeyr had done thirty years before (1973: 534–5). The place that Wilcken's book still occupies in the debate is entirely characteristic of the state of research. When, in 1974, E. N. Borza gathered studies revolving around the question of the fortunate and/or unfortunate consequences of Alexander's conquest ("Civilizer or Destroyer"), he decided to introduce the question of the economic impact: to this end, once again Wilcken 1931 was introduced as the only one authoritative contributor (Borza 1974: 149–59: "The Economic View"). In implicit or explicit opposition to Wilcken and his modernist approach, other historians, not necessarily all with a Marxist[31] orientation, have insisted on the conqueror's ambitions, which were solely aimed at introducing levies, and thus insisted on the absence of any economic development.[32] This, then, brings us back to the vision imposed by Grote more than a century earlier, while at the same time the new approach owes much to the disruption of the relations between Europe and the colonies after 1945 (Briant 2005b: 42–9).[33]

These reflections bring us back to the question of continuity and change. The traditional view of *change* has always been founded on two very closely linked elements: Achaemenid decadence and stagnation as opposed to the economic boom and development triggered by Alexander. It was accepted that the process of Greek revitalization was even more spectacular due to the fact that the Near East was in a state of total prostration. This view persisted as it allowed more forceful argument for the justification of an enterprise which, far from being limited to brutal conquest, was supposed to have brought progress to populations choked by a backward despotism (Briant 2003a: 116–26). Consequently, scholars considered that the peoples of the Persian empire had called for the conquest themselves: "The Near East was being prepared to accept any invader who would offer a firm and efficient administration" (e.g., Olmstead 1948: 487). In short, the history of "Achaemenid decline" and the theme of "oriental backwardness" in contrast to the

---

[29]   See bibliographical references in Briant 2005c: 124–5, and Wiemer 2005.

[30]   The same is true for Lane Fox 2006, though it is explicitly dedicated to the problem of the imperial succession from the Achaemenids to Alexander.

[31]   See, e.g., the discussion by Kreissig 1982: 62–74 that, also in citing Finley (64), denounced in many different ways the conclusions found in "*bourgeois* historiography." For the Marxist point of view, see Jähne 1978 (a discussion based on a combined review of the works of the Russian scholar Shofman 1976, Schachermeyr 1973, Wirth 1973, and Seibert 1972).

[32]   See, e.g., Welles's formula: "Alexander's economy was like that of Republican Rome, based on plunder. War was his source of profit and income . . . He was not concerned with the needs of a trader" (Welles 1965: 226 = Borza 1974: 140).

[33]   For my own position, see Briant 1982: 475–89 (where I argue against the thesis of "Asian stagnation" cherished by Marx), and, most recently, Briant 2005c: 73–84 (with a few changes from the 1st edn. of 1974).

Greek world is a captivating but overlooked chapter in the history of "orientalism" in the sense defined by Edward Said (see Briant 2000b).

The above study has also demonstrated the great conceptual rigidity of models and interpretations. One has the impression that the discussion is still going on around the same two alternatives sprung from the clash between Montesquieu/ Droysen and Grote, but already introduced by Plutarch in the *De fortuna Alexandri*: was Alexander simply a man of war or was he also a political visionary? Did he conquer the Achaemenid empire only for booty and to gather levies from its populations, or did he also have the vision of transforming, if only partially, certain elements of economic life in the countries of the Near East? Did the the Greco-Macedonians by taking control empty the riches of the conquered lands,[34] or did Alexander, directly or indirectly, trigger a new economic lifestyle? So stated, the question will probably never receive an accurately founded response, because it clearly remains too narrowly focused on the personality of the conqueror, or indeed around his postulated demiurgic capacities.

Moreover, the documentation specifically covering the period 334–323 remains very inadequate. Even though attentive and critical rereading of the literary sources can still and always will provoke fruitful debates,[35] it cannot respond to questions that the Classical authors never considered. And though, on the other hand, cunei-form documentation has shed new light on the relations between Alexander and the Babylonians,[36] the small number of tablets dating to the reign of Alexander does not allow us to address the economic lifestyle of Babylon during the period 331–323, except in a partial way, focusing on isolated cases.[37] As for archaeological documen-tation, it remains practically absent (with the notable exception of Macedonia).

The only usable extensive corpus is that of the numismatic documentation. Studies of money and coinage are good examples of what one might hope for in the future, focusing less on the explanation of isolated episodes[38] rather than on general explanations situated in a *longue durée* context. The recent synthesis by G. Le Rider introduces essential points for historical reflection as it replaces the image of an Alexander deciding, right from the start, to unify all minting within his empire, with the image of an Alexander who, following the example of his Achaemenid predecessors, ordered the issue of an imperial coinage while preserving regional and local mintings (Le Rider 2003). Nevertheless, many questions remain unanswered, not only on the quantitative magnitude of Alexander's minting (Callataÿ 1989), but also on the impact that they had on economic life. Le Rider's

[34] See, e.g., Bosworth 2000b: 49: "The conquerors created a desert and called it empire" (the author explicitly places himself in the tradition of Niebuhr and Grote: see Briant 2005b: 49–62).
[35] See the debate, ongoing since 1775, on the consequences of the destruction of the cataracts in the Tigris by Alexander – fortunate in the eyes of some (reopening of navigable routes), detrimental for others (suppression of instruments to regulate the flow of water); see also Briant 2006c: 43–67 and 2008.
[36] See Briant 2003a: 79–84, 562–5, with bibliography.
[37] See the various papers bearing on this region in Briant and Joannès 2006.
[38] On this reservation see Briant 2003a: 52–61, 71–7, 563–4.

thesis undermines the narrow and almost mechanical link that has traditionally been established (since the eighteenth century) between money circulation and economic development. Furthermore, the knowledge that one has today of the daily and frequent use of weighed silver in Babylon in economic exchanges forces one to qualify also the opposition (expressed in the strictest terms by Droysen and his followers) between "a natural economy," synonymous with stagnation (during the time of the Great Kings), and a "monetary economy," synonymous with economic and commercial development (under the influence of Alexander's conquest).[39]

Historians of Alexander must thus widen their scope of vision and use fully the advancements of Achaemenid historiography: it is in this manner that the documents from the time of Alexander, including the pieces of information offered by literary sources, will take on a new historical significance. This suggestion is not new, since one of the first scholars to plead for a scientific evaluation of the Achaemenid era was Michael Rostovtzeff in the many studies that he published in the early years of the twentieth century. In a review article, which first appeared in Russian in 1913,[40] he emphasized that the history of the Hellenistic world could not be removed from the context of Near Eastern history in *longue durée*. In his opinion, there existed an urgent prerequisite which he formulated in the following terms:

> To understand the fundamental organization of the great Persian Empire and, more importantly, to reach a detailed comprehension of the specifics of the reigns of each Persian satrap, in particular those of the satraps of Asia Minor and Syria, including Judea, the Arabic tribes, the Phoenician cities and the temple-states of northern Syria and the confines of Asia Minor, as well as the ancient centers of power, Assyria and Babylon. (1913 [1994]: 15–16)

The difference is that, today, our knowledge of the way the Achaemenid empire functioned, at the global level and in its regional variations, is much more precise. One can even say that at this point the historiography of Alexander can still progress, because it lies at the junction of two of the fields of research that have made the greatest progress in the last quarter-century: Macedonian history and Achaemenid history. The progress made in Achaemenid history allows, in particular, a review of the thesis of stagnation, aided by tools that are of much greater diagnostic value than those used in decades past.

No one thinks that an "economic history of Alexander's reign" will ever be written, or that a synthesis on the economic transformations generated in the short term by the Macedonian conquest can be given. Still, significant progress is conceivable, with two conditions: one has, on the one hand, to liberate oneself from preconceived models and from theories that lack any basis in documentary evidence,

---

[39] See now the discussion by Le Rider and de Callataÿ 2006, with my remarks in Briant 2006a: 314–16.

[40] The article was translated into Italian in 1994, preceded by an introduction by A. Marcone. On Rostovtzeff's place in the historiography of the transition from Achemenids to the Hellenistic kings, see Briant 2000b: 32–4.

and, on the other hand, to integrate reflections on Alexander into the context of both the Macedonian and the Achaemenid *longue durée*. As I have often insisted, posing the problem in its fullest extent requires its examination from the wider perspective of the transition from the Achaemenid empire to the Hellenistic kingdoms.[41] In other terms, one must "break" the predetermined, even overdetermined, periodization centered on the year 334, and approach the history of Alexander as part of a historical period that had its own dynamic, one that encompasses the entire second half of the fourth century in an area spanning from the Indus to the Balkans.

[41] See most recently Briant 2006a, 2006c, and Briant and Joannès 2006.

10

Alexander and his "Terrible Mother"

Elizabeth D. Carney

W. W. Tarn famously doubted that Alexander "ever cared for any woman except his terrible mother."[1] More than a generation later Peter Walcott made Olympias, Alexander's mother, the prime suspect in an article entitled "Plato's Mother and Other Terrible Women."[2] In the years since Tarn passed this judgment, scholars have rejected virtually every other aspect of his interpretation of Alexander's life and reign, but I suspect that many would still agree with his take on Olympias and her relationship with her son. This is so despite an important ambiguity in Tarn's assessment: did he mean that Olympias was a terrible person or a terrible mother?

My own view is that Olympias, her son Alexander, and her husband Philip II were all, in various ways, "terrible." (One might make a similar judgment about a number of their associates and enemies. Murder and violence were commonplace at the Macedonian court and had been for generations.) On the other hand, I do not believe that Olympias was a terrible mother. In fact, in the context of ancient Macedonia and Hellenic culture more generally, I think she was a good one. Her son achieved supreme excellence by the standards of his society and it is difficult not to connect both his achievements and some of his character traits that, even in his own world, seemed negative to the character and values of both his parents.

My concern in this essay is to consider the relationship between Alexander and his mother. This is a particularly daunting task because, though some documentary evidence survives that is relevant to any discussion of their dealings with each other, most of what we know on this topic comes from anecdotes preserved in much later – and usually misogynistic – literary sources, which often seem to use stories about Olympias as a way of venting resentment against Macedonian power. These same sources may also bear traces of the propaganda wars that mirrored and supported

---

[1] Tarn i. 76.
[2] Walcott 1987.

the actual wars of the Successors, battles in which, in the early stages, Olympias was a participant.[3]

Olympias,[4] a daughter of a former Molossian king, was betrothed and then married to Philip II of Macedonia by her uncle Arybbas, the current ruler of the Molossians. Olympias' dynasty, the Aeacids, claimed descent from Achilles, just as the Argeads took Heracles as their ancestor. Like the Argeads, her dynasty had Hellenized and functioned as patrons of major Greek writers, but Molossia was a more remote region than Macedonia, though similar in some respects to its more prosperous neighbor. Like Philip's other marriages, that to Olympias was clearly a political alliance, in this case between two northern rulers with some common interests. By the time Olympias married Philip, around 357, he had already taken at least three and probably four other wives. Philip would acquire two additional wives much later in his reign.[5]

Thus, Olympias was involved in a polygamous marriage and Alexander grew up in court with many women and royal children. Arguably, Olympias was more distinguished by birth than Philip's other wives, but the fact that she bore Philip a son, Alexander, in 356[6] was a more important element in Olympias' position than her high birth. (Soon after Alexander's birth, she also bore Philip a daughter, Cleopatra.) Despite his many wives, Philip had only one other son, Arrhidaeus (usually called Philip Arrhidaeus since he later took his father's name). Though Alexander and Arrhidaeus were close in age and so might have seemed equally likely successors, Arrhidaeus suffered from a sort of mental disability.[7] It is likely that by the time Alexander had reached his early teens (and possibly sooner), Philip had begun to treat him as his presumptive heir and Olympias had therefore acquired greater prestige than his other wives.[8] In Macedonian monarchy at this time, however, there was no formal position as chief wife (in fact, no title for royal women of any sort) nor was there anything like the institutionalized role of Prince of Wales for the king's presumed heir. Thus, though Alexander and his mother became dominant at court, their situation was, by definition, uncertain and both were highly vulnerable to changes in court factions or in Philip's preferences. He could always marry again and produce another male heir whom he might then prefer.

In Alexander's early years, Olympias played an important role in his life for a number of reasons. In the Hellenic world, mothers were generally responsible for

---

[3]   See Carney 2006: 125–37 for a discussion of the extant sources on Olympias.

[4]   On the life of Olympias, see Heckel 83; Carney 2006.

[5]   Our main source on the marriages of Philip II is Satyrus *ap.* Ath. 13.557b–e. For a discussion of the order and dates of his marriages, see Tronson 1984; Carney 2000b: 52–75.

[6]   Hamilton 1965 remains a good source for ancient references to Alexander's early life but its interpretation is now somewhat out of date.

[7]   Heckel 52–3; Carney 2001; Greenwalt 1985.

[8]   My discussion of the factors affecting the status of royal wives stresses the production of children as the most important factor and then birth (including family connections). Many scholars would focus on a royal woman's ethnicity; this point of view is particularly relevant to discussions of the insult Attalus made to Alexander (see below). I am less certain that ethnicity was a major factor in the ranking of wives. See discussion and references in Carney 2000b: 26–7.

the care of both girls and boys until they were 7 or so. Alexander did have a wet nurse, Lanice, a member of the Macedonian elite. Though Alexander developed and maintained close ties to Lanice's family,[9] nothing suggests that this detracted from his relationship with his mother. Almost certainly, he was closer to Olympias than to Philip. For one thing, his father was frequently absent on campaign;[10] Olympias would have been a constant presence in a way that Philip was not. As a consequence, Alexander probably spent more time with his mother, even after his early childhood, than might youths whose fathers were less absent.

In the period before his teens, Alexander may have spent more time with his mother's kin and supporters than with his father. Whether they lived in a physically separate structure or simply had a suite of rooms in the palace, Olympias, Alexander, and Cleopatra formed a family subunit at court, but one with a number of supporters and Molossian connections. Olympias' brother joined the Argead court at some point and remained there until Philip helped to put him on the Molossian throne. Alexander's chief tutor was a kinsman of Olympias named Leonidas (Plu. *Alex.* 5.4, 22.4, 25.5),[11] a choice surely meant to honor Olympias and her family; possibly the choice of Leonidas also reflected Olympias' influence on Philip. Leonidas favored an education heavy on austerity and military training; he supposedly checked to make sure that Olympias was not smuggling forbidden luxuries to her son. Another early tutor, Lysimachus of Acarnania (Plu. *Alex.* 5.4), was quite possibly also chosen through the influence of Olympias and her family.[12] Lysimachus stressed Alexander's Aeacid descent rather than the Heraclid line of Philip: he called himself "Phoenix," Alexander "Achilles," and Philip "Peleus" (Plu. *Alex.* 5.5), thus turning Philip himself into an honorary Aeacid. In a patriarchal and patrilineal world like that of fourth-century Greece, Alexander's identification of himself as an Aeacid (and the tendency of the sources to stress this identification) is striking. Arrian (1.11.8) has Alexander say that he was descended from the *genos* (clan) of Neoptolemus.[13]

Philip's toleration, one might almost say encouragement, of this distinctive non-Macedonian identity of Alexander's, an identity clearly tied to Olympias' *oikos* (house), is not unique to his treatment of Alexander. We know that he apparently allowed his Illyrian wife Audata to bring up their daughter Cynnane in a fashion very much at odds with Macedonian expectations about women; Cynnane was trained to fight as a warrior (indeed she apparently fought in at least one battle during her father's reign) and would train her daughter in turn.[14] Exactly why Philip

---

[9] See Heckel 145.

[10] Mortensen 1997: 168, fig. 5 has a helpful chart of Philip's probable absences between Alexander's birth in 356 and 340 (when he was 16 and functioned as regent). It suggests that Philip was gone for months every year during this period but one and that he was virtually never there when Alexander was between 13 and 16.

[11] Heckel 146–7.

[12] Heckel 153.

[13] See Carney 2006: 28 n. 50.

[14] On Audata, Cynnane, and Adea Eurydice, daughter of Cynnane, see Carney 2000b: 57–8, 69–70, 129–31, 132–7.

seems to have invited these alternate identities in the children of his wives by non-Macedonian women is not clear, but it did give them a sense of themselves that was not exclusively grounded in court politics and the current succession pecking order.

Alexander's lineage meant more to him than simple prestige or high birth. While his emulation of heroes certainly included his father's supposed ancestor Heracles,[15] it was his mother's mythical forebear who proved the more compelling model for his behavior. Though Macedonian society and monarchy was generally more Homeric in its value system and institutions – for instance, *hetairoi* (Companions) accompanied Macedonian kings as they did Homeric ones – than the cultures of southern Greece,[16] Olympias' focus on her ancestry was certainly the origin of Alexander's tendency to explain himself through Achilles. Aristotle doubtless influenced this aspect of Alexander's life as well (Plu. *Alex.* 8.2; Str. 13.1.27), but Olympias and his tutors were the first to focus on it.[17]

Hellenic culture, beginning at least with Homer, was notoriously competitive: an *agon* (contest, trial) existed for virtually every kind of human endeavor and only through victory in an *agon* could *aretē* be achieved and *timē* assigned. In effect, one could not simply be good; one had to be better than others. These agonistic values were responsible for both remarkable achievements and for destructive behavior and devaluation of cooperative behavior and compromise. Achilles epitomized the *aretē* ideal: he was supreme in warfare, brave, young, unyielding, and comparatively uninterested in common goals and activities. Of course, Achilles was famously fated to face a choice of a short and glorious life or a long and inglorious one and naturally chose the former. While, as I have suggested, Olympias and tutors chosen from her family's sphere of influence were probably the first to instil the image of Achilles and the values of Homer in Alexander, the inculcation of these values would surely have met with approval from Philip. Rather than being the warped standards of a woman who could "realize her own thwarted ambitions only vicariously through her offspring,"[18] these were cultural norms, if carried to an extreme degree of success in the case of Alexander and Philip. Indeed, father and son competed with each other in many ways: "emulation and resentment"[19] characterized the relationship between father and son, even after Philip's death (see further below).

A story attributed to Theophrastus (*ap.* Athen. 10.435a) asserts that Olympias and Philip also shared a similar point of view about another parental concern,

---

[15] Huttner 1997: 86–123.

[16] See Cohen 1995.

[17] Ameling 1988; Carney 2000a: 274–85. See also Cohen 1995.

[18] Walcott 1987: 13 and *passim*. He seems to understand the *aretē* ethic quite narrowly, as somehow the product of mothers whose husbands had failed to succeed and therefore turned to their sons. Though he sees Alexander as his prime Greek historical example, he seems to forget that Philip II was hardly a failure and Olympias, whatever her personal feelings about him, was unlikely to think that he was.

[19] Fredricksmeyer 1990. While I do not agree with every argument in Fredricksmeyer 1990, it is generally a compelling portrait of the father–son relationship and an excellent source of references to incidents in the relationship.

Alexander's sexuality. According to Theophrastus, Alexander was not interested in matters sexual, and his parents, fearing he might be womanish, arranged a sexual relationship with a beautiful *hetaira*, Callixeina. Theophrastus actually pictures Olympias nagging Alexander to have sex. The tale, however entertaining, does not inspire much confidence in its truth. Apart from the three wives Alexander ultimately took and the two sons he sired, it is certain that he had at least one non-obligatory sexual relationship with a man (Bagoas) and one with a woman (Barsine), and probably many more, including a long-term emotional tie to Hephaestion (see Ogden, ch. 11). He may well have been more interested in power than sex, but he was hardly a "mama's boy" in any clinical sense.[20] Whatever the truth of Theophrastus' account, it does represent Olympias and Philip acting in agreement and concert as parents and that appears to have been true, at least up until the period after the battle of Chaeroneia in 338.

Despite the larger world Alexander began to enter as he began his teens (studies under Aristotle away from the court at Mieza, time as regent during his father's absence, his prominent role in the great victory of Chaeroneia),[21] a fundamental fact of his life kept him tied to his mother (and to much lesser degree, his full sister). His mother's status, even her safety, derived from his existence and from his position as heir presumptive. Generally, royal women had more influence as kings' mothers than they had as kings' wives; this was particularly true in a situation where a king could have many wives but, of course, only one mother. Not surprisingly, royal mothers acted as succession advocates for their sons. (Full sisters tended to function as part of the succession unit as well; the kind of marriage a sister might make would be determined, in good part, by her brother's success.) Philip's mother, for instance, took dramatic public action to safeguard the throne for her remaining sons (Aeschin. 2.26–9).

In the competitive situation created by royal polygamy, a king's son inescapably grew closer to his mother than to his father because the former was his succession advocate since, as we have seen, her status derived from her son's success whereas his father had or could have more sons and might prefer one of them. A king's preference could change; an aging monarch might begin to find a younger son more preferable to one of adult or nearly adult years; the more youthful son postponed thoughts of debility and death (a famous example of this would be Lysimachus' rejection of his adult son Agathocles in favor of his younger son Ptolemy[22]). Plutarch (*Mor.* 178e–f) tells a story (surely fictional) in which Alexander complains to Philip because he was producing children by many women and Philip orders him, by means of this contest for royal power, to prove he was worthy to rule because of himself, not just Philip. While dubious at best from a historical point of view,

[20]   As some scholars assume. For instance, Wirth 1973: 120 speaks of his "mother complex."
[21]   On Alexander's studies with Aristotle at Mieza, see discussion and references in Carney 2003a: 49–59. On his role as regent (or perhaps co-regent with Antipater), see Plu. *Alex.* 9.1; Theopompus, *FGrH* 115 F217; Isoc. *Ep.* 4; and discussion in Hamilton 1969: 22. On Chaeroneia and his role in the diplomacy following the battle, see D.S. 16.86.1–4; Plu. *Alex.* 9.2; Just. 9.4.5.
[22]   Lund 1992: 196–8.

the anecdote provides a fairly accurate picture of how Argeads gained and then retained their hold on the throne and it recognizes an essential truth about relations between royal fathers and sons. A king's son always had reason to distrust his father, even when he seemed currently on good terms, but he could count on his mother since her self-interest and his own were, at least until he became the king, more or less identical. Almost certainly, the situation that bred political closeness between mother and son also generated emotional closeness. The royal Macedonian court was a frightening place; having someone you could always count on was critical and doubtless inspired affection.

Still, though retaining a certain amount of paranoia was healthy for royal wives and children (after all, there usually was someone out to get them!), the comparative uncertainty about their position that may have characterized the early years of Olympias' marriage and Alexander's childhood had, probably about the time Alexander neared or reached his teens, surely dwindled. Arrhidaeus' mental limits were now obvious and Philip had surely signaled his intention to have Alexander succeed him by his very public choice of Aristotle as Alexander's tutor, by entrusting the kingdom to Alexander when he was only 16, and by Alexander's command of the cavalry at Chaeronea and his diplomatic role in the negotiations after the great victory.

Despite claims to the contrary, we know nothing about relations between Philip and Olympias at any period before 338: perhaps they were always distant or hostile, perhaps first they were passionate and later antagonistic, perhaps not. People were pragmatic, not romantic, about marriage in the ancient world – it was to produce children – and particularly so about royal marriages since their origins were so often political. The fact that a marriage was polygamous would only intensify this situation. Whatever their personal feelings, public relations between Philip and Olympias, so far as we can tell, remained good.[23] The Macedonian and Hellenic world was patriarchal and, of course, a double standard applied: quite apart from other wives, Philip had many lovers, female and male, possibly including Olympias' own brother. This need not mean that Alexander's family life, in his teens, was particularly stressful because of tension between his parents. There is no evidence that Olympias was ever sexually jealous[24] and if she ever were, nearly twenty years of

[23]   Apart from the general good treatment of her son that Philip displayed and that would, of course, have benefited dealings between the two, there are some chance references that imply a continuing connection to Philip: letters between the two (Ath. 10.435a; Plu. *Demetr.* 22.2) and shopping done for Olympias by Philip's agents in Athens (Dem. 18.137). Plu. *Mor.* 799e, in reference to the same correspondence the Athenians happened upon, says that they chose not to break the seal of a letter from an absent husband to his "affectionate" wife.

[24]   Plu. *Mor.* 141b–c has Olympias summon a Thessalian woman (possibly one of Philip's Thessalian wives) with whom Philip had an erotic relationship. Since the woman was suspected of using drugs on Philip, it is not clear whether Olympias was initially acting out of sexual jealousy, concern for Philip's welfare, or the general need to be alert to the ever changing favorites of the king. In any event, Plutarch praises her for being a model wife because, once she met the woman, she was charmed by her and discounted the hostile stories. Her clear jealousy of Philip's last bride, Cleopatra, appears only in the context of the challenge to Alexander's role as heir and so appears to be political rather than sexual jealousy.

marriage to Philip would surely have muted such feelings. There is good evidence that she was, however, quite jealous of her son's position. But, until soon after Chaeroneia, she had no obvious reason for concern there. Indeed, the monument that Philip apparently commissioned soon after the battle to commemorate his victory, the Philippeum, also commemorated the comfortable dynastic status quo: inside the building were statues that appeared to be made of gold and ivory, thus imitating images of the gods, of Philip, his father Amyntas III, his mother Eurydice, Alexander, and Olympias. Philip planned to place this structure at Olympia, within the sacred precincts, a dynastic statement aimed at a Panhellenic audience. Olympias and Alexander could hardly have asked for a clearer validation of their status or one directed at a larger audience. Ironically, within months of Philip's decision to have the Philippeum constructed, the dynastic unity and stability it projected had shattered.[25]

Had a situation not occurred which jeopardized Alexander's succession to the throne, it is possible that the mother–son relationship would not have remained as important during Alexander's later life. Certainly, events transpired that inevitably tied his fate and hers together and inspired in both tremendous uncertainty and anger. The sudden and unexpected fall from favor that both experienced colored all their future political dealings and surely inclined both to suspicion and to vengeance. Roughly eight years of what passed for security at the Argead court had lulled them into a kind of calm that neither would again manage to entertain.

Trouble for Alexander and Olympias began as a consequence of Philip's decision to marry yet again, this time to a young Macedonian woman, Cleopatra, the ward of her uncle Attalus.[26] Philip's decision to marry yet again (this was his seventh marriage) seems unremarkable in itself: many Macedonians contracted marriages in the period just before the beginning of the invasion of the Persian empire, in hope of leaving sons behind; Philip himself had only one viable son, a son who may have been going to accompany his father on campaign and Argead kings rarely died in bed so there was clear need for more dynastic backup; Attalus, though we know nothing about his career before this period, was certainly prominent in the last years of Philip's reign and so this marriage, like the earlier ones, was some sort of political alliance as well. It was not, however, the marriage itself that caused the trouble. Philip had married at least one woman, perhaps two, after his marriage to Olympias, with no obvious upset and no child from a new marriage could possibly jeopardize the more or less adult Alexander's position in the succession for many years. Alexander attended the symposium connected to Philip's wedding, a sign that he considered his father's latest marriage innocuous. It was not the marriage itself but events at the symposium that precipitated dynastic meltdown.

After the men had been drinking for a while (if Cleopatra, Olympias, or any royal women were present, their presence is not mentioned by any ancient author) and

[25]   Schultz 2007a, 2007b; Carney 2007.
[26]   See Carney 2006: 31–7 for discussion and references to the marriage, sympotic quarrel, and subsequent reconciliation.

Attalus and Philip and probably Alexander too were quite drunk, the guardian of the bride, Attalus, called upon the Macedonians to beg the gods that from the marriage of Philip and Cleopatra might come a "*gnesion . . . diadochon tes basileias*" (genuine or legitimate successor to the kingdom or rule; Plu. *Alex.* 9.4–5). Another source (Satyr. *ap.* Ath. 13.557d–e) preserves a similar account that employs the same term *gnesios*. Justin (9.7.2–3) tells a different story, one that has Alexander start the argument because he was concerned that a son born from this marriage would be a rival. For a variety of reasons, Justin's account has generally been considered less credible than the other tradition.[27] Whatever the literal intent of Attalus' insult (some believed it attacked Olympias' and thus Alexander's Molossian ethnicity, some Olympias' sexual fidelity, and I think it was, in effect, comparative – a son by Cleopatra, in Attalus' view, would be more genuine or legitimate than Alexander), it was, however drunken, an assertion of self-interest. Not surprisingly, we hear that Alexander threw a wine cup at Attalus (and perhaps he at Alexander; Satyr. *ap.* Ath. 13.557d–e). What is surprising is not Attalus' bravado, but Philip's reaction. According to Plutarch (and Just. 9.7.4), Philip not only did not support his son but actually attempted to attack him with his sword and was foiled only by his own drunkenness or the efforts of his friends. Even if he did not actually draw his sword on Alexander, Philip apparently allowed this public questioning of Alexander's ability to inherit. Alexander left the symposium and the kingdom, in company with his mother. Alexander left Olympias with her brother, now king of Molossia, but he himself went on to stay among the Illyrians, traditional enemies of Macedonia but also kinfolk.[28]

Alexander and Olympias went into self-imposed exile (Philip did not send them into exile) because of Attalus' insult and what it implied about Philip's intentions. Whatever Attalus had intended by using the term *gnesios*, it was a term that dishonored Olympias and her clan. Justin claims that Olympias wanted her brother the king to go to war with Philip (9.7.7); naturally that did not happen, but Attalus had treated their lineage with contempt; not only Olympias but the Aeacid dynasty had been publicly humiliated. Not surprisingly, particularly because of the imminence of Philip's departure for Asia, a public reconciliation was patched together (Plu. *Alex.* 9.6; *Mor.* 70b, 179c; Just. 9.7.6). Alexander and his mother returned to Macedonia (Plu. *Mor.* 179c). Plutarch (*Alex.* 10.1–3) alone tells a story that suggests that, despite the formal *rapprochement*, Alexander and Olympias remained extremely anxious about Alexander's ability to succeed: supposedly, on the advice of Olympias and other friends, Alexander tried to substitute himself for his brother Arrhidaeus as groom in a projected marriage with the daughter of a critical ruler in Asia Minor, Pixodarus. Apparently Alexander, Olympias, and the rest understood the marriage as a sign that his brother was now the favored choice to succeed Philip. When Philip found out what Alexander had done, he was furious and sent

---

[27]   Justin mistakenly believes that Philip divorced Olympias before he married Cleopatra and generally seems confused about polygamy at the Macedonian court.
[28]   Just. 9.7.5 and Plu. *Alex.* 9.5 have Alexander go with his mother to Epirus and then on to the Illyrians whereas Satyrus *ap.* Ath. 13.557e seems to imply that they left separately.

several of Alexander's friends into exile. If this incident is historical, Alexander and Olympias were still acting as a succession unit but in this case, as opposed to Attalus' insult, their judgment seems questionable. The insult, with its public destruction of the *timē* of mother and son (Arr. 3.6.5), in effect, required that they depart so that Philip would then have to publicly restore their *timē*. In the Pixodarus incident, even if their reading of the significance of the projected marriage were correct, they actually made matters worse; more likely they caused a problem where none had really existed. It is hard not to conclude that the earlier episode had so shaken their confidence in Alexander's position that they overreacted.[29]

Whatever the truth of the Pixodarus affair, Philip certainly did do something dramatic to symbolize the reconciliation and assuage damaged Aeacid pride (*contra* Weber, ch. 5, p. 86): he arranged a marriage between his daughter by Olympias, Cleopatra, and Olympias' brother, the king of Molossia. Moreover, he turned the wedding into an international event and festival, obviously intending to showcase the newly restored harmony of the royal family as well as the wealth and power of Macedonia on the eve of the great Asian expedition (D.S. 16.91.4–6). Unfortunately for Philip, his assassin saw this ancient media event as the perfect occasion for the murder of the king. The identity of Philip's assassin – Pausanias, a bodyguard and former lover of the king – is known but, since Pausanias was killed very soon after the assassination, we can only speculate as to whether he acted alone (he did have strong personal motivation) or in concert with others at court (Arist. *Pol.* 1311b; D.S. 16.93–4; Just. 9.6.4–7.14). Regicide was common in Macedonia but, with one exception, it had previously involved other members of the dynasty. Inevitably, suspicion fell on Alexander and Olympias, particularly because of their recent troubles with Philip (Plu. *Alex.* 10.4; Just. 9.8.1–14). Olympias and Alexander both later demonstrated their willingness to commit murder and Philip had, after all, threatened his son, either directly or indirectly. Even though the baby Cleopatra, Philip's bride, had so recently given birth to was probably female[30] and thus Alexander faced no immediate threat to his succession, his succession did appear to be years in the future. The death of Philip meant that Alexander got to lead the expedition; we do not even know if Philip had planned to take him. More generally, killing Philip would have ended the chronic insecurity of their position. Obviously Alexander and Olympias were capable of murder and had clear motivation. Philip had many enemies and Pausanias may have acted alone. We cannot rule Alexander and Olympias out but neither is there enough evidence to assume that they were guilty. What is impossible to believe is that either instigated the assassination

---

[29] One wonders if Plutarch's picture – however subjective – of Olympias as "jealous, stubborn, and difficult" (*Alex.* 9.3), clearly made in the general context of the last troubled years of Philip's reign, is actually more specific and refers to her role in the Pixodarus incident, though the characterization appears a bit before the Pixodarus incident.

[30] Satyrus *ap.* Ath. 13.557e says it was girl named Europa, Justin (9.7.12) says the baby Olympias killed was female (see below), but Paus. 8.7.7 says the baby was male and Just. 11.2.3 elsewhere speaks of a boy Caranus who seems to be a son of Cleopatra. See Heckel 1979 for the view that Satyrus' testimony is preferable.

without the knowledge and consent of the other. So far as we know, in all the other events connected to the succession troubles at the end of Philip's reign, they had acted together. Besides, it would have been too risky for either to surprise the other on the day of assassination.[31]

The less than two-year period between Philip's murder and Alexander's departure for Asia was a transitional one for the relationship of Alexander and Olympias. In Macedonia typically instability followed the death of a king. Alexander had to prove himself against the Illyrians and possible Greek defectors from the alliance Philip had constructed and he did just that and was recognized as the new *hegemon*. He had to blame the assassination on someone, so he found appropriate Macedonian candidates, people whose absence happened to be convenient from his own point of view, and eliminated them. In addition to dealing with these threats to the stability of the kingdom and projected expedition,[32] Alexander chose to deal with someone he clearly considered an enemy, Attalus. At the time of Philip's murder, Attalus was in Asia along with Parmenion, helping to command the preliminary force Philip had sent to Asia. Alexander had him eliminated, apparently with the collusion of Parmenion. Since Attalus had questioned Alexander's worthiness to rule, his death can hardly have come as a surprise (see Heckel, ch. 4).[33]

Cleopatra, Philip's last bride, and her baby were killed as well. Only one of the major narratives of Alexander's reign mentions the deaths of mother and child; two categorically different accounts from two late and dubious sources are extant (Just. 9.7.12; Paus. 8.7.7). Clearly, the murder was not a public act. Both accounts assert that Olympias had Cleopatra murdered and this seems quite likely: just as Olympias and Alexander had functioned as a succession unit, so had Attalus and his niece. Death, like virtually everything else in the Greek world was gendered; men were supposed to die in public, the victims of sharp weapons, while women died in private, within the world of women and might most nobly (assuming they were of high birth) hang themselves. So Alexander arranged the death of their male enemy and Olympias the death of their female enemy. Their house, their clan, had been insulted and they paid the insult back. Plutarch (*Alex.* 10.4), who does not directly mention the death of Cleopatra (let alone her child), does say that Alexander was angry with his mother because, during his absence, she had treated Cleopatra savagely. It is difficult to know what to make of this passage: is Plutarch euphemistically referring to Cleopatra's murder? If so, why the euphemism? Is it plausible that Alexander did not know that Olympias was going to do this? Even if Plutarch thought that Alexander was sincere in his approval, apparently others did not; in

---

[31]   On the assassination of Philip see, generally, Heckel 182 and Carney 2006: 38–9.

[32]   See Bosworth 1988a: 25–35 for a general narrative of events after Phillip's death and before Alexander's departure.

[33]   See Heckel 62 for events leading to the death of Attalus, who may or may not have plotted against Alexander after Philip's death. Just. 11.5.1 claimed that Alexander killed all of Cleopatra's relatives before he left for Asia whereas Heckel argues that it was only Attalus. The chronological order of the deaths of Attalus and Cleopatra is uncertain; my own view is that she was killed soon after Philip's murder and that Attalus' death came somewhat later.

this same passage Plutarch includes a reference to sources that have Alexander quote a line from the *Medea* (289) that implies Alexander was encouraging Pausanias to bring about the deaths of Cleopatra, Philip, and Attalus. Justin, having mentioned only Olympias in his narrative of the murder, has Alexander, after the killing of Cleitus, regret various murders including that of Cleopatra and his "brothers" (Just. 12.6.14). The great likelihood is that mother and son planned the elimination of their enemies together. Granted the dominance of Judeo-Christian ethics in modern culture, vengeance has a bad name. In the Greek world, where the axiom was that one should help one's friends and harm one's enemies, something close to the reverse applied. Moreover, for members of the Macedonian elite, eliminating enemies was a practical matter, not simply an issue of emotional satisfaction. If they were dead, they couldn't plot against you. Both Cleopatra and her baby could have formed a faction or been used by a faction to jeopardize Alexander's hold on the throne, not just in 336, but even years later.

By the time of Alexander's departure for Asia, he was secure on the throne and no longer needed his mother's advocacy as he had before. Inevitably their relationship grew more complex: Alexander was now an adult, less in need of political support, and pursuing his own policies. Distance doubtless complicated this situation. Mother and son never saw each other again and their experiences, during the years of his reign, were quite different. It is unlikely, however, that either Alexander or his mother entertained the notion that Olympias would go east with her son. Macedonian monarchs did not generally take their wives with them and both mother and son probably thought that Olympias would be more useful on the Greek peninsula than traveling with her son's court. It was a position that entailed a greater possibility for the exercise of power, but also greater vulnerability.

Both power and vulnerability were a possibility because of the arrangement Alexander left behind him. Clearly Antipater had some sort of general administrative and military responsibility for Macedonia and the Greek peninsula, but even early on Olympias had some sort of public responsibility, possibly deriving from a role in dynastic ritual. In any case, though there is evidence for no previous enmity, Antipater and Olympias now began to squabble and complain about each other in letters to Alexander. In the early years of his reign Alexander needed Antipater to send reinforcements and deal with real and potential revolts. Apparently because she was losing out in the struggle for authority with Antipater, Olympias left Macedonia for her homeland of Molossia. Olympias' brother the king had died on campaign and it would appear that she and her daughter ruled Molossia together for some time.[34] By the later years of Alexander's reign, Antipater's influence was waning and Olympias' increasing. Plutarch says (apparently in terms of the last year or two of Alexander's reign) that mother and daughter formed a faction together, Olympias taking Molossia and her daughter Macedonia (Plu. *Alex.* 68.3). Plutarch has Alexander essentially ignoring the situation, other than joking about it, apparently indifferent to what came of it. Of course, Alexander called Antipater to

---

[34] The evidence for Olympias' whereabouts and position is confusing; see Carney 2006: 52–3.

Babylon, planning to replace him with Craterus, but Antipater, at the time of Alexander's death, had not budged. It would appear that Olympias had lost the first battle but won the war with Antipater (or would have, had Alexander lived).

In some respects, Olympias and Alexander's relationship during this period was conventional. He sent his mother (and sister) plunder and Olympias made rich dedications with it at Delphi (Plu. *Alex.* 25.4; *SIG*³ 1.252N.5ff.). She made offerings at Athens to Hygieia (Hyp. *Eux.* 19), probably on her son's behalf. There are, however, a number of indications that Olympias' relationship with her son was not only emotional but political. Olympias and her daughter both received grain shipments in times of grain scarcity, in effect functioning as heads of state, possibly in concert with Alexander (*SEG* ix. 2).[35] At times, Olympias acted as though she had some official position (D.S. 17.108.7) and contemporaries sometimes spoke about her as though she did (Hyp. *Eux.* 20). Our sources refer to frequent correspondence between Olympias and Alexander and periodically quote from or paraphrase their letters. The authenticity of this epistolary exchange is uncertain and has typically been addressed on a case-by-case basis.[36] In any event, aside from references to the Olympias–Antipater feud, our sources indicate that Olympias fairly frequently warned her son against people she considered a threat and more generally against policies she felt threatened his interests. Like some of Alexander's male courtiers, Olympias was clearly jealous and competitive; doubtless Alexander was familiar with this point of view. According to Plutarch (*Alex.* 39.7), Alexander did not permit his mother to interfere in campaigns or public affairs and she complained about this. Plutarch's judgment is problematic on several grounds, not least of which is the fact that Olympias clearly did involve herself in public affairs. Moreover, it is difficult to know how Alexander (or his mother) might have defined interference.

Whereas many people take Plutarch at his word and assume that Alexander never paid attention to his mother's political advice, they do often believe that she did influence her son in terms of his claims to be the son of Zeus. What little ancient evidence survives is ambiguous. Plutarch (*Alex.* 3.2) cites two traditions: Eratosthenes for the notion that Olympias told Alexander that he was the son of a god before he left Macedonia, but others have Olympias denying that she had any role and joking that he was slandering her to Hera.[37] This claim of divine sonship, apparently first asserted publicly in Egypt after his visit to the oracle of Zeus Ammon, moved him in the direction of what would become divine monarchy. Argeads (and other elite families and dynasties in the Greek world) had always claimed descent from

---

[35]   See discussion and references in Carney 2006: 50–1. Those on the list were the ones who paid for the grain; whether Olympias and Cleopatra used Alexander's funds or their own, acted independently or at his behest, it is significant that only they are mentioned; the inscriptions highlight their benefactions.

[36]   Carney 2000b: 87 nn. 11–12 for doubts about their viability. The *Alexander Romance* includes many clearly fictional letters, something it would be wise to recall.

[37]   In addition, Arr. 4.10.2 claimed that Callisthenes referred to Olympias' lies about Alexander's birth. See further Carney 2006: 102–3.

the gods, but asserting that one's father was a god was another matter, particularly since such an assertion meant denying that Philip II was his father. Indeed, divine sonship was clearly unpopular with many Macedonians for exactly this reason. Even if we assume that Olympias, after 338, loathed Philip, we should not assume that she would have been the one to advocate divine sonship, especially early in her son's reign. The insult of Attalus was still fresh in everyone's mind and any woman had to avoid any implication that she had slept with anyone other than her husband. Olympias was the one who first inspired the heroic values her son embraced, the sort of world view that might make divine parentage imaginable, but the specific notion was probably Alexander's, not hers. Curtius alone (9.6.26, 10.5.30) asserts that Alexander planned to deify his mother after her death; this could be true but it could also be an anachronistic Roman understanding of the situation. Whatever the specifics, it does seem likely that the Homeric values of Olympias and Alexander contributed to an understanding of Alexander as divinized.

Did Olympias generally have influence with Alexander? Her influence was certainly not automatic, as the situation with Antipater demonstrates. She always had access to the king and it is likely that Alexander, though clearly recognizing that she pursued her own self-interest as well as his own, must have valued her as an independent source of information (as indicated by the report that he generally kept the content of her letters secret; Plu. *Alex.* 395; *Mor.* 180d, 33a, 340a), one whose interests were close to his own though hardly identical with them. Even Plutarch (*Alex.* 39.7) conceded that she had more influence than Antipater, in the end, and events tend to bear that out. Our tradition heavily depends on Plutarch, who is demonstrably hostile to Olympias, pictures Alexander as a fond and dutiful son, but one who at times found his mother overbearing. Some of this may be Plutarch or that Alexander needed to play to Greek convention and deny that Olympias or any other royal woman had a role in public affairs, but some of it could be real.

For Olympias, as for everyone else, the death of her son was entirely unexpected, almost unimaginable. His death meant that Olympias was vulnerable in a way she could never have been during her son's reign and her actions suggest that she was well aware of her danger. She claimed that Antipater and his sons had poisoned Alexander (D.S. 19.11.8; Plu. *Alex.* 77.1). Doubtless she believed it: they had motive and opportunity and she hated them. She was not the only one who found it hard to believe that the invincible and still young Alexander had died of natural causes. To the degree she was able, Olympias attempted to punish the clan of Antipater for the betrayal of which she believed they were guilty. Olympias clearly saw herself as the custodian of her son's memory. In the end she risked and lost her life as part of what would ultimately prove a disastrous military attempt to insure the throne for Alexander's son, Alexander IV. Just as during Alexander's life Olympias had spent her time in fierce pursuit of her son's and her own self-interest, after his death her pursuit of her grandson's and her own self-interest brought about her own.[38]

---

[38] See Carney 2006: 60–87 for her actions after Alexander's death.

Making judgments about the nature of other people's relationships is always an act of imagination to some degree, and making such a determination about a relationship more than 2,000 years in the past, one that existed in a radically different culture, is far more speculative, particularly in the absence of evidence deriving directly from the two parties. The *Alexander Romance* paints a highly sentimental picture of an idealized and loving relationship between Alexander and Olympias; in effect, it implies that Tarn was right, that Olympias really was the only woman he loved. Perhaps that is the truth. What is more certain is that she was the only woman he could trust.

11

Alexander's Sex Life

Daniel Ogden

Alexander has never seemed quite the same since the twentieth century's discovery of "that horrid thing which Freud calls sex,"[1] and the development of the notion that one's sexuality was somehow a vital determinant of or an indispensable key to the understanding of one's nature and one's identity. At time of writing much of the attention given to Alexander on the Internet is from gay-interest websites attempting to appropriate historical figures or find role models of gravitas. The bulk of the press reaction to Oliver Stone's recent movie *Alexander* (Warner Brothers, 2004) has focused on his representation of the king's sexuality (this is the first mainstream movie to be frank about Alexander's homosexual adventures, although it declines to enact them with the vigor it reserves for his heterosexual ones).[2] It may defy belief that there could be public demonstrations and riots over any point of ancient history in the modern world, but such there were in Thessaloniki in 2002 over precisely the issue of homosexuality in the ancient Macedonian court.[3]

[1] Nancy Mitford, attributing the phrase, perhaps erroneously, to E. F. Benson's marvelous Lucia, at Benson 1977: x.

[2] For an account of the discussions behind the portrayal of Alexander's sexuality in this movie, see Lane Fox 2004: 27–8 (where we also learn that Lane Fox's 1973 Alexander book was once marketed as "the dashing story of the spellbinding young gay who conquered the world"), 33–4, 40–1, 53–4, 67, 69.

[3] The events took place on Wednesday, October 16, 2002 at the Institute for Balkan Studies' Seventh International Symposium on Ancient Macedon (the conference that gives rise to the proceedings *Ancient Macedonia/Archaia Makedonia*) in and around the Hall of the Society for Macedonian Studies in Thessaloniki. Advance publicity had attracted the wrath of the local "nationalist" (to spare other words) party, Laos, to that evening's session, and the leaders duly arrived with mob and camera crew in train. Some forty police were deployed to protect the delegates. The principal incitement was Kate Mortensen's paper on "Homosexuality at the Macedonian Court," but offense was taken also at the adjacent papers, my own on "A War of Witches at the Court of Philip II?" (Philip could never have had any part of such an unchristian thing) and Ernst Badian's on "The Death of Philip II" (Badian's crime was to have doubted the Hellenism of the ancient Macedonians in earlier work). The three of

The problem of Alexander's sex life first came to the fore in English-language scholarship over half a century ago, in 1948, when the great W. W. Tarn included an extraordinary appendix entitled "Alexander's Attitude to Sex" in his biography *Alexander the Great*.[4] The appendix was in some ways old-fashioned, but in other ways rather ahead of its time. It was old-fashioned in that the Victorian Tarn (his more casual detractors give less attention than they should to the fact that he was born as early as 1869) strove, understandably, to preserve an image of Alexander that those of good Christian family values could continue to admire.[5] So, despite copious and lucid *prima facie* indications in the source tradition that Alexander enjoyed numerous affairs both homosexual and heterosexual, and also that he practiced polygamy, Tarn strove to project him rather as a man who found the necessity for sex tedious and regrettable, but who was securely heterosexual when necessity called, and disinclined to extramarital adventure.[6] But, for all this, Tarn may be considered ahead of his time for his implicit assumption of the importance of Alexander's sexuality for the understanding of the man and his achievements.[7]

Tarn's attempt "to straighten the matter out"[8] and to close the question down was to have the opposite effect to that intended. This was not simply because the time for the question of Alexander's sexuality had come and Tarn's discussion bestowed a counter-productive legitimacy upon the subject, but it was also because Tarn's strength of feeling led him to compromise his own remarkable philology in striking fashion. The mishandling of evidence and argument alike conferred a rare notoriety on the appendix, which has been particularly celebrated since Badian's dissection of it in 1958, the year after Tarn's death, in an article subtitled "a study in method."[9] Then Tarn's regretted subject received a further fillip in the late 1970s, as the sexual liberation of the 1960s belatedly arrived in the world of Classical scholarship. Ground-breaking and popularizing studies of sexual codes of practice in the ancient world, starting with Dover's seminal *Greek Homosexuality*, conferred

---

us were branded as "agents of Skopje." Accounts of the events, of varying degrees of accuracy, and commentaries upon them may be found in the Greek newspapers for the following days. Here I confine myself to quoting from a down-market "nationalist" organ *Stochos* ("Target," appropriately), for Thursday, October 17: "So who are these three anti-Greeks? Daniel Ogden has written tens of books in order to demonstrate that the ancient Greeks lived in a Dark Age of magic, prostitution, homosexuality, bastard children, adultery, etc." (p. 8). What I take to be the now canonical "nationalist" account of the affair may be found at Georgiades 2002: 191–9 (with care!).

[4] Tarn ii. 319–26.

[5] For Tarn ii, esp. 399–449, Alexander was in any case a Jesus before Jesus, most notably in the ambitions he attributed to him for "The Unity of Mankind."

[6] Tarn also attempted, in similar style, to deny the existence of Alexander's "mistress" Barsine, the mother of his son Heracles (Tarn ii. 330–8; answered by Brunt 1975). For the possibility that Barsine should be seen as Alexander's wife, see Brosius 1996: 78 and Ogden 1999: 42–3.

[7] Tarn ii. 319 saw himself as reacting to the brief philological review of the sources for Alexander's love life in Berve's *Alexanderreich* (Berve i. 10–11).

[8] Tarn ii. 319.

[9] Badian 1958b.

new legitimacy on the study of Alexander's sex life and seemed to offer new possibilities for insight into it.[10] And it is against the context of these that investigations of Alexander's sexuality, almost inevitably inconclusive ones, continue to be published.[11]

But nothing more of substance is ever going to be established about the historical sexuality of Alexander the Great. Indeed, we have no particular reason to suppose that his sexuality was even understood by his contemporaries. Who, I ask again, is to know the secrets of the boudoir?[12] One may go so far as to wonder whether it was understood by the man himself. And even if it was, we have no prospect whatsoever of recovering that understanding.[13] And so far as the sources for Alexander are concerned, or what I would prefer to call "the literary tradition about Alexander," we continue to run up against the problem that sex and sexuality always were just "too good to think with," just as they still are. So statements about Alexander's sexuality in our texts may tell us much about the literary tradition itself, or about the agendas of its individual writers, but they can tell us little of the man's historical sexuality. In illustration of this I shall devote the final pages of this paper to a study of Curtius' portrayal of Alexander's relationship with Bagoas. But the best we can hope to do from the *historical* perspective is to gain access to and to reconstruct the general, public patterns or modes of sexuality in the society[14] within which Alexander lived and to locate what is said of Alexander's own sex life within these, and this will constitute the focus of the bulk of this paper.

Alexander's Girls

First, let us briefly review the data.[15] The tradition provides credible testimony to four significant relationships with women on Alexander's part. In around 332 he began a relationship with Barsine (Berve, no. 206; Heckel 70), the Hellenized daughter of the Persian noble Artabazus (Berve, no. 152; Heckel 55).[16] The

[10]   Dover 1978; note also Buffière 1980; Foucault 1984; Halperin 1990; Halperin et al. 1990; Winkler 1990; and Davidson 1997 (a substantial new study specifically devoted to Greek homosexuality is awaited from the last).

[11]   E.g., Reames-Zimmermann 1999.

[12]   See Ogden 1996b: 110.

[13]   I recall the (unpublished) observations of Elizabeth Rawson, erstwhile Fellow and Tutor in Ancient History at Corpus Christi College, Oxford, who protested that the only minds of the ancient world we could even aspire to know were those of Cicero and St. Augustine, this by virtue of the voluminous and ostensibly personal nature of the writings they had left behind.

[14]   Perhaps we should say "societies," not least when we think of the Persian court context of Bagoas. For discussion of Persian court eunuchism see Llewellyn-Jones 2002 and Briant 1996: 279–97.

[15]   For a recent review of the women of Alexander's court, see Carney 2003b, only a relatively limited part of which, however, is devoted to Alexander's sexual partners (242–52), subsequent to Carney 2000b: 97–113.

[16]   Plu. *Alex.* 21; *Eum.* 1. For Barsine, subsequent to Tarn and Brunt as cited above, see now Carney 2000b: 101–5, 149–50; 2003b: 243–5.

relationship endured for five years or more, for it was not until 327 that she bore Alexander the first of his children we know of, Heracles (Berve, no. 353; Heckel 138).[17] And it was in 327 also that Alexander married the partner most celebrated and romanticized in his tradition, the captive Bactrian noblewoman Roxane (Berve, no. 688; Heckel 241–2).[18] A delightful example of this romanticization may be found above all in Lucian's ecphrasis of Aetion's painting *The Wedding of Roxane and Alexander*, which showed one team of beaming putti-cupids helping Roxane to undress for her first night with Alexander, while another played with Alexander's discarded armor.[19] She miscarried or gave birth to a short-lived son at the Hydaspes in 326,[20] and was eight months pregnant on Alexander's death in 323 with the future Alexander IV.[21] At the mass marriages Alexander organized for his companions with Persian noblewomen at Susa in 324 he himself took on two wives at once: Barsine-Stateira (Berve, no. 722; Heckel 256–7), eldest daughter of the last and overthrown Persian king Darius III, and Parysatis (Berve, no. 607; Heckel 192), youngest daughter of the penultimate Persian king Artaxerxes III Ochus.[22]

The most general and significant frame against which these relationships should be contextualized is that of Macedonian royal polygamy. We can be sure that Alexander kept his wives in polygamy (as opposed to serial monogamy) for two principal reasons. First, the marrying of two women on the same day and at the same ceremony, as Alexander did at Susa, is peculiarly difficult to reconcile with all but the most economical of approaches to monogamy. Second, Roxane was not only pregnant with Alexander's child after the subsequent marriages to Barsine-Stateira and Parysatis, but she was clearly still installed at the center of his life as he died, since she tended him on his deathbed.[23]

This phenomenon of Macedonian royal polygamy, long suppressed in the scholarship of ancient Macedon, in defiance of numerous direct and explicit testimonies, and many more indirect ones, is now generally accepted.[24] The most graphic of all

[17] D.S. 20.20.2: Heracles was "about 17" in 309; *pace* Just. 14.6, 14.13, and 15.2.3, implying a birth date for Heracles as late as 324; see also Ogden 1999: 42–3.

[18] See, in particular, Arr. 4.19.5–6, 4.20.4; Plu. *Alex.* 47; *Mor.* 332c–e, 338d; Str. C517; Curt. 8.4.21–30, 8.5.7; D.S. 17.30, 18.3.3; Just. 12.15.9, 13.2.5–9. The motif of love-at-first-sight romance is strong in these texts. For Roxane see Carney 2000b: 105–7, 146–8; 2003b: 245–6. For the wedding, see, above all, Renard and Servais 1955.

[19] Lucian, *Herodotus* or *Aetion* 4–6. As Kilburn 1959 notes, the motif of the putti playing with discarded armor was to be adopted by Botticelli in his *Venus and Mars* (National Gallery, London, NG915). See also Lucian, *Eikones* 7.

[20] *Metz Epitome* 70.

[21] Just. 13.2.5; cf. Curt. 10.6.9 (six months) and, for the child's birth, Arr. *Succ. FGrH* 156 F9.

[22] Arr. 7.4.4–8; D.S. 17.107.6; Plu. *Alex.* 70; *Mor.* 329d–e, 338d; Just. 12.10.9–10; Memnon *FGrH* 434 F4.4; App. *Syr.* 5. For the marriages to Barsine-Stateira and Parysatis, see Carney 2000b: 108–12; 2003b: 246–8.

[23] *Metz Epitome* 101–2, 110, 112. Note (suggestively, but admittedly inconclusively) the allusion made by the ghost of Philip II to his son's "so many marriages" in Lucian's *Dialogues of the Dead*, 397 (a case, of course, of the pot calling the kettle black).

[24] See Greenwalt 1989; Ogden 1999: ix–xix (for the suppression of polygamy in the scholarship of ancient Macedon), 3–51 (for detailed discussion of the phenomenon); and Carney 2000b: *passim*, the culmination of her many careful articles on the women of the Macedonian dynasty.

the testimonies to Macedonian royal polygamy (but far from the only one) is found in a fragment of Satyrus the Peripatetic preserved by Athenaeus actually in the context of a discussion of polygamy. Here Satyrus lists seven wives of Philip II, in the order of acquisition, and repeatedly uses terms that indicate that the wives were acquired additionally to each other.[25] Satyrus (or perhaps Athenaeus, introducing the quotation) is the only ancient writer to give a rationale for such polygamy, and it is a military-diplomatic one: "Philip . . . used to make his marriages in accordance with war." We might wish to offer other additional reasons. One might be the display of the king's unique status, or of his exceptional level of wealth. Another might be the desire to sire as many children as possible, perhaps again as a marker of status, or perhaps for use. Since Macedonian kings and their princes were warriors who led from the front, it was advisable to have as many sons as possible; and girls offered the opportunity of making diplomatic marriage alliances. Another reason again might be the fact that murderous competition between polygamously held wives and their respective lines of offspring tended to deplete the numbers of princes that could aspire to compete for the throne on their father's death. Hence, paradoxically, it must always have seemed advisable to marry yet more women and father yet more children: polygamy was a tiger too dangerous for its riders to dismount.[26]

Alexander's polygamous marriages accordingly fell into an established cultural pattern within the Macedonian court (as they did indeed in the Persian court annexed by Alexander),[27] and we cannot proceed in any direct way from the fact of them to conclusions about Alexander's own sexuality. And, other considerations apart, a military-diplomatic purpose can be easily advanced in the case of each of the unions. The union with Barsine may have gratified Parmenion and may further have been an attempt to conciliate the Persian aristocracy.[28] The union with Roxane may have placated Bactria.[29] The Susa marriages expressed Alexander's claim to be the successor to the Achaemenids, and in any case took place in the context of a larger policy to integrate the Macedonian and Persian nobilities.[30]

But the record of Alexander's wives and sirings does, perhaps, give the lie to one particular trend in the ancient tradition, the one that represents Alexander as extremely restrained or even undermotivated in sex.[31] This is the trend that represents Alexander as a *gynnis*, an "effeminate," or probably more accurately, a "eunuch."[32] In similar vein Plutarch speaks of Alexander's restraint with the beautiful captured womenfolk of Darius, demonstrating his self-control

---

[25]   Satyrus F21 Kumaniecki at Ath. 557b–e. Note also Plu. *Comp. Demetr. Ant.* 4. See Ogden 1999: xv, 17–20.

[26]   See Ogden 1999: ix–xxi.

[27]   Brosius 1996: esp. 35–7.

[28]   Curt. 3.13.12–14 and Just. 11.10.2; Brosius 1996: 87–8; Ogden 1999: 42; Carney 2003b: 244–5.

[29]   Renard and Servais 1955: 33; Lane Fox 1973: 317, 535; Bosworth 1980b: 11; Ogden 1999: 44.

[30]   Lane Fox 1973: 474; Brosius 1996: 176–9; Ogden 1999: 44–5; Carney 2000b: 108.

[31]   This is made much of by Tarn ii. 322–6.

[32]   Ath. 435a, incorporating Hieronymus of Rhodes F38 Wehrli and Theophrastus F578 Fortenbaugh. I hope to publish a more detailed treatment of this fascinating text soon.

(τὸ; κρατεῖν ἑαυτοῦ), and indeed claims that he knew no other woman prior to
Barsine.[33] By contrast, Alexander's father Philip has the name of having been
reasonably vigorous in his siring career, and yet, according to one way of looking
at the figures, Alexander was more vigorous still. We can compare Philip and
Alexander from similar baselines, as both men acquired the partners from whom
they begat their first attested offspring at the age of 24. Philip, born in 382, seems
to have married Audata, the mother of Cynna (and indeed his second wife, Phila)
in 358. Alexander, born in 356, acquired Barsine, mother of Heracles, in 332. Philip
lived on twenty-two years beyond the baseline, dying at 46 in 336. Within this time
he sired six children, according to the Satyrus fragment referred to above, and many
scholars would like to add a seventh, the Caranus referred to by Justin, to this total.[34]
Seven attested impregnations in twenty-two years produces an attested impregnation rate of one every 3.1 years. Alexander lived just eight years beyond his baseline,
dying at 32 in 323. As we have seen, he had, as the tradition knows, given rise to
three attested impregnations by the time of his death in 323: Heracles by Barsine,
Roxane's miscarriage at the Hydaspes,[35] and Alexander IV, also by Roxane. Three
attested pregnancies in eight years produces an attested impregnation rate of one
every 2.7 years, which is actually slightly superior to that of his father's.

The tradition celebrates in addition several supposedly casual liaisons between
Alexander and various women. Indeed Alexander, *gynnis* or otherwise, is associated
with more women in the tradition than is any other Macedonian king. While it may
well be that a historical event of some sort underlies some of these liaisons, the
accounts of them are so obviously and heavily fictionalized that they can offer us
nothing in the attempt to reconstuct even the broader sexual codes of the Macedonian court in which Alexander lived, let alone in the attempt to reconstruct Alexander's own sexuality.

The accounts may be briefly reviewed.[36] They fall into two broad categories, the
first of which is courtesans, of whom three are found. Already from Cleitarchus,
Alexander was associated with Thais, the courtesan who came to be associated
with Ptolemy in Alexandria, and bore him the children Lagus, Leontiscus, and
Eirene. She it was, supposedly, who supposedly instigated and enacted the burning
of Persepolis.[37] It is possible that her inclusion in the traditions relating to the cam-

[33]   Plu. *Alex.* 21; cf. Curt. 5.6.8, 10.5.32. Curt. 6.5.32 tells us that Alexander was rather less ardent than
the Amazon queen Thalestris, with whom he agreed to mate. Alexander's sexual restraint was more
often commented on in the context of dealings with boys, however: see Plu. *Mor.* 338d; *Alex.* 22; Ath.
603b (incorporating Dicaearchus F23 Wehrli and a fragment of Carystius' *Historika Hypomnemata*).
[34]   Just. 11.2.3.
[35]   A miscarriage could, I suppose, have been attributed to some sort of deficiency in virility on the
father's part.
[36]   See Ogden 1999: 42; Reames-Zimmerman 1999: 89–90.
[37]   Ath. 576de (including Cleitarchus, *FGrH* 137 F11); Plu. *Alex.* 38; D.S. 17.72; and Curt. 5.7.2–11;
Berve, no. 359; Peremans and Van't Dack 1950–81: no. 14723; Lane Fox 1973: 262–4, 529; and Ogden
1999: index s.v. There is no mention of Thais' involvement in the burning of the palace at Arr. 3.18.11.
If her role in it had been a historical one, then it is possible that Ptolemy passed over it in silence in
the history of which Arrian made so much use.

paign court was retrospective. According to Theophrastus, Callixeina, a Thessalian courtesan, was introduced to the adolescent Alexander by Philip and Olympias in order to cure him of or divert him from his *gynnis* condition. Credible or otherwise, it is noteworthy that this tale was developed very soon after Alexander's death, with Theophrastus writing in the late fourth century or very early third.[38] Aelian tells that the artist Apelles, a highly romanticized figure,[39] "loved the concubine [*pallake*] of Alexander, whose name was Pancaste, and she was Larisan by birth. They say that she was the first woman Alexander had sex with."[40] Pancaste looks rather like a doublet of Callixeina: both hail from Thessaly; both have a courtesan-like designation; and both are, ostensibly, the first woman with whom Alexander has sex.[41]

The second category consists of the recurring motif of the queen transitorily encountered by Alexander in the course of his campaign, who uses him as stud to beget children. The most striking and prominent example of this motif is that of Thal(l)estris, the Amazon queen who supposedly presented herself to Alexander "for the sake of child-making" (παιδοποιίας ἕνεκεν). She was mentioned by Cleitarchus, and was already so established in the Alexander tradition when Aristobulus and Ptolemy wrote that they felt the need to deny it, as, reportedly, did no less an authority than King Lysimachus.[42] According to Justin, Cleophis or Cleophylis, the queen of Indian Beira (which Arrian calls Bazira), ransomed her captured citadel by sleeping with the king and going on to bear a son she named "Alexander."[43] This narrative is in turn perhaps a calque on the Thalestris tradition. It also seems to have been remodeled to reenact the Augustan version of Cleopatra VII's relationships with Caesar and Antony, the queen supposedly ransoming back Egypt from them by sleeping with them and bearing them children (and in Caesar's case a child that shared his name). Justin reports that Cleophis acquired the name of "royal whore" (*scortum regium*) among the Indians, a designation which may reflect "the harlot queen of old Canopus."[44] Two further episodes perhaps reflect

[38] Ath. 435a, incorporating Hieronymus of Rhodes F38 Wehrli and Theophrastus F578 Fortenbaugh.

[39] Cf., again, Lucian *Herodotus* or *Aetion*.

[40] Ael. *VH* 12.34; cf. Reames-Zimmerman 1999: 89 (where the reference is given incorrectly as 7.34).

[41] We find a version of this same story also at Plin. *HN* 35.86, where the concubine's name is given rather as Campaspe. Here we are not explicitly told that Campaspe was Alexander's first love, but we are told that she was his favorite. In an act of magnanimity, Alexander handed her over to Apelles.

[42] Plu. *Alex.* 46 cites many writers on both sides of the debate, including Cleitarchus, *FGrH* 137 F16; Ptolemy, *FGrH* 138 F28; and Aristobulus, *FGrH* 139 F21. See also D.S. 17.77.1–3 (from whom the quote; he is the earliest preserved writer to name the queen Thallestris); Curt. 6.5.24–32; Just. 12.3.5–7 (additionally supplying the alternative name Minythyia). Arr. 7.13.2–3 soberly alludes to, but denies (because omitted by Ptolemy and Aristobulus), accounts according to which Atropates, the satrap of Media, produced 300 Amazon women for Alexander in 324. See Hamilton 1969 on §46 and Brunt 1976–83: app. 21.

[43] Just. 12.7.9–11. Orosius 3.19.1 also has Cleophis sleeping with Alexander (*concubitu regnum redemit*), but Curt. 8.10.35 gives no indication of this or that her son was his. See also Berve, no. 435. For Bazira, see Arr. 4.27–8.

[44] See Yardley and Develin 1994: 115, and, for Augustan propaganda against Cleopatra, Propertius 3.11.39; Plin. *HN* 9.119.

the "pull" of this motif also. Arrian tells that Ada of Alinda adopted Alexander himself as her own son,[45] while the late and ostentatiously fictional Pseudo-Callisthenic *Alexander Romance* gives us Candace, the Ethiopian queen expressing a desire for sons like Alexander.[46]

Thalestris and her Amazons are particularly interesting. In presenting herself to Alexander for stud purposes, she is right at home in the context of the richly elaborated Amazon myths and traditions. Various accounts of their society describe their casual use of men for mere insemination.[47] However, if one surveys the copious literary remains of the complex of Classical Amazon myths in general, one sees that these accounts agree that the Amazons had been completely exterminated in the remote past. The invasion of the Athens of Theseus had been their last, disastrous stand, though some, under Penthesilea, had struggled on into the time of the Trojan War, to disappear at that point for ever.[48] The function of the myth, in this respect, was to distance such a threateningly topsy-turvy, women-on-top world from all that was familiar, near, historical, and real. So, for all that Alexander had progressed far beyond the Amazons' traditional homeland of Themiscyra, adjacent to the Thermodon, the generation of the notion that he came to encounter Amazons themselves, whatever its historical starting point (Atropates?)[49] was in striking defiance of a great weight of established tradition.[50]

Alexander's Boys

Let us again begin with a brief review of the data. Alexander is given sexual relationships with three men in the tradition, Hephaestion, Bagoas, Excipinus(?), and perhaps Hector son of Parmenion, although the evidence for the last two is vestigial.[51] A substantial number of texts represent Alexander's relationship with Hephaestion as particularly close.[52] A more limited number assert or strongly imply

[45]   Arr. 1.23.8; however, Carney 2003b: 248–9 treats the Ada episode as historical.
[46]   Ps.-Callisthenes, *Alexander Romance* 3.18, possibly a dim reflection of Alexander's rather different encounter with Ada of Alinda, as narrated at Arr. 1.23.8.
[47]   E.g., Hdt. 4.113; D.S. 3.53; Str. C504.
[48]   Lys. 2.4; Isoc. 4.24, 68–70; D.S. 2.45–6, 3.52, 4.16; Just. 2.4.
[49]   See above n. 42. Hamilton 1969 on §46 sees the origin of the Alexander–Amazon tale in the Scythian king's offer of a daughter to Alexander (Arr. 4.15.1; Curt. 8.1.9–10).
[50]   See Ogden 1996b: 182–6 for a more detailed justification of the views expressed here, and the principal literary ancient references to Amazons beyond those associated with Alexander. See now also Blok 1997.
[51]   Excipinus will be treated below. The case for Hector (Berve, no. 295) depends on Curt. 4.8.7–9. Here we are told that this lad was in the very flower of his youth (pederastic phraseology) and particularly dear to Alexander (*eximio aetatis flore, in paucis Alexandro carus*), and that when he drowned Alexander was deeply upset and gave him a magnificent funeral, seemingly anticipating that given to Hephaestion. This, I take it, is the evidence that leads Hammond 1981: 265 to posit an affair between the two. Jul. *EP.* 59 implies that Alexander was in some way responsible for Hector's death.
[52]   For Hephaestion, see Berve, no. 357; Heckel 1992: 65–90; Reames-Zimmerman 1999.

that they had a sexual relationship. The most explicit, although far from unproblematic, of these is Arrian's decontextualized observation:

> (Note) that Alexander garlanded the tomb of Achilles and Hephaestion that of Patroclus, the latter riddling that he too was a beloved of Alexander, in just the same way as Patroclus was of Achilles. (Aelian, *Varia Historia* 12.7)[53]

Next in importance is a passing reference in Arrian's *Dissertationes* [sc. *Epicteteae*] *ab Arriano digestae*, which presumably reflects, in the first instance, the words of Epictetus rather than of Arrian.[54] Although it does not mention Hephaestion by name, it does say that Alexander ordered the temples of Asclepius to be burned when his ἐρώμενος died.[55] This is likely to be a reference to the roughly similar measures that Arrian tells us in his own voice that Alexander took after Hephaestion's 324 death in the *Anabasis*.[56] Justin seems to imply that Hephaestion was Alexander's ἐρώμενος in observing that he was dear to Alexander because of his beauty and his boyishness and because of the services he performed for him (from which sexual services cannot be absolutely excluded): *formae, pueritiae, obsequiis*.[57] Curtius uniquely speaks of a man, whose name, according to one MS, was Excipinus,[58] in terms which similarly strongly imply that he was an ἐρώμενος of Alexander but which also make it clear that he served as a sort of replacement for Hephaestion: "... Excipinus, still quite young and beloved to Alexander because of the flower of his youth. Although he equalled Hephaestion in the beauty of his body, he was certainly not equal to him in manly charm." This is the only reference in the tradition to Excipinus.[59]

---

[53] I hope to deal with the complexities of this text in further study.
[54] For this text see Stadter 1980: 26–7; Reames-Zimmerman 1999: 90.
[55] Arrian's *Dissertationes* [sc. *Epicteteae*] *ab Arriano digestae* 2.22.17–18. The reference is wrongly given (for all that it is critical to her piece) at Reames-Zimmerman 1999: 90 (as 2.12.17–18).
[56] Arr. 7.14.5.
[57] Just. 12.12.11.
[58] Curt. 7.9.19. Among the MSS, C offers *excipinon*, P *escipinon*. Hedicke suggested Euxenippus, and is followed by, e.g., the Loeb (Rolfe 1946) and Reames-Zimmerman 1999: 91. The difficulties of the reading or construing of the name hardly militate against the man's existence, *pace* Tarn ii. 321. Cf. Reames-Zimmerman 1999: 91–2.
[59] I list the other texts that imply a sexual relationship between Alexander and Hephaestion:

- In the spurious and undated, but no doubt late, *Letters* of Diogenes, we find a brief note addressed to Alexander: "If you want to become a respectable man, throw off the bit of string you have on your head and come to me. But there is no way you can, for you are controlled by Hephaestion's thighs" (*Diogenis Sinopensis Epistulae* 24.1 Hercher). This is ostensibly a homoerotic reference (as noted by Reames-Zimmerman 1999: 90–1, who, however, seems to be unaware of the spurious nature of this text).
- D.S. 17.114.1–2 tells that Alexander honored Hephaestion in life most of all his friends, even though Craterus had a love to rival Hephaestion's. Alexander is said to have described Craterus as merely "king-loving," whereas Hephaestion was "Alexander-loving."
- At Lucian *Dialogues of the Dead* 397 Philip makes a scornful *praeteritio* of Alexander's errors, as we have seen, "making so many marriages and loving Hephaestion to excess." The word ὑπεραγαπῶν

If the relationship was indeed a sexual one, then it can be contextualized in this regard against known homosexual relationships in and around the Macedonian court. The sensitivities associated with them had often erupted into regicide. Aristotle tells that the killers of Archelaus, Crateuas and Hellenocrates of Larissa, had been former *eromenoi* of the king.[60] He also tells that Amyntas the Little had been killed by Derdas after taunting him with his "youthfulness," which is probably a euphemistic description of the misuse of an *eromenos*.[61] Diodorus tells how Philip was famously killed by a former *eromenos* Pausanias, in the finale of a complex dispute which also involved another of Philip's *eromenoi*, also called Pausanias.[62] However, Alexander's relationship with Hephaestion is likely to have fallen more particularly into the pattern of homosexual relationships between age-peers that are typical of the military elites, and the training bodies for those elites, found in a number of Greek societies, notably Sparta and Thebes. In the case of Macedon, the initial breeding ground for such relationships appears to have been the corps of the Royal Pages (*basilikoi paides*).[63] Alexander and Hephaestion were, so far as we can tell, exact contemporaries. Curtius tells that they were brought up together.[64] We hear of other peer relationships formed among the Royal Pages. Two of the boys involved in the Conspiracy of the Pages were Hermolaus and Sostratus. Arrian explicitly declares that Sostratus was the same age as Hermolaus and his ἐραστής.[65] Also involved in the plot was another Page, Epimenes. Arrian refers also to his

---

does not necessarily entail sexual love in itself. While it may be thought that sexual love must be referred to here for the criticism to have any force, the criticism could perhaps relate merely to the excessive mourning for Hephaestion. I am baffled by Reames-Zimmerman's reference (1999: 92), to this homily as "typically Stoic." Lucian was an agnostic philosopher, with preferences – literary preferences, at any rate – for Epicureanism and Cynicism.

These texts, taken together, amount to a good circumstantial case that a strand at any rate of the ancient traditions regarded Hephaestion as Alexander's ἐρώμενος, in the familiar fashion of Classical Athenian-style Greek pederasty, which was structured, *inter alia*, by an age difference between the lover and the beloved. For the notion that these traditions may have begun during Hephaestion's lifetime, in the malicious gossip of his rivals, see Heckel 1992: 84. It is a great pity to have lost Ephippus of Olynthus' pamphlet "On the Death of Alexander and of Hephaestion," *FGrH* 126, for which see Pearson 1960: 61–8 and Heckel 1992: 87.

[60] Arist. *Pol.* 1311b8–35.
[61] Arist. *Pol.* 1311b4.
[62] D.S. 16.93–4. Philip also supposedly made an ἐρώμενος of Olympias' brother Alexander of Epirus, according to Just. 8.6.4–8. Philip had himself been the *eromenos* of the Pammenes during his hostage-ship in Thebes: *Suda* s.v. Κάρανος; cf. Philip's supposed supportive remarks about the homosexual activities of the Theban Sacred Band after Chaeroneia at Plu. *Pel.* 18.
[63] Ogden 1996b: 111–19 (the military context homosexuality at Sparta and Thebes), 120–1 (the Macedonian Royal Pages), and 121–3 (Alexander). For homosexuality in the Macedonian court, see now also now Reames-Zimmerman 1999: 87–8, and Mortensen (forthcoming).
[64] Curt. 3.12.16–17: *cum ipso pariter eductus.* See also *Alexander Romance* 1.18 and Julius Valerius, *Res Gestae Alexandri Magni* 1.10. See Berve ii. 169 and Heckel 1992: 66–8; *pace* Tarn ii. 57 and Reames-Zimmerman 1999: 91.
[65] Arr. 4.13.3; cf. also Plu. *Alex.* 55 and Curt. 8.6–8.

lover, Charicles, and it is likely, from context, that this Charicles was also one of the Pages.[66] In a passage of scurrilous, humorous abuse of the Macedonian Companions, Theopompus spoke of them having sex with each other, for all that they were all bearded.[67]

However, we cannot invoke this sort of contextualization – peer homosexuality in a military context – for the relationship Alexander is held to have had with the Persian eunuch Bagoas. Indeed, this is a relationship that we cannot hope to contextualize at all, since there was no known history of eunuchism at the Macedonian court. But, as with Hephaestion, the tradition appears to represent him consistently in the role of a Classical, Athenian-style *eromenos* to Alexander. What we hear in fact consists of seven (or possibly just six) testimonies, two of which substantially overlap.[68]

We are told emphatically that Alexander had a sexual relationship with the eunuch by Plutarch in the context of his tale about the theater (whatever kind of theater it was)[69] in Gedrosia:

---

[66] Arr. 4.13.7. See Berve, no. 824 and Ogden 1996b: 121 for his status as a Page; caution from Reames-Zimmerman 1999: 88.

[67] Theopompus, *FGrH* 115 F225a, at Plb. 8.9.9–12.

[68] Even so we hear rather more than either Tarn ii. 320 (although he subsequently contradicts himself) and Stoneman 1997: 52 allow. The references are collected at Berve, nos. 194 and 195.

The uncertain testimony is that of Arrian (*Indica* 18.8), which discusses the appointments Alexander makes for his fleet on the banks of the Hydaspes. A protracted list is given, among which is the brief notice: "And indeed he even had a Persian as a trierarch, Bagoas, son of Pharnouches." It is not clear whether this Bagoas is to be identified with Alexander's eunuch friend, whose patronymic we are not otherwise given (for the contention that we are dealing with two different Bagoases here, see Berve, nos. 194, 195, 768; Tarn ii. 322). Bagoas was in any case a common (Hellenized version of a) Persian name, one commonly, but not exclusively, attached to eunuchs (For other eunuch Bagoases, see Plin. *HN* 13.41; Ov. *Am.* 2.2.1; cf., more generally, Badian 1958b: 144.) But what gives most pause for thought is the consideration that Arrian draws attention to the fact that Bagoas was given a command *even though* he was a Persian, and not *even though* he was a eunuch, which might have been considered a greater object of note, a greater obstacle to military command, and indeed to subsume the quality of "Persianness." Berve, no. 768 insisted on distinguishing the two, but on the spurious grounds that the eunuch Bagoas could not have used such a patronymic as deriving from the slave class (not obviously true of Persian society), and that the trierarch ought to have been older than the eunuch. But we know nothing of the eunuch's age: Curtius' reference (6.5.22–3) to his *pueritia* may as much address the undeveloped nature of his body or indeed his role as *eromenos* as it does any actual age. Nor is it clear that the Pharnouches identified as the father of Bagoas the trierarch is to be identified with the Lycian Pharnouches, whom one would have expected to have been Persian.

A relatively uninformative testimony is a fragment of Eumenes of Cardia preserved by Aelian, which tells us that Alexander had dinner with Bagoas on the 27th of the Macedonian month of Dios at his house, which was ten stades distant from his palace (Ael. *VH* 3.23, incorporating Eumenes of Cardia, *FGrH* 117 F2a). But the importance of this text is that it tells us that a source particularly close to Alexander vouched for the reality of Bagoas. For this reason Tarn ii. 322 n. 3 contended that this referred to another Bagoas. It appears from the organization of the index at Hammond 1981: 343 that Hammond identifies this Bagoas with the Lycian trierarch, and distinguishes him from the eunuch.

[69] See Tarn ii. 322; Badian 1958: 151.

When Alexander arrived at the palace of Gedrosia,[70] he restored the army with a festival. It is said that he got drunk and watched choral competitions. His beloved (ἐρώμενον) Bagoas won in the dancing and he traversed the theater in his costume and sat down beside him. Seeing this, the Macedonians applauded and shouted out, bidding Alexander kiss him, until he embraced him and kissed him deeply (περιβαλὼν κατεφίλησεν).[71] (Plu. *Alex.* 67.8)

The tale originated, as it seems, with Dicaearchus in *c.*320 (this is the overlapping testimony):[72]

Alexander the king loved boys to distraction (φιλόπαις . . . ἐκμανῶς). At any rate, Dicaearchus says in his *Sacrifice at Ilium* that he was so enthralled with (ἡττᾶσθαι) the eunuch Bagoas that in the view of the entire theater he bent back and kissed him deeply, and when the audience shouted approval and applauded, he did as they bid and bent back and kissed him again. (Ath. 603b, incorporating Dicaearchus F23 Wehrli)

But even in this story, Bagoas is nothing more than a cypher, and while we must concede that we are told that he had a sexual relationship with Alexander, we are given nothing with which to color in this outline.

For such color, we depend on Curtius, who gives us two developed narrative episodes featuring the eunuch, but the value of such color, for the historical reconstruction of Alexander's love life is almost nil, because the impact of an elaborate structuring upon it can be clearly detected. To make the case, I shall devote the remainder of this piece to a more detailed analysis of Curtius' material. Several of the more important texts and narratives bearing upon Alexander's sexuality could sustain similar treatment. First, in book 6, Bagoas is given to Alexander among the gifts of Darius' chiliarch Narbazanes:

. . . amongst which was Bagoas, a eunuch of exceptional appearance and in the very flower of boyhood, with whom Darius had had a relationship, and with whom Alexander soon had one; and was because he was most greatly moved by Bagoas' prayers that he spared Narbazanes. (Curt. 6.5.22–3)[73]

And then in book 10[74] we are told, at greater length, of the story of Darius' general Orsines (or Orxines). He meets Alexander's advance in Pasargadae and gives the

---

[70]   The palace will have been at Pura, but Plutarch may have mistakenly transposed Gedrosia and Carmania: see Tarn ii. 322; Badian 1958: 151–2.

[71]   Hammond 1981: 322 sweetly observes that "to kiss an actor even twice was no more a homosexual act than it would be in acting circles today"(!).

[72]   Tarn ii. 93 contended that the figure of Bagoas was invented out of nothing by Dicaearchus, to be elaborated by Curtius.

[73]   For discussion of this passage, see Tarn ii. 320, stiffened by Badian 1958: 145.

[74]   McKechnie 1999 concludes that the fictive element in this book of Curtius is high.

king and his friends gifts, so winning them over initially, but his generosity was his undoing (10.1.22–42):

> For when he had honored all the king's friends with gifts beyond their prayers, he had no honor for the eunuch Bagoas, who had enslaved him to himself by giving up his body to him. Some people advised Orsines that Bagoas was dear to the king, but he replied that he was honoring the friends of the king, not his prostitutes, and it was not customary for the Persians to consider as male those rendered effeminate by fornication.[75] On hearing this, the eunuch directed the power he had attained by means of outrage and disgrace against an innocent and most honorable person. (Curt. 10.1.25–7)[76]

Curtius goes on to explain how Bagoas drips poisonous thoughts about Orsines into the king's ears and sets up Persian stooges to incriminate him:

> And the most shameless prostitute, not forgetting deception even in the midst of fornication and the passive experience of disgrace, whenever he had inflamed the king's love for him, accused Orsines sometimes of greed, sometimes even of disloyalty. (Curt. 10.1.29)

Bagoas is given direct speech, in which he tells Alexander that Orsines has plundered the wealth he has given to him from the tomb of Cyrus, and then brings in his stooges to support his allegations (10.1.33–5). The king accordingly has Orsines executed (10.1.36–8).

> Not content with the execution of an innocent man, the eunuch himself struck Orsines as he was about to be killed. Orsines looked at him and said "I had heard that women had once ruled in Asia, but this is something new: that a eunuch should rule!" (Curt. 10.1.37)

Curtius concludes his narrative of the Orsines episode with comments on Alexander's decline. A little earlier he had not been able to execute Alexander of Lyncestus, despite clear evidence, but now:

> At the end of his life he has so far declined from his own nature that, despite once having a mind resistant to lust, he now, at the whim of a prostitute, gave kingdoms to some and took life from others. (Curt. 10.1.40–2)[77]

---

[75] I find the Rolfe 1946 Loeb translation here implausible: "it was not the custom of the Persians to mate with males who made females of themselves by prostitution." This seems to depend upon construing *ducere* in a sense extrapolated from *ducere uxorem*, "marry."

[76] Discussion at Tarn ii. 321, importantly modified by Badian 1958: 147–50.

[77] Tarn ii. 98, 319, 321 makes much of the fact that in Curtius' narrative the Bagoas figure serves to highlight Alexander's increasing decadence: the point is a good one, whatever the shortcomings of Tarn's general approach to the traditions of Alexander's homosexuality. See also Hammond 1981: 322.

Curtius, we should note, is emphatic about the fact that Alexander had a sexual relationship with Bagoas (*obsequio corporis devinxerat sibi; ne in stupro quidem et dedecoris patientia fraudis oblitum, quotiens amorem regis in se accenderat*). The general tenor of Curtius' material is consonant with the generalization made by Plutarch, which constitutes our final, vague, testimony for Bagoas: "Alexander freely allowed the Hagnons and the Bagoases and the Hagesiases and the Demetriuses to derail him as they performed *proskynesis* before him, dressed him up, manipulated him as if he were some barbarian effigy."[78] However, the general tenor seems to be contradicted by Curtius' summary analysis of Alexander's character. The basic line is that his good qualities derived from nature, his bad ones from his fortune and his youth:

> He was moderate in his immoderate desires. He had sex only within the limits of natural desire. He experienced no pleasure save that which is allowed. And these qualities were certainly the gifts of his character/nature. (Curt. 10.5.32)[79]

These remarks are platitudes based upon Peripatetic notions of *enkrateia*. That they sit so ill with the story Curtius has recently completed suggest that the story has a certain momentum and internal logic of its own.

The key point, and one that has seemingly evaded attention, is that there is a tight set of responses between the Narbazanes tale and the Orsines tale. In both episodes a surrendering Persian general meets Alexander's advance, begging to be spared. Both men seek to insure this by giving lavish gifts. In the Orsines episode Bagoas himself effects the decision to spare; in the second he himself effects the decision to kill. The parallelism between the episodes certainly helps to convey a decline of a sort in Alexander, and this is almost explicit in Curtius' words. But the story is also very much one of Bagoas' own thwarted aspiration, and makes much of the motif of the gift: it is Bagoas' aspiration to progress from the status of a gift himself, an owned slave, to one who receives gifts.

There are more fundamental issues at stake too, and these are revealed by Orsines' first insult to Bagoas: "he was honoring the friends of the king, not his prostitutes, and it was not customary for the Persians to consider as male those rendered effeminate by fornication." The last phrase is a little odd: it might be thought that Bagoas had been rendered effeminate by castration rather more than by fornication, but the Classical Greeks had certainly been familiar with the idea that an excessive devotion to sex, whether homosexual, as in the case of Aeschines' Timarchus (also, supposedly, a prostitute),[80] or indeed heterosexual, as in the case of the adulterer,[81] rendered one effeminate, and this seems to be the idea here. But the key point lies in the *non sequitur* between the two parts of Orsines' insult:

[78]   Plu. *Mor.* 65d, *How to distinguish a flatter from a friend.*
[79]   See, more generally, Curt. 10.5.26–36 and Arr. 7.28–30.
[80]   Aeschin. 1 (*Against Timarchus*); see also Dover 1978: *passim* and Fisher 2001.
[81]   For the effeminacy of the adulterer, see, e.g., Hom. *Il.* 6.321–2, 503–14 (Paris); A. A. 1633–5, 1643–5 (Aegisthus); see Dover 1978: 106 for the effeminate representation of adulterers on vases.

another premise needs to be supplied, to the effect that only males are worthy of gifts. And so we see that Bagoas' craving for gifts does not merely proceed from greed or a desire to aggrandize himself, but from a desire to recover or at any rate symbolically restore his lost manhood. While the eunuch may seek power (*potentiam . . . quaesitam*) as a simulacrum of masculinity, he can achieve it only through a feminizing act. The observation delivered by Orsines before he dies, *regnare castratum*, is at one level to be read literally, as an indictment of the condition of Alexander's regime. Bagoas has come to such a position of influence with Alexander that he effectively rules Asia (one may also wonder whether Alexander himself might fit the bill as metaphorical *castratus regnans*, emasculated by his subjection to Bagoas). But *regnare castratum* is also an insult, a bitter paradox, honed for the Bagoas who has just hit Orsines: for all that he may rule, he remains castrated.

Accordingly, these two episodes intertwine tragic arcs for both Orsines and, more to the point, Bagoas himself. The story, I submit, is simply too good, and should not be used to draw any conclusions about the nature of Alexander's relationship with Bagoas, or about the development of it. The language applied to Bagoas on the whole indicates that the tradition integrated him into Alexander's story in the role of a Classical, Athenian-style *eromenos*, however old he was in fact: Curtius refers to his *pueritia*, Plutarch refers to him as an ἐρώμενος, and Athenaeus introduces his reference to him with the claim that Alexander was φιλόπαις . . . ἐκμανῶς, as we have seen.[82] The curious remarks attributed to Orsines in his initial insult (*nec moris esse Persis mares ducere qui stupro effeminarentur*), however, perhaps rather cast Bagoas in the role of the adult *kinaidos*, rendered effeminate by his craving for (homosexual) sex rather than by the knife.

The general conclusion of this piece may strike some as curiously close to the Tarnism with which we began, in that it has attempted to remove much of the most colorful and engaging material in the Alexander tradition bearing upon Alexander's sexuality from the debate about his sexuality as a historical phenomenon. While I, in contrast to Tarn, am inclined to accept Alexander's heterosexual "promiscuity" (insofar as this concept has any real significance) and homosexual encounters, it is not because I have significantly greater confidence in the historical value of the individual relevant parts of the Alexander tradition. It is rather because the tradition's representation of Alexander's sex life, in outline, if not in detail, allows it to conform to the patterns of sex life reconstructable for Philip before him and for other Macedonian kings. In short, a continent, strictly heterosexual and non-"promiscuous" Alexander is ultimately harder to understand and explain in historical context than the opposite.

[82] Buffière 1980: 30–4 treats the practice, in Greek context, as a variation of pederasty.

12

Heroes, Cults, and Divinity

Boris Dreyer

This chapter provides an overview of the known cults for Alexander the Great and his closest family and adherents. With regard to Alexander, Bosworth observes:

> Beginning as a Heraclid and descendant of heroes, he had become son of Zeus and competitor with the heroes. Finally he had become a god manifest on earth, to be honored with all the appurtenances of cult. The precedent for the worship of a living man was firmly established, and cults were offered to his Successors with greater frequency and magnificence.

The core question that remains for the current scholarly debate is to what extent the various ways of putting the king on par with heroes and gods were actually contemporary. There is also a need to clarify in detail which of the cults and festivities in the various cities were actually desired by Alexander[1] and which were introduced during his lifetime.[2] The available evidence, almost without exception, dates to the period after Alexander's death. The arguments for dating these phenomena within the lifetime of the king are no more than indices. The same is true of the explanations advanced regarding the motives for establishing these honors. There is also a debate as to the extent to which deification stems from oriental/Persian or Egyptian influences on Alexander, and/or whether deification of a living person is reconcilable with Greek thought.[3]

It is in this context that the disputes over Alexander's attempt in the year 328 to introduce *proskynesis* must be seen. Hephaestion had prepared the attempt, with the

---

[1] E.g., Bosworth 1988a: 288, with n. 15.

[2] Habicht 1956: 17–36.

[3] Habicht 1956; 1970; Badian 1981; Bosworth 1988a: 278–90; Seibert 1994: 192–206; Gehrke 2003a: 157–8. On the abundant literature discussing the divinity of Alexander and the relationship between Alexander and the Greeks, see Ferguson 1912–13; Schnabel 1925; 1926; Stier 1939: 391–5; Balsdon 1950; Taeger 1957; Bosworth 1977; Rosen 1978; Fredricksmeyer 1979–80, 1981; Zahrnt 1996, 2003; Faraguna 2003; Nowotka 2003; Wiemer 2005: 163–4.

court historian Callisthenes refusing full implementation. *Proskynesis*, the forms and variants of which are still intensely disputed,[4] was a specific form of symbolic obeisance by the "subjects" (of various legal and social categories) before the Achaemenid ruler, whose tradition Alexander considered himself part of as time progressed (especially from 330) – much to the chagrin of his Macedonian and Greek followers.

In the ceremony that Alexander aimed to introduce, an important role was played by the altar whose eternal flame would cease to burn only when the Great King died (or, as Alexander ordered, on Hephaestion's death in 324). The king received the guest in the antechamber by drinking from a bowl, which he then passed to the guest. The guest emptied the bowl and bowed (or knelt) before the altar of the eternal flame. Then he would kiss the king on the mouth. Callisthenes' act of impropriety, for which he fell into disfavor (his final fall from grace occurred in connection with the Pages' Conspiracy; see Heckel, ch. 4), was his attempt to omit the genuflection in front of the altar when the king was distracted. However, when his refusal was detected, the attempt at introducing *proskynesis* failed and was never repeated.[5] But apart from that, because the Great King had never been divine in the Achaemenid empire, *proskynesis* could not serve as preparation for divine kingship, according to Persian custom. "Greek authors apparently agree that the Persian monarch was not regarded as divine by his subjects and that *proskynesis* was not an act of worship. None the less it evoked widespread abhorrence."[6]

Even if *proskynesis* could not serve as a means of deification, Alexander stylized his descent from heroes and gods from an early date. The king identified himself especially with Heracles, Achilles, and Dionysus in two respects:[7] on the maternal side he traced his lineage via the Epirote Molossians to the hero Achilles; the Argeads, the ruling house in Macedonia, traced their ancestry back to Heracles. Furthermore, it is abundantly evident from his actions that his motive was to repeat what Achilles, Heracles, and Dionysus had done, or indeed to improve upon their acts.[8] After crossing the Hellespont Alexander visited Ilium (see also below) and paid sacrifice at the tomb of Priam to do penance for the actions of his "ancestor" Achilles.[9] He granted favors to the Cilician Mallians based on their common descent from Argos,[10] and personally led his army into

---

[4] Seibert 1994: 143–4, 202–4.

[5] This was recorded by Chares of Mytilene, the court chamberlain of Alexander on the march: Plu. *Alex.* 54.5–6; Arr. 4.12.3–5; *FGrH* 125 F14.

[6] Discussed at length by Bosworth 1988a: 284–7, at 284. His conclusion that the ceremony aimed to prepare Alexander's deification is based on those sources in which *proskynesis* was discussed at court, including Callisthenes' speech against it: Plu. *Alex.* 54.3; Arr. 4.10.5; Curt. 8.5.9. The content, however, seems to be ahistorical. Macedonian opposition to the ceremony followed from their displeasure at being equated with Persian "barbarians."

[7] On the identification with Dionysus and Heracles, see Seibert 1994: 204–6.

[8] Bosworth 1988a: 281–2.

[9] Arr. 1.11.8. The visit was motivated by the mythological-historical obligation of Alexander (he also visited Achilles' tomb): Str. 13.1.27 C594; Bringmann and von Steuben 1995, nos. 246–8. For an overview of Alexander and Achilles see Ameling 1988: 657–92.

[10] Arr. 2.5.9.

Figure 12.1 Shrine of the Bark: dedicatory inscription of Alexander the Great praising the god Amun-Ra four times, while the nomes bring offerings, *c.*330–325 BC. Egypt, Thebes: Luxor Temple. Oriental Institute, The University of Chicago. 38387/N. 43812/CHFN 9246. Photo: The Oriental Institute.

battles in the Hindu Kush, exposing himself to great danger, in order to match up to the models he wished to emulate, namely Heracles and Dionysus,[11] though the latter was relevant only to the eastern part of the campaign. One of the aims of his march through the Gedrosian desert was to compete with Cyrus and Semiramis.[12] Alexander also frequently appeared in robes and disguises that

[11] In 327/6 he besieged the Aornus mountain, where Heracles, according to myth, had failed: Arr. 4.28.2, 30.4; Curt. 8.11.2.
[12] Schepens 1989.

obviously referred to attributes of the gods that he admired (Hermes and Artemis among others).[13]

In modern scholarship, however, there are keen debates as to whether the king felt himself to be an incarnation of Dionysus (as the one who successfully reached India), or whether he would not become a Neos Dionysus until after his death. Such identifications, especially in the latter case, depend on how they are presented in the ancient tradition and how far modern accounts rely on the different ancient versions.

The "vulgate" tradition was associated with Callisthenes' positive image of Alexander, which started with Cleitarchus' hymnic, transfiguring depiction of the king, which can in turn be found in relatively true-to-original form in the seventeenth book of Diodorus and where an intensification of the Dionysian elements can also be discerned. In the first century, during the period in which the Roman republic was threatened by Mithridates VI Eupator, there was a tendency toward a negative portrayal of Alexander, as reflected by Curtius Rufus in the early imperial age.[14] Whatever historical links to Dionysus remain here serve primarily to illustrate the negative characterization of a drunkard. This negative portrayal, however, also had begun immediately after the death of the king in the satirical text of Ephippus, which has as its general theme the deification of Hephaestion and Alexander. The text ridicules comparison with Heracles and his *apotheosis*, contrasting this with Alexander's unhistorical demise after drinking from the "Cup of Heracles" during a heavy drinking session.[15]

As son of the god Zeus, Alexander was raised to the sphere of the gods by the priests of Ammon at the oracular site in the oasis of Siwah.[16] He had identified himself as son of Zeus before that, and it was something his mother had also repeatedly emphasized.[17] The various reports on the Siwah oasis, which contain strong divergences, reflect varying levels of motivation and bias.[18] The report by Ptolemy in Arrian[19] describes in relatively sober and reserved terms the march, after the founding of Alexandria, to the oasis greatly revered among the Greeks, where Alexander performed a sacrifice to Zeus Basileus. Callisthenes and Cleitarchus embellished this (basic) version, which was familiar with and downplayed the extravagant versions. Cleitarchus, who lived in Alexandria at the time of Ptolemy I, had the founding of Alexandria (April 7, 331) follow the inspirational visit to

[13] *FGrH* 126 F5; Bosworth 1988a: 287–8.
[14] Lehmann 1971: 23ff.
[15] *FGrH* 126 F3; see Bosworth 1988a: 287; Lauffer 1993: 186–7 n. 32.
[16] Kienast 1988; for debate on the research see Seibert 1994: 116–25; Bosworth 1988a: 282–4. This oracle was highly rated by the Greeks (see Hdt 2.50–7).
[17] Plu. *Alex.* 3.3.
[18] There are also a wide range of motives for Alexander's actions, including his urge (*pothos*) to surpass his mythological and genealogical models, Perseus and Heracles (Str. 17.1.43 = Callisthenes, *FGrH* 124 F14; Arr. 3.3.1–2).
[19] Arr. 3.3.1–4.5. Aristobulus' account differs from Ptolemy's on the return route; see Lauffer 1993: 88–9. About the same time reports arrived in Memphis from the oracle of the Branchidae at Miletos and of the Sibyl in Erythrae. They confirmed Alexander as the son of Zeus.

the oasis,[20] which he elevates to a processional oracle according to Egyptian custom.

According to Callisthenes,[21] Alexander alone (without his entourage) was allowed into the sanctum of "the father" Zeus by the Egyptian priests, who greeted him, the liberator from the Persian yoke, as the son of Ammon (the Greeks equated Zeus Ammon with the Egyptian Amun Re), that is, as the ruler of Upper and Lower Egypt.[22] After the visit references to his being the son of a god did not cease.[23] Thus, there would be many occasions on which to establish cults for the son of Zeus.

However, other reasons for dedicating cults to Alexander existed even before this, that is, during the liberation of the cities of Asia Minor.[24] The reasons or pretexts for creating a cult cannot be determined directly from the sources except in the rarest of cases, because they reflect the thinking of later periods.[25] They may document the cult directly or indirectly, but it is with hindsight, long after Alexander's death. Nothing demonstrates the popularity of the ruler and the feeling of commitment toward him more than the fact that his cults were being preserved even in the Augustan period and the second century AD. However, we can confidently assume that most of the documented cults had their origins during the lifetime of the conqueror.

Two major occasions for establishing a cult can be identified. The first was the liberation of the Greek cities on the mainland of Asia Minor from the yoke of Persian domination during Alexander's campaign, beginning in 334/3 (particularly up to the year 332, when Alexander's gains were irreversible).[26] These cities viewed the year 334 as the beginning of a new epoch, which confirms the high esteem in which Alexander's actions were held.[27] These comprised the liberation not only from the Persian yoke, but also from the tyrannies and oligarchies it entailed,[28] the

---

[20]   D.S. 17.49–51.

[21]   *FGrH* 124 F14 = Str. 17.1.43 C814; Plu. *Alex.* 27.

[22]   To the Greek cities in Asia Minor Alexander presented himself as liberator, and he affirmed the indigenous traditions (e.g., Sardis: Bringmann and von Steuben 1995: no. 258; Arr. 1.17.3–4; in Caria, Ada, the widow of Mausolus whom Pixodarus had deposed, adopted Alexander (Arr. 1.23.7–8); see below on Halicarnassus); in Egypt, after being crowned pharaoh, Alexander worshiped the Apis bull in Memphis, unlike Cambyses who supposedly killed it (Arr. 3.1.4).

[23]   Bosworth 1988a: 283.

[24]   In the year 335, just before Alexander's own campaign in Asia Minor, the war in Asia Minor under Parmenion (initiated by Philip) was in crisis, as the propaganda of revenge made little impression on the cities of Asia Minor.

[25]   Habicht 1956; see also afterword of 2nd edn. (1970); Laufer 1993: 181.

[26]   See Habicht 1956: 22–5 for the introduction of Alexander cults in Asia Minor between 334 and 331; the reasons Habicht elaborates for the establishment of the cults are treated skeptically by Badian 1981: 59–63, who argues for an introduction in the last four years of Alexander.

[27]   *SIG*[3] 278; *I. Priene* 3.4, 4.4, 6.4, 7.4. In Priene, the *stephanophoroi* became *eponymoi* magistrates in the year 334: *I. Priene* 2.4. In Miletos, Alexander became the *stephanophoros eponymos* in the same or the following year. From that time on the *stephanophoroi* were inscribed on stone: *I. Milet* 122 II, 81 with commentary; for the other date, see commentary of Herrmann 1997: 166. A decree in Colophon (Robert 1936: 158–68) honored Alexander's actions of 334 as the beginning of a new era; see Meritt 1935: 361, 6–7.

[28]   Arr. 1.17.11, 3.2.4ff.; Curt. 4.8.11; Rhodes–Osborne, no. 83.

collection of tribute,[29] and the introduction of democracy. The second occasion (prepared by the first) at which cults were established was Alexander's own desire for deification; this involved primarily the cities of the Greek mainland (see below).[30]

One notable example occurs in Alexandria by Egypt (the official designation of the city). Here it was probably only *after* Alexander's death that a foundation cult for him was established, with a place of worship at his tomb where the anniversary of his death was celebrated.[31]

Asia Minor and Aegean Islands

During his conquest of Asia Minor, Alexander acted according to fixed principles. In the non-Greek areas, he encouraged traditional forms of rule and administration. In the Greek cities he had set out to liberate, he promoted the establishment of democracy which he supported with administrative reorganization. Examples of these follow.

As with the most important cities of Caria, Alexander sent delegates to free the cities of Ionia and Aeolia, abolishing the oligarchies that ruled them and the tribute paid to the Persians, and reestablishing their ancestral laws and constitutions.[32] Alexandrian games with contests and sacrifices were celebrated by the *koinon*, presumably on Alexander's birthday.[33] During the early principate, the festival in Alexandria marking the king's birthday was always celebrated near Teos,[34] whereas previously – demonstrably in the third century – the event was hosted alternately by the member states of the *koinon*. That the event existed in Alexander's lifetime is not disputed. This league celebration should be distinguished from the Alexander cults that have been shown to exist in the separate member states of the *koinon*.

In Ilium there is documentary evidence for the existence of the *phyle* (tribe) Alexandris in this city.[35] Thus there existed a cult for the king. Because of the

[29] D.S. 17.24.1; Arr. 1.18.2.

[30] Arr. 7.23.2.

[31] Habicht 1956: 36; 1970: 252. The cult has to be separated from the dynasty cult which referred to Alexander. Habicht supposed that the death of Alexander preceded the establishment of the cult, because *basileus* was omitted in the title of the priest: Plaumann 1920: esp. 85; Jul. Val. 3.60; *SEG* ii. 849. In the other cities founded by Alexander no cult is known, although it is likely they existed. In these cases Alexander also established democracies.

[32] Arr. 1.18.1–2 (when Alexander was in Ephesus). In order to block up the harbors for the Persian fleet, he started freeing the important cities along the south coast of Asia Minor (Arr. 1.24.5–6; 26.5–27.4; 2.5.5–9) as soon as he gained Halicarnassus in Caria (with the exception of Salmakis: D.S. 17.27.6).

[33] *OGIS* 222, 24–5 (third century); Str. 14.644 (Augustan era); also Le Bas and Waddington 1870: 1540 (Erythrae, Augustan era; see also Robert 1929: 148).

[34] Str. 14.644.

[35] *CIG* 3615; Brückner 1902: 472, no. 79; 576; see also Frisch 1975: no. 122, with the alternative to equate the *eponymos* of the *phyle* to Paris.

mythical significance of Ilium and Alexander's self-identification with Achilles, the
king had provided repeated favors to the city since his stay there in 334.[36] These
favors included intensive building activities[37] that changed the shape of the city to
such an extent that a tribal reorganization of the citizen-body is plausible. The king
donated gifts for the consecration of the temple of Athena, declared the city to be
autonomous, and freed it from paying tribute. According to sources, Alexander had
other great plans for the city. It is also likely that there was a founder's cult for
Alexander in the city.[38]

The cult of Alexander in Erythrae, for which there is considerable documentation, was also established during his lifetime, as suggested at least by the king's title
associated with the cult. Under Alexander's rule, the city was freed from paying
tribute and became independent.[39] The gratitude shown by the city was great, even
though the plan to cut through the isthmus was not implemented in the end.[40] In
332/1, the sibyl of Erythrae announced that Alexander was the son of Zeus.[41]
Around 270, the sale of the priesthood of King Alexander is epigraphically documented.[42] Habicht argues that the outlays for sacrifices to Alexander after 200 were
intended for the city's own cult, not for the cult of the *koinon*.[43] An inscription
was found on the base of a statue in which *agones* are referred to as Alexandreia.[44]
Correctly ascribing this reference is not so easy. An Alexandrian priest, however,
still existed in the third century AD.[45]

The assumption that a cult for Alexander existed in Teos derives from a suggestion by Rostovtzeff concerning an inscription dating from the second century,[46]
according to which the *theos* (god) mentioned is supposed to be Alexander. The
surrounding area (including Smyrna and Clazomenae) had profited by Alexander's
projects. Though these were left uncompleted, there would be a reason for such an
inscription.[47] However, the proposed reconstruction of the text cannot be upheld,
on account of the remaining letters in the lacuna, and so the origins of the Teos
inscription remain by no means certain.

A cult for Alexander has been shown to have existed in Ephesus. A document
dating from AD 102–16 in the reign of Trajan, takes the form of a *laudatio* for
T. Statilius Kriton.[48] Kriton was the personal physician to the emperor himself, a

---

[36]   Arr. 1.12.1ff.; Plu. *Alex.* 15; D.S. 17.17.3; Just. 11.5.12; Instinsky 1949: 54ff.; Zahrnt 1996: 129–47.
[37]   Str. 13.593.
[38]   Habicht 1956: 21.
[39]   The city still referred to this status in the time of Antiochus I: Welles, *RC* 15, 21ff.
[40]   Paus. 2.1.5; Plin. *NH* 5.116.
[41]   Callisthenes, *FGrH* 124 F14.
[42]   *SIG*³ 1014, 111; date discussed by Robert 1933; Sokolowski 1946: 548; Engelmann and Merkelbach:
no. 201, n. 78.
[43]   Habicht 1956: 19, 93–4.
[44]   Fontrier 1903: 232, no. 2.
[45]   *IGR* iv. 1543, with *OGIS* 3 n. 2.
[46]   Rostovtzeff 1935: 62, with *OGIS* 246, 12.
[47]   Paus. 7.5.1–2; Plin. *NH* 5.117; on the Alexandreia of the Ionian *koinon* see above.
[48]   *SEG* iv. 521.

procurator, and thus priest, of Alexander and of Augustus' grandsons Gaius and Lucius. This physician was frequently consulted and enjoyed great influence. The link to the Alexander cult of the Augustan period demonstrates the enormous importance of the cult over the centuries. An Alexandrian renaissance began even during (and because of) the reign of Trajan (also in historiography, with Arrian writing his account of the "historical" Alexander and referring to the works of Ptolemy and Aristobulus). The title of "king" suggests the cult was instituted during Alexander's lifetime (see above, on the cult in Alexandria), presumably on the occasion of his presence in the city in summer 334. According to Arrian, Alexander had released the city from paying tribute and had given it its freedom.[49] He introduced democracy and restored to their homes the citizens who had fled from Memnon of Rhodes. The divinity of the king during his lifetime is also suggested by the anecdote by Artemidorus of Ephesus, cited in Strabo.[50] According to this story, the Ephesians addressed Alexander as a god, although the context seems to be anachronistic. During Alexander's lifetime, a painting by Apelles[51] was erected in the Artemision in Ephesus, which Alexander had refurbished.[52] Although tribute no longer had to be paid, it was replaced by sacrificial offerings. This provided the basis, in 334, for a characteristic element of, and motive for, the subsequent ruler cult in Greek cities of Asia Minor (see Priene).

Among the Greeks of Asia Minor, Philip's Panhellenic propaganda[53] fell on fertile ground, at least by the time of Parmenion's expeditionary campaign (in 336). The Artemision had already housed a statue of Philip II, but this had been removed by the pro-Persian oligarchs before the city was captured by Alexander and democracy restored.[54] The tyrants of Eresus on Lesbos took similar action against the altars of Zeus Philippios, that is, of Philip, shortly before and perhaps even during the campaign in 334.[55]

Philip's cults then were treated accordingly by the Achaemenids and their allies, oligarchs, or tyrants in Asia Minor. When Alexander marched into Ephesus, the

---

[49] Arr. 1.17.10–12; Bringmann and von Steuben 1995: no. 263.

[50] Str. 14.1.22 C640–1; Bringmann and von Steuben 1995: no. 264.

[51] Plin. *HN* 35.92; Cic. *Verr.* 4.135; Ael. *VH* 2.3; Plu. *Alex.* 4.3; Plu. *Mor.* 335a. Berve 2.53–4 dated this to the year 331.

[52] Str. 14.1.22 C641; Alexander was one of the first rulers who guaranteed and extended the territory of an asylum (ibid.), in the case of the Artemision (which became common until the Roman period); but the Ephesians declined Alexander's offer to meet all expenses for the temple, because he demanded credit for it in the dedicatory inscription (as it became common later on honoring the activities of *euergetai*: see above); this was contrary to the case of Priene.

[53] Isocrates was the propagator of these ideas and connected them with Philip: Isoc. *Ep.* 3.5; see also Balsdon 1950. These ideas included the settlement of the uprooted masses of exiles of mainland Greece. Even in this respect Alexander quit the ground of his father's policy with the Exiles' Decree (see below).

[54] Habicht 1956 interpreted this as a cult; but see now Habicht 1970: 245 for a different view. On the removal of Philip's statue see Arr. 1.17.10–11.

[55] Tod 191, ll. 1–2 and 43–4 = *OGIS* 8a. Rhodes–Osborne 83 argue against Heisserer 1980, who suggested that the plurality of the altars for Zeus Philippios could be explained by the fact that the tyrants ruled in the neighboring cities Antissa and Eresus and that altars were in both cities.

exiled citizens who had taken Philip's side and had fled Memnon and his forces (see above) were able to return.[56] Until his death in 333, Memnon posed the greatest, though not always the most dangerous, Persian threat to Alexander.

It is possible that Memnon had suppressed a pro-Macedonian, democratic government that had been able to form under the influence of Philip's troops in 336.[57] In Eresus on Lesbos, Philip had played a role in toppling the tyrants and restoring democracy in the year 343; in 337 Eresus was admitted to the League of Corinth. The gratitude of the liberated city, as seen in cult of Philip established no later than 336, is just as understandable as the destructive hatred of the two sets of tyrants who were installed in power by Memnon soon after 335 and again in 333. Cult honors for Philip had to be renewed when these tyrannic regimes fell and (as in Ephesus) when honors for Alexander were established.

Epigraphic evidence shows that Alexander gave the city of Priene its freedom in 334 and showered gifts on the city and temple.[58] Unlike the Ephesians, the Prienians did not oppose Alexander's dedicating of their temple of Athena.[59] The city, however, did not join the League of Corinth and this encouraged the pro-Macedonian oligarchs. Established by Alexander's father, Philip, the League was not well liked among mainland Greeks, and for some Aegean Greeks Persian dominion according to the settlement of King's Peace of 386 remained an attractive alternative until 332.[60] Therefore, Alexander distanced himself from the League, liberating the Greek cities in Asia Minor and in many cases establishing democracies. This sharply contrasts with the actions of Philip who preferred oligarchic regimes, as did Antipater, Alexander's deputy in Greece, although this was contrary to Alexander's orders.

Additionally, Alexander granted the citizens of Priene other favors, even if he was not necessarily present in the city in person; honors were also bestowed by the city on Antigonus Monophthalmus,[61] Alexander's proxy. It would not be plausible to expect cult honors for Alexander[62] later than those for Antigonus.

It has been suggested that the idea to reestablish Priene completely can be traced back to Alexander. Contrary to this, Helga Botermann argues that Alexander arranged only for the completion of a building project that was already under construction by the indigenous Hecatomnids. In other words. he deliberately adhered to local traditions and fulfilled popular expectations.[63] The honors accorded Alexander were therefore a consequence of his good deeds and thus anticipate the subsequent cult of the Greek city ruler. This role of benefactor (*euergetes*) was

[56]   Arr. 1.17.10.

[57]   Berve ii. 251.

[58]   *I. Priene* 1 and 156 = *OGIS* 1 and *SIG*³ 277 = Tod 185 and 184 = Rhodes–Osborne 86; Botermann 1994. For the dedication of the temple of Athena Polias see Bringmann and von Steuben 1995: no. 268.

[59]   In Xanthos, Lycia, dedications of Alexander are attested: *SEG* xxx. 1533.

[60]   Arr. 2.1.4.

[61]   *SIG*³ 278 = *I. Priene* 2.

[62]   *I. Priene* 108, 75.

[63]   Botermann 1994. In Caria, Alexander respected the traditions by allowing himself to be adopted by the widow Ada (see above).

known to the Greeks almost only theoretically up to this time. Isocrates, in his pamphlet-speech *Philippos,* attributes this role to Philip, Alexander's father, outlining Philip's ideal relationship to the Greeks and his future tasks in organizing the Panhellenic program against the Persian empire.[64] This program consisted of three steps: freedom for the Greeks in Asia Minor; the conquest of Asia Minor if possible, in order to settle Greeks there; and, most important of all, the subjection of the Persian empire.[65] Therefore, the role of the future *pambasileus* (on this see below) and his relationship to Greek cities is rooted in Greek intellectual thought of the fourth century.

One document dating from the second century informs us that a dilapidated Alexandreion was restored with private wealth; the Hieron on West Gate Street may have been that building. In any case, a statuette of Alexander, identified with the cult, has been found on that site.[66]

In Magnesia-on-the-Maeander the founding document for the festival of Artemis Leukophryene in 206 refers to the Alexandreia, that is, the games of Alexander.[67] The reason for mentioning the Alexander festival in this context remains unclear. Since the city did not belong to the Ionian *koinon*, it is quite probable that these Alexander festivities were not those conducted by the *koinon*. Alexander had not visited the city in the year 334, but delegates from the city of Magnesia had traveled to Alexander in Ephesus in order to surrender the city to him.[68]

When the gymnasium in Bargylia and its statue of the king were refurbished in the third century, the cult for Alexander was also revived.[69] The gymnasium substituted for the lack of a temple.[70] Just as the gymnasium and the theater become a "second agora," one can also observe that the municipal theater housed cult altars dedicated to the king – as a substitute for a sacred temple.

Contrary to earlier assumptions, the Dionysia and the Alexandreia on Rhodes were also organizationally separate. There were priests[71] as well as separate festivities.[72] These were amalgamated before 129, because at that time the festivals were held together,[73] and there is much documentary evidence for their combination.[74] However, the Alexander festival did not lose its autonomy and the person being revered was never equated with Dionysus. Tragic plays and chariot races were organized in Alexander's honor.[75]

---

[64] Isoc. 5.76, 114–15, where Heracles, the *euergetes Hellados* and ancestor of the Argeads, is the model for his actions.

[65] Isoc. 5.120.

[66] Habicht 1956: 18.

[67] *I. Magnesia* 16.

[68] Arr. 1.18.1. Tralles of Caria also sent an embassy (see above).

[69] *OGIS* 3, with n. 2.

[70] Habicht 1956: 143–4.

[71] Segre 1941: 29–39, at 30, l. 14.

[72] D.S. 20.84.3; Blinkenberg 1941: no. 197F, l. 5: after 156 BC.

[73] Blinkenberg 1941: ii. 1, no. 233, ll. 8ff.

[74] Habicht 1956: 26 n. 7.

[75] *IGR* iv. 1116; Habicht 1956: n. 151.

Since 332, there had been intensive relations between the Rhodian republic and Alexander,[76] although the extent of the favors bestowed by Alexander has been exaggerated in the legends propagated by Rhodes from the end of the third century onward.[77] The legendary descriptions of an exclusively good relationship are qualified by the news that the citizens of Rhodes had driven out the Macedonian garrison after the death of the king, thus regaining their freedom.[78] So the question as to when the cult for Alexander was established cannot be answered with any certainty.

F. Salviat has edited a law from Thasos dating from the last quarter of the fourth century, which contains a provision that, among other things, imposed limits on trials on festival days.[79] The list of festivals also includes the Alexandreia, which was celebrated on the king's birthday (6th day in the month of Hecatombaion) – as in the Ionian *koinon*. This is one of the earliest documents providing evidence of festivities in honor of Alexander. It appears to be either a consequence of the desire for deification expressed by Alexander in the year 324 (see below), or perhaps already a reaction to the Asia Minor campaign in 334, especially in cases of spontaneous introductions – as in the case of the cities in Asia Minor – and celebrations on his birthday. However, it is also possible that the celebrations were introduced after his death.[80]

The famous regulations in Mytilene on Lesbos probably also belong to an early period (about 332),[81] as in the case with Chios.[82] These followed the Persian naval offensive, which in spite of its (limited) successes could be regarded a failure as Alexander continued his campaign and conquered all the major harbors of the Levant.[83] If this early, not uncontested, date of the document could be confirmed, its contents would be a link between the first and the second period of honors for Alexander, chronologically and geographically. In addition to the care that the well-informed Alexander showed during the settlements – as in the cases of Philippi (331), Chios (334), and later Tegea (324) – the regulations in l. 46 seem to include cultic veneration for the king.[84]

[76]   Arr. 2.20.2; Curt. 4.5.9, 8.12; Just. 11.11.1; Plu. *Alex.* 32. Dedication of Alexander at Lindos: Blinkenberg 1941: ii. 1, no. 2 §38; Bringmann and von Steuben 1995: no. 194. Berve i. 247–8, also on the relationship between Rhodes and Alexander according to the novel of Alexander.

[77]   D.S. 20.81.3; Ps.-Call. 3.33.2 (p. 138 Kroll); Merkelbach 1954: 123–51. Pugliese Carratelli 1949: 154–71 argues that Alexander influenced the Rhodian constitution democratically and therefore became a second founder.

[78]   D.S. 18.8.1.

[79]   1958: 193–267, esp. 244–8.

[80]   Salviat 1958: 247.

[81]   Rhodes–Osborne 85. On the date see, e.g., Worthington 1990; Zahrnt 2003: 416.

[82]   *SIG*[3] 283 = Rhodes–Osborne 84; cf. no. 87. No. 84 deals with the establishment of a democratic constitution. The king himself assumes the role of a *diallaktes*, as in Ephesus and Mytilene. This role introduced the cities to the idea of the *euergetes* ruler so common in the Hellenistic era, a role similar to that of a deity of an oracle (see below).

[83]   Arr. 2.5.7; Curt. 4.5.13–22; Worthington 2004a.

[84]   Rhodes–Osborne, no. 85, ll. 44–6. But the reading is uncertain (in *OGIS* ii. 46): see discussion in Rhodes–Osborne 428.

The Greek Mainland

Alexander's desire for deification, complemented by Hephaestion's secondary ascription as *theos paredros*, or "assistant deity," was intensely debated in 324, especially in Athens. Alexander's ancestors had already been accorded cult honors in the cities of Macedonia, namely Amyntas III in Pydna and Philip II in Amphipolis and Philippi. A *scholion* to Demosthenes indicates a shrine to Amyntas (an Amynteion) in Pydna, into which the inhabitants of the city fled from Philip II.[85] The occasion and time at which the Amyntas cult was established are unclear. It survived Athenian rule and certainly the period after its being stormed by Philip. Aristeides also refers in his report to a temple to Amyntas in Pydna and to divine honors for Philip II in Amphipolis.[86]

This means that the cult for Philip in Amphipolis was already in existence before the city was taken in the year 357. It was introduced after he came to the throne in 360/59. In that year the Macedonian occupation that Perdiccas III had installed against the threat from Athens was withdrawn.[87] The withdrawal of his army was carried out by Philip as an act of *rapprochement* toward Athens. However, the regime in power when the city was stormed by Philip in 357 was hostile to the Macedonian king.[88] The result was an oligarchic overthrow.[89] Thus, it is possible that establishment of the cult was prompted by withdrawal of the occupying Macedonian forces.

In Philippi (Krenides), which had been renamed by Philip in the year 358/7,[90] the dating of an Alexander scroll after a priest has been thought to indicate a cult for Philip, which seems likely in a city bearing his name. This epigraphic letter was found with other inscriptions in a sacrificial pit, possibly an area of cult worship, considered by Picard to be a *heroon* to Philip.[91] At any rate, there were at least two *temene* of Philip II in Philippi.[92]

After the Macedonian victory in 338/7, Philip II received several distinctions in Athens, at the initiative of Demades. These included citizen's rights and the erection of a statue in the Odeion. Apsines, however, claims that Demades did not arrange for Philip to be decreed the thirteenth god.[93]

---

[85]   D. 1.5; on the circumstances by which Philip II took the city and violated the asylum, see D. 1.5, 20.63; cf. D.S. 16.8.2; D. 12.21, 23.

[86]   Aristid. *Symachikos* A (or. 38), vol. I 715D.

[87]   D.S. 16.3.3–4.1; Polyaen. 4.2.17.

[88]   D.S. 16.8.2.

[89]   Habicht 1956: 13; Badian 1981: 39–41.

[90]   D.S. 16.8.6.

[91]   Picard 1938: 334–5. During the marriage of Cleopatra, Philip's statue was carried as the thirteenth god with the other Olympians.

[92]   *SEG* xlviii. 708, 835. It has been suggested that the building where was found a letter sent by Philippi's envoys reporting a decision by Alexander concerning the city's territory (*c.*330: see below) may have related to the cult of Philip II (*SEG* xxxviii. 658).

[93]   *Rhet.* 1. 221 Spengel-Hammer; see also the discussion in Schaefer 1887: iii. 32 n. 1.

In contrast, the cultic veneration of Alexander in Athens is documented by a fragment of a speech by Hypereides.[94] Hence, the cult for Alexander in fact existed before the end of the year 322, the date of the speech.[95] It is clear from the fragment that a cult image, an altar, and a temple were erected in Athens in honor of Alexander. It is also generally assumed that the "servants who were celebrated as heroes" referred to Hephaestion, who was also revered as *theos paredros*, the "assistant deity" for Alexander. The establishment of this cult shortly before the ruler's death is very likely already due to this fact alone. On the other hand, revering him as a deity was certainly not part of the honoring of Alexander between 338 and 335 in Athens:[96] Hypereides definitely speaks of such a cult being established a short time before.

A debate over the establishment of cults at the king's behest is documented for Athens and Sparta.[97] It is certain that revering the king was practiced in several Greek communities.[98] An unspecified number of unnamed cities in Babylon worshiped Alexander as a god. The delegates had the specific title of *theoroi*, that is, they were delegates who sought contact with the god (and not *presbeutai*, as was normal in interstate communications).[99]

The motive behind deification in Athens is known. It was hoped that by deifying the king, Alexander would be lenient in the Samos issue and resolve in Athens's favor the dispute over the Athenian cleruchy on the island.[100] Based on the statement by Hypereides, Habicht has argued that the Alexander and the Hephaestion cults in Athens must be seen as a single entity, and that they were introduced simultaneously.[101] His argument runs as follows. By desiring a cult for Hephaestion in Athens, Alexander was also striving indirectly for his own deification. According to the Ammon oracle consulted by Alexander (in the spring of 323), Hephaestion,

---

[94]   Hyp. 6.21.

[95]   The later legend is that Alexander was worshiped as "Neos Dionysus" or as god additionally to the twelve traditional gods of Athens (see above about the identification with Dionysus).

[96]   Arr. 1.1.3; Paus. 1.9.4.

[97]   Balsdon 1950: 383. On attitudes regarding Alexander's deification in Athens see Lycurgus in [Plu.] *Mor.* 842d and Demosthenes (Din. 1.94). On the wording of the (anachronistic) decision of Alexander's deification in Sparta, see Ael. *VH* 2.19; cf. Plu. *Mor.* 219e; Bosworth 1988a: 289. It is reasonable to suppose that the introduction of the cults in other cities of Greece was easier than in cities like Athens and Sparta which were hostile toward Alexander.

[98]   Lucian, *Mort. dial.* 13.2. For a possible cult-building for Alexander in Megalopolis see Paus. 8.32.1.

[99]   Arr. 7.23.2; about the term *theoroi*, see the honors of Athens for the Antigonids in 307: Plu. *Demetr.* 11. This Athenian way became a model for the manner of worship and in general for the relationship between democratic cities and rulers, who renounced the formal surrender of the city. Aristotle introduced this concept of treatment of a city by the *pambasileus* which was practiced by Alexander for the first time (see below; and on the *euergetes* king see above).

[100]   On the role of Demosthenes, who had already contacted Nicanor during the Olympic Games in August 324 immediately after the publication of the Exiles' Decree, see Lehmann 2005: 207–15. His position during the negotiations was soon weakened because of his involvement in the Harpalus affair.

[101]   Habicht 1956: 29; 1970: 246ff. confirms that the cults for Alexander and Hephaestion in Athens were introduced simultaneously.

who had died in October 324,[102] was to be revered as a hero. Even before that, Alexander had ordered that Hephaestion be revered in the *chora barbaros* and the army camp.[103] Athens too had previously decided – in the winter of 324/3, before the oracle of Ammon spoke – that Hephaestion be revered.[104] Hephaestion was also referred to generally as an "assistant deity," as a *theos paredros*, in Diodorus and Lucian.[105] A cult of Hephaestion in Athens was therefore based on a superordinate Alexander cult. The two cults can therefore be assumed to have coexisted as a single cult,[106] whereby, according to Hypereides, Hephaestion as servant was accorded reverence as a hero.[107] This joint cult is comparable to that of Achilles and Patroclus, who had a common tomb and were jointly revered by a cult[108] which had existed, allegedly, since 334, when Hephaestion and Alexander visited Ilium.[109] This close association of Alexander and Hephaestion in a joint cult is also indirectly addressed in the Ephippus pamphlet, written shortly after Alexander's death, because their divinity stood in sharp contrast to their mortality as humans and to the humiliating manner in which Alexander died (chronic alcoholism).[110] Habicht believed additionally that the joint cult could also be identified in Alexandria, where statuettes for Alexander and Hephaestion were found.[111] This would mean that the joint cult for Alexander and Hephaestion was established in early 323 in Athens, before the arrival in Babylon of the delegates who did not worship the king as a divinity before April 323 according to Habicht.[112]

Habicht thus took an emphatic position against the hypothesis that the Exiles' Decree, already known when announced to the Greeks by Nicanor at the Olympic Games, was legally based on the deification of Alexander that had already been effected.[113] However, there is not necessarily a temporal relationship between the

---

[102]   Habicht 1956: 33–6 argues that Harpalus arrived at Athens in September/October (Berve ii. 78 n. 2; *contra* Treves 1934: 515 – May/June 324). Demosthenes changed his mind during the Harpalus lawsuit which lasted six months (Din. 1.45) in the second half of the year 324 (Hyp. 1, col. 31), shortly before the condemnation in January 323.

[103]   Arr. 7.14.7; D.S. 17.115.6; Just. 12.12.12; cf. Arr. 7.14.9; D.S. 17.115.1; Lucian, *Cal.* 17.

[104]   Treves 1939.

[105]   D.S. 17.115.6; Lucian, *Cal.* 17.

[106]   Habicht 1956: 31.

[107]   The sources do not differentiate between *hero* and *god*: Arr. 7.14.7; Just. 12.12.12; Lucian, *Cal.* 17; Arr. 7.23.6; Plu. *Alex.* 2; D.S. 17.115.6.

[108]   Str. 13.596.

[109]   Arr. 1.12.1; 7.14.4, 16.8; Ael. *VH* 12.7.

[110]   *FGrH* 126; but the version that has Alexander succumb to the same fate as Heracles endured longer (*OGIS* 4.5; D.S. 18.56.2).

[111]   Gebauer 1938–9: 67–8.

[112]   Arr. 7.23.2.

[113]   Habicht 1956: 228–9. In 1970: 273–4 Habicht tried to confirm this by arguing that the Olympic Games were celebrated on August 4 (Sealey 1960). But Habicht's main argument for the establishment of the cult of Alexander in the winter fails, because he has to concede (following Bickerman) that cults of Alexander and Hephaestion were not introduced simultaneously. On the Exiles' Decree: Curt. 10.2.4–7; D.S. 17.119.1, 18.8.2–4; Just. 13.5.3–4; Din. 1.82–103; cf. *SIG*³ 312, l. 11–15; Badian 1961: 41–3. The grateful exiles of Corinth erected a statue in Alexander's honor in Olympia, where the king was equated with Zeus (Paus. 5.25.1).

two cults in the Hypereides fragment. Habicht actually retracted his hypothesis of a joint cult in 1970 (in the afterword to the second edition).[114] He did not state the implications of his unsuccessful argument for the existence of a joint cult, though.

It was Ed. Meyer who had originally suspected that Alexander demanded deification by the cities of the Greek homeland in order to give a legitimate and lasting form to his "ruling position."[115] Habicht distances himself from this view and tends to believe instead that Alexander expressed such a wish in indirect form – by demanding that Hephaestion be revered as an assistant deity.[116]

Regulating the relationship between the Greek city-state and the ruler appears to have been a serious and increasing problem (pending since 334), or at least was considered as such by contemporaries. Given the need for protection on the part of the communities, and the overwhelming power of rulers like Alexander, it was necessary to regulate in which form the ruler could approach the formally free cities from his superordinated position, without damaging the inner structure and workings of the community.[117] It has to be doubted that there was any systemizing will on the part of Alexander to create a superordinate hierarchical level, in the sense of a general deification. However, as the sources show, not only in the case of Alexander, but also in that of the Antigonids in 307, the acknowledgment of a divine ruler figure acting for the benefit of the city was essentially acceptable to Greek cities. The Seleucids under Antiochus III pursued this principle the most rigorously.[118]

In this case, commands from the ruler were like an oracle in nature. The Greeks had been familiar with such a superordinate, divine level of command since the archaic period.[119] It was no coincidence that, since the days of Alexander, the emissaries of the cities who were sent out to receive the ruler's instructions, were called *theoroi*.[120] The ruler, who now took the place previously occupied by traditional protecting gods, was tolerable for a free Greek as long as he acted in the long term for the benefit of the communities.[121] Abuse of his position was "conceptually"

---

[114]   Habicht 1970: 249–50. In Diodorus and Lucian the *theos paredros* was "nicht der beigestellte, sondern der Beistand leistende Gott" (according to Taeger in Habicht 1970: 250 n. 10).

[115]   Meyer 1910; 1924: 265–314. Meyer rated this ruling position as the basis for his command concerning the exiles in August 324.

[116]   Habicht 1956: 225–9, 1970: 272–3; following him: Wiemer 2005: 163–5.

[117]   See, e.g., *Ithyphallikos*, Ath. 6.253b based on: Duris, *FGrH* 76 F13; cf. Demochares, *FGrH* 75 F2; Dreyer 1999: 115ff.

[118]   Dreyer 2007b: 300–20.

[119]   See the leading function of the Apollo of Delphi in the era of the Greek colonization, contrary to the argument of Habicht 1956: 227.

[120]   There is no irony in Arrian (7.23.2); cf. Habicht 1970: 247–8.

[121]   This role is attested for Alexander in the case of Tegea (*SIG*[3] 306 = Rhodes–Osborne 101, 324); Mitylene (*OGIS* 2 = Rhodes–Osborne 85); Chios (*SIG*[3] 283 = Tod 192 = Rhodes–Osborne 84). It shows the well-informed and extraordinary (deified) pretensions of Alexander, which may be regarded as preparation for his intervention in Philippi (about December 331; cf. Hatzopoulos 1987: 436–9, at 438ff. (no. 714); *SEG* xxxiv. 664; *SEG* xlviii. 835, perhaps in regard to the cult of Philip II; cf. *SEG*

impossible, because the "new god" could give his instructions, which acquired the quality of an oracle, only when requested, and with the welfare of the inquiring city in mind. These instructions were "merely" suitable as fundamental decisions on essential issues, and were not to be obtained for day-to-day policy-making in a city. That the rulers of the *oikumene* had to keep the whole community in mind was necessarily to the benefit of the individual communities, since the ruler of the *oikumene* himself was not called into question.

This absolute ruler was theoretically conceived by Aristotle – with an eye to Alexander, of course – as an opposite form to tyranny. In the third and fourth book of his *Politics*, Aristotle termed this form of rule *pambasileia*.[122] Such a ruler ἄρχει πάντων κατὰ τὴν ἑαυτοῦ βούλησιν (1287a 8–9), but not in the negative sense of a tyranny, which Aristotle explicitly contrasts to such *pambasileia* as ἀντίστροφος (1295a 18). The tyrant rules without any duty of accountability (ἀνυπεύθυνος ἄρχει) and merely for his own benefit (πρὸς τὸ αὐτῆς συμφέρον, ἀλλὰ μὴ πρὸς τὸ τῶν ἀρχομένων). His rule therefore appears to be no longer tolerable for any free person (οὐθεὶς γὰρ ἑκὼν ὑπομένει τῶν ἐλευθέρων τὴν τοιαύτην ἀρχήν). In the documentary sources as well (Iasos, Amyzon, Teos), one finds the same concept of *pambasileia* – positively expressed of course – for Antiochus III over all men.

The charismatic king[123] therefore acted purely for the benefit of the (Greek) communities, as *euergetes*, in the sense of fostering traditional political forms (usually democracy). It was therefore a *topos* that any royal directives that violated the constitution of the cities had to be invalid.[124] For this reason, it was standard procedure that deification by the city had to be preceded by the ruler bestowing favors. This meant it was formally voluntary; in any case, the voluntary nature of deification was a desired objective and was purchased at a high "price" for the ruler. However, deification could also be demanded of the cities directly (by the king himself, but mostly through a royal functionary).[125] In this form, it came close to the dynastic ruler cult,[126] which was reserved, in formal legal terms, for the

---

xxxviii. 658) and in the responsibilities of Antipater who was continuously quarreling with Olympias (Plu. *Mor.* 180d) and struggling in the war with Agis of Sparta.
[122] In *Pol.* 1285b 36, the owner of the *pambasileia* is conceded the supreme decision; cf. *Rhet.* 1365b 37–1366a 2 and Hdt. 3.80.3; see also *Pol.* 1287a 8; in *Pol.* 1295a 18, the *pambasileia* is the positive counterpart of the third kind of kingship, the tyranny. This sort of kingship is not only negatively rated, but also as not Greek. The *pambasileia*, on the contrary, is honest, unselfish, tolerable for free men; one can see which considerations are connected with the cult of the worshiped king, who is under certain circumstances tolerable for free cities.
[123] Gehrke 1982; see the definition in Weber 1922: ch. 3, §10.
[124] Plu. *Mor.* 183e: Ἀντίοχος ὁ τρίτος ἔγραψε ταῖς πόλεσιν, ἄν τι γράψῃ παρὰ τοὺς νόμους κελεύων γενέσθαι, μὴ προσέχειν ὡς ἠγνοηκότι.
[125] In the areas in Asia Minor dominated originally by the Ptolemies: for Caria and Cilicia, see Dreyer 2002: 119–38, at n. 87; for Amyzon (*passim*), Kildara, Arsinoe, see Dreyer 2007b: 281 and Pfeiffer 2008: 33–46.
[126] Contrary to Habicht 1956: 226–7. He argues that the city cult for living rulers had no ruling and hierarchic quality, because the city always had the initiative, and that this quality never existed under

dependent regions. However, since this is documented at a relatively late stage, the possibility must be conceded that the substance of the ruler cult in the cities (i.e., the "institutionalization" of the ruler's dominance over a formally free city) became inflated to an increasingly apparent extent. Habicht himself admits, however, that the initiative for establishing the cults in the Greek mainland came originally from Alexander.[127] And in every case in the time of the Successors of Alexander the introduction of the formally voluntary city cult was connected with a change in hegemony.

All endeavors to establish a more or less voluntarily practiced deification of Alexander in Athens and other cities in Greece were quashed by the Lamian War (323/2) after the death of Alexander and, following the victory of the central Macedonian government, were not reestablished because the government, distancing itself from Alexander, returned to forms of rule previously practiced under Philip.

In contrast, cults established for relatives of Alexander after his death are known: these include the cult of Philip III Arrhidaeus and Alexander IV on Samos, and the cult of Eurydice in Cassandreia.[128] An *agon* for Philip III and Alexander IV on Samos was mentioned in the second half of 321.[129] The festivities had been established not long before – following the expulsion of the Athenian cleruchy and after the return of the exiled Samians. Perdiccas had made this decision on behalf of the kings, although Polyperchon retracted it in 319 on behalf of the same. That probably meant the end of the festival.

The cult for Eurydice in Cassandreia is mentioned by Polyaenus (6.7.2). After the death of her son Ptolemy Ceraunus in 279, Eurydice had relinquished power of her own accord. After granting the city its freedom, she was pushed aside by Apollodorus, who intended to establish his own tyranny. He founded a festival for Eurydice and gave citizenship rights to the soldiers of the Macedonian garrison. He then used this garrison to establish a tyranny, which in the end was eliminated by Antigonus Gonatas. After the peace agreement between Gonatas and Antiochus in 278, Apollodorus' tyranny became precarious. The cult therefore dates to between the years 279 and 278. The cult would actually be an indicator for the royal cult in the cities lacking any implications of dominance by a ruler,[130] had it not been explicitly manipulated by Apollodorus and used to establish his own dominance.

---

the successors of Alexander. On the connection of city cult of living rulers and dynasty cult, see Gauthier 1989: 73ff., who describes the development of the city cult for Laodice to the dynasty cult for Laodice; see also Dreyer 2007b: 239–59

[127]   Habicht 1956: 229. The kind of benefit by the ruler for the city can be seen in the cult *epitheton* of the worshiped ruler.

[128]   Habicht 1970: 252–5.

[129]   Habicht 1957: 156ff., no. 1.

[130]   Habicht 1970: 272.

13

Alexander's Image in the Age of the Successors

Alexander Meeus

The history of Alexander the Great did not end with his death.[1] His generals, striving for personal power in the vacuum he left, immediately saw the benefit of exploiting his name. Many scholars, however, hold that in the era of the Successors Alexander was rather unpopular, and that his father Philip was the king the Diadochi tried to connect themselves to. Cassander is especially assumed to have promoted Philip's memory while denigrating Alexander's. These scholars presume that a distinction was made between Philip's branch of the royal family and Alexander's. The main advocate of this view is Malcolm Errington (1976: 145–51), but others have put forward similar arguments.[2] In discussing the various marriage proposals to Alexander's sister Cleopatra, Errington (1976: 151–2) writes:

> Cassander, who would inevitably have been most concerned by any attempt to exploit Cleopatra, decided to build his influence and power on Philip and the Argead house in general rather than on Alexander in particular – which may indeed, have possibly been the attraction of Cleopatra all along. His lasting marriage with Philip's daughter Thessalonice, his restoration of Thebes, and his treatment and finally murder of Alexander IV and Roxane after Olympias had already been removed, his honourable burial of Philip Arrhidaeus, Eurydice and Cynane all point in the same direction.

One may well wonder whether the distinction between the two branches of the family so emphatically stressed by Errington makes sense. After all, Alexander was the son of Philip, and thus belonged to the same family branch.

In this essay I shall first analyze the evidence for the popularity of the Argead dynasty with the Macedonian people, mostly the soldiers, in the age of the

---

[1] Cf. Errington 1976: 138: "The immediate political importance of Alexander did not end with his death"; Dahmen 2007: 1: "Much of Alexander's importance lies in his posthumous fame."
[2] E.g., Müller 1973: 64; Bosworth 1986: 11–12; Wirth 1989: 206; Stewart 1993: 149–50 with n. 86; Billows 1995: 39 with n. 42; Badian 1999: 84; Landucci Gattinoni 2003: 81–3, 145. The most substantial reaction to this view came from Goukowski 1978: 105–11.

Successors, also investigating whether there are any traces of a preference for Philip or Alexander. After that, I shall look at the use the Successors made of the names of Philip and Alexander in their quest for legitimacy.

Argead popularity among the Diadochi generally seems to be underestimated. One reason for this is that most of the Diadochi are considered separatists who were not interested in maintaining Alexander's empire.[3] This opinion mostly affects the interpretation of Alexander's image, since, if this is so, he need not have been as important as his father, especially in Macedon itself. In the last decades several scholars have recognized that there was no opposition between separatist and unitarist Successors.[4] If a Successor had wanted to control Alexander's entire legacy, one would have expected him to try to establish some sort of connection with the late king. This problem exceeds the scope of the present essay, but it is clear that it is a factor which should be taken into account when investigating how the Diadochi used the names of their Argead predecessors.

Another question beyond the scope of this essay is the breadth of popularity Philip and Alexander enjoyed before that fateful day in June 323. Events such as the Cleitus episode or the mutiny at Opis show that there is much to be said about this issue.[5] Alexander's dealings with the Persians seem to be the main problem in this respect. It is clear that many Macedonians resented Alexander's orientalization policy,[6] but things might have changed somewhat when the king died. The chaos after his death may well have inspired Macedonians to remember Alexander's reign in a more positive way. The generals might even have realized the need to give the Persians some part in the administration of the empire. The often repeated view that after Alexander's death all the marshals except Seleucus repudiated their Persian wives is ill-founded.[7] Seleucus is the only one we know of, but on the other hand, only in Craterus' case is divorce attested.[8] With hindsight this might seem a natural thing for Alexander's successor in Asia to have done,[9] but Seleucus had decided to stay married to Apame long before he knew he was going to establish an Asian

---

[3]   See Wheatley, ch. 3. Others who have recently advocated this view include: Hammond 1999b; Erskine 2002: 163–73; Plantzos 2002; Landucci Gattinoni 2003: 146; Grainger 2007: 103.

[4]   Carney 1988: 402; Lund 1992: 51–2; Adams 2006; Meeus 2007; D.S. 20.37.4; Nepos, *Eum.* 2.3–4. Cf. also Gruen 1985, who argues that there was no opposition between unitarians and separatists but also that no one aimed at controlling Alexander's entire empire; Bosworth 2002: 246–7. The cause of the eventual break-up of Alexander's empire was not that some strove for separatism, but that none of the Successors achieved the elimination of all his rivals. Cf. Heckel 2002b, arguing for the same cause for the disintegration of the empire from a different point of view, esp. 86–7: "equality in both competence and authority led to the disintegration of the newly-won empire. Ironically, the very talent, the military potential and the large pool of candidates for supreme office made the survival of the empire virtually impossible."

[5]   On the Cleitus episode see Tritle 2003; on Opis see Carney 1996.

[6]   Plu. *Eum.* 6.3; Plu. *Al.* 47.9; Bosworth 1980a: 7; Heckel 2003b: 215; Roisman 2003b: 292–3.

[7]   This view has been expressed, e.g., by Tarn ii. 434; Briant 1972: 61; Brosius 2003a: 176–8; Holt 2003: 17. Will 1979: 273 and Ogden 1999: 69 at least note the uncertainty.

[8]   Memnon, *FGrH* 434 F4.4.

[9]   Ogden 1999: 119.

empire or even that he would become satrap of Babylonia. In spite of their initial lack of popularity, Alexander's half-Asian sons Alexander and Heracles did not fail to attract popular support later (see below). Curtius (10.10.13) claims that Alexander's body was embalmed by Egyptian and Babylonian priests and the Diadochi in Babylon seem to have decided to bury their late king at Siwah.[10] Both Leonnatus and Craterus, and maybe some of the other Successors as well, tried to imitate Alexander's persona (see further below). For example, they seem not to have shunned the Persian elements of Alexander's attire.[11] In the epigram accompanying Craterus' lion hunt monument in Delphi, Alexander is called *Asias basileus*, in this context a highly remarkable statement for a Macedonian traditionalist.[12] Peucestas entertained a very close relationship with the Persians, and his example was followed by Ptolemy, Seleucus, Alcetas, and Eumenes.[13] Nor do the Successors seem to have been as reluctant to work with Asian and Egyptian troops as scholars have often thought.[14] Indeed, any astute politician would recognize that one cannot completely ignore the major part of the population. From all this, it should be clear that the attitude of the Macedonians toward the conquered peoples after Alexander's death is a problem that begs further study and a more balanced analysis. In any case, any putative resentment of Alexander's orientalization cannot be used as an argument to dismiss a priori the possibility of his popularity after death.[15]

The reactions to Alexander's death are the first element to consider. The sources present two opposite versions. According to the first, transmitted by Arrian (7.26.1), Curtius (10.5.1–16, 10.6.3) and Justin (12.15.2–3), the Macedonians grieved over their king as he lay dying and after he had died. The second version is found in Justin's rather long description of the reaction to Alexander's death (13.1.7–8, 2.1), where he states that the Macedonians were delighted at his passing. Since this contradicts his own comments elsewhere, most likely this is Justin's own rhetorical and dramatic elaboration.[16] No other source mentions any joyful sentiments among the Macedonians. The lack of enthusiasm for Roxane's child can be explained by the fact that it would be half-Asian and that it was unborn. The uncertainty was no attractive prospect for the soldiers being so far from home without a leader.[17] This is one of the reasons why they even seemed prepared to accept Perdiccas as king, and it does not necessarily tell us anything about their affection for the Argeads or Alexander in particular.

---

[10] D.S. 18.3.5; Just. 13.4.6; Heckel 1992: 160 n. 516; Bosworth 2002: 13 n. 30. D.S. 18.28.3 shows that the Successors had originally intended to bury Alexander at Siwah.

[11] Goukowski 1978: 86.

[12] *ISE* ii, no. 73, v. 8.

[13] Briant 1972: 60–1.

[14] Schachermeyr 1970: 23–4; Briant 1972: 60–73; Rodriguez 2004.

[15] Even before his death, it seems that any conflict between Alexander and his soldiers did not diminish the latter's respect for their king: Anson 1991: 245.

[16] Boerma 1979: 99–100.

[17] On the soldiers feeling ill at ease: Errington 1970: 50; Mooren 1983: 235.

The soldiers' support for Arrhidaeus' accession should not be seen as an indication of Philip's popularity over Alexander.[18] The troops wanted a leader as soon as possible, and within the Argead house there was no other choice. With Arrhidaeus on the throne under the supervision of a capable regent, their concerns for the immediate future would be gone. The decision to rename their new king Philip clearly indicates Macedonian reverence for Philip II, but need not be the result of any dislike of Alexander.[19] The soldiers' enthusiasm for the incapable Arrhidaeus as ruler of their empire does show their strong loyalty to the Argead clan (Curt. 10.7.15).

Alexander's body and his relics had a high symbolic value during the struggle in Babylon. Curtius (10.6.4) describes how in the first meeting after the king's death Perdiccas had Alexander's throne placed clearly in view, with Alexander's diadem, robe, and arms displayed on it.[20] Then he added the dead king's signet ring, a gesture probably even more theatrical than Curtius' description of it, but one involving an evident message: Perdiccas' claim to preeminence as Alexander had given him the ring.[21] The whole scene apparently made a deep impression on those present.[22] As the meeting proceeded, Aristonus proposed to appoint Perdiccas king because Alexander had given him his ring, and many Macedonians agreed with him (Curt. 10.6.16–18). Surely the view that Perdiccas enjoyed Alexander's preference was not the only reason for the success of Aristonus' proposal. If Perdiccas became king, the Macedonians at least had a capable leader to solve the crisis caused by Alexander's unexpected death.[23] It proved impossible, however, to reach a consensus acceptable to both the nobles and the common soldiers, and for a time the threat of civil war was very real. The elite retreated to the chamber where Alexander's body lay, and the first struggle over the king's remains ensued, in which the nobles had to yield to the numerical superiority of the rank and file (Curt. 10.7.16–19).

The episode of the Hypomnemata likewise testifies to the feelings the Macedonians had for Alexander. Diodorus (18.4.3) writes that Perdiccas did not want to take a decision which might detract from Alexander's glory on his own:[24]

[18]   *Pace* Errington 1976: 146.
[19]   Arrhidaeus' name change: D.S. 18.2.4; Curt. 10.7.7; Arr. *Succ.* 1.1; Just. 13.3.1; App. *Syr.* 52; *Heid. Epit.* 1.1; Greenwalt 1999. Cf. also Carney 2001.
[20]   On the value of Curtius' account of the events at Babylon: Errington 1970: 72–5; Bosworth 2003a: 175–86; Meeus 2008.
[21]   For Alexander handing his ring to Perdiccas: Curt. 10.5.4; D.S. 17.117.3, 18.2.4; Just. 12.15.12; *LM* 112; Luc. *Dial. Mort.* 13.391; Nepos, *Eum.* 2.1. The historicity of the event has sometimes been doubted, but I see no good reason for this; cf. Rathmann 2005: 9–26. In any case, the episode under discussion shows that Perdiccas claimed – whether justly or not – that Alexander had done so.
[22]   Errington 1976: 139.
[23]   Thus I do not agree with Errington's view (1975: 139) that the exploitation of Alexander's memory failed to be effective because "other more immediate problems were more important" to the Macedonian soldiers. Actually for them both aspects must have made Perdiccas a rather good candidate at the moment, especially since he seems to have been related to the royal house: Curt. 10.7.8. It was Perdiccas' wavering that cost him the throne, but his wavering was well advised because none of the nobles would have accepted his authority: Mooren 1983: 236–7; Meeus 2008b; cf. Heckel 2002b on the competition among the Successors.
[24]   Anson 1991: 238.

But that he might not appear to be arbitrarily detracting anything from the glory of Alexander, he laid these matters before the common assembly of Macedonians for consideration.[25]

According to Diodorus (18.4.6), the Macedonians cancelled Alexander's last plans, although they thought favorably of them:

When these memoranda had been read out, the Macedonians although they applauded the name of Alexander, nevertheless saw that the projects were extravagant and impracticable and decided to carry out none of those that have been mentioned.

Justin provides further testimony to Alexander's popularity with the soldiers when discussing the Argyraspids (14.2.7):

But after Alexander the Argyraspides had little respect for any leader, for after all the memories of the great king, they thought it an indignity to serve under others.

Although this is obviously a rhetorical exaggeration, and the Silver-Shields did serve under other generals, it is not unlikely that such sentiments existed among the Macedonians.[26] Having remained loyal to the Argead house, they might well have been filled with nostalgia for the days when they were actually led by their kings instead of regents or other officers. Moreover, the Argyraspids' obedience to the generals was often qualified and their support of Eumenes clearly resulted from Polyperchon's role as regent for the Argeads, and Eumenes' display of respect for Alexander.[27]

The continuing support for the Argead cause is indeed proven by many events. In 322 Philip's daughter Cynnane crossed to Asia in order to marry her daughter Adea to King Arrhidaeus. Perdiccas felt his power threatened and had Cynnane killed, thus enraging the Macedonian soldiers. The only way to placate them was to let Adea marry Arrhidaeus after all.[28] Errington (1976: 146) argues that this incident is another proof that "direct blood-relationship to Alexander was at first less important in practice to influential sections of Macedonian opinion than the general factor of relationship to the royal house of the Argeads, in particular with Philip."

I have already pointed out that this is a false dichotomy, and in no way does the event suggest anything about a lack of interest for Alexander. Moreover, Polyaenus'

---

[25]   All translations are from the Loeb Classical Library, except those from Justin, quoted from Yardley Develin 1994, and Polyaenus, quoted from Krentz and Wheeler 1994.

[26]   Anson 1991: 246.

[27]   D.S. 18.61.3; Anson 2004: 148; see also below. That they betrayed him in the end is no argument to the contrary, as their allegiance to their own families would surely take priority. Cf. Anson 2004: 255: "[T]he argyraspids surrendered Eumenes to gain the return of their families and property, the ultimate bribe."

[28]   Polyaen. 8.60; Arr. *Succ.* 1.22–3.

account (8.60) of Cynnane's expedition explicitly says that the princess was regarded as related to both:

> When Alcetas opposed her with his force, the Macedonians, upon seeing Philip's daughter and Alexander's sister, felt ashamed and changed their minds.

Furthermore, such negative response from the Macedonians to the murder of an Argead seems to have been the normal reaction in all instances. When Cassander had Olympias killed, he was afraid of the reaction of the people (D.S. 19.52.4), even if Alexander's mother had become less popular because of her harsh and violent actions (D.S. 19.11.9; Just. 14.6.1–2). Later, when he eliminated Alexander IV and Roxane, he concealed it (D.S. 19.105.2). Antigonus acted in the same way after the death of Cleopatra (see further below), trying to blame others and honoring her with a royal burial (D.S. 20.37.6). Just like Cynnane's, the publicly known royal murder of Thessalonice backfired immediately (Plu. *Demetr.* 37.2). In Triparadeisus Adea, now named Eurydice, successfully used her influence on the soldiers against the regents Peithon and Arrhidaeus, and even Antipater had problems asserting his authority under her attacks. If a young girl had such an effect on the army, it is clear that the Argeads meant a lot to them.[29]

In 318 Ptolemy sent messengers to the Macedonians urging them not to obey Eumenes, who had been sentenced to death by the Macedonian army, but they could not be convinced, because the royal house had sanctioned the Cardian's appointment:

> But no one paid attention to him because the kings and Polyperchon their guardian and also Olympias, the mother of Alexander, had written to them that they should serve Eumenes in every way, since he was commander-in-chief of the kingdom. (D.S. 18.62.2)

It is remarkable, however, that when a little later Antigonus did the same (D.S. 18.63.2), the Macedonians did not ignore his orders with the same determination, and even they were in great dismay. The only plausible reason for this seems to be that Antigonus threatened them with punishments if they did not do as he asked, while in Ptolemy's case such intimidation is at least not mentioned by Diodorus. In any case, allegiance to the royal house again prevailed, in spite of the soldiers' fear of Antigonus.[30]

Olympias was held in high esteem because she was the wife of Philip and the mother of Alexander. Both kings are often mentioned when our sources explain the respect for Olympias. Thus, when describing the proceeding of Perdiccas' council on the eve of the First Diadoch War, Justin (13.6.11–12) says:

[29]   D.S. 18.39.2–4; Arr. *Succ.* 1.31–3; Carney 2000: 132–4.
[30]   "While the Macedonian troops were showing signs of their true mercenary nature, the old traditions of loyalty to the Argead house were still strong" (Anson 2004: 155).

Some were in favour of transferring the theatre of operations to Macedonia, the very source and heart of the empire: there they would have Olympias, mother of Alexander, to add significant support to their cause, as well as the favour of the citizens because of the names of Alexander and Philip.

Cassander, when looking for a way to get rid of Alexander's mother, tried to convince the families of those who had fallen victim to Olympias' harsh and violent conduct to accuse her in front of an assembly of the Macedonians. At the same time he also sought other means to kill her, because he was afraid that the people would not condemn her:

> As Olympias, however, refused to flee but on the contrary was ready to be judged before all the Macedonians, Cassander, fearing that the crowd might change its mind if it heard the queen defend herself and was reminded of all the benefits conferred on the nation by Alexander and Philip, sent to her two hundred soldiers who were best fitted for such a task, ordering them to slay her as soon as possible. (D.S. 19.51.4)

In 317 Adea-Eurydice was ready to face Olympias in battle, but her soldiers went over to Olympias before the fighting even began. The sources explain this event in the same vein: Diodorus (19.11.2) gives only Alexander's memory as the reason, while Justin (14.5.10) says that it was Philip's memory or Alexander's greatness. Both passages seem to stem from the same source which actually mentioned both Alexander and Philip.[31]

Some time after the peace of 311 the popular support for Alexander IV's personal rule increased to such an extent that Cassander saw it as a serious threat and had the boy secretly eliminated. Not much later, about 309, the same happened to Heracles when Cassander feared that his troops would join the cause of the young pretender. Justin, who seems to have confused the deaths of both boys, expressly says that the name of Heracles' late father was the reason for the support he received.[32]

Even in the later years of the Diadochi the names of Philip and Alexander were still remembered. When describing how Demetrius as king of Macedon refused to hear petitioners, Plutarch (*Demetr.* 42.3) says:

> And they called to mind, or listened to those who called to mind, how reasonable Philip used to be in such matters, and how accessible.

Although variants of the accompanying anecdote of the old woman telling Demetrius not to be king if he had no time to listen to the people are also told of Philip himself, Antipater, and Hadrian,[33] Demetrius' inaccessibility and the

---

[31]   On the common source of Diodorus and Justin, see Reuss 1876: 23–35; Hornblower 1981: 65–7.
[32]   Alexander IV: D.S. 19.105.2–3. Heracles: D.S. 20.20.3, 20.28.1; Just 15.2.3. For Justin's confusion: Schachermeyr 1920.
[33]   Philip: Plu. *Mor.* 179c; Antipater: Stob. 3.13.48; Hadrian: Cassius Dio 69.6.3.

perceived contrast with Philip might well be historical. Bosworth has shown that this attitude toward his subjects probably was one of the reasons why Demetrius lost popular support.[34] It is not surprising that the Macedonians referred to Philip rather than to Alexander in this context: Philip was the king they had known so well, while Alexander had spent his period of government almost entirely on campaign, far away from those who had stayed in Macedon. At any rate this episode in Plutarch need not mean that Alexander was less popular: the Macedonians in the motherland simply were less familiar with his practices in hearing the people.

Yet another story in Plutarch shows that the Macedonians still thought highly of Alexander at this time. Set in the context of the war between Demetrius and Pyrrhus *c.*290, the Macedonians scorned Demetrius' efforts to imitate Alexander's actions and images, preferring Pyrrhus who showed himself equal to Alexander's battlefield glories.[35] Such a judgment clearly argues for the respect of later generations for Alexander's achievements.

Thus, the sources provide no evidence for the view that the Macedonians would have preferred Philip over Alexander. They seem to have had affectionate memories of both kings. Although other factors, such as the prospect of success and loot, were important as well, it is clear that allegiance to the royal house still influenced the Macedonian soldiers in their choice of whom to side with. Therefore, it would be rather surprising if the Successors did not use a positive image of both of them in their propaganda. I shall now consider how the Diadochi used the names of their Argead predecessors in their wars over Alexander's empire.[36]

Confirmation of Plutarch's statement that Craterus and Leonnatus among the Diadochi modeled themselves after Alexander is found in two fragments of Arrian (*Succ.* F12, F19). Given that Plutarch mentions a comparison between Pyrrhus and other generals, we can assume that some of the Successors who survived into the third century also desired to imitate Alexander's image. Such flamboyant displays are clear indication that the Diadochi deemed a connection with Alexander to be useful.

One of the most important means for political exploitation of Alexander's memory was his body. The one who could bury the dead king legitimized himself as the true heir to Alexander.[37] We have already seen that immediately after Alexander's death a row between nobles and infantrymen ensued around his body. Two years later, when Alexander's funeral carriage was ready to be transported to the king's final resting place, the struggle became more serious. The Babylonian settlement stipulated that Alexander was to be buried at Ammon's sanctuary in Siwah. It seems, however, that in the mean time Perdiccas had decided to take the royal remains to Macedonia, to entomb him at the traditional burial spot at Aegae.[38]

[34] Bosworth 2002: 256–9.
[35] Plu. *Demetr.* 41.5; Plu. *Pyrrh.* 8.2.
[36] See also: Briant 1973a: 129–31; Errington 1976: 138–58; Hammond, in Hammond–Walbank 123–4, 194; Völcker-Janssen 1993: 20–4; Billows 1995: 33–40; Bosworth 2002: 246–78, *passim.*
[37] Schubert 1914: 180–1; Briant 1973a: 130, 318; Greenwalt 1988: 41; Hammond 1989a: 219–20; Stewart 1993: 222; Whitehorne 1994: 64–5; Erskine 2002: 171; Schäfer 2002: 59–60.
[38] Paus. 1.6.3; cf. Arr. *Succ.* 1.25.

Ptolemy, however, was in contact with Arrhidaeus, the man entrusted with the task of escorting the funeral cortege. On arrival at Damascus, he delivered the body to Ptolemy who was waiting for him there. Perdiccas sent out an expedition to regain possession of the dead king, but his men came too late (Arr. *Succ.* F24.1). Ptolemy buried Alexander in Memphis, and later transferred his body to Alexandria.

Many scholars have discussed the significance of this event to both Perdiccas and Ptolemy, and they usually do not attribute the same motives to the satrap of Egypt as to the regent. While Perdiccas is thought to have aimed at legitimizing his personal power over the entire empire, Ptolemy's goal is mostly interpreted as neutralizing the important symbol of the empire's unity or substantiating his claim to rule the Ptolemaic empire.[39] The last notion is especially anachronistic: in 321 there was no Ptolemaic empire. Although Ptolemy was clearly striving for the establishment of a personal power base in Egypt, to the outside world his territory remained a satrapy like any other and his authority that of any other satrap. Moreover, at a time when most people must still have considered Alexander's realm one united empire, it would have been ridiculous to use the most powerful political symbol there was to legitimize one's rule over such a small portion of it. It is hard to see how in the agonistic Macedonian society anyone would have taken Ptolemy seriously if he claimed to be the most worthy to succeed to Alexander and to surpass all his rivals, while at same time he limited his rule to Egypt alone. After the successful hijacking of Alexander's body, Ptolemy held games and sacrifices in honor of the deceased king, and many soldiers decided to join his cause. Diodorus lists Ptolemy's honoring of Alexander as one of the reasons for his increased appeal (D.S. 18.28.4–6). Perdiccas, however, did not leave it at this. Although he had planned to depose Ptolemy before, he now seems to have considered an expedition against Egypt an absolute priority (Arr. *Succ.* F24.1). The propagandistic value of Alexander's body was too high to let a rival exploit it.

The sources often note that so and so had campaigned with Alexander. Such phrases as *tōn Alexandrō synestrateumenōn* not only distinguished such individuals for their military experience, but also because of the status the claim provided.[40] The career of Lysimachus testifies strongly to the usefulness of the claim of having campaigned with Alexander. Bosworth has convincingly argued that before the battle of Ipsus in 301 Lysimachus did not have a strong foundation for his claim to kingship other than the services he had rendered to Alexander during the Asian campaign. That his kingship was accepted nonetheless shows once more how strong the effect of a connection to Alexander was.[41]

---

[39] Most extensively Errington 1976: 141–3; Erskine 2002: 163–73; Rader 2003: 151–61.

[40] The cases which clearly show its value as an asset of status are: D.S. 18.7.3, 18.48.4, 19.15.1, 19.46.2, 19.51.1; Just 13.4.10, 16.1.12, 24.4.10; Plu. *Demetr.* 44.4; Nepos, *Eum.* 7.1; Plu. *Pyrrh.* 12.6; *ISE* ii, no. 73, ll. 7–8; *SEG* xxi (1965), no. 310. Cf. D.S. 19.55.3, 19.56.1, 19.69.1, 19.81.5, 19.82.1, 19.90.3–4; Plu. *Eum.* 1.6; Plu. *Demetr.* 5.2. See Seibert 1969: 152–6; Errington 1976: 159–62; Rosen 1979: 463; Billows 1995: 34, 36.

[41] Bosworth 2002: 274–8.

The following example illustrates how the Successors made use of this distinction. In 317 a large coalition of satraps from the eastern parts of the empire together with Eumenes and the Argyraspids was ready to fight it out with Antigonus. In an army with so many generals, however, tensions unavoidably arose about who was to be in charge:

> Peucestes thought that because of the number of soldiers who followed him on the campaign and because of his high rank under Alexander he ought to have the supreme command. (D.S. 19.15.1)

In the end Alexander's memory did offer the solution, but certainly not as Peucestas would have imagined. Eumenes came up with the idea of holding daily meetings in a tent passing for Alexander's.[42] Thus all would participate in the decision-making process as peers, with Alexander watching over them. Every morning a sacrifice was offered to the deceased king.[43] Clearly, Eumenes was not so much concerned with reverence for Alexander as with finding a way to end the power struggle to his advantage. However, what matters for our purpose is that the appeal to Alexander's memory apparently did not miss its effect, as Eumenes' proposal was accepted. Peucestas, not giving in so easily, tried to outdo the Cardian by lavishly feasting the army in a setting clearly inspired by Alexander's mass marriage ceremony at Susa, with the guests sitting in concentric circles.[44] In the middle were placed altars "for the gods and Alexander and Philip" (D.S. 19.22.3).

Eumenes claimed that the idea for the meetings in Alexander's tent came from the deceased king himself, who had appeared to him in a dream.[45] This was not the only time Alexander came to Eumenes in his sleep, and Pyrrhus, Demetrius, and Seleucus also had dreams of Alexander appearing to them.[46] The dreams served the purpose of showing that Alexander was on one's side, and not on that of their adversaries. In Demetrius' vision, the late king asked him the Antigonid watchword for the battle at Ipsus. Upon hearing that it was "Zeus and Victory," Alexander went to the other side because they welcomed him, implying that their watchword included his name. For their battle in Cappadocia, both Eumenes and Craterus also had watchwords with Alexander's name in them (Plu. *Eum.* 6.6).

Another story about Eumenes is very instructive. The sources claim that after Antipater's death, Antigonus, becoming more ambitious, aimed at gaining control over the whole of Alexander's realm, and deemed it very useful to have a friend like Eumenes to help him achieve this goal.[47] The Cardian, however, had been condemned to death and Antigonus was besieging him. The latter thus decided to raise

---

[42]   D.S. 18.60.4–61.3, 19.15.3–4; Plu. *Eum.* 13.3–4; Nepos, *Eum.* 7.2–3; Polyaen. 4.8.2; Errington 1976: 140–1; Mooren 1983: 238–9; Schäfer 2002: 19–37; Anson 2004: 150–2.

[43]   D.S. 18.61.1, 19.15.4.

[44]   D.S. 19.22–23.1; Bosworth 2002: 255–6.

[45]   D.S. 18.60.4–5; Plu. *Eum.* 13.5; Polyaen. 4.8.2.

[46]   Plu. *Eum.* 6.5; Plu. *Pyrrh.* 11.2; Plu. *Demetr.* 29.1; D.S. 19.90.4; Weber 1999: 13–18.

[47]   Plu. *Eum.* 12.1; D.S. 18.50.1–4.

the siege and release Eumenes if he would join him. Antigonus prescribed a formula according to which Eumenes had to swear loyalty to him, but the clever Greek made up his own oath pledging allegiance to Olympias and the kings as well. He asked the Macedonians which of the oaths was more just and they preferred his version.[48] There are many problems surrounding this story, and its historicity has been challenged.[49] Even if a fabrication, it is telling that someone deemed it credible that the Macedonians would indeed prefer an oath of loyalty to the royal house and Antigonus instead of to Antigonus alone. It may also be argued that the source aimed to show Eumenes in the best possible light by claiming that the Cardian was loyal to the dynasty.

Ptolemy, a true master of propaganda, reached for his pen to display his connection with Alexander. Nowadays, it is almost generally accepted that he had a political axe to grind in writing his Alexander history.[50] One aspect of his perhaps not so hidden agenda was to show how important a part he had played in Alexander's expedition and how close he had been to the king. Although this is not generally accepted, in my opinion Bosworth's recent demonstration that the so-called *Liber de morte* is also a product of Ptolemaic propaganda is convincing.[51] The included fake Alexander testament presents Ptolemy as the only one who has remained truly loyal to Alexander's will in order to exalt him above all the other Diadochi.

In the declaration of Tyre in 315 Antigonus exploited Macedonian sentiment for the dynasty by persuading them to convict Cassander of assorted crimes. Antigonus accused him of having married Thessalonice by force, of murdering Olympias, and of maltreating Roxane and Alexander IV (D.S. 19.61.1–3). If the Macedonians did not think highly of Alexander, it seems they would have cared even less about the fates of his mother, wife, and son.

When Perdiccas conceived the plan to marry Cleopatra, his main motivation was that she would bring him the support of the Macedonians (D.S. 18.23.3). If Diodorus' testimony (20.37.3–4) is valid, the same thought inspired all leading men after Alexander's death who wooed Cleopatra at one time or another:

> She was the sister of Alexander the conqueror of Persia and daughter of Philip, son of Amyntas, and had been the wife of Alexander who made an expedition into Italy. Because of the distinction of her descent Cassander and Lysimachus, as well as Antigonus and Ptolemy and in general all the leaders who were most important after Alexander's death, sought her hand; for each of them, hoping that the Macedonians would follow the lead of this marriage, was seeking alliance with the royal house in order thus to gain supreme power for himself.

[48] Plu. *Eum.* 12.1–4.
[49] Briant 1973b: 69–79; Anson 1977; Bosworth 1992c: 66–7.
[50] E.g., Badian 1964: 256–8; Errington 1969; Goukowski 1978: 141–5; Rosen 1979: 462–72; Bosworth 1996: 41–53; Schepens 1998: 91; Bingen 2007: 20–3. *Contra*: Roisman 1984.
[51] Bosworth 2000a; for a different interpretation see Heckel 1988.

There is no reason to doubt Diodorus' statement about the number of proposals Cleopatra received. We know Ptolemy wanted to marry her, because she was killed when attempting to reach him (D.S. 20.37.3–5). Antigonus had Cleopatra in his power for many years (D.S. 20.37.3–5) and it is very likely that he or his son wanted to marry her as well. No further information is available on Cassander and Lysimachus, but the former married another daughter of Philip, Thessalonice (D.S. 19.52.1–2; Just. 14.6.13), and it is not unlikely that he would have aimed at Cleopatra first. Besides these men, Leonnatus (Plu. *Eum.* 3.9) and Perdiccas (D.S. 18.23.3) also aimed at marrying Cleopatra.

Some scholars have questioned Cleopatra's importance as none of the Successors actually married her and Antigonus eventually had her killed.[52] There might have been more to it, however.[53] Cleopatra was not left unmarried because nobody wanted her, but because two potential husbands, Leonnatus and Perdiccas, died before any marriage could take place. With Ptolemy, it was Cleopatra who met a violent death before she reached the bridegroom. In the cases of Lysimachus, Cassander, and Antigonus, Cleopatra might well have refused the proposals, deeming them not in her own interest. Some hold that Antigonus had her killed because it did not really matter whether she was alive or not,[54] but the reason seems rather to be that it mattered too much whom she married to allow her to marry a rival. Similarly, Alexander's sons Alexander and Heracles were killed because their existence was considered a threat, due to the popular support they attracted from the Macedonians. In the context of Eumenes' visit after Triparadeisus Justin (14.1.7–8) confirms that Cleopatra held such prestige:

> He [Eumenes] next moved on to Sardis and Alexander the Great's sister, Cleopatra, with the intention of using her influence to secure the loyalty of his centurions and senior officers, who would think that royal authority rested on the side favoured by Alexander's sister. Such was the respect that Alexander's greatness commanded that even women were used as a path to the prestige conferred by his hallowed name.

The battle of Ipsus certainly did not mark an end to the political usefulness of the memory of Philip and Alexander. When Demetrius Poliorcetes seized Macedonia in 294, Justin (16.1.12–17) mentions a speech in which Demetrius argued that he had the best claim to the throne of Macedon because his father Antigonus had served with Philip and Alexander on all their campaigns and had held the guardianship for Alexander's children.[55] Demetrius also argued that Cassander's sons were deserving of their fates because their father had brought the Argead dynasty to extinction, an argument which features in Plutarch's account (*Demetr.* 37.2), and,

---

[52] E.g., Errington 1976: 148; Völcker-Jansen 1993: 18; Carney 2000b: 151.
[53] For a reappraisal of Cleopatra's importance: Meeus 2008a; see also Whitehorne 1994: 61–9. Carney 1988 is skeptical of Cleopatra's significance to the Successors.
[54] Carney 2000b: 151.
[55] There is no good reason to doubt the historicity of the substance of the speech: Bosworth 2002: 251–2 with n. 22.

if the spirits of the dead had any awareness, Philip and Alexander would surely prefer to see their avengers on the throne, rather than those who murdered them and their family, as the rulers of Macedon. (Just. 16.1.17)

Apparently such arguments did not misfire, as Justin concludes:

This appeased the people, and Demetrius was declared king of Macedon. (Just. 16.1.18)

In Plutarch's narrative (*Pyrrh.* 12.6) of the later war between Lysimachus and Pyrrhus, Lysimachus uses his connection to Alexander to get the Macedonians on his side:

by letters and conferences he corrupted the leading Macedonians, upbraiding them because they had chosen as lord and master a man who was a foreigner, whose ancestors had always been subject to Macedonia, and were thrusting the friends and familiars of Alexander out of the country. After many had thus been won over, Pyrrhus took alarm and departed. . . .

Of course, that Lysimachus had just seized Pyrrhus' provisions will not have been inconsequential, but it is nonetheless interesting to see that Lysimachus still deemed his connection to Alexander useful in trying to get the Macedonians over to his side in 285.

The Successors also honored Alexander by founding cities named after him (Str. 13.1.26). Appian (*Syr.* 57) lists two cities founded by Seleucus which were named after Alexander; after Ipsus, Lysimachus refounded Antigoneia Troas as Alexandria (Str. 13.1.26), while Antigonus might have been responsible for the foundation of Alexandria-by-Issus. Ptolemy did not found his own Alexandria, but he spent great efforts on the development of Alexandria in Egypt.[56]

As Wheatley (see ch. 3) has also noted, the coinage of the Diadochi has all too often been neglected by historians. It provides important evidence for the attitude of the Successors toward Alexander's memory: coins represent the official view of the issuing authority, but the lack of context makes their iconographic messages often difficult to interpret. The study of Alexander's image through the coins of the Successors actually requires an essay of its own, but here I list only some basic facts.[57] In the first years after his death, coinage bearing Alexander's name continued to be struck in almost all mints throughout the empire.[58] Antigonus and Cassander even upheld the issuing of coins with the name of Alexander after they had themselves become kings, an obvious statement of political continuity. After his father's death, Demetrius still struck Alexander drachms, but now in his own name.[59]

---

[56] Billows 1990: 298.

[57] See Stewart 1993: *passim*; Arnold-Biucchi 2006; Dahmen 2007.

[58] Mørkholm 1991: 56; Price 1991.

[59] Mørkholm 1991: 59, 61.

Cassander's brother Alexarchus, founder of a utopian city called Uranopolis, also issued Alexander tetradrachms.[60]

The first to introduce a new coinage was Ptolemy: shortly after 321 he started striking coins depicting Alexander wearing an elephant scalp and the ram's horns of Ammon, to which were added a few years later a fillet which is usually interpreted as a Dionysiac headband, and the Aegis of Zeus.[61] About 304, after his assumption of kingship, Ptolemy started minting gold staters with his portrait on the obverse and Alexander standing in a quadriga of elephants with a thunderbolt in his hand.[62] On his bronze coins, which were smaller denominations meant for local use only, Ptolemy depicted Alexander with the fillet and the ram's horns.[63] From c.300 Ptolemy no longer issued gold and silver coins bearing Alexander's image.[64]

Seleucus, who at first continued minting posthumous Alexander coins, introduced new types after his assumption of the kingship. Some of these featured Alexander's portrait: he also used the Alexander with elephant scalp iconography, while another issue depicts a hero, possibly Alexander, with a leopard skin helmet decorated with bull's horns and ears. Even after Ipsus some of his coins were struck in the name of Alexander.[65]

Lysimachus did not control a mint before his foundation of Lysimacheia c.305, but apparently he was supplied with coinage by Cassander before that date.[66] Before Ipsus Lysimachus hardly struck any coins of his own. Thereafter he first issued some traditional Alexander drachms in Alexander's name but with his own badge, the forepart of a lion. About 297 he introduced his famous coinage showing Alexander with the diadem and ram's horns.[67]

Now that it appears that there is no evidence for a preference of Philip over Alexander, let us look at Cassander's policy as interpreted by Errington and others. Although some ancient authors had represented Cassander's actions as partial to Philip (D.S. 17.118.2; Paus. 9.7.2), certain scholars have rightly pointed out that it would have been politically harmful for Cassander to have conducted an anti-Alexander policy.[68] It is indeed true that Cassander killed Olympias, Roxane and Alexander IV, and Heracles, that he gave an honorable burial to Arrhidaeus, Eurydice, and Cynnane, that he married Thessalonice and restored Thebes, but is

---

[60] Mørkholm 1991: 60.
[61] Davis and Kraay: 36; Mørkholm 1991: 63–4; Stewart 1993: 233–42; Dahmen 2007: 10–11, 42, 112–14. A recently discovered golden coin from the Mir Zakah hoard, belonging to the so-called Elephant medallions group (on which see Holt 2003; Le Rider 2003: 329–33; Dahmen 2007: 6–9), also depicts Alexander with the elephant scalp. If genuine, this coin would be Ptolemy's source of inspiration, but its authenticity is highly doubtful: see Dahmen 2007: 9 with n. 13.
[62] Mørkholm 1991: 65; Dahmen 2007: 12–13.
[63] Dahmen 2007: 13.
[64] Mørkholm 1991: 65; Dahmen 2007: 12–13.
[65] Mørkholm 1991: 71–3; Houghton and Lorber 2002: 5–9 (with due reservations about the identification of the helmeted hero as Alexander); Arnold-Biucchi 2006: 36–7; Dahmen 2007: 14–15.
[66] Mørkholm 1991: 60–1.
[67] Mørkholm 1991: 81; Arnold-Biucchi 2006: 36; Dahmen 2007: 16–17.
[68] Goukowski 1978: 105–8; Bosworth 1986: 11; Koulakiotis 2006: 95.

this necessarily a policy aimed at promoting Philip's memory to the detriment of Alexander's? Cassander became politically active in his own name after the death of his father, Antipater. His father's decision not to appoint him regent immediately made him an enemy of Polyperchon (D.S. 18.48.4–49.1). The latter appealed to Olympias for help, as she was the natural enemy of his two main opponents, Queen Eurydice and Cassander (D.S. 18.49.4, 57.2). For Cassander, in turn, it was logical to side with Eurydice against Olympias, especially after she had offered him the regency (Just. 14.5.3). Given that Olympias had killed his brother Nicanor and destroyed the tomb of another brother, Iolaus (D.S. 19.11.8), and tried to set the Macedonians against him (D.S. 19.35), Cassander's murder of Alexander's mother needs no ideological explanation.

At the same time, Cassander tried to capitalize on the royal burial for Arrhidaeus, Eurydice, and Cynnane (D.S. 19.52.5; Ath. 4.155a). This was in itself an important opportunity for public display and legitimation, and need not necessarily have been explicitly aimed at promoting Philip's memory. Neither is there any reason why Alexander's memory would have been excluded from the event. Cassander's contemporaneous marriage with Thessalonice (D.S. 19.52.1) was a further step in his quest for legitimacy, but probably she was only his second choice, after Cleopatra. There is no reason to assume that a preference for Philip over Alexander played any part here, and Diodorus mentions that she was both Philip's daughter and Alexander's half-sister.

The restoration of Thebes, although already represented as an anti-Alexander measure in antiquity (D.S. 17.118.2; Paus. 9.7.2), seems to have been intended to gain glory and support among the Greeks, not to be an attack against Alexander (D.S. 19.53.2, 54.1–2). The murders of Roxane, Alexander IV, and Heracles came at a time when popular support for their accession became a grave threat to Cassander's own power (see above). If he had not killed them, they might well have permanently ended his hopes of seizing the throne for himself. Throughout Macedonian history Argeads had been killed by other Argeads simply because they were contestants for the throne.[69] Cassander merely continued this practice. Moreover, Goukowsky has pointed out that there certainly was no *damnatio memoriae* of Alexander in Macedon under Cassander: people could refer to their deeds under Alexander; Aristobulus started writing his Alexander history; the deme of Thessaloniki named after Alexander's horse, Bucephalas, might well have gotten its name from Cassander; one of his sons was named Alexander, and he commissioned a painting of a battle of Alexander by Philoxenus.[70]

The stories of Cassander's hatred of Alexander most likely emanated from the propaganda of his rivals.[71] Many scholars accept most or all of Plutarch's catalog of anecdotes illustrating the enmity between Cassander and Alexander, or at least

[69] Cf. Carney 1983.

[70] Goukowski 1978: 108–11.

[71] Goukowski 1978: 105–8. For the stories: Plu. *Alex.* 74.2–6; Plu. *Mor.* 180–1; cf. D.S. 17.118.2; Paus. 9.7.2.

assume that the hatred on which the anecdotes are based is a fact.[72] The first one, however, of Cassander laughing when he saw Asians performing *proskynesis* before Alexander seems to have been modeled on a similar anecdote about Leonnatus.[73] The story of Cassander being so frightened by a statue of Alexander that he started trembling so badly he could hardly recover would have been credible if it concerned a 4-year-old, but seems rather ridiculous when a ruthless Macedonian warlord is involved. That an argument ensued between Cassander and the king after an embassy had complained about Antipater is in itself not unlikely, but it does not prove any hatred. The statement that Alexander "was particularly afraid of Antipater and of his sons, one of whom, Iolaus, was his chief cupbearer" (Plu. *Alex.* 74.2) refutes itself. Who would have as cup-bearer one whom he feared at a time when poison was such a popular murder weapon? The tensions between Alexander and Antipater too seem to have been greatly overstated as a result of the propaganda wars of the Diadochi. Arrian (7.12.5–7) denies that Alexander would have called his regent to Asia out of mistrust, and indeed certain scholars have argued convincingly that the relationship between Antipater and the king was good.[74] Thus, we see how the Successors were interested not only in stressing their connection with Alexander for their own political benefit, but also in presenting their rivals as enemies of Alexander.

The result of this investigation shows that Alexander enjoyed great popularity after his death and that the Successors did all they could to exploit his name. Their propagandistic choices were determined by expediency rather than by ideology: they referred to Philip, Alexander, and the other Argeads as it suited their cause at the moment. Political realities and existing enmities often played a part in determining the propagandistic claims a Successor could plausibly make, but there seems to be no trace of any absolute preference for either Philip or Alexander.[75]

---

[72]   E.g., Bendinelli 1965; Hamilton 1969: 206; Bosworth 1986: 11–12; Billows 1995: 39 with n. 42; Badian 1999: 84.

[73]   Hamilton 1969: 206; Heckel 1978.

[74]   Griffith 1965; Ashton 1992: 126–7; Baynham 1994: 343–6. For a recent statement of the opposite view see Heckel 1999.

[75]   I am much indebted to Professor Hans Hauben, Professor Hubert Meeus, Dr. Karolien Geens, and Mr. Bert Saerens who commented on earlier versions of this essay. I would also like to thank the editors for their criticisms and suggestions.

14

Roman Alexanders:

Epistemology and Identity

Diana Spencer

Introduction: Reception and Knowledge:
Making Up Alexander

Thinking about Alexander the Great means thinking about a character generated by the cultural politics of the Roman world. Roman culture is saturated with themes that scream "Alexander" – knowing glances and nods to a foreign king who became deeply embedded in the experience of being Roman in the first and second centuries BC and AD. In fact his importance for Rome was so intense that Roman texts (in the broadest sense) have drowned out most earlier (and contemporary) accounts of Alexander, leaving us with a figure that is almost wholly modeled by Roman anxieties, interests, and enthusiasms.[1]

Imperialist, monomaniac, alcoholic, narcissist, mystic, visionary: the seductive combination of fascination and horror which fed the posthumous Alexander industry seems already to have been present, in embryo, in his own publicity machine.[2] From the very start, thinking about Alexander has been influenced and invigorated by his reputation as a man who understood the vital importance of fame for increasing one's authority. For Romans living through the turbulent late republic, emphasis on individual celebrity and the ability to position oneself as an outstanding

---

[1] For the backstory of how and why Alexander keyed so elegantly into Rome's political and cultural concerns in the second and first centuries, see Spencer 2002: 9–38. On the lost histories of Alexander, see Pearson 1960, and more briefly, in summary form Baynham 2003: 3–13. An excellent introduction to the major narratives of Alexander from the early Roman empire is Atkinson 2000b. This essay focuses on the allusive and pervasive impact of Alexander on the popular imagination, rather than dealing with the narratives for which Alexander is the primary focus.

[2] Most straightforwardly, we can see this in the control exercised over "official" images, characterized by the works of Lysippus and Apelles. The wide-ranging impact of Alexander's tightly controlled iconography is discussed in detail in Stewart 1993. The most useful recent discussion is Stewart 2003; see also Moreno 1993, Killerich 1993, and Nielsen 1993; see also Mihalopoulos, ch. 15.

personality were setting politics along a track that would eventually lead to the principate. In this particular political and cultural climate at Rome – a world view intensely influenced by the modes of authority deployed by the Hellenistic kingdoms that succeeded Alexander – his significance as an underlying and at times even explicitly invoked model is difficult to overestimate.

Taking Scipio Africanus as a notional starting point, and concluding with Hadrian, this essay suggests that we read Rome's Alexander as an inevitable precursor to and even by-product of Roman imperialism in the late republic. Furthermore, this approach makes cultural consciousness of "Alexander" (Alexander-as-meme) central – with hindsight at least – to the political changes that transformed Rome into a superpower. Perhaps it is an overstatement to assert that *all* Roman questions and answers inevitably lead to Alexander, but through a three-part examination of Rome's cultural permeability to Alexander during the late republic and early empire, we may find that placing Alexander at the heart of Roman systems of interrogating, understanding, and categorizing the world is less tendentious than it might, at first glance, seem.[3] This essay commences with the figures that we tend to identify as prime candidates for being Alexander at Rome. Focusing, then, on the significance of Alexander's campaign historian Callisthenes for Roman interest in Alexander we can think through why control of historical narrative is such an important feature of Alexander's mythography. Finally, I suggest that we conclude with "Alexander" as a mode for the systematization of knowledge at Rome. Taken together, these approaches show how Roman voices and spaces speak directly about Alexander as an epistemological model for politics, culture, and identity.

Being Alexander the Great – A Roman Complex?

Identifying particular Romans as potential "Alexanders" is only the start of the interpretive process that faces us when we explore the place of Alexander the Great in Roman self-fashioning. We are also faced with another dilemma: to what extent are comparisons with Romans primarily about "Alexander," or their Roman protagonists, or indeed the authors themselves? After all, Cicero likening Caesar to Alexander is rather different from Plutarch or Appian doing so. Pompey is perhaps the most obvious starting point, if only because he gained the same sobriquet *magnus* which so sets Alexander apart, but he is certainly not the only late republi-

---

[3]   Though approaching the topic from a wide variety of angles (e.g., *Quellenforschung*, historiography, biography, cultural studies, literary criticism) the second half of the twentieth century onward has seen a dramatic growth in reception of Alexander at Rome. The most recent extended study is Spencer 2002 (which includes an extensive bibliography). Isager 1993 offers a concise summary of Roman Alexanders from Pompey to Vespasian, but the breadth of coverage allows for little detailed engagement. Other exciting and challenging approaches to Alexander reception in antiquity include three collections (Sordi 1984b; Croisille 1990b; Carlsen et al. 1993) and a handful of individual essays (e.g., Ceauçescu 1974; Green 1989a; Baynham 2003).

can "Alexander." We can, in fact, commence with a brief glance back to the place of Alexander in retroactive accounts of Scipio Africanus, a figure whose struggle against Punic (i.e., Phoenician) Carthage, and whose mythical qualities and legendary chastity are all complicated by the nostalgia of hindsight. The supposed *proskynesis* of the waves before Scipio at New Carthage, facilitating the city's fall and echoing the story of the sea's deference to Alexander at Mt. Climax, is a particular case in point.[4]

Eventually, it is left to Juvenal (*Satires* 10.133–73) to turn the Scipionic model on its head. Rather than *comparing* Scipio with Alexander, or alluding to Alexander-style behavior on his part, he reinvents Alexander as the culture monster Hannibal. By identifying Alexander with Rome's evil genius, the general who commanded Carthage (the only superpower seriously to threaten Rome itself), Juvenal binds Alexander's dangerous possibilities into a story of Rome's imperializing success, transforming Scipio, the "Roman" Alexander and conqueror of Hannibal, into a new and improved version.[5] Despite the cynical and even horrified overtones that typify accounts of post-republican Alexanders – and the attendant complications of reading Scipio through the voices of authors living in a wholly different world – exploring the kinds of things that make these potential Alexanders stand out offers a fascinating insight into how History and identity were being fashioned.

Pompey and the Beginning of the End

Although reception of Pompey's Alexander qualities are colored by the political maneuverings of Marius and Sulla at the beginning of the first century, he does seem to have been the first Roman to encourage widespread and explicit comparisons between himself and Alexander.[6] Pompey's links with the influential Stoic philosopher Posidonius of Rhodes (whose interests also extended to history and political theory),[7] might well have attracted Pompey to aspects of Alexander's image

[4] On Scipio and Alexander see, e.g., Livy 26.19.5–7 and Dio 16.38–9, 17.63 (conversations with Jupiter and divine father); Livy 35.14.6–7 (conversation with Hannibal, about Alexander); Livy 26.50, Dio 16.43, and Gell. 7.8.1–6 (chastity of, at New Carthage – on this, see Spencer 2002: 172–5); Sil. Ital. *Punica* 13.762–76 (Alexander as his compromised, dead adviser – on this, see Spencer 2002: 162–3). For echoes of Alexander in Scipio's success at New Carthage, see Plb. 10.8.6–10.9.3, 10.11.6–8, 10.14.7–12; Livy 26.45.8–9 (cf. Plu. *Alex.* 17.3–5; Arr. 1.26.1–2). Scipio's acclamation as *Inuictus* connects him at least associatively with Alexander, the ultimate invincible leader (see, e.g., Ennius *Operis incerti fragmenta annalibus fortasse tribuenda* 5 (var. 3) V, in Skutsch 1985; and posthumously, Cic. *Verr.* 4.82; *Rep.* 6.9; Livy 38.51.5); this also drags him forward into subsequent usage by Pompey and Caesar. A succinct account of Scipio's associations with Alexander can be found at Green 1989a: 201–2; see also Spencer 2002: 168–9.

[5] For a more detailed discussion, see Spencer 2002: 157–9.

[6] Although, as Isager 1993: 76 acknowledges, much of our detail on Pompey's *imitation* is a function of later texts. Plutarch (with hindsight, of course) offers examples of Pompey attracting mockery rather than glamor from his association with Alexander, e.g., *Pomp.* 2.2; *Caes.* 7.1.

[7] On Posidonius and Pompey see, e.g., Str. 11.1.6; Cic. *Tusc. Disp.* 2.61; Plin. *HN* 7.112.

Figure 14.1   Pompey the Great, Roman, first century BC. Carlsberg Glyptotek, Copenhagen. Photo: Alinari/Art Resource, New York.

beyond those of military glamor and personal style. Alexander's potential as a model for intellectual inquiry, imperializing topography and cultural colonialism offers an important subtext to accounts of Pompey's eastern achievements. Pompey's three Triumphs (over Hiarbas, Sertorius, and Mithridates) located him as the conqueror (albeit for Rome) of the three continents. As master of the world and the man who defined the boundaries of the world and Rome, we can see how significant public images of world domination must have been for his image, and in particular for any attempts to position him(self) as Alexander's successor on the world stage.[8]

One way in which Pompey may have tried to combine both intellectual and military aspects of Alexander's authority was in his sponsorship of Theophanes of Mytilene as a personal historian (on which see Strabo 1.1.6); more generally, one might also see traces of it in his creation of a cultural and intellectual milieu that could secure control over his reception.[9] By modeling his arch-enemy Mithridates

---

[8]   For the representation of *oikoumene* in the Triumph in 61, see Dio 37.21.2; on Pompey as world conqueror see, e.g., Cic. *Pro Sest.* 129; *Pro Balb.* 9.16; Manilius, *Astronomica* 1.793; Plu. *Pomp.* 45.6.
[9]   Franklin 2003 offers a useful summary of Pompeian "ideology."

of Pontus as a new Hannibal, Pompey might nod to Scipio while also – potentially – demonstrating a cause for war not dissimilar to Alexander's campaign of retribution against Persia. Just like Alexander, Pompey could disseminate a version of his campaign that transformed it into a civilizing mission, spreading law and order, and extending the boundaries of science and knowledge.[10] Contemporary responses to this self-promotion, and a rigorous program of public and monumental texts, make it seem likely that this was self-association – indeed, *imitation* – rather than simply a process of ascribing Alexander-style qualities after the fact. We can see this at work in Pompey's foundation of eponymous cities (e.g., Pompeiopolis in Cilicia), the trophy he erected in the wake of his victory over Sertorius (adorned with his statue and an inscription enumerating his conquest of 876 cities), and the similar iconographic program at his theater, developing his identification as *kosmokrator*.[11]

Breathless and admiring comments on Pompey's magnificence in Pliny's *Naturalis historia* are doubtless colored both by (Antonine) hindsight and Pompey's successful image-making as a man guided (at least in part) by scientific and intellectual principles; but the glamor of Alexander is rarely far away.[12] However apocryphal it may have been, the story of Pompey driving through Rome in triumph in 61, wearing Alexander's cloak (which he just happened to have found among Mithridates' belongings) was far too good to pass up.[13] Likewise, his retrospectively reported attempt to harness four elephants to his chariot for the Triumph awarded after his victory over Hiarbas – thwarted only because the arch spanning the route was just too narrow – offers a tantalizing and irresistible set of connections to Alexander's self-positioning as eastern conqueror that even Paul Zanker (1988: 10) was unable to resist.[14] A Tiberian era slant on Alexander's problematic associations may be surfacing in Valerius Maximus (6.2.7), who recounts a story of M. Favonius accusing Pompey, in 60, of wearing a diadem and aiming to turn Rome into a monarchy. Writing in the fourth century AD, Ammianus Marcellinus (17.11.4) suggests that Favonius had in fact misinterpreted a "bandage" that Pompey was

---

[10] Plu. *Pomp.* 37.3 makes Theophanes responsible for black propaganda on Pompey's behalf. For Pompey's self-fashioning as Alexander, see in particular Sall. *Hist.* 3.88M. Green 1989b: 291 n. 40 provides a range of references. Pompey's entourage included Theophanes, Lenaeus (a Greek freedman and rhetorician), and the antiquarian and polymath Varro, and he also seems to have kept up contact with Posidonius (an influential Stoic philosopher and historian from Rhodes, with interests in political theory). On the significance of exploration and science as Pompeian themes in general, see e.g., Plin. *HN* 6.51–2, 12.20, 12.111. On Lenaeus' study of Mithridates' medical texts see, e.g., Plin. *HN* 25.5. On Theophanes see, e.g., Cic. *Pro Arch.* 24; Str. 11.2.2, 11.4.2, 11.5.1, 11.14.4, 11.14.11; Plu. *Pomp.* 35, 36; a connection between Pompey and Theophanes is discussed by Gold 1985.

[11] For Pompeiopolis, see Str. 8.7.5; Plu. *Pomp.* 28; Dio 36.37.6; App. *BM* 115. Cf., e.g., Arr. 5.29; D.S. 17.95.1 for parallelism with Alexander. On his theater, see Plin. *HN* 36.41; Suet. *Ner.* 46.1. For imagery of world mastery in connection with Pompey and Caesar, see Weinstock 1971: 50–3.

[12] See, e.g., Plin. *HN* 7.95, 7.97; Sall. *Hist.* 3.88M; Cic. *Ad Att.* 2.13.2; Plu. *Pomp.* 2.2.

[13] Appian (*BM* 117) and Zanker (1988: 10) certainly want to believe it. See Dio. 59.17.3 and Suet. *Calig.* 52 on Caligula and Alexander's breastplate.

[14] For accounts of the Triumph see, e.g., Plin. *HN* 8.4; Plu. *Pomp.* 14.6.

using to cover an ulcer. It is unclear how diadem-like a bandage could really be! As such later anecdotes suggest, the glory and sparkle of being Alexander at Rome has a flip side, and we see his charm continuing to unravel if we turn to Caesar and Crassus.[15]

Caesar and Crassus

Conquests in the east gave body to Pompey's status as Rome's Alexander, and without this tangible military glory, positioning himself as conqueror of Alexander's "east" (Rome's notional antithesis) and attempting to play up a physical resemblance to Alexander would have been more likely to tend toward bathos rather than glamor. Nevertheless, Pompey's eventual political decline at Rome suggests that deploying "Alexander" qualities at home might prove rather more complicated than being a glamorously reported and victorious "Alexander" in Asia Minor. Our impression of Pompey's career as, ultimately, a failure, suggests that invoking Alexander at Rome was likely to drag overtones of despotism and monarchy into the heart of an empire that still defined itself as a place from which kings were excluded.

What we now term the "First Triumvirate," an unofficial coalition between Pompey, Caesar, and M. Licinius Crassus, drew together three men for whom Alexander proved to be an increasingly problematic running mate. The late 60s were colored by jostling for power between Caesar and Crassus, whilst Pompey was cutting a swathe through Rome's eastern problems. Caesar's tactical transformation of the west into a theater of empire to match the sexiness of Pompey's (and Alexander's) eastern exploits left Crassus in search of a conquest to match them. Perhaps it was in an attempt to claim conquistadorial charisma for himself that he launched an expedition against the Parthian empire. For a man attempting to shed the role of financier, this was a bold maneuver.[16] Pompey's defeat of Mithridates had dragged Alexander's military glamor firmly into his repertoire of attributes, but Mithridates was still only king of Pontus – not a name to conjure with. The Parthians, on the other hand, could be identified fairly straightforwardly as the successors to the Persian empire. And that would, of course, make their conqueror into Alexander. Crassus enjoyed some early success in Mesopotamia in 54, but it was at Carrhae, the following year, that the decisive battle was seared onto Rome's imagination. Crassus' army was wiped out, he was killed, and those

---

[15]   Green (1989a: 198) is hugely doubtful that Pompey's botched Alexandrophilia would have made the Macedonian an attractive model for Caesar, but I suspect that synchronicity between Pompey and Caesar and Pompey's (ultimate) failure may have made outdoing Pompey/Alexander even more (rather than less) attractive.

[16]   The nickname "Moneybags" (*Diues*) that Crassus acquired is rather less alluring than Pompey's "Great." It is interesting that, rather than gaining a tag, "Caesar" instead *becomes* one in the principate (and after).

soldiers who survived ended up settling in Parthia as POWs. Perhaps even more disastrously, the legionary standards were lost.[17] This calamity haunted Roman policy in the east, and was still continuing to overshadow attitudes to expansive imperialism in the second century AD. Suddenly, rather than offering an exciting, wealthy new world for Roman flexing of military supremacy, the "east" became a zone which might put Romans at a disadvantage – physically and psychologically.

We can see all of these complex associations playing themselves out in Julius Caesar's subsequent career, but before looking briefly at their potential impact on his assassination, it is worth setting the scene. Stories of Caesar as the gods' favorite seem to have associated him with Hellenistic patterns of divinely favored monarchy, which themselves look back to the complex relationship between Alexander and the Successor kingdoms and are echoed in elite image-making in late republican Rome.[18] Caesar's famous lightning strike warfare (*celeritas bellandi*) becomes a key element in the positive connection between the two men, even if we have no clear or contemporary evidence that this was a consciously "Alexander"-style tactic on Caesar's part.[19] Plutarch's decision to pair Caesar and Alexander in his series of "parallel" *Lives* is both telling and infuriating. It makes it clear that this kind of comparison was, at least by the late first century AD, acceptable and even straight-forward, but his apparent assumption that readers will know the background to the comparison makes it difficult to analyze how it might have worked in the mid first century, and in the aftermath of Caesar's assassination. Still, even Peter Green, usually doubtful of the contemporaneity of links between Caesar and Alexander, sees echoes of self-fashioning in Caesar's supposed regret when faced with a statue of Alexander in the temple of Hercules at Gades (69) for his own paucity of achievement (at a similar age).[20]

Cicero's self-conscious attempts to work up a letter of advice to Caesar, modeled on Aristotle's guidance of Alexander, show us one way in which even after Pompey,

[17]   Comparisons with Rome's catastrophic defeat by Hannibal at Cannae may not be too far from the mark, as suggested later in Hor. *Carm.* 3.5. Eventually, Augustus managed to negotiate their return, and the standards were lodged in the temple of Mars Ultor in the Forum Augustum at Rome in 2 BC.

[18]   Appian (*BC* 2.149), e.g., includes what seems to be Callisthenes' story of Alexander's "miraculous" passage along the coast beneath Mt. Climax in Pamphylia (*FGrH* 124 F31; Arr. 1.26.1–2; Plu. *Alex.* 17.3–5) in his comparison of Alexander and Caesar. As noted above, this story gets attached to Scipio at his successful siege of New Carthage. Cf. Cicero (*De imp. Cn. Pompei* 10.28; 16.47, 48) on Pompey, and the need for a general to have *felicitas*. Weinstock 1971 draws together a vast array of associations with Alexander that color Caesar's progress to deification (although his encyclopedic tendencies lead to some uncritical readings). Wiseman 1974 and Zanker 1988: 5–25 offer important discussions of late republican aristocratic self-aggrandizement.

[19]   Plutarch tells us that Caesar studied Alexander's campaigns (*Caes.* 11), while speed forms an important narrative strand in Curtius' Alexander (e.g., 4.4.1–2; 5.1.36). Appian makes a direct comparison (2.21.149–54), as does Velleius (2.41.1). Strabo, writing under Augustus tells us that Caesar was *philalexandros* (13.1.27).

[20]   Green 1989a: 195: Suet. *Iul.* 7; cf. Plu. *Caes.* 11.

Alexander could be redrafted as a positive political model.[21] The virtue of *clementia* (forgiveness) is perhaps the other obvious example.[22] *Clementia* connects Caesar directly to Scipio and Pompey, but also ties him posthumously to Augustus' program of post-civil war renewal at Rome.[23] It is in accounts and texts of the years leading up to 44 that we see Alexander's potential as a popularity winner at Rome breaking down, and this coincides with a gradual ratcheting up of negative associations with Caesar. We find Caesar's style increasingly being characterized as more ostentatiously autocratic, and his authority as being less and less clearly dependent upon traditional codes of political practice and the *mos maiorum*. The corollary to these trends is a nexus of associations between Caesar and tropes of monarchy, tyranny, luxury, and self-interest. This in turn may be paralleled in the recurrence of *dominatio* and *libertas* in political rhetoric.[24]

Clementia suggests moral as well as military authority, and combined with a developing network of visual tags which connected Caesar to monarchical style, it is unsurprising that his political enemies had little difficulty in making his plans for a campaign against Parthia into an aspirational blueprint for a return of the trappings of autocracy to Rome. We gain a vivid (if rather belated) picture from a series of authors, suggesting that Caesar wore a "regal" purple toga, a laurel wreath, and a style of boot associated with Etruscan kingship; he was even portrayed on contemporary coins, an honor typically associated with dead "heroes" (or at least notionally heroic ancestors) or gods.[25] Taken in conjunction with the events of early February 44 – when Caesar, sitting on a gold seat at the foot of a statue of himself, was waited on by senators in front of his temple of Venus Genetrix, he is reported to have refused to rise to meet them; infamously, then, at the Lupercalia festival he supposedly acted out a scene of "refusing" a diadem from Antony – the assassination in March of that year seems (narratologically) almost inevitable.[26]

---

[21]   Cic. *Ad Att.* 12.40.1–2, 13.26.2, 13.27.1, 13.28.1–3. Weinstock 1971: 188 thinks (*ex silentio*) that Caesar himself may have "suggested" the comparison to Cicero; Green 1989a: 205 dismisses this. Spencer 2002: 57, 61–3 discusses these letters.

[22]   On the role of *clementia* in modeling Roman Alexanders, see Spencer 2002: 170–5, 229 n. 20. On *clementia* and Cicero's *Pro Marcello*, see Spencer 2002: 58–61.

[23]   On imperial virtues, see Fears 1981.

[24]   Useful texts are referenced by Wirszubski 1960, esp. 52, 62, 103–5.

[25]   Caesar's changing image (and detailed references to texts) is summarized by Gelzer 1968: 278–9, 308–9, 315–23. Weinstock 1971: 188–9 locates Caesar's use of the red boots of the Alban kings very explicitly in Alexander's shadow, linking this to problems associated with Alexander's "Medizing" changes of dress. On the significance of genealogies, mythical and otherwise, in late republican image-making, see Wiseman 1974.

[26]   See, e.g., App. *BC* 2.106–9; Suet. *Iul.* 76, 79; Plu. *Caes.* 61. Despite Pompey's successful post-Sullan reinvention of Venus as his protector, Caesar's explicit annexation of her as his ancestor raised far more disturbing implications. Suddenly, this was more than divine favor for an individual/family, it implied a divine plan which raised the Julii far above fellow citizens, and raised the specter of hereditary power monopolized by one family, whose success was integral to the prosperity and destiny of Rome itself. Green 1989a: 206–7 succinctly (if dismissively) summarizes what he terms "the dim area of merely circumstantial evidence" on Alexander and Caesar (206). Although the textual evidence is complex and at times contradictory, Wiseman 1974 introduces a persuasive vision of a Rome in which vying for

Antony and Augustus: From Republic to Empire

Being Alexander in the wake of Caesar was a fraught enterprise, so it is unsurprising that his direct, named heir, Octavian, distanced himself from the taint that being Alexander carried. Antony, however, was trapped – whether by himself or by enemy propaganda it is not entirely clear, since we have little trace of the kinds of anti-Octavianic rhetoric that his supporters may have indulged in, but are well supplied with propaganda from the winning side. In effect, our story of Alexander from the years before Actium (31) is a story concocted by Octavian and his partisans, with occasional glimpses into the ways in which Antony might have retaliated or set his own agenda.[27] Antony's use of solar imagery, both on coins, and for his son (with Cleopatra), Alexander Helios, connects into the kind of astral symbolism that characterized deification in the wake of Alexander, and that was almost certainly implicit in the anxieties concerning a waning of the sun and the comet that followed Caesar's death.[28] But while this kind of imagery was gaining currency in the late republic, Antony's liaison with Cleopatra and his Parthian expedition located him in much more problematic territory. In effect, by choosing the "east" as his operational field, and leaving the west to Octavian (and, more tenuously, to Lepidus), Antony commenced a process of self-fashioning as yet another Roman Alexander that was to have disastrous consequences.

Excessive drinking and partying is a feature of late republican invective that used Alexander as a frightening model, and became closely identified with Antony. This is summarized neatly by the Younger Seneca (*Ep.* 83.25) when he tells us that drunkenness, a love of wine, and Cleopatra drove Antony into foreign vices and ruined him – in effect, it is a combination that Seneca claims turned him into a barbaric, oriental despot.[29] Sex, surprisingly, is not typically a feature of Roman invective against Alexander, but I suspect this is because drunkenness is used to such eloquent effect as a way of modeling effeminacy, bodily weakness, and mental

---

famous "ancestors" was almost a commonplace, against which backdrop annexation of Alexander – in particular, a deified Alexander – seems highly likely.

[27] Cicero's *Philippics* and Antony's *De ebrietate sua* are the most obvious examples, but a storied charade in which Octavian hosted a "banquet" of the Olympian gods (with himself as Apollo) also crops up (see Suet. *Aug.* 70). On this in particular, see Gurval 1995: 94–8; his account of Antonian propaganda (1995: 92–3) is useful, and should be read in conjunction with Scott 1929 and 1933; Huzar 1978: 233–52; Zanker 1988: 57–65; and Ramsey 2001. Pollini 1990 and Gurval 1995 take an alternative approach to Zanker on pre-Actian propaganda, playing down the likelihood of Octavian partaking even semi-publicly in tropes of deification. On changes in Octavianic coinage, see Zanker 1988: 53–7 and Gurval 1995: 52–65. Despite all this, Cicero's understanding of Alexander is still double-edged enough to allow him to figure early on in the struggle as a positive example for giving power to the *young* Octavian (*Phil.* 5.17.48).

[28] Antony and Cleopatra's daughter, named Cleopatra Selene, continues the theme. On stars and Sol/Helios in connection with Caesar, Weinstock 1971: 370–84 provides a clear overview; cf. Gurval 1996 on the *sidus Iulium* and Augustus.

[29] On Alexander in this epistle, see Spencer 2002: 91–3.

degeneracy. Obsession with sexual pleasure can then become another feature of the lifestyle that a drunken degenerate might enjoy. What this style of polemic against Antony makes clear is that alien and debauched imagery was applied to Antony as part of a coherent oppositional model to "Romanness" – a bundle of qualities laid claim to by Octavian.[30]

The "east," in these terms, is less a place than a state of mind, and it is for this reason that Antony's self-association with Dionysus, Hercules, and of course Alexander was all too successful, and eventually disastrous.[31] Within Roman popular consciousness, it is clear that Antony could plausibly reinvent himself as the conquistadorial, civilizing successor to Dionysus and Hercules, just as Alexander seems to have done. But since this *imaginary* eastern realm was also one in which excess, luxury, despotism, and gender inversion exercised an aggressively seductive hold on everyone who crossed over, Antony's susceptibility to the dark side of the comparisons was inevitable.[32] And not just with hindsight. By associating himself with Apollo, Octavian allowed himself the luxury of joining battle on a divine front, whereby the gods of the "west" were inevitably more powerful than those of the "east." By contrast Antony was enslaved to barbarian Cleopatra and Egyptian Osiris, and, tellingly, was said to want to shift the imperial capital from Rome to Alexandria.[33]

In the light of this, controlling connections with and reception of Alexander at Rome takes on a deadly seriousness. Most importantly, it must have been evident that, to succeed, it was vital not to become marginalized as a Roman playing at Alexander in a decadent eastern ghetto. Positive Alexander imagery (military success, divine favor, charisma, popularity) needed to be assimilated into mainstream Roman understanding of successful imperialism, and neutralized. This required the exercise of *clementia*, as Octavian demonstrated effectively, and a process of redefinition and appropriation that attempted to write explicit references to "Alexander" out of the newly developing ideology of the principate. This new political model demanded a sense of combined mastery of east and west, which we

[30] On Alexander, degeneracy, and Antony, see Spencer 2002: 193–5, and more generally on the years after 44, Zanker 1988: 33–77.

[31] On the "east" and the "other," see Romm 1992 and Evans 2003. On receptions of Hercules, see Anderson 1928 and Galinsky 1972.

[32] Hercules' enslavement by Omphale was easily rewritable as Antony and Cleopatra. We see echoes of Alexander's (and Antony's) problematization of Hercules in Commodus' claims to be him, and, indeed to refound Rome as *colonia Commodiana* in the AD 190s. Dionysus' role as a civilizing imperialist could be countered with the asocial and wilderness associations of his cult and worship. Seneca, *Ep.* 83 is particularly interesting in this respect, since it tacitly acknowledges the tension between the sacral and "truth-telling" connotations of wine, and its dangerous, boundary-breaking effects (see Spencer 2006b). Cf. the elder Pliny on Pompey and Alexander (*HN* 7.95). Gurval 1995: 189–208 focuses on the implications of the propagandist battle of Actium. Kienast 1969: 441–5 discusses Antony's dynasticism in terms of Alexander.

[33] Examples of parallelism involving divine mimesis include Verg. *Aen.* 8.678–713 and Prop. 4.6. Gurval's (1995: 98–131) discussion of Apollo and Augustus is comprehensive, and he also offers an interesting reading of Prop. 4.6.

see expressed strategically by Virgil's comment (via Anchises) that Augustus' *imperium* would encompass the annual passages of the constellations and the sun (*Aen.* 6.795–6). That said, Alexander does not wholly disappear, and he continues to crop up as a reference point for the early years of the Augustan principate in particular. Later accounts tell us, for example, that Octavian apparently spared Alexandria because of its founder's magnificence, and went on to use Alexander's image on his personal seal ring.[34] Nevertheless, as the reality of autocracy at Rome became increasingly apparent, in particular after 27, Livy's programmatic deconstruction of Alexander as a viable or even interesting enemy for Rome sets a formal limit to speculation.[35] Given Augustus' decision to set limits to Roman imperialism, the danger of invoking a despotic, degenerate Alexander rather than his positive achievements probably insured his slippage out of contemporary political currency.[36]

Germanicus: The Perfect Prince

Despite, or perhaps because of, the anxieties about how to succeed (or be successful) after Alexander that clustered around accounts of his death, Alexander never figures explicitly in Augustus' strategies for engineering the succession of power and keeping it within his own family, in what was notionally *not* a hereditary monarchy. Instead, parallels with Alexander reemerge around the person of Germanicus. The elder Pliny is delighted to recount a connection between Alexander, Augustus, and Germanicus which transforms all three into fellow equestrians (a nice Roman touch) – Alexander's affection for his horse, Bucephalas, is legendary, and Augustus did not quite manage to outdo the gift of a city (Bucephalia) as a monument. That said, Pliny tells us that Augustus' horse did receive a funeral mound, and that Germanicus composed a poem about it (*HN* 8.154–5). Horses (and their monarchical associations) continue to be important for Alexander at Rome, but Pliny's story is only a foretaste of Tacitus' complex introduction of Alexander to Germanicus' death in the *Annals*.[37] When Germanicus engaged in what Tacitus traces as a kind of Alexander-style progress through Rome's eastern empire, he was picking up on

---

[34]   Dio 51.16.3–5 recounts the story of Octavian's explanation of why he spared Alexandria, and his trip to Alexander's tomb. Cf. Suet. *Aug.* 18.1.

[35]   See Spencer 2002: 41–53 on Livy's Alexander (9.18); see also Morello 2002 on the rhetoric of the extract.

[36]   Kienast 1969: 432–43 and Eder 1990: 89–101 offer useful readings of how Alexander–Augustus comparisons work (see the more expansive overview in García Moreno 1990). After AD 20 Alexander slips out of focus (with the exception of allusions such as Virgil's (above) and, e.g., Hor. *Carm.* 2.1.232–44) until he briefly recurs in the iconography and rhetoric surrounding the dedication of the temple of Mars Ultor (2 BC), in which the standards recovered from the Parthians were lodged, and Gaius Caesar's Parthian mission in 1. See Spencer 2002: 191 and Isager 1993: 79.

[37]   Tac. *Ann.* 2.72–3, 82–3. On the importance of horsey connections at Rome, see Spencer 2007. Statius' commemoration of Domitian's big horse is discussed below.

a motif that other authors also notice, but that reaches its most impressive development in the *Annals*.[38]

Tacitus transforms Germanicus into a glorious might-have-been whose brief perfection is undercut by increasingly problematic clusters of association with Alexander. In Athens (2.53) and Alexandria (2.59.3) we find Tacitus characterizing Germanicus as gradually shedding what he terms his "Caesarian" dignity; taken together with Germanicus' acceptance of a crown in Parthia, we can see how echoes of Caesar and Antony (his splendidly legitimating ancestors 2.53.1–3) saturate this eastern tour. Alexander looms disastrously over the whole series of episodes, offering a knowing foretaste of Germanicus' ultimate fate – to die young, amid rumors of foul play, leaving a distraught and helpless nation.[39] The perfection that characterizes Tacitus' Germanicus also hints at his lack of feasibility as a savior for Rome in the long term – he is (perhaps like the young Alexander) too good to be true. By dying young, Germanicus makes possible the elaborate comparison with Babylon after Alexander that characterizes responses to his death (2.82–3), but this use of Alexander also fulfills an important narratological function in the *Annals*. It allows Tacitus to represent this as a turning point, after which aiming for the perfect, idealized autocrat is recognizably impossible, and can lead only to the excessive disasters of Caligula and Nero (and perhaps by implication, Domitian).

Caligula, Nero, and Domitian: Alexander the Degenerate Despot

In Germanicus, Tacitus offers a glimpse of an idealized young Alexander, but his hindsight should remind us that much of our disquiet concerning Roman Alexanders is also refracted through authors from the mid to late first century AD. Looking forward to Caligula, Nero, and Domitian, we see familiar motifs recurring, but in the context of insane or excessive devotion to and (over)identification with Alexander and of an increasing inability to set and respect boundaries, whether personal, bodily, political, or imperial, or indeed between divine and mortal identity.[40] We also see sexual excess being mapped onto a generalizing notion of barbarous and infectious luxury, which slots into a pattern of deception and treachery that has its roots in versions of Alexander worked out in more detail in Q. Curtius

[38] E.g., Vell. Pat. 2.129; Suet. *Tib.* 52. For an overview of Alexander in the *Annals*, with particular emphasis on Germanicus and Corbulo, see Spencer 2002: 191–3, 199–200; and on Germanicus and mutiny 202–3. Malissard 1990 is particularly good on Tacitus' "eulogy" of Germanicus. See also Aalders 1961; Shotter 1968; Ross 1973; Rutland 1987; Pelling 1993; Gissel 2001.
[39] A useful comparative for Tacitus' account is Q. Curtius Rufus' version of the aftermath of Alexander's death (10.5.7–16), but see also Just. 13.1.1–6.
[40] André 1990 provides a helpful overview of what we might term "Julio-Claudian" *imitatio Alexandri*.

Rufus' narrative.[41] Finally, an atmosphere of secrecy and lies, a world in which even intimate personal relationships can be misleading, is at the heart of the younger Seneca's (political) philosophy, underpins Lucan's epic account of the previous century's civil war and Tacitus' *Annals*, filters through Suetonius' *Lives* of the Caesars, and colors the Alexander who emerges in this era.

In stories of Caligula, comparisons with Alexander take on a whole new meaning. The association is no longer between an aristocratic, would-be Roman Alexander and Alexander, the prototype for imperializing monarchy. Instead we are presented with a ready-made Roman emperor who appears to embrace Alexander without any concern for the ways in which explicit association and comparisons might have caused problems in the past. Reports of Caligula's enthusiastic assumption of the role of Alexander show just how quickly the principate developed from tentatively expressed "republican" autocracy to monarchy by another name. We can see responses to Caligula's brand of autocracy (and its complications, particularly in the wake of senatorial responses to Tiberius) in accounts of Caligula's preemptive celebration of a Triumph – wearing Alexander's breastplate – *before* risking the vagaries of military campaign. By purloining Alexander's body armor, Caligula thereby makes tomb-robbing a prelude to his other transgressive excesses.[42] An attempt to make his horse, Incitatus, a consul (Suet. *Calig.* 55.3), may look back to Augustus' horse and Germanicus' poem as much as to Alexander's memorialization of Bucephalas, but it also fits in with a pattern of dissolving socio-cultural boundaries, and even breaches in the dividing line between sanity and insanity that seethe through accounts of Caligula's principate.

Boundary-breaking, of course, could still just about be read in a positive and even culturally assertive light vis-à-vis Alexander's "civilization" of the east, despite problematic associations with Caligula. With Nero, however, we see how even this can assume traumatic overtones. Nero's self-fashioning in Alexander's style is on display in accounts of his explicitly aggressive policy toward Parthia, and his problematic relationship with his general Corbulo.[43] Nero's manipulation of a confrontation with Tiridates, using Corbulo as a field-general, highlights the kinds of

---

[41] Curtius' date and identity are not securely fixed, but it is likely that he was writing in the late first century AD. His account is unique in that it provides the only (almost completely) extant treatment of Alexander in Latin. Baynham 1998a provides a full-scale discussion of his entire history of Alexander. For Curtius, Callisthenes, and Rome, see below. On Alexander's rhetoric in Curtius' account of the Pages' Conspiracy, see Spencer 2002: 135–8; on Orientalism and topography in Curtius, see Spencer 2005b.

[42] For the Triumph and breastplate, see Suet. *Calig.* 52.3; Dio 59.17.3. Isager 1993: 81 takes this as a record of actual *imitatio Alexandri* on Caligula's part, but I think it is more indicative of how deeply embedded Alexander had become in Roman political consciousness. It would be almost impossible to conceptualize ways of characterizing a mad, bad ruler without dipping into tropes recalling Alexander.

[43] On Corbulo and Nero, see Spencer 2002: 199–200 (including bibliographical references). The accounts of Tacitus and Cassius Dio are worth comparing (e.g., Tac. *Ann.* 13.6–7, 13.35, 14.20–2, 14.23.1; Dio 62.19.2–4, 62.23.5, 63.6.4). In Elsner and Masters 1994, the complexity of disentangling the historical Nero from the monster is addressed.

tension that attempting to be emperor *and* Alexander could set up – sending a deputy to lead the armies was a fraught undertaking, and as the aftermath of Nero's death demonstrated, it was from the ranks of successful commanders that imperial succession would be determined. Any anxiety on Nero's part concerning Corbulo's potential to be *too* successful was probably well placed. The highly stage-managed "submission" of Tiridates (AD 66) in Rome further demonstrates the impossible situation Nero faced once he had decided on imperial expansion into the east: he could not risk leaving the capital for long periods of time, but still needed to make Corbulo's victory into his own Triumph. Tacitus' narrative makes great play with echoes of Alexander, but eastern maneuvers are not the only way in which Alexander contaminates our understanding of Nero, and vice versa.

Suetonius' account of Nero's highlights (*Ner.* 19) includes a mention of his plan to tour Alexandria and Achaea, and in addition, to send a newly constituted "phalanx of Alexander the Great" (composed of six-foot-tall Italian recruits) out into Alexander territory (the Caspian Gates). Being able to command a whole series of subordinate "Alexanders," ordering them to conquer at one's command, almost puts Nero back among the intellectual games played by Livy when he speculated that Alexander would always lose to Rome because he was one man, whereas Rome comprised an endless succession of super-Alexanders (9.18.8–19). In conjunction with Tacitus' complex characterization of Tiridates as both Alexander and Darius, and the philhellenism with which Nero is so disastrously associated, the younger Seneca's obsession with Alexander as an ethical model comes as no surprise.[44]

Domenico Lassandro (1984) provides an overview of how Alexander fits into Seneca's works, though he stops short of arguing (as I do) that Seneca's use of Alexander drags "Nero" in implicitly, even when he seems to be absent. As Jacob Isager rightly suggests, Seneca's Alexander, in both his good and his bad qualities (patron of the arts, hands-on commander, monomaniacal despot), is strikingly similar to the kinds of post-Neronian critiques of the emperor which make up most of our knowledge of his principate.[45] What this suggests is that by the time we reach the AD 70s, rhetorics of imperial praise and criticism are persistently – if implicitly – dragging Alexander into the frame, and vice versa; this makes the elder Pliny's exclusion of any mention of direct connections between Alexander and any of the post-Augustan emperors particularly fascinating.[46] Traced through Pliny's epistemological imperialism, we find a golden Alexander prefiguring and even propping up Augustus, while others (Antony, Caligula, Nero) take the fall for all that is wrong in Rome.

---

[44]   On Nero's philhellenism, see Alcock 1994.

[45]   Isager 1993: 82. Too 1994 discusses the complex didactic between Nero and Seneca in the *epistulae morales*. On a range of Senecan passages, see also Spencer 2002: 69–79, 89–94, 97–112. On *Ep.* 83 in particular, see Spencer 2006b.

[46]   See Isager 1993: 83. But Isager is vastly overstating the case when he says, conclusively, that after Nero "the model of Alexander seems so abused and emptied of positive connotations that we find no comparison between Alexander and Vespasian." Surely the dark side of Alexander, that which ought not to be invoked, is ever present in the kinds of things which are not said about Vespasian?

Domitian's place in the parade of Roman Alexanders locates him at the intersection between man and god, artiste and patron, Princeps and Dominus. Statius, in his collection of ostensibly occasional poems (*Siluae*), conjures up an Alexander who is endlessly susceptible to revision (*Silv.* 1.1.84–90) – here, Alexander astride Bucephalas is frozen into Roman space in the Forum, before metamorphosing into Caesar and ending up in a dramatic face-off with the vast new equestrian Domitian. Alexander/Caesar's inevitable displacement by Domitian makes clear the precarious nature of imperial identity and authority, and this opening poem leaves us in little doubt of its credentials as a statement of imperial passivity vis-à-vis immediate and longer-term control of reception. The torment and betrayal that suffuse Alexander's relationship with his statue of Hercules (*Silv.* 4.6) dispel any lingering uncertainties about the implications of Alexander for Domitianic Rome.[47] Here, With Domitian's transgressive but irresistible demand to be characterized as *dominus et deus* we see the logical conclusion of drawing Alexander into Roman political rhetoric. Curtius' vigorous denunciation of Alexander's "enslavement" of the freedom-loving Macedonian people, and his attempts to introduce oriental subservience and even worship into relations between ruler and ruled key neatly into the kinds of post-Neronian rhetorics of *dominatio* (and *damnatio memoriae*) that cluster posthumously around Domitian.[48]

Picking up on Augustus' visit to Alexander's tomb and Caligula's tomb-robbing, we find that from Nero to Domitian, death and afterlife and even the perils of immortality are rarely far from Alexander. Lucan's Alexander (*BC* 10.20–52), like the later Alexanders of Silius Italicus,[49] Statius, and Juvenal (*Sat.* 10.171–3), is a function of a world dangerously obsessed with the dead past. This simultaneous sense of closure and anxiety about what kind of world will ensue, reflects and also models elite concerns in the face of the melt-down after Nero, and the continuing instability that culminated in Domitian's own death.[50]

Trajan and Hadrian: Parthia and Civilization

Trajan and Hadrian mark the formal conclusion to this series of Roman Alexanders, and as a pair, they encapsulate the promise of triumph and disaster that characterizes Alexander's Roman imagery.[51] Nerva's smooth accession belied Tacitus'

[47]   On these two poems, see Spencer 2002: 151–4, 184–7 (discussed with Vell. Pat. 1.11.2–5 on the Granicus sculpture group) and Newlands 2002: 46–87.

[48]   See, e.g., Curt. 4.7.30–1; 8.7.1, 14. Domitian, unsurprisingly, did not die peacefully. He was stabbed to death by a group of conspirators who included his wife, Domitia, and the next emperor, Nerva.

[49]   Alexander figures as an ineffectual ghost – Sil. *Pun.* 13.762–76, likely to have been composed before Domitian's death in AD 96. See Spencer 2002: 162–3.

[50]   On Lucan's configuration of Rome's Mediterranean as a toxically historical theme park, where playing at Troy, Alexander, or even Caesar is all that is left, see Spencer 2005a. We can look forward, eventually, to Caracalla's sepulchral tourism in Alexandria, as recounted by Dio (78.7.2).

[51]   Useful biographies of Trajan and Hadrian are Bennett 2001 and Birley 1997.

packaging of his combination of autocracy and liberty (*Agricola* 3) and his speedy
adoption of Trajan as his heir put a stop to threats of another descent into anarchy.
Trajan's title *Optimus*, granted in AD 114, connects him not just with Capitoline
Jupiter (Optimus Maximus) but also acknowledges the implicit dangers of Greatness.[52] Meritocracy versus magnificence: we might see in this unspoken choice of
honorifics an attempt to reinvest Rome's emperors with some of the military kudos
that Alexander might still connote. Reopening this military interface with Alexander
also plays up Trajan's best qualities as an imaginative and ambitious commander.
Moving from triumph over Dacia in the early years of the second century AD,
Trajan's parabola through Arabia, Armenia, and on into Mesopotamia locates him
squarely in a world where comparisons with Alexander are inevitable.[53] Ideologically, the younger Pliny's *Panegyric* maps out how inescapable this process of
Alexandrification has become, and the connections are made explicit in Dio
Chrysostom's orations *On Kingship*.

   Establishing a co-principate with Jupiter, whereby Domitian's formulation
dominus et deus becomes literally the case (Trajan and Jupiter ruling in partnership),
side-steps (temporarily at least) the uncomfortable aspects of emperor worship that
Domitian had bungled in Alexander's shadow. Ancient authors highlight the
significance of the conquistadorial trajectory from Alexander through Caesar and
Antony to Trajan for interpreting these Parthian wars, but with Hadrian we see an
interesting footnote to this optimistic assertion of Rome's authority over the eastern
world. Hadrian's ethnographic and intellectual interests were catholic, and his
empire in microcosm at Tivoli might be interpreted as a pleasure palace for a dilet-
tante, a cabinet of wonders allowing him to enjoy the marvels of the whole world
from a space in which imperial self-fashioning could reflect (on) Rome at a distance.
His quasi-touristic approach to empire certainly looks back to the intellectual
and scientific modes of conquest that informed the elder Pliny's textual empire-
building, and cluster around Pompey's military success. Yet although Hadrian spent
just over half of his reign traveling, his peregrinations were administrative and
even personally motivated, rather than expansive. Hadrian's principate, then, was
susceptible to some of the rhetorics of assimilation (or "going native") that were
attached to Alexander's progress into Persia, Antony's relationship with Cleopatra,
and Germanicus' tour of the east and Egypt. Hadrian's fascination with Egyptian

[52]   As Zecchini 1984: 197–9 observes.
[53]   On Trajan and Alexander as fellow conquerors see, e.g., Bennett 2001: 189, 198, 199. A coda to the
lure of Alexander's footsteps can be found in Caracalla's restless and relentless warfare (AD 213–17),
conducted ostentatiously in the wake of Alexander's trajectory. Historical irony makes it inevitable that,
granted the titles Germanicus Maximus and Parthicus Maximus, he comes to a sticky end. That he met
it at the hands of one of the Praetorians, near Carrhae, scene of Crassus' debacle (and the explicit trigger
for Rome's Parthian complex), is particularly apt. Connections between M. Aurelius Antoninus (as he
was officially styled, although he had himself called Elagabalus (Heliogabalus), named for the Emesan
mountain and sun god), Severus Alexander and Alexander (the Great) focus first on deification and
its disastrous consequences, and then imperialism. Severus failed to measure up to Artaxerxes (king of
Persia from AD 227). He was eventually assassinated by mutineers in Germany (AD 235). The *Scriptores
historiae Augustae* are particularly eager to play up associations.

cults in particular, leading to the posthumous deification of his friend (and probably lover) Antinous, seem to have interesting echoes of the propaganda surrounding Actium. It is also likely that connecting Hadrian with Egypt could have hinted at Alexander's quest for deification at Siwah, and Lucan's implicit syncresis of Cato and Alexander in a weirdly surreal and dangerous Libya, and at Siwah (*BC* 9.564–86).

Authorial (Self-)Fashioning and Making History: Callisthenes and Rome

One of the most fascinating voices that almost (but not quite) speaks to us about Alexander belongs to the man whom Alexander himself commissioned to write up an account of his expeditionary campaign: Aristotle's nephew Callisthenes. Bluntly told, his story seems fairly unremarkable – he accompanies Alexander across Asia only to fall foul of the king's increasingly uncertain temper, becomes embroiled in a plot against his life, and loses his own life as a consequence. But this summary barely touches upon the enduring afterlife that Callisthenes achieved in Roman stories of Alexander; thinking about reasons for his prominence locates us at the heart of the most topical political, cultural, and intellectual (never mind personal) cruces that faced the (would-be) movers and shakers of late republican and early imperial Rome. Writing (and, indeed, commissioning) History is never a culturally neutral activity. Engaging with the process of producing narrative history demands, at the very least, an acceptance that historians are involved in a complex series of implicit and/or explicit position statements concerning the nature of the account that they compose. For our purposes, asking why Alexander's decision to commission an up-to-the-minute narrative of his achievements was so significant for Rome sends us back, in the first instance, to the potential crisis of Hellenic identity, threatened by Macedonian military supremacy.

Alexander succeeded his father Philip just as the Greek world was getting to grips with Macedon as the new superpower. What particularly complicated the relationship between Macedon and the rest of Greece in the mid fourth century was that despite Philip's (and then Alexander)'s undeniable achievement in enforcing a Macedonian hegemony over the other Greek states, Macedon continued to be perceived as a barbarous, primitive backwater (see Zahrnt, ch. 1). We will never know, of course, what complex of reasons led to the elegant, propagandist solution that Philip kick-started and Alexander took to its ultimate conclusion: selling the new and uneasy coalition as a way of finally striking back at Persia to "punish" the empire for its invasions of Greece. In this light, Alexander's country could be redefined as "Greek," positioning Macedon at the head of a retaliatory and even culturally imperialistic crusade against an aggressive and tyrannous eastern threat. Callisthenes' role in the process of realignment of identities is worked out against this backdrop. Although his execution on a charge of treason is not directly connected (as far as we know) to what he wrote in his history of the campaign, nevertheless our image of him, filtered through Roman voices, makes it clear that writing history is tantamount to articulating control over the (im)mortality of one's subject.

Famously, reception of Alexander has immortalized him as a man who believed himself descended from both Heracles and Zeus. With Achilles thrown into the mix, this makes for a heady cocktail of ancestry. From these three, it is (the Homeric) Achilles' role in modeling what "Alexander" signifies that resonates directly in Roman receptions, and it is to Roman interest in connecting Callisthenes and Achilles jointly to Alexander, indeed in foregrounding Callisthenes' role in this aspect of Alexander's story, that I now turn. The figure of Callisthenes' opens up, for Roman authors, strategically interesting ways of focusing on and exploring relationships between historiography, autocracy, and individual responsibility.[54] Reading Roman interest in connecting Alexander to Achilles via Callisthenes in these terms makes evident the complexity and wider significance of Rome's engagement with Alexander. Speaking in 62, on behalf of the poet A. Licinius Archias (whose right to citizenship was in doubt), Cicero paints a picture of Alexander's success and enduring greatness as wholly attributable to his correct understanding of the symbiotic relationship between Achilles and Homer. This is a relationship, Cicero stresses, which is replicated at Rome in Pompey's support and patronage of the historian Theophanes of Mytilene.[55] Moreover, this speech implicitly suggests that Alexander's "greatness" exists only because of his subsequent decision to surround himself with a posse of writers who would Homerize him along similar lines.

Seven years later, Cicero returned to the same motif in an edgy and politically complex letter to the historian L. Lucceius (*Ad Fam.* 5.12).[56] Here, Cicero's own reputation and afterlife hang in the balance; specifically, his urgent need to insure that the history being written by Lucceius provides a favorable account of Cicero's consulship, and his execution of the Catilinarian conspirators. What was implicit in his speech for Archias becomes bluntly explicit here – this is a win–win scenario for historian and subject. Alexander we are told, believed that art glorified both artist and subject; by the end of Cicero's proposition, Lucceius himself has been turned into a great (*magnus*) and illustrious man (*Ad Fam.* 5.12.6–7). Cicero's contention that creative association with great men of action allows writers and

---

[54] As Waldemar Heckel has pointed out, the historic Callisthenes cannot have played a part in the fullest development of the Alexander–Achilles comparison – his death *before* that of Hephaestion rules him out of a direct involvement in creating the parallels between Hephaestion and Patroclus that vividly color accounts of Alexander's response to the loss of his friend. We might also wonder how much of the scenario at Troy, before Achilles' tomb, is a retrospectively applied *topos*.

[55] Cic. *Pro Arch.* 24. For a more extended discussion, see Spencer 2002: 122–4. It is ironic that Pompey's promotion of Theophanes ultimately led to his posthumous deification (as Zeus Eleutherios Theophanes) at Mytilene. We can assume that Cicero did not envisage the historian out-Alexandering his subject in quite such a dramatic way!

[56] It is intriguing to note that Cicero also contacted Posidonius (60 BC), in effect triangulating the relationship with Pompey, asking him to polish up his own account of the Catilinarian conspiracy (*Ad Att.* 2.1.2).

artists to take on something of their attributes draws a direct line between Homer and Achilles, Callisthenes and Alexander, Theophanes and Pompey, and Lucceius and himself. In making this connection, Cicero is locating Roman quests for individual *gloria* and posthumous renown in a tradition that is also intimately concerned with understanding and modeling one's place in the world, whether as a state (Macedon, Rome) or an individual (Alexander, Pompey, Cicero). In order to insure a satisfactory, successful, and credible outcome, individuals and nations must control their representation, and that demands advance understanding of the desired narrative momentum.

Like Alexander (and Macedon), Rome in the third, second, and even first centuries was struggling to articulate a wholly satisfactory story of how and why it was *more* than a hugely successful military superpower. Cultural anxieties were understandable when faced with the highly developed intellectual and artistic milieus of the Hellenistic kingdoms of the Successors to Alexander's empire, the mythopoetics of Greek historiography, and indeed the philosophical and political heritage still peddled by Athens. Rome lacked a developed tradition of History-making which would explain to the Mediterranean world at large why Roman imperialism was both right and inevitable. Perhaps more nebulously, Rome also lacked a rationale for dealing with (relatively) sudden wealth and luxury – the delightful rewards of empire that were increasingly changing what Romans perceived to have been their traditional austerity and way of life.

If we turn this position back to Callisthenes, from a Roman perspective we might now redefine him as one of Alexander's coping strategies for unifying the Hellenic world, creating a successful strategic account of how and why Macedon was the leading state, and guaranteeing his own personal Greatness.[57] Where this goes wrong, of course, is that the historical Callisthenes attempted to capture the center stage of History, and involved himself directly in a conspiracy against Alexander. For late republican intellectuals and politicians this presents a certain tension. As I have suggested, Roman readings of Callisthenes' story as a primer for resistance to Alexander make him a useful model for men such as Cicero (and even Pompey) to deploy. Patronizing or encouraging a historian who, unlike Callisthenes, does not rebel might then suggest that one has avoided the worst of Alexander's excesses, but it also opens up for consideration the possibility that writers can have a serious and long-term impact on politics and posterity that goes far beyond the written word. Moreover, although Alexander's positive qualities seem initially to have been prominent in his reception in republican Rome, Callisthenes' fate might offer a disturbing counterpoint to Alexander's potential to stand for unalloyed "greatness" and "republican" (or consensus-based) monarchy. So we find that although before Antony, Alexander stands primarily as a successful self-fashioner, a man who promotes the idea of a cultural program that combines politics and military achievement in one overarching narrative package, a change takes place as the principate develops into a "hereditary" autocracy.

---

[57] On what it means to have "the Great" tagged after one's name, see Spencer 2002: 2–5.

Instead of focusing on how one goes about creating and acting the role of being Alexander the Great, Romans become increasingly fascinated (and horrified) by how one responds to an uncontrollable subject who no longer seems confinable in neatly packaged story-lines. Developing Callisthenes' role as a figure of resistance to tyranny and political oppression, indeed using him as a means of interrogating the kinds of freedom and discourse that are available to subjects (rather than citizens), could become a serious and even potentially dangerous proposition. It eventually offered one way for political philosophers to question models of citizenship and identity in Neronian Rome, but it also raised the specter of what happens when the relationship between an author and his subject breaks down.

Two first-century AD Roman authors whose interest in Callisthenes' fall from favor is particularly illuminating are Curtius Rufus and the elder Seneca.[58] Curtius' lengthy account of Callisthenes' downfall is interwoven into a narrative that is increasingly driven by suspicion, megalomania, plots, and treason, rather than by magnificent achievements or even the marvels of the east. In his Callisthenes we find characterization and language that are increasingly evocative of Roman senatorial anxieties in the face of ever more absolute autocracy.[59] Simultaneously, Macedonian resistance to (what Curtius represents as) Alexander's ever more "orientalized" behavior, is configured in strikingly Roman terms. In effect, Curtius' stalwart, luxury-hating and down-to-earth Macedonians take on many characteristics that suggest they act as stand-ins for Romans in his conception of the story. And Callisthenes functions as a focus for narratological expressions of dissent.[60] These come dramatically to a head with Alexander's attempt to introduce *proskynesis* – a Persian gesture of obeisance to a social superior which Roman authors tend to interpret as full-body prostration on the ground, and to deprecate as an indication that the recipient was being worshiped as a god.[61] Callisthenes' intensely Roman refusal to perform *proskynesis* in Curtius' story is couched in terms that instantly key into Roman rhetorical contestations of identity. Curtius' positioning of Alexander, eavesdropping on Callisthenes from behind a curtain, hammers home the kind of ideal response he is attempting to generate (8.5.21). Callisthenes' response to *proskynesis*, in Curtius' narrative, makes it plain that Alexander's monarchy is

---

[58]   The elder Seneca (*c.*50 BC–*c.* AD 40) was a historian and rhetorician, originally from Corduba in Spain.

[59]   E.g., Curt. 8.5.13–20.

[60]   See Spencer 2002: 94–7 (on Curt. 6.2.1–5); and on this, in general, 178, 189–90, 194; also Baynham 1998a: 71–2 (Callisthenes as an Alexander historian), 51–2 (on the Pages' Conspiracy), 192–5 (on Callisthenes' resistance to *proskynesis*).

[61]   On Callisthenes' downfall: Curt. 8.5.5–8.23. For a range of versions of the *proskynesis* story, see Arr. 4.10.5–12; Curt. 8.5.5–21; Just. 12.7.1–3; Val. Max. 7.2 ext. 11. In the wake of Augustus' and subsequent deifications this story takes on the most urgent political and ethical implications for a Roman audience, and Romans will, no doubt, have expected accounts of Alexander to take a position on this event and its aftermath.

increasingly losing touch with the kinds of "democratic" style of rule that initially characterize idealizing versions of Macedonian autocracy.[62]

Turning to the elder Seneca's interest in Callisthenes, we find ourselves confronted with a discourse positioned at the heart of elite citizen identity. Learning to manipulate and control the citizen body using public speech was central to senatorial self-fashioning in the republic, and continued, even if solipsistically, to function as a model for citizen excellence in the principate. It is likely that Seneca put together his anthology of epideictic *declamationes* (known as *suasoriae*) for his sons late in his life, and in doing so he was both looking back to exemplary practitioners of oratory, and also collecting up a package of themes on which young Roman aristocrats could be expected to have something to say.[63] So far, so straightforward. But Seneca had more than an antiquarian's interest in the epistemology of declamatory identity. Alongside his catalogues of *suasoriae* and *controuersiae* he also wrote a highly topical history of Rome from the civil wars to his own time, and his *suasoriae* are suffused with a sense of poignancy suggesting a genre and discourse already in a process of decline.[64] This indicates, I think, that he was wholly aware of the biting significance that performing Alexander might have for a young Roman aristocrat.

The first sample theme in Seneca's collection of *suasoriae* is the practicability of Alexander's desire to explore the Ocean that bounded the world. Here, "quoting" the Augustan rhetorician L. Cestius Pius, Seneca boldly sets out a model for public speech (and thereby personal autonomy and identity) under a tyranny (1.5). This practical handbook for courtiers presents us with an uneasy sense that by the first century AD, "Alexander" has become shorthand for inappropriate self-importance, delusions of grandeur, political crassness, and (murderous) lack of proportion in interpersonal relationships.[65] Moreover, "Cestius'" ability to conflate the stories of Callisthenes' execution for treason and Cleitus' murder for a pointed (and drunken) joke at Alexander's expense, suggests that "Alexander" has taken on a Roman life and identity that no longer requires a direct connection to a consistent biographical

---

[62]   See, e.g., Curt. 6.6.2, 9; 8.5.5; 8.7.13–14; Just. 11.11; also Spencer 2002: 178. It is interesting that the accounts of Arrian and Plutarch (e.g., Arr. 4.12.7, 4.14.1; Plu. *Alex.* 55.4–5) are far more ambivalent about the role of Callisthenes in his own downfall. On narratological complexity in Curtius' portrait of Callisthenes, see Spencer 2002: 136–7.

[63]   His sons were Seneca (known as the Younger, who went on to become tutor and then adviser to Nero), and M. Annaeus Mela, father of the poet Lucan. Like his uncle Seneca, Lucan came to grief under Nero despite what seems at first to have been a close relationship; both committed suicide in AD 65. Typically, *suasoriae* positioned their speakers in the realms of familiar and popular insoluble dilemmas, giving them an opportunity to cut their teeth on persuasive and advisory rhetoric in a notionally "safe" political and pop-cultural framework.

[64]   See Griffin 1992: 33.

[65]   Seneca the Younger's comment that all Alexander's achievements were pointless in the wake of his murder of Callisthenes is particularly poignant in the light of Nero's role in his death (*NQ* 6.23.3; concluding: *nihil tam mannum erit quam scelus*" – there will be nothing in which [Alexander] is great, other than villainy).

tradition. In effect, Seneca's representation of Callisthenes in this *suasoria* demonstrates problems of breakdown in category that have significant implications for
understanding cultural change at Rome, and Alexander's role in this process.
"Cestius" tells his audience that Callisthenes' death (speared by Alexander) is a
result of an unwise joke (*urbanitas*) that *ichor* rather than blood should flow from
a wound received by the king. Callisthenes is described as both teacher (*praeceptor*)
and philosopher to Alexander, but his death here is a function of his having stepped
beyond both roles, taking on the guise of (satirical) commentator. This demonstrates the ambiguity inherent in the relationship between subject (willing or
otherwise) and authors, and between advisers and advisees. And at Rome, the
relationship between authorship and advisory, didactic discourse was extremely
close.[66]

Alexander and the Sum of All Knowledge

The characters that make up our set of Roman Alexanders do not, as I have been
suggesting, exist in a cultural vacuum. Alexander is implicitly and explicitly embedded in Roman intellectual taxonomies and gradual development of a self-conscious
imperial world view. While this weaves in and out of the characters and texts that
I have been discussing, it is also on display in the burgeoning field of scientific and
technical writing that Roman authors make distinctively their own from the late
republic onward. Three authors in particular demonstrate Alexander's centrality to
Roman epistemology: Vitruvius, Strabo, and the elder Pliny.[67] It is in their attempts
to categorize, describe, and lay claim to a controlling understanding of the world
(and Rome's place in it) that Alexander's impact is embedded in the longest term.[68]
When Vitruvius recounts Alexander's topographical near-metamorphosis into Mt.
Athos, he is not just providing Romans with a concrete example of how supreme
commanders have a dramatic effect on their landscapes; he is also offering a narratological reification of the psychological impact of imperialism on how reality is
experienced.

[66] On Alexander and the power play involved in advisory rhetoric, discussed in relation to Seneca
and Cicero, see Spencer 2006b.
[67] Vitruvius prospered as an architect (and engineer) for Caesar, but is most famous for his *De archi-
tectura* (dedicated to Octavian). This work nods to the Hellenistic trend to compose philosophically
and theoretically engaged humane "handbooks" that offer aids to conceptual understanding of practical
topics. Strabo's *Geographia* (probably composed under Augustus and Tiberius) is particularly interested in the ethical implications of landscape and the relationship between landscapes and empires.
The elder Pliny owed much of his political success to the Flavians. He wrote extensively on a diverse
range of topics, but of particular interest here is his *Naturalis historia*.
[68] See also, e.g., Sen. *QNat* 3 *pr.* 5; 5.18.10–12. As Lassandro 1984: 162 observes, Alexander's appearance at *QNat* 6.23.3 is an extremely rare occurrence of Seneca using the *QNat* as a vehicle for authorial
comment. For an overview of the kinds of Alexander narratives that all these authors might have had
access to, see Atkinson 2000b and Baynham 2003. On natural history, see French 1994.

Alexander is rarely far from Strabo's concerns in his opening imperial bench-marking statement. For Strabo, Alexander's campaigns connect the newly and increasingly Roman Mediterranean (17.1.6–13 on Alexandria and Egypt, from "then" to "now") with the mythic worlds of Troy (1.3.3, 13.1.27) and the Amazons (11.5.4–5) while also locating him squarely at the start of the process of scientific inquiry into space and territory that drives his own intellectual plan of campaign (1.2.1).[69] We can see this in his fixation on Alexander as a man who supported and promoted the process of mapping as a key strand in conquest: in order to refashion a new identity for conquered peoples, it was vitally important to understand and control how they are and have been categorized and defined (1.4.9, 2.1.6). Ultimately, we see in Strabo an understanding that Alexander himself, in turn, is trans-formed into a benchmark for later attempts to measure the world (2.1.24, 3.5.5). Strabo's Alexander is at once self-aggrandizing (11.7.4) and gullible – and thereby flawed in his conception of the world (15.1.28).[70]

In Pliny's *Naturalis historia* we can see how time and space combine to portray Rome's empire as a kind of magnificent diorama, a spectacular show that acknowledges the lure of the circus, but presents us instead with an imperial panopticon, ordered by a narrative of intellectual and scientific inquiry. When Pliny tells us (*HN* 2.5) that Vespasian was the world's greatest ruler ever, he was doing more than simply nodding to the newest *über*-patron (father of Titus, Pliny's addressee). He is also setting up a taxonomic model that cuts to the heart of Roman understanding of the world; in effect the empire in Vespasian's shadow will be defined and categorized inasmuch as it relates to knowledge required by Rome at its center. A side effect (perhaps) of this model is that Pliny's focus is forced out to the edges of the empire, the places that generate the stories that are directly relevant to Rome's glorious progress (27.1). By synthesizing, assess-ing, and outdoing previous (and Greek) attempts to understand the natural world and to locate the role of nature firmly as a function and feature of Rome's pacification of the world, Pliny makes himself a worthy match for the military men who previously controlled exploration and thereby acquisition of knowl-edge.[71] Just as Pompey, in Pliny's account, matches Alexander and almost equals Hercules and Father Liber in the brilliance of his exploits (*HN* 7.95, 96), Pliny

---

[69] Other instances of Strabo's obsessive cataloging of Alexander as subject and inquirer into natural history include 14.3.9 (the tides at Mt. Climax), 15.1.25 (the "wrong" Nile), 15.1.29 (from "wild" nature to Bucephalus), 15.1.31 (dogs), 15.1.35 (the Ganges), 16.1.9 (destruction of the artificial cataracts on the Euphrates), 16.1.11 (general interest in water management), 16.1.15 (experiments with naphtha).

[70] This rather terse survey is only a sample of Alexander's ubiquity in Strabo, and of particular impor-tance is his appearance at 15.1.26 (in the wake of Strabo's programmatic comments at 15.1.2–10).

[71] E.g., Plin. *HN* 3.20 (a record of the peoples conquered by Rome, listed on a triumphal arch), 6.31 (Augustus' intelligence operations against Armenia), 6.35, 12.8 (Nero's exploratory foray into Ethio-pia), 5.1 (strategic survey of the transalpine region), 6.35 (Juba's fact-finding impulses). This trend comes to its logical conclusion in the mid second century AD with Greek-speaking Aelius Aristides' summation of the whole world as a single city, Rome (*Oration* 26, "Regarding Rome"; e.g., 6, 8, 11, 63, 102; Alexander figures particularly at *Oration* 26.24–8). On Aristides' place in modeling Antonine Alexanders see Zecchini 1984: 199–204.

implicitly suggests that on Rome's behalf, he reconquers the world and holds it fast for Rome.[72]

The mutability of the world, the transience of physical features, forms an important strand in Pliny's rationale – without a structured record of the processes of change and the ability to create historically aware accounts that can capture and control (intellectually, at least) this process, no empire can last. Alexander's flawed understanding and faulty epistemology mean that although he tries frantically to achieve an empire founded on knowledge, his lack of structure and control over the wide-ranging kinds of information that poured in mirrors his lack of rationale for sustainable empire-building.[73] Human progress, in Pliny, means learning to understand, use, and control the natural world, and in these terms, transmission of this knowledge is vital to the imperializing mission. Papyrus, according to Pliny, began to be transformed into paper only with Alexander's foundation of Alexandria (*HN* 13.27).[74]

This essay concludes, then, with paper; and in particular, the close relationship between the reception of Alexander, the hermeneutics of classical identity, and the physical processes by which knowledge was transmitted.

---

[72] Pompey's *Magnus*, Pliny tells us, was the *spolia* (booty) he received on conquering the whole of Africa.

[73] See, e.g., *HN* 6.31 on the stranded "Alexandria," abandoned by the sea.

[74] Other significant examples of Alexander's importance for the world according to Pliny can be found at *HN* 35.93–4 (Apelles in the temple of Mars Ultor), 8.44 (Alexander commissions a natural history of all animal life, from Aristotle), 8.149–50 (Alexander discovering a breed of hunting dog which will attack nothing more humble than lions or elephants), 6.61 (in order to understand India one must follow in the footsteps (*uestigia*) of Alexander).

15

The Construction of a New Ideal
The Official Portraiture of Alexander the Great

Catie Mihalopoulos

The Hellenistic era marks an important shift in postclassical Greek social, political, and artistic beliefs. The person most responsible for shaping and developing the political and religious ideals distinguishing this period was Alexander the Great. His political and military achievements established him as an icon for the Hellenistic world. He became a symbol of power, intelligence, beauty, and fortune.

Nothing is more reflective of these qualities than the numerous examples of Alexander's portraits. An enormous variety of styles and types has been discovered throughout the Greco-Roman world. The surviving evidence of these works is scanty. It is, nevertheless, extremely important in understanding the construction of a new ideal in official portraiture. The sculpted image of Alexander had become much more than a representation of his physical appearance. His portraits were the direct reflection of a political and social order which he had established. The personal character revealed through his portraiture conveyed the increasing emphasis on the individual and his *tyche* (fate). Furthermore, the production of these images can also be viewed as a prominent vehicle for political propaganda and a way of expressing the monarch's achievements and power. The extensive variety of Alexander's representations made him more a paradigm than a person. The official image of Alexander, therefore, is an essential element that distinguishes the art of the Hellenistic period, which set a powerful standard for future tradition and subsequent royal and private portraiture.

Son of Philip II and Olympias, Alexander stands in the first rank of the world's great military commanders. Identified by his massive leonine hair, idealized face, and upturned eyes, Alexander was the first Greek ruler who understood and exploited the propagandistic powers of official portraiture. One of the earliest portraits of Alexander representing him as a youth, dating from 340–330, is found today in the Acropolis Museum in Athens (see fig. 1.1).[1] This portrait shows

---

[1] Museum inv. no. 1331. Found in 1886 near the Erechtheion on the Athenian Acropolis, this portrait is made of Pentelic marble (H: 0.35 m). See Pandermalis 2004: 18, no. 1; Harrison 2001; Stewart 1993: 106–13; Brouskari 1974: 184. I would like to thank Mark Rose, Executive Editor, *Archaeology Magazine*, for his generous gift of the Onassis Foundation Catalogue, *Alexander the Great: Treasures from an Epic Era of Hellenism* (2004).

Figure 15.1   The Getty Alexander, *c.*325–320 BC. J. Paul Getty Museum, Malibu. Acc. no. 73.AA 27. Photo: The J. Paul Getty Museum.

Alexander as a dreamy-looking youth. His eyes are deep set, his eyebrows are strong, and he has a rounded face and fleshy lips. In sharp contrast, his hair locks, which are summarily shaped into a massive mane, produce a strong chiaroscuro. Here, this portrait conflates Attic ideology, legend, and history. Alexander is clean-shaven and is depicted as the Homeric hero Achilles.[2] A second example of the youthful Alexander, said to have originated from Megara and now at the J. Paul Getty Museum in Malibu, dates to about 325–320 (fig. 15.1).[3] This portrait shows

[2]   For an extensive discussion on Alexander as the new Achilles see Stewart 1993: 78–86.

[3]   Museum inv. no. 73.AA.27. This particular work has undergone some restoration, perhaps during antiquity; however, some scholars regard the work as a fake. Stewart 1993: 52–3 gives a list of portraits commissioned during and after Alexander's time. These include: (1) Alexander, the Granikos Group by Lysippus after 334; (2) Alexander with the thunderbolt by Apelles, dedicated at Ephesus after 334; (3) the reliefs in the Shrine of Amun at Luxor, *c.*331–323; (4) the equestrian statue of Alexander as the founder (*ktistes*) of the city of Alexandria, *c.*331; (5) statues on the battlefield of the Hydaspes, *c.*326; (6) a failed proposal to carve Mt. Athos into a portrait of Alexander; (7) several bronzes of Alexander (the lance type) by Lysippus; (8) several paintings by Apelles; (9) several gems by Pyrgoteles. Commissioned by the court: (1) Alexander and Darius in battle, painted by Philoxenus for Cassander, *c.*306?; (2) Alexander on satrapal coinage of Memphis. Cities also commissioned portraits of Alexander:

Alexander with his head turned slightly to the left. He has strong eyebrows, a prominent nose, and a rounded jaw; his mouth is fleshy. There is juxtaposition between the modeled face and the chiaroscuro created by his leonine hair. The Acropolis portrait and the Getty Alexander share similarities in the youthful expression of the monarch who appears to be rendered as a variation of images that connect him with the Homeric hero Achilles.[4] Pausanias tells us that in 338 Philip II commissioned a gallery of portraits to be placed in the Sanctuary of Zeus at Olympia.[5] These statues were made of gold and ivory, thus, chryselephantine, and one of them depicted Alexander at age 16. The portraits commissioned by Philip are said to have been created by the artist Leochares, who was famous for his sculptures of the gods. According to this account, Alexander's image was projected even before he became king of Macedonia.[6]

Alexander spent his life on the battlefield with his troops, while Macedonia was governed in his name by Antipater. He was rarely in the vicinity of his subjects, and when the inhabitants of a state are not often reminded that there is a ruler in charge it can be a difficult task to retain loyal subjects. The absence of a powerful political icon increases the possibility of rebellion, especially when it is an empire that has recently been conquered as had Persia. Perpetuating his image in his place of birth at Aegae (modern Vergina) in Macedonia would not have been much of a problem since his victories brought fame and glory to the Macedonians. The eastern peoples, however, whom he had defeated and absorbed into his empire, would not have been so pleased or concerned to hear news of his continuing conquests. The need for an official powerful image became particularly important toward the end of his life, especially after his withdrawal from India.[7] In order to maintain his unconquered image in the minds of his subjects, he needed some way to remind them of his past achievements. The implementation of a persuasive portrait iconography in the form of statues, paintings, and subsequently coins conveying the existence of an omnipotent leader became a very effective iconic sign.[8] These visual signifiers reminded the empire that there was in fact a powerful monarch present who, if disobeyed, would punish all who broke the law. It was at this moment that the art of propaganda was crystallizing at a rapid pace.[9] To paraphrase Stewart, Alexander's portraiture was a constructed new ideal adhering to the rules of the new Hellenistic

e.g., (1) Alexander and Philip, Athens, *c.*338; (2) the Acropolis Alexander; (3) the proposed Alexander as Invisible God, *c.*324–323; (4) some cult statues for east Greek cities, *c.*323; (5) a statue at Larissa; (6) coins of Leucas and Naucratis. Individual commissions: e.g., (1) battle paintings by Aristides; (2) battle paintings for southern Italian vessels; (3) a painting of the marriage of Alexander to Roxane by Aetion, *c.*324.

[4]   Stewart 1993: nos. 5 and 16.
[5]   Paus. 5.20.9–10.
[6]   Pandermalis 2004: 15.
[7]   On Alexander in India see ch. 2 above.
[8]   Eco 1976: 207. On interpretations of Eco's theory of semiotics regarding this topic, see Stewart 1993: 67.
[9]   There were numerous images of Philip II and Olympias circulating throughout Macedonia, in addition to those now preserved by the finds of Manolis Andronikos at Vergina. See Andronikos 1992.

social ideology. The portraits gave him legitimacy and they were encoded so that they could be interpreted by their audience as imagery of the charismatic ruler. In other words, Alexander's portraits were intended for political and moral interpretation and they became "epideictic *visual* rhetoric."[10]

The official portraiture of Alexander demonstrated a new ideal: the amalgamation of individual characteristics, associated with adopted elements from the Near East and Egypt. Thus, a frequent *modus operandi* involves the ruler as if he were a divinity related with local religious traditions such as the concept of leader of the people he had just conquered. From early in his career, as king (*basileus*) of Macedonia, *hegemon* of the Greeks, successor to the Achaemenids, and finally son of Zeus, Alexander ruled by virtue of what has been called a quasi-constitutional position.[11] Surrounded by Macedonian aristocrats, his "Companions," Alexander shaped a new aristocracy to which his eastern subjects would submit without much struggle. Hence, the personality and energy of the new monarch became determining factors in his subsequent reception and perception of his newly conquered subjects in Asia as well as in Egypt. In pharaonic Egypt the king was a divinity. This belief would later lead to the Ptolemaic ruler cult, but was shaped itself by Alexander's own connection with Egyptian divinities. This is seen in the image of Alexander before Amon-Ra from the so-called Shrine of the Bark at the Temple of Luxor (see fig. 12.1). In winter 332/1 Alexander also took a long march to the desert oracle of Amun at the oasis of Siwah. His own propaganda later announced that the oracle recognized him as the son of Amun, the equivalent to the Greek god Zeus, thus bestowing on Alexander the divine right to rule as Egyptian pharaoh.[12]

The portraiture of Alexander is often divided by scholars into various types. These types were consequently established from images that perpetuated the Hellenistic ruler cult.[13] A variety of these images concentrated on depictions of the monarch as Heracles, Helios, the son of Zeus, and may be considered heroic portraits. Other images, dubbed the equestrian type, show Alexander on horseback as on the so-called Alexander Sarcophagus from the royal necropolis at Sidon (fig. 2.3) and in the Alexander Mosaic from the House of the Faun, Italy (fig. 2.2).[14]

The majority of the so-called royal-derivative portraits were primarily significant in the intentional projection of the idiosyncratic qualities of the *ethos*, *pathos*, and the *arête* of the individual. Hence, these ruler-type portraits represented visual political propaganda and were intended to perpetuate the image, prestige, *tyche*, and the charisma of Alexander. That is to say, these various images functioned in

---

[10] Stewart 1993: 69; my emphasis.
[11] See Tarn. See also Pollitt 1986: 318, app. 2. It is likely that Alexander requested that the Greek cities honor him as a god. See Ael. *VH* 2.19; Hyp. 5, col. 31; Arr. 7.23.2. See also Nock 1928.
[12] Callisthenes *ap.*Str. 17.1.43, 40; Hornblower and Spawforth 27–30; *OCD*³. See also Bell 1985; el-Abdel el-Raqiz 1984; Stewart 1993: no. 53.
[13] Ferguson 1928: 13–22; Nock 1928; Heuss 1937; Wilcken 1938: 298–321; Cerfaux and Tondriau 1957; Taeger 1957; Ritter 1965.
[14] Alexander sarcophagus, Istanbul Archaeological Museum, inv. no. 370; Alexander Mosaic, Naples, Museo Nazionale, inv. no. 10020.

antiquity like popular culture images transmitted today on television and in printed political advertisements. The portraiture of the ruler was an effective and persuasive means of projecting the qualities of the monarch. The artist credited with the creation of this type of ruler portraiture was Lysippus of Sicyon.[15] It is said that Lysippus pioneered a new style in sculpture during the late fourth century, and critics said of his work that "older sculptors made men as they are; he made them as they appear to be."[16]

In addition to individual portraits of Alexander, Lysippus created victory monuments that commemorated the king's battles and subsequent conquests. The most important of these was that commemorating the battle of Granicus.[17] According to Pollitt, the Granicus Monument was transported to Rome by Q. Caecilius Metellus in 146 and no longer survives.[18] The monument commemorating the battle was originally located at Dion, in the great sanctuary of the Olympian Zeus just below Mt. Olympus. According to tradition, Alexander started his campaign following official ceremonial sacrifices. The monument is said to have been a composition depicting the twenty-five Companions who fell during the battle. One of these equestrian statues may have inspired an equestrian statue of Alexander, *Alexander on Horseback*, that no longer survives. Echoes of this now lost masterpiece may be found in the Equestrian Statuette of Herculaneum at the Museo Archeologico Nazionale, Naples (fig. 2.1).

Lysippan Portraits of Alexander the Great

According to Plutarch "it is the statues of Lysippus which best convey Alexander's physical appearance . . . For it was the artist who captured exactly those distinctive features which many of Alexander's successors and friends later tried to imitate, namely the poise of the neck turned slightly to the left and the melting glance of the eyes."[19] Plutarch continues that "Alexander decreed that only Lysippus should be allowed to make his portrait. For only Lysippus, it appears, brought out his real character in the bronze and he also gave form to the essential excellence of his character."[20]

Lysippus' achievement in creating Alexander's portrait is clearly revealed in Plutarch's language. For example, the Lysippan images conveyed first and foremost Alexander's *arête* as well as his *ethos* and *pathos*. According to tradition, Lysippus

[15] According to ancient sources, Alexander was so pleased with the images Lysippus created that he appointed him court sculptor. See Plin. *HN* 7.125; Plu. *Alex.* 4.1; Palagia and Pollitt 1996: 132. For other sources see also Johnson 1927: 301–6; Balsdon 1950; Sjöqvist 1966: 9–10; Badian 1981.

[16] Palagia and Pollitt 1996: 132; see also Johnson 1927; Chamay and Maier 1987.

[17] Gardner 1910: 227; Hammond 1980: 73–88.

[18] Pollitt 1986: 43.

[19] Plu. *Alex.* 4.1–7, *c.*110 AD. See also Stewart 1993: 344.

[20] Plu. *Alex.* 4.1–7.

Figure 15.2   Head of Alexander the Great. Copy of original by Lysippus. Capitoline Museum, Rome. Photo: Alinari/Art Resource, New York.

incorporated Alexander's natural tilt of the neck, a physical peculiarity that caused his head to have a slightly upward angle. No original Lysippan portrait of Alexander survives. Plutarch's artistic vocabulary, however, can be detected in many copies of Alexander, such as the turn of the neck to the left, the upward glance of his eyes and his particular *anastolé* hairstyle that were copied on a number of occasions during and after Alexander's time.[21]

Characteristics associated with Alexander's portraits are also reflected in royal Hellenistic processions, and in the ruler cult of Hellenistic monarchs and subsequent Roman leaders. One of the best-known examples of such sculpture is a marble head generally identified as Alexander that dates to 180, the Alexander from Pergamum, at the Istanbul Archaeological Museum (fig. 15.3).[22] This portrait appears to convey the dramatic artistic elements that have been attributed to Lysippus. Small nuances, however, such as the rounded eyes, the modeled face, and

[21]   The *anastolé* hairstyle refers to the wave-like pattern of hair locks formed above the center of the forehead. For styles in Hellenistic sculpture see Ridgway 1990.
[22]   Museum inv. no. 1138 (cat. 538).

Figure 15.3   Alexander from Pergamum, *c*. third century BC. Archaeological Museum, Istanbul. Photo: Erich Lessing/Art Resource, New York.

the deeply drilled hair locks highly suggest a local Pergamene style.[23] A marble portrait of Alexander discovered in the modern city Gianitsa (Macedonia), now now in the local museum at Pella, is perhaps a truer to life image of Alexander (fig. 15.4).[24] This particular portrait dates from *c*.200–150, the era of the Macedonian kings Philip V and Perseus.[25] There is a lack of dramatic exaggeration as well as a much softer treatment in the creation of the eyes. Such artistic elements can be directly connected with sculpture that dates from the fourth century, that is, the late Classical period. Therefore, the Gianitsa Alexander may indeed be the closest example linked to a Lysippan prototype.

Alexander is also represented in a historical or quasi-historical context in the so-called Alexander Sarcophagus from the royal necropolis at Sidon, now in the

[23]   The Pergamene style is associated with the Hellenistic kings at Pergamum and Halicarnassus in Asia Minor. This artistic development showed the human in full motion, rounded and at times in the round, with rigorous facial characteristics as well as strong chiaroscuro. In addition, the images demonstrated strong emotions and elements of theater. See also Radt 1981; Pollitt 1986; Ridgway 1990.

[24]   Museum inv. no. ΓΛ 15. H: 30 cm.

[25]   Stewart 1993: xxv, no. 97 dates this portrait to *c*.300–270.

Figure 15.4   The Pella Alexander, from Gianitsa, *c.*200–150 BC. Pella Museum, Pella. Sculpture inventory no. ΓΛ 15. Photo: Archaeological Receipts Fund (TAP Service).

Archaeological Museum in Istanbul (figs. 2.3, 2.4, 2.5) depicting a battle scene, possibly that at Issus.[26] The sarcophagus presents us with an image of Alexander created not long after his death. On the sarcophagus, Alexander is shown wearing a lion's head helmet. The sarcophagus may be connected to Abdalonymus who was the last king of the native Sidonian dynasty, and whom Alexander elevated to power.[27] The work is generally referred to as the "Alexander Sarcophagus" and it shows one of the most striking representations of battle that can be connected to Alexander. Traces of color are still evident on the sarcophagus. Two of its four sides show battles between the Macedonians and/or Greeks and the Persians. These

---

[26]   Museum inv. no. 370. L: 3.2 m; W 1.7 m. See Stewart 1993: 294–5, figs. 101–6, with further bibliography. The sarcophagus was perhaps that of Abdalonymus of Sidon. Arr. 2.15.6 reports that, when Alexander reached Sidon, the Sidonians opened their gates and invited him inside "out of their hatred for the Persians and King Darius." Alexander made Abdalonymus king of Sidon after the battle at Issus in 333. See Winter 1912; Schefold and Seidel 1968; Koch 1975; Hammond 1980; and the next note.

[27]   Stewart 1993: 294; but see now Heckel 2006 who argues that the sarcophagus is that of Mazaeus, the Persian nobleman who fought Alexander at Gaugamela but soon after surrendered Babylon to him. Afterward Mazaeus became satrap of Babylon.

images are found on one of the long and one of the short sides of the sarcophagus. The other two corresponding sides show hunting scenes. These reliefs are significant not only for their stylistic quality but also for their subject matter. The elaborate and at times rather complex compositions imply extensive knowledge of pictorial representations as well as exceptional artistic expertise.[28] Additionally, the lion-helmeted horseman may be an elaborate representation of young horsemen found on Attic *stelai* that date from the late fourth century, for example, the Funerary Stele of Dexileus (*c.*390) at the Kerameikos Museum in Athens.[29] Furthermore, the hunting friezes can be a vivid documentation of the political importance attributed to the hunting of lions and the subsequent repetitive motifs of the hunt seen in Hellenistic art. The long side of the sarcophagus, showing a battle scene distinctively portraying a lion-helmeted horseman, associates Alexander with Heracles.[30] The figure of the lion-helmeted horseman may be considered a heroic portrait of Alexander portrayed as the fierce warrior, clearly conscious of his ability to exercise his control and power. Moreover, the symbolic signifier of the lion's head may also imply Alexander's divine-like qualities.

The facial characteristics of Alexander appear to be those described by Plutarch; they are also similar to those of the herm of Alexander, the so-called Azara Herm, found in Tivoli and now at the Louvre.[31] A Greco-Roman copy after a fourth-century original statue believed to have been modeled after a close representation of Alexander (fig. 15.5). Inscribed ΑΛΕΞΑΝΔΡΟΣ ΦΙΛΙΠΠΟΥ ΜΑΚ[ΕΔΩΝ] (Alexander the Macedonian son of Philip), its subject is clearly identified.[32] Though the Azara Herm is much worn, with some restorations and in poor condition, aspects of this portrait of Alexander surely go back to a Lysippan prototype as seen in the characteristic *anastolé* hairstyle. This signature style would reappear later in the portrait of the Roman general and politician Pompey the Great, as seen in the example now at the Ny Carlsberg Glyptotek, Copenhagen (fig. 14.1).[33]

Finally, many scholars agree that the image of Alexander on the Alexander Sarcophagus reflects an amalgamation of the ruler portrait that was created by Lysippus and Apelles. Equestrian-type statues were widely copied throughout history. Though Alexander was not the first person depicted on horseback, later examples of equestrian portraits were perhaps styled after these Alexander prototypes. Examples of these include the Roman emperor Marcus Aurelius, the Byzantine emperor Justinian, and the medieval Frankish king Charlemagne, the emperor who restored the idea of Rome in his celebrated coronation on Christmas Day 800. A much later

[28] Especially see on mosaics located at Pella and Aegae (modern Vergina), dating from the fourth century, such as that signed by Gnosis, showing a stag hunt and two males (see below).

[29] Pedley 2002: 313, no. 9.38.

[30] Suhr 1979: 86.

[31] Museum inv. no. MA 436, originally dated *c.*330. See Stewart 1993: nos. 45, 46.

[32] Museum inv. no. MA 436. H: 68 cm. The eyebrows, nose, and lips are restored, dated *c.*330 BC; Stewart 1993: nos. 45, 46.

[33] Claudian copy of an original discovered in the Licinian tomb on the Via Salaria in 1885, dated *c.*60–50; H: 0.26 m.

Figure 15.5   Alexander the Great, so-called "Alexander Azara." First-century BC copy of original bust (*c.*320 BC) by Leochares. Louvre, Paris. Photo: Erich Lessing/Art Resource, New York.

example is David's famous painting of Napoleon crossing the Alps (*Bonaparte, Calm on a Fiery Steed, Crossing the Alps*, 1801).[34]

One of the best-known works of art discovered at Pella is the mosaic that shows a stag hunt, signed by Gnosis, dated to *c.*300 (fig. 15.6).[35] This mosaic depicts a hunt, a popular theme in works of art associated with the Macedonian court. Royal hunting scenes have a long tradition in the Near East and Egypt and were popularized in the west by Alexander following his conquest of Persia.[36] Some have seen in this mosaic Alexander and his companion Hephaestion.[37] The mosaic shows two armed and nude men hunting a stag with a dog. The focus of the composition is on the stag under attack by the dog. The artist has brought drama and excitement

[34]   At the Musée Nationale du Château de Malmaison, Rueil. See Toman 2000: 376.
[35]   Moreno 2001: 102, pls. 48 and 49, argues that the mosaic is a copy of an original painting by Melanthius or Apelles.
[36]   A famous such scene is the relief sculpture at the London Museum from about 660–636, titled *King Ashurbanipal Hunting a Lion at Nineveh.* For Alexander hunting lions, see Stamatiou 1988: 209–17. See also the wall painting on the facade of "Philip's Tomb," in Andronikos 1992: 100–19, figs. 58–63.
[37]   Moreno 2001.

Figure 15.6 The Stag Hunt, Gnosis, *c.*300 BC. Pella Museum, Pella. Photo: Archaeological Receipts Fund (TAP Service).

to the work as the stag is shown bleeding from the attacking dog. While the two hunters are positioned symmetrically, the stag and the dog are placed in what is defined as a pyramidal composition. This particular artistic arrangement was later favored by Italian Renaissance artists such as Raphael in his *Madonna del Cardellino*,[38] as well as in Leonardo da Vinci's *Virgin of the Rocks*.[39]

Gnosis was technically proficient in the artistic conventions employed by his late Classical contemporaries. One may recall the *Abduction of Persephone by Hades* in the Tomb of Persephone at Vergina dated *c.*340.[40] In the abduction scene the anonymous artist has made clear that what was to become Hellenistic art comprehends fully the idea of the modern concept *di sotto in sù*, first used by Mantegna on the ceiling of the Camera degli Sposi in 1474 in Mantua.[41]

The Gnosis mosaic shares artistic essentials that are analogous to those found on the Hades and Persephone wall painting. In addition, one may argue that Gnosis understood the shared artistic vocabulary that was to be developed and eventually practiced by artists throughout the Hellenistic world. There is an element of the *koine*, which is highly prevalent during the Hellenistic era. These works of art share

[38] Galleria degli Uffizi, Florence; date: 1505–6. De la Croix et al. 1991: 646, no. 17-15.
[39] Louvre, Paris; date: *c.*1485. De la Croix et al. 1991: 635, no. 17-1.
[40] Andronikos 1992: 90–1, no. 49.
[41] Ducal Palace, Mantua; date: 1474. De la Croix et al. 1991: 629, no. 16-65.

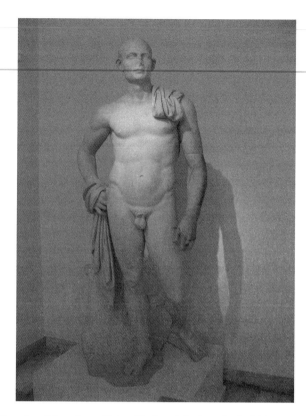

Figure 15.7   Pseudo-athlete from Delos. National Archaeological Museum, Athens. Photo: courtesy of John Pollini.

many commonly understood constructs that distinguish the art of the Hellenistic era from other periods. These constructs relate to the ways in which artists observed nature and the societal ideals that were embedded into the Hellenistic populace, such as *pothos, ponos, pathos*, all of which in turn relate to the theatricality of the epoch, or to the spreading stylistic advantages in individual portraiture.

It is during the Hellenistic era, for example, that we find the fully developed idea of the human condition: it can be a depiction of a fortunate individual, such as the Pseudo-Athlete from Delos (fig. 15.7),[42] or an individual depicted in tragic circumstances and shows his distress and fear, as in the *Laocöon*. M. Robertson argues that what characterizes Hellenistic art is a combination of new emphases as well as continuity: it can be found in the so-called philosopher portraits, in the erotic representations of divinities and humans alike, as well as in the psychological portraits of the period.[43] The Gnosis mosaic appears to embrace several elements that can be distinguished as Hellenistic. For example, the movement and torsion seen in the representation of the two young men is mirrored in the stag and the dog in the middle of the composition.

[42]   Stewart 1993.
[43]   Robertson 1993: 97–101; Pollitt 1986.

Additionally, Gnosis applies a subtle gradation of shade to project the illusion that the figures have a rounded and solid form. The dark background of the composition sets the stage for illuminating the figures, as well as their presence and domination within it. Both hunters are shown wearing a *chlamys*,[44] which billows in the wind, suggesting rapid movement. There is an obvious counterbalance in the representation of their weapons, which are placed on a diagonal, as well as in an opposing but symmetrical manner. The figure on the right holds a sword while that on the left holds an ax. The legs of the two hunters are shown tense and they repeat the same counterbalance to the right and the left of the composition. An interesting signifier is included in this otherwise standard hunting scene: the hat in the upper right of the composition. This hat is a *petasos*, symbolic of travelers.[45] If one were to take the right figure as Alexander, then the *petasos* may imply that the youth was not at Pella, because the monarch was away from Macedonia, a traveler in his newly conquered empire. Pollitt notes that the mosaic may have decorated the royal residence at Pella or simply the home of important Macedonian noble: it may have been at the house of Cassander, who ruled *c.*316–297, or perhaps of Antigonus Gonatas, who ruled 272–239.[46] Moreno gives several reasons for his identification of the two youths. According to him, in Macedonia the *petasos* was a hat emblematic of royal rank and so should depict Alexander. The youth on the left of the composition is armed with a double ax, the weapon used by Hephaestus, the divine namesake of Hephaestion.[47]

An exceptional work of art, the Alexander Mosaic from the House of the Faun in Pompeii is thought by some to depict the battle at Issus (fig. 2.2). Moreno, however, asserts that the scene in fact commemorates the subsequent rout of the Persians at Gaugamela, near Nineveh in Iraq today,[48] as suggested by the accounts of Ptolemy and Aristobulus of Cassandreia.[49] The mosaic is believed by some to be a copy of a monumental Greek original painting by Philoxenus of Eretria (possibly Apelles).[50] According to Moreno, the Alexander Mosaic was augmented during antiquity and was restored at the time it was inserted into the floor of an *exedra* in the House of the Faun, the residence of the Satrii family.[51]

---

[44] For the dress and styles of young men in antiquity see Geddes 1987.

[45] Geddes 1987. For images of young men on white-ground *lekythoi*, see Tzahou-Alexandri 1998: 89.

[46] Pollitt 1986: 40–2, no. 35.

[47] Moreno 2001: 102–4. See Moreno 2001 for bibliography on the two youths, note nos. 73, 74. See also Plin. *HN* 35.80; Plu. *Arat.* 12.3.

[48] Moreno 2001. For an extensive discussion of this interpretation of the mosaic see Moreno 2001 and Zevi 1998. See also Plu. *Alex.* 31.6; Devine 1985, 1986; Cohen 1997.

[49] Winter 1909; Rumpf 1962; Moreno 2001.

[50] Fuhrmann 1931. The original painting is believed to have been a private commission by Cassander. Some scholars believe that Apelles made the original during Alexander's lifetime. Others name a Helen as the artist of the painting.

[51] See Stewart 1993: app. 4 for bibliography; Moreno 2001. *Archaeology Magazine* (2006): 36–9 shows images of the restoration of the mosaic. See also Andreae 1977; Zevi 1988; Dondener 1990; Cohen 1997; Zevi and Pedicini 1998.

The tesserated mosaic was quite influential when it was discovered in Italy in 1831.[52]

This is revealed in Goethe's contemporary description that "the present and the future will not succeed in commenting correctly on this artistic marvel, and we must always return, after having studied and explained it, to simple, pure wonder."[53] At first glance the composition appears to be as chaotic as the spears of the warriors that form several diagonals in the background, especially those created by the Macedonian *sarissai*. To the left of the composition is a lifeless tree, placed off-center behind Alexander and his men. Greeks associated death with dead trees and their subsequent inclusion in the composition conveys an omen of death.[54] A different interpretation about the inclusion of the dead tree, and one that agrees partially with Moreno's, is that made by F. Zevi, who maintains that the dead tree recalls Arabic sources that refer to Gaugamela as the "Battle of the Desiccated Tree." According to this interpretation, these sources, which date after Hellenistic times, claim that Alexander lost his helmet at Gaugamela. This piece of information may point to the location of the battle, since Alexander in this mosaic is shown bareheaded.[55] In this work, Alexander is depicted charging toward Darius and impaling a Persian warrior trying to protect his king. On the right side of the composition, artistic knowledge and understanding of perspective and foreshortening is clearly demonstrated. The extreme foreshortening here showing a horse from the rear does not appear again until the Renaissance, as seen, for example, in Paolo Uccello's *The Battle of San Romano* (*c*.1445) at the National Gallery, London.[56]

The scene of the Alexander Mosaic offers a historical account of Alexander's military success and the creation of his empire. It illustrates his heroism and bravery in battle, his *arête*, a Greek ideal, and exudes *pathos*, a Hellenistic trend in the visual tradition. Darius and his men, on the other hand, express fear and anguish which is clearly visible in their faces. Darius dramatically turns back, gazing at Alexander who slays one of his soldiers. In addition, Darius is shown dressed in Persian attire (as understood by late fourth-century Greek artists), which includes leggings, or pants.[57] In previous representations of battles, such as *Amazonomachies* (battles between the Greeks and the Amazons), which intend to illustrate the "other," Amazons are dressed in leggings. This eastern form of dress often signified the effeminacy and the inadequacy of the opponent, and it was intentionally incorporated to show the "other" as being uncivilized and disruptive of the civilized Greek cosmos. *Amazonomachy* was part of the common artistic repertoire employed by

---

[52]   Mosaics made of *tesserae* appear during the second century; Macedonian mosaics were made of pebbles.

[53]   Cited in Moreno 2001: 11.

[54]   See also the Niobid Painter.

[55]   Zevi 1988; Zevi and Pedicini 1998.

[56]   Tempera on wood; Gardner 1991: 601, pls. 16–29.

[57]   The Greeks did not think leggings acceptable attire for civilized people. For reception and interpretations of encoded images see Eco 1976 and 1990.

Greek artists. This visual signifier was commonly located on the architectural decorations of temples such as the Temple of Zeus at Olympia, the Parthenon on the
Athenian Acropolis, and in the interior frieze of the Temple of Apollo Epicurius
at Bassae.

Images of Alexander by Apelles

A different form of portraiture associated with Alexander is the *Zeus Keraunaios*.[58]
Variations of this type appear to derive from a famous painting by Apelles, the court
painter of Alexander, showing Alexander seated and holding a thunderbolt in his
right raised hand. A painting in the House of the Vettii at Pompeii may be a copy
of this lost painting.[59] The young man is shown with his head turned slightly to the
left, and with a detailed coiffure of the *anastolé* hairstyle. Additionally, the lower
part of the body is covered by a *himation* and the figure's feet rest on a small stool.
Throughout the ancient world, an individual seated on a *klismós* with the feet on a
stool suggested a person of high status. Additionally, the *himation* itself suggests a
subject of either divine or at very least demigod status.

According to Pliny, it was Apelles who created the image of Alexander appearing
as *Zeus Keraunophoros*.[60] The artist is said to have created such a painting of Alexander that was placed at the great sanctuary in the Temple of Artemis at Ephesus.[61]
Aelian, writing in the third century AD, reports that an image of Alexander was to
be seen in this famous and important temple.[62] If Aelian's account is accurate, then
the Temple of Artemis would have been the perfect location to display an image of
the deceased young monarch. Pliny recounts that two images of Alexander by
Apelles were also exhibited in the Forum of Augustus.[63]

A number of images of Alexander portray him with his head twisted to one side,
face uplifted, and with expressive facial features. A good example of this emotionally
charged image or *Pathosbild* is exemplified in the Pergamene head, previously discussed (fig. 15.3). A more idealized version of this *pathos* image is a portrait of
Alexander as Helios at the Capitoline Museum in Rome, dating from about the
second century (fig. 15.8). This image was perhaps based on a Hellenistic prototype
and some scholars regard it as a portrait of Helios and not Alexander as Helios.[64]
The supposed portrait of Alexander as Helios combines soft modeling of the face
and a more flamboyant coiffure of leonine locks. The head is dramatically twisted

---

[58]   See Mingazzini 1961: 7–17; Frel 1979; Archer 1981; Pollitt 1986: 23; Frel 1987.
[59]   See plates in Stewart 1993: no. 65; Pollitt 1986: no. 23. The image sits in the winter *triclinium* of
the House of the Vettii at Pompeii, west wall.
[60]   Plin. *HN* 7.125.
[61]   Pollitt 1986: 22–3.
[62]   Ael. *VH* 2.3. See also Stewart 1993: 377.
[63]   Plin. *HN* 35.94.
[64]   See Pollitt 1986: 28–9, no. 17.

Figure 15.8   Alexander Helios. Hellenistic bust. Capitoline Museum, Rome. Photo: Alinari/
Art Resource, New York.

to the left, thus creating a forceful movement that is further exaggerated by the
chiaroscuro created by his full mane of hair. The curls of the hair are fluid, one
thick strand cascading on top of the other, generating a waterfall type of movement
that frames the highly polished face. This adaptation may exaggerate the features
of some Lysippan prototype and introduces elements of the so-called Hellenistic
Baroque style of c.200–100.[65] Additionally the portrait is most likely indicative of
the eclectic taste of the time, as the smooth surfaces and the hard lines are created
in the neoclassical tradition of the time.[66]

Alexander's divine-like images embody serenity, exemplifying the ruler as the
son of Zeus. This style, expressed in the divine images of the monarch deriving from
Apellan prototypes, is intended to perpetuate the transcended human limitations
of the otherwise mortal ruler. Emotionally charged images, on the other hand, as
seen in the Lysippan prototypes and those descending from them, are associated
with the heroism of figures from the Greek past and now Alexander.

[65] Hellenistic Baroque is a subdivision within the artistic development during the Hellenistic era. It
often combines theatrical elements, as well as much *pathos* (strong emotion) as seen in the *Laoцöon*,
attributed by Pliny to the Rhodian sculptors Hagesander, Polydorus, and Athenodorus, dating from the
second to the first centuries BC or the first century AD in the Vatican Museum, Rome. See Pollitt 1986
and Ridgway 1990.
[66] The so-called neoclassical tradition in Hellenistic sculpture takes its name from works of art that
were created by artists who were consciously reviving and imitating forms of the Classical period,
c.480–340. Some of these works include the colossal statue of *Athena from Pergamum* (c.175), at the
Staatliche Museen zu Berlin, or the *Aphrodite of Melos* (c.150–125) in the Louvre, Paris. See Pollitt 1986:
164–72.

Figure 15.9   Neisos Gem. Hermitage Museum, St. Petersburg.

Varia and Concluding Remarks

Gem-cutters were extremely important in the perpetuation of the heroic images of leaders from Alexander on. According to Pliny, Pyrgoteles was the gem engraver of Alexander's court.[67] An example of Greek glyptic art representing Alexander is the Neisos Gem, probably dating from the second century, and inscribed ΝΕΙΣΟΥ by the artist, at the Hermitage (fig. 15.9).[68] This private work of art is made of carnelian and represents Alexander holding a thunderbolt in his left hand and a sheathed sword in his right hand. The figure appears to be a variant of the Alexander with lance type attributed to Lysippus.[69] Although the ancient sources do not give an extensive description about this type, a number of scholars have written about it. It appears the Alexander with a lance type was created by Lysippus in response to the painting by Apelles showing Alexander with a thunderbolt. There are a number

[67]   Plin. *HN* 35.94. See also Zanker 1968; Pollitt 1986.
[68]   Museum inv. no. 609.
[69]   Plu. *De Is. et Os.* 24; Plu. *De Alex. fort.* 2.2–3; Stewart 1993: 395, 404, 405.

of replicas of Alexander with a lance that survive.[70] The Neisos Gem shows Alexander's forearm covered by an aegis, his right hand resting on a shield. To his right stands the eagle of Zeus. This specific representation of Alexander seems to incorporate a Zeus-like image, which informed a number of other types produced in later times. The fusion of heroic and godlike types may be indicative of later stages in Alexander's life when his divinity was officially worshiped. Gems with such images of Alexander appear to reflect public works of art and perpetuate his memory in the private sphere.

Privately commissioned gems with images of Alexander may also have served as prototypes in the production of coins.[71] The multitude of artistic representations, including the production of coins, that were created during and after the lifetime of Alexander, aided in the creation and subsequent perpetuation of the memory of Alexander and then later of the Diadochi, as well as subsequent Roman leaders.

When considering the real changes that were brought about by the appearance of Alexander in the political landscape of the ancient Greek world and his conquered territories, we must ask the question: what do we mean by Hellenistic? When these changes are considered, we are led to conclude that Alexander was the catalyst that caused what was Hellenic, or Greek, to be transformed into Hellenistic *koiné*. In a seminal chapter in Peter Green's *Hellenistic History and Culture*, M. Robertson asks "What is Hellenistic about Hellenistic Art?" Robertson discusses the multivalent nature of Hellenistic art and Hellenistic ideals as viewed by scholars and the general public. Furthermore, he asks, what is not Classical (Greek) in Hellenistic art? Robertson is unable to decide the precise moment that Hellenistic style came into being. It appears, however, that Alexander's ascension to the throne represents an important moment in the creation of Hellenistic ideology. What used to be the individual as part of the collective, that is the *demos*, was completely altered by individualism and self-projection under the leadership of a monarch. To quote Robertson: "in the changed world of the Hellenistic kingdoms, and directly influenced by the change, philosophical skepticism becomes more cogent . . . Gods are present for all to see in the mortal kings, while the traditional gods become much more dubious entities, and, even if they exist, of much less significance than a universally recognized and overriding power of fortune."[72]

J. J. Pollitt, on the other hand, has shown that there are five different elements that distinguish Hellenistic art from other periods: (1) an obsession with one's fortune; (2) the theatrical mentality of the people; (3) individualism; (4) a cosmopolitan outlook; (5) a scholarly mentality. Pollitt's discussion about these five

---

[70] Stewart 1993: 163–71 divides the statuettes with a lance into three types: the Fouquet type, the Nelidow type, and the Stanford type.

[71] For numismatic production relating to Alexander and his Successors see Bellinger 1963; Davis and Kraay 1973; Smith 1989; Mørkholm 1991; Price 1991; Stewart 1993; Holt 2003; Pandermalis 2004; Kroll, 2007.

[72] Robertson 1993: 89.

particular characteristics shows that "they are interdependent and together constitute something like a Hellenistic *Zeitgeist*."[73]

In conclusion, the artistic development which occurred during and after the time
of Alexander shaped a new ideal in the material culture of the Greek mainland and
the Mediterranean world. The construction of individual objects demonstrates a
mutual understanding of what has been described as *koiné*. This intellectual shift
was the result of a number of factors, including those described by Pollitt. In several
instances one can detect a strong sense of individualization and idealization of a
deified mortal in portraiture, in keeping with a new interest in naturalism. In addition, the inclination for dramatic subject matter, as well as the fate of mortals takes
center-stage in the new world of Hellenistic theater and theatricality. Alexander's
new world is converted into an all-inclusive stage in which a chosen leader becomes
the protagonist. In this climate, there was a proliferation of war monuments that
perpetuated the virtues of the victor, as seen in the Nike of Samothrace, *c.*200.[74]
Furthermore, artistic creations are paid for and dictated by private patrons, for
example, the Pseudo-Athlete from Delos (fig. 15.7).[75] Subsequently, Alexander's
new world order serves as the basis of the Greco-Roman tradition which was to be
reborn and transformed from the Renaissance onward.

[73]   Pollitt 1986: 1.
[74]   Now in the Louvre. See Pollitt 1986: 114–16, 296.
[75]   Kleiner 1992: 34–5, no. 11. See also Stewart 1993.

16

Power, Passion, and Patrons

Alexander, Charles Le Brun, and Oliver Stone

E. J. Baynham

It might be helpful to give some background to this chapter.[1] One focus of this volume is the Macedonian conqueror's *Nachleben* and how he has been perceived in western culture, and when I was initially approached by the editors, I thought that Charles Le Brun's spectacular series of Alexander paintings which he produced for King Louis XIV of France between 1660 and *c.*1668–73 would be an appealing topic.[2]

Following on from these early conceptions, Oliver Stone's movie *Alexander* appeared – to an overwhelmingly hostile critical reception (some of it unfair and misguided) and box office failure in several countries.[3] It seemed to me that Stone and Le Brun offer some interesting parallels; both are artists, albeit in different media, and both have an objective in historical narrative in a primarily visual context. Fundamentally, both are storytellers. Both saw Alexander as an iconic figure and as a hero, although their respective interpretations of the "heroic" appear to coincide in some aspects and differ vastly on others. The artist and the director

[1] I am grateful to the editors of this volume, Professors Waldemar Heckel and Lawrence Tritle, also to art historians Dr. Christopher Allen and Ms. Raichel Le Goff, as well as Professor A. B. Bosworth, for reading earlier drafts of the chapter, and finally to Dr. Fiona Greenland and Professor Robin Lane Fox, who have shared so much information and insight about the film *Alexander*.
[2] The chronology of the series is controversial: see Hartle 1957: 91ff., esp. n. 7. Le Brun's most influential modern biographer, Henry Jouin, gives two different dates for Le Brun's first Alexander painting, *The Queens of Persia before Darius*: 1660 (Jouin 1889: 133–4) and 1661 (221 n. 1). Most modern art historians accept 1660–1, but see Bryson 1981: 52, who places it a year later in 1662. The issue is not insignificant because it relates to whether Le Brun received his first commission from Louis before or after the king took direct control of the throne. Hartle argues that Le Brun's last painting in the series, *Alexander and Porus*, inspired Racine's *Alexandre le grand* and must have been completed before 1665; *contra*: Gareau 1992: 220; Posner 1959: 241–2. Bibliography on each of Le Brun's Alexander series can be found in Gareau 1992; for a catalogue of Le Brun's works, see Thuillier and Montagu 1963.
[3] The version of *Alexander* referred to here is that released in 2004, not *Alexander: Director's Cut* or the more recent *Alexander Revisited: The Final Cut*.

emphasize Alexander's bravery on the field, Le Brun by his vivid depictions of Alexander's face in battle, Stone by the recurring theme that the Macedonian king was "beyond fear" and hence, in that respect, was truly "liberated." There is also a strong affiliation between war and masculinity in both Le Brun's paintings and Stone's film. The most powerful emotional bond is the one between the king and his comrade-in-arms, Hephaestion, whereas the strongest female characters, Olympias and Roxane, are shown as fiercely loving, but also possessive and ultimately treacherous.

Ironically, Alexander is often depicted in early modern European art with rather feminine features, and owing to an apparent iconographical misidentification of an earlier image, Le Brun's most famous painting, *The Queens of Persia before Alexander*, shows the Macedonian conqueror as particularly girlish. The Persian women are shown with great tenderness and sympathy, but despite their prominence, they are mere foils to the painting's main message – Alexander's power and his clemency.[4]

For Le Brun and the Sun King, Alexander offered a noble role model – but only as one part of a rich and complex culture of propaganda directed at the glorification of the French monarch.[5] For Stone, Alexander remains a deeply flawed character – for all his magnificence, charisma, and ability to inspire devotion and strong passion in others.

One should, of course, note that neither Le Brun nor Oliver Stone worked entirely on his own. The annual televised Academy Awards ceremony offers a notorious example of effusive acknowledgment from gushing recipients, which reminds the viewer that the production of any large-scale film involves hundreds of people, from ground support staff to key financiers and technical experts. But the director is the guiding mind, and in a very early exchange between Stone and his historical adviser, Robin Lane Fox, the former remarked that he had to have a scene in his mind, "right down to the details."[6] Likewise, a large staff of assistant painters would have worked on several of Le Brun's vast canvases, as his duties as First Painter included substantial administrative commitments. However, he probably painted the most important particulars personally, and both the preliminary drawings and the overall concept of the scene and its realization would have been his own.

The Hollywood director and French court painter faced similar broad problems in terms of the parameters of their respective media. Cinema is not "history" any more than history painting, which in Le Brun's time was considered the highest expression of the genre.[7] The whole of Alexander's life and reign cannot be shown on celluloid (or on the stage) in less than three hours, any more than it can be shown on a single canvas. Le Brun was not trying to tell a new story so much as to represent episodes – either from ancient history, classical literature, or the

---

[4]   See below, pp. 305–6.

[5]   On the careful creation of Louis's image, see the excellent study by Burke (1992). On the importance of Alexander the Great at Louis's court, see also Hartle 1957, 1970.

[6]   Lane Fox 2004: 25.

[7]   On the high status of history painting in the seventeenth century see Allen 2003: 12–13.

Scriptures – which were already well known to his audience. Although he was working within a historical framework for the Alexander series, he was essentially creating a work of drama,[8] with his own interpretation of characters and their motives – not unlike a director and a cast of actors.

The problem of selection – what to omit and what to highlight – has challenged other dramatists and film directors. Terence Rattigan's 1948 stage play on Alexander, *Adventure Story*, is performed as a series of vignettes from the king's entire reign with little linkage. Robert Rossen's 1956 film *Alexander the Great* (starring Richard Burton) concentrated on Alexander's early life, with comparatively little attention given to the invasions of northeast Asia and India.

Stone's approach was to use a "narrator-mediator" – Alexander's general Ptolemy (played by Anthony Hopkins), in his old age as king of Egypt, who as he dictates his official history of Alexander to his secretary Cadmus (David Bedella), nevertheless offers an insider's details, in much the same way as Robert Graves' Roman emperor Claudius in the well-known novels. Such a device provides exposition and can bridge gaps; the film can omit or merely refer to some important events in Alexander's life, while depicting others.[9] There is also a certain degree of historical and dramatic neatness. Ptolemy's history, although lost, was a dominant part of the ancient Alexander tradition; likewise, Ptolemy's "unofficial" version offers Stone a good opportunity for imaginative, dramatic speculation. It is perhaps not surprising that *Alexander's* Ptolemy says nothing which appears either in attested fragments of the real Ptolemy Soter's history of Alexander, or in Arrian, for whom Ptolemy was a major source. The line between what Cadmus is supposed to be writing down and what is off the record is deliberately blurred. Cadmus himself is a fictitious creation – a kind of scholar's joke on Lane Fox's part,[10] which underscores the artificial nature of the film. Stone and Lane Fox are reminding the audience that *Alexander* is entertainment.

However, there are inevitable and obvious historical inaccuracies in both Le Brun's and Stone's visions of the Macedonian conqueror. The historicity of Le Brun's paintings, and especially his debt to the ancient writers, will be discussed further on in this chapter; suffice to say for now that we can highlight anachronisms in weaponry, equipment and costume. Le Brun's Persians are a mixture: they sometimes wear turbans, sometimes appear dressed in flowing tunics or Greek-style chitons. Also, in keeping with early modern European artistic portrayals of ancient military dress, Alexander and his Macedonians wear tunics, cuirasses, and helmets that often look more generically Roman than Greek. Ancient iconographical sources on the Persians were even more limited; there were some descriptions of Persian dress, accessories, and regalia in literary sources like Herodotus, Curtius, and Xenophon. But western knowledge of the remains of the great Achaemenid palace complex at Persepolis, with its carved reliefs of kings, nobles, and tribute-bearers,

---

[8] Allen 2003: 13.

[9] See Crowdus 2005: 12.

[10] Lane Fox 2004: 25. In Greek legendary tradition, Cadmus brought the alphabet to Greece from Phoenicia.

lay a century in the future;[11] likewise the Alexander Mosaic – a major iconographical source for Macedonian and Persian weaponry and dress – was not discovered until 1831.[12] Although Le Brun himself endorsed the principle of artistic freedom, he was also interested in reproducing authentic details.[13] Our ancient writers tell us that the Persians were great archers and that the Great King's costume was purple and white; in Le Brun's painting of the *Battle of Arbela*, the Persian King Darius, perched high in his elaborate chariot, carries a bow and wears blue and white. In 1719 the Abbé Dubos commented that for his depiction of Alexander in *The Queens of Persia* Le Brun had based his portrait on a medal which had been inscribed with the Macedonian's name on the back, but which in fact was a head of the Roman goddess Minerva. According to Dubos, Le Brun realized his error and gave subsequent depictions of Alexander a more masculine appearance, using a bust from Alexandria that was on display at Versailles.[14]

Unlike Le Brun, Stone's team had the benefit of being able to draw on a considerable body of archaeological research, and for the most part, the film does try to create an authentic look. There are pure flights of fancy – such as the paintings decorating the walls of Philip II's secret cavern, where the king supposedly initiates the young prince into ancient mythological traditions. The cavern scene was Stone's own contribution and, typically, he also had a considerable part in drafting the film's script.[15] Also again, given how frequently Stone explores the protagonist's often tortuous relationship with parents or parental figures,[16] it is perhaps not surprising that one of *Alexander*'s central themes is the king's relationship with his parents, especially his passionate, snake-loving mother, Olympias. It is no coincidence that we see a grinning Medea dispatching her children in one scene on the cave wall.

Elsewhere, *Alexander* displays conflation and blatant changes in locations and personalities, which mostly seem to have been due to artistic whim, pragmatic concerns, and financial considerations. Historically, Antigonus, one of Alexander's

---

[11]   The first European expedition was by the Danish scholar Carsten Niebuhr (1733–1815) who was part of a Danish and Swedish team. Niebuhr's journey to Persia and the Near East lasted around seven years, from 1761 to 1767 and, remarkably, he was the only survivor – even the local guides who accompanied the Europeans died from infections.

[12]   See Cohen 1997: 1.

[13]   During the 1660s several acrimonious disputes took place at the Royal Academy of Painting and Sculpture over what was appropriate for depiction in history painting, one example of which were the debates between Le Brun and several colleagues over whether Poussin should have included camels in his painting of a story from the Scriptures, *Israelites Gathering Manna in the Desert*. Le Brun defended Poussin's decision to omit the animals on artistic grounds; however, when pushed in a second debate, he went back to the text of the Old Testament and claimed that as the camels were not mentioned in the camp of the Israelites, Poussin's exclusion of them had not broken the letter of the Bible (see Bryson 1981: 32–3). For an introduction to the Academy's perception of artistic guidelines for its professional practitioners, see Duro 1997: 1–17.

[14]   See Duro 1997: 78–9; Gareau 1992: 110.

[15]   Stone won early acclaim for his screenplay work – an Academy Award for *Midnight Express* (1978) – and his films are usually written or co-written by him (see Kunz 1997: xii).

[16]   Kunz 1997: xvi.

marshals and a contemporary of his father, Philip II, was left as satrap of Phrygia from 333 until Alexander's death. He never accompanied Alexander on much of his conquests of the Persian empire and India, but became a powerful player in the wars of the Successors after the king's death. In Stone's film, Antigonus is with Alexander throughout. Why? Simply because the director liked the idea of a one-eyed general – it adds to the film's ambiance.[17] Ironically, there was a historical character who was also one-eyed, and who did go on the expedition. His name was Antigenes, but he was not as senior a marshal as Antigonus.[18] Second, Stone's team used two Dutch Friesian horses to play the part of Bucephalas, Alexander's stallion. The standard color of the Friesian breed is black (we are told by Arrian (5.19.6) that Bucephalas was black), but characterized by "feathered" legs (long, trailing hair around the fetlocks), so typical of heavier northern European types. Feathered legs do not appear in any ancient equine iconography – not even on the stocky Persian Nisaean. However, Dutch Friesians are hardy, sweet-natured, and reliable animals – all highly desirable qualities on film location, and they look wonderful on screen.

Finally and perhaps more revealing is this: according to Lane Fox, *Alexander*'s budget allowed for only two set-piece battles. Stone wanted a contrast between the two clashes in terms of location, style of fighting, and spectacle.[19] So they chose Alexander's final battle against Darius at Gaugamela (as opposed to Granicus or Issus) for the spectacle of an open plains confrontation between two large armies, supposedly totaling over 100,000 (in reality, the human element was supplied by the main cast and about 1,500 extras from the Moroccan army – the rest were digitally created). The other battle had to be completely different, and India seemed an obvious choice (the film location was actually Thailand). Stone conflates the battle against the Indian rajah Porus on the Hydaspes river in 326 with Alexander's near-fatal wounding during the Macedonian assault on a Malli fortress near the Hydraotes in 325. Instead of alluvial plain, Stone's battle takes place in thick, eerie jungle (which recalls the director's Vietnam masterpiece, *Platoon*), in patchy, broken light, and with Porus's elephant force, carrying howdahs and garish decorations, emerging suddenly like nightmarish monsters. It is visually very impressive and very dramatic, but hardly history. Interestingly, the climax of the engagement – Alexander on Bucephalas lunging at Porus on his elephant vividly recalls an actual piece of ancient fiction, expressed in both the famous Porus medallions and the *Alexander Romance* – that the Macedonian and the Indian prince fought a personal duel.[20]

---

[17] Lane Fox 2004: 159.

[18] On Antigenes the One-Eyed, see Plu. *Alex.* 70.4–6; cf. *Mor.* 339c. He was one of Philip II's men, who had lost his eye at the siege of Perinthus long before, in 340; in the *Moralia* the name is given as Atarrhias. Both men were hypaspist officers who were promoted to command late in 331 (Curt. 5.2.5). I am grateful to A. B. Bosworth for access to his forthcoming commentary on Arrian, vol. iii, 7.5.2 *ad loc.*

[19] Lane Fox 2004: 99.

[20] See Baynham 1995; Bosworth 1996: 6–8; on the Porus medallions see more recently Holt 2003. There is also a secondary tradition in Arrian (5.14.4–5) that Alexander and Bucephalas were both wounded (fatally in Bucephalas' case) by Porus' son.

Figure 16.1 Charles Le Brun, *The Family of Darius before Alexander* (detail), *c*.1660. Versailles, Chateaux de Versailles et de Trianon. Photo © RMN/Gérard Blot.

Figure 16.2 Charles Le Brun, *The Triumph of Alexander*. Louvre, Paris. Photo © RMN/Daniel Arnaudet/Gérard Blot.

However, both Le Brun and Stone owe a considerable debt to the ancient historical sources, for all that they adapted the material to suit their own interpretations.
The relationship between the ancient texts and the artist is one theme I wish to
explore in this chapter. It should be acknowledged here that Le Brun's composition
was also heavily influenced by the work of other artists. One art historian has
described the *Battles of Alexander* series as "enormous pastiches," drawn from the
work of painters like Pietro da Cortona or Rubens.[21] Le Brun's design and the
arrangement of his figures in his *Battle of Arbela* is similar to Cortona's *Victory over
Darius* (*c.*1640)[22] and in particular two details stand out; an eagle, representing
Zeus' favor (mentioned by Plutarch and Curtius[23]) flies above Alexander's head in
the middle of the fighting in both works, and Le Brun's fleeing Persian, looking
back over his shoulder in horror on the far right, mimics a young man running in
front of Darius' chariot in Cortona's painting. The eagle's iconographic appeal has
continued in modern times. In Stone's *Alexander* the bird becomes something of a
symbol of Alexander himself, or at least his good fortune. At Gaugamela the eagle
soars and the camera and the eagle become one; thus offering the audience a spectacular aerial view of the battlefield, which enables us to appreciate both the scope
of an ancient clash and its chaos. As Alexander's fortune declines, the eagle ceases
to follow him (it disappears as the army prepares to cross the Hindu Kush into
India); finally, when an aging Olympias realizes Alexander is dead, an eagle and a
snake, locked together in a struggle outside her window, fatally wound each other
and crash to the ground.

But it is unlikely that Le Brun and his contemporaries viewed derivation from
existing works in the negative way that we do. In Le Brun's famous lecture to the
Academy on the *Expression of the Passions*, which the artist presented most likely
in 1668, he happily lifts entire passages from René Descartes's *Traité sur les
passions de l'ane* without apparent formal acknowledgment.[24] *Imitatio* – as with
the ancient world – meant that one alluded to or borrowed from one's peers
(and played on the audience's recognition of the parallels), but ideally one also
surpassed one's predecessors. An assessment of Le Brun's overall originality is
beyond my focus, however; it is also evident that in particular paintings the artist
either showed adaptation of certain details which are attested in the ancient
traditions, but which do not seem to appear in other artists' work (like the elephant
in *Alexander's Entry into Babylon*[25]) or else were inspired by the written sources –
as in his brilliant and subtle demonstration of the friendship between Alexander
and Hephaestion.

---

[21] See Allen 2003: 140; cf. the comments by the French critic, P. Marcel, "tableaux de chevalet dému-
surés et confus," in Posner 1959: 237 with n. 4.

[22] See Briganti 1962: 81; Frommel and Schütze 1998: 70.

[23] Plu. *Alex.* 33.2–3; Curt. 4.15.26–7.

[24] On the lecture's date, see Montagu 1994: 141–3; see also 157–62 for the relevant extracts from
Descartes's work alongside corresponding sections from Le Brun's lecture.

[25] See below, p. 308.

A subsidiary theme in this discussion is the motif of passion, both as a physical expression of emotion and in a more broadly romantic sense – which is particular to both Le Brun's work and the film *Alexander*. Passion both drives and destroys Stone's protagonist; jealous Roxane, feeling secure because of her pregnancy, strikes at the man whom Alexander loves most, while his restless, relentless desire for conquest eventually exhausts even his most loyal followers, causing them to murder him (at least in old Ptolemy's account to Cadmus – which he tells his scribe not to record). My last concern is the question of patronage, and the extent to which an artistic vision is driven by the desires of the paymaster. *Alexander*'s projected budget was US$150 million, and its funding was raised from a wide range of sources, including US, British, French, German, and Japanese investors.[26] Stone's task was to make money – and both the film's producer, Moritz Borman, and Warner Brothers studio seem to have had different ideas from the director as to box office appeal. One of *Alexander*'s more notorious aspects, at least in popular opinion, was its emphasis on the king's bisexuality. In fact, the movie is quite coy – expressing the sexual relationship between Hephaestion and Alexander merely through manly hugs, soulful looks, or the occasional romantic remark – the actual sex scenes, such as Philip's rape of Olympias or Alexander's wedding night, are rough and aggressively heterosexual. In a recent article in *Cineaste*, Stone was asked whether he had to cut any of the homoerotic material and replied, "I wasn't forced to cut anything. There was some Bagoas stuff that we trimmed, but it wasn't crucial and it distracted from the more important relationship with Hephaestion."[27]

We know from Curtius that Bagoas was a young Persian eunuch and a concubine of Darius, whom Alexander took into his entourage after the surrender of one of Darius' generals and assassins, Nabarzanes. According to Curtius (6.5.22, 10.1.26–8) he became Alexander's lover, and a highly influential figure at court. There is some evidence (Plu. *Alex.* 67.6–7) suggesting that Alexander's relationship with the beautiful youth was not only well known to his Macedonian followers but approved; at a dancing contest in Carmania, Bagoas won a prize and the Macedonians, cheering loudly, called upon the king to kiss the victor. Bagoas appears in the film in a non-speaking role, and there is only a hint of any sexual relationship between the king and his Persian servant. Anything more explicit was abandoned possibly due to studio pressure about US audience reaction, but in denying the sexuality of Bagoas the film appears to have followed a similar, censorious, path as W. W. Tarn, who effectively tried to write Bagoas out of history (see Ogden, ch. 11).[28]

As First Painter to Louis XIV, Le Brun perhaps had the greater artistic freedom in the realization of his vision and the ideas of his patrons, Louis's powerful minister and Le Brun's chief supporter, Jean Baptiste Colbert, and ultimately the king himself. It is difficult to know whether Le Brun's patrons were highly prescriptive.

---

[26]   US$11 million was also needed for pre-production expenses; see Lane Fox 2004: 59, 60–2.

[27]   Crowdus 2005: 23.

[28]   See Tarn ii. 319–29, esp. 320–3. Tarn's views were refuted by Badian in a ground-breaking article (Badian 1958b).

He would have had to present a portfolio of preliminary sketches for approval, and the lavish, romantic tone of the artist's *Alexander* series is consistent with the way the Macedonian is portrayed in contemporary literary works, like Racine's *Alexandre le grand* – as we shall see. But how much Racine was influenced by Le Brun – or how much both men were left to express the monarch's general propaganda, as opposed to being given specific directions, is hard to determine. Apparently the young Louis XIV went *chaque jour* (daily) to visit Le Brun's studio at Fontainebleau when he was working on his first royal commission, *The Queens of Persia before Alexander*,[29] and certainly there are examples elsewhere of a patron's intrusion. We have detailed correspondence from the powerful and wealthy patron, Isabella d'Este (1466–1519) to the artist Pietro Perugino, commissioning a painting (*Battle of Love and Chastity*) based on Philostratus' *Eikones*, which carefully outlines her interpretation (or that of her humanists') of the text, and how she wanted the scene executed. She was clearly a patron who insisted on a lot of control. But even if Colbert or the Sun King had been as demanding – and the evidence suggests they were not[30] – there were ways in which the First Painter may have been able to modify their wishes, just as Perugino was able to (at least to some degree) with Isabella. She originally wanted "several thousand cupids," but Perugino's painting depicts fewer than twenty.[31]

However, it is significant that Le Brun himself was given his letters of nobility in 1662 shortly after he was appointed to the position of First Painter. This post meant that the incumbent was responsible for all paintings and decoration undertaken by the crown for the adornment of royal residences – which for Le Brun included the redecoration of the Louvre, the king's chateau at Marly, and the palace of Versailles. He was also made director of the Gobelins factory, which was commissioned with producing tapestries, furniture, and metalwork for the King. When Le Brun was put in charge, the factory had a staff of about 200 weavers and fifty painters; this number increased considerably, especially as the expansion and decoration of Versailles got under way.[32] Colbert was apparently extremely deferential to Le Brun, and certain contemporaries refer to the First Painter as having established a kind of tyranny, due to Colbert's unwavering support. Although some artists did work independently for Louis, Le Brun became an important patron in his own right and it was difficult for artists who were not on good terms with him (such as his great rival Pierre Mignard) to get commissions.[33]

Thus, while one reason for the formation of the Royal Academy for Painting and Sculpture in 1648 was to allow artists control over their own work, the Academy under Colbert and Louis XIV also became an instrument of the state cultural

---

[29] See Pericolo 2004: 274; cf. Duro 1997: 81; Allen 2003: 137.

[30] Burke 1992: 54.

[31] Le Goff 2006: ch. 2.

[32] Bryson 1981: 30–1.

[33] The famous Italian sculptor Bernini described Colbert deferring to Le Brun as though the latter were "his mistress": see Burke 1992: 54–6 with nn. 27–8.

apparatus.[34] Le Brun's task was to please his superiors and, provided he did that, he seems to have been left to get on with it, and this is amply supported by his long tenure in office. He did not lose influence until Colbert died; even then, he retained his title as First Painter, although Colbert's successor elevated Mignard and Le Brun himself retired from court in 1688.

It might be helpful to set Le Brun's work within a broader historical context. A. B. Bosworth once commented to me that when the world had produced one megalomaniac (such as Alexander the Great), it was inevitable that another would try to imitate and surpass him. Roman generals like Pompey and Julius Caesar were credited with some celebrated instances of Alexander *imitatio*, as were several Roman emperors, and Alexander became a cultural myth in Roman literature.[35] With a monarch like Louis XIV of France, whose famous epithet, the "Sun King," does not suggest a shy or reclusive figure, we are in truly ostentatious territory in relation to identification with the Macedonian conqueror. Louis XIV's association with past heroes did not stop with Alexander; at various times he was also called "a new Augustus (finding Paris brick and leaving it marble), a new Charlemagne, a new Clovis, a new Constantine, a new Justinian (codifying the law), a new St. Louis, a new Solomon and a new Theodosius (for destroying the heresy of the Protestants)."[36]

While the promotion of Alexander the Great in literature and art at Louis's court in the seventeenth century is hardly a new or unexplored area, the Macedonian king's popularity as an artistic subject from the fifteenth to the seventeenth centuries is striking. This was a time when Europe was dominated by great dynastic monarchies in the countries holding the balance of power, which were not only embroiled in interminable religious conflicts but were also (directly or indirectly) contesting the rich opportunities offered in the New World, the African continent, and the Far East. During the seventeenth century, there was something like only seven years of peace in France alone.

The aristocracy, princes, and *condottieri,* in addition to their own education, were surrounded by humanists and *cortegiani* who were themselves steeped in the Classical revival of the Renaissance and who often offered Classical parallels to flatter their patrons. Thus within such a world of autocrats, aristocracy, and virtual continuous warfare, it is perhaps not surprising that Alexander provided inspiration for the court painters and poets of powerful European (mostly French and Italian) royal and noble families.

Alexander as the great conqueror, particularly his magnificent triumphs over Darius and the Persians, offered an obvious field of representation; a relatively early example is Albrecht Aldörfer's (1480–1538) portrayal of Alexander and the Persian Great King at the battle of Issus, now in the Munich Pinakothek. Other aspects of Alexander's life were portrayed, the artists at times deriving inspiration directly

---

[34]   Duro 1997: 82; Allen 2003: 17.
[35]   See Spencer 2002; also ch. 14.
[36]   Burke 1992: 35.

from the historical traditions. Raphael (1483–1520) executed a wall painting depicting Alexander ordering his copy of the *Iliad* to be stored in Darius' precious casket that was part of the booty captured from Issus (Plu. *Alex.* 26.1); although in this interpretation, the artist's emphasis is more on the king and his anxious attendants than on the appropriately ostentatious box. Alexander's apparent courtly or heroic ethics and chivalry were also celebrated: hence the painting now in the Louvre by Domenico Zampieri (1581–1641) showing Alexander's compassionate treatment of Timocleia, the Theban noblewoman who was raped by a Thracian soldier and who consequently pushed her assailant down a well (Plu. *Alex.* 12.3–4).[37]

Louis XIV lavished enormous expenditure on the arts and his reign was particularly rich in culture. Like his predecessors, the king fostered theatrical and literary talent, taking into his service actors and playwrights like Molière, Jean Racine, and Pierre Corneille. La Fontaine was appointed as First Poet. Le Brun was the king's senior by some twenty years and had already earned the patronage of Louis's mother, Anne of Austria, and of Cardinal Mazarin. According to Le Brun's pupil and earliest biographer, Claude Nivelon (*Vie de Charles Le Brun et description détaillée de ses ouvrages*, fol. 145)[38] the artist successfully realized a religious dream which the queen had had on canvas (*Christ on the Cross Surrounded by Angels*), which in turn brought the artist other commissions from not only the queen mother herself but also from other wealthy French nobles.

However, it should also be noted that Le Brun, himself the son of a well-known sculptor, began his career at a much earlier age when his work was noticed by Chancellor Séguier; he also received recommendation from the great Nicholas Poussin who at the time held the position of First Painter to Louis XIII. In 1648 Le Brun, at the age of 29, founded the French Royal Academy of Painting and Sculpture, an organization that broke away from the old institution of La Maitrise, with its innate conservatism and restricted membership.[39] Le Brun also decorated the sumptuous palace of France's minister for finance, Nicolas Fouquet at Vaux-le-Vicomte. Fouquet had spent four years and over 18 million francs building his dream home, at a time when the annual revenue of the country was about 30 million francs. According to a famous anecdote, Louis XIV was so outraged by his minister's extravagance that he decided to arrest him at his own house-warming party but was persuaded by his mother that such a gesture was not appropriate behavior for a guest;[40] however, Fouquet was arrested a few days later and spent the rest of his life in prison. Like Alexander's general Philotas or Henry VIII's Cardinal Wolsey, Fouquet discovered it was dangerous to upstage a king.

The Queens of Persia before Alexander, or *The Tent of Darius* as it is alternatively known, is one of Le Brun's most famous and influential paintings, which did much

---

[37] There is another version of the same episode by Pietro della Vecchia (*c.*1640); see Spencer 2002: 40.

[38] Gareau 1992: 23 with n. 15; cf. Pericolo 2004: 278–81.

[39] Jouin 1889: 69; Allen 2003: 124ff.

[40] Gareau 1992: 28–9; cf. Allen 2003: 134.

to secure his favor with the king; it was most likely commissioned at his palace of Fontainebleau in 1660, a year before Louis assumed direct control of the throne, which he did when he was about 21. The painting displays Alexander's encounter with Darius' family who were taken captive at Issus in 333, and his respect for them. The story was well represented in the Alexander traditions, with a surprising degree of corroboration in detail between at least three sources.[41] Arrian (2.12.7) includes the vulgate version (given by Curtius and Diodorus) as a *logos* (a tale) but explicitly says he approves of Alexander's conduct. The gist of the episode is that after the battle of Issus, the young conqueror, attended by his best friend and probable lover Hephaestion, visited the captive royal family in their tent, which had been placed behind the line of the Persian king's army. Darius III had taken his family along when he went on campaign, possibly because his hold on the throne was insecure, and he feared that they might have been seized as hostages during his absence.[42]

According to the tradition, the Persian queen mother, Sisygambis, mistook Hephaestion for Alexander because he was the taller, and performed obeisance to him. When her mistake was pointed out, the elderly lady in her confusion and horror tried to bow to Alexander, but he picked her up and, indicating Hephaestion, said, "You did not make a mistake mother; for this man is Alexander too" ("Non errasti," inquit, "mater; nam et hic Alexander est": Curt. 3.12.17).

This scene had been portrayed earlier by Paolo Veronese, the sixteenth-century Italian decorative artist, and Le Brun would almost certainly have known the painting, although there were several other artists' interpretations of the scene.[43] Veronese located the meeting in a palace. Oliver Stone visualized the occasion in Babylon, gives Sisygambis' role to Darius' daughter, and conflates their meeting with Alexander's historically attested encounter in 326 with another monarch, the Indian king Porus – where Alexander asks how Porus would like to be treated – to which the latter replies, "Like a king." Evidently Stone did not want to waste an aphorism that had enthralled Arrian and Plutarch,[44] but his focus (as noted earlier) in the Indian battle was on Alexander's desire to rally his frightened men by attacking Porus personally. Porus is the enemy in this context (as he is in the *Alexander Romance*); there is to be no reconciliation.

For his own version of the encounter between Alexander and Darius' family, Le Brun followed the ancient historical tradition and used the setting of a tent (see fig. 16.1). The tent of the royal women is a fairly modest affair, lashed to a tree on its left corner, which in turn forms a backdrop for Hephaestion and Alexander as they

[41] See D.S. 17.37.3–38.7; Curt. 3.12.1–26; Plu. *Alex.* 21; Just. 11.9.12–16. On the tradition, see Bosworth 1980b: 220–2; Atkinson 1980: 248–9.
[42] Badian 2000a: 82–3.
[43] Caravaggio depicted the episode in brown ink and brown wash in the late sixteenth century, in *Alexander and the Family of Darius and Scene with Prisoners*; Pierre Mignard, Le Brun's great rival, also painted his own version in 1689: see Posner 1959: 237 n. 3.
[44] Arr. 5.19.2; Plu. *Alex.* 60.14–15. See Bosworth 1995: 308–10.

approach from the viewer's left. In the far left corner of the painting, Le Brun partially depicts another tent, larger and more richly decorated (presumably the Great King's field quarters). It is debatable whether the artist could have known how elaborate an Achaemenid royal pavilion would have been. Athenaeus quotes Chares (*FGrH* 81 F41), one of Alexander's courtiers, on the Susa marriage tents, which were said to be even more extravagant than those of the Persians. It is possible that these descriptions were brought to the First Painter's notice. But he also brings other imaginative insights to the picture. The painting was described in 1663 by the Royal Academy's scribe André Félibien, whose pamphlet did much to enhance its fame. More importantly, since the painting has now lost much of its original color, tiny detail, and texture through cleaning, Félibien's commentary offers valuable information.[45]

Hephaestion in a red cloak stands on the left, a little behind Alexander, and the Persian queen mother remains bowed down in front of him. Alexander appears to be directing his attention to the younger women and, as Félibien noted, Le Brun toned down his colors because he did not want the viewer distracted by too much brightness.[46] Further to this, art historians have pointed out that the direction of the light actually falls not upon the rich red of Hephaestion's cloak, but on the lighter, softer colors – the blues, apricots, and pinks of Darius' womenfolk.[47] Darius' wife Stateira holds her young son Ochus in her arms (see Curt. 3.11.24, 12.17; D.S. 17.36.2); both of them look pleadingly at Alexander. Le Brun's Persian women are deliberate portrayals of particular emotions or passions.[48] Darius' two daughters kneel beside Stateira; one wipes her eyes on her dress and the other anxiously joins her hands in supplication. Behind them are handmaidens in turbans and eunuchs; one of the latter lies prostrate in the foreground with his forehead in the dust.[49]

However, the painting works on a deeper level than mere depiction of emotion. The composition emphasizes the ideal of the hero and, in particular, Alexander's generosity, magnanimity, self-control or *continentia*, and especially his *clementia*. Alexander did not rape or kill his suppliants, especially those of high rank. In particular, as the Romans knew well, *clementia* underscores power. *Clementia*, or the capacity to bestow mercy was the trait of a monarch; it implied one man's elevated position above others. Le Brun may have taken some of his inspiration from Quintus Curtius' description of the episode, but even with direct attestation, it is always difficult to know how much an artist consulted the sources directly, as opposed to merely receiving paraphrased material from others. Certainly Curtius' history was

[45] Gareau 1992: 196; Montagu 1994: 43 with n. 63; Duro 1997: 79. Félibien's pamphlet, *Les Reines des Perses aux pieds d'Alexandre, peinture du Cabinet du Roy* (Paris, 1663), was translated into English as early 1703 by William Parsons, who explains in his preface that he has included both French and English texts, "since it [French] is of late Years become as Universal as its Monarch would be." Louis XIV was still alive at that time. Unfortunately I have not been able to consult Félibien's other works first-hand.

[46] Gareau 1992: 197; Duro 1997: 78.

[47] Duro 1997: 79.

[48] Allen 2003: 137–8; Gareau 1992: 196.

[49] Félibien 1663, cited in Gareau 1992: 196; cf. Parsons 1703: 11.

available in French translation at least as early as 1614 (Le Brun was born in 1619),[50] and Arrian and Plutarch were translated even earlier. Elsewhere, Le Brun seems to show relatively detailed knowledge of other ancient sources like Josephus.[51] Moreover, Félibien attended a lot of the Academy's lectures and recorded the discussion of its members afterward, which tended to touch on a range of topics, from theoretical and technical questions to the biblical Scriptures, other literature, and higher aesthetic issues. Assuming that Félibien has given us a faithful representation of the table-talk, it is clear that Le Brun and his colleagues were well educated and erudite men. If Le Brun had read Curtius himself, he would have known that Alexander's display of *continentia* and *clementia* inspired a rhetorical flourish from the historian where he says that Alexander was at a high point of his virtue; at that time he outshone all previous kings in self-control and clemency; the tragedy was that as his reign and triumphs increased he was unable to resist being corrupted by his good fortune.[52]

Le Brun's message thus becomes intriguingly ambivalent: he is flattering his patron Louis by emphasizing the power and virtue of kingship, particularly at a time when that young man was planning to assume absolute control himself,[53] yet at the same time he is also sending a warning. Whether or not Quatorze ever read Curtius is unknown (he seems to have recommended Justin to be put on the school curriculum for his son by his mistress),[54] *The Queens of Per*sia impressed the king sufficiently enough for him to make Le Brun the official master of all court iconography – much in the same way that the Roman emperor Augustus extolled Virgil and Horace as court poets. As we saw earlier, Augustus offered another parallel for the Sun King; Racine's dedication to his (1665) play *Alexandre le grand* admonishes Louis "that history is full of young conquerors and that much more unusual is the accession of a king who at the age of Alexander behaves like an Augustus."[55]

Despite the idealism (which is a feature of Le Brun's work and partly dictated by contemporary artistic principles), there is also subtle symbolism, particularly in expression and gesture. Alexander's open hand reveals his clemency, while the other, resting on Hephaestion, shows that he is a favorite.[56] Moreover, the artist has allowed his audience to see how Sisygambis could make a mistake; in short, the viewer has to figure out who Alexander is.[57] The two men are dressed in similar

[50]   According to the Library of Congress catalog, a translation of Curtius by N. Seguier was published in French and Latin in 1614; Vaugelas' Latin text with Freinsheim's supplements, translated into French by M. du Ryer in 1665 appears to have been more popular; it was reissued in Paris in 1668, 1680, 1681, 1682, and again in Amsterdam (its original place of publication) in 1684 and 1699. On the textual transmission of Curtius in general, see Baynham 1998a: 2–5.
[51]   Joseph. *AJ* 2.5; see Montagu 1994: 46 with n. 85.
[52]   Curt. 3.12.18–25; see Baynham 1998a: 125–8.
[53]   Duro 1997: 80.
[54]   See Angliviel de La Baumelle 1752: i. 121–5; also Ranum and Ranum 1972: 105ff.
[55]   Burke 1992: 37; see also 196–7.
[56]   Félibien 1663, cited in Gareau 1992: 196; see also Parsons 1703: 11.
[57]   Bryson 1981: 53.

costumes; Hephaestion wears a scarlet cloak, whereas Alexander's is a lighter shade ("carnation" in Félibien's description), but embroidered with a gold border, and his cuirass is silver.[58] Hephaestion is a little taller (again as our sources tell us);[59] nevertheless, Le Brun has also cleverly signaled he is not the king. According to Félibien, Alexander's cloak is fastened with a clasp of diamonds, whereas Hephaestion wears an agate cameo bearing Alexander's portrait. Alexander is his beloved, which also recalls Plutarch's comment (*Alex.* 47.10) that whereas Craterus was *philobasileus* ("lover of the king"), Hephaestion was *philalexandros* ("lover of Alexander").

La Fontaine celebrated Le Brun as France's Apelles, thus playing on one of Alexander's best-known artists, but allusions to the Macedonian king had been fashionable from when Louis was still a child; as early as 1639 the Dauphin's birth was welcomed as that of "a new Alexander" and even in 1672 when Louis was about 34, he was celebrated as "the invincible Alexander" as France was faring well in war against the Dutch at the time.[60]

But it is significant that the greatest period of Alexander's promotion falls mostly within the 1660s and early 1670s, the first ten years or so of Louis's personal reign, when the king was still in his twenties. In addition to *The Queens of Persia*, Le Brun painted four other episodes: *The Passage of the Granicus*, *The Battle of Arbela*, *The Defeat of Porus*, and *Alexander's Entrance into Babylon*. Alexander was an attractive and pertinent symbol: the identification of youth, display, and conquest offered paramount opportunities for comparison. And that which was not strictly historical could be adapted in the interests of audience entertainment and aesthetic propriety, where a higher priority was placed on verisimilitude rather than accuracy.

The French nobility valued glory, both military and amorous. Thus in contemporary dramatic productions Alexander was portrayed (somewhat incongruously, it might seem to us) as much an ardent lover as a great general. For instance, in Racine's *Alexandre le grand*, the king, following a victory, rushes off the battlefield to seek out the coy queen Cléofile (Cleophis of the historical traditions) and, declaring his passion, protests that she fails to understand his violent desire for her (III. vi. 883–4). At a later point in the text, he assures her that he will be back to see her after another "another victory" ("Encore une victoire, je reviens, Madame . . .": V. i. 1348).[61]

Alexander was more than a role model for Louis – at times there was outright identification. Some scholars have pointed to the contemporary political allegories inherent between Racine's *Alexandre* and the Sun King; moreover Louis actually performed the role of Alexander in a production called *Le Ballet royal pour la naissance de Vénus* in 1665.[62] Also in 1665, the king finally persuaded the famous Italian

---

[58] Parsons 1703: 5.
[59] Curt. 3.12.17; cf. 6.5.29; D.S. 17.37.5.
[60] Ferrier-Caverivière 1981: 17 ("l'invincible Alexandre," 133).
[61] Racine 1990: III. vi. 911–12; cf. V. i. 1348; see also Hartle 1957: 389 with n. 8.
[62] Cf. Ferrier-Caverivière 1981: 67; Hartle 1957: 387.

sculptor Bernini to come to Paris to carve a portrait bust in marble (now at Versailles); from the start Bernini compared Louis's head to that of Alexander and expressed the allusion through physical and psychological affinities.[63]

Each of Le Brun's canvases is quite large. *The Queens of Persia* is nearly 3 m high by 4.5 m wide. Le Brun was often accorded a big wall to decorate – the dimensions of the gaudy *Triumph of Alexander* are 4.5 m by 7.07 m while those celebrating Alexander's battles, *The Passage of the Granicus*, *The Battle of Arbela*, and *Alexander and Porus* are all around 4.7 m by 12.6 m. The Alexander paintings were also produced as tapestries by the Gobelins. Perhaps because the features of Alexander also bore an idealized (if vague) resemblance to his own, Louis XIV insured that copies of the tapestries were given to his brother, to the Duc de Lorraine, to a minister of the king of Denmark, and to Mlle. de Montpensier.[64]

The Triumph of Alexander, or *Alexander's Entry into Babylon*, now in the Louvre depicts Alexander's march into Babylon when the Persian satrap Mazaeus surrendered the city in 331 (fig. 16.2). Its precise date is uncertain (some time between 1661 and 1665) but it was evidently painted quite rapidly. The extent to which Le Brun (as opposed to his staff) worked on its execution himself is debatable; the memoirs of the Academy of Painting record the artist as being heavily involved with the administration of the king's various decorative projects at the time.[65]

But as noted earlier, the concept was probably Le Brun's, and in many details he was again quite faithful to the sources, particularly Curtius (5.1.17–18) who testifies that the event was a carefully organized pageant. One notes the presence of the Hanging Gardens in the background (see Curt. 5.1.32–3), and the flowers and garlands which Bagophanes, guardian of the citadel, had strewn along the road (5.1.20). Although the elephant, with its ears decorated with jewels and richly caparisoned in blue and silver, pulling Alexander's chariot is not mentioned in Curtius, we know that elephants were part of the booty captured at the battle of Gaugamela (Arr. 3.15.6). However, probably more than any other painting in the Alexander series, *Alexander's Entry into Babylon* best expresses that grandeur and magnificence, calculated to overwhelm the viewer, which the king's court was so anxious to convey. Everything is so big in the *The Entry into Babylon* – even the rump of Hephaestion's horse. Likewise in Stone's *Alexander* the king's climactic entry into a reconstructed Babylon (both the Pinewood studio set and digital recreation) is lush and visually stunning, but here, unlike in Le Brun's version where a youthful Alexander, a little off-center, alone in a huge cream and gold chariot, dressed in gold and carrying a golden scepter, turns to face the viewer, Colin Farrell, his fellow actors, and the extras are dwarfed by the towering architecture. Babylon is a turning point in Alexander's fortunes. It is also where he died.

[63]   See Hibbard 1965: 176–8; cf. Cronin 1964: 155.
[64]   Hartle 1957: 90 n. 1.
[65]   Gareau 1992: 202.

The Passage of the Granicus (now in the Louvre) is another colossal work that was probably begun around the same time as *The Triumph of Alexander*. In addition to commemorating Alexander's military prowess, the painting is also interesting for what it reveals about Le Brun's artistic techniques and theories. The subject is Alexander's first battle against the combined Persian satrapal forces of Lydia, Ionia, and Hellespontine Phrygia. According to Arrian (1.13.2) and Plutarch (*Alex.* 16), the Persians had drawn up their line on the opposite bank of the river Granicus and, contrary to advice, Alexander immediately offered them battle, charging across the stream and up the opposite bank. Again, Le Brun has portrayed certain attested details like Alexander's white plumed helmet (Plu. *Alex.* 16). He also depicts the Persian horses heavily covered in blankets, a detail which he possibly obtained from Xenophon's descriptions.[66]

Le Brun's keen interest in facial expressions, demonstrated elsewhere by his specialized studies of anatomical configuration and by his famous lecture, is expressed here in the intense aggression of Alexander. In a poignant touch, even Bucephalas, either half-crazed by fear or his master's ardor, is shown biting Alexander's opponent Rhoesaces (often interpreted as Memnon in this painting) on the back. In the king's face we see the military *gloire* that the French court so passionately sought. Ironically, in another age, the DVD cover of *Alexander* shows a rearing Bucephalas with Farrell on its back in fierce battle cry, open-mouthed, displaying dazzlingly white teeth, and wearing a helmet shaped like Heracles' lion-skin cap.

Le Brun evidently planned other Alexander paintings, since a collection of preliminary sketches for subjects like the death of Darius' wife, the death of Darius, and Alexander and Coenus (i.e., the mutiny on the Hyphasis) was preserved among his folios. It is possible that he continued to give some attention to realizing the drawings on canvas throughout his long career, but was prevented or distracted by other projects.

However, it is also probably fair to say that the image of Alexander became time-expired. There were probably several reasons for this. Although as late as 1699 a magnificent display of fireworks staged by the municipality of Paris celebrated past heroic role models like Alexander and Charlemagne,[67] by about 1680 antiquity lost the importance that it had enjoyed earlier in the 1660s and 1670s, and Louis's image-makers relied less on allegory.[68] Not only, as he grew older, did Louis XIV want himself glorified, rather than identifying with another's glory, but his military campaigns were not always so successful. It is a sad reminder that by 1688 (the year before Le Brun died), the country's economy was so exhausted by war that Louis himself was forced to melt down much of his own gold and silver masterpieces, thereby destroying a large section of Le Brun's work. As a further irony, some years after Le Brun's death, the Gobelins factory was forced to shut down from 1694 to 1699.

[66] Xen. *Cyr.* 8.8.19.
[67] Burke 1992: 115.
[68] Burke 1992: 126, 131, 197.

Yet Le Brun's Alexander series survives: lavish, sweeping, colorful, cluttered, and romantic – to individual delight or distaste, but certainly as a legitimate part of the cultural heritage of France's Grand Siècle. The paintings were meant to be read as stories and although they can be appreciated by an uninformed viewer, they also function on a more sophisticated level. They demand a certain amount of attention, and reward the viewer who invests time in them. Stone's *Alexander* likewise deserves some consideration. However, it seems to have become the victim of *damnatio memoriae*, conspicuously absent from a montage of film clips at the 2006 Academy Awards that commemorated great historical personages, whose stories have been told on the wide screen. It remains to be seen whether *Alexander* will become a cinema classic or consigned to oblivion.

Bibliography

Aalders, G. J. D. 1961. "Germanicus und Alexander der Grosse." *Historia* 10: 382–4.

Abbott, J. 1848. *Alexander the Great.* New York.

Abdel el-Raqiz, M. 1984. *Die Darstellungen und texte des Sanktuars Alexanders des Grossen im Tempel von Luxor.* Deutsches Archäologisches Institut Kairo, Archäologische Veröffentlichungen 16. Cairo.

Adams, W. L. 2003. "The Episode of Philotas: An Insight," in Heckel and Tritle, 113–16.

Adams, W. L. 2006. "The Hellenistic Kingdoms," in Bugh, 28–51.

Adams, W. L., and E. N. Borza, eds. 1982. *Philip II, Alexander the Great, and the Macedonian Heritage.* Lanham, MD.

Adcock, F. E. 1957. *The Greek and Macedonian Art of War.* Berkeley, CA.

Africa, T. 1982. "Worms and the Death of Kings: A Cautionary Note on Disease and History." *CA* 1: 1–17.

Aharoni, Y., ed. 1981. *Arad Inscriptions.* Jerusalem.

Ahituv, S., and A. Yardeni. 2004. "Seventeen Aramaic Texts on Ostraka from Idumea: The Late Persian Period to the Early Hellenistic Periods." *Maarav* 11/1: 7–23.

Alcock, S. E. 1994. "Nero at Play? The Emperor's Grecian Odyssey," in Elsner and Masters, 98–111.

Alessandrì, S., ed. 1994. Ἱστορίη: *Studi offerti dagli allievi a G. Nenci in occasione del suo settantesimo compleanno.* Galatina, Italy.

Alfieri Tonini, T. 2002. "Basileus Alexandros," in Michelotto, 1–13.

Allen, C. 2003. *French Painting in the Golden Age.* London.

Alonso Troncoso, V. 1995. "Ultimatum et déclaration de guerre dans la Grèce classique," in *Les relations internationales: Actes du Colloque de Strasbourg 15–17 juin 1993.* Paris, 211–95.

Alonso Troncoso, V. 1997. Καθότι ἂν ἐπαγγέλωσιν – παοαγγέλωσιν: *Sobre una cláusula del derecho griego de los tratados,* in *Xaire: II reunión de historiadores del mundo griego antiguo (Sevilla, 18–21 de diciembre de 1995).* Seville, 181–91.

Alonso Troncoso, V. 2000. "La paideia del principe en el tiempo de los Diadocos." *AHB* 14: 22–34.

Alonso Troncoso, V. 2003a. *L'institution de l'hégémonie entre la coutume et le droit écrit*, in *Symposion 1999: Vorträge zur griechischen und hellenistichen Rechtsgeschichte, La Coruña 6–9 September 1999*. Cologne, 339–54.

Alonso Troncoso, V. 2003b. "La KOINH EIPHNH ateniese del 371 y el sistema griego de alianzas." *EC* 71: 353–77.

Amadasi-Guzzo, M. G. 1998. "L'Idumée entre la fin de l'epoque perse et la début de la période héllenistique: nouveaux ostraca araméens." *Orientalia* 67: 532–8. (Review article of Lemaire 1996 and Eph'al and Naveh 1996.)

Amandry, M., and S. Hurter, eds. 1999. *Travaux de numismatique grecque offerts à G. Le Rider*. London.

Ameilhon, M. 1766. *Histoire du commerce et de la navigation des Égyptiens sous le règne des Ptolémées*. Paris.

Ameling, W. 1988. "Alexander und Achilleus: Eine Bestandsaufnahme," in Will and Heinrichs, ii. 657–92.

Amigues, S. 2003. "Pour la table du Grand roi." *Journal des Savants*: 3–59.

Anderson, A. R. 1928. "Heracles and his Successors: A Study of a Heroic Ideal and the Recurrence of a Heroic Type." *HSCPh* 39: 7–58.

Andreae, B. 1977. *Das Alexandermosaik aus Pompeji*. Recklinghausen, Germany.

André, J. M. 1990. "Alexandre le Grand, modèle et repoussoir du prince (d'Auguste à Neron)," in Croisille, 11–24.

Andronikos, M. 1992. *Vergina: The Royal Tombs and the Ancient City*. Athens.

Aneziri, S. 2003. *Die Vereine der dionysischen Techniten im Kontext der hellenistischen Gesellschaft: Untersuchungen zur Geschichte, Organisation und Wirkung der hellenist-ischen Technitenvereine*. Stuttgart, Germany.

Angliviel de La Baumelle, L. 1752. *Lettres de Madame de Maintenon*. Nancy, France.

Anson, E. M. 1977. "The Siege at Nora: A Source Conflict." *GRBS* 18: 251–6.

Anson, E. M. 1989. "The Persian Fleet in 334." *CPh* 84: 44–9.

Anson, E. M. 1991. "The Evolution of the Macedonian Army Assembly (330–315 B.C.)." *Historia* 40: 230–47.

Anson, E. M. 2002–3. "The Dating of Perdiccas' Death and the Assembly at Triparadeisus." *GRBS* 43: 373–90.

Anson, E. M. 2004. *Eumenes of Cardia: A Greek among Macedonians*. Leiden.

Anson, E. M. 2005a. "Idumaean Ostraca and Early Hellenistic Chronology." *JAOS* 125: 263–6.

Anson, E. M. 2005b. "Note on the First Regnal Year of Philip III (Arrhidaeus)." *JCS* 57: 127–9.

Anson, E. M. 2006. "Dating the Deaths of Eumenes and Olympias." *AHB* 20: 1–8.

Anson, E. M. 2007. "Early Hellenistic Chronology: The Cuneiform Evidence," in Heckel et al., 193–8.

Archer, W. 1981. "The Paintings of the Casa dei Vettii in Pompeii." Ph.D. dissertation. University of Virginia.

Arnold-Biucchi, C. 2006. *Alexander's Coins and Alexander's Image*. Cambridge, MA.

Ashley, J. R. 1998. *The Macedonian Empire: The Era of Warfare under Philip II and Alexander the Great, 359–323 BC*. Jefferson, NC.

Ashton, N. G. 1983. "The Lamian War: A False Start?" *Antichthon* 17: 47–63.

Ashton, N. G. 1984. "The Lamian War – *stat magni nominis umbra*." *JHS* 104: 152–7.

Ashton, N. G. 1992. "Craterus from 324 to 321 B.C." *AM* 5: 125–31.

Ashton, R., and S. Hurter, eds. 1998. *Studies in Greek Numismatics in Memory of M. J. Price*. London.

Ashton, R. H. J., et al. 2002. "The Pixodarus Hoard (CH 9.241)," in Meadows and Wartenberg, 159–243.

Atkinson, J. E. 1980. *A Commentary on Q. Curtius Rufus'* Historiae Alexandri Magni *Books 3 and 4*. Amsterdam.

Atkinson, J. E. 1994. *A Commentary on Q. Curtius Rufus'* Historiae Alexandri Magni *Books 5 to 7.2*. Amsterdam.

Atkinson, J. E. 2000a. *Curzio Rufo, Storie di Alessandro Magno*. Milan.

Atkinson, J. E. 2000b. "Originality and its Limits in the Alexander Sources of the Early Empire," in Bosworth and Baynham, 307–25.

Auberger, J. 2001. *Historiens d'Alexandre*. Paris.

Aucello, E. 1957. "La politica dei Diadochi e l'ultimatum del 314 av. Cr." *RFIC* 35: 382–404.

Austin, M. M. 1981. *The Hellenistic World from Alexander to the Roman Conquest*. Cambridge.

Austin, M. M. 1986. "Hellenistic Kings, War and the Economy." *CQ* 36: 450–66.

Badian, E. 1958a. "Alexander the Great and the Unity of Mankind." *Historia* 7: 425–44.

Badian, E. 1958b. "The Eunuch Bagoas." *CQ* 8: 144–57.

Badian, E. 1960. "The Death of Parmenio." *TAPhA* 91: 324–38.

Badian, E. 1961. "Harpalus." *JHS* 81: 16–43.

Badian, E. 1963. "The Murder of Philip II." *Phoenix* 17: 244–50.

Badian, E. 1964. *Studies in Greek and Roman History*. Oxford.

Badian, E. 1966a. "Alexander the Great and the Greeks of Asia," in Badian 1966b, 37–69.

Badian, E., ed. 1966b. *Ancient Society and Institutions: Studies Presented to Victor Ehrenberg on his 75th birthday*. Oxford.

Badian, E. 1967. "Agis III." *Hermes* 95: 170–92.

Badian, E., ed. 1976a. *Alexandre le Grand: image et réalité*. Geneva.

Badian, E. 1976b. "A Comma in the History of Samos." *ZPE* 23: 289–94.

Badian, E. 1977. "A Document from Artaxerxes IV?" in Kinzl, 40–50.

Badian, E. 1981. "The Deification of Alexander the Great," in Dell, 27–71.

Badian, E. 1987. "Alexander and Peucelaotis." *CQ* 37: 117–28.

Badian, E. 1994. "Agis III: Revisions and Reflections," in Worthington 1994b, 258–92.

Badian, E. 1999. "A Note on the 'Alexander Mosaic,'" in Titchener and Moorten, 75–92.

Badian, E. 2000a. "Conspiracies," in Bosworth and Baynham, 50–95.

Badian, E. 2000b. "Darius III." *HSCPh* 100: 241–68.

Baker, H. D., and M. Jursa, eds. 2005. *Approaching the Babylonian Economy*. AOAT 330. Münster.

Balcer, J. M. 1978. "Alexander's Burning of Persepolis." *IA* 13: 119–33.

Balsdon, J. P. V. D. 1950. "The Divinity of Alexander the Great." *Historia* 1: 363–88; repr. in Griffith 1966: 179–204.

Bar-Kochva, B. 1976. *The Seleucid Army*. Cambridge.

Bartlett, J. R. 1999. "Edomites and Idumeans." *PEQ* 131: 102–14.

Barzanò, A., C. Bearzot, F. Landucci, L. Prandi, and G. Zecchini, eds. 2003. *Modelli eroici dall'antichità alla cultura europea*. Rome.

Baynham, E. J. 1994. "Antipater: Manager of Kings," in Worthington 1994b, 331–56.

Baynham, E. J. 1995. "Who Put the Romance in the Alexander Romance?" *AHB* 9: 1–13.

Baynham, E. J. 1998a. *Alexander the Great: The Unique History of Quintus Curtius*. Ann Arbor, MI.

Baynham, E. J. 1998b. "Why didn't Alexander Marry before Leaving Macedonia? Observations on Factional Politics at Alexander's Court 336–334 B.C." *RhM* 141: 141–52.

Baynham, E. J. 2003. "The Ancient Evidence for Alexander the Great," in Roisman 2003a, 3–29.

Bearzot, C. 1985. *Focione tra storia e trasfigurazione ideale*. Milan.

Bearzot, C. 1992. *Storia e storiografia ellenistica in Pausania il Periegeta*. Venice.

Bearzot, C., F. Landucci, and G. Zecchini, eds. 2003. *Gli stati territoriali nel mondo antico*. Milan.

Bedford, P. R. 2001. *Temple Restoration in Early Achaemenid Judah*. Leiden.

Bedford, P. R. 2007. "The Persian Near East," in Scheidel et al., 302–29.

Bell, B. 1985. "The Luxor Temple and the Cult of the Royal Ka." *JNES* 44: 251–94.

Bellinger, A. 1963. *Essays on the Coinage of Alexander the Great*. New York.

Bencivenni, A. 2003. *Progetti di riforme costituzionali nelle epigrafi greche dei secoli IV–II a.C.* Bologna.

Bendinelli, G. 1965. "Cassandro di Macedonia nella Vita plutarchea di Alessandro Magno." *RFIC* 93: 150–64.

Bengtson, H. 1975. *Die Staatsverträge des Altertums*, vol. ii. 2nd edn. Munich.

Bennett, J. 2001. *Trajan, Optimus Princeps: A Life and Times*, 2nd edn. London.

Benson, E. F. 1977. *Make Way for Lucia: The Complete Lucia, including Queen Lucia, Lucia in London, Miss Mapp, The Male Impersonator, Mapp and Lucia, The Worshipful Lucia, and Trouble for Lucia*. Intro. Nancy Mitford. New York.

Benveniste, É. 1958. "Une bilingue gréco-araméenne d'Asoka, IV: les données iraniennes." *JA* 246: 36–48.

Berghaus, I.-J. 1797. *Geschichte der Schiffahrtskunde bey den vornehmsten Völker des Alterthums*, vols. i–ii. Leipzig.

Bergmann, B., and C. Kondoleon, eds. 1999. *The Art of Spectacle*. Washington, DC.

Bertoli, M. 2003. "Sviluppi del concetto di 'autonomia' tra IV e III secolo a.C.," in Bearzot et al., 87–110.

Bianchi Bandinelli, R., ed. 1989. *Storia e civiltà dei Greci*, vol. v. Milan.

Bieber, M. 1964. *Alexander the Great in Greek and Roman Art*. Chicago.

Bikerman, E. 1940. "La lettre d'Alexandre aux bannis grecs." *REA* 42: 25–35.

Bikerman, E. 1944–5. "L'européanisation de l'Orient classique: à propos du livre de Michel Rostovtzeff." *Renaissance* 2: 381–92.

Bilde, P., et al., eds. 1996. *Aspects of Hellenistic Kingship*. Studies in Hellenistic Civilization 7. Aarhus, Denmark.

Billows, R. A. 1990. *Antigonus the One-Eyed and the Creation of the Hellenistic State*. Berkeley, CA.

Billows, R. A. 1995. *Kings and Colonists: Aspects of Macedonian Imperialism*. Leiden.

Bingen, J. 2007. "Ptolemy I and the Quest for Legitimacy," in Bingen and Bagnall, 15–30.

Bingen, J., and R. Bagnall, eds. 2007. *Hellenistic Egypt: Monarchy, Society, Economy, Culture*. Edinburgh.

Birley, A. R. 1997. *Hadrian: The Restless Emperor*. London.

Blackwell, C. W. 1999. *In the Absence of Alexander*. New York.

Blakolmer, F., and J. Borchardt, eds. 1996. *Fremde Zeiten: Festschrift für Jürgen Borchardt zum 60. Geburtstag am 25. Februar 1995*. Vienna.

Blinkenberg, C. 1941. *Lindos*. 2 vols. Berlin and Copenhagen.

Bloedow, E. F. 1998. "The Significance of the Greek Athletes and Artists at Memphis in Alexander's Strategy after the Battle of Issus." *QUCC* 58: 129–42.

Blok, J. 1997. *The Early Amazons*. Leiden.

Blum, H. 1998. *Purpur als Statussymbol in der griechischen Welt*. Bonn.

Boardman, J. 1991[1974]. *Athenian Black Figure Vases*. London.

Boardman, J., J. Griffin, and O. Murray, eds. 1988. *The Oxford History of the Classical World*. Oxford.

Boerma, R. N. H. 1979. *Justinus' Boeken over de Diadochen: Een historisch Commentaar, Boek 13–15 cap. 2 met een inleidung op de bronnen voor de periode 323–302 v.C.* Amsterdam.

Boiy, T. 2000. "Dating Methods during the Early Hellenistic Period." *JCS* 52: 115–21.

Boiy, T. 2002a. "Early Hellenistic Chronography in Cuneiform Tradition." *ZPE* 138: 249–55.

Boiy, T. 2002b. "Royal Titulature in Hellenistic Babylonia." *ZA* 92: 241–57.

Boiy, T. 2005. "Alexander Dates in Lydian Inscriptions." *Kadmos* 44: 165–74.

Boiy, T. 2006. "Aspects chronologiques de la période de transition (350–300)," in Briant and Joannès, 37–100.

Boiy, T. 2007a. *Between High and Low: A Chronology of the Early Hellenistic Period*. Oikumene 5. Frankfurt.

Boiy, T. 2007b. "Cuneiform Tablets and Aramaic Ostraca: Between the Low and High Chronologies for the Early Diadoch Period," in Heckel et al., 199–207.

Borchhardt, J. 1993. "Lykische Heroa und die Pyra des Hephaistion in Babylon," in Borchhardt and Dobesch, 252–9.

Borchhardt, J., and G. Dobesch, eds. 1993. *Akten des II. internationalen Lykien-Symposions*, vol. i. Vienna.

Borza, E. 1967. "An Introduction to Alexander Studies," in Wilcken, ix–xxviii.

Borza, E. 1971. "The End of Agis' Revolt." *CPh* 66: 230–5.

Borza, E., ed. 1974. *The Impact of Alexander the Great: Civilizer or Destroyer?* Hinsdale, IL.

Borza, E. 1983. "The Symposium at Alexander's Court." *AM* 3: 45–55.

Borza, E. 1989. "Significato politico, economico e sociale dell'impresa di Alessandro," in Bianchi Bandinelli, 122–67.

Borza, E. 1990. *In the Shadow of Olympus: The Emergence of Macedon*. Princeton, NJ.

Borza, E. 1996. "Greeks and Macedonians in the Age of Alexander: The Source Traditions," in Wallace and Harris, 122–39.

Borza, E. 1999. *Before Alexander: Constructing Early Macedonia*. Claremont, CA.

Bossuet, J. B. 1681. *Discours sur l'histoire universelle à Monseigneur de Dauphin: pour expliquer la suite de la religion et les changements des empires*. Paris.

Bosworth, A. B. 1971a. "The Death of Alexander the Great: Rumour and Propaganda." *CQ* 21: 112–36.

Bosworth, A. B. 1971b. "Philip II and Upper Macedonia." *CQ* 21: 93–105.

Bosworth, A. B. 1973. "ΑΣΘΕΤΑΙΡΟΙ." *CQ* 23: 245–53.

Bosworth, A. B. 1977. "Alexander and Ammon," in Kinzl 51–75.

Bosworth, A. B. 1980a. "Alexander and the Iranians." *JHS* 100: 1–21.

Bosworth, A. B. 1980b. *A Historical Commentary on Arrian's History of Alexander*, vol. i: *Commentary on Books I–III*. Oxford.

Bosworth, A. B. 1981. "A Missing Year in the History of Alexander." *JHS* 101: 17–39.

Bosworth, A. B. 1983. "The Indian Satrapies under Alexander the Great." *Antichthon* 17: 37–46.

Bosworth, A. B. 1985. Review of W. Will, *Athen und Alexander: Untersuchungen zur Geschichte der Stadt von 338 bis 322 v. Chr.* (Munich, 1983). *Gnomon* 57: 435.

Bosworth, A. B. 1986. "Alexander the Great and the Decline of Macedon." *JHS* 106: 1–12.

Bosworth, A. B. 1988a. *Conquest and Empire: The Reign of Alexander the Great.* Cambridge.

Bosworth, A. B. 1988b. *From Arrian to Alexander: Studies in Historical Interpretation.* Oxford.

Bosworth, A. B. 1992a. "*Autonomia*: The Use and Abuse of Political Terminology." *SIFC* 10: 122–52.

Bosworth, A. B. 1992b. "History and Artifice in Plutarch's *Eumenes*," in Stadter, 56–89.

Bosworth, A. B. 1992c. "Philip III Arrhidaeus and the Chronology of the Successors." *Chiron* 22: 55–81.

Bosworth, A. B. 1994a. *Alexander the Great, Part 2: Greece and the Conquered Territories,* in *CAH*² vi. 846–59.

Bosworth, A. B. 1994b. "A New Macedonian Prince." *CQ* 44: 57–65.

Bosworth, A. B. 1995. *A Historical Commentary on Arrian's History of Alexander,* vol. ii: *Commentary on Books IV–V.* Oxford.

Bosworth, A. B. 1996. *Alexander and the East.* Oxford.

Bosworth, A. B. 1998. "Alessandro: l'impero universale e le città greche," in Settis, 47–80.

Bosworth, A. B. 2000a. "Ptolemy and the Will of Alexander," in Bosworth and Baynham, 207–41.

Bosworth, A. B. 2000b. "A Tale of Two Empires: Hernán Cortés and Alexander the Great," in Bosworth and Baynham, 23–49.

Bosworth, A. B. 2002. *The Legacy of Alexander: Politics, Warfare, and Propaganda under the Successors.* Oxford.

Bosworth, A. B. 2003a. "*Plus ça change . . .* Ancient Historians and their Sources." *CA* 22: 167–97.

Bosworth, A. B. 2003b. "Why did Athens Lose the Lamian War?" in Palagia and Tracy, 14–22.

Bosworth, A. B., and E. J. Baynham, eds. 2000. *Alexander the Great in Fact and Fiction.* Oxford.

Botermann, H. 1994. "Wer baute das neue Priene? Zur Interpretation der Inschriften von Priene Nr. 1 und 156." *Hermes* 122: 162–87.

Boucharlat, R. 2001. "The Palace and the Royal Achaemenid City: Two Case Studies – Pasargadae and Susa," in Nielsen, 113–23.

Boucharlat, R. 2006. "Le destin des résidences et sites perses d'Iran dans la seconde moitié du IVe siècle av. J.C.," in Briant and Joannès, 433–70.

Boucharlat, R. Forthcoming. "Les travaux des successeurs de Darius à Suse," in Perrot.

Bradford, A. S. 1992. *Philip II of Macedon: A Life from the Ancient Sources.* Westport, CT.

Bravo, B. 1968. *Philologie, histoire, philosophie de l'histoire: étude sur Droysen, historien de l'Antiquité.* Warsaw.

Breloer, B. 1941. *Alexanders Bund mit Poros: Indien von Dareios zu Sandrokottos.* Sammlung orientalistischen Arbeiten 9. Leipzig.

Breniquet, C., and C. Kepinski, eds. 2001. *Études mésopotamiennes: recueil de textes offert à J.-L. Huot.* Paris.

Briant, P. 1972. "D'Alexandre le Grand aux diadoques: le cas d'Eumenes de Kardia (I)." *REA* 74: 32–73.

Briant, P. 1973a. *Antigone le Borgne.* Paris.

Briant, P. 1973b. "D'Alexandre le Grand aux diadoques: le cas d'Eumène de Kardia (II). Suite et fin." *REA* 75: 43–81.

Briant, P. 1974. *Alexandre le Grand*. 1st edn. Paris.

Briant, P. 1976. "'Brigandage', conquête et dissidence en Asie achéménide et hellénistique." *DHA* 2: 163–259.

Briant, P. 1979a. "Des Achéménides aux rois hellénistiques: continuités et ruptures." *ASNP* 1375–414 (= Briant 1982, 293–330).

Briant, P. 1979b. "Impérialismes antiques et idéologie coloniale dans la France contemporaine: Alexandre le Grand modèle colonial." *Dialogues d'histoire ancienne* 5 (= Briant 1982: 281–90).

Briant, P. 1982. *États et pasteurs au Moyen-Orient ancient*. Paris.

Briant, P. 1984. *L'Asie centrale et les royaumes proche-orientaux du premier millénaire*. Paris.

Briant, P. 1988. "Le nomadisme du Grand Roi." *IA* 23: 253–73.

Briant, P. 1989. "Table du roi, tribut et redistribution chez les Achemenides," in Briant and Herrenschmidt, 35–44.

Briant, P. 1991. "Chasses royales macedoniennes et chasses royales perses: le théme de la chasse au lion sur La Chasse de Vergina." *DHA* 17: 211–55.

Briant, P. 1993a. "Alexandre à Sardes," in Carlsen et al., 13–27

Briant, P. 1993b. "Les chasses d'Alexandre." *AM* 5/1: 267–77.

Briant, P. 1996. *Histoire de l'empire perse: de Cyrus à Alexandre*. Paris.

Briant, P. 1998. "Cités et satrapes dans l'empire achéménide: Xanthos et Pixôdaros." *CRAI* 305–40.

Briant, P. 1999. "L'histoire de l'empire achéménide aujourd'hui: l'historien et ses documents." *Annales HSS* 5: 1127–36.

Briant, P. 2000a. "Histoire impériale et histoire régionale: à propos de l'histoire de Juda dans l'empire achéménide," in Lemaire and Sæbø, 235–45.

Briant, P. 2000b. *Leçon inaugurale au Collège de France*. Paris.

Briant, P. 2000c. "Numismatique, frappes monétaires et histoire en Asie mineure achéménide (quelques remarques de conclusion)," in Casabonne, 265–74.

Briant, P. 2000d. "Quelques remarques sur Michael Rostovtzeff et le passage du monde achéménide au monde hellénistique." At www.achemenet.com/pdf/souspresse/briant/rostovtzef.pdf

Briant, P., ed. 2001a. *Irrigation et drainage dans l'Antiquité: qanāts et canalisations souterraines en Iran, en Égypte et en Iran*. Persika 2. Paris.

Briant, P. 2001b. "Polybe X. 28 et les qanāts: le témoignage et ses limites," in Briant 2001a, 15–40.

Briant, P. 2002a. "L'État, la terre et l'eau entre Nil et Syr-Darya: remarques introductives." *Annales HSS* 57/3: 517–29.

Briant, P. 2002b. "Guerre et succession dynastique chez les Achéménides: entre 'coutume perse' et violence armée," in Chianotis and Ducrey, 39–49.

Briant, P. 2002c. "History and Ideology: The Greeks and Persian Decadence," in Harrison, 193–210.

Briant, P. 2003a. *Darius dans l'ombre d'Alexandre*. Paris.

Briant, P. 2003b. "Histoire et archéologie d'un texte: la *Lettre de Darius à Gadatas* entre Perses, Grecs et Romains," in Giorgieri et al., 107–44.

Briant, P. 2003c. "New Trends in Achaemenid History." *AHB* 17: 33–47.

Briant, P. 2003d. "La tradition gréco-romaine sur Alexandre le Grand dans l'Europe moderne et contemporaine: quelques réflexions sur la permanence et l'adaptabilité des modèles interprétatifs," in Haagsma et al., 161–80.

Briant, P. 2005a. "Alexander the Great and the Enlightenment: William Robertson (1721–1793), the Empire and the Road to India." *Cromohs* 10: 1–9.

Briant, P. 2005b. "Alexandre et l'hellénisation de l'Asie: l'histoire au passé et au présent." *Studi Ellenistici* 16: 9–69.

Briant, P. 2005c. *Alexandre le Grand.* 6th edn. Paris.

Briant, P. 2005d. "Alexandre le Grand aujourd'hui (iii): Alexandre le Grand 'grand économiste': mythe, histoire, historiographie." *Annuaire du Collège de France* 105: 585–99.

Briant, P. 2005e. "Milestones in the Development of Achaemenid Historiography in the Time of Ernst Herzfeld (1879–1948)," in Gunter and Hauser, 263–80.

Briant, P. 2005–6. "Montesquieu, Mably et Alexandre le Grand: aux sources de l'histoire hellénistique." *Revue Montesquieu* 8: 151–85.

Briant, P. 2006a. "L'Asie mineure en transition," in Briant and Joannès, 309–51.

Briant, P. 2006b. "L'économie royale entre privé et public," in Descat, 339–54.

Briant, P. 2006c. "Retour sur Alexandre et les *katarraktes* du Tigre: l'histoire d'un dossier (*première partie*)." *Studi Ellenistici* (Pisa) 19: 9–75.

Briant, P. 2007a. "Michael Rostovtzeff et le passage du monde achéménide au monde hellénistique." *Studi Ellenistici* 20: 137–54.

Briant, P. 2007b. "Montesquieu et ses sources: Alexandre, l'empire perse, les Guèbres et l'irrigation." Studies on Voltaire. Oxford.

Briant, P. 2008. "Retour sur Alexandre et les *katarraktes* du Tigre: l'histoire d'un dossier (*suite et fin*)." *Studi Ellenistici* 20: 155–218.

Briant, P. Forthcoming. "Suse et l'Élam dans l'empire achéménide," in Perrot.

Briant, P., and M. Chauveau, eds. Forthcoming. *Organisation des pouvoirs et contacts culturels dans les pays de l'empire achéménide.* Persika 13. Paris.

Briant, P., and C. Herrenschmidt, eds. 1989. *Le Tribut dans l'Empire Perse.* Paris.

Briant, P., and F. Joannès, eds. 2006. *La transition entre l'empire achéménide et les royaumes hellénistiques (v. 350–300).* Persika 9. Paris.

Briant, P., W. F. M. Henkelman, and M. W. Stolper, eds. 2008. *Les Archives des Fortifications de Persépolis dans le contexte de l'empire achéménide et de ses prédécesseurs.* Persika 12. Paris.

Briganti, G. 1962. *Pietro da Cortona.* Florence.

Bringmann, K., and H. von Steuben. 1995. *Schenkungen hellenistischer Herrscher an griechische Städte und Heiligtümer,* vol. i: *Zeugnisse und Kommentare.* Berlin.

Broilo, F., ed. 1985. *Xenia: scritti in onore di Piero Treves.* Rome.

Brosius, M. 1996. *Women in Ancient Persia, 559–331 B.C.* Oxford.

Brosius, M. 2003a. "Alexander and the Persians," in Roisman, 169–93.

Brosius, M. 2003b. "Why Persia Became the Enemy of Macedon," in Henkelman and Kuhrt, 227–38.

Brosius, M. 2006. Review of Briant 2003a. *Gnomon* 78: 426–30.

Brosius, M., and A. Kuhrt, eds. 1998. *Studies in Persian History: Essays in Memory of David M. Lewis.* Leiden (= AchH 11).

Brouskari, M. 1974. *Musée de l'Acropole.* Athens.

Brown, T. S. 1947. "Hieronymus of Cardia." *AHR* 53: 684–96.

Brown, T. S. 1977. "Alexander and Greek Athletics, in Fact and in Fiction," in Kinzl, 76–88.

Brückner, A. 1902. "Die 1894 gefundenen Inschriften," in Dörpfeld, 447–62.

Brun, P. 2000. *L'orateur Démade.* Ausonius Scripta Antiqua 3. Bordeaux.

Brunschwig, J. 1992. "The Anaxarchus Case: An Essay on Survival." *PBA* 82: 59–88.

Brunt, P. A. 1963. "Alexander's Macedonian Cavalry." *JHS* 83: 27–46.

Brunt, P. A. 1975. "Alexander, Barsine and Heracles." *RF* 103: 22–35.

Brunt, P. A., ed. and trans. 1976–83. *Arrian: History of Alexander and Indica*. 2 vols. Loeb Classical Library. Cambridge, MA.

Bryson, N. 1981. *Word and Image: French Painting of the Ancien Régime*. Cambridge.

Buck, C. D., and W. Petersen. 1945. *A Reverse Index of Greek Nouns and Adjectives*. Chicago.

Buckler, J. 1989. *Philip II and the Sacred War*. Mnemosyne suppl. 109. Leiden.

Buckler, J. 1994. "Philip II, the Greeks, and the King 346–336 B.C." *ICS* 19: 99–122.

Buckler, J. 1996. "Philip's Designs on Greece," in Wallace and Harris, 77–97.

Buckler, J. 2003. *Aegean Greece in the Fourth Century B.C.* Leiden.

Buffière, F. 1980. *Eros adolescent: la pederasty dans la Grèce antique*. Paris.

Bugh, G. R., ed. 2006. *The Cambridge Companion to the Hellenistic World*. Cambridge.

Bultrighini, U., ed. 2005. *Democrazia et antidemocrazia nel mondo antico*. Alexandria.

Burke, P. 1992. *The Fabrication of Louis XIV*. New Haven, CT.

Burstein, S. M. 1976. *Outpost of Hellenism: The Emergence of Heraclea on the Black Sea*. Berkeley, CA.

Burstein, S. M. 1991. "Pharaoh Alexander: A Scholarly Myth." *AncSoc* 22: 139–45.

Burstein, S. M. 2000. "Prelude to Alexander: The Reign of Khababash." *AHB* 14: 149–54.

Callataÿ, F. de. 1989. "Les trésors achéménides et les monnayages d'Alexandre: espèces immobilisées ou espèces circulantes?" *REA* 91: 259–64.

Calmeyer, P. 1990a. "Die Orientalen auf Thorwaldsens Alexanderfries." *AchH* 5: 91–120.

Calmeyer, P. 1990b. "Das Persepolis der Spätzeit." *AchH* 4: 7–36.

Cargill, J. 1995. *Athenian Settlements of the Fourth Century BC*. Mnemosyne suppl. 145. Leiden.

Carlsen, J., B. Due, O. S. Due, and B. Poulsen, eds. 1993. *Alexander the Great: Reality and Myth*. Rome.

Carney, E. 1983. "Regicide in Macedonia." *PP* 38: 260–71.

Carney, E. 1988. "The Sisters of Alexander the Great: Royal Relicts." *Historia* 37: 385–404.

Carney, E. 1995. "Women and *Basileia*: Legitimacy and Female Political Action in Macedonia." *CJ* 90: 369–91.

Carney, E. 1996. "Macedonians and Mutiny: Discipline and Indiscipline in the Army of Philip and Alexander." *CP* 91: 19–44.

Carney, E. 2000a. "Artifice and Alexander History," in Bosworth and Baynham, 263–85.

Carney, E. 2000b. *Women and Monarchy in Macedonia*. Norman, OK.

Carney, E. 2001. "The Trouble with Arrhidaeus." *AHB* 15: 63–89.

Carney, E. 2002. "Hunting and the Macedonian Elite: Sharing the Rivalry of the Chase (Arrian 4. 13. 1)," in Ogden, 59–80.

Carney, E. 2003a. "Elite Education and High Culture in Macedonia," in Heckel and Tritle, 47–63.

Carney, E. 2003b. "Women in Alexander's Court," in Roisman, 227–52.

Carney, E. 2006. *Olympias, Mother of Alexander the Great*. London.

Carney, E. 2007. "The Philippeum, Women, and the Formation of a Dynastic Image," in Heckel et al., 27–60.

Carter, J. B., and S. P. Morris, eds. 1995. *The Ages of Homer: A Tribute to Emily Townsend Vermeule*. Austin, TX.

Cartledge, P. 2004. *Alexander the Great: The Hunt for a New Past*. London.

Casabonne, O., ed. 2000. *Mécanismes et innovations monétaires dans l'Anatolie achéménide: numismatique et histoire. Actes de la Table Ronde Internationale d'Istanbul, 22–23 mai 1997*. Varia Anatolica 12. Istanbul.

Casabonne, O. 2004. *La Cilicie à l'époque achéménide*. Persika 3. Paris.

Casson, L. 1974. *Travel in the Ancient World*. London.

Cau, N. 1999–2000. "L'uso delle formule di datazione nelle iscrizioni licie." *EVO* 22–3: 179–88.

Cawkwell, G. L. 1961. "A Note on Ps. Demosthenes 17. 20." *Phoenix* 15: 74–8.

Cawkwell, G. L. 1978. *Philip of Macedon*. London.

Ceauçescu, P. 1974. "La double image d'Alexandre le Grand à Rome: essai d'une explication politique." *StudClas* 16:153–68.

Cerfaux, L., and J. Tondriau, eds. 1957. *Le culte des souverains*. Tournai, Belgium.

Chamay J., and J.-L. Maier, eds. 1987. *Lysippe et son influence*. Hellas et Roma 5. Geneva.

Chamoux, F. 2003. *Hellenistic Civilisation*. Malden, MA.

Chauveau, M., and Thiers, C. 2006. "L'Égypte en transition: des Perses aux Macédoniens," in Briant and Joannès, 375–404.

Chianotis, A., and P. Ducrey, eds. 2002. *Army and Power in the Ancient World*. Stuttgart.

Cogan, M., and D. Kahn, eds. 2008. *Treasures on Camels' Humps: Historical and Literary Studies from the Ancient Near East presented to Israel Eph'al*. Jerusalem.

Cohen, A. 1995. "Alexander and Achilles: Macedonians and 'Myceneans'," in Carter and Morris, 483–505.

Cohen, A. 1997. *The Alexander Mosaic: Stories of Victory and Defeat*. Cambridge.

Cohen, R. 1939a. "Alexandre et la conquête de l'Orient," in Glotz, 1–253.

Cohen, R. 1939b. *La Grèce et l'hellénisation du monde antique*. Paris.

Cohler, Anne M., Basia C. Miller, and Harold S. Stone, eds. 1989. *Montesquieu: The Spirit of the Laws*. Cambridge.

Collart, P. 1937. *Philippes, ville de Macédoine*. 2 vols. Paris.

Collingwood, R. G. 1946. *The Idea of History*. Oxford.

Collins, A. W. 2001. "The Office of Chiliarch under Alexander and the Successors." *Phoenix* 55: 259–83.

Corradi, G. 1929. *Studi ellenistici*. Turin.

Croisille, J. M. 1990a. "Alexandre chez Lucain: l'image du tyran. Notes sur Ph. X.1–52," in Croisille 1990b, 266–76.

Croisille, J. M., ed. 1990b. *Neronia IV Alejandro Magno, modelo de los emperadores romanos*. Actes du IVe colloque international de la SIEN, Collection Latomus 209. Brussels.

Croix, H. de la, R. G. Tansey, and D. Kirkpatrick, eds. 1991. *Gardner's Art through the Ages*, 9th edn. Ft. Worth, TX.

Cronin, V. 1964. *Louis XIV*. London.

Crowdus, G. 2005. "Dramatizing Issues that Historians Don't Address." *Cineaste* 30: 12–23.

Culasso Gastaldi, E. 1984. *Sul trattato con Alessandro (polis, monarchia macedone e memoria demostenica)*. Padua.

Culasso Gastaldi, E. 2003. "Eroi della città: Eufrone di Sicione e Licurgo di Atene," in Barzanò et al., 65–98.

Dahmen, K. 2007. *The Legend of Alexander the Great on Greek and Roman Coins*. London.

Dani, A. H. 1994. "Alexander and his Successors in Central Asia. Part I: Alexander's Campaign in Central Asia," in J. Harmatta, B. N. Puri, and G. F. Etemadi (eds.), *History of Civilizations of Central Asia*, vol. ii. Paris, 167–88.

Davidson, J. 1997. *Courtesans and Fishcakes: The Consuming Passions of Classical Athens*. London.

Davies, J. K. 1971. *Athenian Propertied Families*. Oxford.

Davis, N., and C. Kraay. 1973. *The Hellenistic Kingdoms: Portrait Coins in History*. London.

Debord, P. 1999. *L'Asie Mineure au IVème siècle (412–323): pouvoirs et jeux politiques*. Ausonius Etudes 3. Bordeaux.

Decleva Caizzi, F. 1981. *Pirrone Testimonianze*. Naples.

Dell, H. J., ed. 1981. *Ancient Macedonian Studies in Honor of Charles F. Edson*. Thessaloniki.

Del Monte, G. F. 1997. *Testi dalla Babilonia Ellenistica*, vol. i: *Testi Cronografici*. Studi Ellenistici 9. Pisa.

Demangeon, A. 1923. *L'Empire britannique: étude de géographie coloniale*. Paris.

Demangeon, A. 1925. *The British Empire: A Study in Colonial Geography*. London.

Depuydt, L. 1997. "The Time of Death of Alexander the Great: 11 June 323 B.C. (-322), ca. 4:00–5:00 pm." *Die Welt des Orients* 28: 117–35.

Descat, R., ed. 2006a. *Approches de l'économie séleucide*. Entretiens d'archéologie et d'histoire 7. Saint-Bertrand-de-Comminges, France.

Descat, R. 2006b. "Aspects d'une transition. L'économie du monde égéen (350–300)," in Briant and Joannès, 353–73.

de Sélincourt, A., trans. 1971. *Arrian: The Campaigns of Alexander*. Rev. with new intro. by J. R. Hamilton. London.

Deutsch, R., ed. 2003. *Shlomo: Studies in Epigraphy, Iconography, History and Archaeology in Honor of Shlomo Moussaief*. Tel Aviv.

Devauchelle, D. 1995. "Réflexions sur les documents égyptiens datés de la deuxième domination perse." *Trans.* 10: 35–43.

Develin, R. 1981. "The Murder of Philip II." *Antichthon* 15: 86–99.

Devine, A. M. 1985. "Grand Tactics at the Battle of Issus." *AncW* 12: 39–59.

Devine, A. M. 1986. "The Battle at Gaugamela: A Tactical and Source-Critical Study." *AncW* 13: 87–115.

Devine, A. M. 1987. "The Battle of the Hydaspes: A Tactical and Source-Critical Study." *AncW* 16: 91–113.

Dixon, M. D. 2007. *Corinth, Greek Freedom, and the Diadochoi, 323–301 B.C.*, in Heckel et al., 151–78.

Domingo Gygax, M. 2001. *Untersuchungen zu den lykischen Gemeinwesen in klassischer und hellenistischer Zeit*. Antiquitas, R.1, Bd. 49. Bonn.

Dondener, M. 1990. "Das Alexandermosaik: ein antikes Importstück," in *Akten des 13. Internationaler Kongresses für Klassischen Archäologie*. Berlin and Mainz.

Dörpfeld, W. 1968 [1902]. *Troja und Ilion: Ergebnisse der Ausgrabungen in den vorhistorischen und historischen Schichten von Ilion, 1870–1894*. Athens; repr. Darmstadt.

Dover, K. J. 1978. *Greek Homosexuality*. London.

Downey, G. 1961. *A History of Antioch in Syria from Seleucus to the Arab Conquest*. Princeton, NJ.

Dreyer, B. 1999. *Untersuchungen zur Geschichte des spätklassischen Athen*. Stuttgart.

Dreyer, B. 2002. "Der Raubvertrag des Jahres 203/2 v. Chr.: Das Inschriftenfragment von Bargylia und der Brief von Amyzon." *EA* 34: 119–38.

Dreyer, B. 2007a. "The Arrian Parchment in Gothenburg: New Digital Processing Methods and Initial Results," in Heckel et al., 243–63.

Dreyer, B. 2007b. *Die römische Nobiltätsherrschaft und Antiochos III*. Frankfurt am Main.

Drougou, S. 1997. "Das antike Theater von Vergina. Bemerkungen zu Gestalt und Funktion in der antiken Hauptstadt Makedoniens." *MDAI(A)* 112: 281–305.

Droysen, J.-G. 1833. *Geschichte Alexanders des Grossen*. Berlin.

Droysen, J.-G. 1877. *Geschichte Alexanders des Grossen*. 2nd edn. 2 vols. Gotha.

Droysen, J.-G. 1883. *Histoire de l'hellénisme*, vol. i: *Histoire d'Alexandre le Grand*. Trans. from 2nd German edn. (Droysen 1877). Paris.

Droysen, J.-G. 1893–4. *Kleine Schriften zur Alten Geschichte*. 2 vols. Leipzig.

Durand, X. 1997. *Des Grecs en Palestine au IIIe siècle av. J.C.: le dossier syrien des archives de Zénon de Caunos (261–252)*. Paris.

Duro, P. 1997. *The Academy and the Limits of Painting in Seventeenth Century France*. Cambridge.

Duruy, V. 1858. *Abrégé d'histoire grecque*, classe de 5è, prog. 1857. Paris.

Dušek, J. 2007. *Les manuscrits araméens du Wadi Daliyeh et la Samarie vers 450–332 av. J.C.* Leiden.

Eadie, J. W., and J. Ober, eds. 1985. *The Craft of the Ancient Historian: Essays in Honor of Chester G. Starr*. Lanham, MD.

Eco, U. 1976. *A Theory of Semiotics*. Bloomington, IN.

Eco, U. 1990. *The Limits of Interpretation*. Bloomington, IN.

Eder, W. 1990. "Augustus and the Power of Tradition: The Augustan Principate as Binding Link between Republic and Empire," in Raaflaub and Toher, 71–122.

Eggermont, P. H. L. 1970. "Alexander's Campaigns in Gandhara and Ptolemy's List of Indo-Scythian Towns." *OLP* 1: 63–123.

Eggermont, P. H. L. 1975. *Alexander's Campaigns in Sind and Baluchistan and the Siege of the Brahmin Town of Harmatelia*. Leuven.

Eggermont, P. H. L. 1984. "Indien und die hellenistischen Königreiche: Zusammenschau einer westöstlichen Gesellschaft zwischen 550 und 150 v. Chr.," in Ozols and Thewalt, 74–83.

Ehrenberg, V. 1938. *Alexander and the Greeks*. Trans. Ruth Fraenkel von Velsen. Oxford.

Ehrhardt, C. T. H. R. 1973. "The Coins of Cassander." *JNFA* 2: 25–32.

Eisenstadt, S. 1969. *The Political System of Empire*. New York.

Elayi, J. 2005. *Le monnayage d' 'Abd'Aštart Ier/Straton de Sidon: un roi phénicien entre Orient et Occident*. Trans. suppl. 12. Paris.

Elayi, J., and A.-G. Elayi. 2004a. "Le monnayage sidonien de Mazday." *Trans.* 27: 155–62.

Elayi, J., and A.-G. Elayi. 2004b. "La scène du char sur les monnaies d'époque perse." *Trans.* 27: 89–108.

Elayi, J., and J. Sapin (eds.). 2000. *Quinze ans de recherche (1985–2000) sur la Transeuphratène à l'époque perse*. Trans. suppl. 8. Paris.

Ellis, J. R. 1971. "Amyntas Perdikka, Philip II, and Alexander the Great." *JHS* 91: 15–24.

Ellis, J. R. 1976. *Philip II and Macedonian Imperialism*. London.

Ellis, J. R. 1982. "Philip and the Peace of Philokrates," in Adams and Borza, 42–59.

Ellis, J. R. 1994. "Macedonian Hegemony Created." *CAH*[2] vi. 760–90.

Ellis, W. 1994. *Ptolemy of Egypt*. London.

Elsner, J., and J. Masters, eds. 1994. *Reflections of Nero: Culture, History and Representation*. London.

Engelmann, H., and R. Merkelbach. 1973. *Die Inschriften von Erythrai und Klazomenai*. Vol. ii of *Inschriften griechischer Städte aus Kleinasien*. Bonn.

Engels, D. W. 1978a. *Alexander the Great and the Logistics of the Macedonian Army*. Berkeley, CA.

Engels, D. W. 1978b. "A Note on Alexander's Death." *CPh* 73: 224–8.

Eph'al, I. 1998. "Changes in Palestine during the Persian Period in Light of Epigraphic Sources." *IEJ* 48: 106–19.

Eph'al, I., and J. Naveh, eds. 1996. *Aramaic Ostraca of the Fourth Century BC from Idumaea.* Jerusalem.

Errington, R. M. 1969. "Bias in Ptolemy's History of Alexander." *CQ* 19: 233–42.

Errington, R. M. 1970. "From Babylon to Triparadeisos: 323–320 B.C." *JHS* 90: 49–77.

Errington, R. M. 1974. "Macedonian 'Royal Style' and its Historical Significance." *JHS* 94: 20–37.

Errington, R. M. 1975b. "Samos and the Lamian War." *Chiron* 5: 51–7.

Errington, R. M. 1976. "Alexander in the Hellenistic World," in Badian 1976a, 137–79.

Errington, R. M. 1981. "Review-Discussion: Four Interpretations of Philip II." *AJAH* 6: 69–88.

Errington, R. M. 1990. *A History of Macedonia.* Berkeley, CA.

Erskine, A. 1989. "The 'Pezêtairoi' of Philip II and Alexander III." *Historia* 38: 385–94.

Erskine, A. 2002. "Life after Death: Alexandria and the Body of Alexander." *G&R* 49: 163–79.

Eshel, E. 2007. "The Onomasticon of Mareshah in the Persian and Hellenistic Periods," in Lipschits et al., 145–56.

Evans, R. 2003. "Searching for Paradise: Landscape, Utopia, and Rome." Special issue: "Center and Periphery in the Roman World," *Arethusa* 36: 285–307.

Faraguna, M. 1992. "*Atene nell'età di Alessandro: problemi politici, economici, finanziari.*" *Atti dell' Accademia Nazionale dei Lincei. Memorie,* ser. 9, 2: 165–447.

Faraguna, M. 2003. "Alexander and the Greeks," in Roisman, 99–130.

Fears, J. R. 1974. "The Stoic View of the Career and Character of Alexander the Great." *Philologus* 118: 113–30.

Fears, J. R. 1975. "Pausanias the Assassin of Philip II," *Athenaeum* 53: 111–35.

Fears, J. R. 1981. "The Cult of Virtues and Imperial Roman Ideology." *ANRW* 2. 17. 2: 827–948.

Ferguson, W. S. 1912–13. "Legalized Absolutism en route from Greece to Rome." *AHR* 18: 29–47.

Ferguson, W. S. 1928. "The Leading Ideas of the New Period," in *CAH* vii. 1–40.

Ferrier-Caverivière, N. 1981. *L'Image de Louis XIV dans littérature française de 1660 a 1715.* Paris.

Finkel, I. L., and R. J. van der Spek. *Babylonian Chronicles of the Hellenistic Period.* (www. livius.org/cg-cm/chronicles/chron00.html)

Fisher, N. R. E., ed. 2001. *Aeschines: Against Timarchus.* Oxford.

Flower, M. 2000. "Alexander and Panhellenism," in Bosworth and Baynham, 96–135.

Flower, M. 2007. "Not Great Man History: Reconceptualizing a Course on Alexander the Great." *Classical World* 100: 417–23.

Fontrier, A. 1903. "Inscriptions d'Érythrées." *REA* 5: 231–3.

Foucault, M. 1984. *L' usage des plaisirs.* Paris. Translated as *The Use of Pleasure,* New York, 1985.

Francfort, H. P., and Lecomte, O. 2002. "Irrigation et société en Asie centrale des origines à l'époque achéménide." *Annales HSS* 57/3: 625–63.

Franco, C. 1993. *Il regno di Lisimaco: strutture amministrative e rapporti con le città.* Pisa.

Fraser, P. M. 1996. *The Cities of Alexander the Great.* Oxford.

Franklin, C. 2003. "To What Extent did Posidonius and Theophanes Record Pompeian Ideology?" s.v. "Romanization." *Digressus* suppl. 1: 99–110.

Fredricksmeyer, E. A. 1979–80. "Three Notes on Alexander's Deification." *AJAH* 4: 1–9.

Fredricksmeyer, E. A. 1981. "On the Background of the Ruler Cult," in Dell, 145–56.

Fredricksmeyer, E. A. 1982. "On the Final Aims of Philip II," in Adams and Borza, 85–98.

Fredricksmeyer, E. A. 1990. "Alexander and Philip: Emulation and Resentment." *CJ* 85: 300–15.

Fredricksmeyer, E. A. 2000. "Alexander the Great and the Kingship of Asia," in Bosworth and Baynham, 136–66.

Freemann, D. S. 1993. *Lee*. Abridged by R. Harwell, with new foreword by J. M. McPhearson. New York.

Frei, P. 1996. "Zentralgewalt und Lokalautonomie im Achämenidenreich," in Frei and Koch 1996b, 5–131.

Frei, P., and K. Koch, eds. 1996. *Reichsidee und Reichsorganisation im Perserreich*, Zw. Aufl. OBO 55, Freiburg-Göttingen.

Frei, P., and C. Marek. 1997. "Die Karisch-griechische Bilingue von Kaunos." *Kadmos* 26: 1–89.

Frei-Stolba, R., A. Bielman, and O. Bianchi, eds. 2003. *Les femmes antiques entre sphère privée et sphère publique*. Bern.

Frel, J. 1979. *Antiquities at the J. Paul Getty Museum: A Checklist: Sculpture*, vol. i: *Greek Originals*. Malibu, CA.

Frel, J. 1987. "Alexander with a Lance," in Chamay and Maier, 77–9.

French, R. 1994. *Ancient Natural History*. London.

French, V., and P. Dixon 1986. "The Pixodarus Affair: Another View." *AncW* 13: 73–86.

Fried, L. 2004. *The Priest and the Great King: Temple–Palace Relations in the Persian Period*. Winona Lake, IN.

Frisch, P. 1975. *Inschriften von Ilion*. Vol. iii of *Inschriften griechisher Städte aus Kleinasien*. Bonn.

Frommel, C. L., and S. Schütze. 1998. *Pietro da Cortona: atti del convegno internazionale Roma-Firenze 12–15 Novembre 1997*. Rome.

Fuhrmann, M. 1931. *Philoxenos von Eretria*. Göttingen.

Fuller, J. F. C. 1960. *The Generalship of Alexander the Great*. New York.

Funck, B. 1996. "Beobachtungen zum Begriff des Herrscherpalastes und seiner machtpolitischen Funktion im hellenistischen Raum. Prolegomena zur Typologie der hellenistischen Herrschaftssprache," in Hoepfner and Brands, 44–55.

Gadaleta, A. P. 2001. "Efippo storico di Alessandro: testimonianze e frammenti." *AFLFB* 44: 97–144.

Galinsky, G. K. 1972. *The Herakles Theme: The Adaptations of the Hero in Literature from Homer to the Twentieth Century*. Oxford.

García Moreno, L. A. 1990. "Alejandro Magno y la politica exterior de Augusto," in Croisille, 132–42.

Gardin, J.-C. 1997. "À propos de l'entité politique bactrienne." *Topoi* suppl. 1: 263–77.

Gardner, F. 1910. *Six Greek Sculptors*. Oxford.

Gareau, M. 1992. *Charles Le Brun, First Painter to Louis XIV*. New York.

Gargiulo, T. 2004. "E il Citerone esultava: una nota al Romanzo di Alessandro (I 46, 11)." *QS* 60: 109–115.

Garvin, E. E. 2003. "Darius III and Homeland Defense," in Heckel and Tritle, 87–111.

Gauger, J.-D. 1977. "Zu einem offenen Problem des hellenistischen Hoftitelsystems: Ein persischer Ehrentitel, syngenēs?" in Lippold and Himmelmann-Wildschütz, 137–58.

Gauthier, P. 1989. *Sardes* II. Geneva.

Gauthier, P. 2001. "Xanthus." *REG/Bull. Epig.* 114: 568–9.

Gebauer, K. 1938–9. "Alexanderbildnis und Alexandertypus." *MDAI(A)* 63–4: 1–106.

Geddes, A. G. 1987. "Rags and Riches: The Costume of Athenian Men in the Fifth Century." *CQ* 37: 307–31.

Gehrke, H.-J. 1982. "Der siegreiche König. Überlegungen zur hellenistischen Monarchie." *AKG* 64: 247–77.

Gehrke, H.-J. 2003a. *Alexander der Große*. Munich.

Gehrke, H.-J. 2003b. *Geschichte des Hellenismus*. 3rd edn. Munich.

Gehrke, H.-J., and E. Wirbelauer, eds. 1994. *Rechtskodifierung und soziale normen im interkulturellen Vergleich*. Tübingen.

Gelzer, M. 1968. *Caesar: Politician and Statesman*. Oxford: Blackwell.

Georgiades, A. A. 2002. *Ομοφιλία στὴν ἀρχαία Ελλάδα – ὁ μῦθος καταρρέει*. 2nd edn. Athens.

Gillies, J. 1831 [1786]. *The History of Greece, its Colonies and Conquests from the Earliest Accounts till the Division of the Macedonian Empire in the East, including the History of Literature, Philosophy, and the Fine Arts.* 2 vols. in 4. London; repr. London, 1831.

Gillingham, J. 1999. *Richard I*. New Haven, CT.

Giorgieri, M., M. Salvini, M.-C. Trémouille, and P. Vanicelli, eds. 2003. *Licia e Lidia prima dell'ellenizzazione (Roma, 11–12 Ottobre 1999)*. Rome.

Gissel, J. A. P. 2001. "Germanicus as an Alexander Figure." *C&M* 52: 277–301.

Glassner, J. J. 1993. *Chroniques mésopotamiens*. Paris.

Glotz, G., ed. 1939. *Histoire grecque*, vol. iv. Paris.

Golan, G. 1988. "The Fate of a Court Historian, Callisthenes." *Athenaeum* 66: 99–120.

Gold, B. 1985. "Pompey and Theophanes of Mitylene." *AJPh* 106: 312–27.

Goldhill, S., and R. Osborne, eds. 1999. *Performance Culture and Athenian Democracy*. Cambridge.

Goldsmith, O. 1825. *Goldsmith's History of Greece*. London.

Goralski, W. J. 1989. "Arrian's *Events after Alexander*: Summary of Photius and Selected Fragments." *AncW* 19: 81–108.

Goukowsky, P. 1978. *Essai sur les origins du mythe d'Alexandre (336–270 av. J.-C.)*, vol. i: *Les origins politiques*. Nancy, France.

Goukowski, P. 1991. "Les maisons princières de Macédoine de Perdiccas II à Philippe II," in Goukowski and Brixhe, 43–66.

Goukowski, P., and C. Brixhe, eds. 1991. *Hellènika Symmikta: histoire, archéologie, épigraphie*. Nancy, France.

Grabbe, L. 2004. *A History of the Jews and Judaism in the Second Temple Period*, vol. i: *Yehud: A History of the Persian Province of Judah*. London.

Graeve, V. von 1970. *Das Alexandersarkophag und seiner Werkstatt*. Istanbuler Forschungen 28. Berlin.

Graf, D. 2000. "Aramaic on the Periphery of the Achaemenid Realm," in *Iberien (Königreich Kartli) und seine Nachbarn in achaimenidischer und nachachaimenidischer Zeit*. Aktens des internationalen Symposiums in T'bilisi, Georgien, vom 28.9.–3.10.1997. *AMIT* 32: 75–92.

Grainger, J. D. 1990. *Seleukos Nikator: Constructing a Hellenistic Kingdom*. London.

Grainger, J. D. 2007. *Alexander the Great Failure: The Collapse of the Macedonian Empire*. London.

Grayson, A. K. 1975. *Assyrian and Babylonian Chronicles*. New York.

Green, P. 1989a. "Caesar and Alexander: *Aemulatio, imitatio, comparatio*," in Green 1989b, 193–209. Originally pub. *AJAH* 3 (1978): 1–26.

Green, P. 1989b. *Classical Bearings: Interpreting Ancient History and Culture*. London.

Green, P. 1990. *From Alexander to Actium: The Historical Evolution of the Hellenistic Age*. Berkeley, CA.

Green, P. 1991. *Alexander of Macedon, 356–323 BC: A Historical Biography*. Berkeley, CA.

Green, P., ed. 1993. *Hellenistic History and Culture*. Berkeley, CA.

Green, P. 2003. "Occupation and Co-existence: The Impact of Macedon on Athens, 323–307," in Palagia and Tracy, 1–7.

Greenhalgh, P. 1980. *Pompey: The Roman Alexander*. London.

Greenwalt, W. S. 1985. "The Search for Arrhidaeus." *AncW* 10: 69–77.

Greenwalt, W. S. 1988. "Argaeus, Ptolemy II and Alexander's Corpse." *AHB* 2: 39–41.

Greenwalt, W. S. 1989. "Polygamy and Succession in Argead Macedonia." *Arethusa* 22: 19–45.

Greenwalt, W. S. 1999. "Argead Name Changes." *AM* 6: 453–62.

Griffin, A. 1984. *Sikyon*. Oxford.

Griffin, M. T. 1992. *Seneca: A Philosopher in Politics*. Oxford.

Griffin, M. T., and J. Barnes, eds. 1989. *Philosophia Togata: Essays on Philosophy and Roman Society*. Oxford.

Griffith, G. T. 1935. *The Mercenaries of the Hellenistic World*. Cambridge.

Griffith, G. T. 1965. "Alexander and Antipater in 323 B.C." *PACA* 8: 12–17.

Griffith, G. T., ed. 1966. *Alexander the Great: The Main Problems*. Cambridge.

Griffith, G. T. 1970. "Philip of Macedon's Early Interventions in Thessaly (358–352 BC)." *CQ* 20: 67–80.

Grote, G. 1846–56. *A History of Greece*. 1st edn. 12 vols. London.

Grote, G. 1862. *A History of Greece*. New edn. 8 vols. London.

Grote, G. 1888. *A History of Greece*. New edn. 10 vols. London.

Gruen, E. S. 1985. "The Coronation of the Diadochoi," in Eadie and Ober, 253–71.

Güllath, B. 1982. *Untersuchungen zur Geschichte Boiotiens in der Zeit Alexanders und der Diadochen*. Frankfurt am Main.

Gunter, A., and S. Hauser, eds. 2005. *Ernst Herzfeld and the Development of Near Eastern Studies, 1900–1950*. Leiden.

Gurval, R. A. 1995. *Actium and Augustus: The Politics and Emotions of Civil War*. Ann Arbor, MI.

Gurval, R. A. 1996. "Caesar's Comet: The Politics and Poetics of an Augustan Myth." *MAAR* 42: 39–71.

Gutschmid, A. von 1882. "Trogus und Timagenes." *RhM* 37: 548–55.

Guzzo, A. 1998. *Orientalia* 67/4: 532–8.

Haagsma, M., et al., eds. 2003. *The Impact of Classical Greece on European and National Identities*. Amsterdam.

Habicht, C. 1956. *Gottmenschentum und griechische Städte*. Munich.

Habicht, C. 1957. "Samische Volksbeschlüsse der hellenistischer Zeit." *MDAI(A)* 72: 152–274.

Habicht, C. 1970. *Gottmenschentum und griechische Städte*. 2nd edn. Munich.

Habicht, C. 1977. "Zwei Angehörige des lynkestischen Königshauses." *AM* 2: 511–16.

Habicht, C. 1996. "Athens, Samos, and Alexander the Great." *PAPhS* 140: 397–405.

Habicht, C. 1997. *Athens from Alexander to Antony*. Cambridge, MA.

Hadley, R. A. 1974. "Royal Propaganda of Seleucus I and Lysimachus." *JHS* 94: 50–65.

Hafner, G. 1978–80. "Der Alexanderkopf aus Pergamon und der 'Aichmophoros' des Lysippos." In *Anadolu* 21 (*Festschrift Akurgal*): 131–42.

Hallof, K. 1999. "Decretum samium *Syll.*³ 312 redivivum." *Klio* 81: 392–6.

Halperin, D. M. 1990. *One Hundred Years of Homosexuality*. London.

Halperin, D. M., J. J. Winkler, and F. I. Zeitlin, eds. 1990. *Before Sexuality: The Construction of Erotic Experience in the Ancient World*. Princeton, NJ.

Hamilton, J. R. 1953. "Alexander and his So-Called Father." *CQ* 3: 151–7.

Hamilton, J. R. 1956. "The Cavalry Battle at the Hydaspes." *JHS* 76: 25–31.

Hamilton, J. R. 1965. "Alexander's Early Life." *G&R* 12: 117–24.

Hamilton, J. R. 1969. *Plutarch,* Alexander: *A Commentary*. Oxford.

Hamilton, J. R. 1972. "Alexander among the Oreitae." *Historia* 21: 603–8.

Hamilton, J. R. 1975. *Alexander the Great*. London.

Hamilton, J. R. 1987. "Alexander's Iranian Policy," in Will and Heinrichs, i. 467–86.

Hammond, N. G. L. 1972. *A History of Macedonia*, vol. i. Oxford.

Hammond, N. G. L. 1980. "The Battle of the Granicus River." *JHS* 100: 73–88.

Hammond, N. G. L. 1981. *Alexander the Great, King, Commander and Statesman*. London.

Hammond, N. G. L. 1983. *Three Historians of Alexander the Great*. Cambridge.

Hammond, N. G. L. 1989a. "Arms and the King: The Insignia of Alexander the Great." *Phoenix* 43: 217–24.

Hammond, N. G. L. 1989b. *The Macedonian State: Origins, Institutions, and History*. Oxford.

Hammond, N. G. L. 1993. *Sources for Alexander the Great*. Cambridge.

Hammond, N. G. L. 1994a. "One or Two Passes at the Cilicia–Syria Border?" *AncW* 25: 15–26.

Hammond, N. G. L. 1994b. *Philip of Macedon*. Baltimore, MD.

Hammond, N. G. L. 1999a. "The Meaning of Arrian VII, 9, 5." *JHS* 119: 166–8.

Hammond, N. G. L. 1999b. "The Nature of the Hellenistic States." *AM* 6: 483–8.

Hannestad, N. 1993. "*Imitatio Alexandri* in Roman Art," in Carlsen et al., 61–9.

Hansen, M. H., and T. H. Nielsen. 2004. *An Inventory of Archaic and Classical Poleis*. Oxford.

Hanson, V. D. 2001. *Carnage and Culture: Landmark Battles in the Rise of Western Power*. New York.

Harris, E. M. 1995. *Aeschines and Athenian Politics*. New York.

Harris, R. I. 1974. "The Search for Identity," in Borza, 113–22.

Harrison, A. R. W. 1971. *The Law of Athens*, vol. ii: *Procedure*. Oxford.

Harrison, E. 2001. "Macedonian Identities in Two Samothracian Coffers," in Pandermalis et al., 285–90.

Harrison, T., ed. 2002. *Greeks and Barbarians*. Edinburgh.

Hartle, R. W. 1957. "Le Brun's Histoire d'Alexandre and Racine's Alexander Le Grand." *Romantic Review* 48: 90–103.

Hartle, R. W. 1970. "The Image of Alexander the Great in Seventeenth Century France." *AM* 387–406.

Hatzopoulos, M. B. 1985. "Le Béotie et la Macédoine a l'époque del l'hégémonie thébaine: le point de vue macédonien," in G. Argoud and P. Roesch (eds.), *Colloques internationaux du CNRS, "La Béotie antique"*. Paris, 247–57.

Hatzopoulos, M. B. 1987. "Macédoine." *REG/Bull. Epig.* 100: 421–40.

Hatzopoulos, M. B. 1991. *Actes de vente d'Amphipolis.* Meletemata 14. Athens.

Hatzopoulos, M. B. 1996. *Macedonian Institutions under the Kings.* 2 vols. Athens.

Hatzopoulos, M. B. 1997. "Alexandre en Perse: la revanche et l'empire." *ZPE* 116: 41–52.

Hatzopoulos, M. B., and L. D. Loukopoulos, eds. 1980. *Philip of Macedon.* Athens.

Hauben, H. 1975–6. "Antigonos' Invasion Plan for his Attack on Egypt in 306 B.C." *OLP* 6–7: 267–71.

Hauben, H. 1976. "The Expansion of Macedonian Sea-Power under Alexander the Great." *AncSoc* 7: 79–105.

Hauben, H. 1977. "The First War of the Successors (321 B.C.): Chronological and Historical Problems." *AncSoc* 8: 85–120.

Heckel, W. 1977. "The Conspiracy *against* Philotas." *Phoenix* 31: 9–20.

Heckel, W. 1978. "Leonnatos, Polyperchon and the Introduction of Proskynesis." *AJPh* 99: 459–61.

Heckel, W. 1979. "Philip II, Kleopatra and Karanos." *RFIC* 107: 385–93.

Heckel, W. 1981. "Some Speculations on the Prosopography of the *Alexanderreich*," *LCM* 6: 63–70.

Heckel, W. 1986a. "Chorienes and Sisimithres." *Athenaeum* 64: 223–6.

Heckel, W. 1986b. "Factions and Politics in the Reign of Alexander the Great." *AM* 4: 293–305.

Heckel, W. 1986c. "*Somatophylakia*: A Macedonian Cursus Honorum." *Phoenix* 40: 279–94.

Heckel, W. 1988. *The Last Days and Testament of Alexander the Great: A Prosopographic Study.* Historia Einzelschriften 56. Stuttgart.

Heckel, W. 1991. "Hephaistion 'the Athenian'." *ZPE* 87: 39–41.

Heckel, W. 1992. *The Marshals of Alexander's Empire.* London.

Heckel, W., comm. 1997. *Justin: Epitome of the Philippic History of Pompeius Trogus*, vol. i: *Books 11–12: Alexander the Great.* Trans. and appendices by J. C. Yardley. Oxford.

Heckel, W. 1999. "The Politics of Antipatros: 324–319 BC." *AM* 6: 489–98.

Heckel, W. 2002a. "The Case of the Missing 'Phrourarch'." *AHB* 16: 57–60.

Heckel, W. 2002b. "The Politics of Distrust: Alexander and his Successors," in Ogden, 81–95.

Heckel, W. 2003a. "Alexander and the 'Limits of the Civilised World'," in Heckel and Tritle, 147–74.

Heckel, W. 2003b. "King and 'Companions': Observations on the Nature of Power in the Reign of Alexander," in Roisman, 197–225.

Heckel, W. 2006. "Mazaeus, Callisthenes and the Alexander Sarcophagus." *Historia* 55: 385–96.

Heckel, W. 2007. *The Conquests of Alexander the Great.* Cambridge.

Heckel, W., and L. A. Tritle, eds. 2003. *Crossroads of History: The Age of Alexander.* Claremont, CA.

Heckel, W., and J. C. Yardley, eds. 2003. *Alexander the Great: Historical Sources in Translation.* Oxford.

Heckel, W., L. A. Tritle, and P. V. Wheatley, eds. 2007. *Alexander's Empire: From Formulation to Decay.* Claremont, CA.

Hedicke, E. 1931. *Q. Curti Rufi Historiarum Alexandri Magni Macedonis libri qui supersunt.* Leipzig.

Heeren, A. D. L. 1830. *De la politique et du commerce des peuples de l'Antiquité.* Trans. from 4th German edn. (1824), vol. i. Paris.

Heeren, A. D. L. 1840. *Historical Researches into the Politics, Intercourse and Trade of the Principal Nations of Antiquity.* Trans. from German (1824), vol. i. London.

Heisserer, A. J. 1980. *Alexander and the Greek: The Epigraphic Evidence.* Norman, OK.

Helly, B. 1995. *L'État thessalien: Aleuas le Roux, les tétrades et les tagoi.* Lyon.

Heltzer, M., and M. Mahul, eds. 2004. *Tᵉshûrôt LaAvishur: Studies in the Bible and the Ancient Near East, in Hebrew and Semitic Languages.* Tel Aviv.

Henderson, J. 2007. "Drama and Democracy," in Samons, 179–95.

Henkelman, W. 2003. "An Elamite Memorial: The *šumar* of Cambyses and Hystaspes," in Henkelman and Kuhrt, 101–72.

Henkelman, W. 2005. "Animal Sacrifice and 'External' Exchange in the Persepolis Fortification Tablets," in Baker and Jursa, 137–65.

Henkelman, W. 2006. *The Others Gods who Are: Studies in Elamite-Iranian Acculturation based on the Persepolis Fortification Texts.* Diss., Leiden, 101–72.

Henkelman, W. Forthcoming. "Consumed before the King: The Table of Darius, that of Irdabama and Irtaštuna, and that of his Satrap Karkiš," in Jacobs and Rollinger.

Henkelman, W., and A. Kuhrt, eds. 2003. *A Persian Perspective: Essays in Memory of Heleen Sancisi-Weerdenburg.* Leiden.

Herrmann, P. 1997. *I Milet, Teil 1 B Nachträge und Übersetzungen zu den Inschriften n. 1–406.* Berlin.

Heuss, A. 1937. *Stadt und Herrscher des Hellenismus.* Leipzig.

Heuss, A. 1954. "Alexander der Grosse und die politische Ideologie des Altertums." *A&A* 4: 65–104.

Hibbard, H. 1965. *Bernini.* Harmondsworth.

Higgins, W. E. 1980. "Aspects of Alexander's Imperial Administration: Some Modern Methods and Views Reviewed." *Athenaeum* 58: 129–52.

Hirzel, R. 1912. *Plutarch.* Leipzig.

Hitchens, Christopher. 2001. *The Trial of Henry Kissinger.* New York.

Hoepfner, W., and G. Brands, eds. 1996. *Basileia: Die Paläste der hellenistischen Könige.* Mainz.

Hoesch, N. 1996. "Alexandermosaik." *Der Neue Pauly*, vol. i. Stuttgart, cols. 454–7.

Hoesch, N. 1996. "Apelles" (4). *Der Neue Pauly*, vol. i. Stuttgart, col. 829.

Hoffmann, O. 1906. *Die Makedonen: Ihre Sprache und ihr Volkstum.* Göttingen.

Högemann, P. 1985. *Alexander der Große und Arabien.* Zetemata 82. Munich.

Högemann, P. 1992. *Das alte Vorderasien und die Achämeniden: Ein Beitrag zur Herodot-Analyse.* Wiesbaden.

Holt, F. L. 1988. *Alexander the Great and Bactria: The Formation of a Greek Frontier in Central Asia. Mnemosyne* suppl. 104. Leiden.

Holt, F. L. 2003. *Alexander the Great and the Mystery of the Elephant Medallions.* Berkeley, CA.

Holt, F. L. 2005. *Into the Land of Bones: Alexander the Great in Afghanistan.* Berkeley, CA.

Hornblower, J. 1981. *Hieronymus of Cardia.* Oxford.

Hornblower, S. 1982. *Mausolus.* Oxford

Hornblower, S., and A. Spawforth, eds. 1998. *The Oxford Companion to Classical Civilization.* Oxford.

Houghton, A., and C. Lorber. 2002. *Seleucid Coins: A Comprehensive Catalogue.* 2 vols. New York.

Huet, P. D. 1713. *Histoire de la navigation et du commerce des Anciens*. Paris; new edn. Lyon, 1763.

Hurwit, J. M. 1982. "Palm Trees and the Pathetic Phalacy in Archaic Greek Poetry and Art." *CJ* 77: 193–9.

Huss, W. 2001. *Ägypten in hellenistischer Zeit 332–30 v.Chr.* Munich.

Huttner, U. 1997. *Die Politische Rolle Der Heraklesgestalt im Griechischen Herrschertum.* Stuttgart.

Huzar, E. G. 1978. *Mark Antony: A Biography*. London.

Instinsky, H. U. 1949. *Alexander der Große am Hellespont*. Godesberg, Germany.

Isager, J. 1991. *Pliny on Art and Society*. Odense.

Isager, J. 1993. "Alexander the Great in Roman Literature from Pompey to Vespasian," in Carlsen et al., 75–84.

Isager, J., ed. 1994. *Hekatomnid Caria and the Ionian Renaissance*. Odense.

Jacobs, B. 1993. "Die Stellung Lykiens innerhalb der achämenidisch-persischen Reichsverwaltung," in Borchhardt and Dobesch, 63–9.

Jacobs, B. 1994. *Die Satrapienverwaltung im Perserreich zur Zeit Darius' III.* Wiesbaden.

Jacobs, B. 1996. "Die Verwandten des Königs' und die Nachkommen der Verschwörer: Überlegungen zu Titeln, Ämtern und Insignien am Achämenidenhof," in Blakolmer and Borchhardt, 273–84.

Jacobs, B., and R. Rollinger, eds. Forthcoming. *Der Achämenidenhof*. Stuttgart.

Jähne, A. 1978. "Alexander der Grosse: Persönlichkeit, Politik, Ökonomie." *Jahrbuch für Wirtschaftsgeschichte* 1: 245–64.

Jasinski, R. 1958. *Vers le vrai Racine*. 2 vols. Paris.

Jehne, M. 1994. *Koine eirene: Untersuchungen zu den Befriedungs- und Stabilisierungsbemühungen in der griechischen Poliswelt des 4. Jahrhunderts v. Chr.* Stuttgart.

Jensen, J., G. Hinge, P. Schultz, and B. Wickkiser, eds. Forthcoming. *Aspects of Ancient Greek Cult: Ritual, Context, Iconography.* Aarhus Studies in Mediterranean Antiquity. Aarhus.

Joannès, F. 2001. "Les débuts de l'époque hellénistique à Larsa," in Briant 2001a: 249–64.

Joannès, F. 2004. *The Age of Empire in Mesopotamia in the First Millennium BC.* Edinburgh.

Johnson, F. P. 1927. *Lysippos*. Durham, NC; repr. New York, 1968.

Jouin, H. 1889. *Charles Le Brun et les arts sous Louis XIV*. Paris.

Judeich, W. 1892. *Kleinasiatische Studien: Untersuchungen zur griechisch-persischen Geschichte des 4. Jahrhunderts v. Chr.* Marburg.

Julien, P. 1914. *Zur Verwaltung der Satrapien unter Alexander dem Großen*. Weida i. Th.

Kaiser, W. B. 1962. "Ein Meister der Glyptik aus dem Umkreis Alexanders des Grossen." *JdI* 77: 227–39.

Karavites, P. 1984. "The Political Use of Eleutheria and Autonomia." *RIDA* 31: 178–91.

Kienast, D. 1969. "Augustus und Alexander." *Gymnasium* 76: 430–56.

Kienast, D. 1973. *Philipp II. von Makedonien und das Reich der Achaimeniden*. Munich.

Kienast, D. 1988. "Alexander, Zeus und Ammon," in Will and Heinrichs, ii. 309–33.

Kilburn, K., ed. and trans. 1959. *Lucian*, vol. vi. Loeb Classical Library. Cambridge, MA.

Killerich, B. 1988. "Physiognomics and the Iconography of Alexander the Great." *SOsl* 53: 51–66.

Killerich, B. 1993. "The Public Image of Alexander the Great," in Carlsen et al., 85–92.

Kinzl, K. H., ed. 1977. *Greece and the Eastern Mediterranean in Ancient History and Prehistory*. Berlin.

Kirchner, J. 1901. *Prosopographia Attica*. 2 vols. Berlin.

Kleiner, D. E. E. 1992. *Roman Sculpture*. New Haven, CT.

Klinkott, H. 2000. *Die Satrapienregister der Alexander- und Diadochenzeit*. Historia Einzelschriften 145. Stuttgart.

Klinkott, H. 2005. *Der Satrap: Ein persischer Amtsträger und seine Handlungsspielräume*. Frankfurt am Main.

Kloner, A., and I. Stern. 2007. "Idumea in the Late Persian Period (Fourth Century B.C.E.)," in Lipschits et al., 139–44.

Knapton, P., M.-R. Sarraf, and J. Curtis. 2001. "An Inscribed Column from Hamadan." *Iran* 39: 98–117.

Koch, G. 1975. *Die antiken Sarcophagreliefs*, vol. xii, part 6: *Meleager*. Berlin.

Koch, H. 1990. *Verwaltung und Wirtschaft im persischen Kernland zur Zeit der Achämeniden*. Wiesbaden.

Konuk, K. 1998. "The Coinage of the Hekatomnids of Caria." D.Phil. dissertation. University of Oxford.

Konuk, K. 2002. "The Hecatomnids," in Ashton et al., 221–9.

Kottsieper, I. 2002, "Zum aramäischen Text der 'Trilingue' von Xanthos und ihrem historischen Hintergrund," in Loretz et al., 209–43.

Koulakiotis, E. 2006. *Genese und Metamorphosen des Alexandermythos im Spiegel der griechischen nichthistoriographischen Überlieferung bis zum 3. Jh. N. Chr. Xenia*. Konstanzer Althistorische Vorträge und Forschungen 47. Constance.

Kraay, C. M., and G. K. Jenkins, eds. 1968. *Essays on Greek Coinage Presented to Stanley Robinson*. Oxford.

Kraft, K. 1971. *Der "rationale" Alexander: Bearbeitet und aus dem Nachlaß herausgegeben von H. Gesche*. Kallmünz, Germany.

Kralli, I. 2006. "Phokion (Phocion)," in *CDCC*, 682.

Kratz, R.-G., ed. 2002. *Religion und Religionskontakte im Zeitalter der Achämeniden*. Gütersloh, Germany.

Kreissig, H. 1982. *Geschichte des Hellenismus*. Berlin.

Krentz, P., and E. L. Wheeler, eds. and trans. 1994. *Polyaenus: Stratagems of War*. 2 vols. Chicago.

Kroll, J. 2007. "The Emergence of Ruler Portraiture on Early Hellenistic Coinage: The Importance of Being Divine," in Schultz and Hoff, 113–22.

Kuhrt, A. 1985. Review of Briant 1984. *JHS* 107: 236–8.

Kuhrt, A. 1987. Review of Frei-Koch, *Reichsidee* (1984). *BiOr* 44: 199–205.

Kuhrt, A. 1990. "Alexander and Babylon." *AchH* 5: 121–30.

Kuhrt, A. 2001. "The Persian Kings and their Subjects: A Unique Relationship?" *OLZ* 96/2: 167–74.

Kunz, D. 1997. *The Films of Oliver Stone*. London.

Labarre, G. 1996. *Les cités de Lesbos aux époques hellénistique et impériale*. Lyon.

Lamberton, R. 2003. "Plutarch's *Phocion*: Melodrama of Mob and Elite in Occupied Athens," in Palagia and Tracy, 8–13.

Landucci Gattinoni, F. 1985. "La pace del 311 a.C. " *CISA* 11: 108–18.

Landucci Gattinoni, F. 1992. *Lysimaco di Tracia: un sovrano nella prospettiva del primo ellenismo*. Milan.

Landucci Gattinoni, F. 1994. "I mercenari nella politica ateniese dell'età di Alessandro: i soldati e ufficiali mercenari ateniesi al servizio della Persia. Parte I." *AncSoc* 25: 33–62.

Landucci Gattinoni, F. 1995. "I mercenari nella politica ateniese dell'età di Alessandro. Parte II." *AncSoc* 26: 59–91.

Landucci Gattinoni, F. 1997. *Duride di Samo*. Rome.

Landucci Gattinoni, F. 2003. *L'arte del potere: vita e opere di Cassandro di Macedonia*. Stuttgart.

Landucci Gattinoni, F. 2004. "L'Etolia nel protoellenismo: la progressiva centralità di una periferia semibarbara," in Vanotti and Perassi, 105–30.

Lane Fox, R. 1973. *Alexander the Great*. London.

Lane Fox, R. 2004. *The Making of Alexander*. London.

Lane Fox, R. 2006. "The Letter to Gadatas," in *XIAKON ΣΥΜΠΟΣΙΟΝ ΕΙΣ ΜΝΗΜΗΝ W. G. Forrest*. Athens, 149–71.

Lane Fox, R. 2007. "Alexander the Great: 'Last of the Achaemenids'?" in Tuplin, 267–311.

Lanzillotta, E. 2000. "Elementi di diritto costituzionale nelle iscrizioni greche del IV secolo." *RFil* 128: 144–54.

Larrère, C. 2002. "Montesquieu et l'histoire du commerce," in M. Porret and C. Vopilhac-Auger (eds.), *Le temps de Montesquieu*. Geneva, 319–35.

Larmour, D., and D. Spencer, eds. 2007. *The Sites of Rome: Time, Space, Memory*. Oxford.

Lassandro, D. 1984. "La figura di Alessandro Magno nell'opera di Seneca," in Sordi 1984a: 155–68.

Lauffer, S. 1993. *Alexander der Große*. 3rd edn. Darmstadt.

Le Bas, P., and W. H. Waddington. 1870. "Voyage archéologique en Grèce et en Asie Mineure, vol. iii: Inscriptions grecques et latines recueillies en Asia Mineure. Paris.

Lefèvre, F. 1998. *L'Amphictionie pyléo-delphique: histoire et institutiones*. Paris.

Le Goff, R. 2006. "The Transmission of the Eikones of the Philostratoi in Western Art." Ph.D. dissertation. University of Newcastle, NSW (Australia).

Lehmann, G. A. 1971. "Tacitus und die 'imitatio Alexandri' des Germanicus Caesar," in Radke, 23–36.

Lehmann, G. A. 1987. "Hieronymos von Kardia und der 'Lamische Krieg'," in Will and Heinrichs, i. 745–64.

Lehmann, G. A. 2005. *Demosthenes: Ein Leben für die Freiheit*. Munich.

Leingärtner, E., trans. and ed. 1968. *Johann Georg Korb: Tagebuch der Reise nach Russland*. Graz, Austria.

Lemaire, A. 1996. *Nouvelles inscriptions araméennes d'Idumée au Musée d'Israël*. Trans. suppl. 3. Paris.

Lemaire, A. 1999a. "Der Beitrag idumäischer Ostraka zur Geschichte Palästinas im Übergang von der persischen zur hellenistischen Zeit." *ZDPV* 115/1: 12–23.

Lemaire, A. 1999b. "Quatre nouveaux ostraca araméens d'Idumée." *Trans.* 18: 71–4.

Lemaire, A. 2000. "Remarques sur certaines légendes monétaires ciliciennes (Ve–IVe s. av. J.C.)," in Casabonne, 129–42.

Lemaire, A. 2002. *Nouvelles inscriptions araméennes d'Idumée* II. *Trans.* suppl. 9. Paris.

Lemaire, A. 2006a. "Administration in Fourth-Century B.C.E. Judah in Light of Epigraphy and Numismatics," in Lipschits and Oeming, 53–74.

Lemaire, A. 2006b. "New Aramaic Ostraca from Idumea and their Historical Interpretation," in Lipschits and Oeming, 413–56.

Lemaire, A. 2006c. "La Transeuphratène en transition," in Briant and Joannès, 405–41.

Lemaire, A., and M. Sæbø, eds. 2000. *Congress Volume Oslo 1998*. Leiden.

Lendering, J. 2005. *Alexander de Grote: De ondergang van het Perzische rijk.* Amsterdam.

Lepore, E. 1955. "Leostene e le origini della guerra lamiaca." *PP* 10: 161–85.

Le Rider, G. 1977. *Le monnayage d'argent et d'or de Philippe II frappé en Macédoine de 359 à 294.* Paris.

Le Rider, G. 2001. *La naissance de la monnaie: pratiques monétaires de l'Orient ancien.* Paris.

Le Rider, G. 2003. *Alexandre le Grand: monnaie, finances et politique.* Paris.

Le Rider, G., and F. de Callataÿ. 2006. *Les Séleucides et les Ptolémées: l'héritage monétaire et financier d'Alexandre le Grand.* Paris.

Le Rider, G., G. K. Jenkins, N. Waggoner, and U. Westermark, eds. 1989. *Kraay-Mørkholm Essays: Numismatic Studies in Memory of C. M. Kraay and O. Mørkholm.* Louvain-la-Neuve, Belgium.

Le Roy, C. 2005. "Vocabulaire grec et institutions locales dans l'Asie mineure achéménide," in Bultrighini, 333–44.

Leuze, O. 1935. *Die Satrapieneinteilung in Syrien und im Zweistromlande von 520 bis 320. Schriften der Königsberger Gelehrten Gesellschaft,* Heft 4. Halle.

Lippold, A., and N. Himmelmann-Wildschütz, eds. 1977. *Bonner Festgabe Johannes Straub.* Bonn.

Lipschits, O., and M. Oeming, eds. 2006. *Judah and the Judeans in the Persian Period.* Winona Lake, IN.

Lipschits, O., G. N. Knoppers, and R. Albertz, eds. 2007. *Judah and the Judeans in the Fourth Century B.C.E.* Winona Lake, IN.

Llewellyn-Jones, L. J. 2002. "Eunuchs and the Royal Harem in Achaemenid Persia (559–331 B.C.)," in Tougher 2002a: 19–50.

Lloyd, A. B., ed. 1996. *Battle in Antiquity.* London.

Lock, R. A. 1972. "The Date of Agis III's War in Greece." *Antichthon* 6: 10–27.

Lonis, R. 1991. "La réintégration des exilés politiques en Grèce: le problème des biens," in Goukowski and Brixhe, 91–109.

Lorenzo, G. de. 1900. *Una probabile copia pompeiana del vitratto di Alessandro magno dipinto da Apelle.* Naples.

Loretz, O., et al., eds. 2002. *Ex Mesopotamia et Syria Lux: Festschrift für Manfried Dietrich zu seinem 65.* AOAT 281. Münster.

Lott, J. B. 1996. "Philip II, Alexander, and the Two Tyrannies at Eresos of *IG* XII. 2. 526." *Phoenix* 50: 26–40.

Lozachmeur, H., and A. Lemaire. 1996. "Nouveaux ostraca araméens d'Idumée (Collection Sh. Moussaïeff)." *Semitica* 46: 123–42.

Luce, T. J., and A. J. Woodman, eds. 1993. *Tacitus and the Tacitean Tradition.* Princeton, NJ.

Lund, H. S. 1992. *Lysimachus: A Study in Early Hellenistic Kingship.* London.

Lyonnet, B. 1997. *Prospections archéologiques en Bactriane orientale (1974–1978) sous la direction de J.-C. Gardin,* vol. ii. Paris.

Mably, Abbé de. 1766. *Observations sur l'histoire de la Grèce, ou Des causes de la Prospérité et des malheurs des Grecs.* Paris.

McCoy, J. M. 1989. "Memnon of Rhodes and the Granicus." *AJPh* 110: 413–33.

MacDermot, B. C., and K. Shippmann. 1999. "Alexander's March from Susa to Persepolis." *IA* 34: 283–308.

Machiavelli, N. 1992. *The Prince.* 2nd rev. edn. Trans. and ed. by R. M. Adams. New York.

McKechnie, P. 1989. *Outsiders in the Greek Cities in the Fourth Century B.C.* London.

McKechnie, P. 1995. "Diodorus Siculus and Hephaestion's Pyre." *CQ* 45: 418–32.

McKechnie, P. 1999. "Manipulation of Themes in Quintus Curtius Rufus Book 10." *Historia* 48: 44–60.

McQueen, E. I. 1978. "Some Notes on the Antimacedonian Movement in the Peloponnese in 331 B.C." *Historia* 27: 40–64.

McQueen, E. I. 1995. *Diodorus Siculus: The Reign of Philip II: The Greek and Macedonian Narrative from Book XVI: A Companion.* London.

Macurdy, G. H. 1932. *Hellenistic Queens: A Study of Woman-Power in Macedonia, Seleucid Syria and Ptolemaic Egypt.* Baltimore, MD.

Madden, J. 1983. "The Palms do not Weep." *CJ* 78: 193–9.

Maddoli, G. 2006. "Pixodaros di Hekatòmnos e la datazione della Trilingue del Letôon." *Athenaeum* 94/2: 601–8.

Maffi, A. 1994. "Regole matrimoniali e successorie nell'iscrizione di Tegea sul rientro degli esuli," in Gehrke and Wirbelauer, 113–34.

Magnetto, A. 1994. "L'intervento di Filippo nel Peloponneso e l'iscrizione *Syll*³ 665," in Alessandrì, 283–308.

Magnetto, A. 1997. *Gli arbitrati interstatali greci.* Pisa.

Malissard, A. 1990. "Germanicus, Alexandre et le début des *Annales* de Tacite: à propos de Tacite, *Annales*, 2.73," in Croisille 1990b, 328–38.

Marasco, G. 1984. *Democare di Leuconoe: politica e cultura in Atene tra IV e III sècolo a.C.* Florence.

Marasco, G. 1985. "Cherone di Pallene: un tiranno del IV sècolo a.C," in Broilo, 111–19.

Marek, C. 2006. *Die Inschriften von Kaunos.* Vestigia 55. Munich.

Mari, M. 2002. *Al di là dell'Olimpo: Macedoni e grandi santuari della Grecia dall'età arcaica al primo ellenismo.* Paris.

Markle, M. M. 1974. "The Strategy of Philip in 346 B.C." *CQ* 24: 253–68.

Marsden, E. W. 1964. *The Campaign of Gaugamela.* Liverpool.

Martin, H. 1960. "The Concept of *Praotês* in Plutarch's *Lives*." *GRBS* 3: 65–73.

Martin, H. 1961. "The Concept of *Philanthropia* in Plutarch's *Lives*." *AJPh* 82: 164–75.

Marwick, A. 1971. *The Nature of History.* New York.

Massie, R. K. 1980. *Peter the Great: His Life and World.* New York.

Mathieu, G. 1929. "Notes sur Athènes à la veille de la guerre lamiaque." *RPh* 55: 159–83.

Mayrhofer, M. 1976. "Kleinasien zwischen Agonie des Perserreiches und hellenistischem Frühling. Ein Inschriftenfund des Jahres 1973." *Anzeiger d. OÄW* 112: 274–82.

Meadows, A., and U. Wartenberg, eds. 2002. *Coin Hoards*, vol. ix. Royal Numismatic Society, special publication no. 35. London.

Meeus, A. 2007. "De territoriale ambities van de diadochen in de eerste jaren na de dood van Alexander de Grote (323–320 v. Chr.)." *Koninklijke Zuidnederlandse Maatschappij voor Taal-en Letterkunde en Geschiedenis* 61.

Meeus, A. 2008a. "Kleopatra and the Diadochoi," in Van Nuffelen.

Meeus, A. 2008b. "The Power Struggle of the Diadochoi in Babylon, 323 B.C." *AncSoc* 38.

Mehl A. 1980–1. "ΔΟΡΙΚΤΗΤΟΣ ΧΩΡΑ: Kritische Bemerkungen zum 'Speerwerb' in Politik und Völkerrecht der hellenistischen Epoche." *AncSoc* 11–12: 173–212.

Mehl A. 1986. *Seleukos Nikator und sein Reich.* Leuven, Belgium.

Melchert, H. C. 2000. "The Trilingual Inscription oft the Létôon: Lycian Version." (www.achemenet.com/pdf/lyciens/letoon.pdf)

Meißner, B. 2000. "Hofmann und Herrscher: was es für die Griechen hieß, Freund eines Königs zu sein." *AKG* 82: 1–36.

Mendels, D. 1984. "Aetolia 331–301: Frustration, Political Power, and Survival." *Historia* 33: 129–80.

Meritt, B. D. 1935. "Inscriptions of Colophon." *AJPh* 56: 358–97.

Merkelbach, R. 1954. *Die Quellen des griechischen Alexanderromans.* Zetemata 9. Munich.

Meyer, Ed. 1910. "Alexander der Große und die Begründung der absoluten Monarchie." *Kleine Schriften* 1: 283–332; 2nd edn. 1924: 265–314.

Michel, D. 1967. *Alexander als Vorbild für Pompeius, C. Caesar, und M. Antonius.* Collection Latomus 94. Brussels.

Michelotto, P. G., ed. 2002. *Logios aner: studi di antichità in memoria di Mario Attilio Levi.* Milan.

Mildenberg, L. 1990–1. "Notes on the Coin Issues of Mazday." *INJ* 11: 9–23.

Mildenberg, L. 1998. "Money Supply under Artaxerxes III Ochus," in Ashton and Hurter, 277–84.

Mildenberg, L. 1999. "Artaxerxes III Ochus (358–338 B.C.). A Note on the Maligned King." *ZDPV* 115: 201–27.

Miller, M. C. J. 1991. "The Regal Coinage of Cassander." *AncW* 22: 49–55.

Milns, R. D. 1968. *Alexander the Great.* London.

Mingazzini, P. 1961. "Una copia dell' Alexandros Keraunophoros di Apelle." *JBerMus* 3: 7–17.

Miron, D. 2000. "Transmitters and Representatives of Power: Royal Women in Ancient Macedonia." *AncSoc* 30: 35–52.

Momigliano, A. 1952. *George Grote and the Study of Greek History: An Inaugural Lecture Delivered at the University of London.* London.

Montagu, J. 1994. *The Expression of the Passions: The Origin and Influence of Charles Le Brun's Conférence sur l'expression générale et particulièr.* New Haven, CT.

Montesquieu, C. de S., baron de. 1989. *The Spirit of the Laws.* Ed. and trans. by A. M. Cohler, B. S. Miller, and H. S. Stone. Cambridge.

Mooren, L. 1983. "The Nature of the Hellenistic Monarchy," in Van't Dack, 205–40.

Morello, R. 2002. "Livy's Alexander Digression (9. 17–19): Counterfactuals and Apologetics." *JRS* 92: 62–85.

Moreno P. 1993. "L'immagine di Alessandro Magno nell'opera di Lysippo e di altri artisti contemporanei," in Carlsen et al., 101–36.

Moreno, P. 2001. *Apelles: The Alexander Mosaic.* Trans. by D. Stanton. Milan.

Moretti, L. 1967. *Iscrizioni Storiche Ellenistiche,* vol. ii. Florence.

Morier, J. 1812. *A Journey through Persia, Armenia and Asia Minor, to Constantinople in the years 1808 and 1809.* London.

Mørkholm, O. 1991. *Early Hellenistic Coinage.* Cambridge.

Mørkholm, O., and N. M. Waggoner, eds. 1979. *Greek Numismatics and Archaeology. Essays in Honor of Margaret Thompson.* Wetteren.

Morrison. J. S. 1987. "Athenian Sea-Power in 323/322 B.C.: Dream and Reality." *JHS* 107: 88–97.

Mortensen, C. 1997. "Olympias: Royal Wife and Mother at the Macedonian Court." Ph.D. dissertation. University of Queensland.

Mortensen, K. Forthcoming. "Homosexuality in the Macedonian Court." *AM* 7.

Mossé, C. 2001. *Alexandre: la destinée du mythe.* Paris.

Mossé, C. 2004. *Alexander: Destiny and Myth.* Trans. by J. Lloyd with foreword by P. Cartledge. Baltimore, MD

Mossman, J. M. 1992. "Plutarch, Pyrrhus and Alexander," in Stadter, 90–108.

Mossman, J. M. 1995. "Tragedy and Epic in Plutarch's *Alexander*," in Scardigli, 209–28.

Müller, H. 2005. "Hemiolios: Eumenes II, Toriaion und die Finanzorganisation des Alexanderreiches." *Chiron* 35: 355–84.

Müller, O. 1973. *Antigonos Monophthalmos und "Das Jahr der Könige."* Bonn.

Müller, S. 2003. *Maßnahmen bei der Herrschaftssicherung gegenüber der makedonischen Opposition bei Alexander dem Großen*. Frankfurt am Main.

Murray, O. 1996. "Hellenistic Royal Symposia," in Bilde et al., 15–26.

Murison, C. L. 1972. "Darius III and the Battle of Issus." *Historia* 21: 399–423.

Musti, D. 2000. "Il tema dell'autonomia nelle Elleniche di Senofonte." *RFIC* 128: 170–81.

Naveh, J. 1979. "The Aramaic Ostraka from Tell Beer-Sheba (Seasons 1971–76)." *Tel-Aviv* 6: 182–95.

Naveh, J. 1981. "The Aramaic Ostraka from Tell-Arad," in Aharoni, 153–76.

Naveh, J., and S. Shaked, forthcoming. *Aramaic Documents from Ancient Bactria*. (Corpus Inscript. Iran. I.V.) London.

Newell, E. T. 1927. *The Coinages of Demetrius Poliorcetes*. London; repr. Chicago, 1978.

Newlands, C. 2002. *Statius' Silvae and the Poetics of Empire*. Cambridge.

Nicolet-Pierre, H. 1979. "Les monnaies des deux derniers satrapes d'Égypte avant la conquête d'Alexandre," in Mørkholm and Waggoner, 221–30.

Nicolet-Pierre, H. 1999. "Argent et or frappés en Babylonie entre 331 et 311 ou de Mazdai à Séleucos," in Amandry and Hurter, 285–305.

Niebuhr, B.-G. 1828[1812]. "Über das zweite Buch der Oekonomika unter der aristotelischen Schriften," in *Kleine historische und philologische Schriften*. Bonn, i. 412–16.

Nielsen. A. M. 1993. "The Mirage of Alexander: A Minimalist View," in Carlsen et al., 137–44.

Nielsen, I. 1994. *Hellenistic Palaces: Tradition and Renewal*. Aarhus, Denmark.

Nielsen, I. 1998. "Royal Banquets: The Development of Royal Banquets and Banqueting Halls from Alexander to the Tetrarchs," in Nielsen and Nielsen, 102–33.

Nielsen, I., ed. 2001. *The Royal Palace Institution in the First Millenium BC: Regional Development and Cultural Interchange between East and West*. Aarhus, Denmark.

Nielsen, I., and H. S. Nielsen, eds. 1998. *Meals in a Social Context: Aspects of the Communal Meal in the Hellenistic and Roman World*. Aarhus, Denmark.

Nock, A. D. 1928. "Notes on Ruler-Cult I–IV: I. Alexander and Dionysus." *JHS* 48: 21–43.

Nowotka, K. 2003. "Freedom of the Greek Cities in Asia Minor in the Age of Alexander the Great." *Klio* 85: 15–41.

Nylander, C. 1983. "The Standard of the Great King: A Problem in the Alexander Mosaic." *Opuscula Romana* 14: 19–37.

Nylander, C. 1993. "Darius III, the Coward King: Point and Counterpoint," in Carlsen et al., 145–59.

Ogden, D. 1996a. *Greek Bastardy in the Classical and Hellenistic Periods*. Oxford.

Ogden, D. 1996b. "Homosexuality and Warfare in Ancient Greece," in Lloyd, 107–68.

Ogden, D. 1999. *Polygamy, Prostitutes and Death: The Hellenistic Dynasties*. London.

Ogden, D., ed. 2002. *The Hellenistic World: New Perspectives*. London.

Olmstead, A. T. 1948. *History of the Persian Empire*. Chicago.

Osborne, M. J. 1981–3. *Naturalization in Athens*. 4 vols. Verhandelingen van de Koninglijke Academie voor Wetenschapen. Letteren en Schone Kunsten van Belgie. Brussels.

Overy, R. 2004. *The Dictators: Hitler's Germany and Stalin's Russia*. London.

Özet, A. 1994. "The Tomb of a Noble Woman from the Hekatomnid Period," in Isager, 88–96.

Ozols, J., and V. Thewalt, eds. 1984. *Aus dem Osten des Alexanderreiches: Völker und Kulturen zwischen Orient und Okzident: Iran, Afghanistan, Pakistan, Indien: Festschrift zum 65. Geburtstag von Klaus Fischer.* Cologne.

Palagia, O. 1986. "Imitation of Herakles in Ruler-Portraiture: A Survey, from Alexander to Maximus Daza." *Boreas* 9: 137–51.

Palagia, O. 2000. "Hephaestion's Pyre and the Royal Hunt of Alexander," in Bosworth and Baynham, 167–206.

Palagia, O., and J. J. Pollitt, eds. 1996. *Personal Styles in Greek Sculpture.* Cambridge.

Palagia, O., and S. V. Tracy, eds. 2003. *The Macedonians in Athens, 322–229 B.C.* Oxford.

Pandermalis, D. 2004. *Alexander the Great: Treasures from an Epic Era of Hellenism.* New York.

Pandermalis, D., M. A. Tiverios, and E. Voutiras, eds. 2001. *Agalma: meletes gia ten archia plastike pros timen tou Giorgou Despine.* Thessalonike.

Parke, H. W. 1933. *Greek Mercenary Soldiers from the Earliest Times to the Battle of Ipsus.* Oxford.

Parke, H. W. 1967. *The Oracles of Zeus: Dodona, Olympia, Ammon.* Oxford.

Parsons, W., trans. 1703. *Monsieur A. Félibien's descriptions of "The Queens of Persia at the feet of Alexander."* London.

Pearson, L. 1960. *The Lost Histories of Alexander the Great.* Philadelphia.

Pecorella Longo, C. 1971. *"Eterie" e gruppi politici nell' Atene del IV sec. a.C.* Florence.

Pedley, J. G. 2002. *Greek Art and Archaeology.* 3rd edn. Upper Saddle River, NJ.

Pelling, C. 1989. "Plutarch: Roman Heroes and Greek Culture," in Griffin and Barnes, 199–232.

Pelling, C. 1993. "Tacitus and Germanicus," in Luce and Woodman, 59–85.

Peremans, W., and E. Van't Dack. 1950–81. *Prosopographia Ptolemaica.* 9 vols. Leuven, Belgium.

Pericolo, L. 2004. *Claude Nivelon Vie de Charles Le Brun et Description Détaillée de ses Ouvrages.* Geneva.

Perlman, S., ed. 1973. *Philip and Athens.* New York.

Perlman, S. 1985. "Greek Diplomatic Tradition and the Corinthian League of Philip of Macedon." *Historia* 34: 153–74.

Perrin, Bernadotte, tr. 1986. *Plutarch's Lives,* vol. xi. Cambridge, MA.

Perrot, J., ed. Forthcoming. *Le palais de Darius à Suse.* Dijon.

Pfeiffer, S. 2008. *Herrscher-und Dynastiekulte im Ptolemäerreich: Systematik und Einordung der Kultformen.* Munich.

Picard, C. 1938. "Un hérôon macédonien à Philippes." *RA* 1: 334–5.

Pickard-Cambridge, A. 1988. *The Dramatic Festivals of Athens.* 2nd edn. rev. by J. Gould and D. M. Lewis. Oxford.

Picon Garcia, V. 1990. "La figura de Alejandro en la biografía latina," in Croisille 1990b, 361–78.

Pitts, M. W., ed. 2002. *Montesquieu and the Spirit of Modernity.* Oxford.

Plácido, D. 1990. "Alejandro y los emperadores romanos en la historiografía griega," in Crosille 1990b, 58–75.

Plantzos, D. 2002. "Alexander of Macedon on a Silver Intaglio." *AK* 45: 71–9.

Plaumann, G. 1920. "Probleme des alexandrinischen Alexanderkultes." *Arch. Pap.* 6: 77–99.

Poddighe, E. 2002. *Nel segno di Antipatro: l'eclissi della democrazia ateniese dal 323/2 al 319/8 a.C.* Rome.

Poddighe, E. 2004. "Una possibile identificazione del paidotriba di Sicione: Ps. Dem. XVII, 16." *QS* 59: 183–96.

Poddighe, E. 2007. "La questione samia tra Alessandro e Atene: 'libertà dei Greci'." *QS* 66: 29–45.

Pollini, J. 1990. "Man or God: Divine Assimilation and Imitation in the Late Republic and Early Principate," in Raaflaub and Toher, 334–63.

Pollitt, J. J. 1986. *Art in the Hellenistic Age*. Cambridge.

Polman, G. H. 1974. "Chronological Biography and *Akme* in Plutarch." *CPh* 69: 169–77.

Porten, B., and A. Yardeni. 2003. "In Preparation of a Corpus of Aramaic Ostraca from the Land of Israel: The House of Yehokal," in Deutsch, 207–23.

Porten, B., and A. Yardeni. 2004. "On Problems of Identity and Chronology in the Idumean Ostraca," in Heltzer and Mahul, 161–83.

Porten, B., and A. Yardeni. 2006. "Social, Economic and Onomastic issues in the Aramaic Ostraca of the fourth Century B.C.E.," in Lipschits and Oeming, 457–88.

Porten, B., and A. Yardeni. 2008. "The Chronology of the Idumean Ostraca in the Decade or so after the Death of Alexander the Great and its Relevance for Historical Events," in M. Cogan and D. Kahn (eds.), *Treasures on Camels' Humps: Historical and Literary Studies from the Ancient Near East presented to Israel Eph'al*. Jerusalem, 237–49.

Posner, D. 1959. "Charles Le Brun's Triumphs of Alexander." *ABull* 41: 237–48.

Prandi, L. 1983. "Alessandro Magno e Chio: considerazioni su *Syll.*[3] 283 e *SEG* XXII, 506." *Aevum* 57: 24–32.

Prandi, L. 1988. *Platea: momenti e problemi della storia di una polis*. Padua.

Prandi, L. 1996. *Fortuna e realtà del'opera di Clitarco*. Stuttgart.

Prandi, L. 1998. "A Few Remarks on the Amyntas 'Conspiracy'," in Will, 91–101.

Price, M. 1991. *The Coinage in the Name of Alexander the Great and Philip Arrhidaeus*. 2 vols. London.

Price, S. 1988. "Greece and Hellenistic World," in Boardman et al., 309–31.

Pugliese Carratelli, G. 1949. "Alessandro e la costituzione rodia." *PP* 4: 149–71.

Raaflaub, K. A., and M. Toher, eds. 1990. *Between Republic and Empire: Interpretations of Augustus and his Principate*. Berkeley, CA.

Racine, J. 1990. *Alexandre Le Grand*. Ed. by M. Hawcroft and V. Worth. Exeter.

Rader, O. B. 2003. *Grab und Herrschaft: Politischer Totekult von Alexander dem Grossen bis Lenin*. Munich.

Radet, G. 1931. *Alexandre le Grand*. Paris.

Radke, G., ed. *Politik und litterarische Kunst im Werk des Tacitus*. Beiheft 1 zu AV-Reihe 14. Stuttgart.

Radt, W. 1981. "Der 'Alexanderkopf' in Istanbul: Ein Kopf aus dem grossen Fries des Pergamon-Altars." *AA* 583–96.

Ramsey, J. T. 2001. "Did Mark Antony Contemplate an Alliance with his Political Enemies in July 44 B.C.E.?" *CPh* 96: 253–68.

Ramusio, G.-B. 1563. *Primo volume e terza editione delle navigationi et viaggi raccolto gia da M. Gio. Battista Ramusio*. Venice.

Ranum, O., and P. Ranum. 1972. *The Century of Louis XIV*. London.

Rathmann, M. 2005. *Perdikkas zwischen 323 und 320: Nachlassverwalter des Alexanderreiches oder Autokrat?* Österreichische Akademie der Wissenschaften. Philosophisch-historische Klasse: Sitzungsberichte 724. Vienna.

Rawson, E. 1989. "Roman Rulers and the Philosophical Adviser," in Griffin and Barnes, 233–57.

Rayfield, D. 2004. *Stalin and his Hangmen*. New York.

Reames-Zimmermann, J. 1999. "An Atypical Affair? Alexander the Great, Hephaistion Amyntoros and the Nature of their Relationship." *AHB* 13: 81–96.

Rehak, P. 1990. "The Statues of Alexander the Great in the Forum Augustum and the Regia." *AJA* 94: 312.

Renard, M., and J. Servais. 1955. "A propos du marriage d'Alexandre et de Roxane." *AC* 24: 29–50.

Reuss, F. 1876. *Hieronymus von Kardia: Studien zur Diadochenzeit*. Berlin.

Ridgway, B. S. 1990. *Hellenistic Sculpture*, vol. i: *The Styles of ca. 331–200 B.C.* Madison, WI.

Rieu, E. V., tr. 1950. *Homer: The Iliad*. Penguin Classics. London.

Ritter, H.-W. 1965. *Diadem und Königsherrschaft: Untersuchungen zu Zeremonien und Rechtsgrundlagen des Herrschaftsantritts bei den Persern, bei Alexander dem Großen und im Hellenismus*. Munich.

Roaf, M. 1983. *Sculptures and Sculptors at Persepolis*. Iran 21. London.

Robert, L. 1929. "Inscriptions agonistique d' Erythrai." *RP* 55: 148–9 (= *Opera Minora* ii. 1114–15).

Robert, L. 1933. "Inscriptions d'Érythrai." *BCH* 57: 467–81.

Robert, L. 1936. "Décrets de Kolophon." *RP* 62: 158–68 (= *Opera Minora* ii. 1237–47).

Robertson, M. 1993. "What is Hellenistic about Hellenistic Art?," in Green, 67–110.

Robertson, W. 1791. *An Historical Disquisition concerning the Knowledge which the Ancients had of India and the Progress of Trade with that Country prior to the Discovery of the Passage to it by the Cape of Good Hope, with an appendix containing observations on the civil policy, the laws and religious institutions of the Indians*. London; repr. Basel, 1792.

Robinson, C. A., Jr. 1953. *The History of Alexander the Great*. 2 vols. Providence, RI.

Rochberg-Halton, R., ed. 1987. *Language, Literature and History: Philological and Historical Studies presented to Erica Reiner*. AOS 67. New Haven, CT.

Rodriguez, P. 2004. "Les Égyptiens dans l'armée de terre ptolémaïque (Diodore XIX, 80.4)." *REG* 117: 104–24.

Roebuck, C. 1948. "The Settlements of Philip II with the Greek States in 338 B.C." *CPh* 43: 73–92.

Rogers, G. M. 2004. *Alexander: The Ambiguity of Greatness*. New York.

Roisman, J. 1984. "Ptolemy and his Rivals in his History of Alexander." *CQ* 34: 373–85.

Roisman, J., ed. 2003a. *Brill's Companion to Alexander the Great*. Leiden.

Roisman, J. 2003b. "Honor in Alexander's Campaign," in Roisman 2003a, 279–321.

Rolfe, J. C., ed. and trans. 1946. *Quintus Curtius: History of Alexander*. 2 vols. Cambridge, MA.

Rollin, C. 1791. *The Life of Alexander the Great King of Macedon, compiled from Ancient History, translated from the French*. Providence, RI.

Rollin, C. 1821. *Oeuvres complètes: nouvelle édition accompagnée d'observations et d'éclaircissements historiques par M. Letronne*. Paris.

Romane J. P. 1987. "Alexander's Siege of Tyre." *AncW* 16: 79–90.

Romane J. P. 1988. "Alexander's Siege of Gaza." *AncW* 18: 21–30.

Romane J. P. 1994. "Alexander's Sieges of Miletus and Halicarnassus." *AncW* 25: 61–76.

Romm, J. S. 1992. *The Edges of the Earth in Ancient Thought*. Princeton, NJ.

Roos, A. G., and G. Wirth, eds. 1967–8. *Flavii Arriani quae exstant omnia*. 2 vols. Leipzig.

Rosen, K. 1978. "Der 'göttliche Alexander', Athen, und Samos." *Historia* 27: 20–40.

Rosen, K. 1979. "Politische Ziele in der frühen hellenistischen Geschichtsschreibung?" *Hermes* 107: 460–77.

Ross, D. O. 1973. "The Tacitean Germanicus." *YClS* 23: 209–27.

Rostovtzeff, M. 1913[1994]. "L'Asia ellenistica all' epoca dei Seleucidi. (A proposito del libro di Bouché-Leclercq, *Histoire des Séleucides*, Paris, 1913)." *Naučnyj Istoričeskii Žurnal* 39–63 (in Russian). Italian translation in *Quaderni di Storia* 40 (1994): 9–31.

Rostovtzeff, M. 1935. "ΠΡΟΓΟΝΟΙ." *JHS* 55: 56–66.

Rostovtzeff, M. 1941. *The Social and Economic History of the Hellenistic World*. 3 vols. Oxford.

Roussel, P. 1932. "Alexandre le Grand." *JS* (Feb.): 49–60.

Rubinsohn, W. Z. 1977. "The 'Philotas Affair': A Reconsideration." *AM* 2: 409–20.

Rubinsohn, W. Z. 1993. "The Philosopher at Court: Intellectuals and Politics in the Time of Alexander the Great." *AM* 5: 1301–27.

Rumpf, A. 1962. "Zum Alexander-Mosaik." *AM* 77: 229–41.

Russell, D. A. 1973. *Plutarch*. New York.

Rutland, L. W. 1987. "The Tacitean Germanicus: Some Suggestions for a Re-evaluation." *RhM* 130: 153–64.

Ruzicka, S. 1985. "A Note on Philip's Persian War," *AJAH* 10: 84–95.

Ruzicka, S. 1992. *Politics of a Persian Dynasty: The Hecatomnids in the Fourth Century B.C.* Norman, OK.

Ruzicka, S. 1997. "The Eastern Greek World," in Tritle, 107–36.

Ryder, T. T. B. 1965. *Koine Eirene: General Peace and Local Independence in Ancient Greece*. Oxford.

Ryder, T. T. B. 1994. "The Diplomatic Skills of Philip II," in Worthington, 228–57.

Sainte-Croix, A. 1775. *Examen critique des anciens historiens d'Alexandre le Grand*. Paris.

Sainte-Croix, A. 1804. *Examen critique des anciens historiens d'Alexandre le Grand*. 2nd edn. Paris.

Sakellariou, M. B. 1980. "Panhellenism: From Concept to Policy," in Hatzopoulos and Loukopoulos, 128–45, 242–5.

Salviat, F. 1958. "Une nouvelle loi Thasienne." *BCH* 82: 193–267.

Samons, L. J., II., ed. 2007. *The Cambridge Companion to the Age of Pericles*. Cambridge.

Sanchez, P. 2001. *L'Amphictionie des Pyles et de Delphes*. Historia Einzelschriften 148. Stuttgart.

Sapin, J. 2004. "La 'frontière' judéo-araméenne au IVe siècle av. J.C." *Trans.* 27: 109–54.

Savalli-Lestrade, I. 2003. "La place des reines à la cour et dans le royaume à l'époque hellénistique," in Frei-Stolba et al., 59–76.

Sawada, Noriko. 1996. "Athenian Politics in the Age of Alexander the Great: A Reconsideration of the Trial of Ctesiphon," *Chiron* 26: 57–84.

Scardigli, B., ed. 1995. *Essays on Plutarch's Lives*. Oxford.

Schachermeyr, F. 1920. "Das Ende des makedonischen Königshauses." *Klio* 16: 332–7.

Schachermeyr, F. 1970. *Alexander in Babylon und die Reichsordnung nach seinem Tode*. Vienna.

Schachermeyr, F. 1973. *Alexander der Grosse: Das Problem seiner Persönlichkeit und seines Wirkens*. Vienna.

Schaefer, A. 1885–7. *Demosthenes und Seine Zeit*. 2nd rev. edn. 3 vols in 2. Leipzig.

Schäfer, C. 2002. *Eumenes von Kardia und der Kampf um die Macht im Alexanderreich*. Frankfurt am Main.

Schäfer, D. Forthcoming. "Persian foes – Ptolemaic Friends? The Persians on the Satrap Stela and in Contemporary Texts," in Briant and Chauveau.

Schefold, K., and M. Seidel. 1968. *Der Alexander-Sarkophag*. Berlin.

Scheidel, W., I. Morris, and R. P. Saller, eds. 2007. *The Cambridge Economic History of the Greco-Roman World*. Cambridge.

Schepens, G. 1989. "Zum Problem der 'Unbesiegbarkeit' Alexanders d. Gr." *AncSoc* 20: 15–53.

Schepens, G. 1998. "Das Alexanderbild in den Historikerfragmenten," in Schuller, 85–99.

Schlosser, F.-C. 1828. *Histoire universelle de l'Antiquité*, vol. ii. Paris.

Schlözer, A.-L. 1761. *Versuch einer allgemeinen Geschichte der Handlung und Seefahrt in den ältesten Zeiten*. Trans. from Swedish original (1758). Rostock, Germany.

Schmidt, E. 1970. *Persepolis*, vol. iii: *The Royal Tombs and Other Monuments*. Chicago.

Schmidt, K. 1999. "The Peace of Antalcidas and the Idea of the *Koine Eirene*: A Panhellenic Peace Movement." *RIDA* 46: 81–96.

Schmitt, H. H. 1969. *Die Staatsverträge des Altertums*, vol. iii. Munich.

Schmitt, O. 1992. *Der Lamische Krieg*. Bonn.

Schmitt, R. 2000. *The Old-Persian Inscriptions of Naqsh-i Rustam and Persepolis* (CII I/1/II), London.

Schmitt, R. 2006. *Iranische Anthroponyme in der erhaltenen Resten von Ktesias' Werk*. Vienna.

Schnabel, P. 1925. "Die Begründung des hellenistischen Königskultes durch Alexander." *Klio* 19: 113–27.

Schnabel, P. 1926. "Zur Frage der Selbstvergötterung Alexanders." *Klio* 20: 179–86.

Schober, L. 1981. *Untersuchungen zur Geschichte Babyloniens und der Oberen Satrapien von 323–303 v. Chr*. Frankfurt am Main.

Scholl, R. 1987. "Alexander der Große und die Sklaverei am Hofe." *Klio* 69: 108–21.

Scholz, P. 1998. *Der Philosoph und die Politik: Die Ausbildung der philosophischen Lebensform und die Entwicklung des Verhältnisses von Philosophie und Politik im 4. und 3. Jh. v. Chr.* Stuttgart.

Schreiber, T. 1903. *Studien über das Bildnis Alexanders des Grossen*. Leipzig.

Schubert, R. 1914. *Die Quellen zur Geschichte der Diadochenzeit*. Leipzig.

Schuller, W., ed. 1998. *Politische Theorie und Praxis im Altertum*. Darmstadt.

Schultz, P. 2007. "Leochares' Argead Portraits in the Philippeion," in Schultz and Hoff, 205–33.

Schultz, P. Forthcoming. "Divine Images and Royal Ideology in the Philippeion at Olympia," in Jensen et al.

Schultz, P., and R. von den Hoff, eds. 2007. *Early Hellenistic Portraiture: Image, Style, Content*. Cambridge.

Schwenk, C. 1985. *Athens in the Age of Alexander: The Dated Laws and Decrees of the "Lykourgan Era," 338–322 B.C.* Chicago.

Scott, K. 1929. "Octavian's Propaganda and Antony's de sua ebrietate." *CPh* 24: 133–41.

Scott, K. 1933. "The Political Propaganda of 44–30 B.C." *MAAR* 11: 7–49.

Scott-Kilvert, I., trans. 1973. *Plutarch. The Age of Alexander: Nine Greek Lives*. Intro. by G. T. Griffith. London.

Sealey, R. 1960. "The Olympic Festival of 324 B.C." *CR* 74: 185–6.

Sealey, R. 1993. *Demosthenes and his Time: A Study in Defeat*. New York.

Sebag-Montefiore, S. 2003. *Stalin: Court of the Red Tsar*. London.

Seel, O. 1971. *Eine römische Weltgeschichte: Studien zum Text der Epitome des Iustinus und zur Historik des Pompejus Trogus*. Nuremberg.

Segre, M. 1941. "Epigraphica." *Bullsoc Arch. Alex.* 34: 29–39.

Seibert, J. 1969. *Untersuchungen zur Geschichte Ptolemaios I*. Munich.

Seibert, J. 1972. *Alexander der Grosse*. Erträge der Forschung 10. Darmstadt.

Seibert, J. 1983. *Das Zeitalter der Diadochen*. Darmstadt.

Seibert, J. 1985. *Die Eroberung des Perserreiches durch Alexander d. Gr. auf kartographischer Grundlage*. Wiesbaden.

Seibert, J. 1988. "Dareios III," in Will and Heinrichs, i. 437–56.

Seibert, J. 1994. *Alexander der Grosse*. 4th edn. Darmstadt.

Seibert, J. 1998. "'Panhellenischer' Kreuzzug, Nationalkrieg, Rachefeldzug oder makedonischer Eroberungskrieg? Überlegungen zu den Ursachen des Krieges gegen Persien," in Will, 5–58.

Service, R. 2004. *Stalin: A Biography*. London.

Settis, S., ed. 1998. *I Greci: Storia cultura arte società*, vol. ii: *Una storia greca. III. Trasformazioni*. Turin.

Shabazi, A. S. 2003. "Irano-Hellenic Notes 3: Iranians and Alexander." *AJAH* n.s. 2: 5–38.

Shaked, S. 2003. "De Khulmi à Nikhšapaya: les données des nouveaux documents araméens de Bactres sur la toponymie de la région (IVe siècle av. n.è.)." *CRAI* 1517–32.

Shaked, S. 2004. *Le satrape de Bactriane et son gouverneur: documents araméens du IVe siècle av. n.è.* Persika 5. Paris.

Shaked, S. 2006. "Are the Aramaic Documents from Ancient Bactria Part of an Archive?" In *Papers presented to the Conference "Les Archives des Fortifications de Persépolis dans le contexte de l'empire achéménide et de ses prédécesseurs" held at the Collège de France November 6th–7th 2006*.

Sherwin-White, S. M., and A. Kuhrt. 1993. *From Samarkhand to Sardis: A New Approach to the Seleucid Empire*. Berkeley, CA.

Shipley, G. 1987. *A History of Samos 800–188 B.C.* Oxford.

Shipley, G. 2000. *The Greek World after Alexander, 323–30 BC*. London.

Shofman, A. S. 1976. *History of Ancient Macedonia* (in Russian). Kazan.

Shotter, D. C. A. 1968. "Tacitus, Tiberius and Germanicus." *Historia* 17: 194–214.

Siganidou, M. 1980. *The Search for Alexander*. Exhibition catalogue. Boston.

Simpson, R. H. 1952. "The Historical Circumstances of the Peace of 311." *JHS* 72: 25–31.

Sisti, F., ed. 2001. *Arriano: Anabasi di Alessandro*, vol. i. Milan.

Sisti, F., and A. Zambrini, eds. 2004. *Arriano: Anabasi di Alessandro*, vol. ii. Milan.

Six, J. 1910. "Apelleisches." *JdI* 25: 147–59.

Six, J. P. 1884. "Le satrape Mazaios." *NC* 3rd ser. 4: 97–159.

Sjöqvist, E. 1966. *Lysippus*. Cincinnati, OH.

Skutsch, O., ed. 1985. *The* Annals *of Q. Ennius*. Oxford.

Smith, R. R. R. 1989. *Hellenistic Royal Portraits*. Oxford.

Smith, S. 1924. *Babylonian Historical Texts relating to the Capture and Downfall of Babylon*. London.

Smith, V. A. 1914. *The Early History of India from 600 BC to the Muhammadan Conquest, including the invasion of Alexander the Great*. 3rd edn. Oxford.

Sokolowski, F. 1946. "Ventes des Prêtrises d'Érythrae." *BCH* 70: 548.

Sordi, M. 1984a. "Alessandro e l'Anfizionia nel 336/5," in Sordi 1984a, 9–13.

Sordi, M., ed. 1984b. *Alessandro Magno tra storia e mito*. Milan.

Sordi, M. 1984c. "L'orazione pseudodemostenica 'Sui patti con Alessandro' e l'atteggiamento dei Greci prima di Isso," in Sordi 1984a, 23–30.

Sordi, M. 1996. "Larissa e la dinastia Alevade." *Aevum* 70: 37–45.

Spann, P. O. 1999. "Alexander at the Beas: Fox in a Lion's Skin," in Titchener and Moorton, 62–74.

Speck, H. 2002. "Alexander at the Persian Gates: A Study in Historiography and Topography." *AJAH* n.s. 1: 1–234.

Spencer, D. 2002. *The Roman Alexander: Reading a Cultural Myth*. Exeter.

Spencer, D. 2005a. "Lucan's Follies: Memory and Ruin in a Civil-War Landscape." *G&R* 52: 46–69.

Spencer, D. 2005b. "Perspective and Poetics in Curtius' Gorgeous East." *AClass* 48: 121–40.

Spencer, D. 2006a. "'Good men who have skill in speaking': Performing Advice in Rome," in Spencer and Theodorakopoulos, 1–29.

Spencer, D. 2006b. "Telling it like is . . . : Seneca, Alexander and the dynamics of epistolary advice," in Spencer and Theodorakopoulos, 79–104.

Spencer, D. 2007. "Rome at a Gallop: Livy, on *Not* Gazing, Jumping or Toppling into the Void," in Larmour and Spencer, 61–101.

Spencer, D., and E. Theodorakopoulos, eds. 2006. *Advice and its Rhetoric in Greece and Rome*. Bari, Italy.

Squillace, G. 2000. "L'ultimo intervento di Filippo II in Tessaglia nella propaganda macedone e antimacedone." *Aevum* 74: 81–94.

Squillace, G. 2004. *Filippo II e Alessandro Magno tra opposizione e consenso*. Soveria Mannelli, Italy.

Stadter, P. A. 1965. *Plutarch's Historical Methods: An Analysis of the Mulierum virtutes*, Cambridge, MA.

Stadter, P. A. 1980. *Arrian of Nicomedeia*. Chapel Hill, NC.

Stadter, P. A., ed. 1992. *Plutarch and the Historical Tradition*. London.

Stagakis, G. S. 1970. "Observations on the 'hetairoi' of Alexander the Great." *AM* 1: 86–102.

Stamatiou, A. 1988. "Alexander the Great as a Lion Hunter." *Praktika tou XII Diethnous synedriou klasikēs archaiologias, Athēna 4–10 Septembriou 1983*, B: 209–17. Athens.

Stein, A. 1929. *On Alexander's Track to the Indus*. London.

Stein, A. 1932. "The Site of Alexander's Passage of the Hydaspes and the Battle with Poros." *GJ* 80: 31–46.

Stein, A. 1942. "Notes on Alexander's Crossing of the Tigris and the Battle of Arbela." *GJ* 100: 155–64.

Stein, A. 1943. "On Alexander's Route into Gedrosia: An Archaelogical Tour in Las Bela." *GJ* 102: 193–227.

Stern, E. 2001. *Archaeology of the Land of the Bible*, vol. ii: *The Assyrian, Babylonian and Persian Periods (732–332 B.C.E.)*. New York.

Stewart, A. 1993. *Faces of Power: Alexander's Image and Hellenistic Politics*. Berkeley, CA.

Stewart, A. 2003. "The Portraiture of Alexander," in Roisman, 31–66.

Stier, H.-E. 1939. "Zum Gottkönigtum Alexanders des Grossen." *Welt als Geschichte* 5: 391–5.

Stolper, M. W. 1987. "Bēlšunu the Satrap," in Rochberg-Halton, 389–402.

Stolper, M. W. 1989a. "The Governor of Babylon and Across-the-River in 486 B.C." *JNES* 48/4: 283–305.

Stolper, M. W. 1989b. "Registration and Taxation of Slave Sales in Achaemenid Babylonia." *ZA* 79: 80–101.

Stoneman, R. 1997. *Alexander the Great*. London.

Strasburger, H. 1952. "Alexanders Zug durch die gedrosische Wüste." *Hermes* 80: 456–93.

Strauss, B. S., and J. Ober. 1990. "Darius III of Persia: Why He Lost and Made Alexander Great," in *The Anatomy of Error: Ancient Military Disasters and their Lessons for Modern Strategists*. New York, 103–31.

Suhr, E. G. 1979. *Sculpted Portraits of Greek Statesmen*. New York.

Taeger, F. 1957. *Charisma: Studien zur Geschichte des antiken Herrscherkultes*. Stuttgart.

Taplin, O. 1999. "Spreading the Word through Performance," in Goldhill and Osborne, 33–57.

Tarn, W. W. 1913. *Antigonos Gonatas*. Oxford.

Tarn, W. W. 1933. *Alexander the Great and the Unity of Mankind*. London.

Tarn, W. W. 1997. *The Greeks in Bactria and India*. Rev. edn. with new preface and bibliography by F. E. Holt. Chicago.

Tataki, A. B. 1998. *The Macedonians Abroad: A Contribution to the Prosopography of Ancient Macedonia*. Athens.

Thirlwall, C. 1838–9. *A History of Greece*, vols. vi–vii. London.

Thompson, M. 1968. "The Mints of Lysimachus," in Kraay and Jenkins, 163–82.

Thuillier, J., and J. Montagu. 1963. *Charles Le Brun 1619–1690*. Versailles.

Tilia, A.-B. 1972. *Studies and Restorations at Persepolis and Other Sites of Fārs*. Rome.

Titchener, F., and R. F. Moorton, Jr., eds. 1999. *The Eye Expanded: Life and the Arts in Greco-Roman Antiquity*. Berkeley, CA.

Tiverios, M. 1996. *Elliniki Techne: Archaia Aggeia*. Athens.

Toman, R. 2000. *Neoclassicism and Romanticism: Architecture, Sculpture, Painting, Drawings, 1750–1848*. Stuttgart.

Too, Y. L. 1994. "Educating Nero: A Reading of Seneca's *Moral Epistles*," in Elsner and Masters, 211–24.

Tougher, S. F., ed. 2002a. *Eunuchs in Antiquity and Beyond*. London.

Tougher, S. F. 2002b. "In or Out? Origins of Court Eunuchs," in Tougher 2002a, 143–60.

Treves, P. 1934. "Chronologie de l'affaire d'Harpale." *REA* 56: 513–20.

Treves, P. 1939. "Hyperides and the Cult of Hephaistion." *CR* 53: 56–7.

Tritle, L. A. 1988. *Phocion the Good*. London.

Tritle, L. A. 1989. "*Epilekoi* at Athens." *AHB* 4: 55–9.

Tritle, L. A. 1992. "Forty Five or What? The Generalships of Phocion." *LCM* 17: 19–23.

Tritle, L. A. 1995. Review of E. M. Harris (1995). *BMCR* 6: 492–8.

Tritle, L. A., ed. 1997. *The Greek World in the Fourth Century: From the Fall of the Athenian Empire to the Successors of Alexander*. London.

Tritle, L. A. 2003. "Alexander and the Killing of Cleitus the Black," in Heckel and Tritle, 127–46.

Tronson, A. 1984. "Satyrus the Peripatetic and the Marriages of Philip II." *JHS* 104: 116–56.

Tronson, A. 1985. "The Relevance of IG II² 329 to the Hellenic League of Alexander the Great." *AncW* 12: 15–19.

True, M., and K. Hamma. 1996. *Alexandria and Alexandrianism*. Malibu, CA.

Tuplin, C., ed. 2007. *Persian Responses: Political and Cultural Interaction with(in) the Achaemenid Empire*. Swansea.

Tzahou-Alexandri, O. E. 1998. *Lefkes Lekythoi tou Zografou tou Achilleos sto Ethniko Archaeologiko Mouseio*. Athens.

Van Alfen, P. G. 2002. "The 'Owls' from the 1989 Syria Hoard with a Review of Pre-Macedonian Coinage in Egypt." *AJN* 2nd ser. 14: 1–57.

van der Spek, B. 1998. "The Chronology of the Wars of Artaxerxes II in the Babylonian Astronomical Diaries," in Brosius and Kuhrt, 239–56.

van der Spek, B. 2003. "Darius III, Alexander the Great and Babylonian Scholarship," in Henkelman and Kuhrt, 289–346.

van der Spek, B., and I. Finkel. Forthcoming. *Babylonian Chronicles of the Hellenistic Period*.

Van Nuffelen, P., ed. 2008. *Faces of Hellenism*. Leuven, Belgium.

Vanotti, G., and C. Perassi, eds. 2004. *In limine: ricerche su marginalità e periferia nel mondo antico*. Milan.

Van't Dack, E., ed. 1983. *Egypt and the Hellenistic World: Proceedings of the International Colloquium, Leuven 24–26 May 1982*. Studia Hellenistica 27. Leuven, Belgium.

Vincent, W. 1797. *The Voyage of Nearchus from the Indus to the Euphrates collected from the original journal preserved by Arrian and illustrated by authorities ancient and modern, containing an account of the first navigation attempted by Europeans in the Indian ocean*. 1 vol. in 4. London; 2nd edn., London, 1807.

Virgilio, B. 2003. *Lancia, diadema e porpora: il re e la regalità ellenistica*. Pisa.

Vogelsang, W. 1985. "Early Historical Arachosia in South East Afghanistan," *IA* 20: 55–99.

Völcker-Janssen, W. 1993. *Kunst und Gesellschaft an den Höfen Alexanders des Großen und seiner Nachfolger*. Munich.

Volpilhac-Auger, C. 2002. "Montesquieu et l'impérialisme grec: Alexandre ou l'art de la conquête," in Pitts, 49–60.

von Hesberg, H. 1996. "Privatheit und Öffentlichkeit der frühhellenistischen Hofarchitektur," in Hoepfner and Brands, 84–96.

von Hesberg, H. 1998. "Riti e produzione artistica delle corti ellenistiche," in Settis, 177–214.

von Hesberg, H. 1999. "The King on Stage," in Bergmann and Kondoleon, 65–76.

Vössing, K. 2004. *Mensa Regia: Das Bankett beim hellenistischen König und beim römischen Kaiser*. Munich.

Voutiras, E. 1998. "Athéna dans les cités de Macédoine." *Kernos* 11: 111–29.

Walbank, F. W. 1967. *A Historical Commentary of Polybius*, vol. ii: *Commentary on Books VII–XVIII*. Oxford.

Walcott, P. 1987. "Plato's Mother and Other Terrible Women." *G&R* 37: 13–31.

Wallace, R. W., and E. M. Harris, eds. 1996. *Transitions to Empire: Essays in Greco-Roman History, 360–146 B.C., in Honor of E. Badian*. Norman, OK.

Wardman, A. E. 1974. *Plutarch's Lives*. London.

Warner, Rex, tr. 1972. *Xenophon: The Persian Expedition*. Penguin Classics. London.

Watts, J. W., ed. 2001. *Persia and Torah: The Theory of Imperial Authorization of the Pentateuch*. Atlanta, GA.

Weber, G. 1992. "Poesie und Poeten an den Höfen vorhellenistischer Monarchen." *Klio* 74: 25–77.

Weber, G. 1993. *Dichtung und höfische Gesellschaft: Die Rezeption von Zeitgeschichte am Hof der ersten drei Ptolemäer*. Stuttgart.

Weber, G. 1997. "Interaktion, Repräsentation und Herrschaft. Der Königshof im Hellenismus," in Winterling, 27–71.

Weber, G. 1999. "Herrscher und Traum in hellenistischer Zeit." *AKG* 81: 1–33.

Weber, M. 1922. *Wirtschaft und Gesellschaft: Grundriss der verstehenden Soziologie*. 5th edn. Tübingen.

Weinstock, S. 1971. *Divus Julius*. Oxford.

Welles, C. B. 1965. "Alexander's Historical Achievement." *G&R* 12: 216–28.

Westlake, H. D. 1935. *Thessaly in the Fourth Century B.C.* London.

Wheatley, P. V. 1995. "Ptolemy Soter's Annexation of Syria, 320 B.C." *CQ* 45: 433–40.

Wheatley, P. V. 1997. "The Lifespan of Demetrius Poliorcetes." *Historia* 46: 19–27.

Wheatley, P. V. 1998. "The Chronology of the Third Diadoch War." *Phoenix* 52: 257–81.

Wheatley, P. V. 1999. "The Young Demetrius Poliorcetes." *AHB* 13: 1–13.

Wheatley, P. V. 2001. "The Antigonid Campaign in Cyprus, 306 B.C." *AncSoc* 31: 133–56.

Wheatley, P. V. 2002. "Antigonus Monophthalmus in Babylonia, 310–308 B.C." *JNES* 61: 39–47.

Wheatley, P. V. 2003. "The Year 22 Tetradrachms of Sidon and the Date of the Battle of Gaza." *ZPE* 144: 268–76.

Wheatley, P. V. 2007. "An Introduction to the Chronological Problems in Early Diadoch Sources and Scholarship," in Heckel et al., 179–92.

Whitby, W. 2004. "Four Notes on Alexander." *Electrum* 8: 35–47.

Whitehead, D. 2000. *Hypereides: The Forensic Speeches*. Oxford.

Whitehorne, J. 1994. *Cleopatras*. London.

Whitfield, J. H. 1992. "Big Words, Exact Meanings," in Machiavelli, 193–206.

Wiemer, H.-U. 2005. *Alexander der Große*. Munich.

Wiesehöfer, J. 1980. "Die 'Freunde' und 'Wohltäter' des Großkönigs." *Studia Iranica* 9: 7–21.

Wiesehöfer, J. 1994. *Das antike Persien von 550 v. Chr. bis 650 n. Chr.* Munich.

Wilcken, U. 1921. "Alexander der Grosse und die hellenistische Wirtschaftt." *Schmollers Jahrbuch* 45/2: 349–420.

Wilcken, U. 1931. *Alexander der Grosse*. Leipzig.

Wilcken, U. 1938. "Zur Entstehung des hellenistischen Königskult." In *Sitzungsberichte der Preussischen Akademie der Wissenschaften*. Berlin.

Wilcken, U. 1967. *Alexander the Great*. Trans. by G. C. Richards; preface by E. N. Borza. New York.

Will, É. 1979. *Histoire politique du monde hellénistique (323–30 av. J.C.)*. 2nd edn. Vol. 1: *De la mort d'Alexandre aux avénements d'Antiochos III et de Philippe V*. Nancy, France.

Will, W. 1982. "Zur Datierung der Rede Ps. Demosthenes XVII." *RhM* 125: 202–12.

Will, W. 1983. *Athen und Alexander: Untersuchungen zur Geschichte der Stadt von 338 bis 322 v. Chr.* Munich.

Will, W., ed. 1998. *Alexander der Grosse: Eine Welteroberung und ihr Hintergrund*. Bonn.

Will, W., and J. Heinrichs, eds. 1988. *Zu Alexander dem Grossen*. 2 vols. Amsterdam.

Willrich, H. 1899. "Wer ließ König Philipp von Makedonien ermorden?" *Hermes* 34: 174–83.

Winkler, J. J. 1990. *The Constraints of Desire*. London.

Winter, F. 1909. *Das Alexandermosaik aus Pompeii*. Strasbourg.

Winter, F. 1912. *Der Alexandersarkophag aus Sidon*. Strasbourg.

Winterling, A., ed. 1997. *Zwischen "Haus" und "Staat": Antike Höfe im Vergleich*. Munich.

Wirth, G. 1971. "Alexander zwischen Gaugamela und Persepolis," *Historia* 20: 617–32.

Wirth, G. 1973. *Alexander der Grosse*. Reinbek bei Hamburg.

Wirth, G. 1976. "Alexander und Rom," in Badian 1976a, 181–210.

Wirth, G. 1989. "Alexander, Kassander und andere Zeitgenossen: Erwägungen zum Problem ihrer Selbstdarstellung." *Tyche* 4: 193–220.

Wirth, G. 1993. *Der Brand von Persepolis: Folgerungen zur Geschichte Alexanders des Großen*. Amsterdam.

Wirszubski, Chaim. 1960. *Libertas as a Political Ideal at Rome during the Late Republic and Early Principate*. Cambridge.

Wiseman, T. P. 1974. "Legendary Genealogies in Late-Republican Rome." *G&R* 21: 153–64.

Wittenburg, A. 1990. *Il ritorno degli esuli a Mitilene, Symposion 1988, Comunicazioni sul diritto greco ed ellenistico*, Siena-Pisa, 267–76.

Wood, M. 1997. *In the Footsteps of Alexander the Great*. Berkeley, CA.

Worthington, I. 1986. "Hyper. 5 *Dem*. 18 and Alexander's Second Directive to the Greeks." *C&M* 37: 115–21.

Worthington, I. 1990. "Alexander the Great and the Date of the Mytilene Decree." *ZPE* 83: 194–214.

Worthington, I. 1992. *A Historical Commentary on Dinarchus: Rhetoric and Cospiracy in Fourth-Century Athens*. Ann Arbor, MI.

Worthington, I. 1994a. "The Harpalus Affair and the Greek Response to the Macedonian Hegemony," in Worthington 1994b, 307–30.

Worthington, I., ed. 1994b. *Ventures into Greek History*. Oxford.

Worthington, I. 2000. Review of Blackwell (1999). *CQ* 50: 188–90.

Worthington, I. 2003. "Alexander's Destruction of Thebes," in Heckel and Tritle, 65–86.

Worthington, I. 2004a. "Alexander the Great and the Greeks in 336? Another Reading of *IG* II^2 329." *ZPE* 147: 68.

Worthington, I. 2004b. *Alexander the Great, Man and God*. London.

Wüst, F. R. 1938. *Philipp II. von Makedonien und Griechenland in den Jahren von 346 bis 338*. Munich.

Yardley, J. C., and R. C. Develin, eds. and trans. 1994. *Justin: Epitome of the Philippic History of Pompeius Trogus*. Atlanta, GA.

Yardley, J. C., and W. Heckel, eds. and trans. 1984. *Quintus Curtius Rufus: The History of Alexander*. Penguin Classics. London.

Zahrnt, M. 1971. *Olynth und die Chalkidier*. Vestigia 14. Munich.

Zahrnt, M. 1983. "Hellas unter persischem Druck? Die griechisch-persischen Beziehungen in der Zeit vom Abschluß des Königsfriedens bis zur Gründung des Korinthischen Bunde." *AKG* 65: 249–306.

Zahrnt, M. 1984. "Die Entwicklung des makedonishen Reiches bis zu den Perserkriegen." *Chiron* 14: 325–68.

Zahrnt, M. 1992. "Der Mardonioszug des Jahres 492 v.Chr. und seine historische Einordnung." *Chiron* 22: 237–79.

Zahrnt, M. 1996. "Alexanders Übergang über den Hellespont." *Chiron* 26: 129–47.

Zahrnt, M. 2003. "Versöhnen oder Spalten? Überlegungen zu Alexanders Verbanntendekret." *Hermes* 123: 407–32.

Zahrnt, M. Forthcoming. "Amyntas III. und die griechischen Mächte." *AM* 7.

Zanker, P. 1968. *Forum Augustum: Das Bildprogram*. Tübingen.

Zanker, P. 1988. *The Power of Images in the Age of Augustus*. Trans. by A. Shapiro. Ann Arbor, MI.

Zecchini, G. 1984. "Alessandro Magno nella cultura dell'età antonina," in Sordi, 195–212.

Zevi, F. 1988. "Die Casa del Fauno in Pompeji und das Alexandermosaik." *MDAI(R)* 105: 21–65.

Zevi, F., and L. Pedicini. 1998. *I mosaici della Case del Fauno a Pompei*. Naples.

Zoepffel, R. 2006. *Aristoteles: Oikonomika*. Schriften zu Hauswirtschaft und Finanzwesen. Übersetzt und erlautert. Berlin.

Index